NINTH EDITION

Research Methods in Education

An Introduction

William Wiersma
Professor Emeritus, University of Toledo

Stephen G. Jurs
Professor Emeritus, University of Toledo

Boston New York San Francisco
Mexico City Montreal Toronto London Madrid Munich Paris
Hong Kong Singapore Tokyo Cape Town Sydney

To Joan and Nancy and
to the memory of Dr. Dennis E. Hinkle—
scholar, teacher, researcher, and friend

Executive Editor: *Paul Smith*
Editorial Assistant: *Anne Whittaker*
Marketing Manager: *Erica DeLuca*
Production Editor: *Mary Beth Finch*
Editorial Production: *Omegatype Typography, Inc.*
Composition Buyer: *Linda Cox*
Manufacturing Buyer: *Linda Morris*
Cover Administrator: *Kristina Mose-Libon*

For related titles and support material, visit our online catalog at www.pearsonhighered.com.

Library of Congress Cataloging-in-Publication Data

Wiersma, William.
Research methods in education: an introduction / William Wiersma, Stephen G. Jurs.
—9th ed.
p. cm.
Includes bibliographical references and index.
ISBN-13: 978-0-205-58192-4 (hardcover)
ISBN-10: 0-205-58192-7 (hardcover)
1. Education—Research. I. Jurs, Stephen G. II. Title.
LB1028.W517 2009
370.7'2—dc22 2007040447

Printed in the United States of America

10 9 8 7 6 5 4 3 2 1 12 11 10 09 08

Allyn and Bacon
is an imprint of

www.pearsonhighered.com

ISBN 10: 0-205-58192-7
ISBN 13: 978-0-205-58192-4

BRIEF CONTENTS

PART ONE The Research Process

PART TWO Research Designs

PART THREE Research Tools

CONTENTS

PART THREE Research Tools

PREFACE

Purpose

The extent and type of research required in graduate programs in education vary in the United States and in countries worldwide. However, in practically all such programs, there are some research requirements, including participation in research activities, for the successful completion of the program. Therefore, a knowledge of research methods, or at least of basic concepts of research methods, is not only useful, but essential. Much of the professional education literature addresses research results. Educators should be familiar with the research results in their specialty areas and the research methods that are used to produce those results.

Audience

Research Methods in Education: An Introduction is written primarily for graduate students in education because the graduate level is usually the point in education at which the student first encounters formal training in research methods. However, because it is an introductory book, it is appropriate at any point at which research methods are introduced in a program. Students in undergraduate programs that emphasize research should find the book useful, even if there is no formal course in research methods. Education draws on several disciplines for its research methods, and for that reason students in related disciplines will find application for the book, especially students in the behavioral sciences. Of course, the book can be used independently as a professional reference.

Approach

The text emphasizes the rationale for commonly used research procedures and the application of these procedures. Research methods are illustrated through numerous examples, some taken from actual research studies. Exercises are provided at the ends of the chapters to enhance learning. The most commonly used, specific types of research are addressed, both quantitative and qualitative. In attempting to provide comprehensive coverage, topics such as reviewing the literature and preparing a research report are discussed. The procedures covered have wide applicability and the ideas presented are general enough to apply in many specific situations.

Organization

The book is organized into three parts. Chapters 1 through 5 focus on the research process. Chapters 6 through 13 are concerned with specific research designs. The final section, Chapters 14 through 17, addresses research tools that can be used in the different research designs.

Part One addresses educational research in general. The introductory chapter describes the nature of educational research and introduces the steps in the research process. Because adequate identification of a research problem is so important, the entire second chapter is devoted to this topic. The chapter also introduces research terminology. Chapter 3 describes how to review the literature, including the identification of information sources. The use of both the library and online sources is emphasized. Chapter 4 provides suggestions about how to prepare a research proposal and a research report. Both content and format issues are addressed. The chapter also includes guidelines for oral presentations of research both at professional conferences and at thesis or dissertation committee meetings. Chapter 5 discusses evaluating research reports. Criteria for evaluating research proposals are given as well as the criteria used in the publications of the American Educational Research Association.

Part Two explains different kinds of research designs that are commonly used in educational research. Chapter 6 discusses the quantitative research perspective. Chapters 7, 8, and 9 are devoted to various types of quantitative research—experimental, quasi-experimental, and nonexperimental quantitative research. Chapter 10 presents the qualitative research perspective. Chapters 11 and 12 discuss different kinds of qualitative research—historical and ethnographic. Finally, Chapter 13 describes mixed methods, which commonly means using both qualitative and quantitative methods in the same study. The chapter also includes introductory descriptions of Delphi studies and structural modeling, two less commonly used research techniques.

Part Three is devoted to certain technical aspects of conducting research that apply to both quantitative and qualitative research studies. Chapter 14 discusses the concept of a random sample and explains various random sampling designs that are used in educational research. The chapter also describes purposeful sampling designs that are used in qualitative research studies. Most research studies involve gathering data of various kinds. Sometimes the researcher uses existing measures (tests and scales) and at other times the researcher has to create the measures. Chapter 15 discusses the reliability and validity of these measures and provides examples of several kinds of measures. The scores or values from these measures are usually statistically analyzed to summarize the results and to provide meaning relative to the original research question. Descriptive statistical techniques are explained in Chapter 16, and inferential statistical techniques are described in Chapter 17.

There are three appendices. The first addresses ethical and legal considerations in conducting research. Student research proposals are usually required to be reviewed by the institutional review board (IRB) at the student's own institution. Students need to know why this is important and what concerns these committees address. The second appendix contains answers to selected end-of-chapter exercises. The final appendix contains five statistical tables for handy reference. A glossary of research methods terms follows Appendix 3.

The content of the chapters is not entirely linear; that is, all chapters are not necessarily dependent on the preceding chapters. The chapters that describe different types of research are quite independent. Instructors can select different chapters and even different topics within chapters and assemble them to suit their own emphases.

The Ninth Edition

The greatest change in the ninth edition is the reordering of the chapters. Several reviewers said that their preferred sequence of chapters in the first part of their course, when using the eighth edition, was 1, 2, 3, 16, 17. This makes a lot of sense because it groups five chapters that are concerned with the overall research process. We have adopted this sequence in the ninth edition. Of course, instructors who prefer the previous sequence of chapters can still teach it that way.

Any new edition contains the usual updating of examples, references, and so forth. Our position on this task is that we want the new examples to be current and to be more interesting to the students than the previous examples were. To that end, we found studies about the correlation between poor reading performance and suicidality, an ethnographic study of a Christian subgroup at a university, and a historical research study on Southern women who attended Northern colleges around 1900, for example.

The data sets that are used to illustrate statistical procedures in Chapters 16 and 17 have all been updated. These sets of data are on the disk that accompanies the textbook and are provided in Excel and SPSS formats. Although this is a research methods textbook and not a statistics text, some formulas have been added to enhance understanding of statistical concepts.

The text contains over one hundred figures, tables, and examples. Diagrams of research designs are used to illustrate their structures and underlying concepts. Important concepts are summarized and set off throughout the book and key concepts are listed at the end of each chapter, so the pedagogical features of the ninth edition should serve the user well. New end-of-chapter exercises have been added to every chapter.

Acknowledgments

Special acknowledgement goes to Dr. Arlen Gullickson of the Evaluation Center, Western Michigan University, for permission to reproduce a cover letter and example items from the 2007 NSF Advanced Technological Education Survey; to Mr. Jeff Simon of the Early Intervention Division of the New York Board of Health for permission to reproduce the Checklist for Growing Children; and to the Morris Rosenberg Foundation of the Department of Sociology at the University of Maryland for permission to reproduce the Rosenberg Self-Esteem Scale. We appreciate the permission of Dr. Edward Nussel and Dr. Philip Rusche to reproduce material from a research project.

We are grateful to the Literary Executor of the late Sir Ronald A. Fisher, F. R. S.; to Dr. Frank Yates, F. R. S.; and to Longman Group Ltd., London, for permission to reprint Tables III, IV, and VII (abridged) from their book *Statistical Tables for Biological, Agricultural, and Medical Research* (6th edition, 1974).

The many insightful comments of the following reviewers were helpful in the revision: Bert Goldman, University of North Carolina, Greensboro; Gholam Kibria, Delaware State University; Mary Lightbody, Otterbein College; Doris L. Prater, University of Houston; and Darla Twale, University of Dayton.

William Wiersma
Stephen G. Jurs

CHAPTER 1

Educational Research

Its Nature and Characteristics

Introduction

Research has become such a prevailing phenomenon of our civilization that all of us are impacted by it. Scholars and practitioners of various levels of sophistication in the academic disciplines and professions engage in research. Students do not progress very far in our formal education system without encountering the necessity to do some type of research. Research is conducted in many, many settings: laboratories, classrooms, libraries, the city streets, and foreign cultures just to mention a few. A lot of research now is done by computer. Some research is of short duration; other research spans long periods of time. Industries, businesses, and funding agencies, such as the Department of Education and the National Institutes of Health, spend vast sums of money on research activity. Yet, much research is done with little funding, "on a shoestring," so to speak. Advances in many fields of endeavor are attributed to research, and for much of this research activity there is the inherent assumption that research fosters improvement.

Graduate students may find it difficult, at least early in a graduate program, to identify with research situations and to key into a process of conducting research. It may be that the only motivation for taking a research methods course and for engaging in research at all is that they are required in the graduate program. Expertise and experience for conducting research are limited. So, the necessity for conducting research provides little direction for how to go about doing it.

When it comes to matters of research, the situation of the average elementary or high school teacher, counselor, or administrator is not much different from that of the graduate student. In fact, a considerable portion of the graduate student population is often made up of school personnel pursuing graduate degrees on a part-time basis. But regardless of degree requirements, research is done for the purpose of explaining and predicting phenomena, and in the case of educational research, those that impact teaching and learning and the operation of the schools. There is an inherent assumption that educational research, by providing a better understanding of the education process, will lead to the improvement of educational practice.

Decision making in the schools is based on a combination of experience, expert opinion, and research results, and the professional educator should be knowledgeable about research methodology and results.

Much educational research is reported in such a way that a knowledge of the methodology is invaluable, and in almost all cases, such knowledge is essential for a meaningful implementation of research results. Although graduate students may have a short-term or immediate need to conduct research for a thesis or dissertation, a long-term result of the research experience should be that they become better professional educators and that they use research results increasingly in decision making.

Education is a complex process. Students and teachers in schools find themselves in complex and fluctuating networks of social interaction. As Berliner (2002) points out, there is any number of interactions operating simultaneously, such as teaching behavior interacting with student characteristics (e.g., motivation). Education is very much context-specific, limiting the generalizability of educational research findings. Indeed, Berliner concludes:

> In my estimation, we have the hardest-to-do science of them all. (p. 18)

Correspondingly, educational research, too, is complex and demanding. However, the broad spectrum of research activities uses various research methods, ranging from relatively simple, single operations to complex combinations of procedures. With organized and concentrated study, the aspiring educational researcher should be able to master necessary research methods. Knowing what to do in specific situations is important. How is the research problem identified? What procedures apply in pursuing the solution of the specific problem? How are the data to be collected and interpreted? How can a satisfactory, lucid report be produced? In the context of a specific research effort, all these questions call for certain skills.

The approach of this text is essentially one of emphasizing the application of procedures. To a large extent, what is done in educational research is based on common sense. We try to structure things so that we can tell what is going on, so that we can understand the information contained in the data. This text discusses general procedures and methods, but the practicing researcher must apply them to the specific situation. To some extent, the idea of a "typical" research project is a misconception. There is no typical project; each has unique problems and conditions. Although there may be considerable similarity among various types of projects, doing a research project is not like baking a cake from a recipe.

The educational researcher should always aim for a respectable, competently done product. However, a researcher should not become discouraged if the results are less than perfect—it is not likely that there has ever been a perfect study. Therefore, any finished product will not be totally exempt from criticism. In doing research, there are potential pitfalls, and errors are likely to occur. Any researcher should be willing to accept the suggestions of peers. Criticism of research should be offered and accepted in a strictly constructive sense for the purpose of improving a particular project or improving future research in the area.

The Nature of Educational Research

Research essentially is an activity, or process, and even though research procedures are many and varied, certain general characteristics help define its nature. Because educational research also has these characteristics, they are described and illustrated here among educational examples. The few general characteristics are as follows:

1. Research is empirical.
2. Research should be systematic.
3. Research should be valid.
4. Research should be reliable.
5. Research can take on a variety of forms.

These characteristics are related in that, as a composite, they describe the nature of research. They are somewhat separated in this discussion to focus on their individual meanings.

The Empirical Nature of Research

A strong empirical approach characterizes educational research. Technically, empiricism is the concept that all knowledge is derived from sense experience that comes from observation and experimentation. But the result of this experience must take some kind of informational form so that knowledge can be generated. Information takes the form of data. There are many forms of data, including test scores, field notes, responses to questionnaire items, and physical performance scores, to mention just four. The researcher works with this data, organizing and analyzing the data to produce knowledge. This knowledge is data-based. By contrast, nonempirical knowledge would come from purely logical conclusions or from the word of authorities.

The Systematic Process of Research

Research is a process, and it should be conducted in such a way that it is **systematic research.** Indeed, many writers describe research as a systematic process. McMillan and Schumacher (1997) define research as "a systematic process of collecting and analyzing information (data) for some purpose" (p. 9), and Kerlinger and Lee (2000) define scientific research as "systematic, controlled, empirical, amoral, public, and critical investigation of natural phenomena guided by theory and hypotheses about the presumed relations among such phenomena" (p. 14).

Certainly, we would like educational research to be systematic, but what can we do to make it so? We can use the approach of scientific inquiry, the search for knowledge through recognized methods of data collection, analysis, and interpretation. Associated with scientific inquiry is the **scientific method,** a research process considered, at least to some extent, to consist of a series of sequential steps. Opinions may vary as to the exact number of steps in the scientific method, but typically anywhere from four to six general steps are identified. These begin with identifying the problem and proceed through interpreting results and drawing conclusions. Five steps are compatible with the scientific method and provide the elements of a general, systematic approach to research: (1) identifying the problem, (2) reviewing information, (3) collecting data, (4) analyzing data, and (5) drawing conclusions. Because the scientific method has been introduced, it merits some comments about its application to educational research.

Although it is called the scientific method, it is a process and it should not be confused with a specific research method such as experimentation. Sometimes there is a tendency for writers to imply, if not state outright, that certain research methods are more "scientific" than others. Feuer, Towne, and Shavelson (2002) make an excellent argument for a scientific culture in which research or science takes place, which reflects the context for the scientific method. Their description:

> Scientific culture is a set of norms and practices and an ethos of honesty, openness, and continuous reflection, including how research quality is judged. (p. 4)

This description and the five steps of the scientific method do not imply any hierarchy of research methods. The issue of research quality depends on how the research was done, not the specific method used.

Returning to the five steps, first, for a research study to be systematic, the nature of the problem to be studied must be defined, even if only in broad terms. Related knowledge is identified, and, in essence, a framework is established in which to conduct the research. Closely related to establishing the framework or foundation for the research is the identification of any necessary assumptions or conditions related to the research problem.

The second step is gathering information about how others have approached or dealt with similar problems. Certainly, one can and should profit from the work of others; it is not necessary to "reinvent the wheel" each time a research problem is attacked. The research literature is the source of such information.

Collecting data relevant to the problem is the third step in systematic research. However, data cannot be collected in any available, haphazard, or ad hoc manner. The process of data collection requires proper organization and control so that the data will enable valid decisions to be made about the research problem at hand. The fourth step is analyzing data in a manner appropriate to the problem. The fifth step is the process of drawing conclusions or making generalizations after the analysis has been made. The conclusions are based on the data and the analysis within the framework of the research study.

The five steps that characterize the systematic nature of the research process can be illustrated as follows:

The process just described is systematic and ordered, but it should not be inferred that research is a lockstep process. There may be overlap and integration among the steps. In some studies, such as an experiment, hypotheses to be tested may be identified when the research problem is defined. In other research studies, those more qualitative in nature, generating hypotheses may not occur until data are collected and then hypotheses may be revised when data are analyzed. So, the specific conditions of the research study impact on the steps but, to some extent, all educational research studies are systematic.

> Educational research is systematic and within a broad framework follows the steps of the scientific method. However, across different types of studies there is extensive flexibility in how the steps are implemented.

The Validity of Educational Research

Regardless of the form research takes or the ends to which it is directed, we want research to be valid—that is, to possess validity. What is validity of research? In general, for something to be valid we want it to be based on fact or evidence, that is, "capable of being justified." Becoming more specific, validity involves two[1] concepts simultaneously, internal validity and external validity. **Internal validity** is the extent to which results can be interpreted accurately, and **external validity** is the extent to which results can be generalized to populations, situations, and conditions. Consider examples illustrating the concepts of validity.

Internal Validity. Suppose a physical education teacher is interested in possible effects of two different exercise programs on the physical performance test scores of eighth-grade boys. The teacher is scheduled for two morning physical education classes and has the option of randomly assigning twenty-eight students to each class. The teacher implements one program in each class for a sixteen-week period and at the end of the period administers the same physical performance test to both classes. This research study has good internal validity. The overall scheme of the study is diagrammed in Figure 1.1.

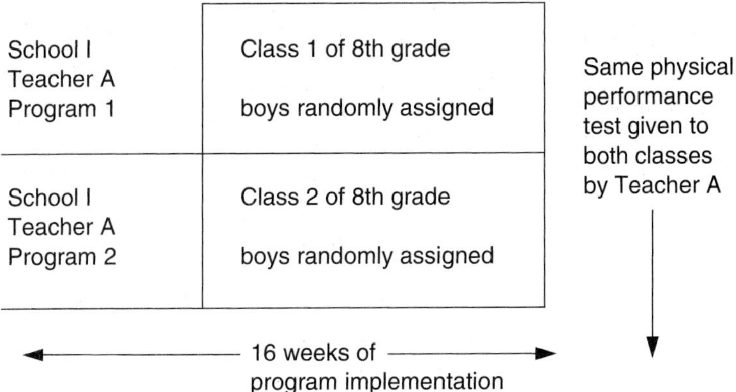

FIGURE 1.1 Overall Scheme of a Hypothetical Research Study That Has High Internal Validity

Why does this study have good internal validity? Because if the physical performance test scores of the two classes differ, say that the mean[2] for Class 2 is much higher than that for Class 1, we can interpret this result with confidence and conclude that Program 2 is the more effective program. Whatever the results, they can be interpreted with confidence, because *overall* the only difference between the two classes is the program. Both are morning classes taught by the same teacher in the same school, and both classes consist of eighth-grade boys. To be sure, any two boys might differ on their inherent physical ability, but fifty-six boys were assigned randomly, twenty-eight to each class. As classes, overall the two classes should be very similar on factors other than the programs that might affect physical performance. For example, possibly some boys get more sleep than others, but overall the averages should be about the same for the two classes. In essence, the random assignment "evens out" the two classes on these other factors, and we say that the groups are equivalent within random fluctuation.

Consider another example, which in contrast presents a situation lacking internal validity. Research is being conducted on the differing effects of three types of materials on performance in eighth-grade science. Three teachers are recruited for participation in the study. The teachers teach in different schools; two have four classes each of eighth-grade science, and the third has three classes. In one school, classes are assigned on the basis of ability grouping. It so happens that the participating teacher in this school has high-ability classes.

Each teacher uses one type of material for a period of nine weeks. The teachers use different materials, and no teacher uses more than one type of material. At the end of nine weeks, the students are tested on science achievement, each teacher using his or her own test. The overall scheme of the research study is presented in Figure 1.2.

		Science Achievement Tested
School I Teacher A Materials 1	4 Classes Heterogeneous Ability	Test constructed by Teacher A
School II Teacher B Materials 2	3 Classes Heterogeneous Ability	Test constructed by Teacher B
School III Teacher C Materials 3	4 Classes High Ability	Test constructed by Teacher C

← 9 Weeks Instruction →

FIGURE 1.2 General Scheme of a Hypothetical Research Study That Lacks Internal Validity

Average science achievement scores are computed for the students taught using each of the three materials. What conclusions can be drawn about the relative effectiveness of the three types of materials? Essentially none. There are numerous factors that may affect the science achievement scores that cannot be separated from possible program effects.

To illustrate this point, suppose the students in School III have the highest average score. Is it because they are high-ability students or because Teacher C is a superior teacher? Or is the test used by Teacher C easier than those used by the other teachers? Or are Materials 3 more effective than the other materials? There is no way these results can be validly interpreted, regardless of the pattern of results. Too many plausible and competing explanations of the results cannot be discounted to be able to conclude that Materials 3 are the most effective. Thus, this research study lacks internal validity because the results cannot be interpreted.

> Internal validity is the extent to which the results of a research study can be interpreted accurately with no plausible alternative explanations.

External Validity. As defined earlier, external validity is the extent to which research results can be generalized. To a large extent, internal validity is a prerequisite for external validity because if results cannot be interpreted it is not likely that they can be generalized. Consider an example.

In a school district that has five elementary schools, a survey is conducted of parents' perceptions of the school—quality of the curriculum, effectiveness of the administration, discipline, and so forth. A telephone interview is developed with well-constructed items and an adequate number of items to cover the school characteristics of interest. Within each elementary school 25 parents of students enrolled are selected randomly and interviewed. For any parents not available or unwilling to be interviewed there is a defined procedure for random replacement. The interviews are conducted and 125 interviews are completed with only six of those being replacements for unavailable parents.

The population to which the results of this study are to be generalized is the population of parents who have children in the five elementary schools. With the manner in which the survey was conducted and the number of completed interviews, the results can be generalized with confidence to this population. The research study has high or good external validity. It is not likely that there would be much interest in generalizing the results to other elementary schools, those in other school systems. If this were done, it would need to be done on a logical basis, providing an argument for the similarity between the parents of students in these schools and those in other school districts.

Consider a second example, again one involving a school survey in which parents are asked about their perceptions of the school. A questionnaire is sent to parents of all the students in a high school of 837 students. One questionnaire is sent to each pair of parents or to the custodial parent in single-parent families. A total of 712 questionnaires are sent but even after two follow-up letters, only 149 completed questionnaires are returned. This is a return rate of about 21 percent. It cannot be argued that the parents returning the questionnaire are representative (or are a representative sample) of the parent population for this school. Essentially, they represent only parents who will return questionnaires in the area served by this high school, and no other population or group of parents. There likely are unknown factors operating, causing the low response rate. The results do not generalize to the parent population of the school and the study is lacking in external validity.

Because external validity can involve generalizations to populations and/or conditions, it is useful to consider another example, admittedly one rather extreme and lacking external validity. A study is conducted on the effect of length of visual exposure on the recall of nonsense symbols. (A nonsense symbol might be five letters randomly sequenced.) The researcher obtains ten volunteers from a graduate student population in educational psychology. There are five different lengths of exposure, so two volunteers are used in each. A volunteer participates in the study by being exposed to twenty nonsense symbols individually; after each exposure, the volunteer is to reproduce the symbol. A total performance score is then generated from the number of symbols correctly reproduced. The overall scheme of this study is shown in Figure 1.3.

Suppose the results show that the performance scores generally increase with increased length of exposure. But to what populations and conditions can this result be generalized? Can it be generalized to elementary or secondary students learning meaningful materials? Can it be generalized to young adults working on meaningful tasks in a highly structured situation? Not likely. The results (for recalling nonsense symbols) may not even be generalizable to the graduate student population, because the participants in the study

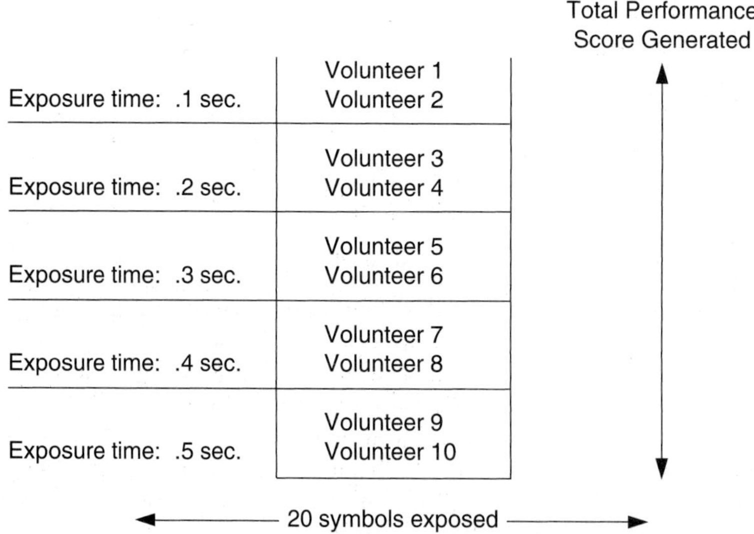

FIGURE 1.3 General Scheme of a Hypothetical Research Study That Lacks External Validity

were volunteers. In summary, the results may be generalizable only to the ten volunteers who recalled the nonsense symbols. The study thus lacks external validity.

External validity is the extent to which research results are generalizable to populations and/or conditions.

It should not be inferred that to have external validity, results must generalize to many and varied populations and conditions. If a study involving only gifted students were conducted, the intent of the study could be to generalize to a gifted student population, not to all students. If a school system were doing a needs assessment, the results might generalize only to that system. Typically, when doing qualitative research, the researcher is not concerned with generalizing beyond the context in which the study was conducted. So, external validity depends on the conditions and purpose of the specific research study.

Validity of research is always a matter of degree. It is practically impossible to attain "perfect" internal and external validity in a study. As will be shown in later chapters, attempts in research design to enhance internal validity may decrease external validity, and vice versa. The researcher attempts to attain a balance so that results can be interpreted with reasonable certainty and still have some useful generalizability.

Validity of research deals with the accurate interpretability of the results (internal validity) and the generalizability of the results (external validity). Both types of validity are matters of degree.

The Reliability of Educational Research

When discussing validity, it is appropriate to consider a related concept—**reliability of research.** *Reliability* refers to the consistency of the research and the extent to which studies can be replicated. We sometimes distinguish between internal and external reliability. *Internal reliability* refers to the extent that data collection, analysis, and interpretations are consistent given the same conditions. For example, if multiple data collectors are used, a question of internal reliability is, "Do the data collectors agree?" Suppose a study of teacher performance is being conducted using a classroom observation inventory for data collection. The question of internal reliability would be, "Do the two or more observers agree when recording the same performance?" This is called the extent of *observer agreement.* If internal reliability is lacking, the data become a function of who collects them rather than what actually happened.

External reliability deals with the issue of whether or not independent researchers can replicate studies in the same or similar settings. Will researchers be able to replicate studies, and, if so, will the results be consistent? If research is reliable, a researcher using the same methods, conditions, and so forth should obtain the results as those found in a prior study. To be replicable, a research study must include adequate descriptions of the procedures and conditions of the research. The amount of definition necessary may vary across studies.

> *Reliability* of research concerns the replicability and consistency of the methods, conditions, and results.

Reliability is a necessary characteristic for validity; that is, a study cannot be valid and lack reliability. If a study is unreliable, we can hardly interpret the results with confidence or generalize them to other populations and conditions. Essentially, reliability and validity establish the credibility of research. Reliability focuses on replicability and validity focuses on the accuracy and generalizability of the findings.

Research Has a Variety of Paradigms

Researchers address a wide variety of research questions and use a vast array of methods, singly or in combination, in their research. Everything from casual observations in the classroom to rigorously controlled conditions in a learning laboratory is called research. Underlying each research study is the researcher's theoretical framework, or paradigm. You might think of a paradigm as a reflection of the researcher's viewpoint on what constitutes valuable research, that is, why and how the research is done. The following is a brief and oversimplified description of several of the more popular paradigms. For a more complete discussion of paradigms, see Mertens (2005).

Positivist. These researchers use the "scientific method" when conducting research. There is one reality and it is the researchers' job to discover it. They formulate statements of the hypothetical relationships among variables and then gather data to see whether their hypotheses are supported or refuted by the data. The goal is to discover the cause-and-effect relationships. Their research is considered to be "value-free."

Postpositivist. Postpositivists believe that the researched relationships among variables may be influenced by values, theories, and conditions that are not included in the research study. Researchers still try to establish causal relationships by manipulating variables to see the effects on other variables, but their goal is to eliminate alternative explanations for the results. Conclusions are stated in terms of probabilities rather than certainty.

Constructionist. Unlike the positivists and the postpositivists, the constructionist does not begin with a theory to be tested, but instead develops theory for testing from the data. Reality is seen as socially constructed. The researcher depends on the participants' interpretations of the situation and tries to capture the participants' language and point of view. Findings are thought to be context-specific. There is also concern of how the researcher's own values may be influencing the research process.

Transformative. The transformative researcher recognizes the political nature of research and attempts to include diverse people in the research so that we have an understanding of whether our research findings are true for all subgroups. The researcher recognizes that the socially constructed reality is influenced by ethnic, gender, cultural, economic, and other factors. Transformative research may also focus on issues that are specific to traditionally underrepresented subgroups.

Many research studies these days are complex, using multiple research methods and borrowing from several paradigms. The important thing for the researcher to be aware of is that there are choices among paradigms. Additionally, some audiences may not believe that all paradigms provide equally strong conclusions. The choice of a paradigm may depend to some extent on what is credible evidence for your primary audience. The more important consideration, though, is that the paradigm is consistent with the research question. The wording of the research question will probably imply the paradigm that best fits the situation.

Classification of Educational Research

There are many ways to classify educational research studies and authors use classification systems of varying degrees of complexity. Essentially, classification systems are valuable to the extent they are useful for enhancing the effectiveness and efficiency by which research is conducted. Three systems are described here, the first based in the goal or purpose of the research; second is the qualitative–quantitative continuum that represents two distinct orientations to phenomena being studied. The third system is a classification of general methods used in educational research.

Basic and Applied Research

Basic and applied research are differentiated by their goals or purposes. The purpose of **applied research** is to solve an immediate, practical problem. Such research is oriented to a specific problem. **Basic research** has a more general orientation: adding to the existing body of knowledge in the discipline. Basic research does not necessarily provide results of immediate, practical use, although such a possibility is not ruled out. If this result does occur, however, it is supplemental, not the primary purpose. On the other hand, in producing a solution to a specific problem, applied research may contribute to the general knowledge of the field. Both basic and applied research are important; one is not necessarily better than the other.

The distinction between applied and basic research should not be overstated. Phillips (2006) explained that research that is conducted for seemingly applied reasons can often lead to further understanding of theory:

> The attempt to unravel the intricacies of educational problems, the attempt to understand the psychology of learning and the developmental process at work in the learner, the attempt to understand the role of scientific findings and values in the making of political decisions

> about educational policy, the attempt to evaluate innovative educational programs and not only to document whether they produce their intended effects but also reveal their (often vitally important) unintended consequences—all these and countless others may be "applied" endeavors, but they also can, and sometimes do, lead to important theoretical understandings. (p. 18)

An example of basic research would be to conduct an experiment concerning learning in a laboratory setting. The purpose of such an experiment would be to contribute to the knowledge about how learning takes place. The experiment might be focused on one or a very limited number of factors associated with learning, such as the differences that result when learning materials are presented in a figural or a verbal manner.

An example of applied research would be to conduct a survey of the elementary school teachers in a school system to determine their preferences and opinions about several available reading programs. The survey would be conducted by a curriculum committee or by the school system's administration, who are concerned with the problem of selecting the reading program or materials to be purchased. The results of the survey would provide information necessary for decisions about the purchase.

Unfortunately, misconceptions have developed with the use of terms *basic* and *applied research.* One such misconception is that basic research is complex and applied research is simple in its methodology. A related misconception is that applied research is carried out by unsophisticated practitioners, whereas basic research is performed by abstract, impractical thinkers. Another misconception is that applied research is often sloppy and haphazard but of great practical value, whereas basic research is precise and exacting but of little or no value in a real situation. As indicated earlier, however, basic and applied research are differentiated not by their complexity or value, but by their goals or purposes.

> Basic and applied research are differentiated by their purposes. The primary purpose of *basic research* is the extension of knowledge; the purpose of *applied research* is the solution of an immediate, practical problem.

One type of applied research is **action research**—research conducted by a teacher, administrator, or other educational professional to aid in decision making in the local school. Action research focuses on the solution of day-to-day problems at the local level. There is little concern about generalizing the results of action research to other educational settings. Often, only a small, accessible population is used, such as the biology classes in a single high school.

Suppose the science teachers in a junior high school are considering whether to use additional group work in conducting experiments or an individual, programmed workbook that simulates experiments. They conduct action research with the students enrolled in the science classes at their school to determine the relative effectiveness and efficiency of the two methods. The teachers are concerned about their own situation; they are not concerned about generalizing to other schools.

Action research has been accused of being less rigorous in terms of design and methods than other educational research, but action research can be of high quality and provide local information that is very credible to local audiences. Often, intact groups are used; in some cases only a single group or an individual is used in the study. Nevertheless, when action research results are combined with what is known from the research literature, the combination can be very convincing to local decision makers.

> *Action research* is usually conducted by teachers, administrators, or other educational professionals for solving a specific problem or for providing information for decision making at the local level.

Some authors, for example McMillan and Schumacher (1997), include a third category of evaluation or evaluative research. For the purposes of this introductory discussion, evaluation research can be considered a part of applied research. Evaluation uses many of the same procedures as research. Typically, the function of evaluation is to assess the merits of a product, program, or practice. The application of the results is at a given site or sites, and this is the primary focus for the evaluation. Evaluation results aid in decision making in a specific situation as with applied research.

> Basic and applied research provide a difference in general orientation based on the purposes of the research. Applied research focuses on solving an immediate problem; basic research more generally focuses on adding to the body of knowledge.

Qualitative and Quantitative Research

Up to this point, the terms **qualitative** and **quantitative research** have been used on occasion, without definition. Although the terms *qualitative* and *quantitative* are generally understood in our society, these terms need some additional explanation with regard to their use as labels for research. McMillan (2003) described them in a simple form:

- Qualitative research stresses a phenomenological model in which multiple realities are rooted in subjects' perceptions. A focus on understanding and meaning is based on verbal narratives and observations rather than numbers. Qualitative research usually takes place in naturally occurring situations, as contrasted with quantitative research, in which behaviors and settings are controlled and manipulated. (p. 9)
- For quantitative research, a major distinction is made between nonexperimental and experimental designs. In nonexperimental research, the investigator has no direct influence on what has been selected to be studied, either because it has already occurred or because it cannot be influenced. . . . It usually means that the study can only describe something or uncover relationships between two or more factors. (p. 9)

- In experimental research, the investigators have control over one or more factors (variables) in the study that may influence the subjects' behavior. . . . The purpose of manipulating a factor is to investigate its causal relationship with another factor. (p. 10)

Qualitative and quantitative research represent two distinctly different approaches to understanding the world, that is, the phenomena being researched. Qualitative research has its origins in descriptive analysis and is essentially an inductive process, reasoning from the specific situation to a general conclusion. Quantitative research, on the other hand, is more closely associated with deduction, reasoning from general principles to specific situations.

As Lancy (1993) points out, qualitative research is typically thought of as a method with a set of procedures for conducting research. From a practical standpoint of doing research this may be a useful approach, but there are underlying differences in the epistemologies of qualitative and quantitative research. They are based on different paradigms, a paradigm being a model consisting of assumptions, concepts, and propositions. Qualitative research in its purest sense follows the paradigm that research should be conducted in the natural setting and that the meanings derived from research are specific to that setting and its conditions. The approach is that of a holistic interpretation of the natural setting.

Quantitative research has its roots in positivism and is more closely associated with the scientific method than is qualitative research. The emphasis is on facts, relationships, and causes. Quantitative researchers place great value on outcomes and products; qualitative researchers have great concern for the impact of the process as well, typically more so than quantitative researchers.

It is not desirable to get sidetracked on a discussion of the role of theory in educational research at this point. That issue, along with a formal definition of theory, merits more elaboration as is done later in the chapter, but a few comments are in order here. Qualitative research does not emphasize a theoretical base for whatever is being studied at the beginning of the research. A theory may develop as the research is conducted; if it does it may be changed, dropped, or refined as the research progresses. If a theory develops based on the data, we have a **grounded theory,** that is, a theory grounded in the data rather than based on some a priori constructed ideas, notions, or system. If no theory emerges, the research will be atheoretical, but will retain its descriptive value.

Quantitative research on the other hand, because of its deductive nature, tends to be more theory-based from the onset. In fact, when theory-testing research is being done it is likely to be quantitative research. Certainly, theories are not always identified explicitly in quantitative research, but the theoretical underpinnings exist in one form or another.

Qualitative research is context-specific with the researcher's role being one of inclusion in the situation. As Smith (1987) indicates, qualitative research is based on the notion of context sensitivity, the belief that the particular physical and social environment has a great bearing on human behavior. Qualitative researchers emphasize a holistic interpretation. They perceive facts and values as inextricably mixed. On the other hand, quantitative researchers look for more context-free generalizations. They are much more willing to focus on individual variables and factors, rather than to concentrate on a holistic interpretation. Typically, quantitative researchers separate facts and values.

Overall, quantitative researchers are more attuned to standardized research procedures and predetermined designs than are qualitative researchers. The latter are more flexible once

TABLE 1.1 Contrasting Characteristics of Qualitative and Quantitative Research

Qualitative		Quantitative
Inductive Inquiry	◄----►	Deductive Inquiry
Understanding Social Phenomena	◄----►	Relationships, Effects, Causes
Atheoretical or Grounded Theory	◄----►	Theory-Based
Holistic Inquiry	◄----►	Focused on Individual Variables
Context-Specific	◄----►	Context-Free (Generalizations)
Observer-Participant	◄----►	Detached Role of Researcher
Narrative Description	◄----►	Statistical Analysis

they are into the research, and qualitative research involves multiple methods more frequently than does quantitative research. Quantitative research has more of a catalog of designs than does qualitative research. The distinction in the way data are presented, mentioned earlier, means that qualitative research relies heavily on narrative description; quantitative research on statistical results.

The distinctions described above between qualitative and quantitative research are due to the different epistemologies underlying the two types of research. There is a difference in purpose between qualitative and quantitative research. Qualitative research is done for the purpose of understanding social phenomena, *social* being used in a broad sense. Quantitative research is done to determine relationships, effects, and causes. The distinguishing characteristics of qualitative and quantitative research are summarized in Table 1.1. This is not necessarily an exhaustive set of distinctions, and additional terms may appear in the literature. But this discussion should provide the reader with a basic conceptualization of the differences. Both approaches are valuable and have relevance for the improvement of education.

> Qualitative and quantitative research have their own characteristics based on different purposes and paradigms underlying the research.

General Methods of Research

In terms of actually doing research it is useful to consider the general methods for research. We talk about doing survey research or historical research, for example, and these imply specific procedures. Five of the most commonly used methods are described below and later an entire chapter is devoted to each method.

Experimental Research. **Experimental research** involves situations in which at least one variable,[3] the *experimental variable,* is deliberately manipulated or varied by the researcher to determine the effects of that variation. This implies that the researcher has the option of determining what the experimental variable will be and the extent to which it is varied. It is possible to have more than one experimental variable in a single experiment. In addition, in order to have what has become to be accepted as a "true experiment," the participants in the experiment must be assigned randomly to the experimental treatments.

Suppose a researcher in health education is interested in the effects of three different exercise periods (periods of varying length) on resting heart rate. Sixty young adults are randomly assigned, 20 to each period. The 60 participants exercise as specified each day: 20 for one-half hour, 20 for 45 minutes, and 20 for 1 hour. The exercise for each period is specified. The exercise program is in effect for two months. The participants are measured on resting heart rate before and after the program so that a measure of change can be taken.

The experimental variable here is the period of exercise. This variable—that is, the three levels of exercise—was constructed by the researcher and then administered to the participants, 20 for each level. If different periods of exercise have an effect on heart rate, this effect should be manifested by differences in the (average) heart rates of the three groups.

Quasi-Experimental Research. **Quasi-experimental research** is similar to experimental research in that one or more experimental variables are involved. However, instead of having participants randomly assigned to experimental treatments, "naturally" assembled groups, such as classes, are used in the research. Members have self-selected themselves into the groups. Single-subject designs that include the use of experimental treatments also are included in quasi-experimental research. Because of the difficulty often encountered when attempting to form groups by random assignment, quasi-experimental research is quite common in education.

Suppose a researcher is studying the effects of an instructional program in logical problem solving on sixth-grade performance on a mathematics concepts test. The experimental treatment is one-half hour of instruction in logical problem solving per day over a ten-week period. The researcher cannot randomly assign sixth-graders to classes, but eight intact classes receive the instructional program and eight classes serve as a comparison group. At the end of ten weeks, the students in the sixteen classes are tested with a common mathematics concepts test.

Nonexperimental Quantitative Research. A variety of research studies can be categorized as nonexperimental quantitative research. Many of these studies are survey research. However, other terms may be used such as **ex post facto research** or *causal–comparative studies.* No experimental variables are manipulated. Variables are studied as they exist in the situation, usually a natural situation. **Survey research,** often associated with studies involving questionnaires or interviews, has a broader definition. It deals with the incidence, distribution, and relationships of educational, psychological, and sociological variables. Some surveys are limited to describing the status quo, whereas others attempt to determine the relationships and effects occurring between variables. If, in such a situation, the variables have occurred, we have what is called ex post facto research.

A researcher conducting a study of the professional practices of college-level counselors in the private colleges of Ohio would be engaged in survey research. One way to do this study would be to construct an appropriate instrument, most likely a questionnaire, that could be completed either by a selected group of counselors or by the entire population of counselors. The responses of the counselors would provide a picture of the professional practices. From this information, the researcher could describe such characteristics as the relative importance (as perceived by the counselors) and the frequency of the practices. The study would emphasize the characteristics of the practices.

Consider an example of a study involving ex post facto research. A study is conducted of the relationship between attitude toward school and achievement of upper elementary school students in various cognitive and skill areas (mathematics, verbal skills, etc.). The researcher would administer to the students included in the study an appropriate attitude inventory and achievement measures for the cognitive and skills areas. No variables are manipulated; that is, the researcher does not administer any treatments to students to change or influence attitude scores or performance scores. The data are collected, and the researcher attempts to identify any effects that may exist and tries to explain how the effects are operating. For example, one question that would undoubtedly be considered is, "Are certain attitude patterns predictive of specific achievement scores, and if so, are the attitudes causing the achievement scores?" Of course, it would be equally appropriate to question whether the achievement scores are causing the attitude patterns.

Historical Research. **Historical research** consists of studying a problem, an issue, a phenomenon, a movement, and so forth, in the past, and information collected from the past serves as the data to be interpreted. Historical researchers cannot relive the past so they must use documents and other artifacts to reconstruct the past through a process of critical inquiry. Historical research consists of describing what was, rather than what is or what effects certain variables may have on others. But historical research is much more than an attempt to reconstruct the past accurately. Historical research involves much interpretation and a projection of results and interpretation onto current issues, problems, procedures, and the like. In the context of education, historical research deals with educational "matters" of the past.

An example of historical research might be a study of federal assistance programs for secondary education during the period 1945–1960. The researcher would inquire about the programs through various sources, such as legislative documents and historical summaries. Then the researcher would describe the programs and consider their possible effects, both good and bad. Specific factors might be considered in tracing the history of these programs, such as their economic impact, and the implications of such impact for educational decision making and policy in the present and for the future. The context would be the events of some past period but the interpretation and implications of the results would not be limited to that period.

Ethnographic Research. **Ethnographic research** is commonly associated with anthropology, but it is finding increasing use in education. An *ethnography* is an in-depth, analytical description of a specific cultural situation, in the broad meaning of *culture*. Put into the context of education, we can define ethnographic research as the process of providing scientific descriptions of educational systems, processes, and phenomena within their specific contexts.

Ethnographic research relies heavily on observation, description, and qualitative judgments or interpretations of whatever phenomena are being studied. It takes place in the natural setting and focuses on processes in an attempt to obtain a holistic picture. Often, ethnographic research does not have a strong theoretical base, and few hypotheses are specified before the research is conducted. Theory and hypotheses are generated as the research proceeds.

Suppose a study of the nature of science instruction in a junior high school is being conducted. The research question is, "What is science instruction like in this school?" Observation is conducted in the science classrooms over the period of the school year. The observers take extensive field notes and interview students and teachers. On the basis of these results, they attempt to provide an accurate description and interpretation of science instruction in the school.

The foregoing examples are brief and quite superficial descriptions of different types of research using methods as the classifying system. Table 1.2 contains a listing of these methods by characteristics and the questions asked. There are other ways of classifying educational research. Some authors use categories such as descriptive research and causal–comparative research. Others may extend the methods to include types such as

TABLE 1.2 Classification of Research by General Methods

Type	Characteristics	Question Asked
Experimental	At least one variable is manipulated to determine the effect of the manipulation. Subjects are randomly assigned to experimental treatments.	What is the effect of the experimental variable?
Quasi-experimental	At least one variable is manipulated to determine the effect of the manipulation. Intact, naturally formed groups are used.	What is the effect of the experimental variable?
Nonexperimental Quantitative	The incidence, relationships, and distributions of variables are studied. Variables are not manipulated but studied as they occur in a natural setting.	What are the characteristics of the variables? What are the relationships and possible effects among the variables?
Historical	A description of past events or facts is developed.	What was or what happened?
Ethnographic	A holistic description of present phenomena is developed.	What is the nature of the phenomena?

case studies. This text does not separate case study as a general research method because case study is recognized more as a way of reporting research and can cut across other types of research. Essentially, a case study involves a detailed examination of a single group, individual, situation, or site. Ethnographic research, when a single group is studied in depth, involves a case study. A single-subject study using quasi-experimental research is a case study.

The different research methods do not fit uniquely into either basic or applied research or into qualitative or quantitative research. For example, at times, experiments may address solving an immediate problem. At other times, they may be conducted primarily for adding to the existing body of knowledge. Methods of research are sometimes more closely associated with the qualitative–quantitative distinction, but this is by no means a "pure" association. For example, ethnographic research is usually considered qualitative but an ethnographic study may involve some quantitative procedures. A lot of survey research is considered quantitative, but some of the procedures commonly associated with surveys, such as interviewing, may be involved in a ethnographic or historical study. So, each classification system should be considered in terms of its own definitions and criteria.

> Classification systems for educational research are valuable to the extent they are useful for distinguishing among different types of research and thus enhancing our understanding of the nature of educational research.

The Role of Theory

The term *theory* is used often in educational research; for example, we talk about *curriculum theory* or *learning theory.* Kerlinger and Lee (2000) define a theory as "a set of interrelated constructs (concepts), definitions and propositions that present a systematic view of phenomena by specifying relations among variables with the purpose of explaining and predicting the phenomena" (p. 11). McMillan (2003) defines a theory as a "set of propositions that explain the relationships among observed phenomena. By providing a more general explanation, the theory can be used in more situations, it has more utility" (pp. 6–7).

> A *theory* is a generalization or series of generalizations by which we attempt to explain some phenomena in a systematic manner.

How are theories obtained or where do we get theories? Certainly one source is the research literature and the conceptual writings in a discipline. For example, theories of learning are often associated with educational psychology. If a theory did not exist or was not well developed, one could conceptualize a theory based on a logical analysis of prior research applied to the phenomenon under study. These approaches might be called "from the top down" as the theory emerges.

Earlier grounded theory was mentioned, and this might be characterized as "from the bottom up" theory development. A grounded theory comes from the inductive analysis of the data as the research is conducted. The theory is grounded in the data and there are no preconceived ideas (at least nothing solidified) about what the theory will be. Suppose research is being done on teacher evaluation practices, and one question raised is, "What theory or theories of teacher evaluation underlie the teacher evaluation practices in the schools?" Using the grounded theory approach, evaluation practices in one or more school systems would be analyzed and the theory or theories would emerge from the data. The use of grounded theory is more closely associated with qualitative than with quantitative research.

The use of theory is more commonly associated with basic research than with applied research, and with quantitative research more than with qualitative research. Sometimes the term *theory-testing research* is used as a part of basic research. Consider an example. An educational psychologist is doing research on the relationship between frequency of encountering instructional materials (for example, word lists or mathematics problem solutions) and retention of the concepts included in the materials. A hypothesis is formulated that increased use enhances retention. Along with this hypothesis are hypotheses about several conditions relating to such factors as the complexity of the materials and the level at which continued use would no longer affect retention. Some relationships among factors may be hypothesized as well. Theory-testing research would enable us to test the theory with its primary and related hypotheses and, presumably, would either confirm or refute the theory, thus providing needed information for revising or extending the theory, if necessary.

What is the **role of theory** and its purpose in research? Basically, theory helps provide a framework by serving as the point of departure for the pursuit of a research problem. The theory identifies the crucial factors. It provides a guide for systematizing and interrelating the various facets of the research. However, besides providing the systematic view of the factors under study, the theory also may very well identify gaps, weak points, and inconsistencies that indicate the need for additional research. Also, the development of the theory may light the way for continued research on the phenomena under study.

In educational research, theory serves a synthesizing function, combining ideas and individual bits of empirical information into a set of constructs that provides for deeper understanding, broader meaning, and wider applicability. In a sense, a theory attaches meaning to facts and places them in proper perspective. Through this process, the theory aids in defining the research problem; that is, it helps identify the proper questions to be asked in the context of the specific project.

As indicated in Kerlinger and Lee's definition (2000), a theory also serves the purposes of explaining and predicting. It suggests an explanation of observed phenomena, and it can also predict as yet unobserved or undiscovered factors by indicating their presence. Operating under the assumption that the theory is consistent, the researcher is then "tipped off" in terms of what to look for.

Another function of theory is to provide one or more generalizations that can be tested and then used in practical applications and further research. This development of generalizations is based on the assumption that generalizations do exist in education (or in any area under study) and that individual observations are special cases of such generalizations.

Conditions under which research is conducted and data are obtained within and across studies tend to be more valuable when incorporated into a meaningful whole. As the facts of the research study, the data derive significance from the theory or theories into which they fit. Conversely, the theories become acceptable to the extent that they enhance the meaning of the data. Through this process, more adequate theories and unobstructed facts are secured; theory stimulates research, and conversely, research stimulates theory development and theory testing. The criterion by which we judge a theory is not its truth or falsity, but rather its usefulness. Theories sometimes decrease in usefulness in the light of new knowledge, and they are combined, replaced, and refined as more knowledge is made available.

A good theory is developed in such a way that the generalizations can be tested. The theory must be compatible with the observations made relative to it and with already existing knowledge. It must adequately explain the events or phenomena under study. The greater the generalizability of the theory, the more useful it will be because of its wider applicability.

Another characteristic of a good theory is reflected in the **law of parsimony,** which holds that a theory should be stated in the simplest form that adequately explains the phenomena. This does not mean that all theories should be simple statements; rather, they should be stated succinctly and precisely, avoiding ambiguities and unnecessary complexity. Important factors must not be overlooked, and the comprehensiveness of the theory must be adequate for its purpose.

The above discussion seems to make a strong case for "theory-based" research, and theories can be very useful, but therein lies the key—theories are valuable only to the extent that they are useful. Education draws on many disciplines and practices for its research base, both content and methods. So, the extent to which theory is valuable depends on the specific purposes and type of research being conducted. Some research studies can benefit more than others from a strong theoretical base. Some studies develop theory from the data of the study itself. Other studies, at least on the surface, appear to be atheoretical, yet make valuable contributions to the research effort. All of this attests to the diversity that makes up educational research.

> A theory provides a framework for conducting research, and it can be used for synthesizing and explaining (through generalizations) research results.

The Activities of the Research Process

The systematic process of research leads to the general activities involved in conducting a research study. These activities are not limited to a specific type of research, such as ethnographic or experimental research, but apply generally. (Activities may receive varying emphasis, however, depending on the type of research.)

In summarizing the general activities involved in conducting a research study, we may appear to be emphasizing the sequential nature of the research process. To a certain extent this is fine, but as mentioned earlier, we do not want to leave the impression that the research process is rigid or completely structured. Activities overlap to some degree, and at times two or more activities can be in process simultaneously. For example, in ethnographic research, hypothesis formulation often takes place throughout the study, from data collection on. In many studies, preliminary analysis begins while data collection is still in process. Nevertheless, it is helpful to impose some order on the various activities.

Figure 1.4 presents a sequential pattern of activities in flowchart form to provide an overview of the various activities. The top row of boxes represents the general activities, and in order to accommodate flexibility in the research process and variations in different types of research, there is some overlap among the activities. For example, an experiment may be conducted for which all hypotheses are formulated and data identified before any data are collected. On the other hand, an ethnographic researcher might be reformulating hypotheses and identifying additional data well into the research process. This characteristic is indicated by the overlapping boxes in the figure.

The lower boxes (broken line) are not activities, but in essence are products of research. The arrows reflect the relationships between the activities and existing knowledge, related theory, and expanded, revised, and new theory and knowledge. Related theory is considered to be a part, but not necessarily all, of the body of knowledge relative to the research problem. Expanded, revised, and new theory, if forthcoming from the research project, then becomes part of the existing body of knowledge, as does new knowledge not considered to be theory. All general activities draw on existing knowledge, but for the

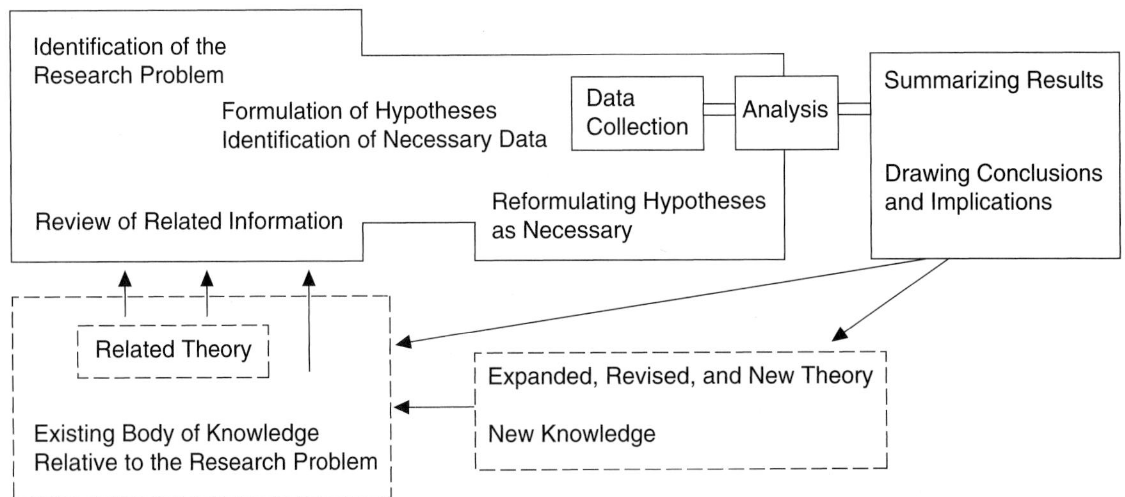

FIGURE 1.4 Sequential Patterns of General Activities in Conducting a Research Study and the Relationship of Such Activities to Existing Knowledge

purpose of this figure, we associate the major impact of the body of knowledge with the research problem.

> The research process may be viewed as a sequence of activities, with the possibility of some overlap and fluctuation among the activities.

At this point, each of the activities will be described in more detail. However, this discussion is introductory and is designed only to provide an overview. In the following chapters, activities are described in detail and illustrated with examples.

Identification of the Research Problem

This is the beginning activity of the research process (at least, it should be), and it is often the most difficult. The problem must be identified with adequate specificity. It is at this point in many studies that hypotheses—tentative "guesses" or conjectures about whatever is being studied—are generated. Variables must be identified and defined adequately for their use in the context of the study so that necessary data can be identified in preparation for data collection. This is done on the basis of existing knowledge. The literature is reviewed for information related to the research problem and to the possible methods for conducting the research, basically to determine what others have done and have discovered that might be useful. The review of literature is a substantial task, and an entire chapter of this book (Chapter 3) is devoted to it.

Data Collection

Before data are collected, any necessary measuring instruments must be identified and perhaps developed; or if the data are going to be contained in a descriptive narrative, the researcher must prepare for taking field notes. If an ethnographic study is being done, the researcher collects the data through various procedures such as interviews and observation. If an experiment is being conducted, the experimental treatments are administered or manipulated just before or during the data collection process. In essence, the experiment is being conducted at this point; the measures are taken. In the case of a survey, measuring instruments, such as achievement tests or questionnaires, are administered. If instruments are developed, they must be pilot tested before the major data collection for the study is undertaken. Then the data must be assembled, coded, and prepared for analysis.

Analysis

Results of the study are generated when analysis is done. Field notes are organized and synthesized at this point. Data are summarized, manipulated, and in essence reduced so they provide necessary information for description and hypotheses testing. If statistical analyses are done, they are completed at this point.

Summarizing Results and Drawing Conclusions

After the data have been analyzed and the results generated, the researcher must decide what information they provide. Results are summarized and tied together, analyses are interpreted, and conclusions are drawn as they relate to the research problem. Conclusions are drawn about hypotheses if hypotheses were tested. The research report is prepared—a task that often requires rewriting. The importance of this task can hardly be overemphasized because it is the way in which the research results add to new knowledge and theory, and are incorporated into the existing body of knowledge.

The culminating activity of drawing conclusions and implications is in one sense the most important, because in essence this was the purpose for doing the research. Yet it is in this activity that many research studies are weak. Graduate students find writing the conclusions sections of theses or dissertations a difficult activity. (However, by no means is this difficulty unique to graduate students.) In the earlier steps, prescribed procedures seem to be followed and it is a matter of doing the tasks. But drawing conclusions requires interpretation, synthesis, and insights, activities that are difficult to specify as tasks. Evidence that drawing conclusions is difficult is the fact that many initial drafts of the final chapter of a dissertation, for example, read like a rewrite of the results chapter.

Although we cannot ensure that drawing conclusions will be insightful, there are suggestions to follow to improve this activity and enhance the value of the research. These suggestions are:

1. Know the area in which the research has been conducted—in essence, know what is in the research literature, not simply have a passing acquaintance.

2. Address the issue of the external validity of the research. (Internal validity should have been established earlier.) Discuss the generalizability of the results and do not hesitate to extend external validity on a logical basis. Make whatever reasonable case possible for generalizing the results. This typically requires a broader perspective than the variables and procedures of the study.

3. Focus on the meaning of the results rather than the results per se.

4. If theory is involved, either existing or if new theory was generated, show explicitly the correspondence between the results and the theory.

5. Search for consistencies between the results and results of other studies, and explain how these consistencies might extend the external validity of research in the area.

6. Search for inconsistencies between the results and results of similar studies, and identify factors that may be causing the inconsistencies.

7. Make the chain of reasoning evident by which the conclusions are reached—do not assume that the reader can read the writer's mind, at least initially; if an error is made, err on the side of overexplanation.

8. If possible, suggest future research that might address unresolved issues, and provide the next logical extension of knowledge.

9. Allow the results to "sit for a few days," that is, do not do anything with them. Then after a week or two, revisit the conclusions and see whether they are as apparent and as reasonable as they seemed earlier.

Summarizing results and drawing conclusions should reflect scholarship throughout. Of course, we want to avoid unwarranted conclusions, but we want to maximize the information from the research results. It is always a good procedure to have one's conclusions reviewed by one or more colleagues familiar with the research in the area.

The naive researcher may attempt to begin the research study by breaking into the sequence at a point such as data collection (a data collector in search of a research problem). Sometimes researchers formulate hypotheses on the basis of some data and then attempt to extract a problem from the hypotheses. Breaking the sequence in this manner tends to result in confusion and inefficiency. Certainly there is flexibility in the research process and there may be overlap and repetition of activities depending on the requirements of the specific research. However, adherence to the process as organized in Figure 1.4 tends to enhance the efficiency of conducting research.

Summary

This chapter provided an overview of the nature of educational research and introduced numerous concepts. In subsequent chapters, concepts and procedures will be expanded and described in detail. The intent of this chapter was to introduce the reader to educational research, thus providing the "big picture."

Three classification systems for educational research were described to give some notions of the breadth and variety in educational research. The terms *basic* and *applied research* have been around a long time and apply to the purpose of the research. Qualitative and quantitative research provide a dichotomy that has different underlying epistemologies and paradigms. That is, they represent different ways of "looking at the world." The third classification system was the general methods, and this system is useful because of the procedures associated with the methods. The purpose of the research dictates the type. Educational research can be put into the context of the scientific method; however, neither educational research nor the scientific method should be viewed as a rigid and invariable lockstep set of procedures.

The general activities of the research process were identified, described, and, in Figure 1.4, interrelated. Educational research involves many activities, some of which are simple, others complex. In fact, an entire continuum is encompassed, from simple to complex. Research is done in many different areas, such as curriculum, learning, and educational administration, to mention just a few. Research takes place at many different levels, from the individual action research conducted at the local school level, to large-scale projects conducted at universities or other agencies. Therefore, the description of educational research must be broad and must include many components. Even broad concepts, when projected into reality, are made up of specifics, however, and it is the specifics of research methods (activities, procedures, underlying reasoning, and so on) that are of major consideration in this text.

KEY CONCEPTS

- Systematic research
- Scientific method
- Internal validity
- External validity
- Reliability of research
- Applied research
- Basic research
- Action research
- Qualitative research
- Quantitative research
- Grounded theory
- Experimental research
- Quasi-experimental research
- Ex post facto research
- Survey research
- Historical research
- Ethnographic research
- Role of theory
- Law of parsimony

EXERCISES

1.1 Identify the primary difference between basic research and applied research.

1.2 Define internal and external validity of a research study.

1.3 Why is it true that if a research study is completely lacking in internal validity, it also lacks external validity?

1.4 For each of the following, identify which type of validity (internal or external) is most likely lacking:

a. An experimenter finds there are four equally plausible interpretations of the results.

b. The possible effects of different materials cannot be separated from the effects of the teachers who use them.

c. A sixth-grade teacher finds the results of a learning experiment do not apply to sixth-graders.

d. In an ethnographic research study for which multiple observers are used, the observers cannot agree on their conclusions.

1.5 Define reliability of research. Describe how reliability might be threatened in (a) an experiment involving four experimenters administering the experimental treatment at different times, and (b) a study of teacher performance using ten different observers.

1.6 What distinguishes an experiment from nonexperimental types of research?

1.7 What do we mean when we say that the general approach of qualitative research is that of inductive inquiry?

1.8 A critic of the schools in a large school system asserts that the procedures for evaluating principals and assistant principals of the system have no theoretical basis. Describe how a researcher would develop a grounded theory of principal evaluation in this system. What might be some of the components of the grounded theory?

1.9 Describe how the focus of historical research differs from that of ethnographic research.

1.10 Develop an argument against the position: "Theory is useless in educational research."

1.11 Use the internet to identify a report for (a) an ethnographic research study and (b) an experiment. Using the information of Table 1.1, identify the contrasting characteristics when comparing the two studies.

1.12 Describe some of the difficulties that would face a teacher who is attempting to conduct an action research study of the effect of using written praise on seventh-grade students' essays as compared to verbal praise.

1.13 Develop an argument either for or against the statement, "The most important step in the research process is the identification of the research problem."

1.14 The research agenda in a field of study often proceeds from descriptive studies, to finding correlates of some variable of interest, to experiments to determine cause-and-effect relationships. Describe three research studies that would follow that pattern on any subject that you choose. Suggested topics would be investigating the school dropout phenomenon, teacher recruitment incentives, and block scheduling.

NOTES

1. Some writers conceptualize validity into more than two concepts, but the two concepts of internal and external validity are adequate for an introductory discussion, and provide a useful distinction when conducting research and interpreting research results.
2. Statistical analyses are discussed later in the text, but it is useful to use some simple statistical concepts for illustration. The mean is a very common measure, and in this case it represents the average score of the class. This is the arithmetic mean, which is the sum of the test scores divided by the number of scores.
3. A *variable* is a characteristic that takes on different values (or conditions) for different individuals. Variables are described in greater detail in Chapter 2.

REFERENCES

Berliner, D. C. (2002). Educational research: The hardest science of all. *Educational Researcher, 31*, 18–20.

Feuer, M. J., Towne, L., and Shavelson, R. J. (2002). Scientific culture and educational research. *Educational Researcher, 31*, 4–14.

Kerlinger, F. N., and Lee, H. B. (2000). *Foundations of behavioral research* (4th ed.). Fort Worth, TX: Harcourt College Publishers.

Lancy, D. F. (1993). *Qualitative research in education: An introduction to the major traditions.* New York: Longman.

McMillan, J. H. (2003). *Educational research: Fundamentals for the consumer* (4th ed.). Boston: Allyn & Bacon.

McMillan, J. H., and Schumacher, S. (1997). *Research in education: A conceptual introduction* (4th ed.). New York: Longman.

Mertens, D. M. (2005). *Research and evaluation in education and psychology: Integrating diversity with quantitative, qualitative, and mixed methods.* Thousand Oaks, CA: Sage Publications.

Phillips, D. C. (2006). Muddying the waters: The many purposes of educational inquiry. In C. F. Conrad and R. C. Serlin (Eds.), *The Sage handbook for research in education: Engaging ideas and enriching inquiry.* Thousand Oaks, CA: Sage Publications.

Smith, M. L. (1987). Publishing qualitative research. *American Educational Research Journal, 24*, 173–183.

CHAPTER 2 Identification of a Research Problem

A good part of the research process deals with obtaining good answers—that is, solutions to research problems. However, the research process involves asking good questions or adequately identifying the problem or the phenomenon to be investigated. This may be a difficult step in the research process because at this point there has been little organization of the study. Adequate identification is necessary to get the research process under way. The extent of detail in problem identification may vary somewhat with the type of research. For example, experimental studies usually have very specific research problems with accompanying hypotheses, whereas ethnographic research has more general problem statements, and hypotheses may be generated throughout the study.

The identification of a research problem involves more than simply providing an ad hoc statement or question about the area of interest. The first step in the identification involves selecting a research topic. Then a specific statement of the problem is generated from the topic. If hypotheses are identified, these along with the statement of the problem involve the use of specific terminology about variables and conditions. Education, like any profession, has a professional language (parts of which are sometimes called jargon), and it is essential that meanings of terms in that language be consistent within the context of the research problem. In this chapter, numerous basic terms are defined, and it is important for the reader to understand those terms because they are part of the foundational language of educational research.

Selection of a Research Problem

The selection of an appropriate research problem is a matter of asking good questions—that is, questions that are relevant and important in the educational context. This general comment may seem reasonable enough, but there are many important educational issues to be researched at any given time. So, how does one go about selecting a research problem?

There are different ways by which research problems are selected, not all of them due to the internal motivation of the researcher, desirable as that may seem. Graduate students seeking research problems in order to complete the requirements for a graduate degree typically zero in on a research problem in one of two ways. They associate themselves closely with the research efforts of one or more professors serving as their mentors, and identify a related problem or one that comprises a subset of that research effort. The assumption is that the reason the students are studying with specific professors is because of mutual interests.

The second way is through discussions with other graduate students, some of whom are farther along in the graduate program and can provide insight into the selection process. Areas of research interest develop over time and when someone initially begins thinking about doing research, the process of selecting a research problem becomes one of successive approximations to defining the problem. A teacher who is in a graduate program may want to do research related to some aspect of classroom instruction. Discussing a possible research problem with colleagues and professors and becoming familiar with the area or topic help in identifying more specifically a researchable problem. But research problems, typically, are not identified overnight. They require becoming informed about a possible topic, thinking about it, and discussing it with others. Problems become modified and refined. Sometimes problems are expanded, sometimes restricted. A related but different direction may be taken. All of this is done to "zero in" on the problem.

Although the selection of a research problem may seem to be somewhat of a "broad" process as described above, there are certain factors that facilitate the process. The research problem should be *interesting* to the researcher and to at least some recognized segment of the education profession. Its place in the context of education should be assured. Originality should also be considered, especially if the research topic is being selected for a thesis, but a completely original research idea is rare. It is more likely that the research will be an extension of some already completed project. The extent of duplication or replication that is desirable in such studies depends on the specific area and the conditions of the research.

Another factor is that the research problem is *significant* for education from either a practical or a theoretical viewpoint. Trivial problems—for example, the percent of elementary students who wear laced or slip-on shoes and the relationship of this choice of footwear to achievement—can be researched procedurally. But such a problem has no theoretical framework and no significance, regardless of what the resulting proportions happen to be. Within recent years there has been an emphasis on school choice directed at improving education. Many research problems can be identified relative to the effects of school choice. A research problem should add to the existing knowledge or contribute to the educational process in a meaningful way.

Not all problems in education are *researchable.* Some are philosophical in nature and can be discussed but not researched. An example is a question such as, "Should the history requirement in the senior high school be one or two courses?" Chances are that if the requirement is two courses, the students will learn more history, but the question remains whether it is important that they have two courses. Answers to such questions are for the most part based on value judgments. If additional conditions are not stipulated, the questions are not researchable.

Even if problems are researchable, doing the research may not be *feasible.* The necessary data for the study may be excessive or may be too difficult to obtain. Ethical considerations may be involved; for example, the testing required to obtain the necessary data may be an invasion of the individual's privacy. Necessary resources, such as laboratory facilities and funds, may not be available. Many of these kinds of conditions can make it impractical to research a specific problem.

Colleges of education in universities often have specific research "thrusts," so to speak. Some colleges may have special interests in curriculum research, research related to mathematics instruction, for example. Others may have interests in teacher performance, policy development in higher education, or the effects of physical training programs, to mention three additional examples. These thrusts can be effective sources for research problems. But there are other sources. The researcher's professional experience and situation can suggest problems, especially in applied research. Current educational issues may generate any number of research problems as can social and political issues related to education. The research literature contains implications for continued research on a topic, and theories from education or disciplines related to education can suggest research problems. For example, organizational theory as applied to education requires research for testing the theory. In summary, research problems are selected in a context that includes multiple factors.

> The selection of a research problem involves reading, discussing, and conceptualizing. Typically, the process is one of successive approximations to the problem as factors related to the problem are considered.

Statement of the Research Problem

Selection of a research problem does not necessarily mean that it is adequately stated. Usually, a problem requires some reworking to get it into a suitable form for the study to proceed effectively. A problem may be stated broadly and then systematically restricted through a review of the literature in the initial stages of the research effort. It is better to work in this direction than to begin with a problem that is too narrow and then attach pieces to expand it.

Research problems may be stated in a declarative or descriptive manner or in question form. Many researchers, possibly the majority, prefer the question form, but either form is acceptable. The question form may aid in focusing the problem, and it is especially effective when subproblems are included within the larger research problem. The most important characteristic of the problem statement is that it must provide adequate focus and direction for the research.

At this point, it might be useful to illustrate some unsatisfactory and satisfactory problem statements. A statement such as "the elementary school curriculum" is far too broad to serve as a problem statement; in fact, it really contains no problem. A satisfactory statement might be: "A study of the effects of elementary school curriculum practices on the reading achievement of fourth-grade students in City A." Or, in question form, we might have: "What are the effects of elementary school curriculum practices on fourth-grade reading achievement in City A?" Following are several examples of original statements and their subsequent restatements into more manageable statements of the problem, including the question form:

Original Creativity of middle school students.

Restatement A study of the relationship between divergent thinking scores and selected characteristics of fifth-, sixth-, and seventh-grade students.

Question form What are the relationships between scores of fifth-, sixth-, and seventh-grade students on a divergent thinking test and scores on (1) a general IQ measure, (2) a reading achievement test, and (3) a measure of physical dexterity?

Original Achievement and teaching techniques.

Restatement A study of the effects of three teaching techniques on science achievement of junior high school students.

Question form Do three different teaching techniques have differing effects on science achievement scores of junior high school students?

Original High school dropouts.

Restatement An ethnographic study of the school environment of regular and learning disabled students to determine factors related to potential dropout.

Question form What factors of the school environment are related to the potential dropout of regular and learning disabled high school students?

Original A history of College A.

Restatement A study of the impact of federal aid to higher education on the expansion of the science and mathematics curriculums in College A during the period 1955–1972.

Question form What was the impact of federal aid on the expansion of the science and mathematics curriculums in College A during 1955–1972?

Original The role of the guidance counselor in the high school.

Restatement A survey of the practices of the guidance counselors in the high schools of City B.

Question form Four questions are given to illustrate the identification of subproblems:

What proportion of guidance counselors' working days is taken up with nonguidance activities?

What are the major strengths of guidance counselors' practices as perceived by the students?

What are the major weaknesses of guidance counselors' practices as perceived by the students?

What practices are perceived by guidance counselors as most effective in advising students about college selection?

A good statement of the problem should provide the researcher with direction in pursuing the research. The statement should indicate the general focus and the educational context of the problem. Key factors should be identified along with a general framework for reporting results. For example, in the first of the preceding restatements, the word *relationship* implies certain procedures and certain types of results. The three grade levels limit and define the population under study, and the term *divergent thinking scores* is certainly more specific than the word *creativity,* which was used in the original statement. Divergent thinking requires a definition such as the score on a specific divergent thinking test.

It should be noted that in the restatements of the problems, considerable definition of terms would be necessary. The selected characteristics in the first example would require identification and definition, and the three teaching techniques of the second example would require definition for the specific situation. Such definitions should accompany the statement of the problem, but they are usually not included in the statement because they would make it excessively long and cumbersome. Assuming that adequate definition accompanies the statement of the problem, there should be no ambiguity about what is to be investigated.

Whether or not research problems are stated in question form depends, to a large extent, on the preference of the researcher. If the question form appears to be helpful, it should be used. Actually, the form for stating the problem is relatively unimportant; what is important is that the statement be precise and definitive, so there is no confusion about what is under study.

It often helps in understanding the nature of the statement of the research problem to consider examples. Following is a list of problem statements, some in question form:

1. A survey of compensatory reading programs in selected school systems of Ohio.

2. What are the effects of cerebral, hemispheric overload on auditory and motor performance in young children?

3. An ethnographic study of science instruction in a girls' college-preparatory high school, grades nine through twelve.

4. What are the relationships between different types of praise and attitude toward school of students in a private elementary school?

5. A survey of the scholastic achievement of students from nine elementary schools entering Junior High School A.

6. What are the effects of age, type of material, and amount of available information on performance on a concept attainment task?

7. A survey of teacher evaluation practices in a four-state region.

8. A study of factors related to the extent of constructivist teaching in grades 1–4 of an elementary school.

9. A study of teacher perceptions of professional development activities offered by regional centers throughout Ohio.

10. A history of federal support for secondary school mathematics instruction offered by the National Science Foundation during the period 1955–1972.

> The statement of the research problem should be concise and should identify the key factors (variables) of the research study.

Constants, Variables, and Operational Definition

By itself, the statement of the problem usually provides only general direction for the research study; it does not include all the specific information. There is some basic terminology that is extremely important in how we communicate specific information about research problems and about research in general. A **constant** is a characteristic or condition that is the same for all individuals in a study. A **variable,** on the other hand, is a characteristic that takes on different values or conditions for different individuals. If a researcher is interested in the effects of two different teaching methods on the science achievement of fifth-grade students, the grade level is a constant, because all individuals involved are fifth-graders. This characteristic is the same for everyone; it is a constant condition of the study.

After the different teaching methods have been implemented, the fifth-graders involved would be measured with a science achievement test. It is very unlikely that all of the fifth-graders would receive the same score on this test, so the score on the science achievement test becomes a variable, because different individuals will have different scores; at least, not all individuals will have the same scores. We would say that science achievement is a variable, but we would mean, specifically, that the score on the science achievement test is a variable.

> A *constant* is a characteristic or condition that is the same for all individuals in a study. A *variable* is a characteristic that takes on different values or conditions for different individuals.

There is another variable in the example above—the teaching method. In contrast to the science achievement test score, which undoubtedly would be measured on a scale with many possible values, teaching method is a categorical variable consisting of only two categories, the two methods. So, we have different kinds of variables and different names or classifications for them. There are many classification systems given in the literature—so many that there is considerable overlap and opportunity for confusion. The names we use are descriptive; they describe the roles that variables play in a research study. The variables described below by no means exhaust the different systems and names that exist, but they are the most useful for communicating about educational research.

Independent and Dependent Variables. Most of the variables in a research study can be identified as independent or dependent variables. The terminology comes from mathematics. In a general sense, it is said that the values of the dependent variable in some way depend on the independent variables.

Dependent variables are the **outcome variables** and are the variables for which we calculate statistics. For example, in a study of the effect of teacher praise on the reading achievement of second-graders, the dependent variable is reading achievement. We might compare the average reading achievement scores of second-graders in different praise conditions such as no praise, oral praise, written praise, and combined oral and written praise. Dependent variables can also be considered the **predicted variables** in a study. The researcher might attempt to predict reading achievement scores from age, gender, free or reduced lunch status, and number of absences. Reading achievement would again be the dependent variable.

There are several kinds of **independent variables.** In the example above about the effect of praise, the researcher is trying to determine whether there is a cause-and-effect relationship, so the kind of praise is varied to see whether it produces different scores on the reading achievement test. We call this a **manipulated independent variable.** The amount and kind of praise is manipulated by the researcher. The researcher could analyze the scores for boys and girls separately to see whether the results are the same for both genders. In this case gender is a **classifying independent variable.** The researcher cannot manipulate gender, but can classify the children according to gender. Finally, in the study to predict reading achievement from student characteristics, the **predictor variables** are the independent variables.

The following example further illustrates the use of variables and constants. In a study conducted to determine the effect of three different teaching methods on achievement in elementary algebra, each of three ninth-grade algebra sections in the same school, taught by the same teacher, is taught using one of the methods. Both boys and girls are included in the study. The constants in the study are grade level, school, and teacher. (This assumes that, except for method, the teacher can hold teaching effectiveness constant.) The independent variables in the study are teaching method and gender of the student. Teaching method has three levels that arbitrarily can be designated methods A, B, and C; gender of the student, of course, has two levels. Achievement in algebra, as measured at the end of the instructional period, is the dependent variable.

Consider other examples of independent and dependent variables:

Example 1: A study of teacher–student classroom interaction in different levels of schooling.

Independent variable: Level of schooling, four categories—primary, intermediate, junior high school, senior high school.

Dependent variable: Score on a classroom observation inventory, which measures teacher–student interaction.

Example 2: A study of the effect of the location of a school upon attitudes toward school of seventh-grade students.

Independent variable: Location of school, three categories—urban, suburban, rural.

Dependent variable: Score on an attitude toward school inventory.

Example 3: A study of the effects of type of material on solving concept attainment problems.

Independent variable: Type of material, two categories—figural, verbal.

Dependent variable: Time required to solve the concept attainment problems.

Example 4: A study of the professional attitudes of men and women teachers.

Independent variable: Gender of the teacher—male, female.

Dependent variable: Score on a professional attitude inventory.

Independent and dependent variables are descriptors of variables commonly used in educational research. The independent variables may be affecting the dependent variables, and in that sense, dependent variables depend on independent variables.

Other Types of Variables. There are other kinds of variables that are frequently referred to in the research literature. A **control variable** is an independent variable other than the independent variable of primary interest whose effects are determined by the researcher. It is included in the analysis in order to get a clearer picture of the effects of the primary independent variable. For example, suppose that a researcher wants to determine the effects of an after-school tutoring program on the mathematics achievement of elementary school children. We know that current achievement is predictable from prior achievement, so it would be wise for the researcher to build prior achievement into the research design as a control variable. Students could be classified into three levels of prior achievement, such as below the 34th percentile, between the 34th and 66th percentiles, and above the 66th percentile on a nationally normed test. Then the analysis could separate the impact of the after-school tutoring program from the impact of prior achievement. Prior achievement is controlled because it is built into the research design.

A **moderator variable** is an independent variable that is not of primary interest that has levels, which when combined with the levels of the independent variable of interest produces different effects. For example, suppose that the researcher designs a study to determine the impact of the lengths of reading passages on the comprehension of the reading passage. The design has three levels of passage length: 100 words, 200 words, and 300 words. The participants in the study are fourth-, fifth-, and sixth-graders. Suppose that the three grade levels all did very well on the 100-word passage, but only the sixth-graders did very well on the 300-word passages. This would mean that successfully comprehending reading passages of different lengths was moderated by grade level.

Note that if grade level were built into the research design, we could also call it a control variable. However, if it were not built into the design, it would be a **confounded variable,** that is, a condition where the effects of two independent variables cannot be separated. The scores on the reading comprehension measure would be a function of both passage length and grade level, and we could not tell how much of the effect were due to each of the variables.

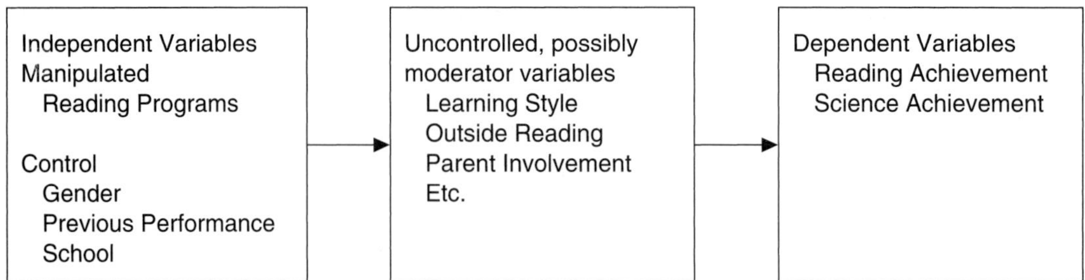

FIGURE 2.1 Different Types of Variables Operating in a Fifth-Grade Achievement Study

Research studies rarely include only one independent variable and one dependent variable. A more typical study would be the following: Suppose a study is done on the effects of three reading programs on fourth-grade reading achievement. The study is done in five schools that are in the same school district. The students' reading achievement scores are grouped by previous performance (high, average, and low) and by gender (boys and girls). The study is later expanded to include the impact on science achievement as well. The variables are summarized in Figure 2.1.

Operational Definition. In any research study, the variables and conditions of the study must be defined operationally. Educators often deal with variables that do not readily manifest themselves. If a school nurse were interested in the weights of first-grade pupils, they could be measured using a common weight scale. Similarly, if we want to measure and quantify ability to learn or reading comprehension, we must have some tool to do so. Perhaps we could set up a chain of definition for ability to learn and thus reach a consensus. But to achieve measurement, we must include the processes or operations that are going to be used to measure the phenomenon or variable under study. Such a definition is called an **operational definition.** In essence, an operational definition of a variable describes how or by what means we are going to measure the variable.

Operational definitions are not only desirable in educational research, they are essential. They define how the variables are measured. We know that creativity is a variable among school-age children, and all people for that matter. But creativity cannot be measured until it has an operational definition. There may be more than one operational definition of a variable such as creativity and herein lies another value of operational definitions. They enable researchers to identify similarities and differences in research studies on the same topic or issue. Some variables are measured in different ways and thus may lead to apparent contradictions in research results. Anxiety is a phenomenon that can take on different operational definitions. If anxiety is defined as the score on a paper-and-pencil test, its relationship to other variables (for example, test performance) may be very different than if it is defined as a galvanic skin response. So, operational definitions provide for the replication of studies and they enhance the interpretations of results. Operational definitions aid in establishing the external validity (or lack of it) of research results, by helping define the limits for generalization.

The following are examples of operational definitions:

1. Ability to learn: score on the LM Form of the Stanford-Binet Intelligence Scale.

2. Science achievement: score on the science subtest on the Iowa Test of Basic Skills.

3. Divergent thinking: score on the Brick Uses Test.

4. Concept attainment performance: time required to solve correctly five concept attainment problems.

Conditions or characteristics of a research study may also require operational definition. For example, if high school seniors are to be surveyed, who is a high school senior? A possible operational definition of a senior is a student who is presently enrolled in a recognized high school, has not yet graduated, but has earned twelve or more high school course credits. In this case, a senior is defined in terms of certain observable or identifiable characteristics.

> An *operational definition* is stipulative in that it specifies the operation or characteristics necessary to identify the variable or condition being defined.

Hypotheses and the Statement of the Problem

Now that the concepts of variables, constants, and operational definitions have been described, we can continue with the elaboration of the specifics of the research study through the use of hypotheses. Attempting to include all specific information in the statement of the problem would make the statement cumbersome and unmanageable, so hypotheses may be developed to provide more specificity and direction. What is the source of hypotheses? They may be derived directly from the statement of the problem, they may be based on the research literature, or in some cases, such as in ethnographic research, they may (at least in part) be generated from data collection and analysis. Ethnographic research also involves foreshadowed problems which, although they are not hypotheses, are statements of what to look for in doing the research. Foreshadowed problems are not replacements for hypotheses, but in ethnographic research they are supplemental to hypotheses and certainly provide direction for the research.

A **hypothesis** is a conjecture or a guess at the solution to a problem or the status of the situation. In a general sense, hypotheses take on some of the characteristics of a theory, which is usually considered a larger set of generalizations about a certain phenomenon. Thus, a theory might include several hypotheses. Logically, the approach is to proceed so a decision can be made about whether or not the hypotheses are tenable. This is called testing the hypothesis; the results of such a test either support or refute the hypothesis.

What are the characteristics of hypotheses? There should be a definite reason for the hypothesis, either from a theory or from some evidence that this is a useful and valuable hypothesis. Typically, a hypothesis states a relationship or effect between variables, and this should be done in as straightforward and clear a manner as possible. Finally, a hypothesis should be testable; indeed, much of research is directed toward testing hypotheses.

A weakness of many hypotheses is that they are too broad to pinpoint the specific problem under study—as, for example, in the following hypothesis: "Bright students have good attitudes toward school." The terms *bright, good,* and *attitudes* represent types of broad, undefined generalities. Some type of vague relationship between brightness and good attitude is implied, but little direction for research is provided. To convert the statement into an acceptable hypothesis, it might be changed to read:

> Students aged nine through eleven who score in the upper 25 percent of their class on the (standardized) IQ test have a higher mean score on the "X-Y-Z Attitude Toward School Inventory" than students who score in the lower 75 percent of the class on the IQ test.

Note that this statement has specificity and that it states an expected relationship (the upper 25 percent on the IQ test have higher mean attitude scores than the lower 75 percent on the IQ test). Assuming that the measurement can be made, the hypothesis is testable.

Another version could be:

> A positive relationship exists between the scores on the (specific) IQ test and the (specific) attitude inventory for students aged nine through eleven.

This statement of the hypothesis is shorter than the initial statement. It includes an expected relationship and it is testable.

In both instances, the hypothesis contains the operational definitions of the variables involved: academic aptitude (brightness) and attitude toward school. These variables are defined by scores on a specific test and a specific inventory. If the operational definitions make the statement of the hypothesis too cumbersome, they can be presented in a separate statement or section. However, the variables should be clearly identified so that the expected relationship is defined—that is, that it will be positive or that the mean of a certain group will be higher than that of another group. The hypothesis is testable; that is, procedures exist for analyzing the data that will give results either supporting or refuting the hypothesis. (However, the two versions presented here would be tested in different ways.) The hypothesis declares the anticipated direction; supposedly, this is not just a wild guess. Assuming that there are reasons that make the hypothesis worthy of testing, then the hypothesis has the desirable characteristics.

> A *hypothesis* is a conjecture or proposition about the solution to a problem, the relationship of two or more variables, or the nature of some phenomenon.

Types and Forms of Hypotheses

Kerlinger and Lee (2000, p. 279) indicate that, in a broad sense, researchers use two types of hypotheses—substantive and statistical. **Substantive hypotheses,** sometimes called

research hypotheses, are tentative statements about the expected outcomes for the variables of the research study. An example of a substantive or research hypothesis is, "As punitive, disciplinary methods are increased in an elementary school, student achievement will decrease." In research in science education, a hypothesis might be: "Laboratory instruction enhances the student's understanding of scientific processes over an instructional approach limited to lecture, discussion, and theoretical problem solution." Notice that the research hypothesis is a directional hypothesis—that is, it indicates the expected direction of the results. The direction is implied by theory or previous research. The hypothesis would not indicate the expected direction of the results in exploratory studies where there is no strong rationale for an expected direction.

When it is time to test whether the data support or refute the research hypothesis, it needs to be translated into a statistical hypothesis.

A **statistical hypothesis** is given in statistical terms. Technically, in the context of inferential statistics, it is a statement about one or more parameters that are measures of the populations under study. Statistical hypotheses often are given in quantitative terms, for example: "The mean reading achievement of the population of third-grade students taught by Method A equals the mean reading achievement of the population taught by Method B."

Let us explain the general form of **statistical hypotheses**[1] further. First, they are concerned with populations. We will use inferential statistics, which are explained in Chapter 17, to draw conclusions about population values even though we have access to only a sample of participants. We may have only fifty students in Method A and fifty students in Method B in our research study, but if the students are randomly representative of the population of third-graders, our conclusions can be statistically projected to all third-graders.

In order to use inferential statistics, we need to translate the research hypothesis into a testable form, which is called the **null hypothesis,** and to generate an **alternative hypothesis.** An alternative hypothesis indicates the situation corresponding to when the null hypothesis is not true. The stated hypothesis will differ depending on whether or not it is a directional research hypothesis.

The null hypothesis states that the population parameter equals some value, such as the population mean on some test equals 85. The corresponding **nondirectional research hypothesis** is that the population mean does not equal 85. Note that this allows for the population mean to be greater than 85 or less than 85. The following example illustrates a nondirectional research hypothesis when two group means are compared.

Nondirectional Research Hypothesis

Null: The mean reading achievement of the population of third-grade students taught by Method A equals the mean reading achievement of the population taught by Method B.

Alternative: The mean reading achievement of the population of third-grade students taught by Method A does not equal the mean reading achievement of the population taught by Method B.

Using a **directional research hypothesis** requires some small but important changes. The alternative hypothesis indicates the direction of the expected result and the null hypothesis contains all other possible outcomes. Consider the earlier example, when the null hypothesis was that the population mean is 85. Suppose that the research hypothesis is that the population mean is greater than 85. The null hypothesis would now state that the population mean is equal to or less than 85. The example below presents the hypotheses for a comparison of two group means when one of the means is expected to exceed the other.

Directional Research Hypothesis

Null: The mean reading achievement of the population of third-grade students taught by Method A equals or is less than the mean reading achievement of the population taught by Method B.

Alternative: The mean reading achievement of the population of third-grade students taught by Method A is greater than the mean reading achievement of the population taught by Method B.

The null and alternative hypotheses include all possible outcomes of the research study. The mean for Method A may turn out to be equal to, greater than, or less than the mean of Method B, and the statistical hypotheses allow for any of those outcomes.

Consider additional examples of hypotheses and their alternatives:

1. The mathematics achievement of high-ability students equals that of average-ability students, or there is no difference between the mathematics achievement of average- and high-ability students.

1a. The mathematics achievement of high-ability students is not equal to that of average-ability students.

2. The reading level of first-grade girls is the same as that of boys.

2a. The reading level of first-grade girls is not equal to that of boys.

3. Science achievement of students taught by inductive inquiry exceeds that of those taught by deductive inquiry.

3a. The science achievement of students taught by inductive inquiry is less than or equal to those taught by deductive inquiry.

4. There is a positive relationship between academic aptitude scores and scores on a social adjustment inventory for junior high school age students.

4a. There is a negative relationship or no relationship between academic aptitude scores and scores on a social adjustment inventory for junior high school age students.

5. Males, ages eighteen through twenty years, participating in Exercise Program A will have greater mean scores on the XY Physical Performance Test, than those participating in Exercise Program B.

5a. Males, ages eighteen through twenty years, participating in Exercise Program A will have mean scores on the XY Physical Performance Test, less than or equal to the mean scores of those participating in Exercise Program B.

Should hypotheses be stated in directional or nondirectional form—or does it make any difference? The form used should be determined by the expected results. If the research literature in the area indicates that we can expect a difference or a direction of results, a directional hypothesis is called for; if the research literature does not present convincing evidence for a direction, or if an exploratory study is being done, a nondirectional hypothesis should be used. Because of the emphasis on null hypotheses in inferential statistics, educational research—and behavioral sciences research in general—has probably overused the nondirectional hypothesis and underused the directional hypothesis.

> *Statistical hypotheses* are used in the analysis of data; *substantive* or *research hypotheses* indicate the direction of results. Hypotheses may be stated in *directional* or *nondirectional* form. The null hypothesis is the hypothesis of no difference or no relationship.

These comments about hypotheses apply more to quantitative research than qualitative research. In quantitative research, hypotheses typically are identified at the beginning of the research study, prior to data collection, and if modified such modification is minimal. On the other hand, hypotheses in qualitative research are much more likely to emerge as the research is being conducted. There may or may not be some tentative, general hypotheses at the outset, but qualitative researchers are very willing to add, delete, modify, and refine hypotheses as data are collected and analyzed. Hypotheses in qualitative research are conjectures, but there is not much concern whether they are directional or null hypotheses. Their wording fits the context of the phenomenon under study.

Foreshadowed problems were mentioned earlier as statements, usually associated with ethnographic research, that supplement hypotheses, at least to get the research underway. Consider the research problem statement given earlier: "An ethnographic study of the school environment of regular and learning disabled students to determine factors related to potential dropout." Examples of foreshadowed problems associated with this statement are:

1. Interaction among regular and learning disabled students during instruction.
2. Role of the teacher in enhancing student learning.
3. Student social systems.
4. Opportunities for student success in the academic subjects.

Note that the foreshadowed problems do not specify anticipated results. Essentially, they identify factors for the researcher to observe as the research gets under way.

Although hypotheses have an important role in educational research and they appear in many studies, all research is not done for the purpose of testing hypotheses. Sometimes, especially in exploratory studies, the nature and characteristics of the data are analyzed without specific hypotheses. In some research, population values may be estimated rather than tested for specific hypotheses about these values. For example, suppose a question in a research study is, "What is the average physical performance level of young adult males on Text XYZ?" If a sample of young adult males is tested, the sample data would be used to obtain estimates of the population average, rather than to test specific hypotheses about that average.

Examples of Hypotheses Related to Problem Statements. A statement of a research problem may have one or more (usually more) hypotheses associated with it. Hypotheses are formulated from the research problem statement and should follow directly from it. Each of the following examples provides a problem statement, hypotheses, and operational definitions or comments on the operational definitions of the variables or conditions. The ethnographic research example (Example 2.3) contains foreshadowed problems, as examples of the phenomenon focused on by the researcher. Two example hypotheses are given, although if there were no basis for hypothesizing about the nature of the phenomenon under study, there would be no initial hypotheses. Example variables are given but they are not categorized as to type. Because ethnographic research takes a holistic and descriptive approach rather than a cause-and-effect approach, we would not be concerned about the distinction between independent and dependent variables. There are not likely to be any control variables in ethnographic research, but there would be many uncontrolled variables, such as the elementary school science backgrounds of the students.

The hypotheses of Example 2.1 are stated in directional form. In Example 2.2, both types of hypothesis are used. Both forms can be used, although a single form is sometimes preferred for consistency.

Example 2.2 would apply to action research, if it were conducted by the third-grade teachers in a single school to help them make a decision about which program to use in the school. Note that the dependent variable in this example is gain score in reading achievement, not simply reading achievement score. To determine gain scores, prior reading achievement scores must be known; therefore, prior reading achievement could be a control variable.

To illustrate the different types of variables discussed earlier in the chapter, the variables are listed and operationally defined as necessary. In each example, the hypotheses, operational definitions, and variables follow directly from the statement of the problem.

EXAMPLE 2.1

Problem Statement

A survey of grading practices and patterns in academic areas of the senior high schools in Ohio.

Hypotheses

1. Average grades in the science areas of chemistry and physics are higher than those in biology and earth science.

2. Average grades in history and other social studies are higher than those in biological and physical sciences.

3. Average grades in advanced mathematics (second-year algebra and beyond) are higher than those in introductory algebra and consumer mathematics.

4. There is a positive relationship between grades received in English courses and those received in foreign language courses.

5. There is a positive relationship between grades received in Algebra II and those received in chemistry.

6. Average grades for courses in academic areas are higher as the size of the high school increases.

Operational Definitions

Academic areas: Sciences, mathematics, English, social studies, history, and foreign languages.

Senior high school: Grades 10, 11, and 12 of any accredited high school in Ohio.

Grades: The possible categories of the letter grading system A, B, C, and so forth, which may be converted to numerical scores.

Size of high school: Total enrollment in grades 10–12; categories are: less than 200 students, 200–499, 500–799, 800–1099, 1100, and greater.

Independent Variables	*Dependent Variables*
Academic areas	Grades
Specific courses in certain areas	Grading patterns/proportions of grades by category
Size of high school	

Possible Control Variables

Type of school

Gender of the student

Location of school

EXAMPLE 2.2

Problem Statement

A study of the effects of two reading programs (A and B) on the reading achievement of third-grade students in School A.

Hypotheses

1. With students of heterogeneous reading achievement, there will be no difference in the mean gains in reading achievement for students taught by Program A and those taught by Program B.

2. For students scoring in the lower 30 percent on prior reading achievement, those taught by Program A will have a greater mean gain than those taught by Program B.

3. For students scoring in the upper 30 percent on prior reading achievement, those taught by Program B will have a greater mean gain than those taught by Program A.

4. For students scoring in the middle 40 percent on prior reading achievement, there will no difference in mean gains for students taught by Program A and those taught by Program B.

Operational Definitions

Individuals included in the study: All third-graders of School A.

Program A: The set of reading materials purchased from Publisher Y and its suggested activities.

Program B: The set of reading materials purchased from Publisher Z and its suggested activities.

Independent Variable	***Dependent Variable***
Reading program—A and B	Gain score in reading achievement—for example, the difference between scores on two forms of a standardized reading test, one form given prior to the study, the second form given after the study

Possible Moderator Variables	***Possible Control Variables***
Teacher	Prior reading achievement
Teaching style	Gender of the student
Learning style	
Student scholastic ability	

EXAMPLE 2.3

Problem Statement

An ethnographic study of the functions of laboratory work in science instruction for junior high school students in School A.

Foreshadowed Problems

1. The interaction among students as laboratory work takes place.
2. The interaction between students and teacher during laboratory work.
3. Student and teacher preparation for laboratory work.
4. The relationship between laboratory work and other aspects of science instruction.

Hypotheses

1. A function of laboratory work is to have students participate in a cooperative activity.
2. More academically able students will monopolize the control of the laboratory work.

Operational Definitions

Participating in the study: All students enrolled in science courses in School A.

Science instruction: All courses including as their emphasis instruction in physical, earth, or biological sciences; the general science and the earth science courses in School A.

Laboratory work: Any activity in which the student is directly involved (either singly or with other students) in conducting experiments, manipulating scientific apparatus, dissecting biological specimens, and so on.

Variables: The functions of laboratory work.

Types of interaction taking place during laboratory work.

Extent of laboratory work.

Type of laboratory work, for example, dissecting animals, physics experiment, and materials analysis.

The timing of laboratory work relative to other instruction in science.

The preceding examples have not exhausted the numbers of possible hypotheses, which depend on the extent and conditions of the research study. In identifying the variables, possible intervening variables are listed. Note that gender is a possible control variable in Example 2.2 and a possible intervening variable in Example 2.1. That is because in Example 2.2 any differential performance between males and females would be determined, whereas in Example 2.1, if there is an effect of gender, it is not separated from the effects of other variables.

Examples from the Research Literature. At this point it is useful to consider a couple of examples of research problem statements and related hypotheses from the research literature. In a study of the effects of a supplemental vocabulary program for third-graders, the *Elements of Reading: Vocabulary,* Apthorp (2006) identified her research problem as follows:

> The challenge for educators to reduce or prevent large achievement gaps is getting children on the right trajectory of vocabulary growth and reading development and helping them maintain that growth. (p. 68)

The author describes the *Elements of Reading: Vocabulary* as a means of addressing this problem and presents three hypotheses in question form.

1. What is the effect of *Elements of Reading: Vocabulary* on classroom practices for teaching vocabulary in reading and language arts?

2. What is the effect of *Elements of Reading: Vocabulary* on children's oral and sight vocabulary?

3. What is the effect of *Elements of Reading: Vocabulary* on children's reading achievement?

The independent variable in this study is the supplemental vocabulary program, specifically the *Elements of Reading: Vocabulary.* There are several dependent variables, or outcomes, that the instructional program was expected to affect: teachers' classroom practices and students' oral vocabulary, sight vocabulary, and reading achievement. Operational definitions for general terms such as *classroom practices* and *reading achievement* are provided elsewhere in the article. The hypotheses are nondirectional. They do not indicate the expected direction of the outcomes, although it would be inconceivable that the researcher would go to all this trouble to conduct a study in which the independent variable were expected to have no impact or a negative impact.

In a study of the relationship between reading problems of adolescents and suicidality and dropping out of school, Daniel et al. (2006) stated their research problem as:

> Therefore, the purpose of this study was to examine the rates and interrelationship of suicidal behaviors and school dropout among youth with poor single word reading ability in comparison to youth with typical reading ability recruited from public schools at age 15. (p. 508)

The authors listed three specific hypotheses that their study addressed. These hypotheses are directional and the directionality had previously been supported in the review of the literature. They further explained the hypotheses by indicating potentially confounding variables that they controlled by the research design or the statistical analysis.

1. Adolescents with poor reading abilities will evidence higher rates of suicidal ideation and suicide attempts over time than adolescents with typical reading abilities. These differences will be apparent after controlling for demographic variables—age, race/ethnicity, socioeconomic status (SES), and gender—and selected psychiatric disorders (e.g., major depressive disorder, conduct and oppositional defiant disorders, and substance use disorders).

2. Adolescents with poor reading abilities will evidence higher rates of school dropout than adolescents with typical reading abilities. These differences will also be apparent after controlling for demographic variables and psychiatric disorders.

3. School dropout will be significantly related to suicidality. This relationship will persist after controlling for demographic variables and psychiatric disorders. (p. 508)

The researchers are looking for relationships among the variables. They are trying to determine whether reading ability, the independent variable, is predictive of suicidality and school dropout, the dependent variables. They strengthened the internal validity of the study by controlling for several demographic variables and psychiatric disorders that are potential alternative explanations for the relationships among the variables. In other words, for example, if they found a strong association between reading ability and suicidality, someone might argue that the relationship really is due to a psychiatric variable such as depression. The critic would say that students who are depressed have lower reading abilities and think about suicide more often. However, by controlling for depressive disorders, the relationship between reading ability and suicidality is not confounded and can be interpreted with confidence.

Note that the third hypothesis uses the word *significantly* when describing the relationship. Strictly speaking, if the researchers are referring to statistical significance, they should use the word *significant* when talking about results from a sample that is taken from a population and not use the term when talking about results for a population. Hypotheses are written about populations. The point is that the researchers should not have used the word *significantly* in the third hypothesis. The reasons why will be clarified in Chapter 17 on inferential statistics.

Summary

This chapter has discussed the identification of a research problem from the initial selection of a problem through the process of generating a workable research problem statement, elaborated with related hypotheses and operational definitions of variables and conditions. It was implied that researchers select research problems in different ways. Certainly, there should be interest in an area of research and internal motivation to pursue the research, but external factors, too, influence the selection of a problem.

The various components for identifying a research problem are connected and their interrelationships can be summarized as in Figure 2.2. The statement of the problem is the springboard for developing the hypotheses, or in the case of ethnographic research, possibly foreshadowed problems in addition to or in lieu of hypotheses. Hypotheses then lead into doing the research. The process of generating hypotheses not only defines the problem more specifically but also can effectively limit the research problem. Hypotheses are stated in the context of variables, operational definitions, and conditions. All of this is done on a base of relevant theory and existing knowledge. Research problems are not identified and pursued in an informational vacuum. They have a place in the educational world—either theoretically or practically, or both.

Hypotheses are not ends in themselves; rather, they are aids in the research process. Occasionally, a report of a research project may seem short on hypotheses. Possibly the researcher was working in an area with very little background information, or perhaps considerable theory development was necessary. In qualitative research, for example, initial hypotheses are often general and limited in number; as the research progresses, however, new hypotheses are generated and prior hypotheses may be revised, retained, or discarded. To the extent possible, hypotheses should be stated concisely and used as the framework for the research.

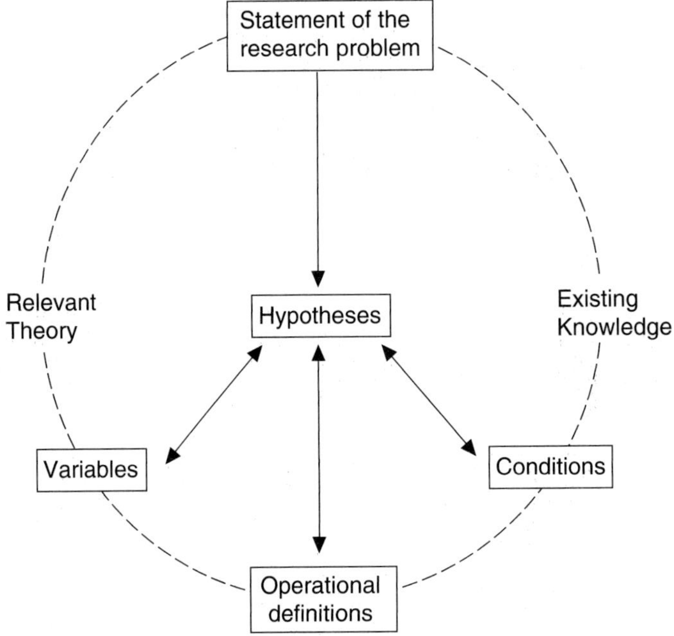

FIGURE 2.2 Connections between the Components for Identifying a Research Problem

The concepts of variables, constants, and operational definition were described in this chapter, but these concepts are used not only when identifying the problem but also throughout the research process. These are extremely important concepts, because they are part of the basic language of research.

The next chapter discusses the review of literature. The placement of the discussion of the review is somewhat arbitrary; it could have appeared before the discussion about identifying the problem, because some review often is done before the problem statement is refined and put into final form. However, the researcher must have some idea of what to look for, so the problem usually is identified before doing any extensive review of the literature.

KEY CONCEPTS

Constant
Variable
Independent variable
Dependent variable
Outcome variable
Predicted variable
Manipulated independent variable
Classifying independent variable
Predictor variable
Control variable
Moderator variable
Confounded variable
Operational definition
Hypothesis
Substantive hypothesis
Research hypothesis
Statistical hypothesis
Null hypothesis
Alternative hypothesis
Nondirectional hypothesis
Directional hypothesis
Foreshadowed problems

EXERCISES

2.1 A study is conducted to determine the effects of three sets of instructional materials on fourth-grade reading achievement. Three random samples of fourth-grade boys are selected within the same school. These three groups are then taught by three different teachers, each teaching only one group and using one set of instructional materials. At the end of ten weeks of instruction, the students are tested on reading achievement. Identify the constant(s), independent variable(s), and dependent variable(s) of this study. Identify possible moderator variables that might be operating in this situation.

2.2 Suppose that, in the study described in Exercise 2.1, the instructional materials are used with six classes each of fourth- and fifth-graders. Both boys and girls are included. The study is conducted at two different schools using three classes of each grade level in each school, each class being taught with a different set of materials. Identify the possible control variable(s) that are now included.

2.3 The problem statement of the study in Exercise 2.2 might be: "A study of the effects of different instructional materials on the reading achievement of fourth- and fifth-graders." Using the variables identified in the first two exercises, develop two or more related hypotheses. The hypotheses may be stated in directional or nondirectional form.

2.4 Suppose an ethnographic research study is to be done on the nature of social behavior of children in a racially integrated kindergarten. Develop four or more foreshadowed problems related to this research. If appropriate, develop one or more hypotheses that might be tested in this study.

2.5 What is the difference between hypotheses stated in a nondirectional or null form and those stated in a directional form?

2.6 A science educator is interested in doing research on whether or not a constructivist approach to science teaching improves science achievement of high school students over other approaches. Would it be more appropriate to use directional or nondirectional hypotheses in this situation? Why? Suppose the research is planned for the biology, chemistry, and physics classes in a single high school with at least two classes in each subject. Identify independent and dependent variables for this situation. For those variables identified, provide operational definitions. Identify one or more constants and one or more possible control variables.

2.7 Suppose a researcher is interested in doing a study on the effects of "online classroom" instruction on scholastic performance of elementary school students. What terms would require operational definitions? Provide examples of operational definitions for these terms.

2.8 For each of the following research problem statements, develop two or more related hypotheses, identify the different possible variables by type, and provide operational definitions for those identified. There is some flexibility in responding to those statements, but please identify any assumptions or special conditions.

a. A survey of parent perceptions of the four elementary schools in a suburban school system.

b. An ethnographic study of the role of the counselor in a large middle school serving inner-city students. You may identify foreshadowed problems in addition to, or in lieu of, hypotheses.
c. A study of the effects of three physical training programs upon the upper-body strength of senior boys in high school.

2.9 A researcher was interested in determining whether physical education should be required in grades 2–6 in a local school district. Write a researchable problem statement related to this issue.

2.10 Statistical analysis revealed that students' test anxiety was negatively correlated with test performance. That is, those with higher levels of test anxiety had lower performance levels on tests. Write a hypothesis that would allow you to decide whether higher test anxiety caused lower test scores. This may require that you imagine an experiment involving these variables.

2.11 A principal hypothesized that student reading achievement was related to parental interest in reading, students' vocabulary size, and the type of reading material that students preferred to read. What is the problem with a hypothesis like this that includes several independent variables in the same hypothesis?

2.12 Use Research Navigator to select a research article from a professional journal. Read the article and try to identify the statement of the problem and any hypothesis that may be tested in the study. Are the variables explicitly identified, and are operational definitions provided when needed?

NOTES

1. The use of statistical hypotheses, including the null hypothesis, is discussed in greater detail in Chapter 17.

REFERENCES

Apthorp, H. S. (2006). Effects of a supplemental vocabulary program in third-grade reading/language arts. *Journal of Educational Research, 100,* 67–71.

Daniel, S. S., Walsh, A. K., Goldston, D. B., Arnold, E. M., Reboussin, B. A., and Wood, F. B. (2006). Suicidality, school dropout, and reading problems among adolescents. *Journal of Learning Disabilities, 39,* 507–514.

Kerlinger, F. N., and Lee, H. B. (2000). *Foundations of behavioral research* (4th ed.). Fort Worth, TX: Harcourt College Publishers.

CHAPTER

3 The Review of the Literature

The selection of the research problem is undoubtedly based to some extent on the literature. It would not be a sufficiently significant problem if it had not ever surfaced in the professional literature. The review of literature is a step in the research process that positions the research problem within the context of the literature as a whole.

A research topic such as school vouchers, for example, would be found in the popular literature such as newspapers and magazines. It would also be found in the professional literature in books, journal articles, and papers presented at professional meetings. The researcher's task is to select relevant sources, to describe the different positions on the issues, and to summarize what is currently known on the topic. Both research articles and opinion pieces will be included when the topic is at all controversial. This is the step in the research process that educates the researcher about the research problem to such an extent that the researcher becomes an authority on the subject.

There are two major parts when reviewing the literature, each with several subparts. The first is the selection of the specific pieces in the literature that will be included in the review of the literature. The second is the actual writing of the review. This chapter is organized around these two activities.

Conducting a Search of the Literature

There are two commonly used approaches to selecting sources from the literature. One is to go straight to the Internet and the second is to go straight to the library. Fortunately, it is usually the case that the library resources are on the Internet. First, let us look at a beginner's search of the Internet.

This can be a frustrating and overwhelming experience because of the sheer volume of information. A search using Yahoo, Google, or another search engine will produce more sources than can be used in a lifetime. Note these results, for example:

Teacher unions	1,360,000 sources
Dropout prevention	1,090,000 sources
Reading instruction	30,000,000 sources

Each site is often linked to other sites, so the pattern of a search can be dictated by links that are in place. Some excellent sites will be found, but many will not be useful. This kind of random walk through the literature is not very systematic and will end when the researcher reaches a point of exhaustion. The results are not likely to be very satisfactory.

This is not to say that the Internet does not offer invaluable information and statistical data to the researcher. It's just that the researcher needs to know which sites to visit. For example, a wealth of data is now available at such websites as: http://nces.ed.gov/ipeds for the Integrated Postsecondary Education Data System, http://nces.ed.gov/timss for the Trends in International Mathematics and Science Study, www.cgcs.org for Council of the Great City Schools database, and each state department of education's website. Be sure to ask subject area specialists for the important websites in their field of study.

The second method, using the library, is the best way for the beginning researcher to start. Today's librarians are well-trained professionals who make the researcher's job easier. Librarians offer introductory sessions on how to use the library, they prepare handouts on how to use research databases and other online indexes, and they are aware of a wide range of potentially relevant literature sources. They are a resource that should not be ignored. The researcher needs to be familiar with what the local library has to offer, what library resources are available online, and how resources at other libraries can be accessed. Reviewing the literature can be a frustrating process without this knowledge. The details of conducting a literature search that are presented in this chapter are meant to be illustrative and may not fit your local situation exactly.

With the amount of information available from a variety of sources, the review of the literature is by no means a trivial task. It is a systematic process that requires careful and perceptive reading and attention to detail. In the review of the literature, the researcher attempts to determine what others have learned about similar research problems and to gather information relevant to the research problem at hand. This process centers on three questions:

1. Where is the information found?
2. What should be done with information after it has been found?
3. What is made of the information?

The first question deals with the specific sources, both electronic and hard copy. For most students, these sources can be found in or obtained through the library and the Internet. Finding the information often involves using reference works such as indexes of periodical literature. Computer searches of databases are very helpful in focusing the search and speeding up the process of sorting through the literature and identifying the potentially most useful sources. The sheer volume of available information on most topics makes a computer search almost imperative for any extensive review.

The second question deals with how information is assembled and summarized. Assuming that the content of a report is relevant to the research problem under study, the information must be retained in a usable manner.

Dealing with the third question is somewhat more abstract. To answer the first two questions, the researcher finds information and sets up a procedure for retaining it. Answering the third question requires making a judgment about the information in a research report. What parts of the reported results are relevant to the research problem? How well was the research conducted? Thus, answering the third question requires a critical analysis of the reports reviewed. In a later chapter there is a discussion of evaluating research reports. Then information from the related reports can be put together.

What is the value of a review of the literature? Besides providing a context for the research study, the review may be useful in any or all of the following ways:

1. More specifically limiting and identifying the research problem and possible hypotheses.
2. Informing the researcher of what has already been done in the area.
3. Providing possible research design and methodological procedures that may be used in the research study.
4. Providing suggestions for possible modifications in the research to avoid unanticipated difficulties.
5. Identifying possible gaps in the research.
6. Providing a backdrop for interpreting the results of the research study.

> The review of related literature serves multiple purposes and is essential to a well-designed research study. It generally comes early in the research process, and it can contribute valuable information to any part of the research study.

The Activities of the Review of the Literature

As Figure 1.4 indicated, the existing body of knowledge relative to the research problem provides information for identifying the problem. In that figure, the general activities of conducting a research study were ordered in their most likely sequence of occurrence. The review of the literature itself consists of several specific activities that, to a large extent, also take place in a sequence. These activities, shown in the **flowchart of activities** in Figure 3.1, are initiated after the research problem has been identified, at least tentatively. The order of activities follows the flow of the arrows in the figure.

Like most activities or steps in a process, there are efficient and inefficient ways to review the literature. Rather than going to the library or the Internet and haphazardly beginning to take notes, the researcher should follow a systematic process, as represented by the activities in the flowchart. Although even this process may involve some inefficiency in locating sources and reports, efficiency will be enhanced by following the process. Another important procedural point in conducting the activities is to do as complete and accurate an initial job as possible for each activity. For example, when a relevant report is located and an abstract is prepared, a complete bibliographic entry for the report should be included and page numbers of potential quotations should be noted. This saves going back later just to complete the bibliography of the reference. If a report is relevant enough to include in the

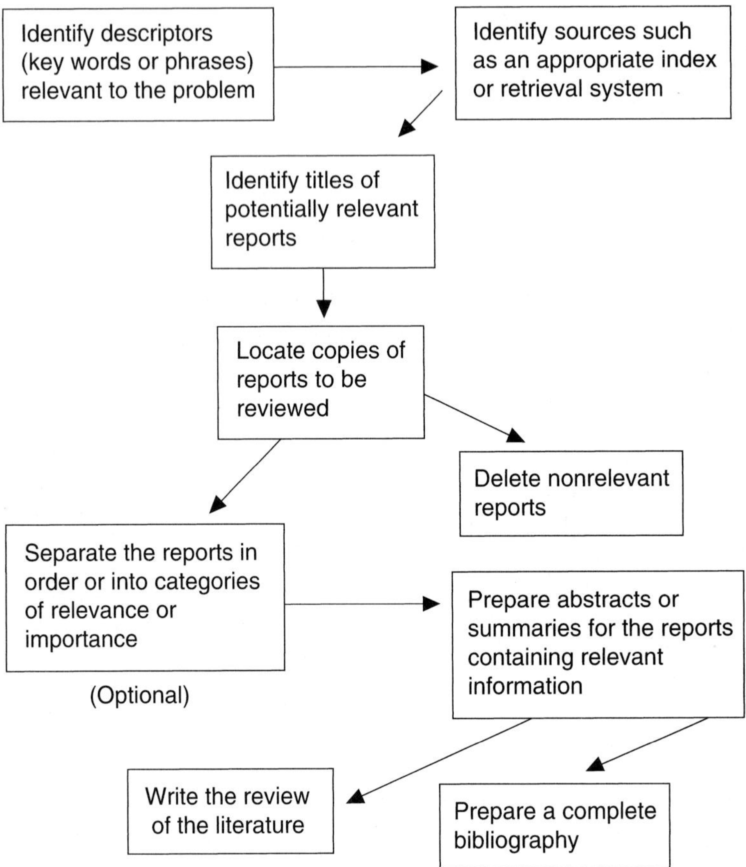

FIGURE 3.1 Flowchart of Activities in the Review of the Literature

review, sufficient information should be obtained from it so that there is no confusion later about what was done (conditions, procedures, individuals involved, etc.) or about the results. Doing the review of literature in the manner suggested not only reduces frustration but also saves time.

Sources of Information

There is no scarcity of reports of research studies related to education. Studies are published in books, periodicals, technical reports, conference proceedings, and academic theses. Most of the recent reports are available in electronic form and can be accessed at your institution's library or from remote sites if you have appropriate authorization. Usually the authorization is offered to all registered students.

The Library

Probably all college and university libraries offer some form of electronic resources in addition to their traditional holdings. Some may be minimal whereas others are very extensive and sophisticated. You should learn how to use library resources effectively either through training sessions that the library offers or through online tutorials that the library has prepared. Do not forget to utilize the library staff. Research librarians are professionals who are very willing to share their expertise.

The library catalog can usually be searched electronically by title, author, subject, or keyword. Professional journals can be accessed online. Large databases containing educational research reports have been produced by private publishers and government agencies and these can also be searched online.

An example of a comprehensive system for literature searches is that of the University of Michigan Library. That system is called MIRLYN, the *MI*chigan *R*esearch *L*ibrar*Y* *N*etwork, and can be accessed at http://mirlyn.lib.umich.edu. Its menu includes a Basic Search (limited to Ann Arbor and Flint), an Advanced Search, Command Language, Browse, a Results List, and Previous Searches. Articles can be searched by title, author, subject, journal name, and call number. The search can be done using words from the title rather than the complete title. The same "words" option can be used with the author, subject, and journal searches. A researcher using a system such as MIRLYN should be able to conduct a literature search much more systematically and more successfully than a general search of the Internet would produce. Most libraries have a system in place to assist researchers. It is important to learn yours.

Periodical Literature

Periodical literature, including professional journals, regularly publish a large volume of research information, although some journals are more oriented to this type of material than others. Unlike the Internet, where anyone can post anything, most of the professional journals have a screening process called "peer review," which requires articles to meet certain standards of quality before they are accepted for publication. It would be impractical to present a comprehensive listing of such periodicals, but some can be mentioned. Of course, the *American Educational Research Journal* (Washington, DC: American Educational Research Association) is a widely used source for information about educational research. The journals of the American Psychological Association, especially the *Journal of Educational Psychology*, often contain reports of education-related research. The *Louisiana Education Research Journal* (Natchitoches: Louisiana Education Research Association) is the official publication of the Louisiana Education Research Association. *The Journal of Educational Measurement* (Washington, DC: National Council on Measurement in Education) often contains reports of research about educational measurement. There are journals such as the *Journal of Research in Science Teaching* (National Association for Research in Science Teaching and Association for the Education of Teachers in Science; New York: Wiley), which covers research on curriculum and teaching in specific areas.

Journals published in other countries also are sources of research information. Examples of such include the *British Journal of Educational Psychology* (London: British Psychological Society) and the *Canadian Education and Research Digest* (Toronto: Canadian Education Association). Most periodicals can be accessed electronically through various databases.

Many journals are now available in electronic format. The American Educational Research Association sponsors links to peer-reviewed, full-text journals that can be accessed from anywhere. The website address is http://aera-cr.asu.edu/ejournals. Journals from the United States and from other countries are available from this site.

Indexes and Abstracts

The primary **periodical index** for educational literature is the *Education Index.* It covers more than 360 educational periodicals. Published since 1929, the *Education Index* is a cumulative author-subject index to educational material in the English language. It provides only bibliographic information. It does not provide an abstract or a summary. It is published monthly except July and August and combined into annual volumes. The entries include literature in periodicals, proceedings, yearbooks, bulletins, monographs, and governmental materials on education and education-related topics. The entries are arranged in alphabetical order in a combined author-keyword index. Under subject headings, such as "Learning, Psychology of," are alphabetically ordered subheadings such as "Attention" and "Conditioned Response." Under these subject headings are references to the related literature, including title, author, and complete bibliographic information. Author entries list all titles of the author's published works that have appeared since the previous volume of the *Education Index.* Because no abstract or summary is provided, not all selected entries may prove valuable when reviewed. The *Education Index* is useful, though, because of the breadth of its coverage.

Numerous indexes and abstracts in other disciplines include education-related research and may be fruitful sources for the review of literature:

> *Psychological Abstracts* is a bimonthly publication that contains abstracts of research reports and articles from over 1000 journals, technical reports, monographs, and scientific documents.
>
> *Exceptional Child Education Resources*, published quarterly by the Council for Exceptional Children, includes reviews from more than 200 periodicals dealing with exceptional children.
>
> *Crime and Penology Abstracts* references current research into school violence, school vandalism, and school absence.
>
> The *Nursing Index* contains references to research into school health, diet, and nutrition, which have implications for education.

Other periodicals that include abstracts that may yield relevant literature on educational topics are:

Sociological Abstracts
Child Development Abstracts
Educational Administration Abstracts

The citation indexes are somewhat different from those just described. The citation index will give all the works that have cited a particular reference. Suppose, for example, that in your review of the literature you have found a particularly important article that was written in 2001. The citation index will list articles that were written since 2001 that cited the important article. This allows the researcher to pursue lines of research that have emanated from that article. A citation index can be especially helpful in locating what other authors had to say about a controversial article. The search is initiated with the author's name and the year of publication. The most widely used citation index for education is the *Social Science Citation Index* (SSCI). The listings are for a given year and then summarized in five-year accumulations.

Indexes and abstracts are available in almost all university libraries, and the procedures for using them are very much the same. The introduction to an index usually contains detailed information about availability and costs of documents and addresses for obtaining information. Detailed information is also provided about codes used in the entries and how to locate references.

ERIC

ERIC is the acronym for the Education Resources Information Center. It is an Internet-based digital library of educational research and information sponsored by the Institute of Education Sciences (IES) of the U.S. Department of Education. ERIC was begun in 1966 and provided a collection of reports and documents to libraries on microfiche. Current technology allows the information to be digitized and made available through the Internet. ERIC now has a growing collection of over 115,000 full-text materials in Adobe PDF format. All documents have complete bibliographic information and an abstract or summary.

The ERIC collection includes more than 1.2 million items indexed since 1966, including journal articles, books, research syntheses, conference papers, technical reports, policy papers, and other education-related materials (www.eric.ed.gov).

An Example Using ERIC. Suppose that you are interested in locating literature on the topic of school vouchers. ERIC can be accessed by typing "ERIC" into any search engine or by using its address, www.eric.ed.gov. This brings you to the ERIC search page, which allows you to search by keyword, title, author, descriptors (from the ERIC Thesaurus), or by the ERIC number. Suppose that we simply put in "school vouchers" as a keyword. This yields 1115 records, the first of which is in Figure 3.2.

It would be impractical to read all 1115 records that resulted from the search. The search should be narrowed in order to focus on the most relevant literature. ERIC allows you to search "within results" with additional keywords. If we limit the results by adding the keyword "court cases" so that we can focus on legal issues pertaining to school vouchers, the search yields only 18 records. The eighth of these is provided in Figure 3.3. Note the drastic

1. The Future of Vouchers: Lessons from the Adoption, Design, and Court Challenges of Florida's Three Voucher Programs (EJ750737)

Author(s): Harris, Douglas N.; Herrington, Carolyn D.; Albee, Amy
Source: Educational Policy, v21 n1 p215–244 2007
Pub Date: 2007-00-00
Pub Type(s): Journal Articles; Reports-Research
Peer-Reviewed: Yes

Descriptors:
Privatization; Educational Vouchers; Accountability; State Legislation; Educational Policy; School Choice

Abstract:
This study considers why Florida has been the most aggressive state in adopting school vouchers. Vouchers are consistent with Florida's tradition of aggressive educational accountability policies, arising from the state's moderate social conservatism, openness to privatization, and state. . . .

FIGURE 3.2 Sample Result from an ERIC Search Using a Keyword

reduction in the results when the second keyword is used. Combining too many keywords, that is, searching too narrowly, can eliminate a lot of pertinent articles.

The ERIC Thesaurus contains the descriptors of the terms used in the ERIC database. If the keyword that you are using is different from the Thesaurus term for the same thing, then the search will not be as effective as it would be if the Thesaurus term were used. Always check to see whether your keywords are in the ERIC Thesaurus.

ERIC is a valuable tool for conducting a literature review. Over 600 journals are indexed in it. It is an efficient way to get to a wide variety of articles, reports, and papers.

8. From the Statehouse to the Schoolhouse: How Legislatures and Courts Shaped Labor Relations for Public Education Employees during the Last Decade. (EJ632409)

Author(s): Strom, David J.; Baxter, Stephanie S.
Source: Journal of Law and Education, v30 n2 p275–304 Apr 2001
Pub Date: 2001-00-00
Pub Type(s): Journal Articles; Legal/Legislative/Regulatory Materials
Peer-Reviewed: N/A

Descriptors:
Charter Schools; Constitutional Law; Court Litigation; Educational Change; Educational Trends; Educational Vouchers; Elementary Secondary Education; Labor Relations; School District Reorganization; School Law; Scope of Bargaining; State Legislation; Tax Credits; Tenure; Unions

Abstract:
Examines six state and federal legislative developments and related court cases that have shaped employment relations in public schools in the 1990s: state takeovers and reconstitutions, vouchers and tuition tax credits, charter schools, legislative efforts to restrict the scope of bargaining. . . .

FIGURE 3.3 Sample Result from an ERIC Search Using Two Keywords

A danger is that the literature reviewer may be so enamored of ERIC that other valuable sources such as books, newspapers, and dissertations are ignored. A thorough review of the literature should go beyond ERIC.

Reports of Meta-Analysis

Meta-analysis is a statistical procedure for synthesizing research results across a number of studies that deal with similar research questions and include similar variables. As Glass (2006) noted in his description of meta-analysis:

> All studies differ. The important question to address is how their findings vary as a function of their differences. Meta-analysis attempts to do this by describing their differences and their findings in quantitative ways that permit statistical analysis of relationships, central tendency, and other interesting quantitative features. (p. 430)

Different studies are made comparable by converting their results to common measures called effect sizes. One of the simplest effect sizes is found by dividing the difference between the mean of the experimental group and the mean of the control group by the standard deviation of the control group. Then, for example, an effect size of 0.50 would indicate that the experimental group outperformed the control group by half of a standard deviation on the dependent variable in that study. In a meta-analysis the researcher would compute the effect sizes from many studies and would then determine the overall average effect size. Another set of analyses would determine whether the size of the effect varied as a function of the quality of the study, the type of dependent variable, the duration of the experimental treatment, and any other variables of interest.

Meta-analyses are useful for summarizing results and for comparing the conditions of the studies that are reviewed. The amount of literature that is available for review is now so huge that meta-analysis is needed to synthesize the many studies. The statistical analysis of results is needed to bring order out of chaos. Meta-analysis can at times bring organization and meaning to mixed results and seemingly contradictory results from different studies. Meta-analyses appear in the periodical literature, but not on any systematic schedule such as is the case with some reviews. Meta-analysis is an ERIC descriptor, so it can be combined with the research topic to search the ERIC database for meta-analyses on the topic.

Review of Educational Research (*RER*)

Some of the most valuable and useful sources of information about a research problem are reviews on various topics and issues. There are reviews published on a regular basis, and others appear in periodicals as appropriate and as needed. One of the most useful is *RER*, issued quarterly by the American Educational Research Association, which publishes critical integrative reviews of research literature bearing on education. From its inception in 1931 through 1969, each issue of the *RER* contained solicited papers organized around a single educational topic or subdivision, such as "Educational and Psychological Testing." Topics were reviewed in three-year cycles; more active topics were reviewed every cycle and less active ones on alternate cycles.

Beginning with Volume 40 (June 1970), the *RER* has published unsolicited reviews of research on topics of the reviewer's own choosing. The papers in both the pre-1970 and post-1970 issues include excellent bibliographies that contain many references to the educational research literature. As an example of topics covered, the reviews that appeared in Volume 73, Number 1 (LeCompte, 2003) were:

"The Effects of Modified School Calendars on Student Achievement and on School and Community Attitudes"

"Workplace Learning and Flexible Delivery"

"Teacher Characteristics and Student Achievement Gains: A Review"

As mentioned above, there are reviews that appear in periodicals on an irregular basis and some of these are of education-related topics. Other disciplines related to education have reviews or review journals—an example is the *Annual Review of Psychology.* Such reviews may be a viable source of information.

Reviews are useful if a researcher wants to locate a substantial quantity of research literature on a broad research topic without conducting an initial search. Reviews are helpful but they do cover broad topics and all of the information contained in a review may not be directly related to the topic at hand. As usual, the researcher must go through the content and retain relevant information.

Theses and Dissertations

Theses and dissertations prepared to meet the requirements for a graduate degree usually contain descriptions of completed research. The university library contains copies of theses completed at that university. To obtain information about dissertations completed at other universities, the most widely used comprehensive source is *Dissertation Abstracts* and its related services.

Dissertation Abstracts was renamed *Dissertation Abstracts International (DAI)* beginning with Volume 30, No. 1 (1969). *DAI* is a reference tool that provides a monthly compilation of abstracts of doctoral dissertations submitted to University Microfilms International (Ann Arbor, Michigan) by some 550 universities in North America and worldwide. There are three sections under which dissertations are abstracted: Humanities and Social Studies (A), the Sciences and Engineering (B), and Worldwide (C). It is published quarterly.

Each of Sections A and B is divided into five main parts, as follows:

Humanities and Social Studies

IA. Communications and the Arts
IIA. Education
IIIA. Language, Literature, and Linguistics
IVA. Philosophy, Religion, and Theology
VA. Social Sciences

Sciences and Engineering

IB. Biological Sciences
IIB. Earth Sciences
IIIB. Health and Environmental Sciences
IVB. Physical Sciences
VB. Psychology

Each main part is divided into numerous subject categories, the names of which are given at the beginning of each volume. Education has thirty-five subject categories, including, for example, "Early Childhood."

Entry to *DAI* is through the keyword title index. Keywords are printed in alphabetical order, followed by the titles of dissertations in which they occur. Keywords may be used in combination. Potentially useful entries can then be followed up in the document resumes section which provides an abstract of the dissertation. If the search goes back to Volume 29 or earlier, the researcher can use the *DAI Retrospective Index*, which contains bibliographic references in nine subject volumes for *DAI* Volumes 1–29. One of those subject volumes is titled *Education.*

Most libraries offer ProQuest to search the *Dissertation Abstracts* databases. Otherwise researchers can use DATRIX to conduct direct dissertation and thesis database searches. The online searches have essentially eliminated searching by hand in the *DAI* volumes.

Books

There are many, many books dealing with educational research and these typically can be found in the reference section or through general circulation of university libraries. In most libraries, a book and its availability can be located quickly through the library's electronic catalog system.

Handbooks that deal with research in a specific area of education can be useful sources of research information. An example of such a handbook is the *Handbook of Research on Science Teaching and Learning* (Gabel, 1994). The *Handbooks of Research on Teaching*, first published in 1963, are comprehensive presentations of research on teaching. Subsequent handbooks are not revisions of earlier editions, but original volumes.

Handbooks contain a lot of information, typically organized in chapters on specific issues and topics. Chapter bibliographies usually are extensive and themselves represent extensive research literature searches. One disadvantage of handbooks that are published infrequently is that they become somewhat dated and may not contain the most recent research in the area.

The *Encyclopedia of Educational Research (EER)* is a project of the American Educational Research Association (AERA) that represents a compendium of research covering five major issues in education. Six editions of the *EER* have been published, the most recent in 1992 (Alkin, 1992). The original edition appeared in 1941, with subsequent editions at approximately ten-year intervals.

The *EER* does not simply catalog the research that has been done on a topic; each entry provides critical evaluation, synthesis, and interpretation of much of the literature on the topic. The entries are prepared by noted educators who are familiar with the literature and research in their chosen topics.

Another publication of AERA is the *Review of Research in Education*, whose purpose is to survey disciplined inquiry in education through critical and synthesizing essays. About ten areas are covered in each issue, categorized under broader topics, such as curriculum. Each article contains a detailed reference list.

This section presented several different sources of research information. Any difficulties encountered at this stage of a literature review are usually due not to lack of information, but to an inability to find the relevant references. Because there is such a large quantity of educational research information, it is important to conduct a systematic search, using the indexes, retrieval systems, reviews, and so forth, that are available. A manual search can be helpful in getting a review started, and it may be adequate for a limited review, but for any comprehensive review, an electronic search is much more efficient.

Computer Searches of Databases

At one time **computer-assisted searches** of databases were a service of libraries and were conducted by professional librarians. Currently anyone with authorization can have access to the library's databases and can conduct the search. Authorization is usually extended to all registered students. Many databases are available. Some are used across libraries and some are unique to an institution. Note the resources at Clemson University, for example.

	ARTICLE INDEXES
ERIC	research in education, 1966–present
PsycINFO	psychology and related fields, 1887–present
Social Sciences Citation Index	social sciences, 1985–present
Expanded Academic	all subject areas, 1980–present
Infotrac OneFile	all subject areas, 1980–present
Current Contents	all subject areas, most recent 2 years
Ingenta Library Gateway	all subject areas, 1988–present
	REFERENCE SOURCES
Mental Measurements Yearbook	information about and reviews of psychological and educational tests and measures, 1985–present
Digest of Educational Statistics	compilation of statistics on American education from kindergarten to graduate school
Children's Literature Comprehensive Database	information about and reviews of children's books and media
K–12 Resources	databases and encyclopedias designed for K–12 students

WorldCat	the combined catalogs of libraries from over 45 countries; contains 47 million+ records
Dissertation Abstracts	dissertation index, all subjects, 1861–present

Because university libraries and other libraries have different databases and different systems for accessing them, the specific procedures and commands when conducting a search vary somewhat. However, most libraries have a brief description of the search process in hard copy or electronic form that any student can follow. These descriptions go by titles such as, "How to Use ERIC." If there is a difficulty with any step in the search, a reference librarian usually is available to provide assistance.

Conducting a Search

Regardless of the specific search process being used, there are overall commonalities in conducting a search, and these are described below in an example searching the ERIC database. The search begins by identifying concepts or terms from the research problem statement and then using the *Thesaurus of ERIC Descriptions* to choose **descriptors** or subject headings that best describe the concepts.

Limiting or Broadening a Search. Before considering a specific research problem, it is useful to consider ways of limiting or broadening a search. Typically, in order to have more focus and to keep the references to a manageable number, we look for ways to limit the search. Ways to limit a search are:

1. Use of the connector *and* between two or more keyword descriptors. In order for a reference to be identified, *both* terms must appear in the reference. This is one of the most common ways of limiting a search.
2. Language—for example, restricted to English references only.
3. Time back—for example, go back only to 1985 or any desired date.
4. Type of publication—for example, limit references to periodicals.
5. Education level—for example, higher education.

Undoubtedly, the most commonly used ways of limiting a search are the first three listed above. However, the others are available if limiting a search in this manner would be useful.

Broadening a search can be done by using the connector *or* between two or more descriptors. This connector will identify references which contain either one or both of the descriptors. Another way to broaden searches is to reverse some of the ways searches are limited. For example, if we had limited time back to 1990 and had not identified adequate references, we could go back to 1980 or any other desired date.

> There are several ways of limiting and broadening searches. Descriptors can be used in combination with the connectors *and* and *or* to limit or broaden a search.

Selecting Studies for the Review of the Literature

The research literature on almost any educational topic is so extensive that it is not likely that all the studies related to a research problem can be included in the review. Also, there are time restrictions on how many studies can be reviewed, and reviews must be brought to closure. How then is a researcher to determine what studies to include in the review, and at what point does further reviewing become unproductive?

One distinction that can be made between references is whether they are primary or secondary sources. A primary source is a report, an article, etc., written by the people who conducted the research. An article in a journal in which the researchers describe their research and report results is a primary source. A secondary source is one written by someone at least one step removed from the research. The authors of a secondary source did not do the research. A meta-analysis is an example of a secondary source. To some extent, primary sources take precedence over secondary sources. It is unlikely that any review would consist entirely of primary sources, but it is desirable to include references for primary sources of research most closely related to the research problem being reviewed.

There are other suggestions that may be helpful for selecting studies for the review. When a search is completed, it can be useful to check the eight or ten most recent references first. For one thing, these are the most current and should reflect the present state of thinking on the topic under study. Another advantage is that recent references will have the most current bibliographies. The reviewer can then determine which prior studies attracted the attention of others working on the same or similar topic. If an earlier reference repeatedly shows up in the bibliographies, it likely merits a review.

The review does not need to be done by "brute force," so to speak. Capitalize on the work others have done. Earlier in this chapter, various handbooks were mentioned. If a handbook contains a chapter on a topic closely related to the research problem being reviewed, the bibliography for that chapter may provide some indication of the importance and relevance of references. Handbook chapters typically include extensive bibliographies, some up to 200 entries. Such bibliographies tend to identify the more recognized authors in the field.

One disadvantage of chapters in handbooks is that they soon become dated and their bibliographies may not be the most current. However, at least early in the review, a computer search could be done from the time the chapter was written until the present. A slightly different approach would be to identify the six or so most often referenced authors in the chapter, and do an author search to see what they have written since the review was completed. Once this activity gets under way, things will begin coming together; authors become associated with the research problem, various methods become apparent, and, hopefully, there will be some consistency across results.

Like chapters in handbooks, reviews and reports of meta-analysis can provide much useful information. These are secondary sources. Of course, the more recent the reference, the more current the information. Whatever the publication date of the reference, the reviewer must bring the review up to date.

It is not unusual to discover mixed results in a review, even contradictory results in some instances. Such results require careful review to determine possible explanations. There may have been differences in the research conditions, and the methods of at least one of the studies may have been deficient. Meta-analyses reports, when available, can be helpful for explaining mixed results. Such reports specify criteria for including studies and usually provide comments about possible reasons for inconsistent results.

When has the review reached the point of "enough"? There is no single answer to this question in terms of number of references reviewed. The number is somewhat determined by the purpose of the review. A review for a journal article typically is considerably shorter than the review for a doctoral dissertation, for example.

There comes a point at which reviewing more references is going to provide little or no more useful information about the research problem. Intuitively, a reviewer pretty much knows when this point is reached. For example, when the patterns of research results of previous studies become consistent and additional studies simply reinforce these patterns, the results information has peaked. The methods used in the research studies may be quite similar and quite adequate for generating the necessary methods for the present study. Adequate here does not mean replicating exactly what has been done, but using the reviewed methods for extending the methods of the present study, possibly even coming up with a new and creative approach to addressing the problem. In general, when the information in the references reviewed seems to stabilize and seems quite complete in the context of the research problem, the review has reached closure. If the research study requires a considerable period, say several months, it will be necessary to update the review periodically to keep it current.

Assembling and Summarizing Information

After locating and reviewing the references from the literature search, the researcher must consider the question, "What should I do with the information?" The initial decision is to determine whether or not the content of the report (article, etc.) is relevant to the research problem under study. If it is not relevant, it can be deleted; if it is relevant, the information it contains must be summarized or somehow put into a usable form so that it is retrievable when the researcher needs it. In Figure 3.1, the separation of reports in order of importance was indicated as an optional activity. Sometimes it may be difficult to do this, because the distinctions between levels of importance may not be clear. Therefore, this activity may be omitted or it may be done after the abstracts or summaries have been prepared.

There are many formats of information-recording procedures that can be used to organize information from the selected studies. Most researchers devise their own methods, but there is software available to help with this task. EndNote[1], Pro Cite, and Take Note are examples of available programs that are designed to assist in the management of information obtained in the literature search.

Whatever method is used, it is important to capture the bibliographic information so that you don't have to return to the original article to retrieve what is missing. A **bibliographic entry** contains the following information: the name(s) of the author(s), the title of the article (report, book, etc.), facts about the publisher or the publication, and, if it is an article in a periodical, the inclusive page numbers. Many colleges and universities require consistency in referencing style. The *Publication Manual of the American Psychological Association* (APA) (2001) is the most commonly used style manual in educational research. It is important, then, that the researcher captures the bibliographic information that is required by the APA referencing system. The format in APA style for an article from a professional journal, for example, is:

> Veldman, D. J., & Sanford, J. P. (1984). The influence of class ability level on student achievement and classroom behavior. *American Educational Research Journal, 21*, 629–644.

The APA Publication Manual referenced at the end of the chapter should be consulted for bibliographic entries for other types of reports.

A complete and accurate bibliographic entry made immediately when the report is used is important because it saves time and possible confusion. To have to look up a report again just because the bibliographic entry is incomplete is frustrating. Also, it is not acceptable to have incorrect entries in the bibliography.

Abstract or Summary

Electronic searches of the literature typically provide abstracts of the reports; however, these may be somewhat limited. So, the researcher, in order to use research results effectively—that is, to fit them into the context of the research problem—must obtain considerable information from the report. The problem of the reported research must be identified along with the conditions under which the results were obtained, and all of this must be related to the research problem under study. Thus, as a report is being reviewed, judgments must be made about the information to be retained, that is, written down.

Rather than just taking notes on research reports, the researcher may prepare an abstract of the report, an extended abstract of the one from the computer search or the abstract that often appears at the beginning of articles in periodicals. An **abstract** is a summary of a research report that contains certain kinds of information. The form of the information should be consistent across the reports reviewed. There are slight variations among the components of an abstract suggested by different authors, but generally some elements of the following information are included:

Bibliographic Entry: An accurate and complete bibliographic entry heads the abstract.

Problem: This is a statement of the research problem of the report being reviewed; it may include statements of hypotheses.

Subjects: The individuals involved in research studies are often called "subjects" of the research; for example, "50 college sophomores enrolled in elementary education, 25 males and 25 females."

Procedures: This section describes how the research was conducted. It includes such items as the measurements used and the analyses performed. This section also may be called "methodology."

Results and Conclusions: This section identifies the relevant results and conclusions of the study. A distinction may be made between results and conclusions—results being whatever occurred, such as certain statistics, and conclusions being what the researcher has made of the results. In long reports with many results and conclusions, it is best to number them.

An *abstract* is a summary that contains the relevant information from a research report according to specified categories.

When abstracting a report, the researcher attempts to condense the relevant information as briefly as possible while including all the necessary details. Although the abstract should be brief, the importance of having all necessary information must be emphasized. It is frustrating and inefficient to find that the information of an abstract is incomplete and that it is necessary to search out the report again. A number of factors affect the length of the abstract, including the length of the report, the complexity of the research, and the extensiveness of the findings. The content of the abstract should be as brief as possible, but include all necessary information. This will usually result in abstracts of varying length when several reports are abstracted.

Organizing Information

Research problems tend to have inherent and identifiable categories on which to group the studies reviewed. Such grouping of the studies facilitates the writing task, so that continuity can be achieved rather than a "back and forth" approach. An outline may be useful, one that includes the main issues or topics of the research problem.

Consider an example research problem—a study of measures of teacher effectiveness obtained through observation. Observation inventories or systems used to measure teacher behavior (and from behavior infer effectiveness) generally can be grouped into two categories: high-inference and low-inference systems. These terms refer to the amount of inference required on the part of the observer when recording the behavior. So, studies could be grouped as to whether either one or both of these systems were used, giving a three-category grouping.

Another possible grouping of studies dealing with teacher effectiveness is the grade level of teaching involved; for example, primary, middle school, high school, or some combination of these levels. Even if the same observation system could be used for all levels, the patterns of results might be quite different depending on the level taught. Most of the studies likely would involve in-service teachers with varying years of experience. But there may be some studies involving teacher education students doing their student teaching. This may be another dichotomy on which the studies could be grouped, in-service teachers or teacher education students being observed. So, there are different ways to group the studies reviewed according to category systems somewhat unique to the research problem.

Studies reviewed can be grouped according to categories that are somewhat unique to the research problem at hand, but that are identifiable. These categories will provide a logical organization of the information.

Interpreting and Using Information

The interpretation of results and other information found in research reports begins when the report is being reviewed. To begin, it is a good idea to skim a report to get an overview, without being too concerned with the specifics. From this overview, a decision can usually be made about the relevance of the report to the research problem being studied. Assuming that a report is relevant, the reviewer can then focus on the specifics and begin the abstracting process.

Critical Review[2]

The review of the literature is not merely a list of studies and findings; it is a critical review of those studies and findings. It is well known that there is considerable variability in the quality and comprehensiveness of reports in the educational research literature. Thus, as a researcher reads a report, it is necessary to take a somewhat critical perspective. But how does one read critically? Reviewing research reports requires an intellectual effort on the part of the reader, and the reader is responsible for having at least some familiarity with the area (not necessarily the research in the area) and some knowledge of research procedures. Indeed, one of the purposes of studying research methods is to better understand the research literature.

Nevertheless, there are characteristics of a report that a reader can look for, and if these characteristics are weak or lacking, the report is suspect. Smith and Glass (1987, p. 2) refer to these as *criteria* or *tools*, and they focus on different types of validity, beginning with logical validity. This validity deals with how the entire research study and report fit together. Do the various parts fit together logically and does the entire report make sense? Do conclusions follow logically from the results or are there inconsistencies? Were the procedures consistent with the research problem?

We have already introduced the concepts of internal and external validity of research. Internal validity deals with adequate and appropriate procedures so that results, including cause-and-effect conclusions, can be interpreted with confidence. Were the research procedures conducted appropriately? Were there possibilities for introducing bias? Are the procedures described adequately so the reader can understand what was done? Was the analysis appropriate?

External validity deals with the generalizability of results. Is the issue of external validity addressed? If so, do the results have adequate generalizability and do the generalizations seem reasonable? Was random selection or random assignment used, and if not, is representativeness argued on a logical basis?

Smith and Glass (1987, p. 4) also include the concept of *construct validity*. Construct validity refers to confounding or misunderstanding the variables in research. The effect of anxiety on performance, for example, varies depending on the type and intensity of the anxiety and the nature of the performance. Understanding the research results depends on understanding how the constructs were defined in a particular study. When constructs are used in research, they should be defined in a way that is consistent with the prevailing thinking and research in the area.

This discussion included several questions, the kinds of questions a researcher has in mind when reading a research report. Many more specific questions could be raised, and those appropriate tend to come to mind as a report is read. This is part of the intellectual exercise of critical review. If a report has gaps in the discussion or the logical validity does not hold up, it will not be usable to the researcher. The internal validity must be adequate for interpreting results. External validity deals with generalizability and, specifically, the relevance of the report to the research problem at hand.

When weaknesses are identified in the research studies or in the logic of the writer of opinion pieces, this should be mentioned and the researcher's conclusions about the knowledge base should be strongly influenced by the quality of the articles that comprise the knowledge base. Strengths and weaknesses of the methods and logic used in the articles should be noted along with the findings and conclusions. The articles and reports are not equally valuable and the reviewer needs to inform the reader of the review of literature of these differences.

> *Critical review* is an intellectual exercise in which the reader must judge the adequacy of the validity of the report.

Writing the Review

The review of the literature often has the following structure:

- An overview of the research problem and the objectives of the review of the literature.
- Historical development of the issues or theories that are considered.
- Major categories of articles (by school of thought, by variable, by context, by research paradigm, or by some other categorization).
- Critical review of articles.
- Differences and similarities of positions and findings.
- Current state of understanding, including gaps in knowledge.

The review is not just a list of quotations extracted from the articles; it is a coherent summary and synthesis of the literature that uses direct quotes sparingly. The writer paraphrases the cited articles to enhance the meaning and the flow of the review.

A well-written review of the literature will adhere to the following guidelines:

1. Select studies that relate most directly to the problem at hand.

2. Tie together the results of the studies so that their relevance is clear. Do not simply provide a compendium of references, devoting a paragraph or two to each without connecting the ideas and results.

3. When conflicting findings are reported across studies—and this is quite common in educational research—carefully examine the variations in the findings and possible explanations for them. Ignoring variation and simply averaging effects loses information and fails to recognize the complexity of the problem.

4. Make the case that the research area reviewed is incomplete or requires extension. This establishes the need for research in this area. (*Note:* This does not make the case that the proposed research is going to meet the need or is of significance.)

5. Although information from the literature must be properly referenced, do not make the review a series of quotations.

6. The review should be organized according to the major points relevant to the problem. Do not force the review into a chronological organization, for example, that may confuse the relevance and continuity among the studies reviewed.

7. Give the reader some indication of the relative importance of results from studies reviewed. Some results have more bearing on the problem than others, and this should be indicated.

8. Provide closure for this section. Do not terminate with comments from the final study reviewed. Provide a summary and pull together the most important points.

There are several kinds of errors that can be made when writing the review of the literature. Dunkin (1996) has summarized them according to the stages of the review process.

The first stage, called the *primary stage*, involves selecting from the literature those studies considered relevant to the topic. The second stage, called the *secondary stage*, involves identifying context, methods, and results of each study. The third and final stage, called the *tertiary stage*, involves summarizing the findings to arrive at generalizations relative to the topics (paraphrased, p. 88).

Across the three stages, Dunkin identifies and describes nine types of errors, simply called Type 1 through Type 9. These are listed below according to the stage in which they occur.

Primary Stage

Type 1. *Unexplained selectivity.* Studies that are relevant are excluded without justification for the exclusion.

Type 2. *Lack of discrimination.* According all studies equal quality, value, or relevance when they are not.

Secondary Stage

Type 3. *Erroneous detailing.* Incorrect statements of the sampling, methods, designs, and other details of the studies reviewed.

Type 4. *Double counting.* Counting different reports from the same project as multiple confirmations of the same results, when in fact there was only one project or study.

Type 5. *Nonrecognition of faulty author conclusions.* Misrepresentation of authors' findings relative to the conclusions of the study. This is a difficult error to detect and may occur if conclusions are accepted uncritically.

Type 6. *Unwarranted attributions.* Reviewers assigning to studies findings or conclusions not justified by the facts of the study.

Type 7. *Suppression of contrary findings.* Ignoring findings contrary to the generalizations the reviewer is attempting to support.

Tertiary Stage

Type 8. *Consequential errors.* Errors in generalizations due to errors made at the primary and secondary stages. The results are erroneous generalizations as consequences of earlier errors.

Type 9. *Failure to marshall all evidence relevant to a generalization.* Failure to recognize results/conclusions of a study that are relevant to a generalization (paraphrased, pp. 88–94).

Dunkin provides more detailed examples of the above errors. Being cognizant of the types of errors most common in literature reviews should help the reviewer avoid them.

Referencing

When information is reported from a source, it must be adequately referenced. A number of acceptable formats for **referencing** may be used, one of which is a footnote at the bottom of the page. Consider the article by Harris, Herrington, and Albee, which we found in the ERIC search, whose citation appears in Figure 3.2. In referencing information from this article, for example, a footnote might be used in the review as follows:

> Harris, Herrington, and Albee[1] have described Florida's educational accountability. . . .

At the bottom of the page the following footnote would appear:

> [1]D. N. Harris, C. Herrington, and A. Albee, The future of vouchers: Lessons from the adoption, design, and court challenges of Florida's three voucher programs. *Educational Policy, 21*, 1 (2007), 215–244.

For the narrative, if there are more than three authors of an article, the last name of the first author may be listed, followed by *et al.* (which means "and others"), rather than writing the names of all authors. A modification of this procedure is to list all of the names the first time the reference is used, then use *et al.* if it is referenced again. This is done simply for brevity. The footnote would contain the names of all authors.

A shorter format for references that does not require the footnote at the bottom of the page can be used. It involves a reference list or bibliography at the end of the chapter or report. One format is the author–date format. Using the sample reference, the author–date format would be:

> Harris, Herrington, and Albee (2007) indicated that social conservatism . . .

Or if the names of the authors are not to be emphasized in the narrative:

> Other researchers (Harris, Herrington, and Albee, 2007) indicate . . .

This format requires an alphabetical listing of references, which should be included in any case. If Harris, Herrington, and Albee were referenced more than once in the bibliography and, if this were the second 2007 reference for Harris, Herrington, and Albee, the reference would be Harris, Herrington, and Albee (2007b). If the page numbers are to be included in the reference, they can follow the year, preceded by a comma.

The short method of referencing can also be used in an author–number format. In this case, the entries in the bibliography are numbered, and the reference number is used instead of the year of publication. The page numbers then follow the reference number if they are included. For example, if the Harris, Herrington, and Albee entry were number 30 in the bibliography, the reference would be:

Harris, Herrington, and Albee (30:220) indicate . . .

or

Other authors (Harris, Herrington, and Albee, 30:220) indicate . . .

The author–date format is generally preferred to the author–number format because in the latter format, if a reference is added or deleted, all numbers of references following the addition or deletion have to be changed. If a reference is added after a good bit of the review is written, the necessary changes will be a bother and a potential source of error.

Referencing can be done in a number of ways—the traditional footnote or shorter methods, using the author–date or author–number formats.

Preparing the Bibliography

Usually, the final step of the review is putting together the **bibliography.** Some journals distinguish between a reference list and a bibliography; a reference list is limited to references cited in the report, whereas a bibliography may also include references for background information or further reading. The American Psychological Association (2001), for example, makes this distinction. Although a bibliography may include entries not cited directly in the review, it is not wise to include a large number of uncited entries.

The entries in a bibliography are ordered alphabetically according to the name of the primary author (the one listed first). This simplifies the task of typing the bibliography, especially if not all of the original sources are used. Abstracts can also be used, although they may be a little cumbersome.

However, if a researcher has available bibliographic software it is not necessary to maintain a hard-copy bibliography. EndNote, Pro Cite, and Take Note are software that will put the entries of a bibliography in APA style, and other styles also, for that matter. So, this type of software can greatly facilitate the task of preparing a bibliography. For special types of entries in a bibliography, the APA Manual referenced at the end of this chapter or any other appropriate style manual may be consulted.

Summary

This chapter described the process of reviewing the literature. A review serves a number of purposes—it puts the research problem in context; it provides information on what has been done; and it often provides information about how to conduct the research, including suggestions for instrumentation and research design.

The extent of a review of the literature depends on a number of factors, but it generally requires some time and attention to detail. Sometimes a researcher might comment, "There isn't anything in the literature on my research problem." What this means is that the researcher has not found a study exactly like the one being contemplated. A review of literature may include studies even indirectly related to the research problem, and it is the reviewer's responsibility to identify their relevance and synthesize the information from the several studies reviewed.

Figure 3.1 generally outlined the activities in a review of the research literature. Although a researcher may return to the literature at times for additional information and may rewrite parts of the review, the activities are generally done in order from top to bottom as in the flowchart in Figure 3.1. A review often occurs early in a research effort; if the study is conducted over an extended time period, additional entries may be necessary to bring the review up to date.

This chapter also provided several suggestions regarding where to find information, how to synthesize it, and what to do about it. Following consistent procedures enhances the review process by speeding the synthesis of information and reducing the likelihood of errors and repetition. In the final analysis, however, the researcher must write the review, organizing it and pulling things together in a way that will make sense to the reader. A well-organized review brings together the information on a single point or on similar ideas, provides some continuity among the results and conclusions of different research reports, and moves logically and smoothly from one point to another. Transition sentences, such as "Considering other factors that may affect teacher effectiveness, we move now to questioning behaviors," can be very helpful in leading the reader from topic to topic. After the review is written, it should be left alone for a week or two and then reread carefully. It will undoubtedly need some rewriting if it is an initial draft, but if it makes sense and there are no gaps or confusing sections, the researcher is well on the way to putting together a good review.

KEY CONCEPTS

Flowchart of activities
Periodical literature
Periodical index
ERIC
Meta-analysis
Computer-assisted search
Descriptors
Bibliographic entry
Abstract
Referencing
Bibliography

EXERCISES

3.1 Select a topic of interest and compile a list of references for this topic using the Education Index. Then use a different search engine for the same search. Compare the differences in the lists of references.

3.2 Suppose a teacher is interested in finding information about the content of mathematics programs for students aged eight to ten in Western European countries and the United States. If the teacher were using the ERIC system, what possible descriptors might be used?

3.3 A review of the literature is being done using a computer search for the following research problem:

> A study of the relationship between teacher classroom behavior and student achievement in science, grades 6–12.

Using the ERIC database, identify descriptors that could be used in the search. What descriptors would broaden the search? What descriptors would narrow the search? Specify combinations of descriptors and the connectors.

3.4 Use the research problem in Exercise 3.3, or a research problem of your own choosing, and conduct a search for references. Use descriptors either singly or in combination.

3.5 Consider the following research problem:

> A study of the relationship between social adjustment and achievement in junior high school level academic areas.

Do a search for *research* reports on this problem. Check about fifteen of the references to determine whether or not they actually deal with research or simply discuss the issue in the research problem. Now, do the same for the following research problem:

> A study of the role of the principal in site-based management.

In comparing the results from the two searches, what do you find with regard to number of references, the nature of the references, and whether or not they describe research studies? (To some extent, the nature of a reference's content can be inferred from the title.)

3.6 Suppose a computer search of the literature is done related to the research problem:

> A study of the effects of different questioning techniques upon achievement in senior high school history courses.

Identify descriptors from the *Thesaurus of ERIC Descriptors* that would be used in searching the ERIC database. Describe the order in which descriptors would be used and also the combinations using the *or* and *and* connectors. How might the search be narrowed? Broadened?

3.7 Do a literature search on student retention policies or on a topic of your choice on Yahoo or Google. Then do a similar search using the research databases that are available through your library. Describe the differences in the results of the two searches.

3.8 Select the name of an educational researcher whose work you admire. Then use the Social Science Citation Index to see how often this researcher's work has been cited.

3.9 Use the research databases through your library to identify six professional journals that are relevant to your research interests.

3.10 Arrange a discussion among several graduate students, some of whom are already working on dissertations or theses. In the discussion, address the following issues:

a. The process by which the research problem was identified.

b. The factors that motivated interest in the research topic.

c. The assistance that can be expected from the graduate program advisor in identifying a research problem.

d. The process by which the research problem was refined, by either narrowing it or broadening it, or by revising it in some manner.

e. The process by which the review of the literature was conducted.

f. The manner in which studies reviewed were grouped for one or more specific research problems.

NOTES

1. The EndNote software may be obtained from the Thomson Corporation. See the EndNote website for ordering information. (www.endnotes.com).
2. A later chapter discusses the evaluation of research reports so the comments here provide only an overview of what is involved in a critical review.

REFERENCES

Alkin, M. C. (Ed.). (1992). *Encyclopedia of educational research* (6th ed.). New York: Macmillan.

American Psychological Association. (2001). *Publication manual of the American Psychological Association* (5th ed.). Washington, DC: American Psychological Association.

Dunkin, M. J. (1996). Types of errors in synthesizing research in education. *Review of Educational Research, 66*, 87–97.

Gabel, D. L. (Ed.). (1994). *Handbook of research on science teaching and learning.* National Science Teachers Association. New York: Macmillan.

Glass, G. V. (2006). Meta-analysis: The quantitative synthesis of research findings. In J. L. Green, G. Camilli, and P. B. Elmore (Eds.), *Handbook of complementary methods in education research.* Mahwah, NJ: Lawrence Erlbaum.

LeCompte, M. D. (Ed.). (2003). *Review of educational research, 73.* Washington, DC: American Educational Research Association.

Smith, M. L., and Glass, G. V. (1987). *Research and evaluation in education and the social sciences.* Englewood Cliffs, NJ: Prentice-Hall.

CHAPTER 4 Communicating About Research

This text emphasizes how to do educational research; it describes the methods and procedures that apply to the various types of research. A part of doing research is communicating about research. Much of the communication takes place through the written word, such as research proposals and reports, although there also is some verbal communication, for example, through presentations at conferences. Formal communication is focused at two points: at the beginning of the research endeavor with a research proposal and at the close with a research report.

Sooner or later, graduate students prepare theses or dissertations, which have been preceded by proposals for the research reported in them. Funding agencies require proposals and reports, and publishing in professional journals is certainly widespread. Thus, the use of the written word in communicating about educational research is extensive.

This chapter discusses two types of written documents: the **research proposal,** which involves writing about intended research, and the **research report,** which describes completed research. Although there is a difference of intent, research proposals and reports do have many common characteristics. Within each there also is variation, especially in length, depending on such factors as the extent of the research, the audience for whom it is being prepared, and, if funded, the requirements of the specific funding agency. Although the general format may be similar, there are some differences between proposals and reports prepared for qualitative research and those for quantitative research. It is not feasible to include an entire proposal, journal article, or dissertation in this chapter, but the focus will be on those characteristics that constitute good proposals and reports.

Graduate students, especially those in doctoral programs, are required to defend their research proposals and completed dissertations, usually before faculty committees. Such defense involves verbal exchange. Presenting papers or giving other presentations at professional conferences and meetings is another form of verbal communication, although it involves more telling and not so much discussion as a dissertation defense. Some suggestions and guidelines are given for these types of communication.

Major Sections of the Research Proposal

Preparing a research proposal involves writing about a proposed rather than a completed research project. In proposal writing, we discuss what research is contemplated, why it is being contemplated, and how we intend to do it. The sections of the research proposal reflect answers to these assertions. The headings and subheadings within the research proposal may differ somewhat for different institutions or agencies. For example, some may require a section entitled "Procedures," others "Description of Activities," and still others "Methodology." Sometimes, a "Narrative" section is suggested for which the writer can supply subheadings. However, there is a general format for the content of a research proposal that develops a logical sequence from the statement of the problem in an adequate context and continues through concluding sections, which often provide a justification for the research. (Concluding sections for proposals submitted to funding agencies usually consist of budgets and résumés of the researchers.)

> *Research proposals* discuss what research is intended, how it is intended to be done, and why the research is intended; the sections of the proposal are then directed to these issues.

Research proposals vary in length depending on a variety of factors, including the magnitude of the proposed research and the complexity of the intended procedures. However, the general format and sectioning of proposals are consistent and an outline for the sections of a research proposal is provided in Figure 4.1. Proposals generally follow this format in order, although in some cases topics may be interchanged. For example, sometimes a major section called "Introduction" is used with such subheadings as "Identification of the Problem" and "Definition of Terms." The significance of the proposed research may be discussed earlier in the proposal. In some instances, a discussion of need for the research is included early in the proposal.

The topics for the major body of the research proposal are contained between the dashed lines in Figure 4.1. Usually, preliminary information is required in the form of a cover page that consists of the title of the proposed research, the names of the investigators, and the institution or agency where it will be conducted. An abstract also may be required.

The same general criteria apply for all sections of a research proposal. Writing should be concise, with continuity between and within the sections. The description of what is to be done should be comprehensive but not wordy. Some proposals submitted to funding agencies have specific limitations on the number of pages and these limitations must be adhered to. The sections should be arranged so that the reader can follow the train of thought. At this point, comments will be made about the various sections.

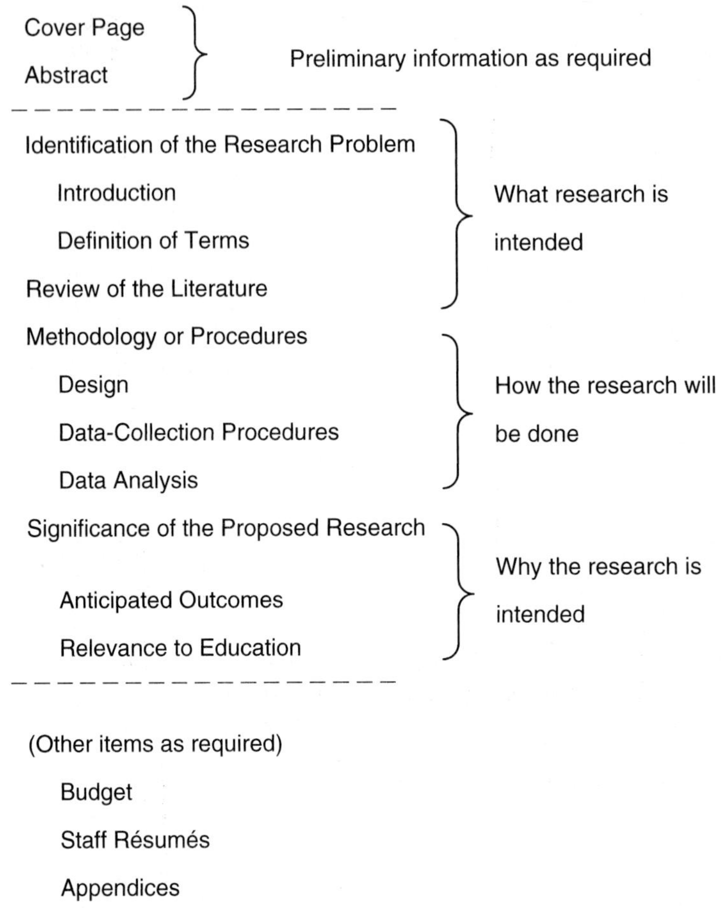

FIGURE 4.1 General Outline for the Sections of a Research Proposal

Identification of the Problem

Considerable discussion about stating **research problems** and hypotheses was presented in an earlier chapter, and those comments are not repeated here. It is important in a proposal that the problem stand out—that the reader can easily recognize it. Sometimes, obscure and poorly formulated problems are masked in an extended discussion, and a reviewer has difficulty recognizing the problem. If that happens, the remainder of the proposal suffers severely in the review. The extent of the elaboration of the problem varies with the magnitude of the intended study. Qualitative research studies tend to have somewhat more general problem statements than those for quantitative research. Experiments and surveys typically have explicit, stated hypotheses, whereas ethnographic research, for example, may have foreshadowed problems.

The statement of the problem typically comes very early in the research proposal. There are usually some introductory comments, possibly including a few references to the related literature, to provide a context for stating the research problem. Then the problem is explicitly identified. The introductory phrase may be one of the following:

> The problem of this proposed research is . . .
> The research question to be addressed is . . .
> The purpose of the research is . . .
> Specifically, the research problem is . . .

The related hypotheses and/or research questions and operational definitions then follow in the proposal, usually quite closely. Occasionally, the hypotheses statements may appear later in the proposal if the measurement and data description might enhance the understanding of the hypotheses. However, unless somewhat unusual data are to be generated and uncommon analysis procedures are to be used, there is no point in separating the statement of the problem and the hypotheses.

Because both research reports and proposals require identification of the problems, examples can be selected from the research literature. In a study comparing the effects of silent reading and reading aloud, Hale et al. (2007) stated that the purpose of the study was to examine the relationship between silent-reading comprehension and aloud-reading comprehension and to determine whether comprehension was systematically affected by reading mode. They were determining whether comprehension scores were higher following reading aloud compared to the scores following reading silently.

The problem statement in a qualitative study is likely to be worded somewhat differently. Andrews and Ridenour (2006) studied the impact of a cultural diversity course on the attitudes and behaviors of students in educational administration.

> We examined gender-awareness training as part of a school administrator preparation program and its effects on students preparing to become school leaders. The question guiding the study was, "What is the impact of an educational administration graduate class in diversity on students' awareness of how gender may play a role in school culture and climate?" (p. 35)

Notice that the problem statement in the qualitative study is open-ended. This allows for discovering many different kinds of effects that were not specified in advance. The problem statement in the quantitative study, on the other hand, looked for improved reading comprehension scores, a precisely defined outcome.

As necessary, terms used in describing the research problem should be defined, especially any terms that otherwise may be ambiguous. However, the identification of the problem should not become too cluttered with operational definitions. Such definitions of variables to be measured can be provided in the methodology section, where the measurement is described, rather than in the statement of the problem, especially if operational definitions are somewhat complex.

Review of the Literature

The **review of the literature** provides the background and context for the research problem. Proposals may vary considerably in the length of the review. Dissertation proposals often contain fifteen or more double-spaced pages in the review. In any event, it is seldom, if ever, possible to include every potentially relevant study in the review. Thus, the proposal writer must be selective.

With survey and experimental research, results from studies reviewed and specific results can be incorporated into the review. For qualitative research, such as ethnographic research, the review will tend to focus on more general or broad concepts. For example, the researcher might identify possible theoretical concepts that may become useful during data collection and analysis. This is a preliminary review but it does identify the conceptual framework with which the researcher enters the field. The review should justify the need for an in-depth descriptive study. Possibly the phenomena have not been studied using a qualitative approach, and the case can be made that such an approach is appropriate and useful. If the approach has been used, it is necessary to identify gaps and deficiencies in other studies.

The significance of the proposed research may be addressed in the review of the literature section. This is appropriate in that the need for the research should be discussed here, and need is related to significance. However, when the case for significance is particularly crucial, such as in a dissertation proposal, it is a good idea to have a special section in addition to any comments about significance in the review. If that section is placed near the end of the proposal, the proposal reader is better informed about the research, and the case for significance may be stronger.

One of the marks of a knowledgeable reviewer is the ability to select pertinent information, tie it together to provide an understandable and accurate background for the problem, and demonstrate the continuity between the ideas in the literature and the research problem. The proposal writer should avoid statements implying that information on the problem is very limited or that the review has revealed no information about the problem. The proposal reader will be very suspicious of such statements (and rightly so) and will likely interpret them as a lack of knowledge on the part of the writer rather than as a gap in the literature. The review of literature should reveal that the writer has a good grasp of the area in which research is intended.

> The review of the literature provides the background and context for the research problem. It should establish the need for the research and indicate that the writer is knowledgeable about the area.

Methods or Procedures

This section of the research proposal will vary considerably depending on the type of proposed research. It will vary not only in content but also in length. To the extent that subheadings are appropriate, it is well to use them. Subheadings such as "Design," "Site

Selection," "Sample," and "Data Analysis" will not only aid the writer in identifying and describing the various activities but also should help the proposal reader understand the continuity of the various activities.

In an ethnographic research proposal this section should address the following issues:

1. Site selection and any sampling, purposeful or random, that will be done at the site;
2. The role of the researcher;
3. Data-collection procedures: observation, interviewing, use of questionnaires, and the application of triangulation or other method-specific techniques;
4. Presentation of data and inductive data analysis;
5. Limitations of the design.

When describing the site selection, the case must be made that the site will provide an appropriate setting for the research. To do this, it is helpful to show the correspondence between the foreshadowed problems and the characteristics of the site. For example, if a foreshadowed problem deals with social interaction, then the site must provide an opportunity to observe social interaction. If key informants are to be used, then make the case why certain types of individuals can assume this role.

The role of the researcher, for example, privileged observer, should be described along with possible data-collection procedures. It should be clear that multiple methods will be used, but the specific methods (items, etc.) will be identified in the field. The anticipated length of the data collection should be stated, along with its intensity. For example, will the researcher be on site every day, three days per week? On a given day will data collection take place for one hour, several hours?

Ethnographic research involves field notes along with other data, so there should be a description of how this information will be analyzed, even if only a general, inductive analysis is described. What are possible category systems or ways of ordering the data? The reader should be given some indication of the extent of the anticipated descriptive analysis, the ethnography that will be the product of this research.

Regardless of the type of research, the limitations of the design should be described. If limitations are not addressed specifically, the proposal reader may well infer that the researcher is expecting results from the study that are not possible. Restricting the statement of the research problem will aid in defining the limits of the design. The extent of generalizability should be addressed in this section. Extensive generalizability typically is more important for quantitative research than for qualitative research.

Ethnographic and historical research are, to a large extent, case studies, not necessarily of individuals, but of a site, an issue, a phenomenon, or an event. As such, it is well to identify the research as a case study, which cues the reader to expect certain design characteristics. For more quantitative research, the design can be described by a specific name. For example:

> A pretest-posttest control group design will be used involving four groups, three experimental and one control, with sex and grade level included as independent variables giving a $4 \times 2 \times 4$ factorial design.

Many designs have relatively common usage in the research literature, and their descriptive titles can be used. A title can be coined for a design so long as it is descriptive and appropriate.

For experiments and surveys, as applicable, the following project activities, materials, and so forth should be described in this section in addition to the general research design:

1. Measurement instruments to be used or developed;
2. Individuals participating in the research (subjects);
3. Sample (design and numbers);
4. Experimental procedure if the intended project is an experiment;
5. Data-collection procedures;
6. Data analysis (specific analyses to be used).

If there are potential weaknesses in the design or potential difficulties in doing the research, the writer should describe what will be done to compensate for or eliminate them. For example, there might be the possibility of extraneous variables being confounded with independent variables. Their possible effects should be discussed, and the discussion should indicate how they will be controlled or eliminated. Occasionally, writers are under the misconception that it is sufficient to identify a difficulty without providing a solution. Identifying a potential problem is not the same as solving it and, certainly, indicating that nothing can be done about the problem is no solution.

The matter of sampling is an example of the need for specific detail. The sampling plan must be viewed in terms of the external and internal validity of the research project. When sampling is used, the researcher invariably is attempting to make inferences to a larger population, so care must be taken in selecting the sample so that it represents the population.

In a study involving a sample of high school seniors from a single state, for example, it is not adequate to say that a random sample of seniors will be selected from the high schools of the state; the sampling plan should be described in detail. Assuming an adequate operational definition of a high school senior, the writer should indicate how all members of the population will be identified. What types of information will be available that will include all seniors who fit the definitions? Are stratifying variables to be used? If so, what are they and why are they important? Will it be necessary to sample through an intermediate unit? What will the replacement procedure be if selected units decline to participate?

These types of questions should be carefully answered. For example, if stratified random sampling with proportional allocation is the sampling design, the stratifying variables should be operationally defined, and it should be clear to the reader that students can be identified in terms of stratifying variables from the population information. It would not be adequate to indicate simply that size of district will be a stratifying variable. The definition of the categories for the stratifying variable would have to be given—for example, less than 2000 students, 2000–5000 students, and so on. Information should be provided about the source, probably a state document, on which the size of the district will be based, and it would be well to provide a rationale for the specific categories of the stratifying variable. A complete description of this type will provide the reader with evidence regarding how and why the sample will be selected.

The discussion of the procedures usually follows a somewhat chronological order of how they will be done. This makes it easier for the reader to recognize the continuity of the various procedures. If the intended research is adequately conceptualized by the proposal writers, they should be able to explain what they intend to do. The important thing is to have an appropriate and complete description.

> The methods or procedures section is really the heart of the research proposal. The activities should be described with as much detail as possible, and the continuity between them should be apparent.

Significance of the Proposed Research

Although empirical results certainly may be important, research is seldom conducted solely for the purpose of generating data. Regardless of the type of research, the study should contribute to the extension of knowledge in the area. Gaps in the existing knowledge may be filled, and the present study may answer questions raised by preceding research studies. Another contribution of a study is the suggestion or identification of questions for future research.

Other anticipated outcomes relate to the practical **significance of the research.** What will the research results mean to the practicing educator? Will the results, regardless of outcome, influence programs or methods? If the research will set the stage for deciding on alternative courses of action for improving education, this can be a significant contribution. What will be improved or changed as the result of the proposed research? How will the results of the study be implemented, and what innovations will come about?

Answers to these questions suggest outcomes that may take different forms. One outcome, in ethnographic research, for example, is a detailed description, an ethnography, of a naturalistic, educational phenomenon. Possibly the description will generate a theoretical explanation of the phenomenon. If such an outcome is anticipated, it should be mentioned in this section.

A revised curriculum or a description of how a segment of a curriculum in a specific area might be changed are examples of outcomes. Another product might be a process for the improvement of learning. A program is a possible product, such as one for dealing with disruptive behavior or reducing the number of dropouts. The research in and of itself may not generate a curriculum or program—these would likely have to be developed after the research is completed—but the research provides the basis for such development. It is important to indicate the potential relevance of the research to such outcomes.

Results of research may be useful for policy formation. For example, a school board may use survey results for determining board policy. When research is conducted on the roles of educational specialists, especially relatively new ones such as computer education specialists, the results can aid in the identification of necessary skills and in the definition of the role.

The case for the relevance to education is made, to some extent, when the need for the research is established through the review of the literature. When discussing the significance of the research, it is important to indicate how the anticipated results of this research will tie in to the research results already reported in the literature. The proposal writer should not hesitate to use previously cited or additional references at this point.

The relevance of the research problem to education is pretty well established through the review of the literature and the background for the problem. The case for the results being relevant to education rests on the effects of the anticipated outcomes. If these outcomes have potential benefit or impact, either practically or theoretically, the case can be made. Because this connection exists, the potential relevance to education depends on the likelihood that the anticipated outcomes will be attained.

> The significance of the proposed research will be established on the basis of the anticipated outcomes, which may be in the form of products or processes.

Other Sections of the Research Proposal

The sections of a research proposal described thus far comprise the major parts or body of the proposal, but other sections may be appropriate for specific proposals. Indeed, funding agencies often require certain routine informational sections and, certainly, a budget. Brief comments on these sections are provided here.

Cover Page. The **cover page** contains introductory information for the proposal: the name of the proposed project, the author of the proposal or principal investigator, and the institution. Some funding agencies have standardized cover pages that may contain additional information, such as a budget total.

Abstract. An **abstract** is a brief summary statement of the proposed research. At the very least, it contains a statement of the research problem. Abstracts usually are limited to a maximum number of words; seldom do they exceed one page.

Budget. When a proposal is submitted to a funding agency, a **budget** is required; it is usually placed near the end of the proposal. When a budget is prepared, the proposal writer should use the guidelines of the funding agency to which the proposal will be submitted and those of the institution through which it is being submitted. This should take care of such matters as overhead and benefit rates. Typical budget categories would include personnel, fringe benefits, supplies, equipment, telephone, data processing, postage, photocopying, printing, and overhead. Failure to follow guidelines usually results in considerable budget recalculation later and, possibly, unanticipated negotiations. An inappropriate or poorly constructed budget may result in rejection of the proposal.

Research conducted for theses and dissertations usually is not externally funded, so budget preparation is not a concern. However, constructing a budget for a dissertation or thesis is a worthwhile exercise because it makes the student aware of the actual costs of doing the research. A graduate student may be doing research for a dissertation through some larger, externally funded project. However, in such situations a separate budget is seldom developed for the dissertation research.

Timeline. A schedule of the research activities is needed to ensure that all of the interrelated activities will occur in a timely manner. The schedule should be realistic and allow for unforeseen delays.

Staff Résumés. **Staff résumés** or vitae consist of summaries of the experience, education, publications, and research activities of individuals who will work on the proposed project. Again, résumés are commonly required for externally funded research.

Appendices. If there is considerable supplementary information that may be relevant to the proposal content, it can be placed in an **appendix.** Appendices contain information that would distract from the continuity of the proposal if it were contained in the main body of the proposal. In a proposal submitted for external funding, an appendix might contain a description of the resources of the researcher's institution, such as the library and computer facilities.

Major Sections of the Research Report

One distinguishing characteristic of the different types of research reports is length. The professional journal article may vary from five to twenty pages, occasionally longer, especially for reports of qualitative research. Restrictions of space for individual publications limit the length of journal articles. Dissertations and technical reports submitted to funding agencies usually are longer, commonly around one hundred pages and, in some cases, considerably longer. (Sometimes appendices contain substantial amounts of supplementary information that increase the length.) The length of a paper prepared for a professional meeting depends on the time allocated for presentation. However, such papers tend to be similar in length to journal articles, and many papers later appear as journal articles.

Even with the different types of research reports, there are some common characteristics in the way they are organized and presented. The sections follow, to some extent, the same sequence as those in a research proposal. However, a research report contains sections dealing with results and conclusions, which are not found in a proposal. In a proposal, there is a great deal of emphasis on how the research will be done. The emphasis for a report shifts to the results and the implications of those results.

> In a *research report,* the writer describes completed research. There are discussions of what research was done, how it was done, and the results and conclusions of the research. The significance of the research also is addressed.

The sections of the research report begin with the identification of the problem and continue through the conclusions and implications. The sections have different formats for different types of reports. For dissertations or long reports, they usually take the form of chapters, whereas journal articles and papers commonly contain headings. Typically, dissertations contain five or so chapters, beginning with an introduction that contains the statement of the research problem, the review of literature, a methods chapter, a results chapter, and a final chapter of conclusions and recommendations. A dissertation about a qualitative research study may be organized differently with more integration of method, results, and conclusions. A journal article runs together the introduction and review and emphasizes the results and conclusions.

The general criteria for preparing a good proposal also apply to writing a good research report. Additional comments on the major sections of a research report are provided here.

Introduction, Including the Statement of the Problem

A dissertation usually has a several-page buildup to the problem statement, providing quite a complete introduction to the research. If hypotheses are appropriate, they too are introduced at this point. Articles in professional journals do not have space for a long buildup to the problem, so the context for the research must be established concisely. This introduction may include a brief review of the literature as well, unless the article deals with historical research or, for some reason, the results of numerous other studies must be brought in.

Problem statements were explained in the section on writing proposals, and another example from the literature is given here. Brand (2006) presents a study of a literature-based program of instruction based on Gardner's theory of multiple intelligences. She presents the purpose of the study and then lists the four hypotheses that will be tested.

> Specifically, the storytelling methods include chant (enlisting musical and linguistic intelligence); felt board and draw talk (enlisting visual-spatial, mathematical, and naturalistic intelligences); pantomime and character imagery (enlisting bodily-kinesthetic and naturalistic intelligences); group role play (enlisting intrapersonal, interpersonal, and musical intelligences); and puppetry (enlisting visual-spatial and bodily-kinesthetic intelligences). These stories, told by the teacher and often accompanied by the children, are used as the foundation upon which sequential and systematic phonics activities are based. (p. 134)

The hypotheses in the study were:

1. Children who receive small-group, literature-based multiple intelligence training will score significantly higher on a measure of Letter Naming Fluency than will an untreated comparison group.
2. Children who receive small-group, literature-based multiple intelligence training will score significantly higher on a measure of Phoneme Segmentation Fluency than will an untreated comparison group.

3. Children who receive small-group, literature-based multiple intelligence training will score significantly higher on a measure of Nonsense Word Fluency than will an untreated comparison group.
4. Children who receive small-group, literature-based multiple intelligence training will score significantly higher on a measure of Word Use Fluency than will an untreated comparison group. (p. 135)

Although the wording of the hypotheses seems to be redundant, it is important to list the hypotheses separately because it is possible that the data will support none of them, all of them, or some combination of them. It would be difficult to draw conclusions if they were all lumped together. The hypotheses contain the word *significantly.* This is a problem because hypotheses are written about populations, not about samples and the word *significant* refers to sample values. This concept is explained in the chapter on inferential statistics.

Review of the Literature

In professional journal articles, the literature review often does not have a separate heading; it is incorporated with the introduction and background. Because of space limitations, the writer must make decisions about which references to include and cite. The pertinent information must then be provided succinctly and tied together to provide a context for the problem.

As indicated earlier, dissertations typically have an entire chapter reserved for the review of the literature, which may cover thirty-five or more double-spaced pages. The headings in the chapter are specific to the study. Of course, the number of headings will vary. Qualitative studies that rely heavily on description tend to have fewer headings than quantitative studies, the latter having as many as ten or twelve headings. The important characteristic is not the number of headings, but the way the headings are placed to partition the review into appropriate segments.

The ideas from the various studies referred to in the review should relate to each other, as should the parts designated by the headings. This is called **transition,** and transition is facilitated by keeping the writing focused on the research problem. A common error is to present ideas from individual studies as little packages within themselves, which makes for a disjointed presentation. A related error is to treat each study in a mechanical way, regardless of relative importance.

The writer should avoid excessive use of quotations. In the context of the research problem, the ideas from several sources usually can be tied together better by the writer's own words than by a series of quotations. The ideas from the review of the literature should be integrated into a logical discussion focusing on the research problem.

The writer is not obligated to discuss information from every source listed in the bibliography. Often, in an article, three or four main points are brought in from an equal number of sources. Additional references may be listed in the bibliography to complement the information from the sources discussed. In the discussion of the review of the literature, the writer should demonstrate an adequate knowledge of the problem and the research related to it. An extensive bibliography with almost no discussion is not evidence of an adequate review of literature.

Methods or Procedures

The parts of this section describe how the research was done. How much description is necessary? A good rule to follow is that the description should be detailed enough so that a reader could replicate the study. Descriptions in dissertations tend to be very detailed, because the writer is demonstrating mastery of the methodology as well as the appropriateness of the methods used.

Methods sections often contain subheadings. For example, in a study by Madrid, Canas, and Ortega-Medina (2007) on the effects of team competition versus team cooperation in classwide peer tutoring, the methods section contains the following subheadings:

Participants and Setting
Bilingual Proficiency
Curriculum
Probes
Design
Procedures (pp. 156–157)

Each of these subsections contains considerable descriptions of the details. This length is often necessary to explain what was done.

In contrast, a study of physical activity opportunities in K–12 public school settings in Nevada by Lounsbery, Bungum, and Smith (2007) had only three subheadings in the methods section:

Subjects
Instrumentation
Statistical Analysis (pp. 31–32)

Although they are quite different, each of these methods sections is well done and appropriate for the study. The point being made is that methods sections may vary considerably, not only in length and content but also in the writing approach. Methods sections in qualitative research reports tend to be more descriptive than those in quantitative reports. For quantitative research, statistical procedures are discussed at some point.

> Methods sections show a lot of variability across research reports in length, content, and the writing approach. The important criterion is that enough information is given so the reader can understand what was done.

The methods section describes instrumentation, data collection, sampling, experimental procedure, materials, and statistical analysis as these topics apply. The order of presenting the various topics in a methods section is somewhat arbitrary. One logical order is the sequence in which the activities of the topics occurred in conducting the research. It is possible that two or more of the activities were worked on simultaneously. However, the research project usually progresses from the development of the design and selection of the participants through data analysis.

Results

Results are the products of data analysis and they come in various forms. They may consist of summary statements synthesized from other documents, as in a historical study, or from field notes, as in ethnographic research. When statistical analysis is used, descriptive statistics and those generated by statistical tests are results.

Consider the qualitative study by Andrews and Ridenour (2006) that was mentioned earlier in this chapter on the effects of a cultural diversity class. After describing the conceptual and theoretical frameworks, the setting, the research design, the educational program intervention, and the analysis of evidence, the results are presented under the following headings:

Profile of Study Participants
Analysis and Interpretation of Student Journals
Blatant Gender Stereotypes
Increased Reflection on and Change in Professional Practice
Awareness of Gender Discrimination and Power Differences
Impact of Gender-Biased Language

The results were organized according to the major findings with considerable discussion of each finding.

Reporting quantitative results is quite straightforward, and tables are often used to summarize results. In a study about how children's achievement-related beliefs could be predicted from their friends' beliefs, both concurrently and over time, Altermatt and Pomerantz (2003) reported many statistical results in five separate tables. They reported both internal consistency and stability reliability coefficients for their measures; the means and standard deviations across three time periods; the correlations between academic performance, competence-related beliefs, and motivational beliefs; and the standardized regression coefficients used in their predictions that were done at the same time and at a later time. The results were summarized and some supplementary analyses were reported in narrative form rather than in tables. The results section was followed by a discussion section. It is typically easier to separate the results and the conclusions in quantitative research than it is in qualitative research. Whether they are separate or not depends on the most effective and understandable method of presentation.

Use of Tables and Figures. Tables can be used effectively for summarizing results, especially if a report involves a large amount of statistical material. The content of a table should be clear to the reader. This may seem to be an obvious statement, but tables are sometimes confusing and puzzle the reader.

Statistical software, spreadsheets, and word processing programs provide the researcher opportunities to create figures that range from the simple to the elaborate. Too many figures or figures that are too complicated can distract and confuse the reader.

Well-crafted figures can enhance the reader's understanding. They should be used sparingly and effectively. A "picture is worth a thousand words," but a poorly designed figure can cost more than a thousand words to explain it.

Figures can be useful ways to describe the steps in processes. The boxes and arrows convey the message much more succinctly than would a lengthy narrative in paragraph form. Figures also depict linkages and relationships more clearly than words would. One way to find out whether the figure or diagram that you created is as clear to others as it is to you, is to have others interpret the figure, telling you what message they think that it conveys.

Pie charts, bar charts, and other charts are also figures that are available on most software. These can be effective visual devices when they are used sparingly. At times their availability leads to their overuse. This can be especially true when numerical results are presented and the researchers think that it is necessary to attach a corresponding figure to every tabled result.

There are some relatively straightforward rules to follow when constructing tables and figures:

1. The title should state specifically what the table or figure contains, including the referent or source of the content.

2. Appropriate subheadings should be included for rows and columns.

3. The number of different types of information a table contains should be limited. For example, means and standard deviations may go together, but correlation coefficients probably would not be included in the same table.

4. Spacing in the table or figure should be such that information is clearly separated. Do not crowd.

5. If possible, tables and figures should be limited to a single page. A table or figure that will fit on one page should not be split over two pages.

6. The table or figure should follow the first reference to it as closely as possible.

7. Table and figure formats should be consistent within a report.

8. An excessive number of lines should not be included in tables. Horizontal lines may be used to set off headings, but vertical lines are seldom necessary. The information should not appear as if it is being "caged."

Figure 4.2 contains a sample results table, showing the title and headings. Note that the title does not simply state that the table includes means and standard deviations; it indicates the source of the means and standard deviations.

> Tables and figures can be used effectively for summarizing results, but their content must be adequately labeled and logically organized.

Table 0.0
Means and Standard Deviations of Fifth-Grade Students on Academic Measures

	Experimental Group 1		*Experimental Group 2*		*Control Group*	
Measure	*Mean*	*Standard Deviation*	*Mean*	*Standard Deviation*	*Mean*	*Standard Deviation*
Reading						
Arithmetic						
Spelling						
Science						
Social Studies						

FIGURE 4.2 Example of Title and Headings for a Table Containing Results

The important concern in writing a results section is to present the results in a clear, well-organized manner. Results can be organized in a number of ways. For example, when reporting on an ethnographic study, one possible organization is around foreshadowed problems. Or the results may be presented in a sequential narrative describing what happened. If several dependent variables are included in the study, the results may be grouped according to dependent variables, for example, grouping achievement measures separately from attitude measures. Sometimes, results are reported in the order of the hypotheses, if there are specific hypotheses. If several experiments were included in a study, the results could be organized in the order in which the experiments occurred. This is often done in dissertations based on a series of experiments. Whatever organization makes the most sense and facilitates the reader's understanding should be used.

Conclusions, Recommendations, and Implications

The final section of the research report consists of the summary, conclusions, implications, and recommendations for further research. The **summary** section usually begins with a brief restatement of the research problem and possibly some comments on the methods that were used.

The **conclusion** section should follow logically from the results and should avoid undesirable repetition of the results section. One common error in dissertations is that the writer is reluctant to draw conclusions and, instead, repeats results and passes them off as conclusions. The number of conclusions drawn depends on the complexity of the results. Supposedly, at least one substantial conclusion can be drawn; otherwise it hardly would be worth conducting, much less reporting, the research.

> The results of a research study are the products of the data analysis. Conclusions are the inferences and the like that the researcher draws from the results.

The following should be done in preparing the conclusions part of a research report:

1. Identify all noteworthy results in order of importance.
2. Interpret these results relative to the research problem and in the context of related research and/or theory; that is, draw conclusions.
3. Discuss other plausible interpretations of the results and explain why these are less likely than the interpretation of item 2.
4. Tie your results in with results from related research studies.
5. Explain any inconsistencies between your results and results from related research studies.
6. Discuss any limitations of your study, such as design limitations or problems in the procedures of conducting the research.
7. Address the external validity of the conclusions, being specific about the generalizability of the conclusions and how generalizability may be limited.

The extent to which each of these items will be addressed depends on the magnitude of the study. Research conducted for a dissertation typically results in several conclusions.

Implications refer to how others, often teachers and administrators, can use the conclusions. If there is evidence that can inform practitioners, it should be made explicit. One of the difficulties with educational research is the lag time between what is found in research and what is put into practice in the schools. A clear implications section, along with proper caveats, might shorten the lag time.

Most dissertations have extensive **recommendations** for future research. These recommendations can sometimes be interpreted as "How I would conduct the study if I could do it all over again." More often, a good study will raise as many questions as it answers, and the researcher is in the best position to see what would be the next steps in the investigation of the phenomenon. Journal articles, because of space limitations, for one reason, usually do not have extensive discussions of recommendations for future research.

This final section of a research report likely will require more rewriting than earlier sections. Transition and continuity between ideas are especially important in this section. A good procedure is to let the report sit for a few days, then go through it again completely and see whether the conclusions still seem reasonable. There also should be a check for possible omissions. Rewriting should take off any "rough edges" and generally improve the quality of writing.

Other Sections of the Research Report

Preliminary sections, such as a title page, a table of contents, and an abstract, often are found in a research report. A bibliography and possibly an appendix often follow the conclusions section. These latter sections are called "backmatter." (A journal article would not contain a table of contents or an appendix and, when published, would not have a separate title page.) The title page usually follows a prescribed format similar to that of the title page of a proposal. Acknowledgments, a table of contents, and any necessary lists are self-explanatory. This leaves the abstract for the preliminary information.

Abstract

The **abstract** of a research report is similar to that of a research proposal, except that it describes what was done instead of what is contemplated. It contains a brief summary of the results. Again, abstracts can vary in length, depending on the report, but they usually do not exceed one double-spaced typed page.

Many professional journals require abstracts for published reports, and these tend to be quite brief, around 120 to 150 words. An example of such an abstract, from Elbaum (2007), is as follows:

> This study compared the performance of students with and without learning disabilities (LD) on a mathematics test using a standard administration procedure and a read-aloud accommodation. Analyses were conducted on the test scores of 625 middle and high school students (n = 388 with LD) on two equivalent 30-item multiple-choice tests. Whereas mean scores for students both with and without LD were higher in the accommodated condition, students without disabilities benefited significantly more from the accommodation (ES = 0.44) than students with LD (ES = 0.20). In addition, effect sizes from the present study were combined meta-analytically with those of previous studies. Results of the meta-analysis revealed that for elementary students, oral accommodations on a mathematics test yielded greater gains for students with LD than for students without disabilities; for secondary students, the converse was true. Findings of the study are discussed in relation to the question of the validity of an oral accommodation on mathematics tests for students both with and without disabilities. (p. 218)

The abstract identifies the participants, the procedures, the analyses, and the results. The rationale for the accommodations and any controversy about using accommodations were not included, but enough of the results were presented that the implications of the study are clear to the reader.

Executive summaries, which are sort of extended abstracts, have become quite popular for extended reports submitted to agencies. An executive summary may be as long as several pages, although a length of two or three pages may be preferred in the interest of brevity. Executive summaries elaborate more on results and conclusions than abstracts. Executive summaries and abstracts are not necessarily easy to write because of condensing the important points of the research into a small space.

Bibliography and Reference List

Toward the end of a research report, following the conclusions section, appears the list of references and, possibly, a **bibliography.** The American Psychological Association (2001) distinguishes between a **reference list** and bibliography as follows:

> Note that a reference list cites works that specifically support a particular article. In contrast, a bibliography cites works for background or for further reading. (p. 215)

Professional journals commonly require reference lists, not bibliographies. An extensive report such as a dissertation would require a bibliography.

A bibliographic entry contains a full description of the work, the name of the first author, inverted with last name first, followed by the names of coauthors. Titles of books, monographs, and journals are italicized. There are slight variations in format, as suggested in different editorial style sources. The *Publication Manual of the American Psychological Association* (2001) provides the following rules for referencing books, magazines, and electronic sources. The APA Manual also contains rules and examples for most other sources that you might use, such as dissertations, monographs, and the like.

Books

- Invert all authors' names; give surnames and initials.
- Put the publication date in parentheses followed by a period.
- Capitalize only the first word of the title and of the subtitle, if any, and any proper nouns; italicize the title.
- Put the edition, if not the first, in parentheses followed by a period.
- List the location of the publisher followed by a colon, then the publisher.
- Finish with a period.

Example

Kowalski, T. J. (2008). *Case studies on educational administration* (5th ed.). Boston: Allyn & Bacon.

Articles

- Invert all authors' names; give surnames and initials.
- Put the publication date in parentheses followed by a period.
- Capitalize only the first word of the title and of the subtitle, if any, and any proper nouns.
- Capitalize and italicize the name of the periodical.
- Italicize the volume number, followed by a comma.
- Put the issue in parentheses, only if the periodical is paginated by issue.
- List the page numbers.
- Finish with a period.

Example

Hopkins, M. H. (2007). Adapting a model for literacy learning to the learning of mathematics. *Reading and Writing Quarterly, 23,* 121–138.

Electronic sources

- Use the rules for articles and books for authors and titles.
- Note that there may not be page numbers.
- Provide the date when the document was last retrieved.
- Provide the complete URL.

Example

Harvard Family Research Project. (2007). Out-of-school time program research and evaluation bibliography. Retrieved April 12, 2007, from www.gse.harvard.edu/hfrp/projects/afterschool/bibliography/tutoring.html

The format used by the American Psychological Association is widely accepted, especially among professional journals in the behavioral sciences.

Entries are placed in the bibliography in alphabetical order, using the last name of the first author. If two or more works by the same author are included, the last name is not repeated in subsequent entries but is substituted for by a long dash, followed by a period. The two or more listings for an author are alphabetized by initial letter of the title, excluding *A, An,* or *The.* If entries include publications of which the author is sole author and others coauthor, those of sole authorship appear first.

Appendix

An appendix is included only if it is necessary, for example, when there are materials that do not fit well in the main body of the report. Several types of materials can be placed in an appendix: self-constructed measuring instruments, such as tests or questionnaires; tables of raw scores; or related data. A large volume of related results tends to make the main report cumbersome and difficult reading, and such results can be placed in the appendix. Separate appendices should be used for different types of materials. The appendices appear at the end of the report, following the references or bibliography.

Putting a Report Together

A research report, especially a long one, is seldom conceptualized and written in one sitting. It usually is helpful to work from an outline. Sections often need reworking and rewriting. Generally, revision is a normal part of the task, and the report usually is improved by subsequent revisions, additions, and deletions. Critical reviews (conducted in a positive sense) of initial drafts by knowledgeable colleagues are helpful. Self-criticism or review is also valuable, but it is usually most valuable after the writer has let the report sit for a short time, perhaps a week to ten days. Explanations may not be so obvious and logical as they seemed to be during the initial writing, and omissions and confusing statements may become more apparent.

There are always several technical considerations when preparing a research report. Correct grammar and spelling and accepted uses of tenses are required. The past tense is used to report research findings, both one's own and those reported by others, for example:

"Students in grades five and seven obtained mean scores of 25.3 and 31.6, respectively." The present tense is used to refer to the presentation of data and well-accepted generalizations, for example, "Table 1 contains the mean of all grades, separated by geographic region."

There are acceptable formats for presenting content in a report. Some institutions and associations have their own requirements about such things as margin size, table format, and presentation of graphs and figures. These are technical concerns, and it is simply a matter of knowing the rules and following them. Most institutions will accept any recognized standard format.

There are a number of publications dealing with format and style for preparing reports. The reference desks of most college and university libraries have copies of several such publications. The content of these manuals, guides, or handbooks includes explicit detail about format and style, including how to handle variations of the usual references and sections. The following are examples of such publications:

American Psychological Association. (2001). *Publication manual of the American Psychological Association* (5th ed.). Washington, DC: American Psychological Association.

Gibaldi, J. (1998). *MLA style manual and guide to scholarly publishing* (2nd ed.). New York: Modern Language Association of America.

Slade, C., and Perrin, R. (2008). *Form and style: Research papers, reports, theses* (13th ed.). Boston: Houghton Mifflin.

Williams, J. M. (2003). *Style: Toward clarity and grace* (7th ed.). New York: Longman.

This chapter provides an overview of communicating about research, but there are entire books written about the preparation of proposals and research reports including dissertations and theses. For those readers who desire additional resources on this topic, the following books may be useful.

Dees, R. (2003). *Writing the modern research paper* (4th ed.). Boston: Longman.

Glatthorn, A. A. (1998). Writing the winning dissertation: A step-by-step guide. Thousand Oaks, CA: Corwin.

Klausmeier, H. J. (2001). *Research writing in education and psychology—from planning to publication: A practical handbook.* Springfield, IL: Charles C. Thomas.

Lester, J., and Lester J. (2006). *Writing research papers: Research Navigator edition* (11th ed.). New York: Longman.

Locke, L. F., Spirduso, W. W., and Silverman, S. J. (2007). *Proposals that work: A guide for planning dissertations and grants proposals* (5th ed.). Newbury Park, CA: Sage.

Meloy, J. M. (2002). *Writing the qualitative dissertation* (2nd ed.). Mahwah, NJ: Lawrence Erlbaum.

Guidelines for Presenting Papers at Meetings

As professionals, educators participate in professional meetings or conferences, examples being the annual meetings of organizations such as the American Educational Research Association (AERA) and the National Council for Measurement in Education (NCME).

At these meetings, participants present papers about research or other professional activities and take part in symposia. Associations typically have a **call for papers,** which goes out in a professional journal several months before the meeting. The call for papers will include forms to be completed. An abstract about the research to be reported on may be required, along with other information about the topic and the presenter. There will be a deadline for responding to the call, and it is important to follow the directions to the letter, so the proposed paper is not rejected on some technicality.

> The first step in getting a presentation accepted for a professional meeting is to respond to the *call for papers* of the association sponsoring the meeting.

Assuming the association's proposal review committee accepts the paper proposal, following are the guidelines for preparing and presenting the paper.

1. Prepare a draft of the paper so that the research described in the paper has closure. Sometimes this research is part of a larger study, but it must not be left hanging, so to speak.

2. Accurately estimate the time required to read the paper. The association will have time limits and these must be honored. It may be possible to have a more extended paper for distribution than what is actually read, but what is read must have continuity and closure.

3. Have one or more colleagues critique the draft of the paper.

4. Prepare a final draft of the paper. (It may be necessary to repeat step 3, depending on the status of the original draft.)

5. Anticipate the size of the audience and prepare enough copies for distribution at the meeting.

6. Familiarize yourself with the content of the paper, so presenting it can be done with audience eye contact.

7. At the meeting, check the room in which the presentation will be given to make sure that any necessary equipment is available. If any AV equipment is necessary, this would have been requested in the response to the call for papers.

8. Arrive at the presentation room several minutes before the session is to begin so that you can meet the chairperson and other presenters.

9. If tables or charts are to be distributed with the presentation, arrange to have them distributed efficiently and without wasting time.

10. When it is your turn, give your presentation in a straightforward manner, speaking at a normal rate. You should be familiar enough with the paper so that you can talk to the audience, not read the paper verbatim. *Do not* attempt to give the presentation from memory or extemporaneously give a condensed version.

11. If for some unforeseen reason time does not allow reading the entire paper, make a decision about what part will be omitted, inform the audience, and mention that the omitted part is covered in the available copies.

12. Let the audience know that copies of the paper are available if they have not been distributed earlier. After the session, remain a few minutes to be sure there are adequate copies of the paper. If you run out of copies, have a sign-up sheet for the names and addresses of those desiring copies. (Be sure to follow up immediately in mailing these copies when you return to your home institution.)

Often presentations will have discussants or reactors to the papers. If this is the case, be sure to send that individual a copy of the paper several weeks in advance. It is very embarrassing to have a discussant fail to react to a paper because it was not sent in time. To the extent possible, it is well to anticipate a discussant's reaction or questions, as well as possible questions from the audience. If the research discussed in the paper was well done, and the paper is written without loose ends, questions should cause no difficulty.

Presentations to Dissertation and Thesis Committees

There are two points in a graduate program when presentations are given to committees of graduate faculty members: the defense of a dissertation (thesis) proposal and the **defense of a dissertation** (thesis). Although these are oral presentations, they are very different from presenting papers at professional meetings. For one thing, committee presentations are much longer; those for dissertation defense typically require about two hours. The audience is usually small, three or four committee members for a dissertation and as few as two for a thesis. The committee members usually have considerable interaction with the graduate student (candidate).

Whether the defense is of a proposal or a dissertation, there are numerous similarities in giving the presentation. For the proposal defense, the candidate makes a case that the intended research is well designed and worthwhile, and that the candidate is knowledgeable about research in the area. For the dissertation defense, the candidate makes a case for the adequacy and importance of the completed research. Either way, the secret to a successful presentation lies in the preparation that takes place before the committee meeting.

The candidate should be very knowledgeable about the research area and research methodology that applies to the research problem. Before the meeting, prepare an organized and efficient presentation that provides the committee members with an overview of the research, highlighting important points. Overhead projectors can be helpful in presenting tables, diagrams, and lists. This introductory presentation should be twenty to thirty minutes in length and should be brought to closure after such time. Do not go on about trivial information or tangential issues in order to use up time.

Knowing the research in the area includes being able to anticipate the relevant questions. The questioning by the committee members usually will proceed in a somewhat predictable sequence. Certain questions will lead to other questions, and, although the exact questions may not be anticipated beforehand, the candidate should have a good idea about their content. With regard to questions, the following are suggested:

1. Listen to the question carefully and answer the question asked. Too often candidates will give prepared responses regardless of whether or not they fit the questions.

2. Respond to a question succinctly but completely. In a dissertation defense, refer to research results if they are appropriate.

3. If you do not understand the question, ask for a repetition or an elaboration of the question.

4. If you do not know the answer to a question, say so. Do not try to bluff through a response.

5. Formulate a response in your mind and select your words carefully. Do not hurry your response. Use precise and appropriate terminology.

With regard to the latter point, precision in the use of terminology is often lacking, especially in terminology about the research methodology. For example, candidates often interchange the use of *sample* and *population* or make statements such as "testing hypotheses at the .05 level of confidence." Lack of precision in using terminology shows incomplete knowledge about the issue.

In the defense of a dissertation proposal, suggestions for improving the research may come from the committee members. Indeed, giving suggestions is one of the functions of committee members. But these suggestions should be viewed as "fine-tuning" rather than major revisions. The candidate should be aware of any research design limitations and must be able to make the case that these limitations will not jeopardize the validity of the research or the successful completion of the research.

In the defense of a dissertation, the candidate should distinguish explicitly between results and conclusions. One of the greatest weaknesses of first drafts of dissertations is the lack of conclusions. Candidates should address the external validity of the research and work from that to conclusions. Drawing conclusions requires effort; it takes a thorough knowledge of the research in an area and a projection of the research results into the appropriate context, usually an educational context.

Recognize the limitations of completed research in the dissertation defense. However, there should not be serious limitations in the research methods. It is not adequate to explain poorly done research by, "I did the best I could." Limitations most likely will apply to the external validity of the research. Any study should have some external validity, or a strong case must be made for why external validity is not of importance.

Overall, the defense of a research proposal or dissertation should be a learning experience for the candidate. It provides the opportunity for a relatively high-level professional discussion. Most candidates are unduly anxious about this experience, although understandably so. The advisor or major professor is unlikely to go ahead with the meeting if the candidate is not prepared for it. Remember that, very likely, the candidate is the most knowledgeable about the research of all the people participating in the defense.

Summary

Communicating about research is generally the concluding activity of a research project. Certainly, much is written about research, either in the form of a proposal for contemplated research or as a research report of completed research. This chapter provided suggestions for writing about research. Also, comments were made that will be helpful to anyone making an oral presentation about research.

Written reports of research take a variety of forms. Among the more common forms are articles in professional journals, research reports, dissertations, and papers distributed at meetings of professional organizations. The form to some extent will determine specifically how the research report is written. For example, the review of related research typically is much longer for a dissertation than the review for a journal article. Research reports for funding agencies may have unique specifications. However, overall, any research report addresses the issues:

What is the context for the research?
How was the research done?
What were the results?
What were the conclusions or the significance of the research?

A proposal for a research study provides a context for the research and describes how the research will be done. Of course, proposals do not contain results and conclusions from the anticipated research, but they may describe conclusions from related studies. Proposals may be prepared for funding agencies, and when this is done they should adhere to the specifications of the funding agencies. An agency soliciting proposals often distributes a "Request for Proposals" (RFP). This is a document that describes the type of research being solicited and contains the specifications for the proposal.

Whether communicating research through a written report or a presentation, it is important to have the description organized so that it is logical and understandable. Use terminology that is appropriate for the area being described. Reports, whether published in written form or given as presentations, typically require revision and refinement. Reviews by colleagues can be helpful. Preparing good research reports is a task that requires considerable time and effort and should be recognized as such.

KEY CONCEPTS

Research proposal
Research report
Research problem
Review of the literature
Significance of the research
Cover page
Abstract
Budget
Staff résumés
Appendix
Transition
Methods section
Summary
Conclusion
Implications
Recommendations
Bibliography
Reference list
Call for papers
Defense of a dissertation

EXERCISES

4.1 Select a research problem of limited magnitude and write a proposal about doing a research project on the problem. Include in your proposal a statement of the problem, a context for the problem, and a brief (about two double-spaced pages) review of the literature. Comment on the anticipated procedures, the analysis that would be used, and the potential significance of the project. Be brief and concise, and pay special attention to the continuity of ideas. Include a bibliography. This is a writing task of the magnitude of a short term paper.

4.2 Locate a research article in your area of interest that deals with an educational topic in your area or one about which you have some knowledge. Read the report through the results (or data analysis) section, but do not read the conclusions. Write a conclusions section of your own. After you have completed your conclusions, compare them to the conclusions of the report.

4.3 Obtain a copy of a research paper presented at a professional meeting. The meeting program of a recently held annual meeting of a professional organization such as AERA (American Educational Research Association) is a good source. Review the paper for its format, completeness, and closure. Compare the sections of the paper with those of a research article on somewhat the same topic. How are they similar and how do they differ?

4.4 Suppose you were conducting a research study in which the scores of school-age children, grades 3–6 inclusive, on a battery of ten academic and skills areas tests (dependent variables) were analyzed. Within each grade, there was an experimental and a control group, with one-half of the students in each group. Means and standard deviations for each grade, separated by experimental and control groups, were calculated. Develop an organization for presenting these results in tables. Provide names and headings for your tables. Number the tests 1 through 10 for convenience.

4.5 In a teacher-education program at a university there are 152 elementary level graduates (grades 1–6) and 103 secondary level graduates (grades 7–12). All graduates near the close of their programs take a common set of professional measures that provide four scores: (1) Professional Relations, (2) Pedagogy–Knowledge, (3) Pedagogy–Application, and (4) History of Education. Other descriptive information of the graduates consists of age, gender, and race. Means and standard deviations can be computed for the professional measures. Develop an organization for providing this information in one or more tables, contrasting the data for elementary- and secondary-level graduates. Be specific about the table title and the headings in the table.

4.6 Consult a form and style manual such as the *Publication Manual of the American Psychological Association* (5th ed.) and indicate the editorial style for entries in a reference list for the following:

a. A book that has a corporate author (rather than one or more persons)
b. An English translation of a book
c. An edited book
d. An article or chapter in an edited book

e. An article in a professional journal that has five authors
f. A revised edition of a book

4.7 Select a master's thesis from your library and compare it to a typical journal article in the same general subject matter in terms of the outline, the length, and the writing style.

4.8 Use ERIC to locate a paper presented at a professional conference. Compare the paper to a journal article in the same general subject matter in terms of the outline, the writing style, and your impression of the quality of the two reports.

REFERENCES

Altermatt, E. R., and Pomerantz, E. M. (2003). The development of competence-related and motivational beliefs: An investigation of similarity and influence among friends. *Journal of Educational Psychology, 95,* 111–123.

American Psychological Association (2001). *Publication manual of the American Psychological Association* (5th ed.). Washington, DC: American Psychological Association.

Andrews, M. L., and Ridenour, C. S. (2006). Gender in schools: A qualitative study of students in educational administration. *Journal of Educational Research, 100,* 35–43.

Brand, S. T. (2006). Facilitating emergent literacy skills: A literature-based, multiple intelligence approach. *Journal of Research in Childhood Education, 21,* 133–148.

Elbaum, B. (2007). Effects of an oral testing accommodation on the mathematics performance of secondary students with and without learning disabilities. *Journal of Special Education, 40,* 218–229.

Hale, A. D., Skinner, C. H., Williams, J., Hawkins, R., Neddenriep, C. E., and Dizer, J. (2007). Comparing comprehension following silent reading and aloud reading across elementary and secondary students: Implication for curriculum-based measurement. *Behavior Analyst Today, 8,* 9–30.

Lounsbery, M., Bungum, T., and Smith, N. (2007). Physical activity opportunity in K–12 public school settings: Nevada. *Journal of Physical Activity and Health, 4,* 30–38.

Madrid, L. D., Canas, M., and Ortega-Medina, M. (2007). Effects of team competition versus team cooperation in classwide peer tutoring. *Journal of Educational Research, 100,* 155–160.

CHAPTER 5 Evaluating Research Reports

With all the articles in professional journals, reports to funding agencies, papers, and so on that deal with some type of educational research, it stands to reason that a very large quantity of research reports is in the professional literature. With a large quantity comes a lot of variation in the quality of reports and the quality of the research on which the reports are based. Journals have varying standards of acceptance for manuscripts submitted for publication. Most journals are what are called "refereed," which means that manuscripts are reviewed and evaluated, usually by two or more reviewers. Before being accepted for publication, the manuscripts must meet certain criteria or standards that may be more implied than explicit. However, because of the numbers of manuscripts submitted, most journals have numerous reviewers so the extent of the manuscript critique depends on the competence of the specific reviewers to whom the manuscript is assigned. Research reports submitted to funding agencies, although they should be critiqued internally at the institution where the research was conducted, often are little more than first drafts of the report. Papers presented at professional association meetings may not be prepared in time for discussant review, and the papers are presented with no revision. Anyone can put anything on the Internet, and it is not surprising that many research reports that are available online have never been refereed, peer reviewed, or critiqued in any way. These "rogue" sources should be used with care. So, there is opportunity for poorly reported research to appear in the literature.

> Just because research is reported in the literature does not ensure that the research was conducted well or reported well.

Types of Errors and Shortcomings in Reports

Conducting research can be a complex process; thus there are numerous kinds of errors and shortcomings possible, both with conducting the research and reporting it. Errors may range all the way from relatively minor **technical errors,** such as an incomplete reference, to **substantive errors** such as the use of an inappropriate design for the research problem. Much educational research is reported in professional journals and certainly the journals are a major source of research information. In a typical dissertation, for example, the number of references to journal articles far outnumbers all other references combined. Also, research for dissertations and funded projects often is reported in reduced form in the journals. So, errors that appear in journal articles are similar to those in other reports.

Twenty years ago, Hall, Ward, and Comer (1988) conducted an evaluation of fifty-four published research articles and found that 42 percent of the articles were:

> judged to be either unacceptable for publication or in need of major revisions to make them acceptable. (p. 186)

The situation is not likely to be much different today.

The most commonly identified error, which really was an omission, was the lack of validity and reliability information about the data-collection instruments, an error that appeared in 43 percent of the articles (p. 188). Tingle, DeSimone, and Covington (2003) found similar results when evaluating the research on eleven school-based smoking prevention programs. They reviewed fourteen studies and found reliability evidence in only four of them and validity evidence in just one (p. 66).

The sections of research reports dealing with methods or procedures are especially susceptible to errors. Research designs may be weak or inappropriate, sampling may have flaws, and the analyses may not be the most appropriate or they may even be wrong. Of course, reports may be so poorly written that, even if the procedures and analyses are correct, there is confusion that leads to misunderstanding.

This brings us to what might be considered **broad deficiencies** in a report. Sometimes reports are not clearly written, and Hall et al. (1988) found this problem in 26 percent of the articles reviewed (p. 188). The organization of the report may be confusing, or it is difficult to follow the logic from procedures to results to conclusions. Results may be presented in a confusing manner, with notation not readily apparent to readers. Lack of transition across the sections can make a report seem disjointed and may lead to reader confusion.

> There are broad types of deficiencies such as confused reporting and lack of continuity that reduce the quality of a research report, even if the research on which the report is based was well conducted.

Critiquing Major Sections of a Research Report

Chapter 4 discusses the characteristics and procedures that make for effective communication about research. When evaluating research reports, we can look for the same characteristics and procedures and raise questions about whether or not they are present. The discussion of Chapter 4 was organized according to the major sections of a research report and the same organization will be followed here.

Introduction

The introduction should contain a statement of the research problem and this statement should be identified clearly and easily for the reader. If hypotheses are appropriate they should be stated. There should be provided enough of a context for the research so that the reader understands the research problem and how it fits in the education world. The **significance of the research** should at least be alluded to or implied. Variables should be identified, although they may not be operationally defined until measurement is discussed in the methods section.

> The introduction should address the questions: What is the research problem, where does it fit in the educational context, and what is its significance?

Review of the Literature

Reviews of the literature for journal articles are limited because of available space, so they require skilled writing to have adequate comprehensiveness for the review. The references reviewed should be clearly relevant to the research problem. If their relevancy seems obscure or missing, the review has a major weakness. Questions to keep in mind when reviewing the literature are:

1. Do the results from the references have a logical flow; that is, are they well organized?
2. Does the researcher "pull together" results and show their relevance to the research problem rather than state them as a series of individual and possibly isolated results?
3. Is there a summary or adequate closure to the review so that it does not conclude abruptly with the results of the final study referenced?
4. Does the review reflect the researcher's understanding of how the results cited in the review are integrated and relate to the research problem or have implications for it?

The review of the literature is susceptible to technical errors. References may not be included in an acceptable format. A referenced study may be omitted from the bibliography. Errors may be made in the spelling of authors' names and dates of publication.

> Relevance to the research problem, organization, continuity across the studies reviewed, and closure are characteristics to be considered when evaluating the review of the literature.

Journal articles especially are limited in the number of possible references, so all or even the most relevant related studies may not appear in the review. Quite often, a reader is not even aware of what may be the most relevant studies. Thus, in terms of evaluating the review, it is best to focus on what is there, not what might have been had other or additional studies been included.

Methods or Procedures

The methods or procedures section probably is the most crucial section when evaluating a report because from this section the reader must obtain an understanding of how the research was done. The research design may have weaknesses for the specific research, or, even worse, the design may be inappropriate for the research problem. Overall, this section should provide enough description so that the reader understands how the research was done, the specific procedures, and the sequence in which they occurred.

There are numerous questions that may be raised when evaluating the methods section, some specific to the type of research.

1. Are the data gathering (measurement) instruments described so that the variables are operationally defined? The validity and reliability of the instruments should be addressed. If a questionnaire was used, do the items have content validity? If a standardized test was used, was it appropriate for the situation and were reliability coefficients reported? In an experiment, was the experimental procedure consistent?

2. Are the data sufficient for testing the hypotheses or for addressing the research problem?

3. Is the design adequately identified, and was it appropriate? For example, if a 2×4 factorial was used, the two independent variables should be identified and be part of the research problem.

4. If sampling was used, is the sampling design described, was it appropriate, and was the number of subjects adequate? If a survey was conducted, is the return rate given? A serious flaw that can occur with reporting questionnaire studies is to fail to give the return rate, or to give it, but then ignore it if it was low.

5. Was the analysis appropriate for the hypotheses or research problem and the data collected? For example, an error may be analyzing data that are only ordinal level with statistical procedures that require interval or ratio level data. If statistical procedures were used, was there enough statistical power to test hypotheses with confidence? For example, in an experiment, does the number of subjects seem adequate?

6. As the research was conducted, does it appear to be free of confounding variables and other factors that may threaten the internal and external validity of the research? In the chapter on experimental research, several such factors were described. If an experiment was conducted in the school setting, for example, was it adequately free from extraneous factors so that the internal validity was not threatened?

7. Is the analysis described so that it is clear to the reader?

8. Does the methods section have adequate closure so that the reader has in mind a composite of how the research was conducted?

> Evaluating the methods or procedures section is a process of focusing on the specifics of how the reported research was conducted, specifics of the instrumentation and data collection, design, and analysis.

Results

One of the major problems with many research reports is that the data are inadequately reported. For example, statistics such as means may be omitted or the means for groups may be given but no variance data are provided. So, the results should be checked for completeness relative to the analyses that were done and relative to results required to address the research problem.

Questions that may be raised when evaluating the results section are:

1. Are the results well organized, clearly identified, and presented so that there is no confusion? For example, are tables used appropriately and without "overloading" of information?

2. Are acceptable formats used for presenting results? If tables are used, are they titled adequately and presented with correct and clear headings?

3. Do the results follow from the analyses? For example, if hypotheses about means were tested, there should be information about *t*-tests or analyses of variance.

4. Are the results comprehensive? If hypotheses were tested, are there results for all hypotheses?

5. Is there adequate information about the conditions of the results such as the levels of significance used if hypotheses were tested? Are the results internally valid, that is, can they be interpreted with confidence?

6. Are the results free of confusing and unidentified symbols? There are conventional symbols widely used and these are appropriate, but if an author uses unique symbols they must be defined.

7. Does the results section have closure with some type of summary? For reports requiring an abstract, much of this statement may appear in the abstract.

> The results should be presented clearly and follow directly from the analyses. They should be complete.

Conclusions, Recommendations, and Implications

The concluding section (sometimes called "Discussion") is the capstone of the research report. A major criterion for evaluating this section is that the conclusions follow from the results, and any recommendations or implications are logical extensions of the conclusions. Additional issues or questions relative to this section are:

1. Are conclusions in fact conclusions and not simply a restatement of the results?

2. Is it clear which conclusions follow from which results?

3. Are possible limitations of the study identified and the results interpreted accordingly?

4. Is the issue of importance to education addressed? Some authors equate statistical significance with practical importance, and this may not be the case.

5. Is external validity or generalizability of the study addressed, and, if so, are the generalizations reasonable and based on the conclusions? Errors with this issue can take two directions. External validity may be ignored so the readers are left to make their own generalizations, or generalizations are given that are not justified by the results.

6. Are there recommendations for continued research, either addressing related research problems or the same problem with extended research?

7. Are the conclusions from the research tied in with research documented in the references? Are conclusions consistent with those of other researchers, and, if not, are possible reasons given for inconsistencies?

8. Does this section have a summary statement?

9. Is there adequate closure for the entire report?

> Conclusions should follow directly from the results, and this section should address external validity of the research, as well as providing closure for the entire report.

Evaluating the major substantive sections of a research report has been discussed above. Other sections such as the reference list are relatively straightforward. The reference list should be complete and presented in an acceptable format. If all the references in the list are old, say none more recent than five or so years, a question may be raised about the recency of the references. Has research in this area been dormant and, if so, why? The author should address this question in the review of literature.

Abstracts usually are brief statements and should be clear and concise. If appendices are included, their content should be identified explicitly, and typically there is at least one reference to each appendix in the body of the report.

Overall Impressions When Evaluating a Report

There are many specific questions that can be raised when evaluating the sections of a research report but there also is the overall impression that impacts the quality of a report. Technically, a report should be "clean," that is, free of spelling errors, use accepted headings and formats, and follow a logical organization. There should be adequate continuity and transition within and between sections so readers get a "complete picture" rather than the feeling of somewhat isolated parts.

Another pitfall of research reports is **inappropriate editorializing.** This may occur through an overuse of value-laden words such as *important* or *interesting.* There may be a tendency to pass off results as important just because the writer says so, rather than establishing the case for importance. The writing in the report should be complete, but also concise. Sometimes, with longer reports, the reader gets the feeling that "filler" is being included. Filler is content that, although not incorrect, adds nothing to the report in terms of substance or quality.

A report should be clearly written and readable. It should be free of unnecessary jargon. All professions have their technical language, and education is no exception, but the jargon should be used only to the extent that it is known and appropriate. Definitions should be provided as necessary, and any assumptions underlying the research and the conclusions drawn from it should be stated.

Overall, the reader should get a feeling of completeness and cohesiveness about the research report. The research should have implicit or explicit importance in the educational context. Although most researchers do not write best sellers, the report should have adequate style and format and be free of technical errors.

The Review Process for Journals

The evaluation of research reports is especially important when the research is considered for publication. Klausmeier (2001) described the range of review processes that journals require:

> Some journals submit manuscripts to stringent review. They receive more manuscripts than they can accept because they are limited in the number of pages they can print yearly. These journals have high rejection rates. Other journals also review the manuscripts received and have firm page allocations; however, they receive fewer manuscripts and have moderate rejection rates. A feature of the preceding journals is that they do not charge authors for publishing their manuscripts. Other journals have relatively low rejection rates. Some of them have per-page or other charges and flexible page arrangements. The manuscripts received may have not been reviewed except by the journal editor. (p. 6)

An example of a typical review form for a journal is presented in Figure 5.1 (http://education.osu.edu/rehabed/eval-form.htm). This particular form is administered through the Internet. Note that care is taken to shield the identity of the reviewer. The Manuscript Evaluation Criteria for this journal are similar to the criteria for most other journals. Though not depicted in Figure 5.1, one important part of the form is the space for reviewer comments. These comments are usually returned to the author to help explain the basis of the ratings and to assist in revisions.

Suggested Disposition

- Accept with minor revisions. The ms requires specific revisions, but they are not substantial. Editors may decide to review the revised manuscript, or send it for re-review to the original review team.

FIGURE 5.1 Manuscript Evaluation Form for a Journal

Rehabilitation Education

Manuscript Evaluation Form

Manuscript number (for printed manuscripts enter 00)
Your rehabed username (e.g., rehabed99) **[Do not use your real name]**
Abbreviated manuscript title (up to 50 characters)
Please rate the manuscript on the following scale:

0 = The manuscript DOES NOT meet this criterion
1 = Manuscript is MARGINAL on this criterion
2 = Manuscript MEETS this criterion
3 = No opinion or does not apply

RATING				**MANUSCRIPT EVALUATION CRITERIA**
0 ❍	1 ❍	2 ❍	3 ❍	The topic is of current interest
0 ❍	1 ❍	2 ❍	3 ❍	The article is prepared according to APA style
0 ❍	1 ❍	2 ❍	3 ❍	The article is based on a sound rationale
0 ❍	1 ❍	2 ❍	3 ❍	The literature review accurately reflects relevant literature
0 ❍	1 ❍	2 ❍	3 ❍	The research design is sound and appropriate
0 ❍	1 ❍	2 ❍	3 ❍	The data analysis is appropriate and done correctly
0 ❍	1 ❍	2 ❍	3 ❍	Conclusions are based on correct interpretation of the data
0 ❍	1 ❍	2 ❍	3 ❍	The article has appropriate implications for rehabilitation educators
0 ❍	1 ❍	2 ❍	3 ❍	The article is readable and generally well written

- Reject but invite resubmission. The ms requires significant revision and cannot be accepted, but the authors should be encouraged to revise and resubmit, or send it for re-review to the original review team.
- Invite resubmission as Gray Matter, Teaching Tip, Research Tip, and so on. (Content is of interest but not a research ms.)
- Reject. The authors need to totally rework the manuscript. The editors may invite submission as a new manuscript, which will then be sent to a new review team.
- Reject due to lack of fit with *Rehabilitation Education.* Submit to another journal. Type the suggested journal here ____________________________
- Reject. The manuscript appears not to be publishable, even with major revisions.

Please send additional comments by either attaching a document to an e-mail message and by including the comments directly in the body of the e-mail message. Send the e-mail to rehabed@osu.edu.

Standards for Publications

The American Educational Research Association has published a set of standards for AERA publications (2006) that applies to both quantitative and qualitative research studies. Its primary audiences for the standards are those who wish to publish in AERA journals and those who serve as reviewers for those journals. The **standards for publication** actually apply very well to all research reports, whether or not they are submitted for publication. The standards could just as easily have been presented in the preceding chapter because they were written for those writing research reports and those who review those reports. Their placement here was arbitrary.

Two principles underlie the standards:

> First, reports of empirical research should be *warranted;* that is, adequate evidence should be provided to justify the results and conclusions. Second, reports of empirical research should be *transparent;* that is, reporting should make explicit the logic of inquiry and activities that led from the development of the initial interest, topic, problem, or research question; through the definition, collection, and analysis of data or empirical evidence; to the articulated outcomes of the study. (p. 33)

The standards are divided into eight general areas with specific standards for each area. The following is a shortened and somewhat paraphrased listing of the standards[1]:

Problem Formulation

1.1 The problem formulation should provide a clear statement of the purpose and scope of the study.

1.2 Reporting should make clear how the study is a contribution to knowledge.

1.3 Reporting should include a review of the relevant scholarship that bears directly on the topic of the report.

1.4 The rationale for the conceptual, methodological, or theoretical orientation of the study should be described and explained.

1.5 The rationale should be provided for the problem formulation as it relates to the group studied.

Design and Logic of the Study

2.1 Research reporting should follow a clear logic of inquiry that allows readers to trace the path from the statement of the problem, to the review of the relevant scholarship, to the research questions, to the description of the site and participants, to the methodology guiding collection and analysis of evidence, to the interpretation and presentation of outcomes and understandings gained from the research process.

2.2 There should be a specific and unambiguous description of the design.

Sources of Evidence

3.1 The units of study (sites, groups, participants, events, or other units) and the means through which they were selected should be adequately described.

3.2 The collection of data or empirical materials should be clearly described, including how and when they were gathered, by whom, and for what purposes.

Measurement and Classification

4.1 The development of measurements and classifications should be clearly described.

4.2 Any classification scheme should be comprehensively described and illustrated with concrete examples.

4.3 When measurement is entailed, reporting should describe data elements and organization in a specific and unambiguous way.

4.4 When transcriptions of audio- or video-recordings are provided, the conventions and symbols used to represent the discourse or characterize the actions or interactions should be clearly described.

4.5 A rationale should be provided for the relevance of a measurement or classification as capturing important characteristics where questions about appropriateness might arise.

Analysis and Interpretation

5.1 The procedures used for analysis should be precisely and transparently described.

5.2 Analytic techniques should be described in sufficient detail to permit understanding of how the data were analyzed.

5.3 The analysis and presentation of the outcomes of the analysis should make clear how they support claims or conclusions drawn in the research.

5.4 Analysis and interpretation should include information about any intended or unintended circumstances that may have significant implications for interpretation of the outcomes, limit their applicability, or compromise their validity.

5.5 The presentation of conclusions should (a) provide a statement of how claims and interpretations address the research problem; (b) show how the conclusions connect to support, elaborate, or challenge conclusions in earlier scholarship; and (c) emphasize the theoretical, practical, or methodological implications of the study.

With quantitative methods, standards 5.6 to 5.10 apply:

5.6 Reporting should clearly state what statistical analyses were conducted, describing them in enough detail that they could be replicated by a competent data analyst.

5.7 Descriptive and inferential statistics should be provided for each of the statistical analyses.

5.8 Any considerations that arose during data collection and processing that might compromise the validity of the statistical analysis or inferences should be reported.

5.9 Any considerations that are identified during the data analysis that might compromise the validity of the statistical analyses or inferences should be reported.

5.10 For each statistical result, it is important to include (a) an index of the quantitative relation between variables, (b) an index of uncertainty, (c) the test statistic and significance level, and (d) a qualitative interpretation of the effect.

With qualitative methods, standards 5.11 to 5.14 apply:

5.11 The process of developing the descriptions, claims, and interpretations should be clearly described.

5.12 The evidence that serves as a warrant for each claim should be presented.

5.13 Practices used to develop and enhance the warrant for the claims should be described, including a search for disconfirming evidence and alternative explanations.

5.14 Interpretive commentary should provide a deeper understanding of the claims.

Generalization
6.1 It is crucial to make clear the specifics of the participants, contexts, activities, data collections, and manipulations involved in the study.

6.2 The author should make clear the intended scope of generalization of the findings of the study.

6.3 The author should make clear the logic by which the findings of the study should apply within the scope of generalization.

Ethics in Reporting
7.1 Ethical considerations involved in data collection, analysis, and reporting should be explicitly addressed.

7.2 Reporting on research should be done in a way that honors consent agreements.

7.3 Reporting should include a description of any potential conflict of interest or biases of the researcher.

7.4 Reporting of research should be accurately stated.

7.5 Data or materials should be maintained so that a qualified researcher could reproduce the analysis or trace the trail of evidence.

7.6 Funding support should be acknowledged in a publication note.

Title, Abstract, and Headings
8.1 The title should clearly convey what the article is about.

8.2 The abstract should provide a summary of the article that is self-contained, concise, and accurate.

8.3 Headings and subheadings should make clear the logic of inquiry underlying the report.

The Evaluation of Proposals

Chapter 4 included the preparation of research proposals, and comments are made here about the evaluation of proposals. A proposal for graduate study research (dissertation or other) typically is reviewed by a professor or a committee of professors. The usual criteria of a relevant problem, evidence of knowledge in the area, appropriate methodology, and good continuity apply when a proposal is reviewed. Funding agencies also develop criteria for the evaluation of proposals, and these often appear in guidelines for proposal preparation.

Evaluation criteria of funding agencies are quite general and similar across agencies. Except for special criteria, such as the reasonableness of the budget, the evaluation criteria of funding agencies are similar to those for any proposal, including a dissertation proposal. The evaluation focuses primarily on two issues: (1) the significance of the proposed research and (2) the quality of the proposed research. The following issues are considered in evaluating proposals relative to those two characteristics.

Significance of the Proposed Research

1. Contribution to basic knowledge relevant to the solution of educational problems
2. Contribution to educational theory
3. Contribution to the development of methodological tools, either for educational practice or research
4. Contribution to the solution of educational problems, either long-range or short-range
5. The potential generalizability of anticipated results
6. The potential of anticipated results to influence the improvement of educational practice

Quality of the Proposed Research

1. The extent to which the writer shows a thorough knowledge of relevant prior research
2. The extent to which prior research is related to the proposed research
3. The comprehensiveness and appropriateness of the research design
4. The appropriateness of the instrumentation and the methodology
5. The appropriateness of the anticipated analyses
6. The likelihood that the proposed research can be completed successfully as described

Funding agencies usually consider the qualifications of the principal investigator and other research project staff, and they may require a statement about facilities and resources available to the researcher. The reasonableness of the budget has already been mentioned. However, this characteristic usually receives few points, because budgets can be negotiated if they do not seem appropriate to fiscal officers of the funding agency.

Implicit criteria also are applied in evaluating any proposal. The writing should be technically correct and neat. The content of the proposal should be well organized, and there should be good continuity from section to section and within sections. Generally accepted formats, including sizes of margins and spacing, should be followed.

The preparation of a good research proposal is no small task and internal evaluation should be a part of that preparation. When submitting a proposal to a funding agency, it is important to follow the proposal preparation guidelines of that agency. Some agencies do not have guidelines; they will accept any standard format. Private foundations and funding programs within large agencies often fund projects for specific purposes or only in certain areas. It is important to be aware of these limitations; there is little point in submitting proposals that do not correspond to agency interest.

> The evaluation of research proposals focuses on two major issues: (1) the significance of the proposed research and (2) the quality of the proposed research.

The review process for proposals is often based on explicit criteria with a certain number of points allowed for each criterion. Figure 5.2 illustrates a typical rating form for proposals. This particular form was used for a Request for Proposals (RFP) to conduct research on teacher education/teacher training in Canada, but the evaluation criteria are the same for most proposals (Canadian Education Statistics Council, 2001).

FIGURE 5.2 Proposal Evaluation Form

Criteria for RFP		
Evaluation Parameters	*Evaluation Criteria*	*Score*
1. Comprehension/ understanding of project	■ General understanding—comprehends essential aspects of the project ■ Needs identification—recognizes challenges/ potential problems in the project ■ Solutions identification—provides creative and insightful, yet feasible, solutions to challenges/problems	/25
2. Methodology and project administration	■ Suitability and soundness of methodology—provides high probability of accomplishing study objectives ■ Technical integrity—based on good research design principles	/25
3. Relevance	■ Applicability of findings to policy and practice—findings address policy questions/issues and/or other pertinent issues related to the five priority subject areas in the RFP	/25
4. Qualifications and experience	■ Education/technical expertise—demonstrates knowledge and expertise required to undertake the project ■ Experience—demonstrates experience in the field of study under consideration	/10
5. Budget	■ Budget—adequate but realistic, given amount of work involved	/10
6. Overall assessment	■ Strategy—proposal provides superior strategy for accomplishing goals of the project ■ Style—clear and concise writing, carefully edited, well-presented concepts, attractive and easily understood layout ■ Overall quality of proposal—provides overall impression that adequate care, attention to detail, and effort went into the planning and creation of the proposal	/5
	Total	/100

Summary

Anyone involved in educational research, sooner or later, and usually sooner, finds it necessary to read research reports about the area of research. In doing so, evaluations are made about the reports and the research on which the reports are based. There is a variety of types of research reports, but certainly one of the major sources for research information is the professional periodical literature.

When evaluating research reports we focus on (1) the content and quality of the individual sections and (2) the overall report, its comprehensiveness, continuity, and so on. Substantive errors, such as an inappropriate design, tend to be more serious than technical errors, such as a misspelled word. Usually, careful editing can eliminate technical errors. Substantive errors are more difficult to deal with and may invalidate the research study.

The criteria for judging the quality of research reports may imply that the writing style has to be mechanical and that the format is dictated. Although a common format makes reading the reports easier because the reader will know where to find certain information, the important thing is that the information is included somewhere and can be easily understood by the reader. The writing style should be one that flows well with smooth transitions between sections. The research report is a means for communicating with target audiences. As such, the emphasis should be on helping the reader understand the research rather than on making the writer look impressive.

The first five chapters have focused on the research process, from developing a statement of the research problem all the way to writing the report of the completed research. The next set of chapters is about the various research designs that are commonly used in educational research. The emphases are on understanding the strengths and weaknesses of the different designs and on selecting the appropriate design for addressing the research problem. Terms that have been used in a general way, such as experimental research and ethnography, will now be explained in detail. Our goal is to fill the beginning researcher's toolkit with research approaches that will fit most research questions.

KEY CONCEPTS

Technical errors
Substantive errors
Broad deficiencies
Significance of research
Inappropriate editorializing
Standards for publication

EXERCISES

5.1 Suppose you are reviewing an article about a study involving survey research. Give examples of two substantive errors that might occur in such an article.

5.2 Identify two substantive errors that may occur in an article about experimental research. In the reported research, college sophomores serve as subjects in a physical performance experiment. Both genders participate. The independent variable of primary interest is the level of training with three different training routines.

5.3 Use Research Navigator to locate an article that reports on research in your area of interest. Evaluate the article using the applicable questions of this chapter. List any deficiencies you find in the article.

5.4 A research article was titled "Johnny's Big Struggle." Explain why the title, although intriguing, is inadequate as a title.

5.5 The AERA Standards for Publications (2006) state that research should be *warranted* and *transparent*. Explain what is meant by these two terms.

5.6 A major criterion used for evaluating research proposals is that the research should be significant. Explain in your own words what would make the proposed research significant.

NOTES

1. From *Educational Researcher* by AERA. Copyright 2006 by Sage Publications Inc. Journals. Reproduced with permission of Sage Publications, Inc., via Copyright Clearance Center.

REFERENCES

American Educational Research Association. (2006). Standards for reporting on empirical social science research in AERA publications. *Educational Researcher, 35,* 33–40.

Canadian Education Statistics Council. (2001). Criteria for RFP. Retrieved September 22, 2003, from http://fcis.oise.utoronto.ca/facultyresearch/Archives/#30563357.1/RFPsymposium2001-E.pdf

Hall, B. W., Ward, A. W., and Comer, C. B. (1988). Published educational research: An empirical study of its quality. *Journal of Educational Research, 81,* 182–189.

Klausmeier, H. J. (2001). *Research writing in education and psychology: From planning to publication.* Springfield, IL: Charles C. Thomas.

Rehabilitation Education. (2003). Manuscript evaluation form. Retrieved September 22, 2003, from http://education.osu.edu/rehabed/evalform.htm

Tingle, L. R., DeSimone, M., and Covington, B. (2003). A meta-evaluation of 11 school-based smoking prevention programs. *Journal of School Health, 73,* 64–67.

CHAPTER

6 Research Design in Quantitative Research

The next several chapters deal with research design considerations, first for quantitative approaches and then for qualitative approaches. Our intention is to provide a wide menu of choices for investigating research questions in education. Your choice of a research design should be based on the research question. Research questions that are concerned with the interrelationships among variables, the predictability of certain outcomes, and the comparison of specific groups are likely to require quantitative research designs. Research questions that are concerned with processes, unanticipated outcomes, and cultural impacts are likely to require qualitative approaches. When there are multiple research questions investigated in a study, the researcher will probably use a combination of quantitative and qualitative techniques. We begin by describing quantitative research designs.

After a researcher has identified a research problem and has completed at least some review of the literature, it is time to develop a *research design*—a plan or strategy for conducting the research. As a plan, research design deals with matters such as selecting participants for the research and preparing for data collection—activities that comprise the research process. Research designs tend to be quite specific to the type of research, and the conditions that determine the specific research design to use are discussed in subsequent chapters. This chapter focuses on general concepts of design in quantitative research, and a later chapter, Chapter 10, does the same for qualitative research. There are process differences between qualitative and quantitative research. Quantitative research has its roots in **positivism,** which Gall, Gall, and Borg (2003) have defined as:

> The epistemological doctrine that physical and social reality is independent of those who observe it, and that observations of this reality, if unbiased, constitute scientific knowledge. (p. 632)

Thus, research design in quantitative research tends to be structured and prescriptive, much more so than in qualitative research. Also, as the name implies, the outcomes of quantitative research typically are to a large extent expressed as numbers, and research design is directed to enabling the researcher to make valid interpretations through comparisons and partitioning of those numbers.

The Purposes of Research Design

To a large extent, the need for research design is implicit. How could we proceed otherwise? There must be a plan by which the specific activities of the research can be conducted and brought to successful closure. Kerlinger and Lee (2000, p. 450) identified two basic purposes of research design: (1) to provide answers to research questions and (2) to control variance. This latter purpose is, to a large extent, unique to quantitative research.

The first purpose is general and straightforward—to provide answers to the specific research questions. But going through the motions of conducting research or engaging in research activities alone will not necessarily yield answers. This relates to a point made in Chapter 1 regarding our concern about making educational research systematic. Research should be valid, which includes being able to interpret results and, through those results, answer the research questions or problems being posed. Good research design assists in understanding and interpreting the results of the study and ensures that a researcher obtains usable results.

It has been said that all research is conducted for the purpose of explaining **variance,** that is, explaining why individuals are different or explaining why their test scores or other characteristics are different. In a broad sense, this may be true, although qualitative researchers may take issue with this assertion. Variance can be evident in a number of ways. For example, variance in elementary school students' achievement, motivation, attitude, age, and family background can be considered. Also, when the variance of any one variable is considered, it may be influenced by any number of factors. Variance in achievement, for example, may be due to aptitude and motivation, to mention two possible factors. Procedures are used in quantitative research design to control variance. **Controlling variance** means creating conditions that allow the researcher to get a clear look at the variable of interest by limiting or eliminating the influence of some variables and explaining the influence of others.

> Explaining or controlling variance is an important part of quantitative research, and research design should address this issue.

The Concept of Controlling Variance

In quantitative research we attempt to quantify variance, and to the extent possible, partition it according to various sources or causes. But, how does variance manifest itself? Consider an example. A high school chemistry teacher is studying the effects of different methods of teaching on achievement in chemistry. The research problem could be stated as follows:

> A study of the effects of teaching method on the performance of high school students enrolled in chemistry.

The problem implies that an experiment will be conducted, because teaching method, the independent variable of primary interest, will be manipulated by the chemistry teacher. Teaching method has three different categories (also called levels), say M_1, M_2, and M_3. The dependent variable is performance on a chemistry achievement test administered after one semester of instruction. Ninety students, all juniors enrolled in the same school and taught by the same teacher, participate in the study. Thirty students are taught by each method. When the students are tested on chemistry achievement, there will be ninety scores, but these ninety scores will not all be the same. There will be a distribution of scores, the scores on the dependent variable, and because these scores are not all identical, this distribution will have variance.

Why are the ninety scores not all identical? This may be due to a variety of causes. The teaching methods may have different effects, and because method is the independent variable, the researcher certainly wants to be able to determine whether or not the three methods have different effects. Some students are undoubtedly more able than others, regardless of the instructional method. Possibly the time of day that instruction takes place has some effect. These are examples of variables that could be used as control variables or might remain as acknowledged, intervening variables as discussed in Chapter 2. There undoubtedly is inherent variation in the way students respond to a chemistry test. Any number of factors might be operating to cause variance in the dependent variable scores.

Consider the variance of the ninety chemistry test scores. As will be seen in the chapters on statistical analysis, variance can be quantified; it is a real, positive number, a number such as 132 or 10,920. A variance of zero would indicate no variance, that is, all scores in a distribution would be identical. The greater the number, the greater the variance; however, when analyzing variance we are more interested in "comparing" relative amounts of variance than in the actual values of the numbers. Suppose the variance of the ninety chemistry test scores is 360. Although variance does not come in circles, it can be quantifiably represented by the area in a circle as in Figure 6.1. The entire area of the circle represents all the variance (360) in the ninety chemistry test scores.

> Variance can be expressed quantitatively as a real, positive number. A variance of zero indicates that all scores in a distribution are identical.

Procedures for Controlling Variance

This section continues the chemistry example and illustrates procedures by which control of variance can be enhanced. The method of instruction is the independent variable of primary interest, and student ability will be considered as another variable to be controlled. There are basically four ways by which variance is controlled:

1. Randomization
2. Building conditions or factors into the design as independent variables

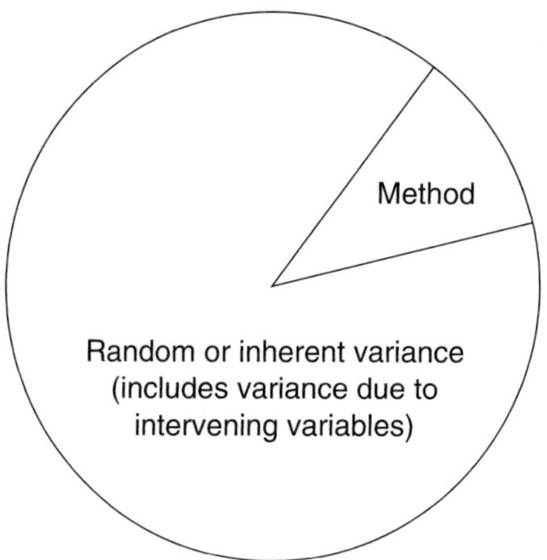

FIGURE 6.1 Quantitative Representation of the Variance of the Ninety Chemistry Test Scores

3. Holding conditions or factors constant
4. Statistical adjustments

The first three procedures are directly involved in structuring the research design. The fourth includes computational manipulations in an attempt to obtain control, so it is done at the analysis stage of the research, although preparation for it must be done when the research is designed.

Randomization. Suppose in the chemistry example that the same teacher will teach the ninety students, having three classes of thirty students each, with each class taught by a different method. The ninety students are a heterogeneous group with respect to ability level, which may well have some effect on their performance on the chemistry test. We would not want to have one group with mostly higher ability students and another with mostly lower ability students. Therefore, thirty students are *randomly assigned* to each of the three methods, as diagrammed in Figure 6.2. This can be done in a number of ways: (1) drawing

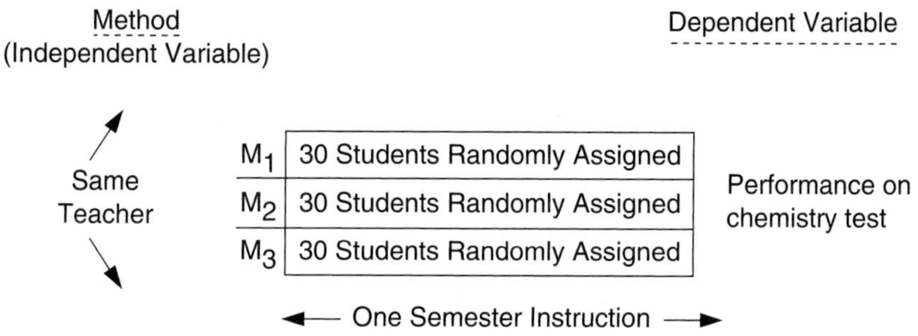

FIGURE 6.2 Research Design Using Randomization to Control for Ability Level

names out of a hat, similar to a lottery drawing, or (2) numbering the students from one to ninety and using a random number generator, such as www.randomizer.org, to determine which students are assigned to which group.

Random assignment to groups causes ability level to be randomly distributed among the three methods. The student with the greatest ability has an equal probability of being assigned to each of the three groups. The same is true for all of the other students. One would expect then that the effect of ability level would be spread evenly across the three groups.

Note two important points about random assignment. First, the randomization essentially equalized the groups with respect to ability level, but it also equalized them with respect to other variables such as motivation, attitude, and prior achievement, to name a few. Second, although this process distributes the effect of ability level evenly, it does not allow the researcher to quantify the influence of ability level on the scores of the chemistry test.

Remember that the chemistry test score is the dependent variable and the variance of all ninety test scores is 360. Suppose that the means[1] of the thirty test scores for the three methods are 89, 75, and 96, respectively, for the methods, M_1, M_2, and M_3, and that the variance accounted for by these differences in means is 50 of the 360. Then the quantitative representation of the variance can be indicated as in Figure 6.1. The entire variance of 360 is partitioned into two parts, that due to method and all the rest, which is **random variance** or inherent variance. This random or inherent variance is the variance among the scores within the groups; hence, it is also called the "within groups" variance. Another term used for this variance is **error variance.**[2] This does not mean that variance is due to some mistake. It simply means variance due to random assignment and any unaccounted for factors that may cause variance within the groups. Quantitatively, in our example, the value of the variance due to method is 50, and the value of the random variance is 310. Random variance contains the variance due to student ability, but, because of randomization, this variance is evenly spread among the three groups.

It can be noted that, in this example, randomization would also control other variables—primarily, variables associated with the students. Motivational level, for example, would be randomly distributed among the three methods or groups. Mathematical knowledge or skill that might well be related to performance in chemistry would also be randomly distributed.

> *Randomization* spreads the effects of other variables evenly across the groups of the study.

Building in Factors as Independent Variables. In the design in Figure 6.2, the students are separated into three groups according to method. If an ability level measure were available—possibly a score on a recent IQ test—the students could also be grouped according to ability level. If the top forty-five students on the ability-level measure were designated as "higher" and the remaining forty-five students as "lower" ability level, ability level would be

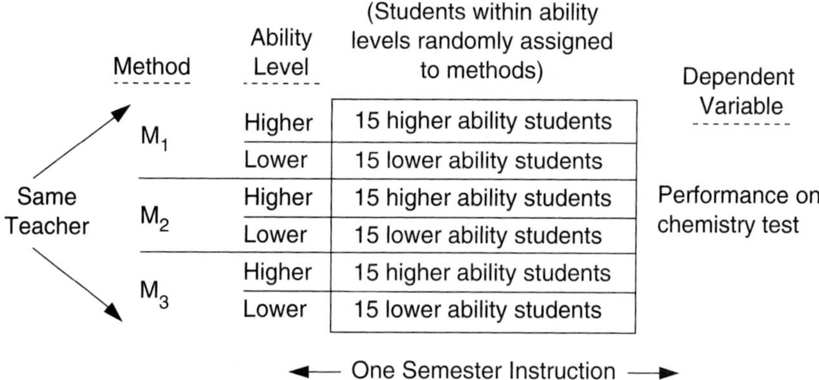

FIGURE 6.3 Research Design with Ability Level Built in as an Independent Variable

an independent variable with two levels. Fifteen students of each of the two ability groupings would be randomly assigned to each method. This design is presented in Figure 6.3. Now it can be determined not only whether there is a difference among methods but also whether there is a difference between the higher and lower ability groups. The variance that might be caused by the ability-level effect can be accounted for. Suppose that ability level accounts for 75 of the variance. (This would be determined from the difference in the two ability-level means of the chemistry scores.) Method[3] still accounts for 50 of the total variance, so the variance due to random variance is now 235 (360 – 50 – 75 = 235). This partitioning of the variance is presented in Figure 6.4.

The division of the students into only two ability-level groups is arbitrary in this example. (Three groups could have been used, designated high, medium, and low.) It should be noted that the researcher arbitrarily formed the groups so that equal numbers were maintained. To do this, the IQ test publisher's definition of higher and lower ability level would not be used (if a definition were available), because a published definition

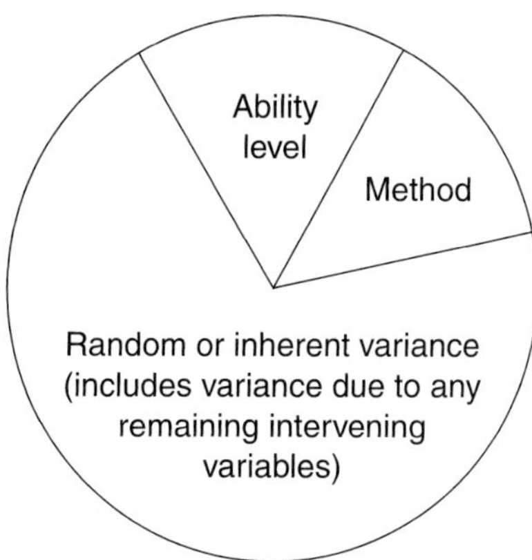

FIGURE 6.4 Quantitative Representation of the Variance of the Ninety Chemistry Test Scores with Ability Level Built in as an Independent Variable

would undoubtedly make for considerable inequality in the numbers of students in each ability level. Indeed, for chemistry, one would expect few, if any, students of low ability level. Instead, the researcher would list the ability scores from lowest to highest and label the top half of the list the higher ability group and the bottom half of the list the lower ability group. This is called a median split.

Building in a variable does allow the researcher to determine the effect of that variable, that is, to determine how much of the variance in the scores is due to that variable. This is referred to as the *variance* accounted for by that variable. In the example, more of the variance has now been explained than when method was the only independent variable. The random variance has been reduced to 235. Then why is this procedure not always used? For one thing, measures on which the individuals can be separated, in this case the ability levels of the chemistry students, are not always available. For example, motivational level may have an effect, but motivation scores would be difficult if not impossible to come by. Therefore, motivational level remains an intervening variable, but it is randomly distributed if random assignment is used. Also, including increasing numbers of independent variables may make the design unnecessarily complicated. Therefore, factors so included are usually those that are expected to cause some variance in the dependent variable scores.

> Building factors into the design as independent variables enables the researcher to determine the effects of those factors. Too many independent variables, however, can unnecessarily complicate the research design.

Holding Factors Constant. Holding a factor constant essentially consists of reducing a variable to a constant. In the chemistry example, the teacher could reduce ability level to a constant if only students with one defined ability level—say, those scoring between 100 and 108 on an IQ test—were included in the study. If ability level does tend to affect performance on the dependent variable, its effect would now be considerably diminished from what it would have been with the entire range of ability level included. Most of the variance in the chemistry test scores due to ability level would have been eliminated. The design would be essentially the same as that in Figure 6.2, except that only students within the designated IQ range would be randomly assigned to the methods. This number would likely be less than thirty per group if the teacher had started with the original ninety students. The variance of the chemistry scores of the remaining students would now change; it would tend to be reduced over what it was for all ninety students because the students now are more homogeneous in ability.

Holding factors constant can have some disadvantages. One has already been indicated: the possible elimination of individuals from the study, causing logistical problems or reducing the amount of data available on the dependent variable. Also, such results generalize only to the restricted group. Thus, external validity is reduced. The chemistry example already has several constants built into the design, such as teacher and length of instruction.

> When a factor is held constant, a potential variable is reduced to a constant. This eliminates, or at least substantially reduces, any effect the factor may have on the dependent variable.

Statistical Control. Statistical control, when used, is attained through computational procedures applied when the data are analyzed, but the variable to be so controlled must still be planned for in conducting the research. For the purposes of this discussion it is not necessary to focus on the statistical procedures; they are taken care of through the analysis, usually done by computer. The important issue here is the concept of how variance can be controlled by this method. Turning again to the chemistry example, assume that an ability measure consisting of performance on a recently administered IQ test is available for all ninety students. It is likely that a relationship exists between performance on the IQ test and performance on the chemistry test such that high scores on one tend to go with high scores on the other and, similarly, low scores on one go with low scores on the other.

If we could somehow adjust the chemistry test scores for this difference in ability level, we would be controlling the effect of student ability on the chemistry test scores. This can be done with a relatively sophisticated statistical procedure. Depending on the strength of the relationship between the chemistry test and IQ test scores, high chemistry test scores would be lowered (by statistical computation) if the students had high ability-level scores, and students with low ability-level scores would have their chemistry scores raised. These adjusted chemistry test scores, now independent of ability level, would then be analyzed. *Independent of ability level* means that the effect of ability level has been removed.

The process of statistical control can be diagrammed as in Figure 6.5. Again, conceptually we can consider the total variance in the ninety chemistry scores. The statistical control would most likely account for more variance than building in student ability as a two-category, independent variable. Measuring students on an IQ test is more sensitive to differences than categorizing students as higher and lower. Suppose the statistical control for ability level accounts for 130 of the original 360 variance in the chemistry test scores. Method still accounts for 50, so the random or inherent variance is now reduced to 180 (360 – 50 – 130 = 180). This is illustrated in Figure 6.6.

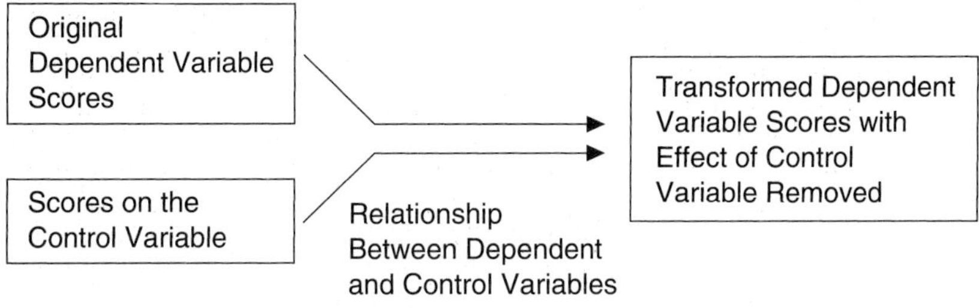

FIGURE 6.5 Conceptual Diagram of Statistical Control

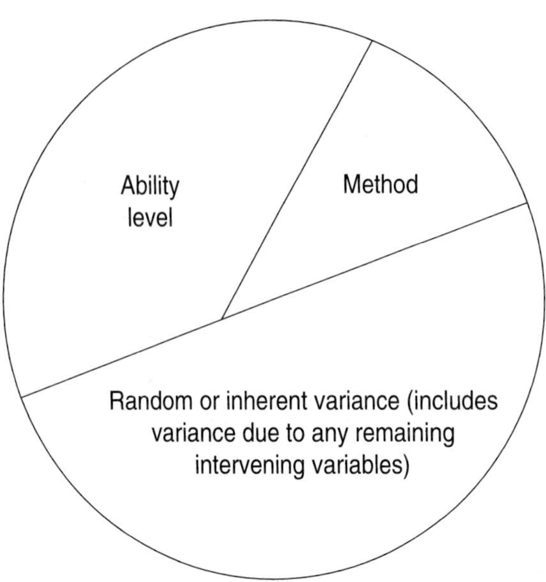

FIGURE 6.6 Quantitative Representation of the Variance of the Ninety Chemistry Test Scores with Ability Level Controlled by Statistical Control

> Statistical control, in essence, consists of adjusting the dependent variable scores to remove the effect of the control variable.

If statistical control is simply a matter of putting an analysis through the computer, why is it not used more frequently? One reason is that it is often difficult to obtain adequate scores on a control variable. Scores must be available for all participants in the research. The scores on the control variable should be obtained prior to conducting the research so that there is no possibility of the scores being affected by the independent variable—in the chemistry example, the teaching method. Then, too, control variables are effective only to the extent that they are related to the dependent variable and account for variance in the scores of that variable. Furthermore, certain statistical assumptions must be met; if they are not tenable, the statistical procedure should not be used.

Using Procedures for Control in Combination. The four procedures for enhancing control can be used singly or in combination. One procedure might be used for controlling one variable and another procedure for a second variable. Extending the chemistry example somewhat will illustrate this point.

Instead of using only 90 students, a large high school in which there are at least 180 chemistry students will be used. Teaching method, with the same three levels, is still the independent variable of primary interest. Two teachers (T_1 and T_2) will be used, because there will be six chemistry classes. It is known that the students come from various science and mathematics backgrounds in the elementary schools they attended and in courses they have taken thus far in high school. (For example, some students may have taken Algebra II, others not.) Scores on an IQ test given to all students when they were in eighth grade are available. There are two other high schools in this district, but there is considerable difference in the composition of the student bodies (for example, socioeconomic background) among the high schools. The four variables (in addition to the independent variable) and their methods of control are as follows:

Variable	*Method of Control*
1. Science background of the students	**1.** Randomization; the 180 students participating in the research are randomly assigned, 60 to each teaching method.
2. Teacher	**2.** Built in as an independent variable; each teacher uses the three teaching methods.
3. School	**3.** Reduced to a constant; students of only one school are included.
4. Ability level	**4.** Statistical control; the IQ test scores are used.

The research design is diagrammed in Figure 6.7. With the relatively high degree of control, if large enough differences occurred among the chemistry test scores of students taught by the three methods, the result would be an indication that the differences are in fact due to the methods. The research design has a high degree of internal validity; the results can be interpreted quite conclusively. However, it should be noted that the generalizability of results may be somewhat limited. Only one school and only two teachers in that school were used. The results generalize only to the extent that the student body and the teachers in this school are representative of some larger population. It may be that the intent is to generalize only to students of this school, but if wider generalization is intended, the external validity of the study must be argued on a logical basis.

When making decisions about the effects of independent variables, the variance they account for is compared with the random or error variance. If the random variance tends to be large because it contains variance caused by extraneous variables, the results may be difficult to interpret or be misinterpreted, thus jeopardizing internal validity. Although randomization does spread the effects of a variable evenly, it does not remove the variance caused by that variable from the random or inherent variance. Some variables, such as learning style of students, cannot be controlled practically by any other manner in most situations in which they might be involved. So, we want to guard against situations in which too much of the variance is unexplained, and therefore methods of controlling variance are used in combinations.

The purpose of controlling variance is to enhance the interpretation of results so the researcher can tell what effects, if any, the independent variables are having. The time to think about control is when the research design is being developed. Carefully designing the research does much to enhance the validity of the research; failing to do so may well lead to uninterpretable or nongeneralizable results.

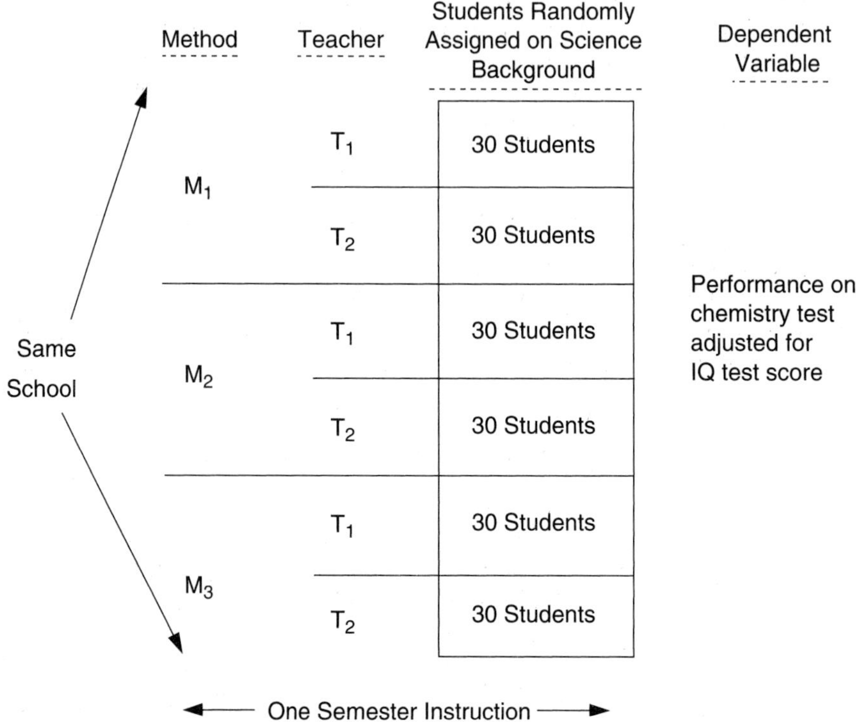

FIGURE 6.7 Diagram of a Research Design in which School, Science Background, Teacher, and Ability Level Are Controlled by Different Control Procedures

> Research design in quantitative research is used to control or explain variance. This is done by using certain research conditions such as random assignment to groups, including additional variables as independent variables, and reducing variables to constants.

Characteristics of Good Research Design

What constitutes a good research design? There are some general answers, such as that the design should be appropriate for the hypotheses or that it should be feasible within available resources. However, to be more specific, four characteristics are discussed that enhance research design. These characteristics are not mutually exclusive; they have some overlap. We want research not only to be "do-able" but also to yield results that can be interpreted with confidence.

Freedom from Bias

One characteristic of a good research design is that it will provide data that allow fair, unbiased comparisons among groups. This means that care has been taken to ensure that any differences between groups can be attributed to the independent variables under study. The data and the statistics computed from them do not vary in any systematic way except as they may be influenced by the independent variables. All other variation stems from random fluctuations.

Unfair comparisons can enter the research in a number of ways, including biased assignment of the individuals to the experimental treatments. For instance, a **bias** would have been introduced in the chemistry example if the higher ability students were all assigned to one teaching method. Random assignment of students to groups would eliminate the bias of putting the higher ability students in one method. (The possibility of a "wildly biased assignment" does exist, but its probability would be very small.) Another unfair comparison would occur when participants volunteer to be in the experimental group and those who did not volunteer are left to serve as a control group. These groups would surely differ in terms of motivation as well as in terms of the independent variable.

Freedom from Confounding

Another way that bias can enter the data is through confounding. Two (or more) independent and/or other variables are **confounded variables** if their effects cannot be separated. A good research design eliminates confounding of variables or keeps it to a minimum so that effects can be separated and results can be interpreted without confusion. In the chemistry example, confounding would occur if three teachers were used, each using only one method, and there were considerable differences in their teaching effectiveness. Then teacher and method would be confounded. If the students of one method scored higher on the chemistry exam than those of the other two methods, we would not know whether the higher performance was due to the method or to the teacher. The effects of teacher and method cannot be separated, because each teacher uses only a single method.

> Two or more variables are *confounded* if their effects cannot be separated.

Control of Extraneous Variables

Although **extraneous variables** are not the variables of primary interest in a research study, they may have an effect on the dependent variable. To control such variables is to be able to identify, balance, minimize, or eliminate their effects. The effects are manifested as they influence the variance in the dependent variable, so the **control of extraneous variables** is accomplished through the control of variance, as described earlier. In the chemistry example, the ability level of the students was considered an extraneous variable, and various approaches to its control were discussed. A good research design controls such variables, rather than confounding their effects with those of other variables or ignoring their effects altogether.

Statistical Precision for Testing Hypotheses

Analyses in quantitative research typically involve some types of statistical procedures, because quantitative research involves numbers and hypotheses that require statistical tests. It is important to have appropriate data with enough precision so hypotheses can be tested with confidence. In a statistical sense, precision is increased as the random or error variance is decreased. **Statistical precision** is increased with larger samples and when additional independent variables are built into the research design. As we discussed in the chemistry example, when additional variables were controlled, the random variance tended to be reduced.

When statistical procedures are used to test hypotheses, for at least some hypotheses, it is necessary to obtain an estimate of random variance from the data. The more precise this estimate, the more sensitive the analysis will be to the effects of the independent variables. That is, the analysis will be more likely to indicate an effect if, in fact, one exists. Extraneous variables inflate the estimate of random variance and tend to make the statistical tests insensitive to existing, real differences.

The research design should provide data for testing all of the hypotheses of the study. Sometimes numerous and complex hypotheses are involved, so the researcher should check the design carefully and identify which part of the design will provide for testing such hypotheses.

Summary

The concepts discussed in this chapter apply to research design in quantitative research. Quantitative research typically has quite a structured design from the outset and there is little, if any, deviation from the design during the study.

In addition to providing answers to research questions, one of the purposes of research design is controlling variance. Controlling variance means being able to explain what is causing it, at least to the point that results can be interpreted with confidence. Variance is controlled in quantitative research by the structure of the design. Four general methods of controlling variance were described and illustrated, and these may be used in combination.

Four characteristics of a good research design in quantitative research, which are by no means independent of each other, were identified. For example, as we construct the design to avoid confounding, we may also be controlling extraneous variables. Although problems inevitably arise while conducting research, they usually can be circumvented or corrected with a well-planned design.

Of necessity, research designs are specific to the types of research. In subsequent chapters different types of research are considered, and each type has its underlying, general design with many possible variations.

Sometimes we talk about "selecting" a research design. Certainly designs are selected, but the variables, conditions, and so forth of a specific study flesh out the design. Thus, it is not correct to infer that selecting a design completes the task of obtaining an adequate research design. The selected design must be translated into the specifics of the study.

KEY CONCEPTS

Positivism
Variance
Controlling variance
Random or error variance
Bias
Confounded variables
Extraneous variables
Control of extraneous variables
Statistical precision

EXERCISES

6.1 Suppose the boys in a senior high school, grades 10–12, are measured on a physical performance test. Identify variables or factors that may contribute to the variance in the performance test scores.

6.2 A study is being conducted in which the dependent variable is student attitude toward school, defined operationally as the score on a specific attitude toward school inventory. There are sixteen elementary schools, four junior high schools, and two senior high schools in the district for which the study is conducted. Random samples of students are selected from all schools and administered the inventory. The independent variable of primary interest is the school, of which there are twenty-two. Considering the four methods of controlling variance described in this chapter, how would variance caused by the following factors be controlled? Suggest one method for each factor.

a. level of school—elementary, junior high, senior high
b. school district
c. gender of the student
d. academic motivation of the student
e. intelligence or ability of the student
f. time of year

6.3 In the research study of Exercise 6.2, are there any variables confounded with the independent variable of primary interest, school? If so, identify examples of such variables.

6.4 The research study of Exercise 6.2 is a survey. Why is this not an experiment?

6.5 Two high school history teachers who each teach two classes of American history have available two different packets of instructional materials. They are interested in whether the materials have differing effects on achievement in history, as measured by the final exam for the course (a common exam for all classes). A specific class will use only one packet of materials, but the teachers have the option of randomly assigning students to classes. In addition to the independent variable of primary interest (materials), it is desirable to control the variance due to (a) learning style of the student, (b) gender or sex of the student, (c) teacher, and (d) ability level of the student.

The students are high school juniors, and no recent IQ test scores are available; but the grade point average (GPA) for the first two years of high school is available. Develop a research design to control the variance due to the four variables. Use at least two of the four basic methods of controlling variance in quantitative research. Diagram the design.

6.6 An educational psychologist is designing an experiment in which three different types of motivational techniques will make up the levels of the independent variable. The dependent variable is performance on a cognitive task that has been shown to be related to an ability-level measure. The participants (subjects) will be sixty randomly selected college freshmen enrolled in an introductory psychology course. Discuss possible variables that might be controlled in this experiment and suggest procedures for enhancing such control.

6.7 Define what is meant by *confounding of variables* and describe a research study in which confounding could occur.

6.8 Locate a quantitative research article in your area of interest. Read the article carefully and attempt to identify the design used for the research. Is there enough description in the article so that you can understand how the research was done? Does the article deal with the variance in the dependent variable and describe how this variance was analyzed? Are issues of internal and external validity addressed?

6.9 Three different reading programs are used in the first grades of three different elementary schools, one program in each school. At the end of the school year the first-graders of the three schools are given a standardized reading test to determine differing effects of the three programs on reading achievement. Discuss how this research design is especially susceptible to confounding. Identify possible confounded variables.

6.10 At a college there are some 500 students about evenly divided between men and women who frequent the college's health and physical exercise center. The center's director plans to conduct a research study of the effects of three levels of physical training (T_1, T_2, T_3) on performance of a physical task. The study can accommodate 150 participants, and these can be selected at random from the 500-plus students. The students range in age from 18 to 27, although there are few students older than 22 years. The three levels of training take place over four weeks, and each participant is involved in only one level. The training levels are self-administered and the physical task is administered in group sessions by the director at the end of the four weeks. The dependent variable is the performance score on the physical task and the independent variable of primary interest is the level of training. Develop a research design for this study including ways to control variance of variables that may affect performance. Diagram the design, indicating numbers of participants, and identify variables being controlled.

6.11 A researcher is interested in investigating the differences in student achievement between public and private elementary schools. Discuss how the issues of freedom from bias, freedom from confounding, control of extraneous variables, and statistical precision for testing hypotheses may or may not affect the comparisons.

6.12 Use the website www.randomizer.org to develop procedures for randomly assigning fifteen students to a treatment group and fifteen students to a control group prior to an experimental intervention.

NOTES

1. In the analysis, each method would be represented by the mean of the thirty test scores of students taught by that method. The mean would be determined by adding the thirty scores and dividing that sum by thirty.
2. *Error variance* is a term commonly used when statistical analyses are done.
3. In practice, the numbers would not quite add this way because as we go from one procedure to the next, the design changes. However, the concept, not the numbers, is important here, so for simplicity we will keep the variance accounted for by method at 50.

REFERENCES

Gall, M. D., Gall, J. P., and Borg, W. B. (2003). *Educational research: An introduction* (7th ed.). Boston: Allyn & Bacon.

Kerlinger, F. N., & Lee, H. B. (2000). *Foundations of behavioral research* (4th ed.). Fort Worth, TX: Harcourt College Publishers.

CHAPTER

7 Experimental Research

The word **experiment** is used quite freely in our society and, therefore, it has a broad, quite familiar meaning. We talk about *experimental programs* and *experimental drugs,* for example. These involve a new approach or procedure or new ingredients to see what the effects will be. When something is tried, we refer to this as an experiment or to the process as experimenting.

In educational research, we use the same basic concept for an experiment; that is, something is tried to determine its effects. That something is one or more independent variables manipulated to determine the effects. An independent variable manipulated in an experiment is called an **experimental variable.**

> An *experiment* is a research situation in which at least one independent variable, called the *experimental variable,* is deliberately manipulated or varied by the researcher.

The Meaning of Experimental Design

In its broadest sense, an **experimental design** is a preconceived plan for conducting an experiment. More specifically, an experimental design is the structure by which variables are positioned, arranged, or built into the experiment. The design includes the independent variable(s), which must include the experimental variable(s) and possibly other variables. Because the measures (the data to be analyzed) are taken on the dependent variable(s), the points in the experiment where these measures are to be taken may also be indicated. Experimental designs are often diagrammed with symbols to indicate the arrangement of the variables and conditions. Such diagrams and their arrangements and symbols have certain meanings, which are explored in this chapter.

Consider an example. An educational psychologist uses three types of instructions—verbal, written, and combination verbal-written—to determine the effects of instruction on performance in solving abstract number problems. The participants in the experiment are college freshmen, twenty of whom are randomly assigned to each type of instruction. A participant comes to a learning laboratory, receives the instructions, and attempts to solve a series of number problems. The dependent variable is the score on the number of problems solved correctly in the series. Each participant goes through the experiment alone, rather than in a group, and the entire activity takes about one hour. The experimental variable is type of instruction, and there are three levels (the different types) of this variable.[1]

The experiment is diagrammed in Figure 7.1. In the upper part of the figure, the entire design is written out. The experimental procedure consists of administering the appropriate instruction and solving the problems. The measures on the dependent variable are collected during the experiment and usually recorded when it is completed. Depending on the experiment, the data may be collected while the experiment is in process or shortly after it is concluded. In this example, the data are collected while the participants are solving the problems.

Below the dotted line in Figure 7.1, the experiment is diagrammed in symbol form.[2] The R indicates random assignment to the three groups, designated by the Gs with subscripts. X is used as the symbol for the introduction or use of an experimental variable, and the subscript on the X simply indicates the level of that variable. In the diagram, the V, W, and C subscripts on the X indicate the type of instructions—verbal, written, and combination. The Os indicate data collection (in a general sense, observation taken), and, in this example, the subscripts on the Os correspond with the numbers of the groups. In this diagram, O_1 indicates the data from Group 1 (G_1) the group that had verbal instructions (X_V). The Os are scores on the dependent variable—in this case, number of correct solutions.

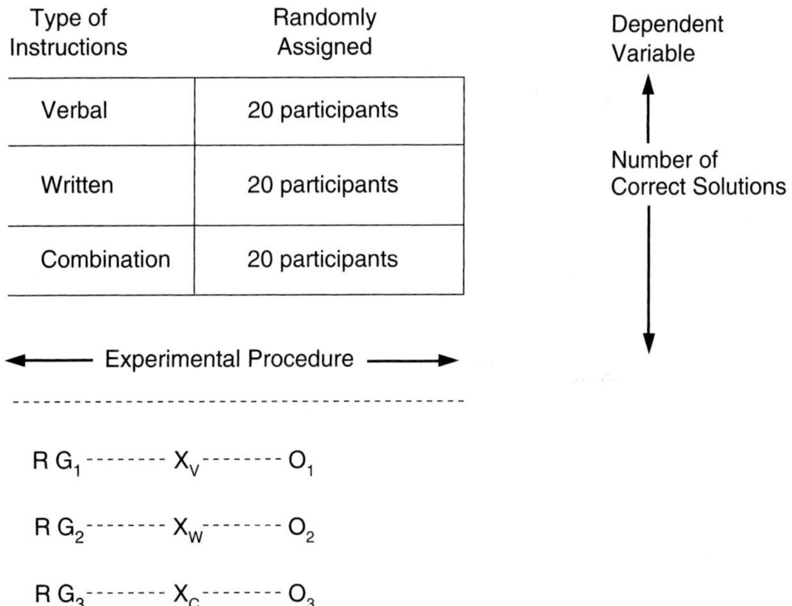

FIGURE 7.1 Experimental Design for the Problem-Solving Experiment

The experiment diagrammed in Figure 7.1 is relatively simple. It contains only one independent variable, the experimental variable. Data are collected only at the close of the experiment. The experimental procedures with the instructions and problem solving might be somewhat complicated, but the design does provide the researcher with considerable control. If, in analyzing the scores, the researcher found those of G_3 to be consistently and considerably higher (more correct solutions) than those of G_1 and G_2, it would be quite conclusive that the combination type of instruction is more effective than the other two types in enhancing this type of problem solution.

Why bother with experimental design? It enables the researcher to interpret and understand the data of an experiment. The purpose of experimental design is no different from the purpose of research design generally—to be able to make sense of the results—and experimental design enhances control. In the example, the researcher can draw conclusions about the effect of type of instructions on problem solving because the design structures the instructions so that their effects are separated and can manifest themselves. Patterns of results can be directly associated with certain effects of the independent variable.

> An *experimental design* is the structure by which variables are positioned or arranged in the experiment.

Experimental Variables

In Chapter 2, various types of variables were discussed. One type introduced was the independent variable, which may have an effect on the dependent variable. Independent variables can take different forms, such as characteristics of the participants or variables that indicate different treatments or procedures to be administered to the participants in the research. An experimental variable is an independent variable; but not all independent variables are experimental variables. In the forgoing example, had the participants been identified according to their sex, so that ten boys and ten girls were administered each type of instruction, the sex of the participant could have been designated an independent variable. However, it is not a manipulated variable. The type of instruction was the experimental variable.

Any number of independent variables can serve as experimental variables. Conceptually, an experimental variable can have any finite number of levels, but in educational research, experimental variables usually have relatively small numbers of levels—perhaps two to five, and rarely more than seven or eight. The levels of the experimental variable are sometimes called **experimental treatments.** The following are some examples of possible experimental variables in educational research:

Experimental Variable	*Possible Levels*
1. Type of instructional organization	**1. a.** team teaching **b.** self-contained classroom
2. Type of materials for concept attainment	**2. a.** verbal **b.** figural

3. Drug dosage for experimental animals	**3. a.** 5 grams **b.** 10 grams **c.** 15 grams
4. Length of time on task with no break	**4. a.** 5 minutes **b.** 10 minutes **c.** 20 minutes **d.** 30 minutes
5. Instructional procedure used in teaching history	**5. a.** lecture **b.** group discussion **c.** individualized instruction
6. Instructional strategy used in teaching third-grade math	**6. a.** constructivist **b.** traditional
7. Length of exercise period (per day)	**7. a.** 15 minutes **b.** 30 minutes **c.** 45 minutes **d.** 60 minutes
8. Type of therapy	**8. a.** medication alone **b.** exercise alone **c.** medication and exercise in combination

For each of the examples of experimental variables, the researcher can manipulate or control the levels of the experimental treatments. This is easier to do for some variables than for others. For example, drug dosage for experimental animals and time on task would be relatively easy to manipulate, compared to the constructivist or traditional strategies of number 6.

Use of the Term *Subject*

In research generally, but especially in experiments, the term **subject** is used to mean someone who participates in an experiment. Subjects are the participants in the experiment, those who receive the experimental treatments. Thus, the subjects of the instructions example were college freshmen. If fifth-grade students were used in an experiment, they would be the subjects. The symbol *S* is used to designate a subject. The term *subject* and the symbol *S* are commonly used in the literature. We will use the term *subject* and the symbol *S* in our examples and figures for the sake of brevity and simplicity. It is more common, though, to use the term *participant* in narrative descriptions of the experiment.

Criteria for a Well-Designed Experiment

Before specific experimental designs are introduced, some general criteria for a well-designed experiment will be considered. Essentially, the characteristics that make for a good research design also apply to the design of an experiment. The criteria are listed here with brief comments for each criterion to explain what it means:

1. *Adequate experimental control*—This means that there are enough constraints on the conditions of the experiment so that the researcher can interpret the results. The experimental design is so structured that if the experimental variable has an effect, it can be detected. **Experimental control** may also mean controlling other variables through randomization or by building them into the design as independent variables.

2. *Lack of artificiality*—This criterion is especially important in educational research if the results of the experiment are to be generalized to a nonexperimental setting—for example, a classroom. It means that the experiment is conducted in such a way that the results will apply to the real educational world. We do not want the artificial or atypical characteristic of an experiment to cause the experimental effects.

3. *Basis for comparison*—There must be some way to make a comparison to determine whether or not there is an experimental effect. In some experiments, a control group is used—a group that does not receive an experimental treatment. The control group in an instructional experiment usually consists of a group of students taught by a traditional method. In a drug experiment with animals, a control group would consist of the animals that receive no drug. Certainly, not all experiments require control groups. Comparisons can be made between two or more experimental treatments and, on occasion, with some external criterion.

4. *Adequate information from the data*—The data must be adequate for testing the hypotheses of the experiment. The data must be such that the necessary statistics can be generated with enough precision to make decisions about the hypotheses.

5. *Uncontaminated data*—The data should adequately reflect the experimental effects. **Contaminated** data are affected by poor measurement or errors in the experimental procedure. The individuals from the various groups should not interact in such a way as to cancel experimental effects or to cause misrepresentation of the experimental effects.

6. *No confounding of relevant variables*—This criterion is closely related to adequate experimental control. There may be other variables operating that have an effect on the dependent variable. If so, these effects must not be misinterpreted as experimental effects. Their effects must be separated or controlled, usually through the experimental design.

7. *Representativeness*—Researchers usually want to generalize the experimental results to some individuals, conditions, methods, and so forth. To obtain representativeness, they commonly include some form of random selection of subjects from the population to which they intend to generalize.

8. *Parsimony*—The criterion of **parsimony** means that, with all other characteristics equal, a simpler design is preferred to a more complex one. Of course, a design must be complex enough for the purposes of the experiment, but complexity is not encouraged for its own sake. The simpler design is usually easier to implement and possibly easier to interpret.

Experiments, like any type of educational research, are susceptible to technical and procedural errors. The development of an appropriate experimental design and its adequate implementation require considerable and careful planning, but they provide the best safeguard against errors. Experimental design requires simultaneous attention to a variety of details. This planning is done prior to conducting the experiment.

Experimental Validity

The criteria of a well-designed experiment can be summarized as the characteristics that enhance experimental validity. In Chapter 1, the validity of educational research was discussed, and the concept of experimental validity is essentially the same. *Experimental validity* is used here as defined by Campbell and Stanley (1963) and by Cook and Campbell (1979) and is considered to be of four types: internal, external, construct, and statistical conclusion.

Internal validity refers to the validity of the cause-and-effect inference linking the independent variable and the dependent variable. It questions whether the experimental treatment really makes a difference in the dependent variable. To answer this question, the researcher must be confident that factors such as extraneous variables have been controlled and are not producing an effect that is being mistaken as an experimental treatment effect.

External validity of an experiment deals with the generalizability of the results of the experiment. To what populations, variables, situations, and so forth do the results generalize? Generally, the more extensively the results can be generalized the more useful the research, given that there is adequate internal validity.

Construct validity deals with the definitions of the independent and the dependent variables in an experiment and in the ways that those variables are operationalized in the experimental setting. The concern is that the constructs that are investigated could be construed to be different constructs.

Statistical conclusion validity refers to the validity of the decision that there is a statistically significant difference between the experimental group and the control group. This is the first step in deciding whether the experimental treatment has had an effect. A mistake at this point will lead to an inaccurate conclusion about the impact of the independent variable on the dependent variable.

> *Experimental validity* is of four types. *Internal validity* is concerned with whether changes in the dependent variable are due to the experimental variable. *External validity* deals with the extent of generalizability of the results. *Construct validity* is about clear and unambiguous identification of the constructs of the independent and the dependent variables. *Statistical conclusion validity* deals with the accuracy of the decision about whether the experimental and control groups differ.

Although the purpose of experimental design is to have experiments high in all types of validity, in some cases securing one type tends to jeopardize the other. As more rigorous controls are applied in the experiment, less carryover can be anticipated between what occurred in the experiment and what would occur in a natural educational setting. For example, in research on instructional techniques, the control of the experiment may be so extensive that an essentially artificial situation is created and only the experimental variables are operating. This would greatly enhance internal validity, but the generalization might be so limited that the results could not be applied to a real classroom situation. This does not imply that it is never desirable to achieve maximum control; the objectives of the experiment dictate the extent of the validity requirements.

Clearly, an experiment whose results are uninterpretable is useless even if wide generalizability would be possible. On the other hand, it is unsatisfactory to do an experiment and then discover that the results cannot be generalized as anticipated in the objectives of the experiment.

Internal validity involves securing adequate control over extraneous variables, selection procedures, measurement procedures, and the like. The experimental design should be developed so the researcher can adequately check on the factors that might threaten the internal validity. To be sure, all possible factors are not operating in all experiments, but the researcher should have some knowledge about the variables and the possible difficulties that may arise in connection with internal validity. Then the experiment can be designed so the results can be interpreted adequately.

External validity certainly concerns the populations to which the researcher expects to generalize the results, but it also may include generalizing the findings to other related independent variables or modifications of the experimental variable. There may be factors such as size of class, type of school, and the like, across which the researcher hopes to generalize. For example, would the results of an experiment being conducted in a suburban school with fourth-grade pupils apply to an inner-city school? To eighth-graders? Most likely not, but again this would depend on the variables and the details of the experiment. The researcher may also desire to generalize to different measurement variations. For example, would the results of an experiment including pretesting be applicable to a classroom situation without pretesting? External validity is concerned with these types of questions.

Construct validity deals with the construct of the independent variable and the construct of the dependent variable. Care must be taken in defining the experimental variable so that others can replicate the study or extend it to different populations or settings. This means that the experimental treatment has to be described so specifically that others will know exactly what was done and true replication is then possible. The definition and measurement of the dependent variable need similar attention to detail. Often, it is wise to use the same definitions and measures that were used in previous studies. This allows the results of your study to be compared directly to the results of related studies.

Statistical conclusion validity is assured when the researcher understands the statistical methods that are used in the research, including the assumptions that underlie the statistics. A large enough sample size is needed to ensure adequate statistical power and the measures should be technically adequate, which, in part, means that the reliability coefficient of the measure of the dependent variable should be high, probably around .90. An appropriate analysis of good measures is essential to a high-quality research design.

Threats to Experimental Validity

Experimental design should enhance experimental validity, but experimental validity does not depend on experimental design alone. The specifics of the experiment have an influence, and a number of things can happen to threaten experimental validity, both internal and external.

Campbell and Stanley (1963) have summarized the **threats to experimental validity,** identifying twelve threats, eight to internal validity and four to external validity. Table 7.1 lists and describes most of these threats and provides an example of how each could occur.

TABLE 7.1 Threats to Experimental Validity

Threat	Example
Internal Validity	
1. History—unanticipated events occurring while the experiment is in progress that affect the dependent variable.	**1.** During a relatively short instructional experiment, one group of subjects misses instruction due to a power failure at the school.
2. Maturation—processes operating within the subject as a function of time.	**2.** In a learning experiment, subject performance begins decreasing after about fifty minutes due to fatigue.
3. Testing—the effect of taking one test on the scores of a subsequent test.	**3.** In an experiment in which performance on a logical reasoning test is the dependent variable, a pretest cues the subjects about the posttest.
4. Instrumentation—an effect due to inconsistent use of the measuring instruments.	**4.** Two examiners in an instructional experiment administered the posttest with different instructions and procedures.
5. Statistical regression—an effect caused by a tendency for subjects selected on the basis of extreme scores to regress toward an average performance on a subsequent test.	**5.** In an experiment involving reading instruction, subjects grouped because of poor pretest reading scores show considerably greater gains than the average and high readers.
6. Selection—an effect due to the groups of subjects not being randomly assigned to groups; a selection factor is operating such that the groups are not equivalent.	**6.** The experimental group in an instructional experiment consists of a high-ability class, while the control group is an average-ability class.
7. Mortality—an effect due to subjects dropping out of the experiment on a nonrandom basis.	**7.** In a health experiment designed to determine the effects of various exercises, those subjects finding exercise most difficult stop participating.
8. Selection-maturation interaction—an effect of maturation not being consistent across the groups because of some selection factor.	**8.** In a problem-solving experiment, intact groups of junior high school students and senior high students are involved. The junior high students tire of the task sooner than the older students.
External Validity	
1. Interaction effect of testing—pretesting interacts with the experimental treatment and causes some effect such that the results will not generalize to an unpretested population.	**1.** In a physical performance experiment, the pretest cues the subjects to respond in a certain way to the experimental treatment that would not be the case if there were no pretest.
2. Interaction effects of selection biases and the experimental treatment—an effect of some selection factor of intact groups interacting with the experimental treatment that would not be the case if the groups were formed randomly.	**2.** The results of an experiment in which teaching method is the experimental treatment is effective with low achievers but is not as effective with high achievers.

(*continued*)

TABLE 7.1 ***(Continued)***

Threat	Example
3. Reactive effects of experimental arrangements—an effect that is due to the artificial or novel experimental setting. (Note that this can also threaten internal validity.)	**3.** An experiment in remedial reading instruction has an effect that does not occur when the remedial reading program is implemented in the regular classroom.
4. Multiple-treatment interference—when the same subjects receive two or more treatments (as in a repeated measures design). There may be a carryover effect between treatments such that the results cannot be generalized to single treatments.	**4.** In a drug experiment the same animals are administered four different drug doses in some sequence. The effects of the second and fourth doses cannot be separated from possible (delayed) effects of preceding doses.
Construct Validity	
1. Inadequate preoperational explication of constructs—insufficient definition of the independent and/or dependent variables.	**1.** Two teachers implement individualized instruction in very different ways because they lack a precise definition of the term.
2. Mono-operation bias—only one form of the experimental variable is implemented.	**2.** An experiment concerning the effect of feedback includes only written feedback.
3. Mono-method bias—only one form of the dependent variable is implemented.	**3.** An experiment on reducing test anxiety uses only a paper-and-pencil self-report of anxiety.
4. Hypothesis-guessing within experimental conditions—participants behave differently when they know they are part of an experiment. (Note that the behavior of subjects can also threaten internal validity.)	**4.** Subjects in an experimental program interact differently when they know they are being studied.
5. Confounding constructs and levels of constructs—drawing conclusions about variables when some levels of the variable are absent.	**5.** A researcher concludes that music enhances exercise programs when this is only true for certain kinds of music.
Statistical Conclusion Validity	
1. Low statistical power—using a sample size that is too small to detect differences between groups.	**1.** A researcher concludes that two instructional approaches are equally effective when an experiment with five students in each group yields no significant differences.
2. Violated assumptions of statistical tests—failing to meet the underlying assumptions.	**2.** A researcher reports means and variances of nominal scaled data such as ethnicity.
3. Fishing and the error rate problem—capitalizing on chance findings.	**3.** A researcher compares two methods on fifty dependent variables and bases conclusions on two significant findings.
4. Reliability of measures—using technically inadequate measures.	**4.** A psychologist finds no difference between boys' and girls' recall of memories of infancy.

Because these are experiments, all examples assume that some experimental treatment has been administered.

The designs discussed in this chapter are general designs and they are fleshed out by the specifics of whatever experiment is being conducted. For this reason it should not be implied that certain designs will guard against all threats to experimental validity. For example, it does not make any difference what design is being used; if measurement breaks down and is inconsistent, instrumentation is a threat.

Experiments that include only one data-collection point, such as those using posttest-only designs, are not threatened by testing. The designs discussed in this chapter meet the criterion of "true" experimental designs as defined by Campbell and Stanley (1963). That is, subjects have been assigned at random to experimental treatments. Thus, differential selection of subjects is not a threat for these designs, but it very well may be for quasi-experimental designs as described in Chapter 6. Random assignment ensures the equivalency of groups prior to administering experimental treatments. Statistical regression is not a threat if the subjects involved are not selected because of extreme scores. But if an experiment is conducted with such subjects, the possibility of this threat should be recognized and addressed. For example, if a statistical regression effect is confounded with the experimental effect, it may be possible to estimate the magnitude of the statistical regression effect from information in the research literature.

The shorter the duration of an experiment, the less likely history is to be a threat to validity. Careful specification and control over the measurement can do much to eliminate problems with instrumentation. If no subjects drop out of the experiment, experimental mortality is no problem. If only posttesting is used after the experimental treatment is completed, there is no opportunity for an undesirable interaction between testing and the experimental treatment. Thus, it is through the planning and the careful conducting of the experiment that the threats to validity are countered. Many times extraneous variables can be controlled as independent variables built into the design. It may not be possible to eliminate all threats, but it is important to recognize and interpret the results accordingly, entertaining alternate explanations of the data if such explanations are plausible.

Experimental designs in educational research are rarely, if ever, perfect. Through experimental design, the researcher attempts to attain adequate validity, both internal and external. Because enhancing one type of validity may tend to jeopardize the other, the researcher often must attempt an adequate balance, essentially by attaining sufficient control to make the results interpretable, while maintaining enough realism so that the results will generalize adequately to the intended situations.

> Experimental validity must be considered in the context of each specific experiment. Attaining validity is not an all-or-nothing outcome. Possible limits to validity should be recognized and countered through the design and the way the experiment is conducted.

The following sections describe a number of designs commonly used in educational research. The designs are diagrammed in general and described, and an example is provided for each design discussed.

Posttest-Only Control Group Design

In discussing experimental designs, two terms, *pretest* and *posttest*, are often used in connection with the data collection. *Pretest* refers to a measure or test given to the subjects prior to the experimental treatment. A *posttest* is a measure taken after the experimental treatment has been applied. Not all designs involve pretesting, but posttesting is necessary to determine the effects of the experimental treatment.

Experimental designs commonly involve two or more groups, one for each of the experimental treatments and possibly a control group. The **posttest-only control group design** in its simplest form involves just two groups, the group that receives the experimental treatment and the control group. The subjects are randomly assigned to the two groups prior to the experiment, and the experimental group receives the experimental treatment. Upon the conclusion of the experimental period, the two groups are measured on the dependent variable under study. Preferably, this measurement is taken immediately after the conclusion of the experiment, especially if the dependent variable is likely to change with the passing of time.

The posttest-only control group design is an efficient design to administer. It does not require pretesting, which for many situations is not desirable or applicable. Pretesting and posttesting require that each individual subject be identified so that pre- and posttest scores can be paired. The posttest-only design requires the subjects to be identified only in terms of their group and, possibly, other independent variables if such variables are included in the design.

The two-group design can be diagrammed as follows:

$$\begin{array}{lll} R\,G_1 & X & O_1 \\ R\,G_2 & — & O_2 \end{array}$$

In this diagram, G indicates group and R indicates that the members of the group are randomly assigned to each group. An X indicates an experimental treatment, a dash, no experimental treatment. The Os indicate a measurement (test, task, or observation) on the dependent variable, and the vertical positioning of the Os indicates when they take place. Because they are vertically aligned, they take place at the same point in the experiment. In this case, they are posttests, because they occur after the experimental treatment.

The posttest-only control group design may be extended to include more than two groups; that is, two or more experimental treatments may be used, increasing the number of groups to three or more. The subjects would be randomly assigned to the groups from the population, and the effects of the various experimental treatments could be investigated by comparing the performances of the groups. In the more general sense, the posttest-only control group design can be diagrammed as follows:

R G_1	X_1	O_1
R G_2	X_2	O_2
•	•	
•	•	
•	•	
R G_k	X_k	O_k
R G_{k+1}	—	O_{k+1}

The subscripts on the Xs indicate the different experimental treatments. The number of these treatments in the specific experiment is k. Note that there is one group, the control group, that does not receive an experimental treatment. If no control group were needed, the design would be called a posttest-only randomized groups design.

EXAMPLE 7.1

A fourth-grade teacher does an experiment on the effects of supplementary instructional materials on reading performance. Two kinds of supplementary instructional materials are to be used; along with the traditional materials, they make up the three levels of the independent (experimental) variable.

The research problem can be stated as follows:

> A study of the effects of kinds of supplementary materials on the reading performance of fourth-grade students.

Fifteen students in fourth grade are randomly assigned to each level of the independent variable; thus, forty-five students participate in the experiment. During daily reading instruction, the fifteen students using each of the supplementary materials work with those materials for twenty minutes. The control group continues working with the traditional materials. After eight weeks of instruction, the students are tested with a reading test. Performance on this test is the dependent variable. The experiment is diagrammed in Figure 7.2. The symbols for the experimental treatments are X_1 and X_2 with a dash for the control group. Referring to the general design, in this case the number of experimental treatments, k, would equal two.

> The *posttest-only control group design* contains as many groups as there are experimental treatments, plus a control or comparison group. Subjects are measured only after the experimental treatments have been applied.

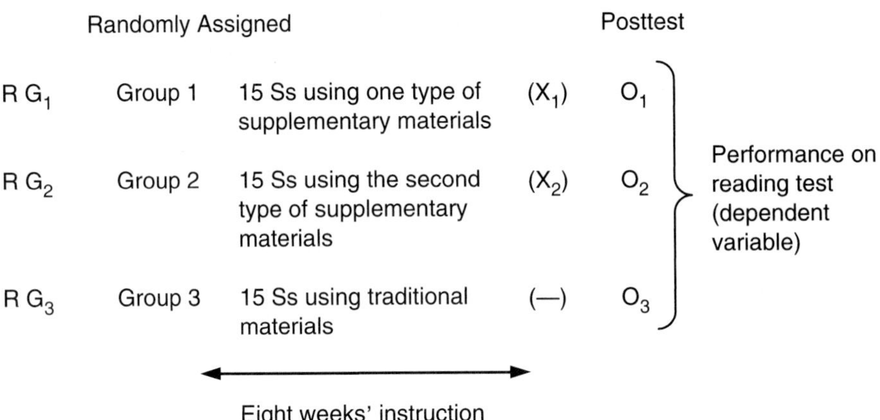

FIGURE 7.2 Diagram of Example 7.1 Posttest-Only Control Group Design, Including Two Experimental Groups and a Control Group

Pretest-Posttest Control Group Design

The addition of a pretest given prior to administering the experimental treatments essentially extends the posttest-only control group design to the **pretest-posttest control group design.** The subjects are randomly assigned to the two or more groups and tested just prior to the experiment on a supposedly relevant antecedent variable, possibly a second form of the test that measures the dependent variable.

What do pretests provide? First, the purpose of pretesting in a randomized, comparative experiment is *not* to assure equivalence of the comparison groups; random assignment of individuals to comparison groups takes care of that. Granted, there could be a "one in a million" random assignment where all the top scorers on the pretest were assigned to the experimental group and all of the bottom scorers to the control group. Having the pretest scores available would reveal that improbable result, which would be a very rare occurrence. Second, pretests on one or more variables can be used as statistical controls in the analysis, as was described in the last chapter. Third, the most common use of pretests is when the pretest is the same measure as the posttest. Then a *gain score* can be calculated by subtracting the pretest score from the posttest score. Although gain scores seem simple enough, they have some real problems. Their complexities are described in a classic paper by Cronbach and Furby (1970). For example, one difficulty is that a 5-point gain at one point on the measurement scale may not have the same meaning as a 5-point gain at another point on the scale. It is often more difficult to go from 95 percent to 100 percent correct on an achievement test than it is to go from 45 percent to 50 percent correct. That is because the items on most tests are not equally difficult. A second problem with gain scores is that even when both the pretest and the posttest are very reliable, the gain score that is calculated is much less reliable than either of them. In spite of these technical problems, gain scores continue to be widely used.

In its simplest form, the pretest-posttest control group design contains two groups—one receiving an experimental treatment, the other not. It is diagrammed as follows:

$$
\begin{array}{llll}
R\ G_1 & O_1 & X & O_2 \\
R\ G_2 & O_3 & \text{—} & O_4
\end{array}
$$

Now there are twice as many Os as in the posttest-only design, so the Os with odd-numbered subscripts indicate pretests and those with even-numbered subscripts indicate posttests.

The pretest-posttest control group design can be extended to include more than two groups. It can be diagrammed in general form as follows:

$$
\begin{array}{llll}
R\ G_1 & O_1 & X_1 & O_2 \\
R\ G_2 & O_3 & X_2 & O_4 \\
\bullet & \bullet & \bullet & \bullet \\
\bullet & \bullet & \bullet & \bullet \\
\bullet & \bullet & \bullet & \bullet \\
R\ G_k & O_{2k-1} & X_k & O_{2k} \\
R\ G_{k+1} & O_{2k+1} & \text{—} & O_{2(k+1)}
\end{array}
$$

The notation indicates k experimental treatments and a comparison group as a control group. If two or more experimental treatments were used and the experiment did not require a control group, the design would be called a pretest-posttest randomized groups design.

EXAMPLE 7.2

A researcher is interested in the effects of length of intense instruction in geometric concepts on performance on a spatial relations test. The research problem can be stated as follows:

> A study of the effects of different length of instruction in geometric concepts on spatial relations performance of high school juniors.

The problem statement clearly implies an experiment, because length of instruction is a variable manipulated by the researcher.

Two parallel forms of the spatial relations test are used—one as the pretest, the other as the posttest. The experiment is set up as follows. Forty high school juniors are randomly selected, with the condition that all have taken a geometry course. The forty students are randomly assigned to four groups of ten each, and the experimental treatments are administered as follows:

G_1 will receive one fifteen-minute period of instruction in three-dimensional geometric concepts.

G_2 will receive two fifteen-minute periods of instruction in three-dimensional geometric concepts.

G_3 will receive three fifteen-minute periods of instruction in three-dimensional geometric concepts.

G_4 (control group) will receive no instruction in three-dimensional geometric concepts.

The members of G_1, G_2, and G_3 will receive the instruction individually in a tutorial situation. (Care must be taken that the instruction is consistent for the members of a group; across groups, the only thing that should vary is the length of instruction.) The entire instruction will be completed over the period of one week. Before anyone receives instruction, the students are pretested; shortly after instruction is completed, the students are posttested. The experiment is diagrammed in Figure 7.3.

The dependent variable in this experiment could be the gain scores between pre- and posttesting. Or the posttest scores could be the dependent variable, adjusted for pretest score. The adjusted scores would be generated through a statistical procedure.

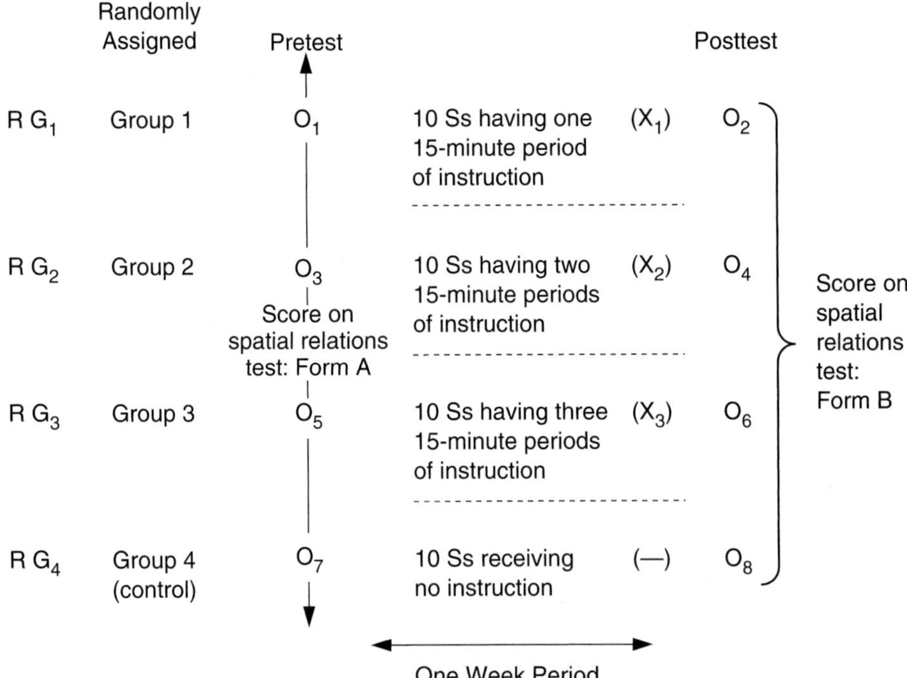

FIGURE 7.3 Diagram of Example 7.2 Pretest-Posttest Control Group Design, Including Three Experimental Groups and a Control Group

Using this design, the researcher can determine whether there are effects on spatial relations test performance from the different amounts of instruction in three-dimensional geometric concepts or, in comparison with the control group, whether instruction has any effects at all.

> The *pretest-posttest control group design* contains as many groups as there are experimental treatments, plus a control group. Subjects are measured before and after receiving the experimental treatments.

Solomon Four-Group Design

Combining the pretest-posttest control group design and the posttest-only control group design in their simplest forms produces a design described by Solomon (1949). This design, in its four-group form, includes two control and two experimental groups, but the experimental groups receive the same experimental treatment. Only one of each of the two types of groups is pretested, and all four groups are posttested at the conclusion of the experimental period. The assignment of subjects to all groups is random.

The diagram for the **Solomon four-group design** is as follows:

R G_1	O_1	X	O_2
R G_2	O_3	—	O_4
R G_3	—	X	O_5
R G_4	—	—	O_6

Because it is a four-group design, only four groups are included and only one experimental treatment is used, the effects of which are determined by comparison of the posttest scores of the experimental and control groups. Because there is only one experimental treatment, no subscript appears on the X. Groups 1 and 3 are experimental groups, Groups 2 and 4, control groups (indicated by the absence of X).

The advantage of the Solomon four-group design is that it enables the researcher to check on possible effects of pretesting, because some groups are pretested and others not. It is possible that pretesting affects the posttest score or that pretesting interacts with the experimental treatment. That is, the effect of the experimental treatment is not the same in pretested and nonpretested groups. Because pretesting is not the rule in actual classroom practice, this is often an important consideration for validity.

EXAMPLE 7.3

An educational psychologist is experimenting with the effects of viewing a problem solutions film on performance on a logical reasoning test. The research problem can be stated as follows:

A study of the effects of viewing a problem solutions film on logical reasoning performance of young adults.

The experimental treatment is viewing the thirty-minute film. The subjects for the experiment are college seniors enrolled in an educational psychology class. The psychologist wants to pre- and posttest so that at least some gain scores can be analyzed. However, there is concern that the pretesting may trigger a certain kind of reaction to the film, such that the subjects being pretested may be cued about what to learn from the film. This is the reason for using the Solomon four-group design rather than a posttest-only design or a pretest-posttest design.

Thirty-two students are used for the experiment, and eight are randomly assigned to each of the four groups of the design. The design is diagrammed in Figure 7.4. The sixteen students in G_1 and G_2 are pretested at a single time. The next day, the sixteen students of the experimental groups view the film. Shortly thereafter, all thirty-two students are posttested. A logical reasoning test is given as the pretest and again as the posttest.

The psychologist can now check on possible effects of pretesting and the interaction of pretesting with the experimental treatment. Herein lies the advantage of the Solomon four-group design over the posttest-only and pretest-posttest control group

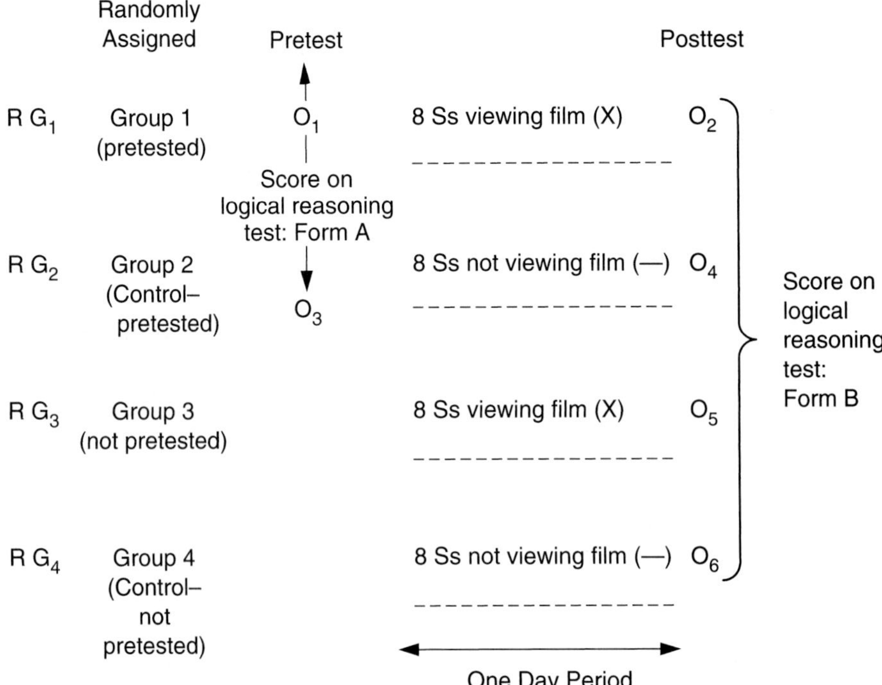

FIGURE 7.4 Diagram of Example 7.3 Solomon Four-Group Design

designs. However, the Solomon four-group design has a disadvantage in that it requires more groups and consequently more subjects. The design can be extended to include more experimental treatments, but for each additional treatment, two additional groups are required—one pretested and the other not. For example, if the experimental variable contained two treatments, six groups would be required; if it had three treatments, eight groups would be required.

> The *Solomon four-group design* is a combination of the posttest-only control group design and the pretest-posttest control group design.

Factorial Designs

The Solomon-four group design actually belongs to a family of designs called **factorial designs.** These designs are used extensively in educational research, because essentially they are the designs when two or more independent variables are included in the design. The basic construction of a factorial design is that all levels of each independent variable are taken in combination with the levels of the other independent variables (technically referred to as *complete factorial).* The design requires a minimum of two independent variables, with at least two levels of each variable. This minimum design is called a two by two (2×2) factorial. The Solomon four-group design fits the 2×2 factorial because it has two independent variables (the experimental variable and the pretesting variable) and each variable has two levels.

Theoretically, there could be any number of independent variables with any number of levels of each. Using the numerical designation for a design, such as 2×4, the number of integers indicates the number of independent variables, and the numerical values of the integers indicate the number of levels for the specific independent variables. These numbers need not be the same for the independent variables. A $2 \times 3 \times 5$ factorial has three independent variables, with two, three, and five levels, respectively. An example that fits this factorial is two teaching methods, three ability levels, and five grades.

The number of different groups involved in a factorial design increases very rapidly with the increase of the number of independent variables and number of levels. The 2×2 factorial has four groups. Adding just one independent variable with two levels would increase this to a $2 \times 2 \times 2$ (denoted by 2^3) factorial with eight groups. If one level is added to each of the independent variables of a 2×2 factorial, resulting in a 3×3 factorial, the number of groups is increased to nine. Because the levels of the independent variable are taken in all combinations, the number of groups is the product of the integers that specify the factorial design. The $2 \times 3 \times 5$ example above would require 30 groups.

The advantages of factorial designs over simpler designs are generally threefold: Factorial design provides the economy of a single design rather than separate designs for each of the independent variables, and it allows the researcher to investigate the interactions between the variables. For many research studies, a knowledge of interaction is of major importance, and investigating the existence of interaction is a primary objective of the study. The third advantage is that, by including additional independent variables and their interactions, the random error variance is reduced. The reduction of random variance increases the probability of finding a significant experimental effect.

Interaction is an effect on the dependent variable such that the effect of one independent variable fails to remain constant over the levels of another. An interaction is present if the joint effect of two independent variables is not equal to their separate (additive) effects. This means that the effect of an independent variable by itself is not the same as when it is taken in combination with the levels of another independent variable. An example of interaction would be if students of different ability levels profited differently from different instructional content. Ability level and instructional content would be the independent variables.

The simplest type of interaction is that of two variables interacting. (This is sometimes called a *first-order interaction.*) More than two independent variables can be involved in an interaction. However, as more independent variables are involved in an interaction, it becomes increasingly complex, and interpretation becomes increasingly difficult.

> *Interaction* in an experiment is an effect on the dependent variable such that the effect of one independent variable changes over the levels of another independent variable.

The factorial design allows for the manipulation or control of more than one independent variable. For this reason, it is often used as a design for enhancing control by including relevant factors as independent variables. Theoretically, the factorial design may be extended to include any finite number of variables and levels. However, complex designs should be considered with caution, one reason being that such a design may not be economically feasible in terms of the available subjects. Also, the interpretation of complex interactions involving more than two independent variables may, for all practical purposes, be impossible. For example, an interaction involving four independent variables—ability level, sex of the subject, instructional method, and type of material—would be very difficult to interpret.

> *Factorial designs* involve two or more independent variables, called *factors*, in a single design. The cells of the design are determined by the levels of the independent variables taken in combination.

As indicated above, factorial designs can become complex and extensive with the inclusion of additional independent variables. Nevertheless, the concept of factorial designs is straightforward and these designs do appear extensively in the research literature. The example below includes only two independent variables and, because it is a 2×3 factorial, requires six groups.

EXAMPLE 7.4

A teacher is interested in the effectiveness of two different types of materials in learning American history—one highly graphic and pictorial, the other more abstract and more verbally detailed. The students available for the experiment are heterogeneous in ability, and academic aptitude test scores are provided for the students. Not only can academic aptitude serve as a control variable, but it is also possible that types of materials are not consistently effective across ability levels. That is, type of material and ability may interact. The research problem can be stated as follows:

> A study of the effects of graphic and verbal materials on American history achievement when used with high-, average-, and low-ability high school students.

The 120 students are categorized into three groups on ability, arbitrarily designated high, average, and low. The 40 students with the highest academic aptitude test scores are designated high, the next 40 average, and the remaining 40, low. Then 20 students from each of the ability levels are randomly assigned to each of the two materials, and the instruction takes place over the period of one semester. The dependent variable is performance on a common history exam covering the content of the materials. The design is diagrammed in Figure 7.5.

The scheme used to diagram the factorial designs is slightly different from the designs diagrammed earlier. The groups are designated in the various cells of the design, rather than only on the rows, and the designation of independent variables is arbitrary. In the example, the types of materials are the experimental treatments, but M (for materials) is used instead of X. It is understood that all six groups of the example are tested at the close of the semester's instruction. Os are not included in the diagram.

In the example, random assignment is used only for assigning students to methods. Obviously, students cannot be assigned ability level at random, because it is a personal characteristic. Also, ability level is arbitrarily defined so that forty students would be in each category. It is not a requirement that the cells of a factorial have equal numbers, but they usually do, because analysis of the data and, to some

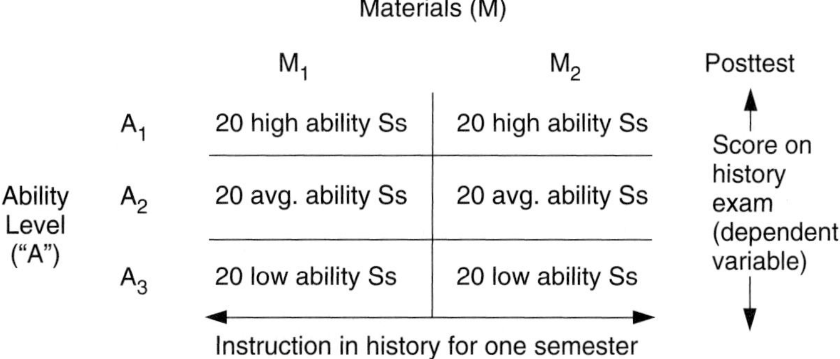

FIGURE 7.5 Diagram of Example 7.4 2 × 3 Factorial Design

extent, interpretation of the results are made less complicated if the cells have equal numbers.

Repeated Measures Designs

Sometimes, when working with educational variables and other variables in the behavioral sciences, it may be difficult to anticipate the time required for an effect to manifest itself. For some variables, the duration of an effect is unknown. Experimental designs can be extended to check on possible delayed effects or to check on the duration of an effect. This can be done by taking additional observations, extended in time, that is, **repeated measures designs.** If we extended the posttest-only control group design in such a manner, a possible diagram of the design would be as follows:

R G_1	X_1	O_1—O_2—O_3
R G_2	—	O_4—O_5—O_6

In this design, observations are taken on both groups after the experimental treatment has been administered to G_1. Then, at specified, regular intervals, subsequent observations are taken on both groups; although, no additional experimental treatments are administered. The length of intervals between observations would depend on the variables under study.

Designs so extended are susceptible to an effect of **multiple observation,** because groups are measured more than once. Earlier observations may have an effect on subsequent ones. Whether or not there is a multiple observation effect depends on the variables involved. Also, as designs are extended in time, they become especially susceptible to history and maturation effects as threats to internal validity.

> *Repeated measures designs* are designs in which the same subject is measured more than once on the dependent variable.

EXAMPLE 7.5

A researcher is studying the effects of three different exercise programs (X_1, X_2, and X_3) on the resting heart rate, measured one minute after a brief, strenuous exercise. The research problem can be stated as follows:

> A study of the effects, and duration of those effects, of three exercise programs on the resting heart rates of young male adults.

A random sample of sixty males, ages eighteen to twenty-two, is selected, and twenty are assigned to each of the three exercise programs. The subjects participate daily for two weeks in their respective programs; later, on the final day of the two weeks, they are measured on heart rate. When the heart rate data are being collected, a subject

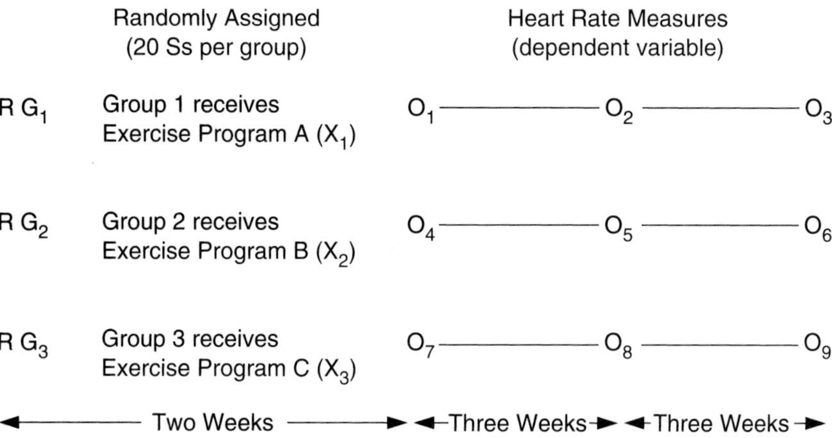

FIGURE 7.6 Diagram of Example 7.5 Repeated Measures Design

exercises strenuously for five minutes and rests for one minute; then the heart rate is measured. After the two-week period, the subjects no longer participate in exercise programs and are instructed not to initiate exercise on their own. They are again measured on heart rate at three-week intervals after the final day of the exercise program. The design is diagrammed in Figure 7.6.

There is little likelihood of a multiple observation effect in this example. Simply having had heart rate measured three weeks earlier should have no effect on subsequent measures of heart rate. There may be a threat to internal validity if subjects continue to exercise on their own after the program has been completed. It would be desirable, almost necessary, to obtain the subjects' commitment prior to conducting the experiment that they will cooperate as instructed throughout the eight-week period of the experiment, including all observation.

Time Series Designs

Campbell and Stanley (1963) classify time series designs as quasi-experimental designs because they discuss the designs as being used with intact groups. However, time series designs can be "true" experimental designs, if the groups are formed randomly and there is provision for a valid comparison, such as a control group. Time series designs involve repeated measurement, usually some measures taken prior to the experimental treatment, and the insertion of the experimental treatment somewhere between two of the measurements.

> Time series designs involve repeated measurement with an experimental treatment inserted between two of the measurements.

EXAMPLE 7.6

A university professor teaches an "Introduction to Education" class that has seventy-eight students. The students have two discussion sections that meet once per week for two hours over the course of the semester. These sections meet for all students at the same time, and beginning with the third week, and at two-week intervals, the students are given exams covering the content of the previous two weeks. Seven such exams are given over the course of the semester. Graduate students conduct the discussion sessions and they rotate among the two groups.

The seventy-eight students are assigned randomly to the two discussion sections, thirty-nine to each section. One section receives the traditional treatment, which is discussion of content covered and educational issues that may be raised. This is the control group. The experimental group receives traditional treatment except, between the second and third exams, the discussion section time is spent viewing and discussing videotapes of school situations. The use of the videotapes is the experimental treatment. The design may be diagrammed as:

$$R\ G_1 \quad O_1—O_2—X—O_3—O_4—O_5—O_6—O_7$$

$$R\ G_2 \quad O_8—O_9———O_{10}—O_{11}—O_{12}—O_{13}—O_{14}$$

The Os are given at the same time; for example, O_1 and O_8 are the same test. The different subscripts are used only to indicate that the Os come from different groups. The horizontal intervals between the Os all represent two weeks.

The primary interest in this example would likely be on the difference between O_3 and O_{10}. However, there might be some delayed effects of the experimental treatment that also could be checked. The differences between O_1 and O_8, and O_2 and O_9, those observations taken prior to the experimental treatment, should be no more than that due to random assignment.

Time series designs can be extended to additional groups and they may also involve multiple insertions of the experimental treatment. Of course, they can be extended in time. However, as designs are extended, they become increasingly susceptible to history and maturation as threats to validity. Time series designs also are discussed in the next chapter because they do find applications with intact groups, and single-subject designs can be viewed as time series designs applied to an individual.

Interpreting Results of Experiments

If an experiment is designed properly, the researcher should be able to draw some conclusions about the existence and nature of an experimental effect. There are any number of specific analyses that are used to analyze experimental data. (Analysis procedures are discussed in later chapters. The role of statistics, both descriptive and inferential, is one of providing analyses; therefore, statistics are very important to the entire research effort.) However, in interpreting results, we want to consider some patterns of the data (the Os in the designs) and what these patterns indicate about the experimental treatment.

The interpretation of results can be approached in two ways: (1) given a certain result (or pattern of Os), what does it mean? and (2) what comparison would be made to determine whether or not a certain kind of effect exists? Sample designs and interpretations are considered below. The notation in the designs is the same as defined previously. Interpretation of results involves making comparisons between Os. Although Os consist of observations, such as pretest or posttest scores, in the design, they also represent group data summarized by computing a mean or some group measure. The symbol = means that these group measures are close to being equal; ≠ means that they are substantially different. (A substantial difference would likely be identified through the use of inferential statistics.[3]) In the examples, the a, b, . . . sets of results are considered independently.

INTERPRETATION EXAMPLE 7.1

A four-group pretest-posttest control group design is used with three different experimental treatments, X_1, X_2, and X_3, and a control treatment. All groups are pretested and posttested. The design is diagrammed as follows:

R G_1	O_1—X_1—O_2
R G_2	O_3—X_2—O_4
R G_3	O_5—X_3—O_6
R G_4	O_7———O_8

a. *Result:* $O_1 \neq O_2$, $O_3 \neq O_4$, $O_5 \neq O_6$, $O_2 = O_4$, but O_2, $O_4 \neq O_6$ and $O_1 = O_3 = O_5 = O_7 = O_8$.

Interpretation: There are effects for all experimental treatments. The effects of X_1 and X_2 are the same, but they are different from that of X_3.

b. *Result:* $O_1 = O_3 = O_4 = O_5 = O_6 = O_7 = O_8$, but $O_1 \neq O_2$.

Interpretation: There are no effects of X_2 and X_3, only an experimental effect for X_1.

c. *Result:* $O_1 = O_3 = O_5 = O_7$ and $O_2 = O_4 = O_6 = O_8$, but $O_1, O_3, O_5, O_7 \neq O_2, O_4, O_6, O_8$.

Interpretation: There are no experimental treatment effects, but something, possibly a maturation effect, is causing a change between pretest and posttest.

d. What comparison would be made to determine whether or not there is a change in subjects independent of the experimental treatment?

Comparison: O_7 and O_8. If $O_7 = O_8$, there is no change; if $O_7 \neq O_8$, there is a change. (Comparisons could also be made between O_1, O_3, O_5, and O_8, because O_1, O_3, O_5, and O_7 are considered equivalent due to random assignment of subjects.)

It should be noted that there is no way to check on the effect of pretesting in this design, because all groups are pretested. There is no nonpretested comparison group. Also, when there are two or more experimental treatments (in this case, three), it is important to distinguish between them because they may have differing effects. The sets of results for the example do not exhaust the possible patterns, but they illustrate possible outcomes.

INTERPRETATION EXAMPLE 7.2

A researcher uses a three-group design. There are two different experimental treatments, X_1 and X_2, and a control treatment. Groups are not pretested, but they are posttested twice, once shortly after the experimental treatments are completed and again later to determine whether there is a delayed effect of the treatments. The design is as follows:

R G_1	X_1—O_1———O_2
R G_2	X_2—O_3———O_4
R G_3	—O_5———O_6

a. *Result:* $O_1 = O_3$, but O_3 and $O_1 \neq O_5$, and $O_2 = O_4 = O_6$.

Interpretation: There are immediate experimental effects, and they are the same for X_1 and X_2. There are no long-term experimental effects.

b. *Result:* $O_1 \neq O_3$, and O_1 and $O_3 \neq O_5$, and $O_2 \neq O_4$, and O_2 and $O_4 \neq O_6$, but $O_1 = O_2$, and $O_3 = O_4$, and $O_5 = O_6$.

Interpretation: There are experimental effects in both the short and the long term, and they are different effects for X_1 and X_2. However, the effects are consistent over time; that is, the short-term and long-term effects are the same.

c. *Result:* $O_1 = O_3 = O_5 = O_6$, but O_2 and $O_4 \neq O_6$, and $O_2 \neq O_4$.

Interpretation: There are no short-term experimental effects. There are different long-term experimental effects for X_1 and X_2.

d. *Result:* $O_1 = O_3$, but $O_1, O_3 \neq O_5$ and $O_1, O_3 \neq O_4$, but $O_2 = O_4$, and O_1 and $O_4 \neq O_6$.

Interpretation: There are short-term experimental effects, and they are the same for X_1 and X_2. There are long-term experimental effects, and they are the same for X_1 and X_2, but they are not the same as the short-term effects.

e. What comparison would be made to determine whether there are any long-term effects and whether they are the same for X_1 and X_2?

Comparison: O_2 and O_4 with O_6. If O_2 and $O_4 \neq O_6$, then long-term experimental effects are indicated; then if $O_2 \neq O_4$, the effects of X_1 and X_2 are *not* the same.

f. What comparison would be made to check whether the passing of time affects the subjects on the dependent variable?

Comparison: O_5 and O_6. These Os come from the control group, which receives no experimental treatment. If $O_5 \neq O_6$, there is some effect due to the passing of time; if $O_5 = O_6$, time has no effect.

g. Is there any way to check on the initial (preexperiment) equivalence of the three groups? Is this of concern? Why or why not?

Answer: Because there were no pretests, there are no preexperimental Os to check equivalence, but this is of no concern, because the groups are considered equivalent due to the random assignment (R).

Other comparisons could be made in the forgoing designs, and, of course, there could be other patterns of results. An important characteristic of design and interpretation of results is that there must be a comparison group for a contrast to check on a possible effect. Therefore, in the first example, because all groups were pretested, an effect of pretesting cannot be checked.

The interpretation of experimental results is a common sense process. The design aids the researcher in structuring the desired comparisons or contrasts so that effects can be checked. In any specific experiment, a knowledge of the variables and possibly of the results of related studies is also helpful in interpreting and understanding the data.

Randomness and Representativeness

In the designs described in this chapter, some aspect of **random selection** or **random assignment** of the subjects was included. By randomly selecting a sample, the sample represents the population from which it was selected. If a number of subjects are randomly assigned to the experimental treatments (including the control treatment, if there is one), then prior to the experiment, the groups of subjects differ only on the basis of random sampling fluctuation. The experimental groups are equivalent because of the random assignment. This characteristic makes for what Campbell and Stanley (1963) call "true" experimental designs.

However, if there is a pool of available subjects and they are randomly assigned to experimental treatments, what population do these subjects represent? Suppose that a researcher uses the 120 students enrolled in a beginning education course as the subjects for an experiment. The students are randomly assigned to experimental treatments, but they have not been randomly selected from some larger population. It could not be argued that they randomly selected themselves into the education course, so what population do they represent? This is a question of external validity that can be answered only by the researcher through a knowledge of the subjects and the variables under study. Do the 120 students represent college students who have been enrolled in beginning education courses during the past several years? Do they represent college students in education generally? Or do they represent young adults generally? Probably not the latter, but cases could possibly be made for the others.

The point being made is that the matter of representativeness, and hence generalizability, must often be argued on a logical basis. It would be nice if there were always the option of random selection from the population under study, but this is not the case. In the example here, if the 120 students participated in a learning experiment, the results would likely have considerable generalizability. They might even generalize to other age groups, depending on the conditions of the experiment.

In some experiments in educational research, intact groups are used. The groups have not been randomly selected, nor have the members been randomly assigned to the groups. For example, this situation occurs when intact classes of students are used in an experiment. When such groups are used, we have what Campbell and Stanley (1963) call a "quasi-experimental" design. (Such designs are discussed in the next chapter.) When groups are initially not equivalent in a random sense, this condition not only influences the generalizability but also may affect the internal validity of the experiment, because there may have been some initial differences between the groups relative to the variables under study.

In summary, it is preferable to have some condition of randomness in designing an experiment, but this is not always possible. Even if random assignment is used, the subjects may not have been randomly selected from some larger population, and generalizability must be argued on a logical basis. (The difference between random selection and random assignment is discussed in the sampling chapter, Chapter 14.) Of course, the case for external validity of any experimental results must be made in the context of the specific variables and conditions of the experiment.

Summary

This chapter provided some of the more general designs used in experimental research. The distinguishing characteristic of experimental research is the manipulation of variables. The experimental design provides the structure for the experiment in which the variables are deliberately manipulated and controlled by the researcher. It might be mistakenly inferred that complexity of design is a desirable characteristic of a more sophisticated experimenter, but a truly sophisticated experimenter need only come up with an experimental design that will do the job—meet the objectives of the research and be adequate for testing the hypotheses. An experiment must have definitely stated hypotheses, and the design should test these hypotheses, providing for the meaningful interpretation of results, whatever the pattern of the data.

At this point, the reader should have an understanding of the underlying reasoning of experimental design and the logic of the various design structures. Characteristics of a good experimental design were discussed early in the chapter. A well-conceived design will not guarantee valid results, but an inappropriate and inadequate design is certain to lead to uninterpretable results and tenuous conclusions, if any can be drawn. The design must be conceived prior to the experimentation, and it should be carefully planned and applied. No postexperiment manipulations, statistical or otherwise, can take the place of a well-conceived experimental design.

KEY CONCEPTS

Experiment
Experimental variable
Experimental design
Experimental treatment
Subjects
Experimental control
Contamination
Parsimony
Internal validity

External validity
Threats to experimental validity
Posttest-only control group design
Pretest-posttest control group design
Solomon four-group design
Factorial design
Repeated measures design
Multiple observations
Random selection
Random assignment

EXERCISES

7.1 Define the concepts of internal and external validity of an experiment. Why do we say that for some experiments, an attempt at increasing one type of validity tends to jeopardize the other type?

7.2 Several teachers plan to do an experiment in the school setting concerning the effects of class size on achievement in chemistry. Class size is an independent variable and has four levels of size—10–14, 18–23, 26–31, and 34–38 students. Four high schools are involved in the study, each with eight chemistry classes, two of each class size. Students can be assigned at random to a class within a school, but students cannot be assigned randomly to a school. Two chemistry teachers are used in each school, each teaching four classes. The dependent variable is chemistry achievement, measured after an instructional period of one semester. Develop and describe one or more experimental designs that would apply to this research study. Consider possible uncontrolled variables and variables that might be controlled. Is there a possibility of confounding of variables? State one or more hypotheses that might be tested by this experiment.

7.3 Discuss in detail an example of an experiment for which the posttest-only control group is appropriate. Consider such points as why you would not need pretests and the number of groups you would include. (You may want to extend the design to more than two groups.) Describe how you would enhance control in your proposed experiment. Also, identify the independent variable(s), dependent variable(s), and constants.

7.4 Discuss the possible gains in internal validity when going from a pretest-posttest control group design to a Solomon four-group design.

7.5 A teacher designs an experiment to determine the effects of programmed learning materials as supplementary aids in an advanced algebra course. The dependent variable is the amount of algebra learned during one semester of instruction. There are eighty-three students enrolled in four advanced algebra classes who are taught by this teacher, and these students were assigned randomly to the classes. The students make up the subjects for the experiment. One group of students has access to the programmed materials; the other group does not. Suggest an experimental design that would apply to this situation. Is it necessary for the teacher to use a pretest? How might the internal validity of the experiment be enhanced? Does this experiment have external validity, and if so, to what extent?

7.6 A five-group, posttest-only control group design is used. There are four experimental treatments and a control treatment. Using the notation introduced in the chapter, the design can be diagrammed as follows:

R G_1	X_1	O_1
R G_2	X_2	O_2
R G_3	X_3	O_3
R G_4	X_4	O_4
R G_5	—	O_5

a. Is there any need to be concerned about the preexperiment equivalency of the groups? Why or why not?

b. Is there any way to check on whether or not groups change on the dependent variable from before the experiment to after the experiment, independent of any experimental treatment? Why or why not?

c. What would you conclude from the following results and comparisons? The equals sign means that the observations are about the same; the not-equals sign means that they are substantially different. (*Note:* Consider only the results given. Do not read into the comparison results not specified.) Consider each set of results independently.

(1) No pair of Os are equal.
(2) $O_1 = O_3$ and $O_2 = O_4$, but $O_1, O_3 \neq O_2, O_4$, and $O_1, O_2, O_3, O_4 \neq O_5$.
(3) $O_1 = O_2$ and $O_3 = O_4 = O_5$, but $O_1, O_2 \neq O_3, O_4, O_5$.
(4) $O_1 = O_2 = O_3, = O_5$, but $O_1, O_2, O_3, O_5 \neq O_4$.

7.7 A researcher uses the following experimental design. It involves six groups and is, in essence, a takeoff on the Solomon four-group design. Only one experimental treatment, X, is involved.

R G_1	O_1	X	O_2	
R G_2	O_3	—	O_4	
R G_3	O_5	X	—	O_6
R G_4	O_7	—	—	O_8
R G_5	—	X	O_9	
R G_6	—	—	O_{10}	

a. What is gained (apparently) by including the middle two groups?

b. What comparisons could be made to determine whether or not there is an effect of pretesting?

c. What would you conclude from the following results and comparisons?

(1) $O_2 = O_9$ and $O_6 = O_8$, but $O_2, O_9 \neq O_6, O_8$.
(2) $O_2 = O_6 = O_9, O_4 = O_8 = O_{10}$, but $O_2, O_6, O_9 \neq O_4, O_8, O_{10}$.
(3) $O_1 = O_2 = O_3$, and $O_3 = O_4$.
(4) $O_2 = O_4 = O_9, O_6 \neq O_2$, and $O_6 \neq O_8$.

7.8 The following design is used, including three groups, all of which are pretested once and posttested twice. Two experimental treatments, X_1 and X_2, are used.

R G_1	O_1	X_1	O_2——O_3
R G_2	O_4	X_2	O_5——O_6
R G_3	O_7	—	O_8——O_9

a. What is gained by including a pretest rather than only posttesting the subjects?
b. Is it possible to check on an effect of pretesting with this design? Why or why not?
c. What comparisons would be made to determine whether there is an experimental effect in the long term?
d. Is it necessary to have the pretest to check on the preexperimental equivalence of the groups? Why or why not?
e. Suppose that $O_7 \neq O_8 \neq O_9$, the observations on the control group. What would you conclude from these results?
f. What would you conclude from the following results and comparisons?

(1) $O_2 = O_5$, but O_2 and $O_5 \neq O_8$, and $O_3 = O_6 = O_9$.
(2) $O_1 \neq O_2$, and $O_4 \neq O_5$, and $O_2 \neq O_5$, but $O_7 = O_8$.
(3) $O_2 = O_5 = O_8$, but $O_3 \neq O_2$ and $O_5 \neq O_6$, and O_3 and $O_6 \neq O_9$.
(4) $O_2 \neq O_5$, and O_2 and $O_5 \neq O_8$, $O_2 \neq O_3$, and $O_5 \neq O_6$, and $O_3 \neq O_6$, and O_3 and $O_6 \neq O_9$, but $O_7 = O_8 = O_9$.

7.9 Summarize the general characteristics of a well-designed experiment. Select one or more research articles that involve experimentation from such publications as the *American Educational Research Journal* or the *Journal of Educational Psychology.* Read the article carefully to determine the design used and the experimental procedure. Does the experiment seem to have high internal validity? Is there any indication of its external validity?

7.10 Identify three advantages to using a repeated measures design when investigating the effect of training parents to assist their children in reading during first grade.

7.11

	T_1	T_2	T_3
M	22	32	38
F	35	30	28

A 2 × 3 factorial design was used to determine the effect of three treatments on the on-task time, assessed as the average number of minutes on task per forty-minute observation. Describe the interaction in words.

7.12 For the design in Exercise 7.11, put in means that would indicate no interaction between treatment and gender.

	T_1	T_2	T_3
M	22	32	38
F			

NOTES

1. The term *levels* is a holdover from the days when experimental variables were often such variables as drug dosages and fertilizer concentrations; that is, there were quantitative levels of the experimental variables. Now the term applies to qualitative and categorical variables, as well as quantitative variables.
2. The symbolism, terminology, and diagramming used here and throughout this chapter and the following chapter are similar to that introduced by D. T. Campbell and J. C. Stanley in "Experimental and Quasi-Experimental Designs for Research on Teaching" in N. L. Gage (Ed.), *Handbook of research on teaching* (Chicago: Rand McNally, 1963), pp. 171–246. More recently this notation is used and extended to more complex designs in W. R. Shadish, T. D. Cook, and D. T. Campbell, (2002), *Experimental and quasi-experimental designs for generalized causal inference* (Boston: Houghton-Mifflin).
3. If inferential statistics are used in analyzing data from such designs, as they usually are, a substantial difference would be one that is statistically significant. Concepts of inferential statistics are discussed in Chapter 17.

REFERENCES

Campbell, D. T., and Stanley, J. C. (1963). Experimental and quasi-experimental designs for research on teaching. In N. L. Gage (Ed.), *Handbook of research on teaching* (pp. 171–246). Chicago: Rand McNally.

Cook, T. D., and Campbell, D. T. (1979). *Quasi-experimentation: Design and analysis issues for field settings.* Chicago: Rand McNally.

Cronbach, L. J., and Furby, L. (1970). How we should measure change—or should we? *Psychological Bulletin, 74*, 66–80.

Solomon, R. L. (1949). An extension of control-group design. *Psychological Bulletin, 46*, 137–150.

CHAPTER 8 Quasi-Experimental Research

The experimental designs discussed in Chapter 7 had a common characteristic of random assignment of subjects to treatments. Random assignment attains equivalence of the groups within the limits of random fluctuation. When conducting educational research, there are many situations in which random assignment of subjects is not an option. A case can be made that some school classes are formed on a random basis if, for example, there are four third-grade classes and every fourth student on the master list is placed in each class. Sometimes there are several sections of university classes that meet at the same time of day and students are assigned to sections on a random basis. A true experimental design can be fashioned in those instances by randomly assigning classrooms to treatments. In most cases though, when the researcher does not have the power to randomly assign subjects to groups, there will be some factors on which the intact groups differ that make them nonequivalent. This is the danger of using groups in which there has not been random assignment. A quasi-experiment is an approximation of a true experiment that uses groups that have not been formed randomly. Such research can make valuable contributions, but it is important that the researcher be especially cautious about interpreting and generalizing results.

Quasi-experimental research involves the use of intact groups of subjects in an experiment, rather than assigning subjects at random to experimental treatments.

The Problems of Validity

Lack of random assignment potentially introduces problems with the validity of the experiment—both internal and external validity. In Chapter 7, it was noted that one of the threats to internal validity is differential selection of subjects. Suppose that two intact classes of fifth-grade students were used in an experiment for which the dependent variable was performance in science, operationally defined as the score on a science test. The classes had initially been formed on the basis of ability grouping, one class with high ability and the other with average ability. The classes receive different experimental treatments. If there were an effect favoring the high-ability class, it would be difficult to argue that the effect was due to the experimental treatment. Ability level and experimental treatment are confounded, and there is no way to interpret an effect with confidence.

Any number of factors might be operating in the formation of intact groups, and it cannot be argued that such groups are randomly representative of larger populations. Random selection and random assignment are processes (described more completely in Chapter 14), and they either have or have not been done. With quasi-experimentation, the lack of random assignment jeopardizes the comparison of groups and the lack of random selection jeopardizes the generalizability of the results.

What is a researcher who uses intact groups to do? For the purposes of generalizability, representativeness must be argued on a logical basis. For internal validity, the researcher must attempt to establish the degree of equivalence between groups. This requires considering characteristics or variables that may be related to the variables under study. For example, if intact classes were involved in an instructional experiment in mathematics, the grade level probably would be included either as a constant or as another independent (control) variable. The researcher would also want evidence that the classes are of comparable ability level. If empirical data such as IQ test scores are available, they can be helpful in checking equivalence of groups. In fact, such data sometimes can be used for statistical control. Even with empirical data, checking and establishing equivalence always involves some subjective judgment on the basis of information about variables and conditions of the experiment. The lack of randomness must be given specific attention when interpreting the results, and the extent to which it can be countered determines the confidence in the internal validity of the experiment.

> When considering problems of validity of quasi-experimental research, limitations should be clearly identified, the equivalence of the groups should be discussed, and possible representativeness and generalizability should be argued on a logical basis.

Posttest-Only, Nonequivalent Control Group Design

Some of the quasi-experimental designs look very much like the experimental designs discussed in the preceding chapter, except that there is no random assignment of subjects to the groups. When the term **nonequivalent groups** is used, it means nonequivalent in a random sense. It does not mean that it will be impossible to make a case for the similarity of the groups on relevant variables or characteristics. Indeed, with quasi-experimental designs, the confidence that can be placed in the validity of results depends in large part on the case that can be made for the similarity of the groups.

Using the notation introduced in the preceding chapter, the **posttest-only, nonequivalent control group design** in its simplest form can be diagrammed as follows:

$$
\begin{array}{ll}
G_1 & X\text{—}O_1 \\
G_2 & \quad\text{—}O_2
\end{array}
$$

The design indicates that one group receives the experimental treatment and another group, serving as a control group, does not receive the experimental treatment. Both groups are posttested at the same time, shortly after the experimental treatment is completed for G_1. The design can be extended to include any number of experimental treatments. For k treatments,

$$
\begin{array}{ll}
G_1 & X_1\text{—}O_1 \\
G_2 & X_2\text{—}O_2 \\
\bullet & \bullet \\
\bullet & \bullet \\
\bullet & \bullet \\
G_k & X_k\text{—}O_k \\
G_{k+1} & \text{——}O_{k+1}
\end{array}
$$

the design requires k + 1 groups. If two or more experimental treatments were used but no control group, the design would be called a posttest-only, nonequivalent multiple-group design.

> The *posttest-only, nonequivalent control group design* contains as many groups as there are experimental treatments, plus a control group. Intact groups are used, and subjects are measured only once, after the experimental treatments have been applied.

The validity of any experiment depends on the specific conditions of the experiment, but experiments using the posttest-only, nonequivalent control group design generally are weak in validity. The difficulty arises from the possibility of selection bias and the lack of pretests prior to the experimental treatments. The design should not be used unless some antecedent data are available that provide information about the extent of similarity between the groups. Such data will not eliminate selection bias if it exists, but they provide information that may avoid a misinterpretation of the results.

EXAMPLE 8.1

A junior high school teacher who has four classes of eighth-grade science conducts a study using three different new approaches plus the traditional approach (control) to teaching the laboratory portion of the course. The teacher uses a different approach for teaching each of the four classes. The dependent variable is performance on an examination given at the end of the semester covering the laboratory content. The research problem can be stated as follows:

> A study of the effects of instructional approach on the performance of eighth-graders on a science laboratory examination.

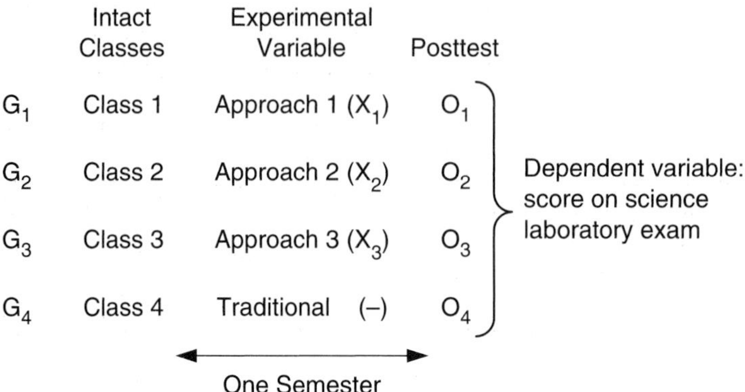

FIGURE 8.1 Diagram of Example 8.1 Posttest-Only, Nonequivalent Control Group Design, with Three Experimental Groups and a Control Group

The design is diagrammed in Figure 8.1.

No pretests were given, but to check on the similarity of the classes, other information was reviewed and the following data were discovered:

1. The proportions of boys and girls are about the same across the classes.
2. The previous seventh-grade science grades of the students were about the same for Classes 1, 2, and 4, but Class 3 students had somewhat higher grades. The same pattern was true for other areas of previous seventh-grade achievement, such as mathematics.
3. Although, for the most part, the school does not group students by ability, there is an honors program in English; because of scheduling restrictions, many of the students in Class 3 are also in the English honors program.

The time of instruction and the teacher are constants in this study. Two classes, 1 and 4, meet in the morning; the other classes meet in the afternoon.

It appears that Classes 1, 2, and 4 are quite similar on variables that may affect performance on the examination. However, Class 3 seems to be a more able class, which will have to be considered when interpreting the results. There is a partial confounding between experimental treatment and ability level, because any one class receives only one treatment.

Example 8.1 Results and Interpretation

Suppose that the following pattern of results appears on the posttest: $O_1 = O_2$, but O_1 and O_2 are greater than O_4, and O_3 is greater than O_1 and O_2.

Interpretation

Approaches 1 and 2 are more effective than the traditional approach, and they appear to be equally effective. These approaches do not seem to be affected by the time of day, because one class meets in the morning and the other in the afternoon. No definite conclusion can be drawn about Approach 3; in fact, it may not be as effective as the traditional approach, and the higher posttest scores of G_3 may be due to the students' abilities.

This example illustrates the fact that there may be alternative explanations with quasi-experimental designs, depending on the pattern of results. It may be that Approach 3 is the most effective approach, explaining the high O3, or it may be that the high O3 is due to the higher ability of G3. Suppose that O3 had been less than O1, O2, and O4. Then it would be quite conclusive that Approach 3 is not as effective as the others, at least not with higher ability students. The similarity of Classes 1, 2, and 4 allows us to be relatively confident about the conclusions for Approaches 1 and 2 and the traditional approach.

Pretest-Posttest, Nonequivalent Control Group Design

The **pretest-posttest, nonequivalent control group design** is similar to the posttest-only, nonequivalent control group design, except that the subjects are also pretested. In its general form, if there are k experimental treatments, it can be diagrammed as follows:

G_1 $\quad O_1$——X_1—O_2

G_2 $\quad O_3$——X_2—O_4

• •

• •

• •

G_k $\quad O_{2k-1}$–X_k—O_{2k}

G_{k+1} $\quad O_{2k+1}$———O_{2k+2}

Only two groups are required, an experimental group and a control group, for the design in its simplest form. If no control group is included, the design is called a pretest-posttest, nonequivalent multiple-group design.

The inclusion of the pretest greatly aids in checking the similarity of the groups, because the pretest scores are on variables that have a strong relationship with the dependent variable. The pretest is administered to all subjects, under consistent conditions, prior to conducting the experiment. Pretest scores also can be used for statistical control, and in some cases gain scores can be generated.

The *pretest-posttest, nonequivalent control group design* aids in checking the extent of group similarity, and the pretest scores may be used for statistical control or for generating gain scores.

EXAMPLE 8.2

An instructional experiment involves the use of two new reading programs and their possible effects on reading achievement in the fourth grade. The new programs are the experimental treatments, and the traditional program is the control treatment. Thirty fourth-grade classrooms in the elementary schools of a single district are to participate, and there is no random assignment. Ten teachers have agreed to use each of the reading programs, the two new programs and the traditional program. Of course, each teacher uses only one program. The students are pretested on Form A of a reading achievement test; the programs are used for an eighteen-week period; and then the students are posttested on Form B of the test. The design is diagrammed in Figure 8.2.

The pretest score is helpful in checking on the similarity of the groups, but it is not the only variable that could be checked. Thirty teachers are involved, and no teacher uses more than one program. Are the groups of ten teachers similar on factors that may affect reading achievement? Although individual teachers may differ, groups of ten teachers may be quite similar when considering all the teachers. One factor to check might be the length of teaching experience of the teachers. If the most experienced teachers were all in one group, a systematic difference between the groups might exist.

If the schools in which the thirty classes are located differ on such factors as socioeconomic regions, this would have to be considered. It would not be satisfactory to have one program limited to schools at a certain socioeconomic level, because there would be confounding between the effect of school and the effect of the reading program. A desirable arrangement would be for each of three schools at a socioeconomic level to use one of the programs. It might be that some schools would have more than one program, although such an arrangement could lead to some contamination of the data due to interaction of students from different classes.

	Intact Classes	Pretest	Experimental Variable	Posttest (dependent variable)
G_1	Class 1 ⋮ Class 10	O_1	New Program 1 (X_1)	O_2
G_2	Class 11 ⋮ Class 20	O_3	New Program 2 (X_2)	O_4
G_3	Class 21 ⋮ Class 30	O_5	Traditional Program (–)	O_6

← Eighteen weeks' instruction →

FIGURE 8.2 Diagram of Example 8.2 Pretest-Posttest, Nonequivalent Control Group Design, with Two Experimental Groups and a Control Group

In Figure 8.2, although there are thirty classes, there are only three pretest Os and three posttest Os. When analyzing results, we initially check the group results, but in an extensive study such as this example, it is usually helpful—and even necessary—to break down or sort out results by making more detailed comparisons, such as the following:

1. Suppose that the pretest scores of classes in a program (group) are similar. Compare the ten posttest scores of the classes within a program. Are these scores close together or are they highly variable? If they are close together, the program appears to be having a consistent effect; if they are highly variable, the inherent variation is overriding any program effect, or the program effect is not consistent across classes within the program.

2. If classes vary on pretest scores, group the classes within a program into two or three categories (high, middle, low) on pretest score. Then check the posttest scores of these categories to determine whether the gains are consistent or different across categories within a program and across programs within a category. For example, suppose that for the classes scoring high on the pretest, the gains for New Program 1 are greater than those for New Program 2 and the traditional program. This is a comparison across programs within a category, and it appears that New Program 1 is the most effective for those students who were initially the most able readers.

3. If the pretest scores of classes are similar, compare the posttest scores of the classes within a program. If they are about the same, external factors such as the teacher or school are having consistent effects; if they are different these external factors are having differing effects.

Example 8.2 Results and Interpretation

Suppose that the following pattern of results appears: $O_1 = O_3 = O_5$, but $O_2 \neq O_4$, and $O_2, O_4 \neq O_6$, but O_4 is greater than O_2 and O_2 is greater than O_6.

Interpretation

Based on pretest results, the groups appear to be quite similar initially. There are program effects: Both new programs are more effective than the traditional program, and New Program 2 is the most effective.

In many experiments involving nonequivalent groups, the design is extended to include control variables as independent variables. (If socioeconomic level could be included in this way, it would be an example of a control variable.) In essence, this extends the design to a factorial design. If some aspect of randomness could be included, the validity of the design would be enhanced. In the example, it would be helpful if the thirty classes could be randomly assigned to the programs. This still would not make for random assignment to the classes, but it would make the ten groups of teachers equivalent on a random basis. Such assignment would tend to equalize the differences among teachers over the experimental and control treatments. When using a quasi-experimental design, we attempt to build as much control as possible into the design. Then available information is used to check the equivalence of the groups. The results must be interpreted and generalized in the context of this information and the conditions of the experiment.

Time Series Designs

Time series designs were introduced in Chapter 7 as experimental designs if the groups can be formed through random assignment and there is a basis for comparison, such as a control group. However, quite commonly, time series designs are used with one or more intact groups, and with this condition they become quasi-experimental designs. The designs involve repeated measurement and an experimental treatment is inserted between two of the measurements for at least one of the groups. Time series designs are useful for situations in which there is periodic, naturally occurring measurement of the dependent variable over time, such as repeated testing in a class. Measurement should be consistent across the observations; with some dependent variables, it may be difficult to attain consistency.

> *Time series designs* as quasi-experimental designs involve repeated measurement of one or more intact groups, with an experimental treatment inserted between two of the measurements of at least one group.

Single-Group Time Series Design

A **single-group time series design** can be diagrammed simply as follows:

$$G \quad O_1—O_2—O_3—X—O_4—O_5$$

As indicated, there is no random assignment of subjects to the group. There can be any feasible number of observations or measurements, and the insertion of X should be done randomly. Observations may coincide with some routine measurement that takes place, such as a test every four weeks in a class.

One characteristic of time series designs is that there are numerous possible patterns of results. This introduces a problem with internal validity, especially with only one group in that there may be alternative explanations for the results other than the effect of the experimental treatment. Figure 8.3 shows three possible patterns of results. The Os on the horizontal axis represent the measurement occasions, and the vertical axis is the scale of the dependent variable.

For any particular experiment and dependent variable, there would be only one pattern. The interpretation of pattern A would be that the experimental treatment appears to have had an effect. There was a slight increase in the scores prior to the experimental treatment, but after the experimental treatment, the rate of increase was greater, especially between O_3 and O_4 and O_5. The smaller rate of increase between O_5 and O_6 may have been due to a diminishing experimental treatment effect with the passing of time.

On the surface, pattern B appears to include no experimental treatment effect. However, the marked increase between the final two measurements might be the result of a delayed effect. If no apparent external event could have produced this effect, an experimental effect is

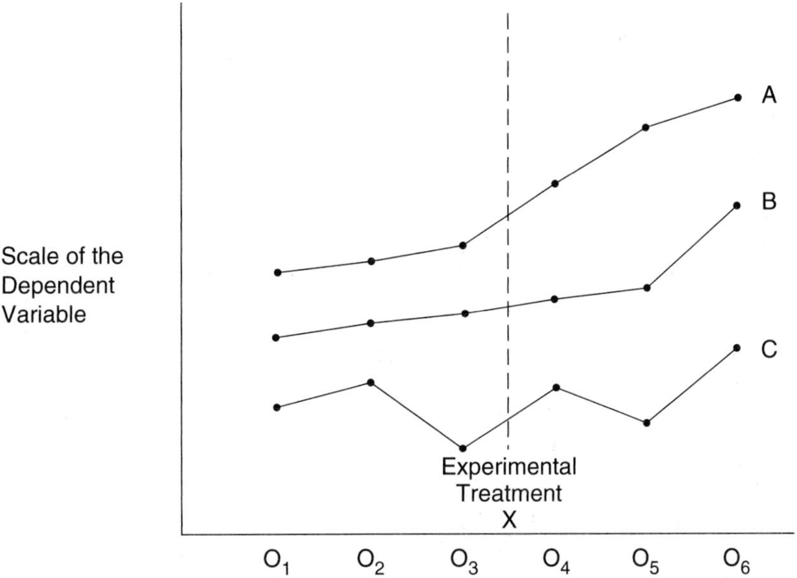

FIGURE 8.3 Possible Results Patterns of a Single-Group Time Series Design

certainly plausible. For this reason, it is important to anticipate the time interval between the introduction of the experimental treatment and the appearance of its effect. For certain variables, the effect in pattern B is about as definite as it is in pattern A. It should be noted that as the time interval increases, the likelihood of an intervening extraneous event also increases.

The erratic pattern C almost excludes the possibility of drawing a conclusion about an experimental treatment effect. Because there is no control group, it is most difficult to infer the pattern without the experimental treatment. The fluctuation between observations may indicate that other factors are operating that override any experimental treatment effect. It is possible that the experiment would require an increase in control before there could be sensitivity to an experimental treatment effect. The conclusion of no experimental treatment effect cannot be drawn from pattern C, however.

The numerous observations of the time designs are useful, not only for locating a possible effect but also for avoiding inference of an effect when there likely is none. Consider pattern C. If O_3 and O_4 were the only measures taken, the researcher would conclude that there is an experimental effect, when the difference in the measurements may well be due to something else. In pattern B, the possible delayed effect would have been missed if only measures O_3 and O_4 (and even O_5) had been taken, so it is important to consider the entire pattern.

EXAMPLE 8.3

A physical therapist is working with a group of twelve patients in an eight-week rehabilitation program. Members of the group receive therapy every day, and the group is tested at the end of each week on a physical performance test. A traditional type of therapy is used, except for the seventh week (determined on a random basis), during which an experimental therapy is administered. The design can be diagrammed as follows:

G O_1—O_2—O_3—O_4—O_5—O_6—X—O_7—O_8

Suppose that the results of this experiment produce the pattern shown in Figure 8.4. How would these results be interpreted? There is strong evidence that the experimental therapy is more effective than the traditional therapy. The pattern of improvement is quite consistent for the first six weeks, but it shows a large increase during the seventh week. Improvement returns to the earlier level during the eighth week. Thus, unless there is some other reason why there would be increased performance during the seventh week, there is a good case for an experimental effect.

In this example, maintaining consistency of measurement poses no problem, because the same physical performance test is used throughout. Consider another situation. An elementary school teacher uses a time series design to check the effects of individual versus group practice on performance in spelling. The class is used as the group. Each week the class is given a certain amount of time for spelling practice (in addition to the instruction), and a test is given every Friday. The usual format for practice is on an individual basis, but during one week over a six-week period, group practice is used as an experimental treatment.

One problem with this example is keeping the difficulty level of the spelling tests consistent. If the test after the group practice is easier than others and the class tends to perform better, the easier test is an alternative explanation for the results. Of course, the amount of practice time should be constant regardless of the practice format.

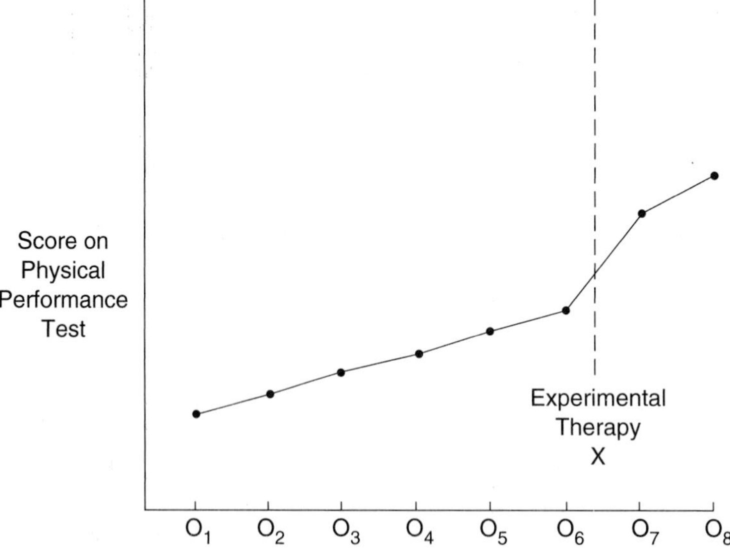

FIGURE 8.4 Pattern of Results for Example 8.3, Using a Single-Group Time Series Design

Multiple-Group Time Series Design

The single-group time series design can be extended to include two or more groups. A common practice is to include a control group in the design, in which case an example design could be diagrammed as follows:

$$
\begin{array}{ll}
G_1 & O_1—O_2—X—O_3—O_4—O_5—O_6—O_7 \\
G_2 & O_8—O_9———O_{10}—O_{11}—O_{12}—O_{13}—O_{14}
\end{array}
$$

Again, any number of observations can be taken, and the experimental treatment is inserted randomly for one group. The groups are measured at the same times.

> The **multiple-group time series design** includes two or more intact groups, one of which may be a control group, and an experimental treatment is inserted for at least one of the groups.

The inclusion of two or more groups strengthens the design because it provides for comparison, thus enhancing internal validity. For example, it provides a check for the possibility of an external event coinciding with the experimental treatment. Suppose that both groups in a control group design demonstrated an unusually large increase for the observations immediately following the administration of the experimental treatment to the experimental group. Because the increase occurred in both groups, it cannot be an experimental effect (because the control group had no experimental treatment), so it is likely due to some external factor that is affecting both groups.

The observations that occur prior to the experimental treatment can be used to check on the similarity of the groups. As with any multiple-group quasi-experimental design, the greater the similarity between the groups, the more confidence can be placed in the conclusions drawn from the results.

EXAMPLE 8.4

A teacher who has three classes of first-year algebra decides to do a study for which the research problem can be stated as follows:

> A study of the effects of different types of feedback on performance in algebra.

During the semester, the teacher gives five equally spaced one-hour exams. The exams are of about the same difficulty overall, because the teacher carefully constructs the exams using items of about equal difficulty levels, even though the tests cover different content as the instruction progresses. Between the second and third tests, the teacher provides positive feedback (X_1) to one class, negative feedback (X_2) to another class, and no feedback (control treatment) to the third class. The experiment is diagrammed in Figure 8.5.

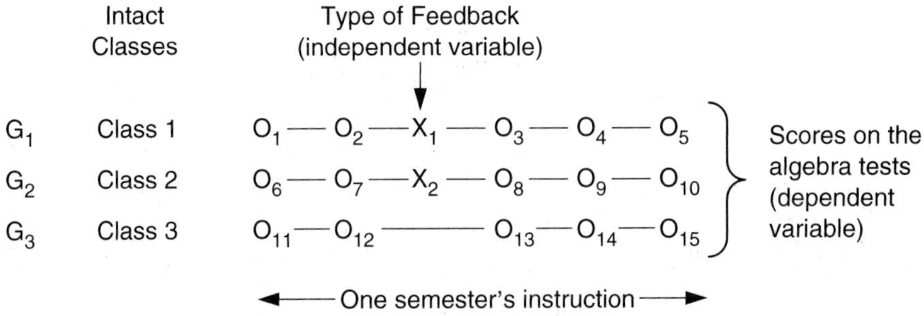

	Intact Classes	Type of Feedback (independent variable) ↓	
G_1	Class 1	O_1 — O_2 — X_1 — O_3 — O_4 — O_5	Scores on the algebra tests (dependent variable)
G_2	Class 2	O_6 — O_7 — X_2 — O_8 — O_9 — O_{10}	
G_3	Class 3	O_{11} — O_{12} ——— O_{13} — O_{14} — O_{15}	

← One semester's instruction →

FIGURE 8.5 Diagram of Example 8.4 Multiple-Group Time Series Design, with Two Experimental Groups and a Control Group

This design enables the teacher to make comparisons, not only between experimental groups but also with a control group. Note that the experimental treatments are applied only between two observations. At this point, we can consider possible patterns of results and interpretations that might be made. Because of the numerous Os, interpreting results requires sorting through them. The following patterns are to be considered independently.

Example 8.4 Results Pattern 1

$O_1 = O_2 = O_5$, and $O_3 = O_4$, but O_3, O_4 are greater than O_1, O_2, O_5, and $O_6 = O_7 = O_9 = O_{10}$, but O_8 is less than O_7, and $O_{11} = O_{12} = O_{13} = O_{14} = O_{15}$, and $O_1 = O_6 = O_{11}$.

Interpretation

Positive feedback (X_1) increases performance, and its effect persists through O_4; negative feedback (X_2) decreases performance, but it has only an immediate effect. Because performance in G_3 is highly consistent, it is unlikely that any external factors are causing changes in performance. Because the initial test scores of the classes were equal, the groups appear to be similar (on algebra test performance) prior to administration of the experimental treatments, even though there was no random assignment to the groups.

Example 8.4 Results Pattern 2

$O_1 = O_2$, and $O_3 = O_4 = O_5$, but O_3, O_4, O_5 are greater than O_1, O_2; $O_6 = O_7 = O_8$, and $O_9 = O_{10}$ are greater than O_6, O_7, O_8; $O_{11} = O_{12} = O_{13}$, and $O_{14} = O_{15}$, but O_{14}, O_{15} are greater than O_{11}, O_{12}, O_{13}; $O_1 = O_6 = O_{11}$, and $O_4 = O_9 = O_{14}$.

Interpretation

Negative feedback (X_2) has no effect, in that the patterns for G_2 and G_3 are the same. Positive feedback (X_1) increases performance; at least it appears to have an immediate effect. It is difficult to infer anything about long-range effects of X_1, in that all classes increased performance at the fourth testing. That consistent increase across classes is most likely due to an external factor. Whatever caused the increase had a persistent effect through the fifth testing. Because initial test scores of the classes were equal, the classes appear to be similar at the beginning of the experiment.

Of course, with numerous observations, such as in the example, a large number of different results patterns are possible. If patterns are erratic, it becomes difficult to draw conclusions—for example, if the Os in classes keep fluctuating. Also, if test scores for classes prior to inserting the experimental treatments are different, there is very likely a selection bias.

Variations in Time Series Designs

The forgoing discussion focused on single-group and multiple-group time series designs—the basic configurations for time series designs. There are variations, however, that can be incorporated into these designs. The number of observations in the series depends on the variables under study, but there should be sufficient observations so that the pattern can become established. One variation is to increase the number of observations in the series, possibly even as high as fifteen or twenty, for long-term experiments or for experiments in which observations can be sequenced closely. Extending the number of observations does increase the likelihood of external factors having an effect if time is extended.

Another variation is to insert the experimental treatment more than once in the series. This variation is more feasible if the series is lengthened. Multiple insertions provide a check on the consistency of an experimental effect if there is one. There are two ways to accomplish multiple insertion of the experimental treatment: (1) include it two or more times on a random basis, or (2) once it is inserted, persist with it for the remainder of the experiment. These two ways can be diagrammed as follows:

1. Multiple, random insertion of X:

$$G \qquad O_1—O_2—X—O_3—O_4—O_5—X—O_6—O_7—O_8$$

2. Persistent insertion of X:

$$G \qquad O_1—O_2—O_3—X—O_4—X—O_5—X—O_6—X—O_7—X—O_8$$

Either one of these approaches could have been used for the experimental treatments in the algebra classes example. The reinforcements, X_1 and X_2, could have been randomly inserted more than once in the series; or after their initial insertion, they could have been continued for the remainder of the semester.

> Variations of multiple insertions can be included in time series designs.

Single-Subject Designs

Most experimentation in educational research involves groups of subjects; that is, we intend to generate results that apply to groups rather than to individuals. However, there are experimental situations in which it is desirable or necessary to use individual subjects—essentially, a sample size of one. In these single-subject situations, the basic experimental approach is to study the individual under both nonexperimental and experimental conditions.

Single-subject research can be useful for teachers who conduct research (probably action research) with individual students. Counselors who work with students on an individual basis may also have applications for **single-subject designs.** Researchers in such areas as rehabilitation and physical therapy encounter situations in which individual research is desirable. Generally, a subject is included in a study because of some condition or problem, and there is no random selection or assignment. Therefore, single-subject designs are usually considered quasi-experimental designs.

Single-subject designs commonly involve repeated measurement, sometimes several measurements of the dependent variable. Measurement is highly standardized and controlled, so that variations in measurement are not interpreted as an experimental effect. The conditions under which the study is conducted are described in detail, not only to enhance the interpretation of results but also to allow decisions about their generalizability.

Single-subject designs are characterized by what is sometimes called the **single-variable rule.** This means that only one variable, the treatment, is changed during the period in which the experimental treatment is applied. During the traditional or baseline treatment and the experimental treatment, all other conditions—such as length of time and number of measurements—are kept the same. This is necessary for interpreting the results so that some other effect is not misinterpreted as an experimental treatment effect.

The period during which the traditional treatment or normal condition is in effect is called the **baseline.** This period should be long enough that the dependent variable attains stability. If a dependent variable is fluctuating and the experimental treatment is applied, it is impossible to determine whether variation in the dependent variable is due to the experimental treatment.

> *Single-subject designs* commonly involve repeated measurements, and they use the *single-variable rule*—changing only one variable at a time.

As with any quasi-experimental design, validity is a major concern in single-subject designs. Internal validity must be established to interpret the results. Alternative explanations of the results (other than an experimental effect) must be considered and, it is hoped, discounted. To deal with alternative explanations, it is necessary to maintain as much control as possible and to understand the nature of other variables that may be operating in the study. External validity depends on the similarities between the research study and other situations, and it must be argued on a logical basis.

A-B Design

Single-subject designs are designated with a somewhat unique notation. The letters *A* and *B* are used to represent conditions; *A* indicates the baseline condition and *B* indicates the experimental treatment condition. Because individual subjects are used, there is no group notation.

The ***A-B* design** is the simplest of the single-subject designs. In general, it can be diagrammed as follows:

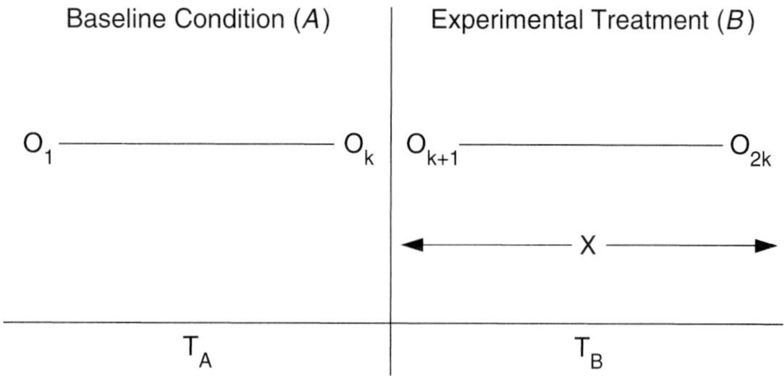

In this design, a single subject is observed under the baseline condition until the dependent variable stabilizes. Then the experimental treatment is introduced and the subject is again observed the same number of times. The T_A and T_B at the bottom of the design represent periods of time, and $T_A = T_B$.

The interpretation of results for the *A-B* design is based on the assumption that the observations would not have changed from those of the baseline condition if the experimental treatment had not been introduced. The design is susceptible to other variables, possibly those associated with history and maturation, causing an effect that may be a threat to internal validity. In a sense, the *A-B* design is the weakest of the single-subject designs with respect to internal validity, because the change between conditions is made only once.

EXAMPLE 8.5

A beginning teacher is having difficulty with classroom management, and an experienced teacher is helping the beginning teacher deal with this problem. The experienced teacher observes the beginning teacher twice per week over a period of four weeks, using a teacher performance observation inventory such as the Classroom Observations Keyed for Effectiveness Research (COKER). This period is the baseline period (*A*), and the data from the eight observations comprise the baseline data. The classroom performance of the teacher is well stabilized during this four-week period.

The experimental treatment (*B*) consists of half-hour consultations between the two teachers, in which the experienced teacher discusses the classroom performance of the beginning teacher and attempts to shift it to behaviors that will improve classroom management. There are nine of these consultations, one before the first observation in condition *B* and then one immediately following each observation. Like condition *A*, condition *B* is in effect for four weeks, and the eight observations of condition *B* are taken under corresponding conditions (same classes, same length of time, same time of day, etc.) as those of condition *A*, the only difference being the experimental treatment. The design for this study is diagrammed in Figure 8.6. The data consist of the observation data using the COKER inventory.

Example 8.5 Results Pattern 1

Observations O_1 through O_8 are stable and show few teacher behaviors that are believed to enhance classroom management. Then, beginning with O_9 through O_{14}, the observations show increasing behavior that would improve classroom management, and O_{14} through O_{16} are stable. The results are plotted in Figure 8.6.

Interpretation

With such a results pattern, there is quite conclusive evidence that the experimental treatment is having the desired effect. There has been an improvement in classroom management to a stability point. However, it is possible that the results are due to a natural maturation of the beginning teacher, although this is quite unlikely as an alternative explanation due to the relatively short time periods.

Example 8.5 Results Pattern 2

There is considerable fluctuation among O_1 through O_5, but O_5 through O_8 are quite stable. O_9 through O_{16} had the same pattern of fluctuation as O_1 through O_5, except that the observations were slightly higher in behaviors that enhance classroom management.

Interpretation

It is practically impossible to make a conclusive interpretation of these results. The beginning teacher's performance is quite unstable, and, although the experimental treatment does seem to improve performance slightly, it does not enhance stability of

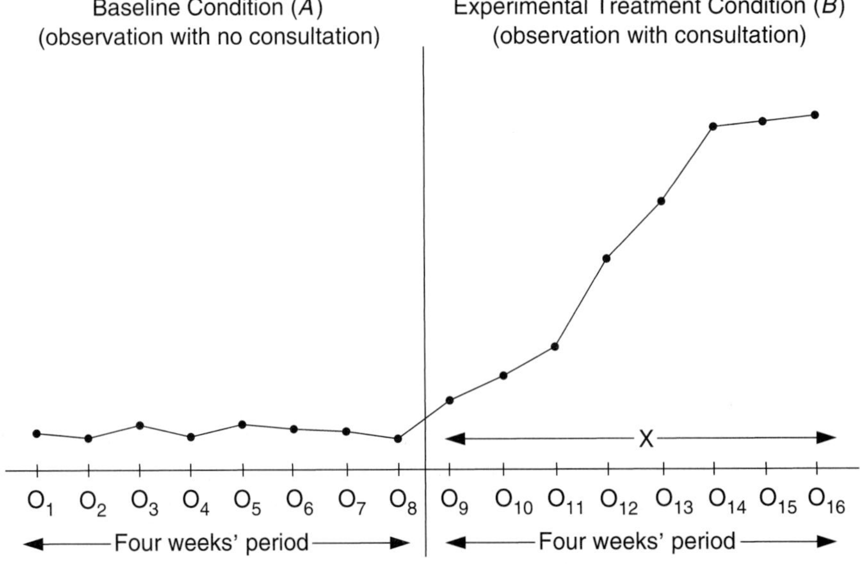

FIGURE 8.6 Diagram of Example 8.5 *A-B*, Single-Subject Design, with Results Pattern 1

performance during the four-week period. Apparently, there are other variables, such as conditions in the classroom or the feelings of the teacher, that have overriding effects.

What about generalizability of results from this study? If Results Pattern 1 had appeared—the results for which we concluded an experimental effect—they would be generalizable to other beginning teachers who have characteristics similar to those of the teacher in this study and who teach under similar conditions. Generalizability would have to be established through detailed description, which makes the case for such similarities. Because the teachers were attempting to solve an immediate local problem, there may not be much concern with generalizability.

A-B-A Design

The ***A-B-A* design** extends the *A-B* design so that another period of the baseline condition is included following the period of experimental treatment. The design also may be called a *reversal* or *withdrawal* design, because the experimental treatment is withdrawn. Except for the change from baseline to experimental treatment and back to baseline condition, other characteristics—such as duration and number of observations—are kept the same. The added period of baseline condition tends to enhance internal validity over the *A-B* design, because the pattern of results is extended. The general design can be diagrammed as follows:

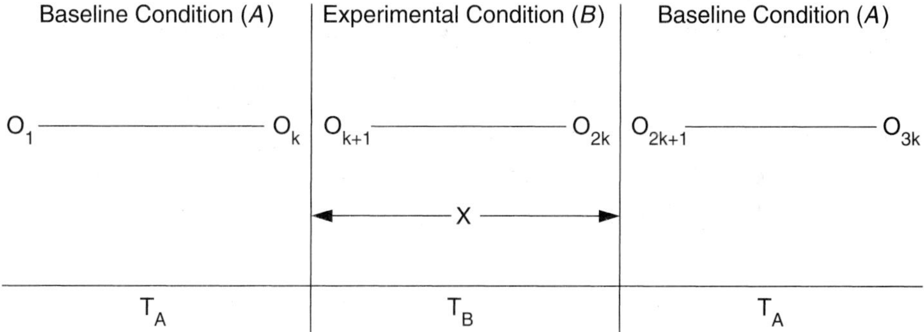

Note that in this design, there are the same number of observations for each duration of condition or treatment. Time would be constant, such that $T_A = T_B$.

EXAMPLE 8.6

A teacher has a student whose classroom behavior is highly negative—characterized by persistent, disruptive interruptions. The teacher keeps a weekly record of disruptive situations caused by this student. The behavior stabilizes over a three-week period, designated the baseline condition. Then for three weeks the teacher requires two individual counseling sessions per week with the student. These sessions, which are considered the experimental treatment, are conducted for one-half hour each on Monday and Thursday. After three weeks, the counseling sessions are discontinued and the teacher continues to collect data on the dependent variable (number of disruptive situations during the week) for another three weeks. Discontinuing the counseling sessions is reverting back to the baseline conditions. No other apparent changes occur between the three-week periods; the class, subjects taught, and so on remain the same. The study is diagrammed in Figure 8.7.

Example 8.6 Results Pattern 1

(Consistent with the symbolism introduced in Chapter 5, = means about the same.) $O_1 = O_2 = O_3 = O_7 = O_8 = O_9$, and $O_4 = O_5 = O_6$, but O_1, O_2, O_3, O_7, O_8, O_9 are greater than O_4, O_5, O_6. (Note that the dependent variable is the number of disruptive situations caused by the student in class, so a low score is preferred.)

Interpretation

The counseling sessions have the desired effect, but it is only an immediate effect. When the sessions are discontinued, the student reverts to the old behavior. It is not likely that an extraneous variable would have an effect that coincided exactly with the experimental treatment.

Example 8.6 Results Pattern 2

$O_1 = O_2 = O_3$, and $O_4 = O_5 = O_6$, and $O_7 = O_8 = O_9$, but O_7, O_8, O_9 are less than O_4, O_5, O_6, which are less than O_1, O_2, O_3.

Interpretation

This pattern of results gives rise to alternative explanations; therefore, we cannot be conclusive about an experimental effect. There may be an experimental treatment

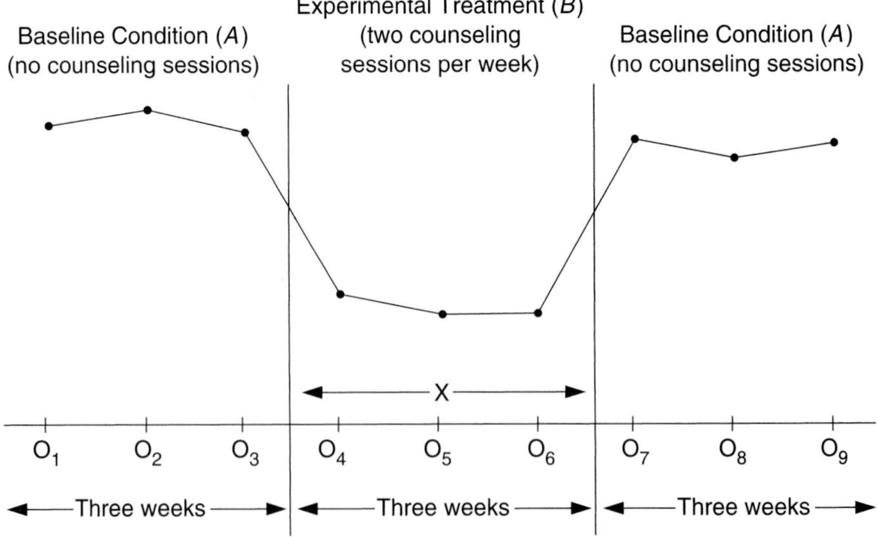

FIGURE 8.7 Diagram of Example 8.6 *A-B-A*, Single-Subject Design, with Results Pattern 1

effect; if there is, it is immediate, but it also has an accelerating long-range effect, which may be difficult to understand. There is a possibility that some other variable associated with maturation is operating. This explanation would be more likely if there was a constant decrease in O_4 through O_9, rather than the single decrease between O_6 and O_7.

There are any number of possible patterns of results. If O_4 through O_9 fluctuated considerably, it would be impossible to conclude anything about an experimental effect. The experimental treatment may be interacting with an extraneous variable, or the behavior may have become unstable and this may or may not have been caused by the experimental treatment.

Action Research and Quasi-Experimental Research

Action research was defined in Chapter 1, not as a separate methodology such as survey research or experimental research, but as research conducted at the local level, typically by a practitioner, focused on solving a specific problem. The concept of action research can be expanded to include collaborative efforts—collaboration, for example, between educators at the local level and personnel from universities or agencies such as regional educational laboratories. Action research can take place in a nonschool setting, such as a hospital, if research is being conducted on an educational program that addresses a local problem. So, action research may involve only one individual such as a teacher conducting research in a classroom, to research involving several individuals.

Action research can utilize any methodology, qualitative, or quantitative, but when experimentation is involved in action research, it most likely will be quasi-experimental in nature. Teachers, counselors, and administrators seldom have the option of random selection of subjects or assigning subjects randomly to treatments. Students may be the subjects of action research because of certain characteristics that they did not acquire at random. A study of teenage pregnancies involves the women of that age that are pregnant and available and willing to participate in the study. Thus, the subjects of action research typically "self-select" themselves into the study for whatever reasons, not because of random assignment.

Many of the examples described earlier in this chapter could be considered examples of action research. Practically all of the single-subject design examples could be examples of action research. Example 8.4 describes a situation of a single teacher conducting action research in a classroom.

The following example shows how quasi-experimental design can be used by a teacher in an action research study.

EXAMPLE 8.7

The Madison Metropolitan School District in Madison, Wisconsin, maintains a Classroom Action Research program to promote and support the research efforts of classroom teachers. An action research study by a high school teacher (Fashing-Bittner, 2001) used a quasi-experimental design to address the question, "How does student selection of vocabulary words impact vocabulary development and comprehension?" The study proceeded in three steps.

Step 1

The comparison groups were two classes of twenty sophomore students who attended class regularly. The first book that was studied was *Of Mice and Men* by John Steinbeck. One class, dubbed the control group, received traditional vocabulary instruction consisting of teacher-selected word lists for which students defined the words and used them in sentences.

The other class, the experimental group, was instructed on how to select vocabulary words that are important to the meaning of the text; that is, the word (1) is not established in student vocabulary; (2) is actually used in the reading selection; (3) must describe a character, important idea, or theme of the text; and (4) is repeated in the text. The teacher modeled how to use these criteria on a vocabulary list that she selected.

Differences on a comprehension test of the book were minimal, but differences on a vocabulary test were substantial. The experimental group's scores averaged over 20 percent better than those of the control group.

Step 2

For the second book, *The Old Man and the Sea* by Ernest Hemingway, the control group was asked to select words that group members thought the class needed to know and passages that were important to the story. The experimental group was asked to select important words using the four criteria noted above. The teacher went over students' selections and reasoning for the first half of the book, and students continued on their own for the second half of the book. Again, differences on a comprehension test were minimal, but the experimental group outscored the control group by an average of 14 percent on the vocabulary test.

Step 3

The final step in the research process was to allow both groups to apply their methods to a third book, *A Patch of Blue* by Elizabeth Kata, without teacher instruction. No vocabulary test was given, but scores on a comprehension test showed a 12 percent average difference favoring the experimental group.

The researcher's conclusion is that "students benefit from vocabulary instruction if they know WHY the word is important whether I explain it or they provide their own reasons." The implications of the study are that from now on she will "put away most word lists, sentences, crossword puzzles, seek-n-finds, Friday vocabulary quizzes, word sorts, affixes and concept circles in order to teach students the importance of words within context so that they not only learn the word but also grasp its meaning as it applies to a larger framework" (online).

This would be classified as a nonequivalent control group, quasi-experimental design because students were not randomly assigned to comparison groups. A critic could argue that the experimental group's superior performance on the tests was due to the makeup of the groups rather than the experimental treatment. Perhaps the students in the experimental classroom were generally brighter than those in the control classroom and did better in most subjects regardless of the instructional strategies used. In this instance the use of a pretest could confirm the initial equivalence of the groups. Unfortunately, a pretest was not used in this case. The conclusions would also be more convincing if the results were replicated in other high schools by other teachers. However, this is the more typical action research scenario, with the study limited to one teacher in one location. In spite of the technical design weaknesses, the results are data-based reasons for this teacher to change instructional strategies, which will undoubtedly improve her instruction and benefit her students.

Summary

This chapter discussed quasi-experimental research, which uses designs in which subjects are not randomly assigned or selected. The lack of randomization poses potential problems for establishing the validity of the research. When intact or naturally formed groups are used, there is a possibility of selection bias being introduced, and the similarity (or lack thereof) of the groups must be considered. In single-subject designs, the subject is usually selected because of some problem or condition associated with that subject. Rarely are the subjects used in single-subject designs selected at random.

Although the use of intact groups or specified subjects may pose threats to validity, they can be used effectively if adequate attention is given to the design of the research. In educational research, it is often impossible to apply random assignment when forming groups. Yet intact groups can provide valuable results, provided such results are interpretable.

When two or more intact groups are used, the credibility of the research depends on the extent to which the groups are similar on relevant variables. Relative to randomness, the groups are nonequivalent, but an argument may be made for their similarity. Therefore, it is important to have antecedent information about the groups, preferably through some kind of pretesting. Generalizability is argued on a logical basis.

Single-subject designs apply when the research centers on individuals rather than on groups—for example, when teachers or counselors are working with individual students. These designs involve multiple observations or measurements, taken across the baseline condition and the experimental treatment condition. Single-subject designs are characterized by extensive control over the administration of the experimental treatment and the collection of data on the subject, but because they are usually conducted in a natural setting, extraneous variables may have effects. Such research commonly involves extensive data collection, and the analysis of results may require considerable sorting through the data. It is often helpful to plot the data to identify the dominant pattern.

Action research is not characterized by a unique methodology, but by its intention or focus—that of addressing a problem usually at the local level. Because action research often involves intact groups, individuals, or at least participants not selected at random and may involve experimental treatments, such research is quasi-experimental. Teachers can conduct action research, for example, as they implement single-subject designs with individual students on remedial instruction or enrichment. When one or more teachers implement experimental procedures with one or more classes, the most likely design will be some type of posttest only or pretest-posttest, quasi-experimental design. We often envision action research as being somewhat limited and conducted by only one or a few educational professionals. But it can be expanded to collaborative efforts that may be quite broad in scope, and it can be conducted in a nonschool setting.

Here and in Chapter 7, the more commonly used designs for experimental and quasi-experimental research have been discussed. However, many variations can be made to accommodate specific research situations. For example, as was discussed in Chapter 7, if a time series design were used with random assignment to the groups, we would then have a "true" experimental design, with some type of repeated observation. The important thing is to have a design that fits the objectives of the experiment, one that provides adequate control so that the results can be interpreted with confidence and generalized as intended.

KEY CONCEPTS

Quasi-experimental research
Nonequivalent groups
Posttest-only, nonequivalent control group design
Pretest-posttest, nonequivalent control group design
Time series designs
Single-group time series design
Multiple-group time series design
Single-subject designs
Single-variable rule
Baseline
A-B design
A-B-A design
Action research

EXERCISES

8.1 The most desirable procedure for obtaining groups for an experiment is random selection or assignment of subjects, yet at times it is necessary to use intact groups and a quasi-experimental design. Discuss some of the difficulties that may be introduced when intact groups are used.

8.2 A biology teacher has three sets of laboratory materials available and decides to use one set with each of three classes over the period of one semester. The research question of interest is whether or not the different materials have differing effects on attainment of laboratory concepts, as measured by a section of the final examination given at the end of the semester. The score on this section of the test is the dependent variable. The classes are heterogeneous in ability, although students have not been randomly assigned to classes. The teacher decides to use a posttest-only, nonequivalent control group design. Diagram the design. How could the teacher apply a pretest-posttest, nonequivalent control group design, and what advantages would this design have over the posttest-only design? What are possible threats to the internal validity of this study? How generalizable are the results?

8.3 A study is conducted in three elementary schools on the effects of intermittent versus massed practice on fifth-grade spelling achievement. The fifth-grade teachers are allowed to use the method they prefer, but any one teacher uses only one method. After an eight-week period, the students are given a common spelling test. Discuss possible problems in interpreting the results of this experiment. Comment on both internal and external validity.

8.4 A teacher conducts a study on third-grade reading achievement with a class. Two methods of instruction are used, but not simultaneously. The students are tested every two weeks, and a particular method is used for each two-week period. The methods are randomly assigned to the two-week periods, and the study continues for an eighteen-week semester. Diagram this study as a time series design. Discuss its strong points and potential weaknesses. What might be a special measurement problem?

8.5 A study is conducted using intact groups to determine the effects of three different training programs. The groups are pretested, and the training programs are implemented for six weeks. The groups are posttested immediately following completion of the programs and again six weeks later. The design can be diagrammed as follows:

G_1 $O_1—X_1—O_2——O_3$

G_2 $O_4—X_2—O_5——O_6$

G_3 $O_7—X_3—O_8——O_9$

Interpret the following sets of results. Consider each independently.

a. $O_1 = O_4 = O_7 = O_3 = O_6 = O_9$, and O_2 is greater than O_1, and O_5 is greater than O_4, and O_8 is greater than O_7, but O_2 is greater than O_5, which is greater than O_8.

b. $O_1 = O_4 = O_7$, and $O_2 = O_5 = O_8 = O_3 = O_6, = O_9$, but $O_1, O_4, O_7, \neq O_2, O_5, O_8, O_3, O_6, O_9$.

c. O_1, O_4, and O_7 are not equal to each other, in that O_1 is greater than O_4, which is greater than O_7; O_2 is greater than O_5, which is greater than O_8, but $O_3 = O_6 = O_9$.

d. Assuming that there is an experimental treatment effect immediately after the program is completed, what comparisons would be made to determine whether there are long-term experimental treatment effects?

e. Is there any way to check on whether or not there is an effect of pretesting in this design? If so, how would it be checked; if not, why not?

8.6 A two-group time series design is used in a health education study in which two senior high school classes participate. The dependent variable is attitude toward health maintenance habits; it is measured at the beginning of the semester and every three weeks during the eighteen-week semester. Thus, each class is measured seven times. An experimental treatment (X), which consists of showing a series of films about the medical effects of poor health habits, is randomly inserted in one three-week period for one of the classes. The design can be diagrammed as follows:

G_1 $O_1—O_2—O_3—X—O_4——O_5——O_6——O_7$

G_2 $O_8—O_9—O_{10}———O_{11}——O_{12}—O_{13}——O_{14}$

Interpret the following possible patterns of results:

a. $O_1 = O_2 = O_3 = O_8 = O_9 = O_{10} = O_{11} = O_{12} = O_{13} = O_{14}$, and O_4 is greater than O_3, but O_4 is less than O_5, which is less than O_6, which is less than O_7. The greater the score on the dependent variable, the more positive the attitude.

b. $O_1 = O_8$, and $O_2 = O_9$, and $O_3 = O_{10}$; none of O_8 through O_{14} are equal, and the pattern is such that the scores increase consistently from O_8 through O_{14}; O_4 is greater than O_3 and O_{11}; O_5 is greater than O_{12}, but $O_6 = O_{13}$, and $O_7 = O_{14}$.

c. What comparisons would be made to check whether or not the normal class instruction is having an effect independent of X?

8.7 A guidance counselor is working with a high school student who, though an able student according to Scholastic Aptitude Test results, is having difficulty in all subjects. The counselor has been meeting with the student once a week for four weeks. The counselor decides to have the student keep a detailed log of how his time is spent when not in school. These logs are then used in the counseling sessions in an attempt to get the student to concentrate more on subject matter. Each week, the counselor receives reports from the student's teachers and synthesizes this information. The logs are used for a four-week period, so this is an *A-B* design. Diagram the design. What pattern of results would be indicative of an experimental treatment (the use of the logs) effect? If there was an experimental treatment effect, how would the patterns of results differ if it was a one-time effect versus a consistent, accumulative effect? Present a pattern of results from which no conclusion could be drawn.

8.8 Describe a situation in an area of your own interest for which a single-subject design would apply.

8.9 Several of the preceding exercises describe research situations that might be considered action research. Identify those exercises and describe why they are examples of action research. When action research is conducted, is it considered to be primarily applied or basic research?

8.10 When using a time series design, identify the advantage of including a group that does not receive the experimental treatment. From a practical standpoint, what are the difficulties of including such a group in most quasi-experimental situations?

8.11 Action research is typically thought of as being of limited scope conducted by one or a few individuals. However, it can be a considerably more extensive effort done as a collaborative study. For example, the collaboration may be between teachers in a school system and educational researchers at a university. In the research literature, identify a report of collaborative action research. Describe why the study was action research. Was it identified as such by the authors of the report?

8.12 The posttest-only, nonequivalent control group design is the weakest of the quasi-experimental designs presented in this chapter. Is the design ever useful? Give an example when this might work in assessing the effectiveness of a teacher professional development program.

8.13 Compare the strengths and weaknesses of the randomized posttest-only control group design of the preceding chapter to the pretest-posttest nonequivalent control group design of this chapter in terms of ease of implementation and the susceptibility to alternate explanations of the results.

REFERENCES

Campbell, D. T., and Stanley, J. C. (1963). Experimental and quasi-experimental designs for research on teaching. In N. L. Gage (Ed.). *Handbook of research on teaching* (pp. 171–246). Chicago: Rand McNally.

Fashing-Bittner, M. C. (2001). *Vocabulary development and comprehension.* Retrieved May 1, 2007, from www.madison.k12.wi.us/sod/car/abstracts/110.pdf.

CHAPTER 9 Nonexperimental Quantitative Research

The preceding two chapters dealt with experimental research. It was noted that, for a research project to be an experiment, at least one independent variable must be manipulated by the researcher according to some preconceived plan. However, many variables in educational settings do not lend themselves to deliberate manipulation. For example, intelligence, aptitude, and socioeconomic background cannot be randomly assigned to individuals or manipulated in an experiment.

Generally, there tends to be less control in nonexperimental research than in experimental research; therefore, interpretation of nonexperimental results may be less straightforward and more susceptible to ambiguity. But this is more a function of the general conditions under which nonexperimental research is conducted than a consequence of one or more independent variables being manipulated in an experiment. Nonexperimental research generally is conducted in a natural setting, with numerous variables operating simultaneously. Nevertheless, nonexperimental research can be carefully designed to enhance not only completion of the research but also interpretation of the results. It is the research problem and the conditions of the research that determine the appropriate methodology.

Nonexperimental Quantitative Research: Its Scope and Description

Nonexperimental quantitative research is probably the single most widely used research type in educational research. It encompasses a wide variety of research studies: all the way from ex post facto studies, which are studies of variables as they occur in natural settings, to status surveys designed to determine the status quo of some variables, situations, or contexts. Ex post facto research may focus on relationships of educational, psychological, and sociological variables, conducted in nonexperimental settings. Studies involving relationships among variables are often called correlational studies. Surveys are used to measure attitudes, opinions, or achievements—any number of variables in natural settings. Survey research has been around a long time and we owe much of its development to the field of sociology.

Nonexperimental quantitative research is broad in scope, ranging from status quo studies to ex post facto research, which may be causal–comparative or correlational in nature.

Ex Post Facto Research

Ex post facto means "from a thing done afterwards," and when ex post facto research is done, variables are studied in retrospect in search of possible relationships and effects. There are no variables deliberately manipulated by the researcher. **Ex post facto research** goes by different names. Krathwohl (1993, p. 514) includes ex post facto research as part of "after-the-fact, natural experiments." These are not experiments in the sense that the researcher manipulates variables, but under natural conditions in which there are operating independent and dependent variables. **Causal–comparative research** is another term sometimes used for this type of research. Essentially, causal–comparative research explores effects between variables in a nonexperimental setting. It is more a way of analyzing research data than a separate research method.

Correlational research that is ex post facto research focuses on the relationships between variables as they occur in natural settings. As will be seen in a later chapter, correlation is an analysis procedure and not a specific research method. Regardless of what it is called, ex post facto research can be considered a part of survey research because of its nonexperimental nature and the way data are collected; in essence, subjects are "surveyed."

Causal–Comparative Research Examples. The educational research literature abounds with examples of ex post facto research, but studies are too long to reproduce in their entirety here. However, it is useful to make some comments about examples of such studies in order to illustrate the nature of ex post facto research, and we begin with a couple of causal–comparative research examples.

The study on suicidality, school dropout, and reading problems among adolescents (Daniel et al., 2006) that was mentioned in the discussion of problem statements in Chapter 2 is an example of a causal–comparative research study. The researchers' goal was to "examine the rates and interrelationship of suicidal behaviors and school dropout among youth with poor single-word reading ability in comparison to youth with typical reading ability" (p. 508). Participants were classified as poor readers or typical readers based on their scores from the Letter-Word Identification subtest of the *Woodcock-Johnson Psycho-educational Battery—Revised.* Their placement into groups was supported by differences on several other reading tests. The 188 students were then tested for suicide ideation and psychiatric disorders using the *Schedule for Affective Disorders and Schizophrenia for School-Age Children—Epidemiologic Version* on two occasions. Information about school dropout and sociodemographic variables was obtained from interviews with the adolescents and their families.

The statistical analysis was quite complex, but essentially it estimated the probability of dropping out of school or experiencing suicide attempts or suicide ideation at a given assessment for participants who had not experienced these events previously (p. 511). Those who were more likely to drop out were poor readers, European Americans rather than minorities, those with lower SES, those with major depression, and those with conduct disorders. Suicidality was related to being a poor reader, being European American, and being older than classmates. Suicidality and dropping out were strongly interrelated. Daniel et al. (2006) concluded that youth with poor reading abilities exhibit significantly more suicidal ideation and suicide attempts and have a much greater chance of not completing secondary school than their peers with typical reading abilities.

Note that the researchers could not have conducted this study as an experiment because you just cannot randomly assign some adolescents to be suicidal or to drop out of school. The dynamics occur in their natural state, and the researchers were limited to making assessments and then statistically analyzing the data to determine the relationships among the variables.

Tsui and Mazzocco (2007) investigated the effects of math anxiety and perfectionism on timed versus untimed math test performance among mathematically gifted sixth-graders. The research literature indicated that students perform less well on timed tests than on untimed tests and students with higher levels of math anxiety generally had lower levels of mathematics achievement. The literature was less clear about the impact of perfectionism. The researchers wanted to learn how these variables interrelate in a sample of gifted sixth-graders.

The independent variables in the study were math anxiety and perfectionism. They were operationally defined as scores on the Mathematics Anxiety Rating Scale-Elementary (MARS-E) and on the Multidimensional Perfectionism Scale (MPS). The dependent variable was the score on a calculations test or, more specifically, the discrepancy between the scores in the timed and untimed conditions. There were two forms of the calculations test so that different items would be used in the timed and untimed conditions. Which form was used and the order of the timed and untimed tests were randomized. Note that the students were tested under different conditions, but there was no intervention or treatment imposed by the researchers.

Recruitment mailings were sent to 226 sixth-graders who qualified for a talent search done by a major university, were enrolled in at least one gifted math program offered by the university, and lived within 35 miles of the investigator's institution. Thirty-six sixth-graders agreed to participate in the study.

The results of the statistical analysis showed the following: (1) The average score on the timed test was lower than on the untimed test, but only when the timed test was administered first. (2) Higher levels of math anxiety and perfectionism were associated with smaller discrepancies between the scores from the timed and untimed conditions. The researchers had hypothesized that higher math anxiety would hinder math performance during timed testing, but they found just the opposite. Higher math anxiety seemed to arouse the gifted students to perform better on the timed test. (3) Students with higher perfectionism scores scored similarly on the timed and untimed tests. Perfectionism may act to arouse gifted students to better performance on both timed and untimed tests. Perfectionism promotes a healthy pursuit of excellence. (4) Perfectionism and math anxiety are positively correlated among gifted sixth-graders.

Although there were variables that were called independent and dependent variables, the ex post facto nature of the design did not allow the researchers to make solid cause-and-effect conclusions (Tsui and Mazzocco, 2007). They could conclude only that they found differences and correlations, most of which were consistent with their hypotheses.

Correlational Research Examples. Bures, Amundsen, and Abrami (2002) report on a study in which they investigated the relationship between student motivation and student acceptance of learning via computer conferencing. The participants in this study were 167 students enrolled in seven undergraduate and one graduate university-level course, and two college-equivalent, grade 12 courses. All courses used common conferencing software, but the computer conferencing software varied somewhat across courses, especially in its use by instructors.

An attitude toward computers questionnaire was administered prior to the courses. The questionnaire also measured traitlike motivational characteristics such as computer conferencing self-efficacy and task-specific motivation, which had three subscales: personal relevance, subjective competence, and task attractiveness. A post-course questionnaire was administered that had three subscales measuring satisfaction with computer conferencing impact on learning processes and products, satisfaction with the process of using computer conferencing, and overall feelings relative to face-to-face instruction. Final grades and available grades for online discussions were obtained. Grades from different institutions required some rescaling to common letter grades.

The analyses included a host of correlation coefficients representing strength of relationships between the variables. The results were reported in the narrative under subheadings listing the variables being correlated. An example of results as reported is:

> Starting with satisfaction, valuing the subject area was not related to satisfaction with cc ($r = 0.189$) but was related to satisfaction with the course ($r = 0.252$). Motivation toward the tasks in a course was related to satisfaction with cc ($r = 0.327$) and also to course satisfaction ($r = 0.365$). (p. 258)

Quite often, when authors report numerous correlation coefficients, they are included in tables, but this form of reporting also was effective. The actual correlation coefficients were reported as indicated above, and correlation as a statistical analysis is discussed in later chapters.

In this study there was no manipulation of variables. Computer conferencing occurred as the various instructors used it. In order to develop models of computer conference learning, the authors used the relationships between variables as represented by the correlations.

In another study Coker (2006) identified predictors of early writing. The participants were 309 low-income children enrolled in sixteen urban elementary schools. Descriptive writing samples were collected yearly as students progressed from first to third grade. The researcher hypothesized that writing development could be predicted by student background, vocabulary knowledge, reading skills, classroom literacy environment, and the first-grade teacher. Measures of each of these variables were either selected or created.

The analysis used individual growth modeling, which essentially tracks the individual student's writing scores and word totals across the years. First, an unconditional growth model is fit to the data. Then the hypothesized predictors are added to the model to see whether they account for the variation in the scores or for the rate of change over time. Predictor variables were retained in the model if their effects were statistically significant. Multiple analyses were conducted when a variable had several indicators such as (1) availability of pencils and paper and (2) range of genres in the classroom library. Separate analyses addressed the interaction of multiple predictors. The major results are presented here.

For the writing scores, it was found that oral vocabulary showed differences at the end of first grade, but this was not a predictor of growth. The same pattern was found for reading skill (letter-word identification). The classroom literacy environment (range of genres in the classroom library) was related to growth. Growth was also related to which first-grade teacher the student had.

The results for word total were somewhat different from those for the writing scores. Student characteristics, classroom literacy environment, and first-grade teacher were again significant predictors, but student oral reading skill and student oral language were not.

The conclusion was that diverse influences have a simultaneous and complex impact on writing development. The study is clearly quantitative and it is longitudinal, extending across three grade levels. There was no manipulated independent variable for which the researcher was trying to establish an effect, as is found in experimental and quasi-experimental research.

The above descriptions of the four examples are brief. Any reader interested in the specifics of the studies can consult the references. Nonexperimental quantitative research can be descriptive, causal–comparative, or correlational. There are many research studies that include all three of these orientations. For example, in a study of classroom cheating a researcher might want to be (1) descriptive, documenting the extent of cheating that takes place; (2) causal–comparative, finding any differences in the prevalence of cheating among high and low achievers; and (3) correlational, identifying a set of variables that predicts the likelihood of cheating.

Survey Research

Practically all adults have been involved in surveys at some time or another. We are familiar with the political polls taken on almost a continuous basis during election years. People are surveyed about attitudes, opinions, perceptions, and often they are asked to evaluate something. General public populations are surveyed as well as more specific populations such as a professional population.

Education has its share of **survey research.** One of the most extensive surveys has been done annually since 1969. It is the Phi Delta Kappa/Gallup Poll of the Public's Attitudes Toward the Public Schools. This is a telephone survey in which the phone numbers are randomly generated so that both listed and unlisted numbers can be contacted. Some of the major results from the thirty-eighth annual survey are these (Rose and Gallup, 2006):

> Forty-nine percent of the respondents gave the schools in their community an A or a B.
> Sixty-four percent gave the school that their oldest child attends an A or a B.

Twenty-one percent gave the nation's schools an A or a B.
Support for vouchers is declining and is in the mid-30 percent range.
There is near-consensus support for the belief that the problems the public schools face result from societal issues and not from the quality of schooling. (pp. 42–43)

This kind of information is useful because it comes from a trusted source and allows for the identification of trends across the years. It presents a national picture of public school issues.

Local school districts also conduct surveys to gather perceptions of how the schools are operating and the community's feedback on issues facing the district. Local needs assessments often use surveys to obtain opinions about what changes should be considered or what needs are currently not being met.

Colleges and universities conduct surveys of their graduates to obtain perceptions of the college experience and the value of the completed program. Education professionals may be surveyed about their opinions about educational issues. Evaluation research studies often include surveys of participants or clients. So, there are many educational research situations for which survey research is the appropriate methodology.

Survey Designs

Survey designs basically are of two types, longitudinal and cross-sectional. These designs are commonly used with samples,[1] although they can be used with an entire population. (When an entire population is included in the survey it is called a **census.**) The two characteristics that distinguish the designs are (1) the points at which data collection takes place and (2) the nature of the sample.

Longitudinal Designs

Longitudinal designs involve the collection of data over time and at specified points in time. Some longitudinal studies are of short duration, and others span a long period, possibly several years. In any event, data for such studies are collected at two or more points in time.

One type of longitudinal design is the **trend study.** In a trend study, a general population is studied over time. Random samples are taken at various points, and these are different samples, but the samples represent the general population. Trend studies often are used for studying attitudes or opinions over an extended period. For example, in a study of a community's changing attitude toward the schools, the general population would be the members of the community. Each time (possibly yearly) attitude is measured, a random sample is selected from the general population. An individual might be selected for more than one sample. The polls conducted over the course of a political campaign are examples of trend studies.

A *trend study* is a longitudinal study in which a general population is studied over time. Usually, the population is sampled, and random samples are measured.

A variation on the trend study is the **cohort study,** which is also a longitudinal design. In a cohort study, a specific rather than a general population is studied, usually by drawing random samples at different points in time rather than including the entire population. The difference between trend and cohort studies can be illustrated by an example. A researcher is interested in studying the attitudes of the teachers in Region A toward professional unions. The survey is conducted every three years for fifteen years. At any given time, the random sample of teachers surveyed is selected from the teacher population at that time. The membership of the population would have changed, at least partly, from the previous time, but at any particular time it is the teacher population (in this case, called a *general population*). A survey conducted in this manner would be an example of a trend study.

If the researcher were interested in studying the attitudes toward professional unions of the 2007, beginning teacher population in Region A, this would involve studying a specific population. Three years later, the next random sample would be drawn from what remains of this population, which in 2010 would be teachers with three years' experience. Although some of the original beginning teachers would have left teaching along the way, the study would include only the attitudes of the population of teachers who were beginning teachers in 2007. A survey conducted in this manner would be an example of a cohort study.

A *cohort study* is a longitudinal study in which a specific population is studied over time.

In some populations that turn over rapidly, the actual members of the population may change almost entirely over time. For example, if a survey of undergraduate attitudes at a college were conducted every four years, there would be a large percentage of change in the actual members of the undergraduate population. However, the undergraduates at each point in time would still be the general population under study.

Trend and cohort studies enable the researcher to study change and process over time. However, because different random samples are selected each time data are collected, the trends are studied for the group, not for individuals. If changes are taking place, the researcher cannot specifically determine which individuals are causing the changes.

One variation on longitudinal designs, the **panel study,** involves collecting data on a sample of individuals at different times. The sample of individuals used is called the *panel,* which should be randomly selected at the outset of the study.

A *panel study* is a longitudinal study in which the same sample is measured two or more times. The sample can represent either a specific or a general population.

One advantage of panel studies is that they enable the researcher not only to measure net change but also to identify the source of change in terms of the specific individuals who are changing. Panel studies also can provide information on the temporal ordering of variables. Such information is important if the researcher is attempting to establish cause and effect, because an effect cannot precede its cause. Suppose we were interested in attitudes toward the central college administration and promotion patterns among college professors. If a full professor has an excellent attitude, is it because of promotion, or was the attitude there before promotion, and did it have some effect on whether or not promotion took place? Without some kind of ordering of what occurred first, there is no way to establish possible cause and effect. (The ordering does not necessarily establish cause and effect; it merely indicates whether or not a cause-and-effect relationship is possible.)

Panel studies have some definite disadvantages, an obvious one being attrition in the panel across the data-collection points. Therefore, panel studies tend to be of relatively short duration compared to other longitudinal studies. Another disadvantage is that the panel study is demanding for both the panel members and the researcher, who must follow up and locate panel members. If the population from which the panel was selected is highly mobile and changing, the original panel may no longer be representative of that population at later data-collection points. Panel studies are most applicable with static populations over short time periods. For example, surveying school board members quarterly over one calendar year might involve a panel study. Another possible disadvantage is that the panel members might become conditioned to certain variables so that they are better at recall or exceptionally skilled in responding. Conditioning can also work the other way, causing panel members to become fatigued, bored, or careless.

Longitudinal designs are used for studying change or status over a period of time. The length of time and the number of data-collection points involved in a specific longitudinal design depend on the objectives of the study. For sampling, the trend study involves different random samples from a general population, the cohort study involves different random samples from a specific population, and the panel study involves a single random sample measured at two or more times.

Cross-Sectional Designs

In contrast to longitudinal designs, **cross-sectional designs** involve the collection of data at one point in time from a random sample representing some given population at that time. A cross-sectional design cannot be used for measuring change in an individual, because an individual is measured only once. However, differences between defined groups in the cross-sectional study may represent changes that take place in a larger defined population. Consider the following example.

Suppose a researcher is conducting a survey of mathematics achievement of senior high school students (grades 10–12) in a city school system or in a geographical region. Mathematics achievement is operationally defined as performance on a comprehensive, standardized mathematics test. A random sample is selected that includes tenth-, eleventh-, and twelfth-graders, and each individual is identified in terms of grade level. Another way of viewing the sampling is that random samples are selected from all grade levels. The sample is tested, and the researcher now has data on the three grades.

Even though the data are collected at the same point in time, because the three grade levels are represented, the data represent the pattern of mathematics achievement in senior high school. The differences between the grade levels represent gains in mathematics achievement across the three years. However, instead of using a single, grade-level population of students and measuring them three times longitudinally as they progress through the grades, three different grade levels are studied simultaneously.

> A *cross-sectional design* involves data collection at one point in time from a sample or from more than one sample representing two or more populations.

Selecting samples from two or more populations simultaneously and conducting a study related to the same research problem is called a *parallel-samples design*. Parallel-samples designs usually appear as cross-sectional designs, although they can be longitudinal. In the latter case, there would be two or more data-collection points, separated by a time interval.

As an example, a parallel-samples design used in a study of attitudes toward professional unions might include samples of teachers, school administrators, and school board members. Each of these three samples could respond to similar, if not identical, attitude inventories or questionnaires. The results of the different samples could then be compared.

Characteristics of different survey designs are summarized in Table 9.1. The cross-sectional designs have some logistical advantages over the longitudinal designs. Data collection is not spread over an extended time period, and potentially difficult follow-up of individuals is not necessary, as it is in a panel study. For these reasons, cross-sectional designs are more practical than longitudinal designs for master's thesis and doctoral dissertation research. If the time interval between data-collection points is very short—for instance, less than three months—a longitudinal design may be feasible for dissertation research. Most longitudinal studies are relatively large scale, however, and many take on the characteristics of continuing research that is conducted over a period of years. The

TABLE 9.1 Characteristics of Survey Designs

Design	Population Studied	How Sampled
Longitudinal		[Two or more data-collection times]
Trend	General	Random samples at each data-collection time
Cohort	Specific	Random samples at each data-collection time
Panel	General or specific	The initial random sample is used throughout the data-collection times
Cross-sectional	General or specific and could include subpopulations[a]	Random samples from all populations at one point in time

[a]If two or more populations are studied simultaneously, this becomes a parallel-samples design.

characteristics of longitudinal and cross-sectional designs can be combined into a complex design that includes sampling two or more populations at two or more times. Comparisons could then be made at a given point in time and also across data-collection times.

The Methodology of Survey Research

The methodology of conducting a survey involves a series of detailed steps, each of which should be carefully planned. The initial step is to define the research problem and to begin developing the survey design. The definition of the research problem should include a good background in the variables to be studied, which of course includes a review of the literature. Variables included in the survey must be operationally defined, and the investigator should have information about the relationships of any sociological and psychological variables that may be involved. This information is valuable for constructing items or selecting measurement instruments, such as tests, for the survey.

The next step is the development of the sampling plan, if it has been decided to sample rather than measure the entire population. Various factors must be considered. The population to be sampled must be defined and the units identified for the sample selection. The sample must be selected so that valid inferences can be made to the population and to any subpopulations. Sampling procedures can be quite complex, and acquiring the sample may require considerable effort and resources.

Although some activities can be conducted simultaneously, the next major step is the preparation for data collection. For surveys involving interviews or questionnaires, this is a major step, because the instruments must be constructed. When data are to be collected using tests or inventories, such as an observation inventory, more than likely instruments will be available. It may also be necessary to train observers or testers.

Certainly, it is necessary to identify the specific types of data that will be generated by the questionnaire early in the construction of the items, and it is also necessary to consider how data will be tabulated, summarized, and analyzed. The procedures by which data are to be analyzed should be identified. Quantitative data analysis may be used, and many surveys involve qualitative data, so both quantitative and qualitative analyses may be necessary. The survey must produce data that can be used to test the research hypotheses or answer the questions raised by the research problem.

Especially for surveys using questionnaires and interviews, background or demographic information about the respondent is important in that it identifies the individual in terms of classifying variables for the analysis. For example, if the responses of men and women are to be analyzed separately or comparatively, it is essential to know the sex of the individual. Surveys vary as to the amount of required background information.

Initial drafts of a questionnaire or interview should be "tried out," so to speak, with a pilot run or trial run. Such a tryout should be done with individuals similar to the intended respondents. The purpose of the pilot run is to check for ambiguity, confusion, and poorly prepared items. Pilot run feedback can be very useful for finalizing the instrument. A pilot run is done with a limited number of individuals, usually five to ten, but seldom more than twenty.

When the measurement instrument is judged to be satisfactory, the data collection begins. The researcher should adhere to the sampling plan when collecting the data. If interviews are used, and depending on the complexity of the interview, there may need to be provision for systematically checking the interviewers. This may be accomplished by having two interviewers interview the same individual. Such a measure of consistency is called **interrater reliability.** For certain types of interviews, it is also well to get a measure of the consistency of a specific interviewer, which is called **intrarater reliability.** This can be accomplished by taping responses and having the interviewer record the responses on two independent occasions.

Data, that is, the responses to the survey, will need to be tabulated and synthesized. For open-ended items, responses will need to be categorized, and category systems must be constructed for this purpose. Such systems may be based on a content analysis or on an a priori system of responses. The translation of data is known as *coding*. This task is greatly facilitated if the information from the questionnaire or interview form can be put directly into the computer.

Data analyses will depend on the nature of the data; to the extent that responses can be quantified, statistical analyses are appropriate. But qualitative description may also be done. Ultimately, the analyses must take forms that allow for testing the hypotheses and answering the research questions of the survey. If inferences are to be drawn to populations, the analyses should provide for them. A number of separate analyses commonly are conducted on the data of a single survey, and separate analyses as well as different types of analyses may be in order. For example, data composed of frequencies on factual information items would be analyzed differently than data from an attitude scale. The former might involve proportions, whereas the latter most likely would involve frequencies or means. Data from teacher interviews requesting their perceptions of social interaction among students might be synthesized through description. The final step of conducting the survey is preparing the report of results and conclusions.

Figure 9.1 summarizes the steps in conducting a survey. The left side of the figure includes the major steps, and the right side shows the activities that come under each step. In some cases, activities overlap into two steps. Not all activities would necessarily be applicable for a specific survey; for example, training of interviewers is necessary only for studies involving interviews.

The successful completion of a survey is not a simple task. Several possible pitfalls and problems can sabotage the survey. One common problem is the failure to allow enough time and resources for the various steps. The sampling procedure can break down, or there may not be enough resources to test and revise the items adequately. The items of the interview or questionnaire may be poorly constructed, resulting in unusable data. Failure to provide the follow-ups is a very obvious but common difficulty, and inadequate procedures for assembling and tabulating the data as the questionnaires are returned are often sources of inefficiency and confusion. Nonresponse may bias the results, and failure to consider the source of nonresponse may lead to unwarranted generalizations. Finally, if the researcher reports results as separate, isolated analyses without some synthesis, it is likely that the maximum information is not being obtained from the survey. Careful planning will go a long way toward avoiding serious difficulties when conducting the survey.

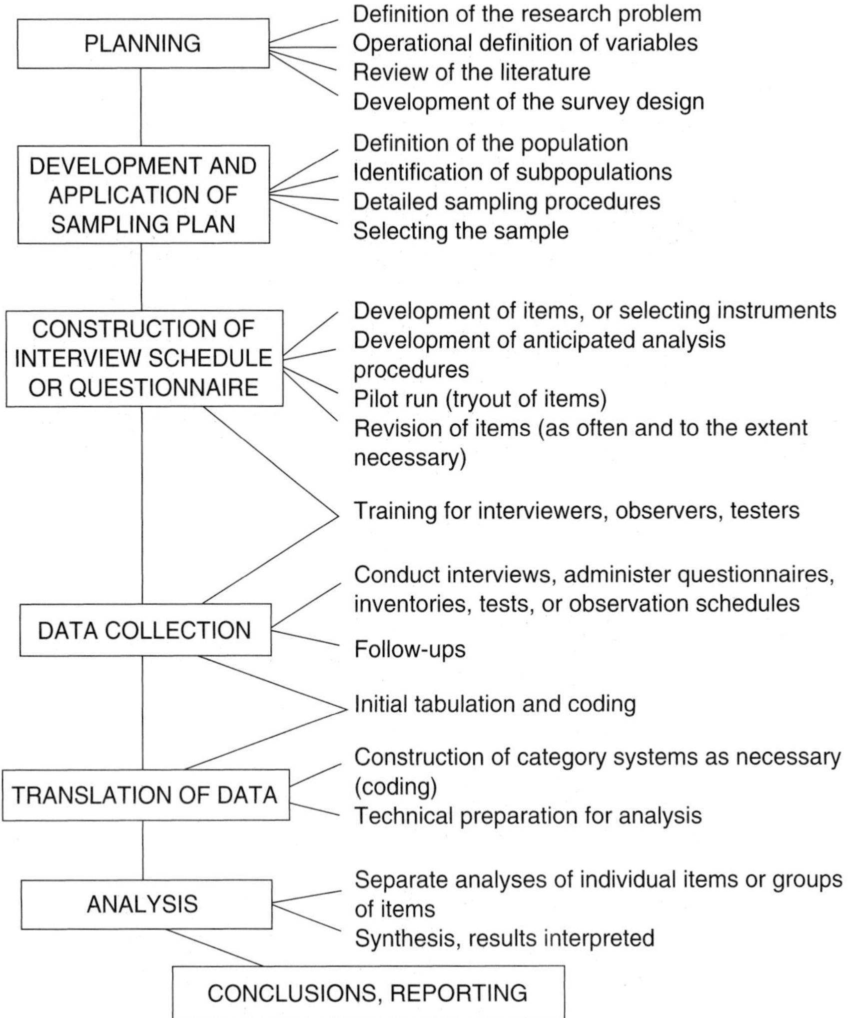

FIGURE 9.1 Flowchart for the Steps in Conducting a Survey

Questionnaire Surveys

One of the distinguishing characteristics among surveys is the method of data collection, and certainly the mailed questionnaire commonly is used for data collection. Questionnaires are used for surveys ranging in magnitude from national surveys to local surveys such as a **community survey** for a school system or even a single school. Questionnaires vary in length and complexity. But whatever the situation, surveys involving questionnaires require a series of sequential activities. The overall scope of these activities is presented in Figure 9.2. As

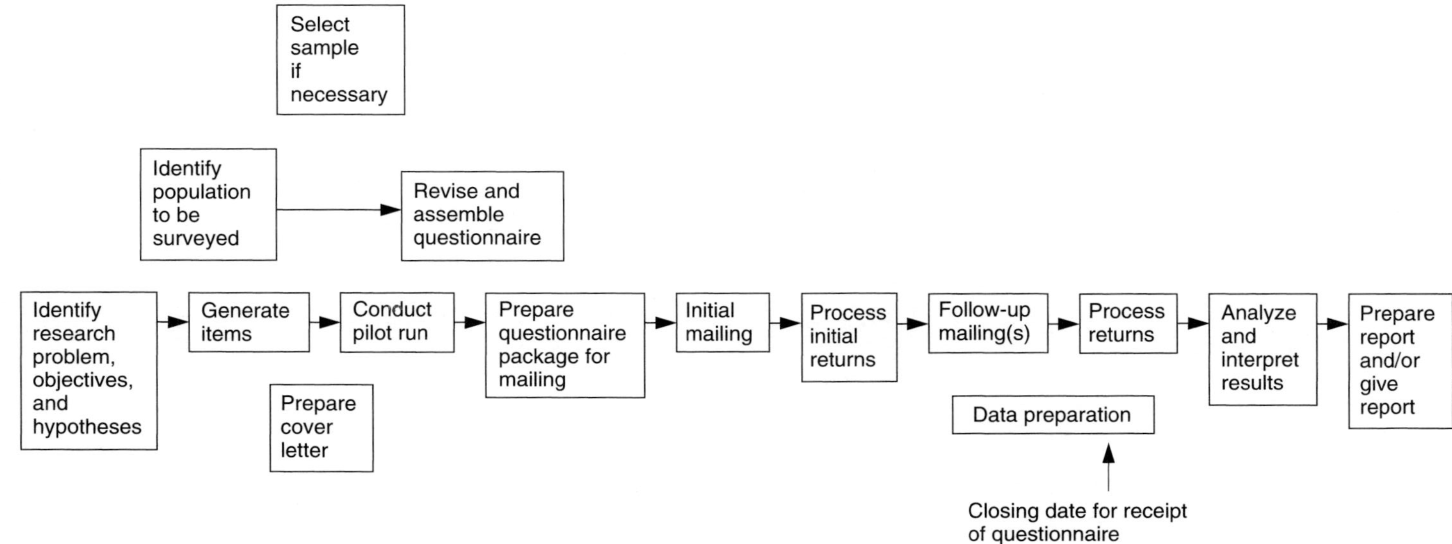

FIGURE 9.2 Sequential Activities of a Questionnaire Survey

indicated on the left side of the figure, early in the process some activities can be conducted concurrently or at least overlap to some extent.

A good bit of the efforts of a questionnaire study are directed toward constructing good items and getting respondents to complete the questionnaire. But all activities are important and require attention to detail. The questions or hypotheses associated with the research study should be identified explicitly. This will facilitate the construction of questionnaire items and avoid both the inclusion of useless items and the omission of necessary items.

Item Construction

Item construction for questionnaires is a straightforward process, but without careful attention to detail, the items may be put together poorly and not provide the necessary data for the study. Before discussing item format, we consider general guidelines for item construction. These are:

1. Except for a few items that may request background or demographic information, the items should directly relate to the research problem, questions, or hypotheses.

2. Items are to be clear and unambiguous. Use terminology that the respondents will understand. Avoid vague words, technical terms, and jargon.

3. Include only one concept in a single item. An example of violating this guideline would be, "Are you in favor of minimum competency testing for students and career ladders for teachers?"

4. Avoid the use of **leading questions.** These are questions with implied assumptions or anticipated outcomes. Often such items suggest a preferred response. An example of a leading question would be, "Are you in favor of relaxed discipline in the schools, even though such discipline undermines the moral development of youth?"

Leading questions may not be as obvious as the one above. Moe (2002) found that the percent endorsing the statement dropped when the Phi Delta Kappa/Gallup Poll item about school vouchers was changed from defining vouchers as "a government-funded program allowing parents to choose among public, private, and parochial schools" to an item asking whether they favored or opposed "allowing students and parents to choose a private school to attend at public expense" (p. 1).

5. Avoid questions loaded with social or professional desirability. In essence, do not ask questions so that certain responses make respondents disapprove of themselves. An example of violating this guideline would be asking a teacher, "Do you have difficulty maintaining a good learning climate in your classroom?"

6. Avoid questions that demand personal or delicate information. These items include requests for specific income information, possibly age of the respondent, or questions about the extent of involvement in illicit activities.

7. Request only information that the respondent is able to provide. All items should fit the informational background of the respondents.

8. Make the reading level of the items appropriate for the respondents. To the extent possible, use "soft" words rather than "hard" words. For example, when surveying teachers use *correction* or *corrective action* rather than *punishment.*

9. Shorter items are preferred to longer items, and simpler items are preferred to complex items. Rather than using a single detailed and complex item, use two or more shorter items.

10. When requesting quantitative information, ask for a specific number (such as an actual frequency) rather than an average. For example, ask, "How often during the past two weeks did you help your child with homework?" *Do not* ask, "On the average, how many times a month do you help your child with homework?"

11. The options for response to an item should be exhaustive; the options should be mutually exclusive. For some items, it is necessary to provide a middle-of-the-road or neutral response, such as "no definite feeling" or "undecided," to avoid forcing the respondent to make an undesirable response.

12. The response options should fit the intent of the item. There is a tendency to overuse the strongly agree to strongly disagree set of response options. Suppose an item is intended to measure level of satisfaction with an educational product. The item stem, "you were very satisfied with Product A," with strongly agree to strongly disagree options does not measure level of satisfaction very well. It measures agreement with "very satisfied." A better item would be, "Rate the extent to which you were satisfied with Product A," and have options from not at all to very satisfied.

13. Avoid unwarranted assumptions. For example, the item "Do you think the teachers of School A are capable of implementing educational reform?" assumes that the teachers of School A want to implement educational reform.

14. To the extent possible, avoid negative items and do not use double negatives. An example of a question in the form of a negative item would be, "Which of the following instructional strategies do you not use?"

These guidelines may seem somewhat extensive, but in fact they are straightforward. Try to make the task of completing the questionnaire as easy as possible for the respondent so that it can be done efficiently and without confusion.

Formulating items is essentially a matter of common sense. The law of parsimony applies: Keep things as simple as possible to obtain the necessary data.

Item Format

There are two general types of items used for questionnaires: (1) selected-response or forced-choice items for which the respondent selects from two or more options, and (2) open-ended items for which the respondent constructs a response. **Selected-response items** enhance consistency of response across respondents; data tabulation generally is straightforward and less time-consuming than for open-ended items. Selected-response items have the disadvantage of possibly "boxing-in" the respondent on the breadth of the response, but if the selected-response items produce the required data, this is not a problem. Adequately constructing selected-response items generally requires more time and effort, primarily because more of them are needed to cover a research topic. But this time is usually well spent and is more than made up when the responses are tabulated and interpreted.

Open-ended items allow the individual more freedom of response because certain feelings or information may be revealed that would not be forthcoming with selected-response items. A disadvantage of open-ended items is that responses tend to be inconsistent in length, and sometimes in content, across respondents. Both questions and responses are susceptible to misinterpretation. Irrelevant information may be included in the response. In any event, responses to open-ended items are usually more difficult to tabulate and synthesize than responses to selected-response items. Selected-response items should be used to the extent that they can obtain relevant information. They also require less effort from the respondents, because they do not need to construct the responses, and responding can be done in less time.

> The two general types of item format are selected-response items with two or more options and open-ended items for which the respondent constructs the response.

Consider the following item formats for a survey on a single topic, attitudes toward mathematics among elementary school students. Sample items are listed in Figure 9.3.

The open-ended format allows for responses that are creative, unique, and not known to the researcher in advance. Open-ended questions are sometimes used in preliminary studies so that the most frequent responses can then be used in the wording of selected-response items in subsequent surveys. The second item looks like an open-ended item but acts like a selected-response item. The student's potential responses are restricted by the wording. The item could just as easily be recast as a selected-response item.

Rating scales, as illustrated in Figure 9.3, are frequently used on surveys because the items can be analyzed separately or the responses to a set of items pertaining to one dimension or topic can be summed to form a score for the entire scale. When some of the items are worded positively (1 = low and 5 = high) and others are worded negatively, it is essential to reverse the scoring on the negatively worded items (to 1 = high and 5 = low) so that when the responses are summed positive responses yield higher scores. Figure 9.3 shows that the number of choices on the rating can vary. Five-point rating scales are used quite often because people can usually discriminate that finely without difficulty. Of course it may be better to use 3-point scales for younger children. Note that a 4-point scale does not allow the respondent to withhold a judgment. Because it forces the respondent to come down on one side or the other, it could distort the responses for someone who really is undecided.

Rankings, as shown in Figure 9.3, have an appeal to those who have not used them. They seem to be simple. They cause the respondent to choose among the things being ranked and they seem easy to analyze. The difficulties arise when respondents don't precisely follow directions, which often happens. When respondents feel fairly equal about

Open-ended question

What feeling do you get when the teacher says, "Now take out your math books?"

Selected-response item posing as an open-ended item

How do you feel about math as compared to science?

Rating scale, 5-point

	Strongly Agree	Agree	Not Sure	Disagree	Strongly Disagree
Math is fun to learn.	1	2	3	4	5
Math is challenging.	1	2	3	4	5
Math frightens me.	1	2	3	4	5

Rating scale, 4-point

	Strongly Agree	Agree	Disagree	Strongly Disagree
Math is fun to learn.	1	2	3	4
Math is challenging.	1	2	3	4

Ranking

Please rank the following subjects from most favorite (1) to least favorite (6)

Language Arts ______
Mathematics ______
Physical Education ______
Reading ______
Science ______
Social Studies ______

FIGURE 9.3 Examples of Item Formats from a Survey of Attitudes Toward Mathematics

two items, they award tied ranks even when the researcher expects the rankings to be made with no tied ranks. Problems also occur when one or more of the items that are to be ranked are left blank. How should the omitted ranks be processed? Should you use only the complete sets of rankings and ignore the rest? The initial appeal of rankings often diminishes when the data are being analyzed.

Pilot Run of the Items. Before preparing the final form of the questionnaire, the items should be tried out with a small group in a **pilot run.** This is a pretesting of the questionnaire, and deficiencies may be uncovered that were not apparent by simply reviewing the items. The group used for the pilot run need not be a random sample of prospective respondents, but the members of the group should be familiar with the variables under study and should be in a position to make valid judgments about the items. A class of students, possibly graduate students, can often serve effectively as a pilot run group. The results of the pilot run should identify misunderstandings, ambiguities, and useless or inadequate items.

Additional items may be suggested, and mechanical difficulties in such matters as data tabulation may be identified. Difficulties with the directions for completing the questionnaire may also be uncovered. On the basis of the pilot run results, necessary revisions should be made for the final form of the questionnaire.

Besides eliminating ambiguities and clarifying directions, a pilot run can avoid results that provide little or no information. The following item, used in a pilot run with twenty-five respondents, is an example. The frequencies of responses are underlined following the category.

> Please indicate your years of teaching experience (to the closest whole year) by checking the appropriate category.
>
> 0–10 <u>21</u> 11–20 <u>3</u> 21–30 <u>1</u> more than 30 <u>0</u>

These results provide little information, because the response categories do not separate the respondents. The possible responses might be changed, with the following results:

> 0–2 <u>7</u> 3–5 <u>5</u> 6–8 <u>4</u> 9–11 <u>5</u> more than 11 <u>4</u>

Now the response categories provide more definitive information about the years of experience of the respondents. The pilot run also provides the opportunity to discuss the items with the members of the pilot run group. This may be done when piloting questionnaire or interview items. The discussion may provide suggestions for item improvement.

> A *pilot run* of the items provides the opportunity to identify confusing and ambiguous language, and to obtain information about possible patterns of results.

The Cover Letter

The **cover letter** is an essential part of any survey involving a questionnaire. It is the mechanism for introducing individuals to the questionnaire and motivating them to respond. The letter should be straightforward, explaining the purpose and potential value of the survey and transmitting the message that an individual's response is important. There should be nothing in the cover letter to arouse suspicions about the purpose or nature of the survey. The individual should be assured that the researcher is interested in the overall responses of the group and that the individual responses will not be singled out. A procedure may be set up by which replies remain anonymous, but in any event the individual should be assured that all responses are confidential.

The matter of who signs the cover letter can be of some importance. The cover letter should be on the letterhead of a professional organization or an institution with which the respondents would be likely to identify, or at least be knowledgeable about. If possible, the letter should be signed by someone in a professional position, who is (or appears to be) associated in some way with the respondents. For example, the cover letter of a questionnaire being sent to guidance counselors about guidance institutes might carry the signature of the institute director on the staff of a university that conducts such institutes. A graduate student who sends out a questionnaire and states that its purpose is data collection for a thesis can expect a limited and disappointing response.

Figure 9.4 contains the cover letter of a survey conducted as part of the external evaluation of the AEL, Inc.[2] The following points can be made about the letter:

1. The purpose of the survey is stated in the first paragraph and the respondent has been selected because of receiving an AEL product.

2. The recipient is informed as to what will be done with the information provided through the questionnaires.

3. Confidentiality is assured.

4. Each questionnaire had a code number in the upper, right-hand corner. The purpose of this number is explained, and in the explanation it is clear that there will be a follow-up of nonrespondents.

5. The importance of response is mentioned in the third paragraph.

6. A time estimate is given for completing the questionnaire. When such an estimate is given it must be an accurate estimate. Underestimates of time annoy respondents when they realize completion of the questionnaire is taking a lot longer than the estimate.

7. A "deadline" is given for the return of the questionnaire, which is about three weeks from the mailing date. This deadline is arbitrary but there should be enough time for recipients to complete the questionnaire, but not so much that they put it aside and forget about it. A return deadline should be specified in all cover letters.

8. The recipient is reminded about the enclosed, postage-paid envelope, and enclosing such an envelope is a requirement.

9. Appreciation for completing the questionnaire is expressed.

10. The cover letter is signed by the person in charge of the external evaluation.

11. This cover letter is addressed to the specific individual by name rather than using a general address such as "Client." Making the request more personal encourages response. A decision must be made whether or not naming individuals on the letters is worth the effort. Also, rather than just indicating, "you received a product," the specific product is named, which should aid the recipient's memory.

12. The letter fits easily on a single page, which essentially is the maximum length for a cover letter.

The cover letter merits careful attention and may require review and revision. It must inform the recipients about the survey and motivate recipients to complete the questionnaire in an accurate and timely manner.

College of Education
The Evaluation Center

Kalamazoo, Michigan 49008-5178
616 387-5895

WESTERN MICHIGAN UNIVERSITY

October 3, 2003

Mr. Aaron Ballard
1516 Scott St.
Covington, KY 41011-3408

Dear Mr. Ballard:

The Evaluation Center at Western Michigan University has been engaged by AEL, Inc., to be its external evaluator. As part of that evaluation, we are surveying people who received a product from AEL during the past 15 months or so. According to our records, you received The Link. We are asking you to complete the enclosed, brief questionnaire concerning your perceptions of this product.

The information provided throught the questionnaires will be presented to the AEL board, the federal government, and AEL staff to help them improve AEL materials and services. Your responses to this survey will be confidential; no individual will be identified with his or her responses. The number on the questionnaire is a code so that we can identify those who have responded. This is to reduce the cost of follow-up and to eliminate the disruption of follow-up for those who have returned the questionnaire.

Your response is very important to the success of this evaluation. The information you provide is important to AEL, not only for program planning, but also in dealing with the funding agency. Completing the questionnaire should require no more than 10 minutes. We very much appreciate your completing and returning the questionnaire by October 20, 2003, in the enclosed, post-paid envelope.

Sincerely,

William Wiersma

William Wiersma, Ph.D.
External Evaluator for AEL

enc.

FIGURE 9.4 Cover Letter Used with Questionnaire Survey

Source: FY03 Report: External Evaluation of AEL, Inc. (December 2003) Kalamazoo, MI. The Evaluation Center, Western Michigan University. Reproduced by permission of the AEL, Inc., and The Evaluation Center.

Questionnaire Format

The questionnaire as a whole should be attractive and easily read. Multicolored printing can be used, although there is little evidence that such printing has much effect on the respondent's motivation. The questionnaire should not be so long that it makes responding a tedious or burdensome task or makes unreasonable demands on the respondent's time. The items should be in a logical sequence to hold the interest of the respondent.

Instructions for completing the questionnaire should be concise and clear, with examples for any complex or difficult items. If more than one item format it used, items with the same format are often grouped together. However, the logical sequence of the items should take priority over item format. That is, when completing the questionnaire, the respondent's chain of thought should be logical and organized, not "jumping around" from concept to concept.

The cover letter should set the stage for responding, and the early part of the questionnaire should begin immediately with the content related to the research problem. Most questionnaires include a section on respondent background or demographic information (for example, information about position, degrees held, etc.). This section should appear near the end of the questionnaire so that the transition from the cover letter is not broken. The items of this section should be selected-response format, and the options for any item should be mutually exclusive and exhaustive.

To the extent that it does not break the logical flow of the questionnaire, any open-ended items should appear toward the end of the questionnaire. Sometimes in questionnaires dealing with several concepts, open-ended items are dispersed throughout the questionnaire. In any event, the questionnaire should not begin with an open-ended item that requires extensive writing. If there are items that may be difficult for the respondent, place them near the end.

The questionnaire layout should not appear crowded, and the items should be easy to respond to. Items and pages should be numbered. An item and its response options must be on the same page, and the options must fit the item. If any special instructions are necessary, such as responding so that the questionnaire can be machine-scored, be sure that these instructions are clear and emphasized. Finally, at the end of the questionnaire, the name and address of the person to whom the questionnaire is to be returned should be given, reminding the respondent to place the questionnaire in the enclosed stamped, self-addressed envelope.

> Questionnaire format should be attractive and straightforward, with the items ordered in a logical sequence. Responding to the items should be convenient and without confusion.

Procedures for Increasing Response Rate

One of the persistent problems with questionnaire studies is the possibility of a high rate of nonresponse. Here, we are referring to unit nonresponse, the failure of an entire questionnaire to be returned. The validity of survey research involving questionnaires depends on the response rate and the quality of response. **Response rate** is the percentage of respondents returning the questionnaire, and *quality of response* depends on the completeness of data. The problem with nonresponse is that it introduces the possibility of bias, because the respondents might not be representative of the group intended to be surveyed.

The possibility of nonresponse is a problem with questionnaire studies because non-response may introduce bias into the data.

Of course, the greater the response rate, the more accurate the results. Most surveys can tolerate some nonresponse, but what are acceptable rates of nonresponse? By strict standards, the response rate should be high enough that conclusions could not be reversed if the nonrespondents all answered the other way. Writers differ on suggested minimum response rates, and the rates may vary depending on the population being surveyed. Generally, however, when surveying a professional population, 70 percent is considered a minimum acceptable response rate. Porter and Whitcomb (2003) say that it is now common for educational researchers to use survey data in which the response rate is less than 50 percent (p. 389). When surveying the general public, the response rate can be expected to be even lower.

Researchers have tried many different ways to increase response rates. Monetary rewards have been used on occasion, but these often are not feasible because of the cost. Hopkins and Gullickson (1992), in a meta-analysis of the effects of monetary gratuities on response rates, concluded that a gratuity can enhance the response rate by as much as around 20 percent. The greater the gratuity, the greater the impact, but even a $1.00 gratuity resulted in approximately a 20 percent increase. Enclosed gratuities were much more effective than promised gratuities. The findings held for both general and professional populations, and were consistent regardless of the saliency of the questionnaire content. Gratuities can have a positive impact even in a follow-up mailing (pp. 6–7).

Porter and Whitcomb (2003) studied the impact of entering the respondents to an online survey into a lottery in which they could win a gift certificate for $50, $100, $150, or $200 to Amazon.com. They surveyed over 9000 students from 3500 high schools. There was a dismal response rate of about 15 percent that was similar for all incentive groups. The conclusion was that the incentives were not effective with this group of students.

It would stand to reason that an attractive, professional-looking questionnaire enhances response. Indeed, in a survey by Clark and Boser (1989) of experts in survey research, over 80 percent indicated high importance of appearance factors. Yet, in a later study by Boser and Clark (1992), focusing on questionnaires mailed to teacher education program graduates, they found factors such as adequate margins and splitting a checklist over two pages were not particularly important to the respondents. However, when expending the effort of putting a questionnaire together, an attractive, professional-looking questionnaire certainly does not reduce the response rate.

Green, Boser, and Hutchinson (1997), in a meta-analysis of over 200 studies about factors that may affect survey response rates, found that the type of population surveyed tends to have an effect. Results indicated that for mail surveys, customers, educators, and students had higher response rates (by as much as one-third) than the general public. Inferred reasons for this result are higher educational levels and possibly more familiarity with forms such as questionnaires. Usually, the content of questionnaires sent to educators is associated with their professional interests and activities, and this relevance is another factor likely to enhance response.

Contacting the respondent prior to mailing the questionnaire is another suggestion for enhancing response. A letter, postcard, or telephone call may be used for the contact. Colton and Kane (1989) conducted a national survey of newly licensed registered nurses. Three groups were used: (1) a control group receiving no prior letter, (2) an experimental group receiving a personalized pre-letter, and (3) an experimental group receiving a nonpersonalized pre-letter. The latter had no inside address and had "Dear Colleague" as the salutation. Otherwise the bodies of the pre-letters were identical. The response for the control group was 51.4 percent, and those for the experimental groups were 63.3 percent and 64.2 percent (p. 4). The group receiving the nonpersonalized letter had the highest response rate. The pre-letters produced higher response rates than the normal mailing alone. This result was consistent with that found by Green et al. (1997), in that precontact tended to have a positive effect. Precontacting respondents is an additional task, but it may be worth considering if a low response rate is anticipated and the size of the sample is manageable for precontacting.

Tollefson, Tracy, and Kaiser (1984) used three time-cue conditions: (1) thirty minutes, (2) fifteen minutes, and (3) no information, for completing a questionnaire that required about twenty-eight minutes for completion in field testing. They found the highest return rate with the thirty-minute cue, which led them to conclude: "While time cues increase the response rates, the time cues need to be matched to the average time required to complete the questionnaire" (p. 9). It can be inferred that individuals will not be tricked by an unrealistic time cue. Although reduced time for completing the questionnaire may increase the return rates, any time cues should be realistic.

Follow-up Procedures. **Follow-ups** are a must for almost all questionnaire surveys, and the follow-up mailing should be timed to arrive at the respondents' addresses a few days after the deadline for return specified in the cover letter. They should be planned for in advance; in some cases, two or more follow-ups may be desirable. The follow-up letter should be pleasant but firm. Jackson and Schuyler (1984) found that fewer responses were received from graduates who received "cute" reminders than from those whose reminders were more businesslike. Again, the follow-up letter should encourage the individual to respond immediately.

> Follow-ups are considered necessary for questionnaire surveys, and they should be planned for in advance.

If financially feasible, a copy of the questionnaire along with a stamped, self-addressed envelope should be included with the follow-up mailing. Sometimes, a postcard reminder can be used effectively, but, if so, it should be sent within a week to ten days of the original mailing. Of course, it is not possible to include another questionnaire with the postcard, and this is a disadvantage. The individual is more likely to respond if a questionnaire is at hand, rather than having to find the one from the original mailing.

There are two approaches to a follow-up: (1) send a letter (or postcard) only to individuals who have not responded, or (2) send a blanket follow-up to everyone. The former approach is much preferred, because it is less expensive and eliminates the possibility of receiving two completed questionnaires from the same person. The latter approach should be used only if the nonrespondents cannot be identified. If the latter approach is used, the individuals must be told not to respond a second time if they have already responded.

Telephone calls, telegrams, or special-delivery letters may also be used for follow-up. However, they are expensive in terms of time and costs and, therefore, are not used extensively. Repeated follow-up mailings can be used, but the percentage gained by repeated follow-ups decreases with each follow-up. Unless response is low or an unusually high response rate is required, repeated follow-ups are not common.

In summary, for enhancing the response rate of mailed questionnaires, the researcher is well advised to construct an attractive, concise questionnaire with an informative cover letter and to provide for timely follow-up. If time cues are given, they should be realistic. A monetary incentive is helpful if this is an option. Of the procedures used to increase the response rate, follow-ups and monetary incentives seem to be the most effective, based on the results of empirical studies.

Identifying Sources of Nonresponse

The difficulty with a high rate of nonresponse is that the data may be biased. Under no circumstances can it simply be assumed that the respondents are a random sample of the original questionnaire recipients. Also, increasing the size of the sample does not counter bias; it only increases the quantity of data.

When the data are biased, they do not represent the group under study. A survey on the need for mathematics teachers, conducted on a statewide basis with the following response, illustrates this point. The central administrations of almost all large school systems responded, but, for some reason, those in small school systems did not return the questionnaire. Therefore, the data on the returned questionnaires indicated an average need for mathematics teachers in excess of the total number of mathematics teachers in most schools throughout the state. Thus, nonresponse can result in a data gap that markedly distorts the real situation. It is very tenuous to assume that nonresponse is randomly distributed throughout the group originally sent questionnaires.

Demographic information can be very useful for identifying possible bias due to nonresponse, and, indeed, frequently demographic items are included specifically for determining sources of nonresponse. The researcher should be able to identify the sources of nonresponse in terms of respondent characteristics that may be related to the variables under study. Do certain subgroups of individuals—for example, men, junior high school teachers, suburban teachers, superintendents of small school systems—have a high nonresponse rate? It generally is not satisfactory to use a questionnaire without having a way of knowing who has returned it. Sources of nonresponse are identified by determining the response rates for categories of demographic variables—for example, secondary teachers versus elementary teachers.

Identifying subgroups with high nonresponse rates does not reveal the feelings of the nonrespondents, but it does identify the nonresponding groups. If nonresponse is associated with a certain type of feeling toward the questionnaire items—that is, nonrespondents have unfavorable attitudes toward them—the sample of responses definitely will be biased, because response and nonresponse are associated with the variables under study. It may be possible to interview a sample of the nonrespondents to acquire information about their characteristics and their reasons for not returning the questionnaire. Checking a sample of nonrespondents involves additional effort, although a sample of twenty-five or so is usually an adequate number.

In some studies, it may be possible to argue that the nonrespondents are neutral in their feelings or disinterested in the issue. If this assumption is tenable, it can be used when interpreting the data, and a higher nonresponse rate would be tolerable before checking with nonrespondents. Such an assumption would more likely be valid when surveying a general public population rather than a professional population.

Nonresponse cannot be ignored, and the researcher must know the sources of the nonresponse. To the extent possible, it is important to determine the reasons for nonresponse.

Incomplete and Possibly Dishonest Responses

Another type of nonresponse is item nonresponse, the failure of the respondent to respond to one or more questionnaire items. Although questionnaire recipients may be directed to respond to all items, there often are some respondents who omit one or more items. An omitted item may not be understood or a respondent may be unsure about the item. If there are just a few omitted items throughout and there does not seem to be any pattern to the omissions, the omissions should cause little difficulty. But, if there are frequent omissions, they merit some checking.

Johnson, Gips, and Rich (1992) have observed that, when respondents are asked to evaluate someone or something, there may be a tendency to omit items more frequently when the evaluation would be less positive than when it would be more positive (p. 1). So, with evaluative items that are frequently omitted, this may be a possibility to be recognized. If open-ended items are frequently omitted, this may be due to respondents simply not wanting to put forth the effort of responding. Or the omissions may be due to some other factor. One way to do an internal check on the responses to other items is to separate the questionnaire into two groups, one with the item answered, the other with it omitted. Then analyze the responses to the other items separately for these two groups. If the results differ, then omitting the item is related to how the respondents responded to the other items.

There is no consistently prescribed method for dealing with omissions. It may be that an item is not easily understood. The researcher should check the extent of omissions and, if it seems noteworthy, look for patterns in the omissions or possible relationships to other variables. For example, if all the omissions of an item were on questionnaires completed by males (gender as one of the demographic information items), this result would be noteworthy.

> Omitted items are a nuisance and, if there seems to be a noteworthy amount of omissions, it is necessary to look for patterns that might explain the cause of omissions. Omissions essentially are nonresponse and may bias the results.

When surveys are conducted about sensitive topics, respondents may be motivated to be less than honest. Drug use is an example of a sensitive topic. Requesting information about any illegal or socially undesirable behavior is always tenuous, but much of this type of information can be obtained only through self-report. Wrona, Sanborn, and Constantine (1992) discussed four methods for identifying dishonest and careless respondents that were surveyed in a student drug-use survey. These four methods were:

1. Impossible response—respondents indicated using a nonexistent drug.
2. Implausible frequency and extent of use.
3. Unlikely response combinations—use of numerous items for inter-item consistency checks.
4. Honesty item—ask the respondent to indicate the extent of honesty in answering the items (pp. 3–4).

A somewhat subjective criterion can be set for excluding a respondent's data. For example, if any one of the four methods identifies a dishonest respondent, the data are excluded. Or if, on an honesty item, a respondent indicates being dishonest, that is quite indicative of dishonest response. Of course, it is undesirable to discard data, but a reduced data set is an improvement over one that contains false information.

For most surveys done as educational research there is probably no reason to believe that the respondents would be dishonest when completing the survey. It is only likely to occur with sensitive issues, or topics such that certain responses reflect badly on the respondents; for example, topics involving behaviors that are against regulations, such as cheating or illegal behaviors. When these topics are addressed, there should be some type of check for dishonest and careless responses.

> There are methods for including an "honesty check" of responses, and one or more of these should be used when addressing sensitive issues in the survey.

Web-Based Surveys

Online surveys are a viable alternative to mailed surveys. Most of the target audiences for **web-based surveys** have access to the Internet. Of course, there are important segments of the population for which an online survey would not be appropriate, and mail or telephone methods would have to be used.

There are advantages for online surveys over mailed questionnaires. The response time can be reduced greatly; the recipient of an online survey can respond immediately on receiving the survey. There is no lag time for mail delivery. There are also no printing and mailing costs. However, there are also disadvantages to online surveys, not the least of which is getting the recipient to recognize the legitimacy of the survey. Assuming that the survey gets through a spam blocker, the recipient still has to recognize the sender or it will be deleted even before it is opened.

Hayslett and Wildemuth (2004) compared the relative effectiveness of web-based versus paper surveys. The researchers compared a paper survey announced and distributed by mail, a web survey announced in advance by mail, and a web survey announced by e-mail. The target audience was comprised of 300 academic reference librarians, a computer-savvy population. Their results were very interesting:

> The "percent usable" response rates were 42.3 percent for the paper survey, 22.9 percent for the web survey with the paper announcement, and 33.1 percent for the web survey with the e-mail announcement. (p. 85)
>
> The average response times were 13.41 days, 6.74 days, and 4.20 days for the same order of groups as above. (p. 86)

The paper survey method had the highest response rate, but the slowest response time. A high response rate is usually more important that a quick response time. The immediacy of getting the information online is usually not important because the data will probably not be analyzed and reported for some time anyway. A ten-day difference between these approaches may not have practical implications. The researchers stated that the hybrid approach of a mailed invitation to a web-based survey was the least effective of the approaches that they used.

Of course, there are many studies of the relative effectiveness of online and paper surveys and the results do vary. In a study by Lee, Frank, Cole, Mikhael, and Miles (2002), in which medical educators were surveyed by e-mail, a 63 percent response rate was attained after four weeks and one blanket follow-up consisting of a short e-mail reminder. Matz (1999) found a 33 percent response rate for a web-based survey and the response rate for the same survey sent as a paper questionnaire was 43 percent. However, in a survey of college students, Mertler and Earley (2003) found a reverse pattern. Those who had received the survey electronically had a response rate of 50 percent, whereas students receiving questionnaires through regular campus mail had a 32 percent response rate. It appears that other factors, such as the importance of the survey content to the recipient, influence response rates more than the method by which the survey is received.

Response rates to web-based surveys vary greatly, and there does not seem to be a consistent advantage in response rates over mailed questionnaires or vice versa.

Montez (2003) conducted a follow-up of nonrespondents to a web-based survey. The original sample consisted of over 400 college deans and they were sent a rather extensive questionnaire about higher education leadership. The response rate was 51 percent, and follow-up e-mails were sent to the nonrespondents. Fifty-five of the nonrespondents sent replies, which gave various reasons for not responding to the survey. These nonrespondents were grouped into five reasons for nonresponding categories:

1. Refused to participate—no specific reason;
2. Refused to participate because of costs to them in time, energy, and resources;
3. Had stepped down from their positions;
4. Choose to answer only surveys from specific organizations or associations;
5. Consciously refused, followed by an explanation of their rationale (pp. 13–14, paraphrased).

As Montez noted, it was still uncertain as to whether these nonresponders were representative of the nonresponding group, because they comprised only about 24 percent of that group. However, these reasons for nonresponse are not unlike reasons for nonresponse when using a mailed questionnaire.

It is difficult to determine specific reasons for nonresponse, but the reasons when conducting web-based surveys likely are similar to those for mailed questionnaires.

Example of an Online Survey. The National Science Foundation provides support to the Advanced Technology Education (ATE) Program to increase the quantity and quality of technicians in strategic advanced technology fields. There are currently over 230 grants that have been awarded to centers and projects, mostly at two-year institutions. Courses, modules, and materials are developed in this program. Teachers are involved in professional development activities and students are enrolled in a wide variety of technical education fields. A part of this initiative is an annual evaluation that has been conducted by the Evaluation Center at Western Michigan University. One component of the evaluation is an online survey that is sent to the directors of the centers and projects to obtain information about their students, educational offerings, products that were developed, collaboration with business and industry, and accomplishments.

The cover page of the online survey is presented in Figure 9.5. This cover letter is shorter than the example that was given for mailed questionnaires because the directors are required to complete the survey by the funding agent, so it can be more direct. A 100 percent response rate is virtually guaranteed. Note that the purpose of the survey and how the

2007 ATE SURVEY
Overview

This survey serves two primary purposes: (1) to provide information about the work of the ATE program and (2) to provide information that will guide possible follow-up studies on specific topics and issues.

Findings from this survey will be used by NSF program staff to prepare their annual reports and make program decisions. ATE projects, centers, and articulation partnerships can use the results of this survey to learn about the activities and findings reported by other ATE grantees and to serve their own information needs. Additional information about the ATE program evaluation, as well as the survey form in pdf and online versions, is available at our Web site at http://ate.wmich.edu.

The survey will be available online in February 2007. The deadline for online and paper survey responses will be March 16, 2007. A complete survey schedule, including reporting dates, will be communicated through our Web site and via e-mail to ATE principal investigators. We will neither report individual survey responses nor attribute any data to a specific respondent. Survey findings and aggregated data across projects and centers will be reported through our Web site, via interactive data displays, and through formal reports to NSF.

We recommend that you review this document before responding so that you will have all the information you need to complete the survey. Any questions regarding this survey should be directed to

Chris L.S. Coryn
ATE Program Evaluation Research Associate
The Evaluation Center, Western Michigan University
269-387-5920
christian.coryn@wmich.edu

Thank you for participating in this survey process.

GENERAL INSTRUCTIONS

1. Sections 1–3 are required for all respondents. These sections address grantee characteristics, organizational practices, and collaborative activities.
2. Sections 4–6 are about materials development, professional development, and program improvement. Only complete those sections where your project or center allocates $100,000 or 30 percent or more of its direct costs to the activity.
3. Focus your responses on the past 12 months only.

FIGURE 9.5 Cover Page for a Web-Based Survey

Source: This material was created as part of Project ATE 07–08, funded by the National Science Foundation, Award #0702981.

information will be used is explained. Details about dates and deadlines are given. Confidentiality of individual responses is promised in the reporting of the results. The general instructions at the bottom of the cover page provide guidance about how to proceed.

A sample item from the 2007 ATE survey is found in Figure 9.6. The focus of the question is on the evaluation data that the project or center used to evaluate its local program. It is a two-part question in that the directors must first check which type of information that they used and then rate that type of data or practice in terms of its usefulness on a 4-point scale. The programming allows only one rating per row. This item is straightforward and easy to respond to. The results can be tabulated quickly and can be aggregated across different groupings of respondents such as centers and projects or two-year schools and four-year schools.

7. How useful were the following types of evaluative data or practices for that evaluation?

Type of Evaluative Data or Practice	Data or Practice We Gathered or Used	Degree of Usefulness			
	Check (✓) those that apply	Not Useful	Somewhat Useful	Useful	Very Useful
Business and industry input to verify the alignment of materials to industry needs					
Student and industry standards or guidelines					
Review by external experts					
Field test of materials internally (i.e., within your project/center)					
Field test of materials externally (i.e., outside your project/center)					
Assessment of student performance in the classroom (learning effects)					
Assessment of student performance in the workforce (work performance effects)					
Other (describe):					

FIGURE 9.6 Sample Item from a Web-Based Survey

Source: This material was created as part of Project ATE 07–08, funded by the National Science Foundation, Award #0702981.

Factors to Consider when Conducting Web-Based Surveys. Web-based surveys provide a viable method of conducting questionnaire surveys; however, they do have limitations and certain conditions will enhance their validity and, correspondingly, their usefulness. Factors to consider include:

1. All members of the population must have e-mail addresses, computer access, and adequate computer skills to respond to the questionnaire. Any population members not having e-mail addresses are excluded from the sample.
2. Due to (1) above, web-based surveys work best with limited, specialized populations that are known to have e-mail addresses.
3. If e-mail addresses are not available, the use of listservs is tenuous, in part because to some extent the population becomes unknown and listservs will not necessarily post the message.
4. Access to the survey should be simple and recipients must be directed to the uniform resource locator (URL). This can be done through e-mail or through a cover letter (Mertler and Earley, 2003, p. 5).
5. As with all questionnaire surveys, one or more follow-ups should be planned and conducted with appropriate time intervals.

There are some guidelines that are specific to web-based surveys that have been written by Dillman (2000). Some of these are listed here to show how they relate to mail surveys, yet how they differ with regard to technical considerations.

Principle 11.10	Introduce the Web questionnaire with a welcome screen that is motivational.
Principle 11.11	Provide a PIN number for limiting access only to people in the sample.
Principle 11.12	Choose for the first question an item that is likely to be interesting to most respondents, easily answered, and fully visible on the welcome screen of the questionnaire.
Principle 11.13	Present each question in a conventional format similar to that used on paper self-administered questionnaires.
Principle 11.14	Restrain the use of color so that figure/ground consistency and readability are maintained, navigational flow is unimpeded, and measurement properties of questions are maintained.
Principle 11.15	Avoid differences in the visual appearance of questions that result from different screen configurations, operating systems, browsers, partial screen displays, and wraparound text.

In summary, web-based surveys have advantages of efficiency over mailed questionnaires when they can be adequately conducted. Web-based surveys are efficient in costs, time, and data transfer. However, there are other factors than how the survey is conducted that seem to have more impact on the response rate. Web-based surveys have their limitations and these should be recognized whenever such a survey is contemplated.

Interview Surveys

Questionnaire surveys are relatively inexpensive for reaching a substantial number of people, but they have some disadvantages associated with nonresponse, and occasionally with careless response. The interview is an effective method of conducting a survey, and the use of an interview has the following advantages over use of a questionnaire:

1. If the interview is granted, there is no problem with nonresponse.
2. The interview provides opportunity for in-depth probing, and elaboration and clarification of terms, if necessary.
3. Completion of the survey can be standardized.
4. There tends to be more success with obtaining responses to open-ended items.
5. It is easier to avoid the omission of items.
6. Interviews can be used with individuals from whom data cannot otherwise be obtained.

With regard to (6) above, collecting information from educationally disadvantaged adults might require an interview, because such persons might lack the motivation to respond to a questionnaire, even if the items were written in an understandable manner.

However, interviews are costly in terms of time and effort. Within recent years, telephone interviewing has received increased usage as a replacement for face-to-face interviews. Telephone interviews typically reduce the cost of the survey, and they have other advantages over face-to-face interviews, as identified later. Interviews must be scheduled if they are face-to-face, because they involve an interchange between two people. Even with telephone interviews, unless the interviews are very brief, it is a good idea to schedule them in advance.

> The use of interviews has some advantages over the use of questionnaires, but interviews are costly in terms of time and effort.

Interview Items

Interview items, like questionnaire items, can be selected-response or open-ended format, and they can vary in the extent of structure. However, unstructured items would more likely be used in an interview than a questionnaire. The reason for this is that unstructured items leave much more interpretation to the respondent. In an interview, this interpretation can be somewhat controlled and directed, but with a questionnaire such direction is not possible. Generally, all respondents in an interview survey are asked the same set of questions. Wording could vary slightly to accommodate different respondents—for example, if students, teachers, and principals were being interviewed in the same survey. A variety of item formats can be used in the same interview, and the interviewer has control over switching formats so there should be no confusion.

Whether items require an open-ended response or a selected response, they should be clearly stated in complete question form, with unambiguous terms that are meaningful to the respondent. Also, terms should have consistent meaning across respondents. The item should give the respondent adequate direction. Sometimes, optional wording or optional probes are given with items, but these should be used with caution. Consider the following open-ended item:

> What do you like best about the schools in this district?

If the respondent hesitates, an optional probe might be given, such as:

> We are interested in things such as the facilities, the quality of instruction, the schedule, the administration, whatever.

If this optional probe is used, those respondents who hesitate are answering a somewhat different question than those who do not receive the optional wording. At least, those who hesitate would be given more structure through the cues. A better approach would be to provide the same amount of structure for all respondents, such as:

> Of the following, which do you feel are strong points of the schools in this district?
>
> **a.** quality of instruction
> **b.** facilities
> **c.** schedule
> **d.** central office administration
> **e.** school (building) administration

Respondents could be invited to list others after the structured list is exhausted.

One of the most comprehensive surveys in education is the annual Phi Delta Kappa/Gallup Poll of the Public's Attitudes Toward the Public Schools. The results of the survey are reported each year in the September or October issue of the *Phi Delta Kappan*. Presently, telephone interviews are used, conducted in all areas of the United States and in all types of communities, during the spring of the year. National samples range from about 1000 to 1600 adults.

The items of the survey focus on the public's perceptions of the job the schools are doing. The items cover not only school performance in providing effective learning experiences but also issues such as promoting understanding and tolerance among students of different racial and ethnic backgrounds. The interview items are quite structured and the results are typically reported as percentages for the various response options. Some items are repeated in selected years, providing a pattern for the responses across the years. Americans are asked yearly to rate the public schools on a scale from A to F.

The Phi Delta Kappa/Gallup Poll provides a great deal of information about the public's perceptions of educational issues. Phi Delta Kappa will allow school districts to use items in local school or community surveys if desired. In this way, comparisons can be made between local and national results. The Phi Delta Kappa Center for Professional

Development and Services makes available materials on conducting polls of attitude and opinion on education.

Conducting the Interview

As with any data-collection process, there must be preparation for conducting the interview. Interviewers must be trained in the procedures for conducting the specific interview, and these procedures must be "standardized" so that the respondents receive as consistent and identical interviews as possible. Because interviewing is demanding of time, unless a survey is very limited, multiple interviewers are used. They need to be trained, and they may need special knowledge for the survey. As with a questionnaire, the interview should be pretested and items revised until they are satisfactory. Interviewers require practice until the interviews are consistent across and within interviewers.

> Training the interviewer is a necessity. When two or more interviewers are used, the consistency in conducting the interview must be checked. In any event, an interviewee's responses should not be the function of the specific interviewer.

To schedule the interview, a mutually convenient time for the potential respondent and the interviewer must be identified. Interviewers should have flexible schedules so they are available at times convenient for the respondents. For example, if those surveyed are not available during the day, it is necessary to concentrate on evenings and weekends for the interviews.

After the interview is scheduled or initiated, it is necessary to obtain the respondent's cooperation. An advance letter informing the respondent about the study can be effective in obtaining cooperation. Such a letter is not only informative but it can also reassure respondents, especially those who are concerned about their personal safety when admitting a stranger. The respondents should be informed about the purposes of the study and the importance of their contributions. Respondents should not be threatened by the interview or the subsequent use of the data. Making the respondent informed and comfortable about the interview does much to enhance cooperation.

Because the interview is a social encounter, it is important that the interviewer establish a good rapport with the respondent. The approach should be businesslike and efficient, friendly but not "chummy." Confidentiality of information should be assured, and the respondent should not be threatened by the questions. The interviewer must know the extent of probing desirable and the extent of elaboration allowed if the respondent has questions. Digressions should be avoided unless they relate directly to the items and are a part of probing for information.

The data-recording procedures used in the interview should be efficiently structured so that they do not interfere with the process of conducting the interview. A tape recorder can retain the entire oral communication, but the interviewer should get the respondent's consent before using one. If taping an interview is not practical or feasible, shorthand records of the interview must be developed. Structured questions may require only a check mark indicating one of several alternative responses, whereas responses to unstructured questions must be recorded briefly but completely, covering all main points. The recording of data should be as inconspicuous as possible and should not arouse suspicions in the respondent; for example, if a short response is given, the interviewer should not engage in extensive writing.

An aid for data recording is the laptop computer. Interviewers capable in its use can record the responses in an unobtrusive manner about as fast as they are given. For the most part, laptops are no more disruptive than interviewer writing and they can provide a complete record of the responses.

> The interview should be structured to obtain the necessary information efficiently in a friendly but businesslike atmosphere. If possible, there should be some accuracy checks on the responses.

Potential Sources of Error

Although the interview is well suited to probing the feelings and perceptions of the individual, the items of the interview itself do not ensure accurate measurement of those feelings. The individual must be able and willing to respond accurately with adequate oral expression; difficulties arise if the individual does not have the information necessary to answer the question or if there is an uneasy feeling about divulging the information. A tendency of the respondent to give inaccurate or incorrect information is called *response effect.* If a response effect exists, it is the difference between the actual response and the true response. The interviewer must be able to recognize misunderstanding and uneasiness and make on-the-spot decisions about any additional probing that may be desirable.

There are potential sources of error when collecting interview data. One of these is the predisposition of the respondent to respond in a certain way, in essence producing a response effect. The respondent may lack motivation to respond, be threatened by the interview, or respond in a way perceived to put himself or herself in the best light. A respondent may give what is perceived to be a socially or professionally preferred response, regardless of his or her true feeling. There is no methodological technique that can ensure the accuracy of the data, but it may be possible to enhance truthful responses and to construct somewhat crude checks. The interviewer must be careful not to imply that there are preferable responses, and controversial questions should be avoided until the proper background and rapport have been established. In the context of the interview, the interviewer may form an opinion about whether the respondent is telling the truth, and it may be possible to construct questions that check on the consistency of responses. In so doing, the interview contains questions that ask essentially the same information, but in somewhat different form or wording, and appear at different points in the interview.

Another possible source of error is the predisposition of the interviewer toward the interviewee. Negative examples are if interviewers are ill at ease in the situation, talk down to the respondent, fail to establish rapport, or have stereotyped the interviewees. Interviewers should be selected carefully to avoid predispositions. To the extent possible, interviewers and interviewees should be matched on variables that may affect responses. For example, if the questions are such that responding to an interviewer of the opposite sex will inhibit response, then make sure that interviewer and interviewee are of the same sex.

Another possible source of error is associated with the procedures used in conducting the interview. There may be inconsistency across interviews. If the interview is too long the respondent may become bored or fatigued. The maximum length for an interview depends on the characteristics of the respondent and the intensity of interest in the interview items. A professional respondent can be interviewed for a longer period than someone from the general public. Generally, other people should not be present while the interview is being conducted. The location of the interview should be convenient and comfortable for both interviewer and respondent.

> There are a number of possible sources of error in interview data: response effect of the interviewee, predispositions of the interviewee, and inconsistent or unfavorable procedures when conducting the interview.

Telephone Interviews[3]

As mentioned earlier, the telephone has received increased use in survey research within recent years, and when appropriate, it can be used effectively. The big advantage of **telephone interviews** over face-to-face interviews is cost—they are only about one-half to one-third as expensive. Generally, the lack of a telephone by potential respondents is no longer a problem (households in some rural areas might be an exception), and it certainly is not a problem with populations of professional respondents. However, in surveying some populations, unlisted numbers may be a problem. Sudman (1981) found that cooperation rates are about the same for telephone and face-to-face interviews, with possibly a slightly higher refusal rate for telephone than for face-to-face interviews. However, the telephone is more effective in locating hard-to-reach respondents. Quite often, professional respondents such as school personnel (teachers, principals, superintendents) are more accessible by telephone than by personal visits.

Telephone interviewing has other advantages over face-to face interviews:

1. Respondents can be sampled from a greater accessible population because travel time to individual respondents is eliminated.
2. Data collection can be centralized, and automatic data entry may be possible.
3. With the central data-collection facility, monitoring for quality control is easier.
4. Data collection and data processing can be done with greater speed.
5. If in-home interviews are conducted, some potential respondents may be threatened by a visit from a stranger, whereas a telephone call would not be threatening.
6. If there is no answer to the call, much less time is lost than if a potential respondent does not keep an interview appointment.

Face-to-face interviews provide greater flexibility in conducting the interview and they can accommodate more complexity and length than telephone interviews. Most interviewees will tire of a telephone interview after twenty-five minutes or so, whereas face-to-face interviews can go longer without fatigue, even up to forty-five minutes to an hour. Visual cues, such as graphs and pictures, can be used in face-to-face interviews. However, if the study requires respondents to react to some written material, this can be accommodated in a telephone interview by first sending the material to the respondent and then obtaining responses by telephone. Surveys that require such materials are seldom used with the general public; they are more applicable to populations of specialized professionals. Even then the researcher runs the risk that the interviewee has not received the necessary materials, or has not reviewed them.

Consider an example. Suppose a survey is being conducted of the school superintendents in a state. This is a specialized, professional population. A random sample is selected for the interview. Rather than traveling around the state conducting interviews, the superintendents selected for the sample could be sent necessary materials in advance and interviewed by telephone at mutually convenient times. The telephone interview would be less costly than a face-to-face interview.

In summarizing the comparison between telephone interviews and face-to-face interviews, Sudman (1981) concluded:

> Response differences between phone and face-to-face procedures are small and can be ignored for most research applications. Using the appropriate methods and experienced interviewers, initial cooperation is the same on telephone and face-to-face interviews. There may be slightly higher refusal or don't know responses and shorter answers to open-ended questions on the phone because respondent suspicions may be higher while motivations to talk are not as great. (p. 8)

Thus, telephone interviews are certainly worth considering as an alternative to face-to-face interviews. They may not be quite as effective with sensitive or controversial questions, but this may be countered by the savings in effort, time, and costs.

> Telephone interviews are less costly than face-to-face interviews. They can be used effectively under conditions that do not require a face-to-face encounter. There is no evidence that cooperation is greatly reduced by the telephone approach.

Summary

A good bit of educational research consists of nonexperimental, quantitative research. This is research in which no variables are manipulated but the research focuses on variables, as they exist in natural situations. Nonexperimental quantitative research is used in a variety of situations to investigate a large number of research problems.

In this chapter we discussed ex post facto research, causal–comparative research, correlational research, and survey research. Practically all nonexperimental quantitative research fits in one or another of these categories, and these categories are not necessarily mutually exclusive. For example, correlation is a statistical analysis and a lot of research studies, surveys, causal–comparative, and so forth, involve computing correlations. In this sense, the title correlational studies is somewhat misleading but it is commonly used in the research literature as a type of research, and it was so identified in this chapter.

A large portion of this chapter was devoted to survey research, an extensively used type of nonexperimental quantitative research. When we think of survey research, we typically think of questionnaires and interviews, although surveys can involve other data-collection methods such as surveys of educational achievement using published tests. Mailed questionnaires are probably used more than interviews because of the time and effort required for conducting interviews. However, telephone interviews have been around for some time and can be effective. Web-based surveys have some advantages over other types of surveys, but they have their limitations and work well only under certain conditions.

Questionnaire surveys have gotten some bad press, partly because questionnaires at times are poorly constructed, and because they are susceptible to excessive nonresponse. A well-designed questionnaire survey requires several steps, from the identification of the research problem to the analysis and interpretation of the data. Careful attention to detail and using procedures to enhance response, especially conducting follow-ups, will do much to overcome the problems of a questionnaire survey.

The interview has an advantage over the questionnaire in that if the interview is granted and if the interviewer is adequately skilled, there should not be any missing or unusable data. Interviews also provide for probing and elaboration, if necessary. But interviews are costly and require the training of interviewers. Interviews must be consistent between interviewers, sometimes called interrater reliability, and within themselves. The latter is called intrarater reliability, and it is the extent to which an interviewer is consistent as he or she conducts two or more interviews. Pilot studies should be done before finalizing the items of either a questionnaire or an interview.

Survey designs were discussed; there are basically two types, longitudinal and cross-sectional. In longitudinal surveys, data are collected at two or more points over a period of time from the populations being studied. Trend, cohort, and panel designs are variations on the longitudinal survey, depending on the population studied. Cross-sectional surveys involve data collection at only one point in time, usually from two or more populations or subpopulations.

The successful completion of a survey is not a simple task. Several possible pitfalls and problems can sabotage the survey. One common problem is the failure to allow enough time and resources for the various steps. The sampling procedure can break down, or there may not be enough resources to test and revise the items adequately. The items of the interview or questionnaire may be poorly constructed, resulting in unusable data. Failure to provide for follow-ups is a very obvious but common difficulty, and inadequate procedures for assembling and tabulating the data as the questionnaires are returned are often sources of inefficiency and confusion. Failure to consider nonrespondents may bias the results and lead to unwarranted generalizations. Finally, if the researcher reports results as separate, isolated analyses without some synthesis, it is likely that the maximum information is not being obtained from the survey. Careful planning is essential for a successful survey; although such planning will not guarantee success, it will go a long way toward attaining this goal.

KEY CONCEPTS

Ex post facto research
Casual–comparative research
Correlational research
Survey research
Survey designs
Census
Longitudinal designs
Trend study
Cohort study
Panel study
Cross-sectional designs
Interrater reliability
Intrarater reliability
Community surveys
Leading questions
Selected-response items
Open-ended items
Pilot run
Cover letter
Response rate
Follow-ups
Web-based surveys
Telephone interviews

EXERCISES

9.1 A study of the effects of class size was conducted as a longitudinal study in Tennessee and the findings are reviewed by Pate-Bain, Achilles, Boyd-Zaharias, and McKenna (1992). The study was ex post facto in nature and included seventy-two schools throughout Tennessee. Of course, the independent variable of primary interest was class size. Without reading the report, identify possible additional independent variables and dependent variables. What is the value of conducting a study on class size as a longitudinal study? (Actually, the Tennessee study was a four-year study.) How often would data be collected on the dependent variables you identified? After completing this exercise it may be useful to compare your conceptualizations of a study with what was done in the Tennessee study.

9.2 In a liberal arts college of approximately 6000 undergraduate students, a study of student attitudes toward the general education requirement is to be conducted. The researcher is also interested in the change of attitude throughout students' college careers. One approach would be to design a longitudinal study, beginning with the present freshman class and surveying a sample of this population at four annual points. Another approach would be to use a cross-sectional design, selecting random samples from the four undergraduate class populations and surveying them at one point in time. Discuss the merits and disadvantages of the two types of designs.

9.3 Suppose that for the study of Exercise 9.2 it is decided to do a longitudinal study beginning with the freshman class. Describe how the survey would be done as a cohort study and as a panel study. Compare the advantages and disadvantages of doing the survey as a cohort study versus a panel study.

9.4 An educational products publishing firm is conducting a five-year longitudinal survey of teacher opinion and use of its products. The survey is conducted in a large city system, and a random sample of teachers is selected to serve as a panel for a panel study. Data will be collected from the panel every six months. What is to be gained by using a panel study as the longitudinal design? Discuss some disadvantages and potential difficulties of this panel study.

9.5 The director of institutional research at a college is concerned about the reasons undergraduates drop out before graduation. Each student who drops out is sent a questionnaire as soon as it is known that he or she is not returning. Construct items that might be used in this questionnaire. Would you use selected-response or open-ended items? Is nonresponse likely to be a problem? Why or why not? Suggest possible ways of following up on nonrespondents.

9.6 The department of guidance and counseling in a state department of education is planning to survey the state's secondary guidance counselors in an attempt to determine their specific professional duties and the time spent weekly on each duty. A random sample of guidance counselors will receive the three-page questionnaire by mail. Prepare a cover letter for this questionnaire. Whose signature (the position, not the individual) would you suggest for the cover letter?

9.7 Suppose that, for the survey in Exercise 9.6, a random sample of one hundred guidance counselors were selected. Under what conditions would it be possible to conduct the survey by telephone? What would be the advantages of doing the survey by telephone? What would be the disadvantages?

9.8 A proficiency testing program is legislated and implemented in the schools of a state. The program provides standards of achievement for the advancement through the high school grades, and finally for graduation from high school. Proficiency must be demonstrated in selected academic subjects. A survey is to be conducted of educator perceptions and opinions about the program. There are different types of educators (teachers, principals, etc.) in the schools. A questionnaire is to be sent to a random sample of educators. Construct six or so items for the questionnaire to determine the extent of knowledge about, and acceptance of, the program. Identify possible dependent variables and independent variables, in addition to the type of educator. What comparisons among groups identified by independent variables might prove useful for policy decisions about the program?

9.9 For the survey suggested in Exercise 9.8, discuss provisions that might be made before sending the questionnaire for identifying sources of nonresponse. In this situation, what factor(s) might encourage educators to respond to the questionnaire? (Do not suggest a gratuity.)

9.10 A local school board wants to conduct a community survey of perceptions of the schools, especially as related to the curriculum, grades 5–12, and the policies of the board relative to student issues such as the dress code. Develop ten or so items appropriate for a questionnaire survey. Would you suggest selected-response or open-ended items? Who (position, not the individual) would you have sign the cover letter for the survey?

9.11 The parents of the students in a single school are to be surveyed about their opinions of a new grading system and report card. Under what conditions would you suggest a longitudinal design over a cross-sectional design, and vice versa? Assume that the school has about 350 students. Would you suggest selecting a random sample of parents or surveying the entire parent population? Why?

9.12 A health educator is designing a survey to determine the eating habits of the high school student population in a city school system that has six high schools. Eating habits deal with factors such as what students eat and drink, and when they do so. Why would this be a difficult study to conduct as a questionnaire survey? Suppose it is decided to use an interview and a random sample of students will be interviewed. Develop three or four example questions for the interview. How would you check on the possibility of careless or dishonest response? Is such response likely to be a problem? If so, why? If not, why not?

9.13 Suppose the teacher certification and licensure division of a state department of education is conducting a statewide survey of teacher evaluation practices throughout the state. There are about 600 school districts throughout the state ranging from large city to quite small, consolidated rural districts. A questionnaire is to be sent to each district. To whom would the questionnaire be sent and what might be done to enhance the response rate? It would be desirable to use selected-response items to the extent possible. Develop five or six items appropriate for this survey.

9.14 Locate an article describing a causal–comparative research study. Identify the research problem and the procedures that comprise the survey part of the study.

9.15 Repeat Exercise 9.14 for a correlational research study.

9.16 The 38th Annual Phi Delta Kappa/Gallup Poll of the Public's Attitudes Toward the Public Schools, as reported in the *Phi Delta Kappan* (September 2006), contained several questions related to the No Child Left Behind (NCLB) Act. As an exercise, review the results relative to these questions and from them draw your conclusions and compare them to those of the report authors. Are there inconsistencies between your conclusions and those of the authors, and, if so, can they be resolved?

9.17 In a correlational study linking school and home factors of fourth-grade children, it was found that the number of books in the child's room was positively correlated with the child's standardized reading test scores.

a. What other variables might account for this correlation?

b. Can we conclude with confidence that increasing the number of books in the children's bedrooms will result in higher reading test scores? Why?

9.18 Contrast experimental research with nonexperimental research in terms of strength of causal conclusions, intrusiveness of the researcher, breadth of researchable topics, and the typical number of subjects included in the analysis.

NOTES

1. Many variations on random sampling and sampling designs are discussed in Chapter 14.
2. AEL, Inc., is a federally funded, regional educational laboratory. AEL is located in Charleston, West Virginia, and serves the four-state region of Kentucky, Tennessee, Virginia, and West Virginia.
3. Many survey or polling agencies now use computer-assisted telephone interviewing (CATI) with sophisticated equipment. However, unless someone specifically is in the survey research business, CATI is not likely to be a feasible option.

REFERENCES

Boser, J. A., and Clark, S. B. (1992). *Desirable mail questionnaire characteristics in teacher education research.* Paper presented at the annual meeting of the American Educational Research Association, San Francisco.

Bures, E. M., Amundsen, C. C., and Abrami, P. C. (2002). Motivation to learn via computer conferencing: Exploring how task-specific motivation and CC expectations are related to student acceptance of learning via CC. *Journal of Educational Computing Research, 27* (3), 249–264.

Clark, S. B., and Boser, J. A. (1989). *Seeking consensus on empirical characteristics of effective mail questionnaires: A first step.* Paper presented at the annual meeting of the American Educational Research Association, San Francisco.

Coker, D. (2006). Impact of first-grade factors on the growth and outcomes of urban schoolchildren's primary grade writing. *Journal of Educational Psychology, 98,* 471–488.

Colton, D. A., and Kane, M. T. (1989). *The effect of preletters on survey study response rates.* Paper presented at the annual meeting of the American Educational Research Association, San Francisco.

Daniel, S. S., Walsh, A. K., Goldston, D. B., Arnold, E. M., Reboussin, B. A., and Wood, F. W. (2006). Suicidality, school dropout, and reading problems among adolescents. *Journal of Learning Disabilities, 39,* 507–514.

Dillman, D. (2000). *Mail and Internet surveys: The tailored design method.* New York: John Wiley.

Evaluation Center. (1998). *FY 97 report: External evaluation of the Appalachia Educational Laboratory.* Kalamazoo, MI: Western Michigan University.

Evaluation Center. (2007). *2007 ATE Survey.* Kalamazoo, MI: Western Michigan University.

Green, K. E., Boser, J. A., and Hutchinson, S. R. (1997). *Effects of population type on mail survey response rates and on the efficacy of response enhancers.* Paper presented at the annual meeting of the American Educational Association, Chicago.

Hayslett, M. H., and Wildemuth, B. M. (2004). Pixels or pencils? The relative effectiveness of Web-based versus paper surveys. *Library and Information Science Research, 26,* 73–93.

Hopkins, K. D., and Gullickson, A. R. (1992). *Response rates in survey research: A meta-analysis of the effects of monetary gratuities.* Paper presented at the annual meeting of the American Educational Research Association, San Francisco.

Jackson, E. E., and Schuyler, N. B. (1984). *Practice makes perfect? Skills gained in seven years of questionnaires.* Paper presented at the annual meeting of the American Educational Research Association, New Orleans.

Johnson, G. A., Gips, C. J., and Rich, C. E. (1992). *"If you can't say something nice." Alternatives for dealing with survey item nonresponse.* Paper presented at the annual meeting of the American Educational Research Association, San Francisco.

Krathwohl, D. R. (1993). *Methods of educational and social science research: An integrated approach.* New York: Longman.

Lee, C., Frank, J. R., Cole, G., Mikhael, N. Z., and Miles, C. H. (2002). *Web-based surveys for data gathering from medical educators: An exploration of the efficacy and impact of follow-up reminders.* Paper presented at the annual meeting of the American Educational Research Association, New Orleans.

Matz, C. M. (1999). *Administration of Web versus paper surveys: Mode effects and response rates.* (Masters thesis, University of North Carolina). (ERIC Document Reproduction Service No. ED/ 439694).

Mertler, C. A., and Earley, M. A. (2003). *A comparison of the psychometric qualities of surveys administered by Web and traditional methods.* Paper presented at the annual meeting of the American Educational Research Association, Chicago.

Moe, T. M. (2002, April). Biased questions in Phi Delta Kappan/Gallup Poll stack the deck against vouchers. Hoover Institution Online. Retrieved October 12, 2007, from www.hoover.org/publications/ednext/pastissues

Montez, J. (2003). *Web surveys as a source of nonresponse explication.* Paper presented at the annual meeting of the American Educational Research Association, Chicago.

Pate-Bain, H., Achilles, C. M., Boyd-Zaharias, J., and McKenna, B. (1992). Class size does make a difference. *Phi Delta Kappan, 74,* 253–256.

Porter, S. R., and Whitcomb, M. E. (2003). The impact of lottery incentives on student survey response rates. *Research in Higher Education, 44,* 389–407.

Rose, L. C., and Gallup, A. M. (2006). The 38th annual Phi Delta Kappa/Gallup poll. *Phi Delta Kappan, 87,* 41–53.

Sudman, S. (1981). *Telephone methods in survey research: The state of the art.* Paper presented at the annual meeting of the American Educational Research Association, Los Angeles.

Tollefson, N., Tracy, D. B., and Kaiser, J. (1984). *Improving response rates and response quality in educational survey research.* Paper presented at the annual meeting of the American Educational Research Association, New Orleans.

Tsui, J. M., and Mazzocco, M. M. M. (2007). Effects of math anxiety and perfectionism on timed versus untimed math testing in mathematically gifted sixth graders. *Roeper Review, 29,* Online. Retrieved October 12, 2007, from http://goliath.ecnext.com/coms2/summary_0199-6160675_ITM

Wrona, M., Sanborn, J., and Constantine, N. (1992). *Identifying dishonest and careless survey respondents.* Paper presented at the annual meeting of the American Educational Research Association, San Francisco.

CHAPTER 10 Research Design in Qualitative Research

Just as with quantitative research, there are different methodologies of qualitative research, but there are common research design characteristics across different types of qualitative research. However, it should be noted that research design in qualitative research, when applied in a specific study, is less structured and generally considered to be more flexible than research design in quantitative research. This has nothing to do with whether designs are good or bad, or whether some are better than others. Research designs differ because of the context, purpose, and nature of the research.

The Epistemology of Qualitative Research

Before discussing the components of qualitative research design, it is useful to consider the epistemology of qualitative research. **Epistemology** is defined as a branch of philosophy that investigates the origin, methods, and limits of human knowledge. Essentially, when we are talking about the epistemology of qualitative research we mean underlying assumptions and basic ideas of how research is conducted. When being introduced to research methods there is a strong tendency to focus on techniques and procedures for getting the research done. This is fine, but it is important to realize that qualitative research is more than techniques; it is an approach to research that has somewhat different underpinnings than quantitative research.

Extensive descriptions can be written, and in fact are written, about the underlying epistemology of qualitative research (see for example, Lancy, 1993). For the purposes of this discussion, the major points can be summarized as follows:

1. Phenomena should be viewed holistically, and complex phenomena cannot be reduced to a few factors or partitioned into independent parts.

2. The researcher operates in a natural setting because of the concern for context and, to the extent possible, should maintain an openness about what will be observed, collected, etc., in order to avoid missing something important. This results in a flexibility in design and even the possibility of an evolving design as the research proceeds.

3. It is the perceptions of those being studied that are important, and, to the extent possible, these perceptions are to be captured in order to obtain an accurate "measure" of reality.

"Meaning" is as perceived or experienced by those being studied; it is not imposed by the researcher.

4. A priori assumptions, and certainly a priori conclusions, are to be avoided in favor of post hoc conclusions. Assumptions and conclusions are subject to change as the research proceeds.

5. Phenomena in the world are perceived as a somewhat loosely constructed model, one in which there is flexibility in prediction, for example, and one that is not run in a mechanistic manner according to a set of laws.

Of course, the points above could be elaborated, and their listing is somewhat repetitive with the discussion of qualitative research in Chapter 1. But the important point is that, regardless of the specific techniques used, qualitative research has its set of underlying assumptions, its perspectives, its epistemology, if you will.

> The epistemology of qualitative research provides the underpinnings for how qualitative research is conducted—how data are collected and analyzed and how conclusions are reached.

Educational research draws its content and methods from a variety of disciplines and traditions. We typically associate qualitative research with historical research and field-based research such as anthropology, and ethnography, which is associated with anthropology. We often think of qualitative research as some type of unified, single approach to conducting research, but, as Jacob (1987) in his review of qualitative research traditions points out, there are diverse traditions, which may be considered subdisciplines, within qualitative research. Although there is commonality across these traditions there are some differences, influenced by the purposes of the research. For the purposes of this discussion it is not necessary to categorize and describe the different subdisciplines; different writers will use differing category systems anyway. However, it is useful to define two of Jacob's (1987) identified traditions to illustrate the point about diversity. Ecological psychology and holistic ethnography are considered below.

Ecological psychology is sort of the natural history component of psychology. It focuses on naturally occurring human behavior and relationships between human behavior and the environment (Schoggen, 1978, p. 33). The individual and the environment are viewed by ecological psychologists as having both subjective and objective components. Thus, in producing detailed descriptions of naturally occurring behavior, ecological psychologists are very willing to conduct quantitative analyses along with the more subjective, qualitative analyses.

Jacob (1987) describes what holistic ethnographers do as:

> Holistic ethnographers seek to describe and analyze all or part of a culture or community by describing the beliefs and practices of the group studied and showing how the various parts contribute to the culture as a unified, consistent whole. (p. 10)

Culture is defined in different ways but in a broad sense refers to what humans have learned that impacts on behavior. The various parts of a culture are assumed to be interdependent. The cultures of bounded groups are studied by **holistic ethnographers.** In educational research, bounded groups might be groups of specified students or teachers, for example.

> Although qualitative research is viewed as a general approach based on its epistemology, we can identify traditions or subdisciplines that have some inherent differences related primarily to the purposes of the research.

Components of Research Design

Although there are different subdisciplines contained within qualitative research, for the purposes of this chapter, general components of qualitative research can be described. It should be kept in mind, however, that the extent to which these components apply will vary across specific research situations.

Qualitative researchers, for the most part, do research in natural settings; they do not manipulate or intervene (except possibly by their presence) in the situation. Therefore, research design requires flexibility and a tolerance for adjustment as the research progresses. Smith and Glass (1987, p. 259) refer to this as a **working design,** similar to what McMillan and Schumacher (1997, p. 393) call an **emergent design.** From the identification of the research problem, decisions must be made about beginning the study. Although the working design runs through the entire study, the components can be separated for discussion purposes, even though there is considerable overlap and integration of the research activities.

Working Design

The working design is the preliminary plan that begins the research. Decisions are made about the subjects or sites to be studied, the length of time for data collection, and possible variables to be considered. For example, an example research problem dealing with dropouts was stated as:

> An ethnographic study of the school environment of regular and learning disabled students to determine factors related to potential dropout.

In order to pursue the research, the specific schools involved must be identified. These schools will not be selected randomly but because of their characteristics and availability. The schools are selected because they are considered typical of schools with high and average dropout rates. This is an example of *purposeful* (also called *purposive*) *sampling*, which means that the units, in this case the two schools, are selected because of their characteristics relative to the phenomenon under study, rather than being selected randomly. Decisions also would be made about whom to interview or observe, for example, students, teachers, and guidance counselors. Is the study going to require a couple of months, six months, or a school year? At least a preliminary decision needs to be made about the length of the study. Some adjustment may need to be made later, but, based on the review of the literature and background information on the problem, a good estimate should be made.

> The *working design* is a preliminary plan for getting the research under way.

Working Hypotheses

Qualitative research uses inductive inquiry, which for data collection means that it commences without any preconceived theories or hypotheses. However, all researchers are influenced by their own backgrounds, and some information is likely to be available about the research problems. Earlier the concept of foreshadowed problems was introduced. Although technically these are not hypotheses statements, foreshadowed problems come in at this point. Questions about the research problem may be introduced. There may be numerous questions, hypotheses, and **foreshadowed problems,** which may be reviewed, deleted, or extended as the data collection and analysis proceed.

Example working hypotheses from a study of dropouts might be:

> As counseling sessions begin earlier and are more direct, the dropout rate decreases. What is the role of the faculty in attempting to reduce the dropout? (question form) Interaction of school administration and students. (foreshadowed problem)

Grounded Theory. An important characteristic of qualitative research is that it is emergent. This means that if the theory emerges from the data it is **grounded theory,** instead of being posed in advance and subjected to hypothesis testing for verification. The researcher's task is to understand the situation, the actors, and the interpersonal dynamics, and this is done through a series of overlapping steps. Key elements are (1) gathering data from observations, conversations, and documents; (2) note taking to capture the issues; (3) constant comparison of issues from different sources of information; (4) identifying codes or categories of themes or ideas embedded in the information; (5) writing memos to yourself about linkages among codes; (6) sorting the information, codes, and memos to clarify the theory; and (7) writing up the results in a way that clearly communicates the theory that has emerged.

The actual process is not that sequential. There is considerable back and forth among the first six steps. There are categories and subcategories. There are issues concerning how much and what kinds of information to gather and when to stop gathering data. To do each of the steps well is a large undertaking requiring skills such as keen perception, effective listening, interpersonal rapport, and organization. The result is a theory of what is happening in the situation that is based on local information and experience.

Data Collection

When preparing for data collection and during actual data collection the qualitative researcher deals with a host of issues, especially if data collection is done in a present situation such as with ethnographic research. The researcher must gain access to the situation, which may require special arrangements. If a researcher is conducting a study in her or his own institution, access may be automatic and data collection can be quite unobtrusive. However, for most situations the researcher needs to gain access more formally and decide on a particular role: Will the researcher be a participant–observer or simply an observer?

Data collection may be interactive or noninteractive, and these terms are what their names imply; interactive techniques involve the researcher interacting with subjects who are being studied, noninteractive techniques lack such interaction. Among the numerous methods of data collection, those most commonly used include observation, interview, collection and review of related documents, taking specimen records, and taking oral histories. Conducting an interview is an example of an interactive data-collection technique. Reviewing historical documents is a noninteractive technique.

In the dropout example, the researchers might engage in the following data-collection activities, although data collection certainly would not be limited to these.

1. Interview students and faculty, including guidance counselors.
2. Observe the interaction taking place between students and between students and faculty.
3. Review school records relative to factors such as grading patterns.
4. If in any way available, interview recent dropouts.

The data record of a qualitative research study can become quite massive with all the interview and observation protocols, document information, and so on. As recommended by some authors (Bogdan and Biklen, 2003), researchers should keep written accounts of their own thoughts about the data being collected. These accounts might include any possible personal bias, changes in the working design, and new hypotheses that are suggested by the data. As Smith and Glass (1987, p. 270) point out, a data record of 1000 pages or more is not unusual. Multiple copies may be useful as the researcher uses one for a chronological record and another for analysis, for example.

> Methods of data collection are interactive or noninteractive depending on whether or not the researcher interacts with the subjects being studied. Observation, interview, and document collection and review are commonly used methods, and taking specimen records and oral histories are possible methods of data collection in qualitative research.

A comment about specimen records and oral histories is in order because these are not as familiar as observation, interview, and document collection. Schoggen (1978) defines a **specimen record** as:

> A narrative description of one person, usually a child, in a natural, noncontrived situation as seen by skilled observers over a substantial time period. (p. 43)

The first task is to record the stream of behavior; then the stream is divided into units and the units analyzed. To some extent, taking a specimen record is a special case of observation because the behavior is recorded though observation. Specimen records are most commonly used in ecological psychology, although they also apply to other qualitative research such as ethnographic studies.

Oral histories typically are interviews taken through the use of a tape recorder. This method eliminates the need for interviewer note taking, and it records the entire conversation. To the extent that any inflections in the comments and subject characteristics come through on a tape recording, these also are captured. Oral histories emphasize open-ended questions allowing the subject wide latitude in providing information. The most effective method of analyzing the interview, and certainly the most efficient, is to listen to the tape rather than to transcribe it.

Data Analysis and Interpretation

Data analysis in qualitative research begins soon after data collection begins, because the researcher checks on working hypotheses, unanticipated results, and the like. In fact, data collection and data analysis usually run together; less data are collected and more analysis is produced as the research progresses. There is considerable overlap of these steps in practice. For example, Moscovici (2003) studied the dynamics of power relations in the schools from information she obtained from people learning to be secondary science teachers in an emergency permit program. Her data consisted of over ninety students' written assignments on the power relationships in their schools, over seventy-five portfolio entries, and responses to over thirty semiformal interviews and fifty informal discussions regarding power relations. The patterns that were developed (working hypotheses) were verified by participants and by people who were not part of the study. Assertions from different sources and from different data-collection methods were contrasted. There were also instances when different participants made observations regarding the same principals, secretaries, parents, and superintendents, which allowed for convergence and contrasts. Tentative findings were presented at various stages of the research in order to get reactions and comments that helped to structure the next steps in the research process.

Qualitative data analysis requires organization of information and data reduction. The data may suggest categories for characterizing information. Comparisons can be made with initial theories or working hypotheses. Early data collection might suggest a hypothesis or theory, and then more data might be collected to support, disconfirm, or extend the hypothesis or theory. Initial descriptions of causes and consequences may be developed. Possible internal and external checks are made. All in all, analysis in qualitative research is a process of successive approximations toward an accurate description and interpretation of the phenomenon. The report of the research is descriptive in nature and contains little technical language. The emphasis is on describing the phenomenon in its context and, on that basis, interpreting the data.

Coding

Qualitative research often produces large quantities of descriptive information from field notes or interviews, for example. The information needs to be organized, and through this organization there should be data reduction. This process is called **coding.** It may be possible in some studies to construct coding categories prior to data review, but more commonly the specific categories emerge from the data. The researcher searches for patterns of thinking or behavior, words or phrases, and events that appear with regularity or for some reason appear noteworthy. The words describing such phenomena become the coding categories. The data analysis of the dropout example would undoubtedly include categorizing the information from several faculty interviews, for example. Faculty likely would have varying perceptions of characteristics of potential dropouts, and faculty may have noted certain behavior patterns, social or academic. If, for example, three or four behavior patterns were evident these could become the categories for coding on behavior of potential dropouts.

> *Coding* is a process of organizing data and obtaining data reduction. In essence, it is the process by which qualitative researchers "see what they have in the data."

Possible Codes. Any number of possible codes may be used, and the coding categories become specific to the research study. The research problem and the purpose of the research influence the particular coding systems. For example, in the dropout study, teachers' perceptions of potential dropout characteristics suggest a basis for coding. Another basis would be potential dropouts' perceptions of school. A third basis would be patterns of potential dropouts' academic performance (behavior) patterns. The coding systems need not be mutually exclusive; in fact, they most likely would not be so. When perception of the subjects about how they perceive the situation is an important factor, as it is in a good bit of qualitative research, coding systems should capture these perceptions. In fact, the perceptions of the subjects about the phenomenon under study is a general code.

Setting or context codes are other general, often useful, codes. As the name implies these codes reflect the context or setting in which the phenomenon under study is observed. In the dropout example, the school environment would fit a setting code and categories might include a vocational school setting, a comprehensive high school setting, and so on. Categories might also include information about factors such as the size of the school.

Another general code, which might be part of subjects' perception codes, is the subjects' perceptions of people or things. In the dropout example, potential dropouts may have different views of their teachers, and these views may differ from those of other students.

Process codes, which focus on the sequence of events and how changes occur, also can be useful. Again in the dropout example, there probably are different ways in which students go about dropping out of school. It would seem reasonable that different sequences of events would precede a learning disabled student dropping out than other students. If these processes exist, they should be captured by the data and their presence can be coded.

The above discussion by no means exhausts the possible general coding systems. The important characteristics of a coding system are (1) the system accurately captures the information in the data relative to what is being coded, and (2) this information is useful in describing and understanding the phenomenon being studied.

> Data analysis in qualitative research is a process of categorization, description, and synthesis. Data reduction is necessary for the description and interpretation of the phenomenon under study.

The components of research design in qualitative research, which coincide closely with conducting the research, can be summarized as in Figure 10.1. It should be emphasized that the steps are highly integrated and interdependent. Qualitative research is very "researcher-dependent." For example, it has been said that for data collection the researcher is the instrument. This means that as data collection is ongoing, and during the entire research process for that matter, the researcher makes decisions about what data to collect,

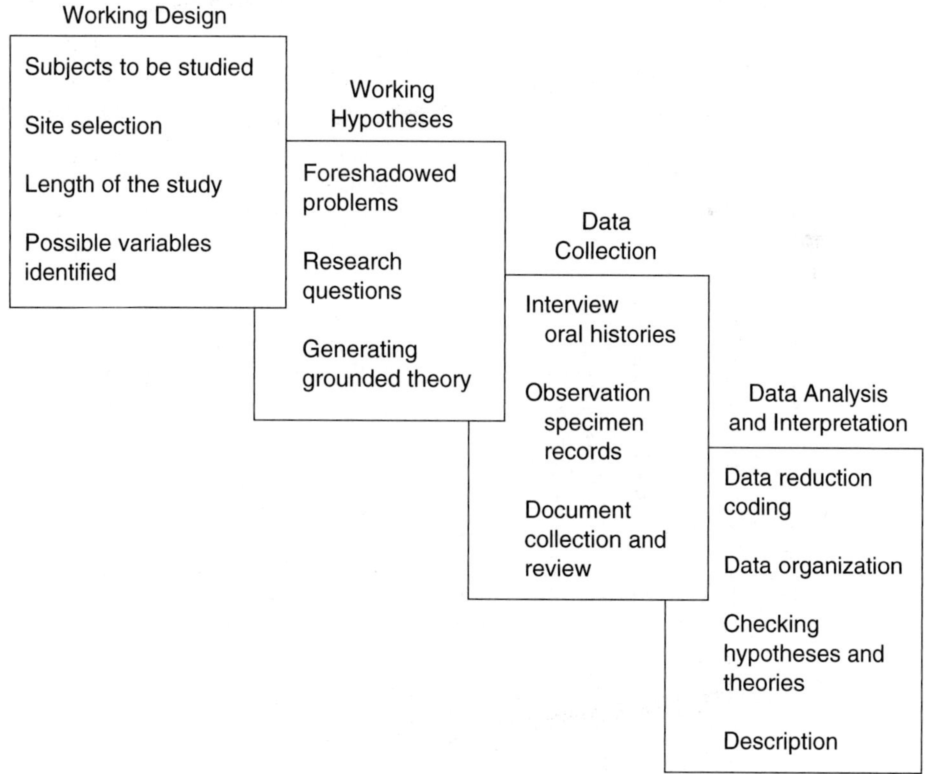

FIGURE 10.1 Components of Research Design in Qualitative Research

whom to interview, and so on. Interviews and observation inventories are less structured and standardized than with quantitative research, so the researcher's perspectives are highly influential in qualitative research.

Coding Examples. It may be useful to consider a couple of coding examples from the literature. Evans (2007) studied how suburban schools changed in response to an increase of at least 20 percent in the number of African American students in the school population. She conducted a multisite case study. She held ninety-minute interviews with superintendents, principals, and teachers in three suburban high schools. She also gathered documents and archival data on the programs, policies, and practices that schools modified or adopted in response to the growing African American population. Within-site analysis resulted in the information being grouped into the following categories:

curriculum and instruction
professional development
discipline
school restructuring
staffing
student support services
student placement
other (p. 328)

From the data in these categories, patterns and key events emerged as indicated by consistent and repetitive themes and ideas. The coding was necessary because without it the sheer volume of information would obscure the patterns. The cross-site analysis compared the results from the within-site analyses. Patterns emerged that reflected the broader themes that appeared to be significant in their impact on school beliefs, behavior, and decision making.

Scribner, Sawyer, Watson, and Myers (2007) investigated the nature of distributed leadership in two teacher teams in a public secondary school. Data came from field notes and video recordings. The researchers' first pass through the data focused on identifying types of discourse between team members to deconstruct dialogue into its constituent elements. They quickly determined that their own initial coding process was generating categories consistent with Searle's taxonomy of speech acts. Rather than force the use of their own coding system, they used Searle's system, which was recognized in the literature. Five broad types of speech were identified:

Representatives convey information.
Expressive utterances express the internal state of being of the speaker.
Directives get the hearer to act or do something.
Commissive speech commits the speaker to do some action.
A declaration marks specific changes in a state of affairs.

This coding system allowed the researchers to understand the interactions among team members. Three important constructs emerged: purpose, autonomy, and patterns of discourse. This study is noteworthy because the categories that emerged from the data matched an already recognized system of codes.

Writing Up Results—Thick Description

The write-up of a qualitative research study is noticeably different from that of a quantitative study and much of that is due to the kind of information that is included in the **thick description** characteristic of qualitative research. Whereas quantitative results are usually limited to the presentation of facts and the tests of hypotheses, qualitative results focus on underlying structures, relationships among entities, influencing factors, and even the "meaning" of events and experiences. Thick description is interpretive; the researcher seeks to interpret how and why individuals and groups behave as they do. For example, in a study of the attitudes of middle school principals and teachers toward school suspensions, thick description would go beyond reporting differences in the average scores of principals and teachers on some rating scale and include how principals view the meaning of "being a middle school principal" and how this may influence their attitudes. Thick description goes behind the scenes to explicate the underlying dynamics of the situation and in doing this provides much more than a surface understanding of the situation.

Types of Designs in Qualitative Research

Case studies are used quite extensively in qualitative research. A case study is a detailed examination of something: a specific event, an organization, or a school system, just to name a few examples. Tracing the historical development of an organization or a certain innovation would be what Bogdan and Biklen (2003) call a "Historical Organizational Case Study." Much of the data would come from documents and interviews. An example of a historical case study is that of Conroy and Sipple (2001). They studied the merger of two previously separate teacher education programs, agriculture and math/science at Cornell University. Documents were reviewed and participants were interviewed. They found that the agriculture faculty perceived that they were treated as second-class citizens by the math/science faculty and that the two groups had very different ideas about what should be stressed in the teacher education program. The merger caused the agriculture educators and the science educators to work with each other and to appreciate each other's strengths and the strengths of their students. Old assumptions were challenged and an integrated program for teacher education was developed.

A case study of a current phenomenon for which observations could be used to supplement documents and interviews is called an observational case study. Jobe and Pope (2002) conducted an observational case study to identify the degree to which student teachers used principles and methods from their university-based methods class in student teaching in English. The English methods class was audiorecoded and observed each day and four target students were observed in that context. The professor was interviewed and asked to make predictions about the student teaching success of the target students. The target students were observed and interviewed on several occasions during student teaching and their cooperating teachers were interviewed. The professor had several themes to his class, such as "making the English class a special place" and engaging the students in writing. The student teachers also embedded themes into their teaching, just as their professor had. The extent to which themes were used was at times limited because of restrictions placed on the student teachers or their choice to teach as their cooperating teacher did. The conclusion of the multisite case study was that the professor and the methods course had a decided impact on the individual teaching styles that the student teachers developed.

Bogdan and Biklen (2003) define an extension of the case study:

> When researchers study two or more subjects, settings, or depositories of data, they are usually doing what we call multi-case studies. (p. 62)

A multicase study may begin as a single case study and then be expanded to two or more cases. The added setting or individuals may be included to enhance the generalizability of the research. Another purpose for multicase studies is for comparative reasons, so that the results of the two or more cases can be compared and contrasted. For enhancing generalizability, the additional sites or cases may involve some diversity in order to provide some range for the observations. If cases are to be compared and contrasted, additional sites or cases may be selected because of the absence or variation in some characteristics.

The descriptive names for case studies are by no means limited to those mentioned above. Terms such as *community studies* are used for a case study of a community, town, or neighborhood. Historians sometimes do a history of a person (usually someone famous or infamous), and these are called life-history case studies. So, there are any number of terms that may be used for case studies, but case studies commonly focus on historical development or involve observation of whatever is the subject of the case study.

> Case study research is used extensively in qualitative research and historical organizational case studies and observational case studies are the two most commonly used designs.

Another approach in qualitative research design is the "multisite study." These studies are exactly what the name implies in that multiple sites or subjects are studied. They differ from multicase studies in that they retain a common focus for the research, but they typically require several or many sites rather than just two or three. Corbin and Strauss (1990) indicate that multisite studies differ from multicase studies in that the former are more oriented toward developing theory. Although there are differences in the orientation and possibly the foci of these designs, the procedures for conducting the research, such as data collection and analyzing data, are often quite similar.

Perspectives for Qualitative Research

Thus far we have identified the components of research design and described some general designs used in qualitative research. Because research is a process, it is useful to think about research design in terms of activities or tasks conducted during the research. There are many different qualitative research studies, each with special considerations depending on the purposes and conditions of the research. It is not feasible to describe all kinds of qualitative research in an overview chapter. However, qualitative research may be approached from two perspectives and the differences in these perspectives have implications for how the research is conducted. One perspective we will call the **funnel approach,** and the other, using the terminology of writers such as Bogdan and Biklen (2003), is described as **modified analytic induction.** This latter approach is not quite a funnel in reverse, although when applied it does arrive at a universal explanation of some sort.

The funnel approach begins with general research questions that initiate the study. The researcher explores possible sites, subjects, sources of data, and procedures for data collection. On the basis of results from initial data collection, the groups/sites/conditions are identified more specifically, thus providing increased focus on the phenomenon under study. This process leads to more narrow data collection, concentrating on those data that reflect the specific phenomenon that has emerged. This process may be repeated, becoming more focused until the conclusions are concentrated on a specific component or a limited number of components of the study. The data collection, analysis, and interpretation has become more focused, directed or narrow, from a more general beginning.

In contrast, the modified analytic induction approach begins with more specific research problems or questions and then attempts to cover all cases of the phenomenon under study to arrive at a comprehensive descriptive model. Data are collected on "cases," some of which fit the model, others that do not fit this initial model. There is a reformulation of the model to accommodate all cases, and more data are collected including a search for cases that do not fit this reformulated model. This process of data collection and reformulating the model is continued until a satisfactory, universal explanation is obtained of the phenomenon under study.

The funnel approach and the modified analytic induction approach are contrasted in Figure 10.2. Note that the descriptors of the approaches deal with the focus of the research. They do not address issues such as specific data-collection procedures. Observation, interviewing, and so on may be used for either approach.

> The funnel approach and the modified analytic induction approach are two contrasting ways in which we can consider the focus of qualitative research design.

The two approaches can be illustrated through examples of hypothetical but possible studies. This will focus on a constructivist approach to instruction in elementary school reading and mathematics, grades 2–4.

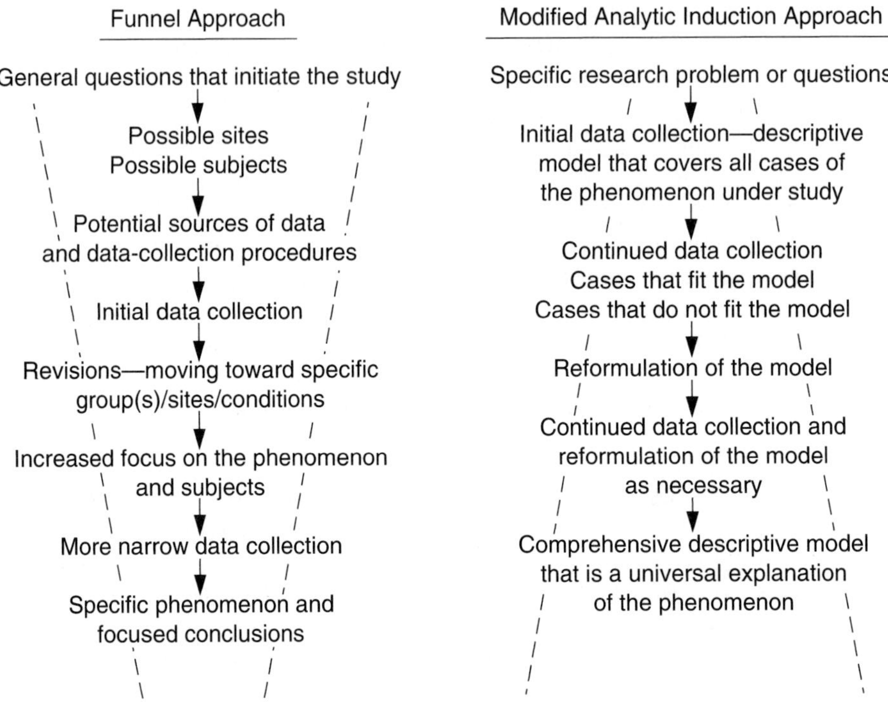

FIGURE 10.2 Contrast Between the Funnel Approach and Modified Analytic Induction Approach

EXAMPLE: FUNNEL APPROACH

The research is conducted on the nature of instruction using a constructivist approach to teaching reading and mathematics in grades 2–4. Three general questions to begin the research might be:

1. What are the achievement patterns of students?
2. How do the teachers and aides plan the instruction?
3. What are the interaction patterns between teachers and students during instruction?

The research is being conducted in a school system that has eight elementary schools. However, the teachers in three of the eight schools have made a decision to implement constructivist teaching, and their professional development for the past year or so has been directed to this type of instruction. The three schools are the possible sites for the research, and the subjects are the grades 2–4 teachers, aides, and students of these schools. To a lesser extent, the principals of the schools also may serve as subjects.

Data are collected through interviews, observation, and review of student records. Initial data are collected through visits to all three schools and on the basis of these visits the following revisions are made:

1. One school is selected as the site for the study because the instruction of the teachers in grades 2–4 in this school most closely corresponds to the conceptual model of constructivist teaching.

2. The phenomenon to be investigated is the interactions between teachers (and/or aides) and students while conducting instruction in reading and mathematics.

3. The planning meetings of the teachers will be observed to identify factors from the planning that may impact the interactions.

4. The principal will be interviewed to determine his or her perceptions of, and possible impact on, constructivist teaching.

The data collection becomes more focused. Classroom instruction and planning meetings are observed. The teachers, aides, selected students, and the principal are interviewed. The data collected are directed to the interaction taking place, especially that between the teachers and students during instruction. The conclusions become focused on this interaction. However, student data, especially achievement in reading and mathematics, are reviewed as outcome measures of the instruction.

It should be noted that the narrowing of the research may go through more than one step. In the example, we went from initial data collection observing instruction in the three schools, to the more intense data collection in a single school, to the conclusion of the study. This process might involve a series of successive approximations. For example, it may be concluded that any extensive or additional interviews with the principal provide little information for the focus of the study.

EXAMPLE: MODIFIED ANALYTIC INDUCTION APPROACH

Again, consider an example in the context of constructivist teaching in an elementary school. The research question is: "What factors make for effective instruction when using a constructivist approach?" The researcher has available the teachers, aides, principals, and students of four elementary schools. The focus of the research will be instruction in reading and mathematics, grades 2–4. The following process is followed:

1. One teacher at each of the three grade levels and the principal in one of the three schools are interviewed in an open-ended manner. An operational, descriptive model of constructivist teaching is developed. The interviews concentrate on the nature of constructivist teaching.

2. The model of Step 1 sets the stage for interviewing the principal, two teachers from each of the three grade levels, and three fourth-grade students from another school. Some information from these interviews fits the previous model; other information does not. On this basis, the model is reformulated.

3. Additional interviews are conducted in all four elementary schools initially identified. Interviews are conducted with nine additional teachers, four aides, and twelve additional students. It is decided that interviewing more principals will not provide additional useful information. With each interview the model is reformulated as necessary.

4. The researcher observes instruction in all four schools at each grade level. The observation is interspersed with conducting the interviews.

5. Teacher planning meetings are observed, at least one in each school, and all grade levels are covered.

6. Patterns of student achievement in reading and mathematics are reviewed.

7. Based on all the data collected, the researcher develops a descriptive model explaining in a universal manner the factors that make for effective constructivist teaching in grades 2–4, reading and mathematics. Essentially, the description is the model, and it is a comprehensive description. The focus of the description is on the teacher–student interaction during instruction but other factors are included such as the type of instructional planning among teachers.

For both examples, the question might be raised, "When has enough data been collected to bring the study to a close?" Sometimes it seems as though data collection in qualitative research can go on and on. In fact, studies may require considerable time and effort, but most researchers can tell when they are reaching, or have passed, the point of **data saturation.** This is the point of diminishing returns for data collection, and additional data collection is not worth the time and effort. Field notes and other data may run several hundred pages, and as mentioned earlier, even over 1000 pages. When this happens, the data saturation point likely has been passed. There is no point in collecting data that will not be analyzed due to a lack of time or other resources.

Reliability and Validity of Qualitative Research

The traditional concepts of **reliability** and **validity** of research may cause some difficulties for qualitative researchers. Because qualitative research occurs in the natural setting it is extremely difficult to replicate studies. Nevertheless, a well-organized, complete persuasive presentation of procedures and results enhances external reliability. The reader should acquire an adequate understanding of the research so that a judgment can be made about its replicability within the limits of the natural context.

Internal reliability, that is, consistency in the research process, can be addressed in a number of ways. Much of qualitative research involves observation by multiple observers as at least part of data collection. Through proper training, consistency across observers can be enhanced, but there typically is some disagreement among observers. One way to obtain a measure of agreement is to complete the ratio of agreements to agreements plus disagreements. Lancy (1993) calls this **concordance.** Another procedure is to have a third observer analyze independently the material that is the source of disagreement. Videotapes can be especially useful for a reanalysis of data recorded thereon. If two or more researchers independently analyze the same data and arrive at similar conclusions, this is strong evidence for internal consistency.

Bogdan and Biklen (2003) comment on reliability of qualitative research:

> Qualitative researchers tend to view reliability as a fit between what they record as data and what actually occurs in the setting under study, rather than the literal consistency across different observations. (p. 36)

Essentially, two or more researchers could have different data and different findings from the same setting. As long as the results are not contradictory, both sets could be reliable.

Internal validity relies on the logical analysis of the results, as the researcher develops the description of the phenomenon under study. Because research is conducted in natural settings, often with complex phenomena, there is not the option of controlling variables, as might be the case in an experiment, for example. Verifying results and conclusions from two or more sources or perspectives enhances internal validity. As with any research, attention to detail is important for doing the research well.

A common question about qualitative research, as indicated by Bogdan and Biklen (2003), is:

> Are qualitative findings generalizable? (p. 32)

This is the question of external validity, and it must be considered with qualifications when applied to specific research studies. When doing qualitative research, the researcher typically is not concerned with broad generalization of results. Rather, external validity is more concerned with the comparability of and the **translatability** of the research. **Comparability** refers to the extent to which adequate theoretical constructs and research procedures are used so that other researchers can understand the results.

For some qualitative research studies the issue of external validity may be left to those who read the report of the study. In essence, it is someone else's task to fit the results into whatever is being considered. If such is the case, the research must be very well documented, as it should be anyway, so that the context, subjects, and so forth can be understood with no confusion or ambiguity. Case study research, for example, often is done without attempting broad or even limited generalization, but readers of the research may find applications to other situations.

There are quite extensive discussions of validity and reliability of qualitative research in texts devoted exclusively to the qualitative research topic. Anyone doing a qualitative research study of the magnitude of a doctoral dissertation, for example, would do well to consult a text such as Miller and Dingwall (1997). This text contains an entire part on validity and credibility.

> Validity of qualitative research for the most part is established on a logical basis, and providing an argument for validity requires well-documented research and a comprehensive description.

Use of Technology in Qualitative Research

The discussion in this chapter thus far has focused on how qualitative research is conceptualized and the components of the research process in qualitative research. But qualitative research typically involves massive quantities of data that require an intensive analysis. The analysis requires content analysis and interpretation. Characteristics, issues, themes, and variables require categorization and coding, and as the analysis and writing proceed, they need to be retrieved and collated for summation and interpretation. Although all of this needs to be conceptualized and defined by the researcher, there are numerous mechanical tasks or phases that can be assisted by available technology.

The major technology that was available to qualitative researchers just a couple of decades ago consisted of tape recorders, scissors, tape, and a copying machine. Interviews would be tape-recorded and then transcribed for analysis. Relevant documents would be photocopied. Pertinent passages would be cut out, sorted, and perhaps color-coded. The analysis would then consist of identifying evidence and themes that supported or refuted the working hypotheses. Sometimes conclusions would emerge from repeated wallowing in the data.

The development of word processing capabilities on computers was a great breakthrough for qualitative researchers. The capabilities far surpassed "electronic scissors and tape." This software allowed researchers to copy passages and to search for words or phrases within documents. They could count the number of times a term appeared and highlight or code selected passages. The mountains of information became much more manageable with word processing programs.

Technological developments also assisted researchers in the field. Field notes could be taken with laptop computers or with handheld electronic devices that downloaded the information into computers. A great deal of data could be gathered very unobtrusively.

It is not surprising then that data analysis programs were developed specifically to assist qualitative researchers. Some of the more common tasks associated with qualitative research that have been programmed for computers are described below.

1. *Coding.* Weaver and Atkinson (1994) describe coding as:

> the strategy whereby data are segmented and tagged according to the researcher's definition of units of meaning, so that those segments which have common or related meaning can be drawn together in one place for analysis. (p. 31)

Coding is not unique to qualitative research. It has the same purpose in quantitative research, that being to structure and facilitate analysis. Coding requires an organized set of categories based on a specified rationale. Coding "themes" or categories commonly are drawn out of the data, often the initial data such as early field notes.

2. *Lexical Searching.* Coding is a form of searching through the data based on categories and retrieving coded segments. Another way of searching is to look for specific words, phrases, combinations, or strings of words. This direct exploration of the data, lexical searching, reveals the dominant terminology used to describe the phenomenon under study.

3. *Hypertext.* This is one of the newer capabilities of qualitative research software. Hypertext essentially is a flexible, database management system. Segments of text in the research data are joined together by electronic links. Hypertext is based on the concept of multidimensional geometry (hyperspace). This concept is extended to hypertext to mean multidimensional text. Human mental processes are multidimensional, and hypertext attempts to imitate these processes by providing a structural representation of data by various links. The data may be explored in various side trails, just as an individual might engage in meaningful digressions when exploring information. In this sense, hypertext may complement the thinking process more closely than typical coding and searching.

Capabilities of Computer Software in Qualitative Research

For the qualitative researcher, it is important to recognize what it is that the computer and software packages can and cannot do. As mentioned above, computers can deal with mechanical tasks but they cannot perform the conceptual tasks requiring the traditional analytic skills of qualitative research. Computer programs are not capable of doing key tasks of interpretation, synthesis, and hypothesis testing. In essence, any task that requires conceptualization and systematic judgment is beyond the capability of the computer.

Of course the computer can be used for word processing in qualitative research, as it can be used when writing about any type of research. The computer can be used for organizing information, and in this way it functions as a database management system. Basically it can keep track of information that is filed and maintained. Beyond that, in general, computers are capable of searching, retrieving, manipulating, arranging, and rearranging descriptive data that previously have been coded or in some way identified by the researcher. Computers can do these tasks quickly and efficiently. For example, computers can expedite time-consuming content analyses when directed by the researcher through the software. Content analysis might include quantifying the number of times an issue was mentioned by people being interviewed.

> Computers used in qualitative research can be useful for conducting mechanical tasks such as searching and arranging descriptive data, but they cannot perform the conceptual tasks.

Computer Software in Qualitative Research

Several computer software programs are available that help the qualitative researcher organize, analyze, and synthesize the vast amount of information that is gathered in a research study. We describe two of the programs used most often.

Atlas.ti. The following description of Atlas.ti was adapted from information on the website www.atlasti.com. Atlas was developed in Germany but is available in many languages, including English. Atlas provides interactive and automatic coding. The researcher enters primary documents that are the text, graphical, audio, or video materials that the researcher wishes to analyze. Text level activities include segmenting the primary documents into quotations, adding comments to passages, and coding passages to facilitate their retrieval. Search, retrieval, and browsing functions are available.

The software allows editing, drag-and-drop linking, and hypertext to analyze threads of conversations. The researcher can use Atlas to diagram conceptual connections in the data. Figures are created that show the linkages among themes and ideas. The relationships between codes, text passages, and notes that the researcher develops can be displayed in diagrams that visually represent the connections.

NVIVO7. One of the earlier qualitative analysis programs was NUD*IST, which evolved to N6, the sixth version of the program. This has been upgraded to NVIVO7. The following description was adapted from information from the website www.qsrinternational.com. NVIVO7 allows tables or images embedded in rich text or Microsoft Word files to be imported and coded for analysis. Source documents can be annotated by the researcher. The researcher's memos can be coded, searched on, and linked to other project items. The researcher can explore how concepts and ideas are related and code evidence of those relations. Text searches can be done and visual models of the interrelationships can be diagrammed.

Which software program to use is, in the big picture, not an important concern. The important idea is that there is software available that allows the qualitative researcher to organize and utilize large amounts of information. It was previously the case that qualitative researchers had to work with hard copy, often multiple copies, which were color-coded, cut apart, sorted in many ways, covered with sticky notes, placed in folders, and more often than not piled on floors or taped to walls. Computerizing these tasks provides for much more efficient analysis of the information. Searches within the information are more thorough than hand searches, and the final product is not going to be determined by when the researcher reaches a point of physical exhaustion.

Summary

This chapter has provided an overview of research design in qualitative research.[1] Qualitative research design is not as prescriptive and structured as quantitative research design. Considerable flexibility is needed in decision making while the research is being conducted, and decisions on specifically how to proceed may be deferred to later stages of the research.

Nevertheless, general components of research design, which reflect the research activities, can be identified and described. In qualitative research there is considerable integration and overlap of these components. The discussion in this chapter described four components from an initial working design through data analysis and interpretation. Two general approaches were also described that showed contrasting directions that may be taken by qualitative researchers.

The chapter concludes with an overview of the use of computers when conducting qualitative research. Computer programs (software) have the capability of assisting with some of the technical tasks, especially those of analysis of descriptive data. However, software will not perform the "thinking" tasks, tasks of conceptualization and interpretation. These later tasks must be done by the researcher and these are the tasks, especially conceptualization, most directly associated with research design.

The following two chapters discuss two types of qualitative research, historical and ethnographic, in detail. Although the issue could be debated, these two types of research probably have the greatest application to education of the various types of qualitative research.

KEY CONCEPTS

Epistemology
Ecological psychology
Holistic ethnography
Working design
Emergent design
Foreshadowed problems
Grounded theory
Specimen record
Oral history
Coding
Thick description
Funnel approach
Modified analytic induction
Data saturation
Reliability
Validity
Concordance
Translatability
Comparability

EXERCISES

10.1 An ethnographic research study is being designed for which the statement of the research problem is, "A study of the principal's role in school-based management at the elementary school level." Develop the working design for this problem by considering the specific decisions that can be made at this initial step of the research design.

10.2 For the research problem of Exercise 10.1, develop three or more working hypotheses. These may include foreshadowed problems and research questions.

10.3 When conducting the research of Exercise 10.1, teachers and the principal undoubtedly would be interviewed and other information would be obtained. Identify possible documents (within the school) that might be collected. What specific situations would merit observation, at least as a starting point?

10.4 A qualitative research study is to be conducted on the nature, efficiency, and effectiveness of site-based management in the schools of a large city district, one that has over seventy schools. Identify or describe each of the following:

a. general questions to initiate the study

b. possible sites, subjects, and potential sources of data

c. how the funnel approach can be used to narrow the focus of this research

d. a specific "phenomenon" that might emerge from this funnel approach

10.5 Compensatory reading programs for deficient readers in the primary grades often emphasize scores on standardized reading tests, and improvement in such scores as measures of program success. Thus, the focus tends to be on quantitative outcomes. However, the argument can be made that qualitative outcomes, for example, attitudes, motivation, and the social-psychological factors of participating in the program, are of significant importance. Suppose a compensatory program is implemented in which small groups (maximum size of six) of deficient readers receive special instruction for one hour during the school day. A student participates in this instruction two times per week. In the elementary schools of a specific school system there are several of these groups. Suppose a qualitative research study is undertaken to determine the nature of the program and the way it is perceived by the students participating in it. Develop the research design, providing specifics for the four components of Figure 10.1. For example, comment on the site selection, considering that there are several groups, possible research questions, kinds of data to be collected, and how obtained, and so on.

10.6 A research study is to be conducted about teachers' perceptions of an effective, fair, and appropriate model for teacher evaluation. The study will be done in a school system that has 218 teachers, grades K–12. The teachers are the subjects of this study. Describe how the modified analytic induction approach would be used to arrive at a comprehensive descriptive model for teacher evaluation as perceived by the teachers. It would not be possible or desirable to interview all 218 teachers. Comment on issues such as how many, and specifically which teachers will be interviewed. Does the concept of grounded theory have any relevance in this situation? If so, how?

10.7 For the research study of Exercise 10.6, develop five specific research questions to get the study under way.

10.8 Use the internet to find a qualitative research study from a professional journal such as the *Anthropology and Education Quarterly* or the *History of Education Quarterly.* In reviewing the article, identify the specifics of the research design used for the research. How is the issue of external validity or generalizability addressed?

10.9 It has been said that "research questions about variables are best addressed by quantitative research methods and that research questions about processes are best addressed by qualitative methods." Do you agree or disagree and why? Provide examples that would illustrate your position regarding this statement.

10.10 Qualitative studies are said to provide different "sight lines" into educational problems and issues when the opinions and perceptions of different groups of informants are assessed through interviews, focus groups, and the review of written documents.

Some people see this as an attempt to document different "realities." Do you believe that the "multiple realities" concept is a fundamental difference between qualitative and quantitative research? Explain your answer.

NOTES

1. For a comprehensive treatment, the reader is referred to the *Handbook of Qualitative Research*, edited by N. K. Denzin and Y. S. Lincoln (Thousand Oaks, CA: Sage Publications, 2000). This book contains chapters by some of the leading authors in qualitative research.

REFERENCES

Bogdan R. C., and Biklen, S. K. (2003). *Qualitative research in education: An introduction to theories and methods* (4th ed.). Boston: Allyn & Bacon.

Conroy, C. A., and Sipple, J. W. (2001). A case study in reform: Integration of teacher education in agriculture with teacher education in mathematics and science. *Journal of Vocational Education Research, 26*, 206–243.

Corbin, J., and Strauss, A. (1990). Grounded theory method: Procedures, canons, and evaluative criteria. *Qualitative Sociology, 13*, 3–21.

Evans, A. E. (2007). Changing faces: Suburban school response to demographic change. *Education and Urban Society, 39*, 315–348.

Jacob, E. (1987). Qualitative research traditions: A review. *Review of Educational Research, 57*, 1–50.

Jobe, L. G., and Pope, C. A. (2002). The English methods class matters: Professor D and the student teachers. *Reading Research and Instruction, 42*, 1–29.

Lancy, D. F. (1993). *Qualitative research in education: An introduction to the major traditions.* New York: Longman.

McMillan J. H., and Schumacher, S. (1997). *Research in education: A conceptual introduction* (4th ed.). New York: Addison Wesley Longman.

Miller, G., and Dingwall, R. (Eds.). (1997). *Context and method in qualitative research.* Thousand Oaks, CA: Sage Publications.

Moscovici, H. (2003, Spring). Secondary science emergency permit teachers' perspectives on power relations in their environments and the effects of these powers on classroom practices. *Teacher Education Quarterly, 30*, 41–53.

Schoggen, P. (1978). Ecological psychology and mental retardation. In G. Sackett (Ed.), *Observing behavior: Vol. 1: Theory and applications in mental retardation* (pp. 33–62). Baltimore: University Park Press.

Scribner, J. P., Sawyer, R. K., Watson, S. T., and Myers, V. L. (2007). Teacher teams and distributed leadership: A study of group discourse and collaboration. *Educational Administration Quarterly, 43*, 67–100.

Smith, M. L., and Glass, G. V. (1987). *Research and evaluation in education and the social sciences.* Englewood Cliffs, NJ: Prentice-Hall.

Weaver, A., and Atkinson, P. (1994). *Microcomputing and qualitative data analysis.* Aldershot, England: Avebury.

CHAPTER

11 Historical Research

Historical research has been around a long time, possibly longer than most other types of research. When we think of historical research, a process of searching for, summarizing, and interpreting information from the past comes to mind. The past may be any time: as recent as within the immediately preceding year or it may go back several centuries. Specifically, historical research is a systematic process of describing, analyzing, and interpreting the past based on information from selected sources as they relate to the topic under study.

> Historical research is a systematic process of searching for the facts and then using the information to describe, analyze, and interpret the past.

For the most part, historical researchers use the methods and reasoning from the qualitative research tradition. Historical research is analytical in that **logical induction** is used in arriving at conclusions. Edson (1986) identifies similarities between historical research and other approaches to qualitative research. These include the importance of context and the study of the wholeness of experience. Historical research is the study of phenomena in natural settings, not in theoretical or experimental settings. However, not all qualitative researchers are historians, and although historical research relies heavily on qualitative research methods, quantitative methods may also be applied in historical research. So, by no means are historical research and qualitative research synonymous.

Historical research may have a variety of foci. We may focus on issues, movements, and concepts in education. The history of the development of the teachers college in the United States would focus on a movement or a concept. However, we could do historical research about a specific teachers college, which would then focus on a specific institution. Biographies of educators would involve historical research. So, historical research can cover a wide spectrum as we consider past aspects of education.

Historical research deals with events of the past, occurring in natural rather than contrived settings. The context of the event must be emphasized in its interpretation. Interpretation takes on special importance in historical research, because the events have occurred, and they occurred before the decision was made to study them. As documents were produced, such as a reporter preparing a newspaper story, interpretation was involved in preparing the document. As the researcher uses the document, interpretation again takes place.

Context and interpretation are essential elements of historical research. Ellenwood (2007) noted:

> History requires a recognition of the importance of understanding the full context of events—the deeper causes and the long-range consequences. Of course there are many versions of the past, and that fact itself also asks that we slow down and think clearly about both the veracity of each version and the subsequent implications for actions. (p. 23)

Interpretation is central to the research process when conducting historical research.

The historical researcher discovers data as the search is conducted through documents and other sources. This is in contrast to experimental research, for example, in which the researcher produces data. This requires the historical researcher to be especially sensitive to the existence of relevant data. It has been said that historical research is both science and art. The science part comes in the systematic process, the procedures of the research, that is used. But as Kaestle (1988a, p. 61) points out, making generalizations is more than inductive reasoning and requires creative interpretation, which invariably reflects the researcher's values and interests. So, producing historical research remains, to a large degree, subjective, and the process of historical research is primarily qualitative in nature.

The Value of Historical Research

Historical research deals with something that is over and done with, so why do it at all? The reason is that historical research in education is useful in a number of ways. Stricker (1992) discusses twelve reasons why the study of history is important and useful. Although the discussion is directed to the study of history at the high school and college levels, some of the reasons are directly relevant to the value of historical research. These reasons summarized and paraphrased are:

1. History is a storehouse of great ideas (p. 296).
2. The past is a bulwark against contemporary confusion and overload (p. 298).
3. Knowledge of the past is essential to understanding and judging current events and participating in current debates (p. 302).
4. History shows what is and is not possible; thus a knowledge of history empowers, especially those with decision-making tasks (p. 305).

Essentially, these reasons make the case that a knowledge of history, gained through historical research, can provide a perspective for decision making about educational problems, and it assists in understanding why things are as they are. Educational reform and even social reform are functions often served by historical research. Issues are often better understood—and probably better dealt with—if the historical perspective is known. Historical research can also be useful for predicting future trends. There is an old adage that those who are unfamiliar with the mistakes of history are doomed to repeat them. Thus, historical research can provide information necessary to avoid previous mistakes.

Historical research is valuable in identifying trends of the past and using such information to predict future patterns and implications for related trends. Thomas and Moran (1992) provide an excellent example of historical research for this purpose. In their study they were testing the idea of superintendents being extremely vulnerable to myriad pressures and criticisms of various special interest groups (p. 22). They followed the career path of a single school executive from 1914 through 1922 as he served in three cities. In the conclusions section of the report the authors summarize their findings and then apply them to the educational scene today, especially with regard to the concern for school reform. In their conclusions they state:

> Far from being weak and vulnerable, Hartwell [the superintendent whose career was followed] found strong support among like-minded, influential career superintendents and conservative business and professional groups. . . . In the context of a period of reforms, punctuated by managerial efforts to dominate the work force, school superintendents constituted a powerful network of executives. Strengthened by their powerful school boards, they could ignore with impunity diverse interest groups, including teachers and working-class citizens demanding greater participation in the educational decision-making process. (pp. 48–49)

Then, in applying the results of their research to today's educational context;

> The events that occurred in early 20th century St. Paul and Buffalo have important implications for contemporary superintendents. The issues and the actors remain much the same as they were in the period of progressive reforms, when superintendents gained and exercised greater control over school affairs. (pp. 49–50)

In the remainder of their discussion they elaborate on this conclusion, recognizing changes between the 1914–1922 period and the present, and the implications of those changes for the school superintendent.

Graham (1980) argues for the contribution the study of history makes to the process of policymaking. **Policymaking** is principally concerned with two questions: "What is right?" and "What will work?" (p. 21). Answering these questions—that is, the formulation of policy—is often done through a judgment call, with the hope that a wise decision has been made. Graham concludes: "I believe that history, perhaps more than any other academic discipline, does make a valuable, though partial contribution. . . . I believe that history's contribution is two-fold: perspective and prevention" (p. 22). In this sense, the contribution of historical research to policymaking is consistent with its value to informed decision making about educational issues and problems.

> The value of historical research covers a wide spectrum, from providing an understanding of the past through accurate description to providing perspectives for decision making and policy formation.

Sources of Information in Historical Research

Because historical research concerns the critical evaluation and interpretation of a defined segment of the past, it is necessary to acquire some records of the period under study. The most common **source material** is some type of written record of the past, such as books, newspapers, periodicals, diaries, letters, minutes of organizational meetings, and so on. However, written documents are not the only sources. Physical remains and objects (relics) of the past are other possible sources. Information may be orally transmitted through such media as folk songs and legends, and pictures, records, and various other audiovisual media can also serve as sources of information about the past.

When doing research of recent history, it may be possible to interview participants that actually were present for certain events. A study of school desegregation efforts and issues during the period 1950 through 1980 would be an example of historical research in which participants in relevant events could be found and interviewed about their experiences.

The sources of historical information are commonly classified as primary and secondary. A **primary source** is an original or firsthand account of the event or experience. A **secondary source** is an account that is at least once removed from the event. A court transcript of a desegregation hearing would be an example of a primary source for a study involving a desegregation problem; a newspaper editorial from another state concerning the problem would be a secondary source.

In a study of Southern women attending Northern colleges near the turn of the twentieth century, Johnson (2007) used several different primary sources. She used the alumnae registers of the colleges; letters to parents, siblings, and other relatives; and data on marriage, number of children, wage work, volunteer work, and primary place of residence. She utilized these sources to find out how the college experience changed these women and how they, in turn, later changed the culture from which they came. These accounts were primary sources. A report on the same topic by another author would be a secondary source. The writings of John Dewey are primary sources of his views, whereas an interpretation by his students would be considered a secondary source.

> *Primary sources* are firsthand accounts of the event or experience under study; *secondary sources* are accounts at least one step removed from the event or experience.

The Methodology of Historical Research

Edson (1986) came to the conclusion that "there is no single, definable method of historical inquiry" (p. 29). Kaestle (1992) supports this conclusion that historical research does not have highly developed methodology around which there is consensus, and historians are continually scavenging other disciplines for methods or theories (p. 362). Certainly, individual researchers vary in their approaches. Some search for historical information until all sources appear to be exhausted, and then begin organizing and interpreting extensive notes. Others work on a "search and write" cycle approaching the issue under study from two or more perspectives. There are any number of variations on specific procedures. Historical research tends to be a rather holistic process in which there is considerable overlap of activities. For example, interpretation runs throughout the process not only when making value judgments about the authenticity of sources but also when deciding the relevance of the sources.

Nevertheless, for the purpose of enhancing understanding of the historical research process, it is useful to describe the methodology in four steps. It is important to keep in mind that the steps may have considerable overlap, and although they can be defined, the steps tend to run together when conducting historical research.

The first step is the identification of the research problem, a typical beginning for any research study. The second and third steps are collection and evaluation of source materials and synthesis of information, respectively. These steps are closely tied together and may involve continued formulation and possible revision of hypotheses. The final step is analysis and interpretation with the formulation of conclusions. This final step includes drawing any generalizations. The four steps are diagrammed in Figure 11.1. The historical method of research is called **historiography.**

Identification of the Research Problem

The statement of the research problem may be such that hypotheses or questions are formulated along with the problem. If hypotheses are stated, they can be viewed as answers to implicit (or explicit) questions, or the problem may be stated as the purpose of the research without any explicitly stated hypotheses or questions.

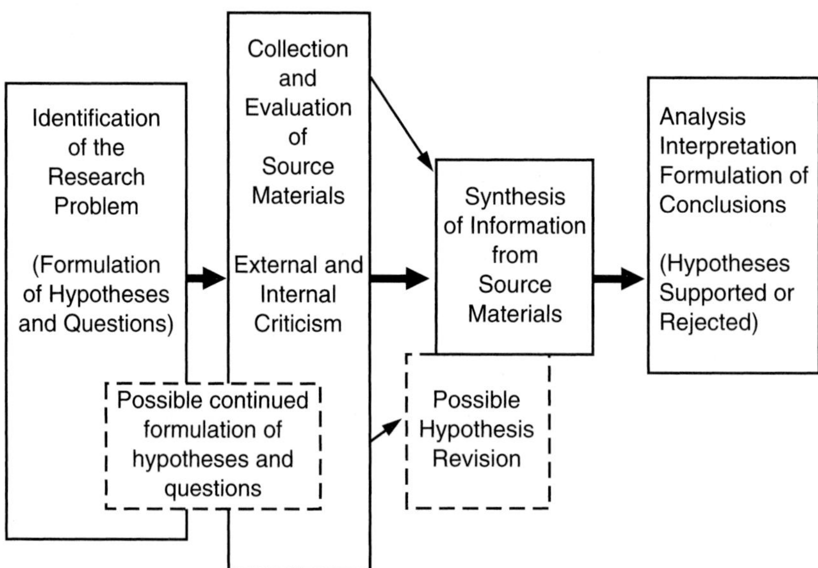

FIGURE 11.1 The Four Steps in the Methodology of Historical Research

An example of the latter is found in a study by Johnson (2007) entitled, "Job Market or Marriage Market? Life Choices for Southern Women Educated at Northern Colleges, 1875–1915." This was a study of how Southern women who enrolled in prestigious Northern colleges were impacted by the very different culture they found in the North. The question that guided the study and a glimpse of what was found is given in the following paragraph:

> Why did these Southern women seek a prestigious and rigorous classical education? While some students desired a professional career, the absence of practical aims for most suggests that they sought the intangibles of a liberal education: a general bettering of themselves, sharpening of their minds, building of their characters, and developing their person to their fullest potential. Many believed that a college education would, in short, make them better women. Thus for many the revolution was unanticipated: they did not realize how much the experience threatened traditional understandings of what it meant to be a Southern lady. Yet, despite most colleges' professed determination to produce a "womanly woman," that is, a charming and domestic wife and mother, exposure to feminist professors and progressive reform opportunities caused Southern women to broaden their ideas of what was proper and appropriate behavior for women. (p. 151)

The implied questions that drove the study included at least these:

1. Why did Southern women choose to attend Northern colleges?
2. How did the roles of women differ in the North and in the South?
3. What were the intended and actual teachings at the colleges?
4. What did these women do after they left college?
5. What was their impact on their Southern communities?

Cutler (1989), in a study of the schoolhouse in American education, listed five questions early in the report, which set the stage for the study. These questions were:

1. When did the schoolhouse become important in American education?
2. Why did it become so significant?
3. Has it become symbolic of our national ideals?
4. Does it remind us of the importance we attach to either the environment or education?
5. Has it lived up to its promise? (p. 1, listed in order but not numbered)

These questions were then answered and defended on the basis of historical perspective. The report includes over eighty references to sources. The use of questions is effective for organizing the content of the report and enhancing the continuity of ideas.

Nelson-Rowe (1991), in reporting on corporation schooling in the early twentieth century and the issues associated with factory-based trade education, states the purpose of the research as:

> This essay examines these issues by focusing on the relationship between corporation schooling and the labor market in the early twentieth century United States. More specifically,

> it explores the labor market concerns that led employers to create such schools, the effects the schools had on the occupational outcomes and wage earnings of graduates, and the extent to which the schools met the needs of the sponsoring companies. (p. 30)

The content of the report focuses on these issues, presenting the evidence and then drawing conclusions from the evidence. Forty-three footnotes provide the references for the research.

In a study that involved considerable quantitative analysis, Galenson (1998) states the purpose as:

> This essay will explore possible ethnic differences in contextual or neighborhood effects on school attendance in early Chicago by extending the previous quantitative analysis in two ways. (p. 18)

The analysis referred to estimated the probability of school attendance for a boy of a given ethnicity as a function of the specific ethnic composition of his neighborhood. For this analysis, 1860 federal census data were used. The previous analysis focused on sons of Irish immigrants. Galenson extended the analysis to determinants of school attendance for sons of native-born Americans and Germans, again using 1860 federal census data. The research problem of this study did not state any specific hypotheses as such.

> Research problems may be stated in a variety of ways for historical research studies. They may or may not include specific hypotheses and/or questions.

When hypotheses are stated, they usually are not stated in a statistical sense, although statistical information from the past could be used to support or refute hypotheses. Rather, in historical research, hypotheses are conjectures about the characteristics, causes, or effects of the situation, issue, or phenomenon under study.

Suppose a study is being conducted on the decline of the humanities curriculum during the seventeenth and eighteenth centuries. Undoubtedly this decline was due to a combination of factors. One hypothesis might be that the elevation of the common person and his or her vernacular through the industrial revolution reduced the importance of the humanities as an avenue to culture. A second hypothesis might be that the advances of science made unwelcome inroads into the curriculum, and this was detrimental to the humanities.

It should be noted that these hypotheses rest on an assumption of fact—that is, that the humanities curriculum did decline during this period. If this assumption were not correct, the hypotheses would have no basis. Having established any necessary assumptions (or facts) and stated the hypotheses, the researcher would then set out to assemble the necessary information to confirm or refute the hypotheses. In the forgoing example, when dealing with the initial hypotheses, the researcher would look for increased use of the common vernacular in the curriculum materials of the period. Different avenues to culture that developed during the period of the relationships between these and the humanities could be investigated. On the basis of the evidence, the hypothesis could be retained or discarded.

Another example would be a study of the historical development of professional education in the United States, specifically as it relates to secondary teachers. Undoubtedly, there would be several hypotheses; one might be that the teachers college developed as an outgrowth of the normal school, due primarily to the inadequate supply of teachers produced by the colleges and universities. The researcher would then collect evidence about the various possible factors that influenced the development of the teachers college. Information would be needed about the supply of and demand for secondary teachers and how this was related to the numbers of teachers produced by colleges and universities. The hypothesis is based on the assumption that the teachers college was an outgrowth of the normal school and considers the inadequate supply not only as a factor, but as the primary factor.

The matter of basing hypotheses on accurate assumptions may seem obvious, but failure to do so can occur, and a false assumption is almost certain to lead to an erroneous conclusion. For example, in the late nineteenth century, many liberal arts colleges took the position that it was unwarranted to grant a baccalaureate to graduates of professional schools. This position was based on the assumption that it was not in the tradition of higher education to award bachelor's degrees for the profession of education. Careful historical research would have revealed that the arts degree of the medieval university originated almost exclusively for teaching purposes.

Kaestle (1988b) identifies four pervasive methodological concerns and one of these, the problem of defining key terms, applies to the identification of the research problem. Some terms generally have vague meanings and this can be a pitfall in discussions and conclusions if terms are not defined more specifically. The term *educational reform* has been around a long time, and it is almost always in vogue, but in any given context its meaning must be specified.

A second potential difficulty with key terms is what Kaestle (1988b) calls presentism, described as:

> the danger of investing key terms from the past with their present connotations, or conversely, applying to past developments present-day terms that did not exist or meant something else at the time. (p. 41)

It could be argued that *school choice, educational objectives,* and *inquiry* are terms whose meanings have changed across the years. If you encountered these terms while doing historical research on some educational issue of the 1840s, they would probably have very different meanings in that context than they have in the present educational landscape. It could be argued that competency-based education and, correspondingly, competency testing have been around for some time. But these terms may not have been used until relatively recently, and over the years the operational meanings likely would have changed had the terms been used.

> When identifying the research problem, and throughout reporting the research, it is important to avoid vague and inconsistent use of key terms.

Collection and Evaluation of Source Materials

The collection of source material does not consist of simply assembling all available documents that appear to have some relevance to the research problem. A basic rule of historical research is to use primary sources whenever it is possible to locate them. The researcher must decide which are primary and which are secondary sources. This requires an analysis of the sources.

External Criticism. Source materials must be subjected to **external criticism,** the tool for establishing the validity of the document. The question to be answered is: Is the document genuine, authentic, and what it seems to be?

> *External criticism* in historical research evaluates the validity of the document—that is, where, when, and by whom it was produced.

Establishing the validity of materials involves several possible factors, any of which could make the document invalid. With written material, the status of the author in the context of the event is important. Was the author an on-the-spot observer, if the document appears to be a primary source? Are factors such as time and place consistent with what is known about the event?

Because the practice of using ghostwriters is common, a document that appears to be the product of a direct observer may in fact be a secondary source. The ghostwriter's unique contributions may inadvertently or deliberately threaten the validity of the document, and there also are possibilities of inadvertent mechanical errors. A word may be mistranslated or an error made in typing or transcribing documents. For source materials produced before the advent of printing, copy errors in reproduced documents are not unusual. Printing has not eliminated the possibility of such errors, but it has reduced their likelihood.

Internal Criticism. The second part of critical evaluation is **internal criticism,** which establishes the meaning of the material along with its trustworthiness. There may be some overlap between external and internal criticism, but the shift in emphasis is from the actual material as a source to the content of the material. To some extent, external criticism precedes internal criticism in the sequence, because there is little point in dealing with the content of the material if its authenticity is doubtful. However, consider the external criticism directed toward the author of what appears to be a historical document. In establishing the author's status, it may very well be necessary to evaluate some of the content. This essentially becomes internal criticism.

> *Internal criticism* in historical research evaluates the meaning, accuracy, and trustworthiness of the content of the document.

The author is an important factor in evaluating the content of a document as well as in establishing the authenticity of the document. A pertinent question of internal criticism is whether the author was predisposed, because of position or otherwise, to present a biased rather than an objective account. Biographies and autobiographies may tend to shift the emphasis from the event to the person. Fictitious details may be included by the author because of some personal factor. An author who was opposed to an existing educational policy might have emphasized different factors than one who was favorable toward the same policy at the same time. For these kinds of situations, the position or status of the author is very important in ascribing meaning to the content.

An analysis of the author's style and use of rhetoric is important for internal criticism. Does the author have a tendency to color the writings by eloquent but misleading phrases? Is part of the writing figurative rather than a record of the real event? If the question of figurative and real meaning arises, the researcher must be able to distinguish between the two. Does the author borrow heavily from documents already in existence at the time of his or her writing? If so, is the document an objective restatement of the facts, or do the author's own interpretations come into the writings? The latter is more likely the case. The researcher should check the reporting of the author for consistency with the earlier sources. This process should also give indications of the separation of fact and interpretation.

The concern for accuracy is basic to all internal criticism (as well as external criticism). There are two parts to the question of the accuracy of a specific author: Was the author competent to give an accurate report and, if competent, was he or she predisposed to do so? A competent reporter may, for some reason, give a distorted account of an event. In checking several authors, there may be inconsistencies even about such facts as the date of a specific event. In such a case, the researcher must weigh the evidence and decide which account is more accurate.

A single document, even a primary source, can seldom stand on its own. Internal criticism involves considerable cross-referencing of several documents. If certain facts are omitted from an account, this should not be interpreted to mean that the author was unaware of them or that they did not occur. Each document should be evaluated in its chronological position—that is, in the light of the documents that preceded it, not in the light of documents that appeared later. If several sources contain the same errors, they are likely to have originated from a common erroneous source. If two sources are contradictory, it is certain that at least one is in error, but it is also possible that both are in error. The discounting of one account does not establish the trustworthiness of another. A specific document may prove valuable for certain parts of the overall research problem and essentially useless for other parts.

Both external and internal criticism are necessary for establishing the credibility and usefulness of the source. If the source is not authentic, it cannot be used. Even if it is authentic, if its content is not relevant to the research problem, it would be useless. The functions of external and internal criticism are summarized in Figure 11.2.

Synthesis of Information

Internal criticism carries over into the third step of the methodology—synthesis of the information. The materials have now been reviewed and their authenticity established, at

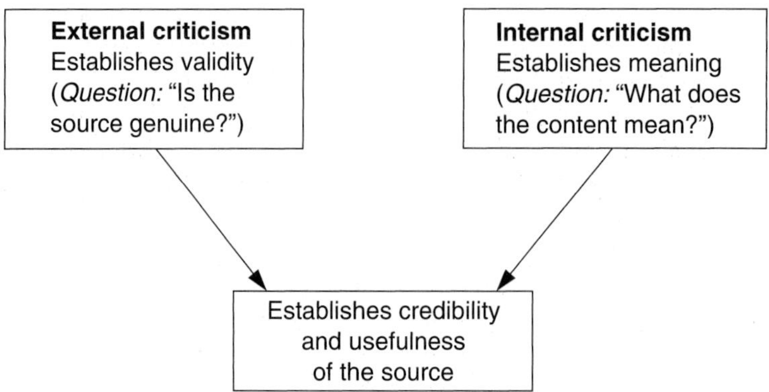

FIGURE 11.2 External and Internal Criticism in the Evaluation of Source Materials for Historical Research

least to the satisfaction of the researcher. The relative value of the various sources must be considered. For example, a primary source may be considered more important than a secondary one. If contradictory accounts appear, the inconsistencies must be resolved, which may require developing a case for discounting one version of the event.

Central ideas or concepts must be pulled together and continuity between them developed. If a substantial period of time—say, several years—is covered by the research study, the ideas often can be organized chronologically. In fact, chronological ordering commonly is required to avoid confusion between possible cause and effect among events. Several accounts of the same event may be included in the source materials. If the accounts are consistent, they provide historical support, and the researcher can summarize the information from these accounts with respect to the point being made.

As the researcher reviews the source materials and synthesizes the information from them, it may be necessary to formulate additional hypotheses or revise initial ones. Evidence may appear that refutes initial hypotheses; unanticipated information may support new hypotheses; and the materials also may generate new questions relevant to the research problem. If hypotheses and questions are not included but the research proceeds from a statement of purpose, it may be advantageous to introduce hypotheses when synthesizing the information. In any event, hypotheses should be introduced when they prove useful, especially as they provide direction for the research and assist in synthesizing information.

Analysis, Interpretation, and Formulating Conclusions

The final step of historical research methodology is characterized by decision making about the research problem. Historical research relies heavily on a logical analysis of the information from the documents. At the final step, the conclusions are formulated, and any hypotheses introduced earlier are either supported or rejected. Of course, it is necessary to make interpretations of the information, and the researcher should recognize the possibility of alternative explanations of the results if such explanations are reasonable. A case should be made for the most likely interpretation, but if other possible interpretations exist, they should at least be recognized. For all interpretations, the author should remain as objective as possible.

Earlier it was mentioned that Kaestle (1988b) identified four methodological problems and one of those primarily was associated with the identification of the research problem. The other three are most directly associated with interpretations and conclusions. They are:

1. Confusion of correlations (or associations) and causes.
2. A lack of distinction between ideas about how people should behave, and how ordinary people in fact behaved.
3. Failure to distinguish between intent and consequences. (pp. 40–41, paraphrased and numbered)

The first problem often is associated with quantitative research, that of interpreting an association or correlation between two variables, as a cause-and-effect relationship. There may be such a relationship, but the simple fact of association does not establish such a relationship.

Evidence about how people actually behaved may be lacking in historical documents. If during a certain period substantial legislation was passed, it cannot be inferred that people were pleased with the laws or even that they obeyed them.

We tend to think that knowing how things turned out gives hindsight a definite advantage over foresight. This may be so, but there may be danger in ascribing consequences to deliberate intentions. For school reforms of the past that have failed, it would be tenuous to conclude that failure was due to the deliberate intentions of educators. Many times other factors, over which educators have little or no control, contribute to failure and change. Also, in many situations, people may not have been aware of potential consequences of their actions.

Historical researchers cannot eliminate all potential difficulties in analysis and interpretation. However, researchers should be aware of potential problems and take these into consideration when interpreting results and drawing conclusions.

It is not practical to include here an entire conclusions section of a historical research report. These sections tend to be lengthy narratives, sometimes having the conclusions interspersed throughout the report. Occasionally, authors will not use headings within the report, although conclusions can be identified in the narrative.

As an example of conclusions drawn from a historical research study, an excerpt is taken from a study of the social history of the school principal in North America that was done by Rousmaniere (2007):

> As educational historians have long argued, the development of a bureaucratic school system in the late 19th and early 20th centuries created a seismic shift in the organizational character of North American schools. In this essay, I have traced the role of the principal in those massive educational changes. I suggest that the peculiar position of the principal as a middle manager with a "dual personality," standing between the classroom and the district,

> provides a fresh insight into how school systems slowly lumbered into their contemporary model. The school principal continues to represent the on-going tension between central and local management, between policy development and policy implementation, and between formal bureaucratic aspects of school administrative work and the informal, relational, and immediate demands of daily school life. However much effort has been made to separate the principal from the teacher and to design it as an authoritative and professional profession, the principalship has remained tethered to the classroom and the teacher. That legacy continues in the workload of contemporary principals who juggle a diverse array of responsibilities from supervision of staff to instructional design to discipline of students to community relations to crisis management. Not surprisingly, there is a shortage of school principals, and also not surprisingly, a shortage of women and people of color expressing interest in the principalship. More historical studies of the school principal may provide further insights into the curious combination of marginality and centrality of the principal in school organization and culture. (p. 22)

The conclusions indicated that what she had found was true in the late nineteenth and early twentieth centuries was also true today. The principal has one foot in the central office and the other foot in the classroom. There is tension associated with maintaining this position with reasonable balance.

Quantitative Methods in Historical Research

As was mentioned earlier, historical research is usually considered a type of qualitative research, but quantitative methods may apply also. Indeed, within recent years there has been an increased use of quantitative methods, motivated in part by the availability of computers for summarizing and quantifying data. Historical research in education enables us to get in touch with the realities of schooling in the past and Kaestle (1988a) identifies this as the "great virtue of quantitative educational history" (p. 65). The description aids in learning about factors such as teacher supply and demand, the role of schooling across communities, and the impact of schooling on the individual. Quantitative methods help provide a description of the realities of schooling in the past.

Descriptive statistics quite commonly appear in historical research studies. These statistics may be percentages, proportions, or means simply describing the distributions of some variable, such as the percentages of 18- and 19-year olds who graduated from high school during a specified period. However, more sophisticated quantitative methods can be used. Galenson (1998) used logit regression in which a binary variable, whether or not the sons of native-born American family heads had attended school in the twelve months preceding the 1860 census, was expressed as a function of five other variables such as the boy's age and his father's occupation.

Sometimes the volume of data from the past is such that sampling is necessary. In a study reported by Ringer (1978), a random sample of entries was selected from major biographical encyclopedias for Germany, France, England, and the United States. The entries were those for males born between 1810 and 1899 who might have reached advanced educational institutions between 1830 and 1930. Perlmann and Margo (1989), in their study

"Who Were America's Teachers?" used two-stage, random sampling. At the first stage, they selected a 50 percent sample of census microfilm reels in 1860 and 1880. Then, at the second stage, they selected sets of pages from each reel. So, random sampling can be used effectively in order to keep the quantity of data manageable.

> Historical research is viewed primarily as qualitative in nature, but quantitative methods may be used effectively for some studies, especially those involving data sets (such as census data) that can be made machine-readable for computers.

Comments on the Reporting of Historical Research

In contrast to reports of experimental or survey research, which typically include generally accepted headings, reports of historical research tend to take on a variety of forms. One form is that of an unbroken narrative, which may enhance the content of ideas. In a study of medical education change at the Stanford University School of Medicine, 1908–1990, Cuban (1997) poses the research problem in question form as:

> Why are there recurring curricular and instructional reforms, and why do these reforms seemingly leave untouched this 2 × 2 model? (p. 83)

The 2 × 2 model referred to consists of two years of preclinical schooling followed by two years of clinical work in hospitals and clinics.

Cuban then uses a series of headings to describe medical education at Stanford University, beginning with a somewhat chronological overview for the period 1908–1990. Then the headings focus on specific redesigns or reforms of the curriculum such as the five-year plan or the all-elective curriculum. These again, are to a large extent, chronological. The final heading is "The Paradox of Change without Reform," which is a long section addressing the answer posed in the question of the research problem.

The Galenson (1998) study referred to earlier used quite different headings than those of Cuban (1997). Galenson provides an introduction followed by four sections with the following headings: The Data, Statistical Estimates of Neighborhood Effects, Ethnicity and Early Chicago's School Systems, and Conclusion. Except for the description of the data, which is only three paragraphs in length, the other sections are quite long. Galenson focuses on a very limited time period, 1860, in contrast to Cuban, who covered a period of about eight decades.

The point is that headings may vary considerably across reports of historical research in terms of both the numbers of headings and their content. The important characteristic is that the headings facilitate the organization of the content and the continuity of ideas. Overall, the research problem typically is identified early in the report, with a supporting context. Hypotheses or questions may be included, or a proposition (which is basically a hypothesis) may be presented that will be supported or refuted. Then the evidence is provided, synthesizing information from several sources. Finally, conclusions are presented, based on the evidence.

> Reports of historical research may vary considerably in the number and content of the headings.

Reports in Professional Journals

A number of professional journals devote at least part of their space to reports of historical research. The most obvious journal for reports of historical research in education is the *History of Education Quarterly,* published by the History of Education Society. Numerous other journals publish reports of historical research, although they are not limited to this area. These journals include:

Educational Studies, published by the American Educational Studies Association

Comparative Education Review, published by the University of Chicago Press

Harvard Education Review, published by Harvard University Press

There are journals that are not specifically oriented to education, but do report historical research and include some educational studies. These journals include:

Historical Research, published by the Institute of Historical Research (an institute in the University of London's Centre for Postgraduate Studies in History)

History, published by the Historical Association

Historical Methods, published by HELDREF Publications and edited by the Department of History of the University of Illinois at Chicago

The latter entry is identified as a journal of quantitative and interdisciplinary history.

An interesting example of historical research that illustrates the research process already described was done by Hines (2003), in which she studied the impact of the elimination of sex segregation on Pi Lambda Theta (PLT) and Phi Delta Kappa (PDK), honorary organizations dedicated to advancing the profession of education. The time period of her study was the late 1960s and the early 1970s, a period of intense focus on women's issues. She began by describing the organizations.

> Deans at university schools of education founded Phi Delta Kappa in 1910 to give university-educated men in education an organizational place separate from women. Within two years, many of these same deans instigated the founding of Pi Lambda Theta to give university-educated women a place separated from those trained at less prestigious normal schools and to avoid the proliferation on university campuses of the coeducational Kappa Delta Pi, another honorary and professional fraternity in education. From their birth, PDK and PLT coexisted cooperatively on university campuses as separate but parallel societies. (Hines, 2003, p. 196)

Primary sources were available to Hines from the records of both organizations. This included entire records of defunct chapters that were sent to PLT headquarters and board meeting minutes and correspondence from both groups. She followed the developments chronologically.

Hines describes the various pressures that surfaced at that time including the emerging women's rights movement, a "generation gap" between the young members of PLT and the organization's leadership, and legal and government initiatives to end sex discrimination, among other things. She describes how "maverick" chapters of PDK initiated women into the organization in defiance of the PDK constitution and how PLT members at those institutions gravitated from PLT to PDK.

Board meeting minutes revealed how the organizations' leadership responded to these pressures. Proposals to merge the groups, to open admissions to both sexes, and to continue the status quo were hotly debated. Hines explains the rationales for each of these proposals as well as the outcomes.

> Phi Delta Kappa's representatives at the 1971 Biennial Council sent a clear message supporting sex segregation. Not only did delegates vote against the coeducation initiative, but they also adopted a resolution allowing the national officers to punish chapters that violated the organization's constitution. (Hines, 2003, p. 204)

Lawsuits were then filed to test the constitutionality of PDK's membership policies. Members of PLT who joined maverick PDK chapters no longer saw a need for a separate women's educational fraternity. And, perhaps even more significantly, the federal government enacted legislation denying federal funds to institutions that engaged in sex discrimination. Noted university administrators responded by examining single-sex organizations on their campuses and at times denying them access to university facilities.

The organizations still opposed the admission of both sexes and instead explored cooperative activities and later explored various ways to merge. PLT members decided that it would not serve their interests to merge in that they would lose power, because PDK was so much larger than PLT, and that it would eliminate their identity. Merging would compromise the position of women.

After extensive debate and the consideration that each chapter might have the option of admitting women members, the 1973 PDK Biennial Council voted to grant full admission to women. Two months later PLT, through a mail ballot, voted to extend membership to men. Interestingly, Hines had access to the ballots in the PLT archives and was able to record comments that were written on the ballots.

After a discussion of the changes that occurred after the votes, she concluded, among other things, that:

> For PLT, that goal of advancing the profession took precedence over any individual or personal goal that may have resulted from women's organizing for feminist ends. . . . Pi Lambda Theta did not thrive but underwent a period of membership loss and financial troubles. In many ways women saw access to the men's organization as success for women; for PLT, with access to professional status achieved and with the end of separatism, the organization lost an important part of its reason to exist. Pi Lambda Theta was not able to maintain either its market or its mission. (Hines, 2003, p. 223)

Hines supported her claims with forty-eight footnotes from a variety of sources including Board of Directors' meeting minutes, chapter correspondence files, committee reports, project reports, books, journal articles, newsletters, newspapers, a dissertation, telephone conversation notes, internal reports, Proceedings of the PDK Biennial Council, and confidential proposals. The writing is clear and well documented. Her conclusions are based on the evidence that she presented.

Reports of historical research in professional journals often tend to be somewhat longer than those of experiments or surveys because historical research requires information from numerous sources that must be included with considerable detail. The information cannot simply be referred to and stated in a sentence or two. Historical research studies usually cover periods of several years (or longer) or deal with issues that involve considerable information. Using all of this information effectively, with good continuity of ideas, tends to increase the length of the report. The number of references cited in a historical research report tends to be quite large, in some cases over one hundred in a report of thirty pages or so in a professional journal.

Summary

Historical research, like any type of research, has some unique characteristics. Because historical research deals with events that have already happened, the historical researcher searches for data rather than producing data. The variables of the past have occurred; they are not subject to manipulation.

Educational research problems investigated by historical research can cover a variety of areas: general educational history, the history of an issue, the history of educational legislation, institutional history, and many others. In some manner, the problems generally deal with either policy or practices, and the nature of history and historical inquiry places this limitation on historical research. In a certain sense, the problems investigated by historical research have an ongoing characteristic. Many important educational issues are initially dealt with by relying on the perspective supplied by the history of the issue. Curriculum change often is viewed in the light of past philosophy, ideas, developments, and curriculums, and historical research is necessary to define the situation of the past and its meaning in the light of the present problem. Interpretations based on historical research thus can aid in defining a course of action for dealing with a present educational problem.

Historical research follows a systematic process, called historiography, from the identification of the research problem through the formulation of conclusions. The process is quite integrated, characterized by a synthesis of information from the source materials. Internal and external criticism are used to establish the validity of source materials. In summary, historical research is a systematic process of reconstructing what happened and interpreting the meaning of events.

As with any period, there presently are many educational issues before the profession and before the public. Historical research in education can provide a perspective for issues, including information that can be used to avoid mistakes. The study of educational trends of the past may be useful for predicting similar or related trends for the future. Policymakers at any level in education can benefit from the contributions of historical research in arriving at decisions.

KEY CONCEPTS

Logical induction	Primary source	External criticism
Policymaking	Secondary source	Internal criticism
Source materials	Historiography	

EXERCISES

11.1 Use the internet to find a historical research study. Review the article carefully, focusing on the author's procedures for collecting information. Consider such things as whether or not primary sources were used. Is there adequate continuity between ideas? Did the author use hypotheses, either explicitly stated or implicit in the statement about the research problem? If so, what are they? Did the evidence used in making decisions about the research problems (or hypotheses) seem adequate?

11.2 For each of the following examples, indicate what type of research is most likely called for: experimental, survey, or historical:

a. An indicator of the likelihood of passing a school district's bond proposal.
b. The effects of drill exercises on the development of computation skills in arithmetic.
c. The basis for the age-graded school.
d. The relationship between psychomotor skills and achievement in academic success.
e. Precedents for the establishment of a dress code.
f. The effect of attitude toward school on achievement in science.
g. The attitude toward school of students enrolled in science courses.

11.3 Suppose you are interested in the history of requirements for graduation from elementary school that involved passing a common test of some kind. The period to be covered is 1900 to 1940, and the history within a single state is being studied. To some extent, this is a study of proficiency testing of the past, although it probably did not go by that name. What sources would you use for information? What are possible primary and secondary sources? Would there be any merit in reviewing educational legislation passed at the state level during the period?

11.4 Identify three or four educational key terms that might be susceptible to a problem of definition when considering these meanings today and what they meant fifty or seventy-five years ago. Are the difficulties in definition due to vagueness or presentism?

11.5 Suppose historical research is being done on the history of teachers' unions during the early days of their formation. Identify possible situations in which there may be problems making a distinction between how we interpret how people may have behaved and how they actually did behave. Would research in this area be susceptible to possible confusion between intent and consequences? If so, how?

11.6 Review an article from a professional journal, such as *Historical Methods,* that involves the use of quantitative methods. Identify the methods used and note how they are used to support the conclusions of the study.

11.7 The study by Hines (2003) relied on the archives and documents of Phi Delta Kappa and Pi Lambda Theta. How would you design a study of the same topic using oral histories? Consider whom you would interview and what difficulties you would encounter. What kind of information would you probably uncover that is not likely to appear in written records?

11.8 Design a study that would be a follow-up to the Hines (2003) study that would research what has happened to Pi Lambda Theta and Phi Delta Kappa since admitting both sexes into the organizations? What time periods would you consider? What sources of information would you use? Would you specify any hypotheses?

11.9 Identify several primary sources and several secondary sources that might be used in a study of desegregation of Alabama schools in the 1960s.

11.10 What would be the difficulties in doing historical research on a recent educational issue such as the No Child Left Behind legislation?

REFERENCES

Cuban, L., (1997). Change without reform: The case of Stanford University School of Medicine, 1908–1990. *American Educational Research Journal, 34*, 83–122.

Cutler III, W. W. (1989). Cathedral of culture: The schoolhouse in American educational thought and practice since 1820. *History of Education Quarterly, 29*, 1–40.

Edson, C. H. (1986). Our past and present: Historical inquiry in education. *Journal of Thought, 21*, 13–27.

Ellenwood, S. (2007). Revisiting character education: From McGuffey to narratives. *Journal of Education, 187,* 21–44.

Galenson, D. W. (1998). Ethnic differences in neighborhood effects on the school attendance of boys in early Chicago. *History of Education Quarterly, 38*, 18–35.

Graham, P. A. (1980). Historians as policy makers. *Educational Researcher, 9*, 21–24.

Hines, L. M. (2003). When parallel paths cross: Competition and the elimination of sex segregation in the educational fraternities, 1969–74. *History of Education Quarterly, 43,* 196–223.

Johnson, J. M. (2007). Job market or marriage market? Life choices for Southern women at Northern colleges, 1875–1915. *History of Education Quarterly, 47,* 149–172.

Kaestle, C. F. (1988a). Recent methodological developments in the history of American education. In R. M. Jaeger (Ed.), *Complementary methods for research in education* (pp. 61–78). Washington, DC: American Educational Research Association.

Kaestle, C. F. (1988b). Research methodology: Historical methods. In J. P. Keeves, (Ed.), *Educational research: Methodology and measurement: An international handbook* (pp. 37–42). Oxford: Pergamon.

Kaestle, C. F. (1992). Standards of evidence in historical research. *History of Education Quarterly, 32,* 361–366.

Nelson-Rowe, S. (1991). Corporation schooling and the labor market at General Electric. *History of Education Quarterly, 31*, 27–46.

Perlmann, J., and Margo, R. (1989). Who were America's teachers? Toward a social history and a data archive. *Historical Methods, 22*, 68–73.

Ringer, F. K. (1978). The education of elites in modern Europe. *History of Education Quarterly, 18,* 159–172.

Rousmaniere, K. (2007). Go to the principal's office: Toward a social history of the school principal in North America. *History of Education Quarterly, 47,* 1–22.

Stricker, F. (1992). Why history? Thinking about the uses of the past. *History Teacher, 25*, 293–312.

Thomas, W. B., and Moran, K. J. (1992). Reconsidering the power of the superintendent in the progressive period. *American Educational Research Journal, 29*, 22–50.

CHAPTER 12

Ethnographic Research

Ethnographic research, which traditionally is associated with anthropology, has been around for a long time. Within the past two or three decades, ethnographic research in the educational context has been receiving increased attention. Undoubtedly, this is in part due to the increased acceptance of, and the increased interest in, qualitative research. Another contributing factor to the interest in ethnographic research has been the realization that there may be problems in education that can best be attacked, and possibly only can be attacked, through an ethnographic research approach. Ethnographic research sometimes goes by other names, such as *field research* or *qualitative research.* Although these terms are to some extent descriptive of ethnographic research, they are not synonymous with it. In this chapter, the nature of ethnographic research is discussed, along with procedures used in ethnographic studies. Also discussed are examples of educational research using ethnographic methodology.

The Nature of Ethnography in Education

The term **ethnography** refers to both a research process and the product of that process. The product is a written account, that is, the ethnography of what was studied. The term *ethnography* comes to us from anthropology. The *Random House Dictionary of the English Language* defines *ethnography* as "a branch of anthropology dealing with the scientific description of individual cultures." Anthropology is considered a science—specifically, the science that deals with the origins, development, and characteristics of humankind, including such factors as social customs, beliefs, and cultural development.

If we project this definition of ethnography into educational research, we can describe the ethnographic research process as:

> The process of providing holistic and scientific descriptions of educational systems, processes, and phenomena within their specific contexts.

This is a broad definition, which is necessary because ethnographic research is applied in a variety of situations. As Wolcott (1988) points out, "no particular research technique is associated exclusively with ethnography" (p. 191). Numerous research procedures are used in ethnographic research, and these can be described, but by themselves these techniques will not produce the desired product: the ethnography of what is under study. Ethnographic research is an inquiry process guided by experience in the research setting.

Although ethnographic research may at times involve quantitative procedures, it is considered a part of qualitative research. As such, its epistemology—that is, its origins and methods—is based in the epistemology of qualitative research.

The Phenomenological Nature

Phenomenology is the study of phenomena; it stresses the careful description of phenomena from the perspective of those experiencing the phenomena. Phenomenologists do not assume that they know what things mean to the people they are observing. If behavior is being observed, the phenomenologist does not simply note that a certain behavior has occurred, but attempts to understand what the behavior means to the persons being studied, and this emphasizes the subjective aspects of the behavior.

Because ethnographic research is phenomenological in nature, it takes on the characteristics of that approach to research. These characteristics include the holistic and naturalistic nature of ethnographic research discussed below, so these characteristics overlap and are separated here only for emphasis. Essentially, the phenomenological approach is based on the concept that reality consists of the meaning of experiences by those being studied. For example, a good case can be made for the position that research on instruction in the schools should, at least in part, be ethnographic research. Consider fourth-grade mathematics instruction. The important focus for the phenomenological approach is to understand what mathematics instruction means—how it is perceived—by the fourth-grade students experiencing such instruction. There is little importance placed on what the educator thinks is going on; the importance is on understanding what the students are experiencing from their perspectives.

> The phenomenological approach emphasizes that the meaning of reality is, in essence, in the "eyes and minds of the beholders," the way the individuals being studied perceive their experiences.

The phenomenological nature of ethnographic research has certain implications for how research is conducted, and these can be listed as:

1. As much as possible, a priori assumptions about the phenomenon under study are avoided.
2. Reality is viewed holistically and complex phenomena are not reduced to a few variables.
3. Data-collection procedures and instruments, although having some structure, should have minimum influence on the phenomena under study.
4. There is an openness to alternative explanations of the phenomenon, which may lead to alternative and changing concepts of reality.

5. Theory, as applicable, should emerge from the data as grounded theory rather than preconceived theories.

With regard to this latter characteristic, Lancy (1993) provides an excellent example of the emergence of **grounded theory.** In a study of parental influence on children's storybook reading, thirty-two parent–child pairs were videotaped as they read to each other. The process of identifying or developing grounded theory is summarized by:

> We had few if any preconceptions of what we would find, only that we hoped that distinct patterns would emerge and that these would be associated with the children's evident ease/difficulty in learning to read. I spent literally dozens of hours viewing these videotapes: developing, using and casting aside various categories until I found two clusters of characteristics, which I called "reductionist" and "expansionist," which accounted for a large portion of the variation among parents' reading/listening styles. (p. 10)

Thus, grounded theory is generated from the data, and developing grounded theory requires insight and understanding, and may require repetitive review of the data. Typically, this is not an easy task. Grounded theory does not lie like nuggets on the surface; it may require difficult extraction.

The Naturalistic Nature

Ethnographic research is conducted in a natural setting: a classroom, a school, a college, or some naturally occurring assembly of individuals. The researcher observes what is happening as it naturally occurs; there is no manipulation of variables, simulation, or externally imposed structure on the situation. Thus, ethnographic research is characterized as **field research,** with the "field" being the natural situation in which the research is conducted. For example, in an ethnographic study of social interaction among students in an integrated school, it would be necessary to observe student behavior in the school. The information could not be limited to teachers' opinion, and any social psychology theory that might apply should be grounded in the data.

Related to ethnographic research is the characteristic of **contextualization,** which requires that all data be interpreted only in the context of the situation or environment in which they were collected. Although all of educational research has a contextual emphasis to some extent, ethnographic research is probably more sensitive to context than other approaches. This has implications for the generalizability of research results. Ethnographic researchers often are not concerned about generalizability; to them, accurate and adequate description of the situation being studied is paramount. Of course, generalizability of results depends on the correspondence between the context under study and other situations.

> Ethnographic research involves *field research* and requires *contextualization*—the interpretation of results in the context of the data collection.

The Holistic and General Perspective

Experimentation and survey research traditionally involve a priori hypothesis formation, followed by specific procedures designed to test hypotheses. In contrast, ethnographic research proceeds from the position that hypotheses may emerge as the data collection occurs. The implication for data analysis is that it will be inductive, rather than deductive, which typically concentrates on testing preconceived hypotheses. The ethnographic researcher attempts to suspend any preconceived ideas or notions that might undesirably influence the interpretation of what is being observed. The researcher concentrates on the entire context and thus maintains a holistic view, rather than focusing on bits and pieces. If hypotheses emerge from the data collection, they are retained for the time being, but an ethnographic researcher is willing to abandon tentative hypotheses if subsequent data collection fails to support them. The results of prior research also are held in abeyance until the researcher is convinced of their relevance to the research situation at hand.

> Ethnographic research takes a general and holistic perspective. Hypotheses are more likely to emerge from the data than to be formulated prior to the research.

Given these characteristics, we can see that ethnographic research consists of naturalistic inquiry with a holistic emphasis. It is a phenomenological approach, emphasizing the subjective nature of behavior. Ethnographic research is conducted in the field setting, based on the premise that the situation influences people's interpretations, thoughts, and actions. The researcher attempts to interpret the situation from the perspective of the individuals being studied. Geertz (1973) characterizes the task of ethnography as "thick description."

To some extent, the methodology of ethnographic research emerges as the research is in progress. As indicated before, no particular research technique is associated exclusively with ethnographic research. But a variety of techniques are used, and it is helpful to put them into a conceptual schema in order to provide a general context for ethnographic research.

A Conceptual Schema for Ethnographic Research

What kinds of research problems, issues, or topics are studied through ethnographic research?[1] Typical ethnographic studies in education might have the following research statements:

1. A study of life in an urban classroom.
2. A study of decision making in an inner-city high school.
3. A study of student life in law school.
4. A study of student relations in an integrated school.
5. A study of peer interactions in racially mixed classrooms of a suburban high school.
6. A study of interaction patterns among faculty in a private prep school.

7. A study of instruction in writing in the elementary school.
8. A study of socialization within a rural high school.

Note that these statements are general. They do not contain phrases such as "the effects of," nor do they imply cause-and-effect relationships. As research statements, they lack specificity, which would be undesirable if an experiment or a survey were anticipated. But ethnographic research does not begin from specified, preconceived hypotheses; it relies heavily on description as the research proceeds. The foregoing sample statements clearly imply description.

Given the nature of ethnographic research, what elements are present in an ethnographic research study? One commonality among ethnographic research studies is the focus on an **organization** or community, usually of a social nature, or some part of a social organization or community. It may be possible to distinguish between an organization and a community. We usually think of organizations as having a hierarchial structure, possibly more so than a community, which may be formed more on the basis of shared values, beliefs, or needs. For the purposes of this discussion, either organization or community may be used as a starting point.

We think of an organization as defined groups of people who interact in regular and structured ways. There is collective social action, based on rules and relations that have been developed by consensus. The behavior of any one group is influenced by how that group interacts with another or several groups. Furthermore, individuals in an organization tend to behave as the members of the groups to which they belong. A school is a social organization, as is a classroom within a school.

> Ethnographic studies focus on *organizations* or *communities* that consist of defined groups of people who interact in regular and structured ways.

In our conceptual schema, we can now begin breaking down an organization into its parts. There are a number of ways this can be done, depending on the criteria used. We will consider two divisions—cultures and perspectives.

An organization can be viewed as consisting of **cultures.** A culture is the context in which the members of an organization function and relate one to another. A culture of a school, for example, can be defined by factors such as:

1. The concept/vision that people have of effective learning
2. The conditions that affect how the teaching–learning process is conducted
3. The rituals, or ceremonies, that mark important school events
4. The heroes/heroines that serve as role models

There is the culture of the school, and within the school, there are cultures such as a student culture (possibly more than one student culture), a faculty culture, and an administrative culture if the school is large enough. In summary, a culture consists of the collective understandings among the members of the group that are related to their particular roles.

Whatever makes up the parts of a culture, there is coherence and consistency among these parts. We will call the parts that make up a culture **perspectives.**

Perspectives direct the behavior of individuals and groups; usually in ethnographic research, group perspectives are studied. The coordinated set of ideas and actions utilized by an individual in dealing with a situation is his or her perspective. Thus, perspectives are situation-specific. A group perspective consists of ideas and actions developed by a group that faces a common problematic situation. Ideas include beliefs and attitudes as well as conceptual schemes about how to deal with the problem.

> Organizations are considered to be composed of *cultures*, and cultures are made up of *perspectives.*

To understand an organization or some part of it, ethnographic research is conducted from the inside, outward. That is, the researcher begins with the perspectives of one or

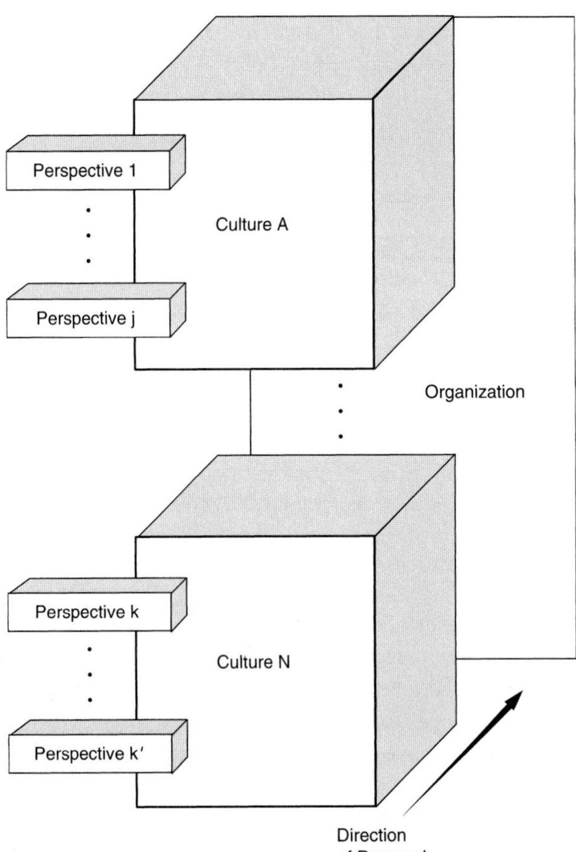

FIGURE 12.1 Conceptual Schema of a General Context for Conducting Ethnographic Research

more defined groups and uses them to describe one or more cultures. The purpose of the research may be to describe only one culture or to describe some aspect of one or more cultures in the organization. Unless the organization is small and sociologically simple, describing the entire organization might be quite ambitious. In the research statements listed earlier, the first implies description of an entire organization, the urban classroom. The second focuses on decision making, an aspect that cuts across cultures in a high school. The third focuses on student culture.

The relationship of perspectives, cultures, and organization is illustrated in Figure 12.1. The perspectives form the cultures, and the cultures make up the organization. The arrow indicates the direction of ethnographic research, beginning with perspectives to describe the cultures, which in turn describe the organization or some part of it.

Figure 12.2 illustrates an application of the conceptual schema to an ethnographic study of student life in law school. As indicated, three cultures are considered. These cultures

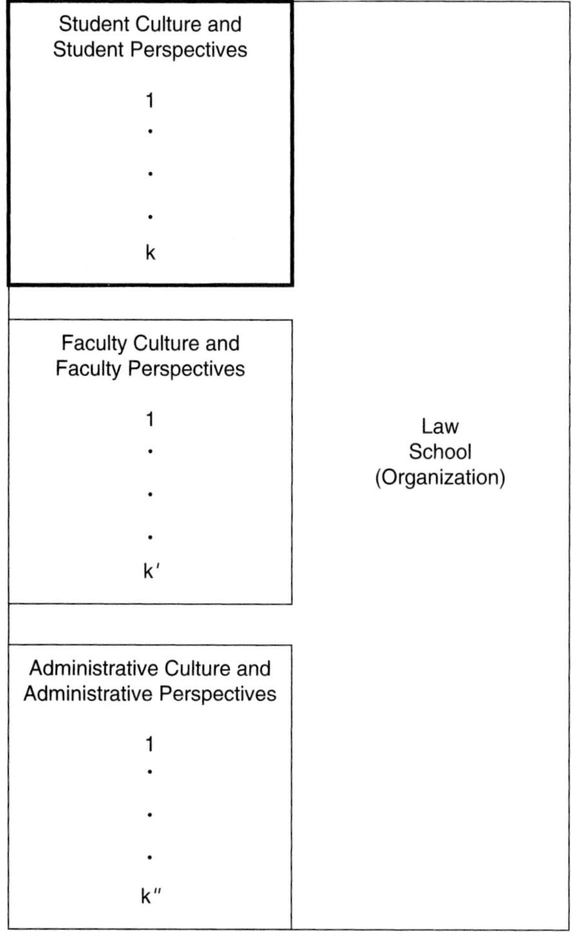

FIGURE 12.2 Sample Application of the Conceptual Schema to an Ethnographic Study of Student Life in Law School

may be made up of different numbers of perspectives—hence the use of k and k′ and k″. This study focuses on a particular culture—the student culture—which is indicated by bold lines. The other two cultures are included because they are likely to affect student culture although they are not the cultures of primary interest.

Thus far, we have discussed ethnographic research primarily in terms of generally conceptualizing the nature of such research. The process has been alluded to, but specific procedures have not been described. At this point, we turn to the process and procedures of conducting ethnographic research.

The Process of Ethnographic Research

One characteristic of the process of ethnographic research is that the activities or procedures are more integrated than the procedures of other research methodologies. In Chapter 1, a sequential pattern of general activities for conducting research was discussed. The activities were quite distinct, generally proceeding from identifying the research problem through drawing conclusions. Although we can identify specific procedures in ethnographic research, the procedures tend to run together or overlap throughout the process. For example, hypotheses may be generated throughout the entire data-collection process rather than being listed first and then tested with collected data. Thus, the ethnographic researcher is little concerned with sequencing specific procedures.

> The process of ethnographic research is an integrated process in which procedures are conducted concurrently.

The activities of the ethnographic research process are diagrammed in Figure 12.3. The layering of the activities in the figure indicates that they overlap and that they may be conducted concurrently. Although ethnographic research does not have distinct sequencing of activities, there is a starting point and an ending point. The identification of the phenomenon to be studied is the starting point, and the study terminates when the final conclusions are drawn. The activities are described and illustrated here in the context of a hypothetical study.

Identification of the Phenomenon to Be Studied

Suppose a study is conducted on:

> The social interaction of students in a racially mixed urban high school.

This statement identifies the phenomenon to be studied as social interaction of high school students, specifically in a racially mixed, urban high school. This is a general statement with few restrictions, but it does provide a starting point. Stated in question form it would be, "What happens socially to students in a racially mixed urban high school?"

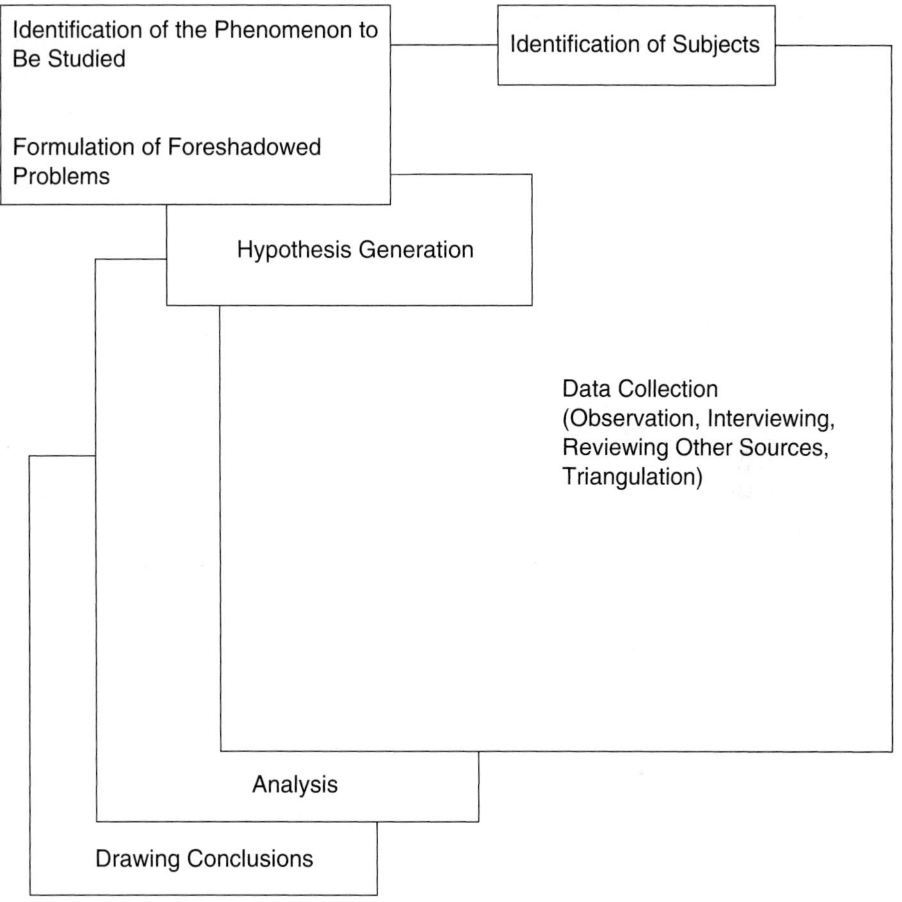

FIGURE 12.3 The Activities of the Ethnographic Research Process

Such a statement usually implies **foreshadowed problems**—somewhat specific factors and issues that apply to the phenomenon and provide a focus for the research. Essentially, there may be any number of foreshadowed problems, depending on the nature and extent of the study. The following are foreshadowed problems associated with the foregoing statement:

1. Interaction among the students across races
2. Interaction among the students across the sexes
3. Faculty social systems
4. Role of the faculty in the social interaction of students
5. Established policies that encourage or discourage social interaction
6. Acceptable codes of social behavior among students

Foreshadowed problems provide the researcher with something to look for. They provide direction, but they should not be considered restrictive. For example, as the study progresses, it might become apparent that grouping patterns for instructional purposes are also relevant, so these patterns would then be analyzed and discussed.

> *Foreshadowed problems* follow from the more general statement of the phenomenon to be studied; they provide a focus for the research.

Identification of Subjects

Because the example deals with social interaction of students, students are the subjects of interest. However, the students are found in a high school and the school was selected because of its characteristics and availability. The results of this study might generalize to other designated urban high schools, but certainly not to all such schools. Generalization would be argued on a logical basis.

Getting back to observing students, it is not possible or necessary to observe everything. So, conditions and restrictions must be considered. Will students be observed:

1. As one class followed through four years, or as four classes simultaneously?
2. From the time they enter the school in the morning until they leave in the afternoon, or only for a specified segment of the day?
3. In class and out of class, participating in such activities as clubs and athletics, or only in specified "academic" activities?
4. Only in instructional situations and in situations such as eating lunch or walking in the halls, or in all the situations of the school day?

These questions illustrate the kinds of things that need to be considered when collecting the data. Decisions about conditions are somewhat arbitrary. The study must be feasible, but it would be undesirable to have restrictions that might distort or mask the phenomenon under study. For the example, the four classes would likely be observed simultaneously; following one class through four years would require a long study. Students would be observed in any situations that involve social interaction. They would be observed in large groups and small groups, some as small as one-on-one interchanges. To facilitate data collection, groups of students (possibly even individuals) would be selected and then observed for a specified period, such as a day or a week.

It would not be possible to observe all students. Although students or groups of students might be selected randomly, they would more likely be selected through purposeful sampling. Purposeful sampling, which is described more fully in Chapter 14, is a procedure of selecting individuals, or in this case small groups, because of certain characteristics relevant to the phenomenon under study. For example, a group might be selected because it contains both boys and girls of several races in a relatively informal setting.

Although the students are certainly the subjects of major concern in this example, other subjects, such as faculty members, also may be observed or interviewed. Faculty may affect the social interaction of the students, and they are a source of information. Again, faculty would most likely be selected through purposeful sampling. Certain faculty may be in a better position to observe social interaction than others. Essentially, the research is a study of the student culture, with a focus on social interaction, but other cultures in the school would undoubtedly contribute relevant information.

> Subjects to be studied must be identified, and typically it is necessary to specify conditions and restrictions so that the study is feasible.

Hypothesis Generation

As the data collection proceeds in an ethnographic study, hypotheses may be formulated and modified. A study may begin with few if any specific hypotheses, but the data may imply hypotheses as the study continues. The ethnographic researcher is very amenable to introducing new hypotheses and discarding hypotheses that are not supported. There are no a priori limits on the number or nature of hypotheses.

A hypothesis that might be formulated in the social interaction example is, "Social interaction across racial lines increases as students become older." This hypothesis would be based on what is observed and initial data might support such a hypothesis, but it might be modified later to state, for example, that the increase occurs only within the sexes. The hypothesis modification procedure may become a process of successive approximations in an attempt to accurately describe the phenomenon under study.

> Hypothesis generation is a continuing activity throughout an ethnographic study. Unlike survey research or experimentation, for which hypotheses are initially specified and then tested, ethnographic research may begin with no hypotheses, and hypotheses may be formulated and modified along the way.

Data Collection

The mainstay of data collection in ethnographic research is observation conducted by the participant–observer, and a basic form of data is field notes. An observer may be identified openly as a researcher or may be in a disguised role. Wolcott (1988, p. 194) distinguishes among different participant–observer styles as active participant, privileged observer, and limited observer. As an active participant, the observer assumes the role of a participant. In the Becker, Geer, Hughes, and Strauss (1961) study, the observers actually assumed the role of medical student. For most ethnographic research in schools, the observer becomes a **privileged observer.** That is, the observer does not assume the role of a participant but has access to the relevant activity for the study. The **limited observer** role would be used when opportunities for observation are restricted and other data-collection techniques, of necessity, take precedence. Limited observers should be used sparingly, if at all, in educational ethnographic research. Wolcott (1988) suggests that the active participant role has been underutilized in educational research and that researchers should attempt to become more active participants rather than passive, albeit privileged, observers.

Not all data collection in an ethnographic study is necessarily conducted through participant observation. Interviews may be conducted with key individuals, and data may be collected through a survey that may support or refute information collected through observation. Written resources such as records may provide data. Like historical researchers, ethnographic researchers prefer primary sources over secondary sources. In fact, because ethnographic research deals with the present, there should be little need for secondary sources. Nonwritten sources such as videotapes, photographs, and artifacts also may provide data.

> Ethnographic research involves a variety of data-collection procedures, the primary procedure being observation.

Observation. Whatever their particular roles, observers try to be as unobtrusive as possible so that they do not interfere with normal activities. An important part of observation relates to the idea of contextualization; that is, to understand behavior, the observer must understand the context in which individuals are thinking and reacting. The observer must have the option of interpreting events. Thus, observation extends beyond objective recording of what happens. The **participant–observer** attempts to assume the role of the individuals under study and to experience their thoughts, feelings, and actions.

> The *participant–observer* attempts to generate the data from the perspective of the individuals being studied.

Observation in ethnographic research is comprehensive, that is, continuing and total. The observer attempts to record all relevant information in an unobtrusive way; consequently, observation is quite unstructured. It is not likely that an observer conducting ethnographic research would have a structured observation inventory. The emphasis is on capturing the perspective of the individuals being observed, which requires careful listening to pick up subtle cues and nuances. Observation is a continuing process; it is not limited to one or two sessions. In the social interaction example, observers might be in the school situation every day, all day, for an extended period—possibly an entire school year.

In the social interaction example, it would be difficult for the observer to assume the role of a student, so observation most likely would be conducted as a privileged observer. Possibly the observer could assume the role of a teacher, which would make him or her a participant from a culture other than the one of primary interest. However, the task of teaching would divert energy from the research effort and also would limit the researcher's mobility about the school.

The recordings made by the observer while actually conducting the observations are called **field notes.** There are two kinds of field notes, *descriptive* and *analytic.* **Descriptive**

field notes, as the name implies, describe the situation and events as they occur. The field notes need to describe when, where, and under what conditions the observation was made. The content of descriptive field notes may be somewhat unorganized and rough. They are usually written as a narrative, which may contain abbreviations, some form of shorthand, and phrases. If positions or movements of subjects are important, the field notes may contain diagrams with arrows. Immediately following the observation, before the details are forgotten, the researchers should synthesize and summarize the descriptive field notes.

Analytic field notes include the inferences and interpretations that are made about what was observed. Descriptive field notes might, for example, note that a particular student raised his hand repeatedly. The corresponding analytic field note could include possible reasons for the hand-raising such as attention-getting, the need for clarification, or the willingness to contribute to a discussion. Analytic field notes would also include questions that are raised that will be addressed in later observations. Figure 12.4 contains a partial observation record that might apply to the social interaction example.

> *Observation* in ethnographic research is continuing and total. It is quite unstructured. Field notes should be synthesized and summarized immediately after the observation.

Videotaping. Within recent years, videotaping has increased as a data-collection procedure. Videotaping has definite advantages when it applies, the overriding advantage being that the situation may be reviewed repeatedly for the purpose of obtaining more information. In the Lancy (1993) example, described earlier, videotaping was very useful for generating grounded theory. It enabled the researchers to review and to repeatedly compare

Time: 11:45 a.m., April 12, 2007
Location: School Cafeteria, Ninth-Grade Students' Lunch Period

Descriptive

The groupings at lunch were almost entirely along gender lines: small groups of boys and small groups of girls. There were only three groupings of couples, two were white, one Hispanic. There was no mixing of the races for girls, but there was some for boys. The boys at tables with mixed races were recognized as athletes who had been teammates. Conversation tended to focus on social rather than academic topics. There was little, if any, interaction from one table to another. Students were orderly regardless of their groupings . . .

Analytic

The pattern of seating at lunch is self-selected and highly structured. It appears that boys are more likely to interact socially across racial lines than girls. The small number of couples could mean that these students do not see the lunchroom as an appropriate setting for this kind of interaction. It is not clear whether the minimal interaction from one table to another is due to school discipline policies or student choice. Question: Will groupings of girls differ in other settings? . . .

FIGURE 12.4 Example of a Partial Observation Record: Descriptive and Analytic Field Notes

the parent–child reading situations. Grounded theory would have been much more difficult to develop based on one in-person observation of each situation.

If focus groups are used, videotaping can be effective. It is difficult for an observer to pick up the entire discussion because of the rate at which it occurs. Also, a videotape allows for a review of the nonverbal behaviors.

But videotaping has some definite disadvantages. It is hardly unobtrusive and the presence of equipment and the process may impact the situation. Another disadvantage is that something may occur that is not in the viewing field, and hence may be missed. For this reason, videotaping is more amenable to relatively compact situations such as a focus group of six or so individuals in which there is limited physical movement of the group members. It is much more difficult to get a holistic picture of everything going on in a classroom or cafeteria, for example. The videotaping equipment must be available and, of course, there is some cost associated with videotaping.

Videotaping does take pressure off taking field notes. In essence, field notes may be taken at leisure as the tapes are reviewed. Given the conditions under which observation is being conducted, and videotaping is an option, a decision can be made whether or not it is feasible or even worthwhile.

Interviewing. Interviewing might be quite open-ended and casual or it might be quite structured. However, in keeping with the phenomenological approach, at least some of the interviewing should be open-ended and informal. Casual and informal interviewing can be done when an occasion presents itself during observation. Questions might be asked of those being observed in an attempt to clarify what is happening or in an attempt to capture the feelings of those observed.

Key informant interviewing is a technique from anthropology in which the term *informant*[2] is defined by Wolcott (1988) as "an individual in whom one invests a disproportionate amount of time because that individual appears to be particularly well informed, articulate, approachable, or available" (p. 195). Wolcott also implies that ethnographic research in education may not be using the key informant to maximum benefit; partly because of the notion that truth resides in large numbers, and partly because of familiarity with education, researchers tend to see themselves as key informants.

Interviewing key informants would apply in the social interaction example. Certain students might be exceptionally well informed about the interaction or highly sensitive to it. Some faculty, such as one or more guidance counselors, also might serve as key informants. The principal or an assistant principal who deals with discipline is another candidate for key informant.

Formal, structured interviews may be conducted with a predefined set of questions. In the social interaction example, a number of students might be interviewed. Faculty and administrators also might be interviewed. Other people, such as cooks, lunchroom attendants, and janitors, might be interviewed to obtain their perceptions of the students' social interaction. Such interviews would be helpful in determining the tone of the social interaction, which might not be entirely apparent from observing behavior.

It is important that the interviewer be a good listener. At no time should interviewers indicate that they are being evaluative of the responses. An expression of genuine interest in what the informant is saying should be maintained. The informants should be at ease and inclined to talk freely. The interviewer should be flexible and ready to respond to whatever in the situation will produce useful information.

Reviewing Other Sources. There may be other sources of data that reflect on the research problem under study. These other sources often consist of records maintained on a routine basis by the organization in which the study is being conducted. Data from standardized achievement tests, attitude inventories, psychological tests, and vocational interest inventories might be useful. In fact, such measures could be administered in connection with the study although it is more common to use data from existing sources. Nonwritten sources such as photographs and films might provide information.

In the example, records of the incidence of discipline infractions involving interchanges between two or more students would be of interest. Such records might support (or fail to support) the observation data and the perceptions of the researchers. Students might be administered an attitude inventory to measure racial and socialization attitudes. (Such an inventory would likely need to be constructed for the study.) Videotapes of students interacting in a social situation would be an example of a nonwritten source.

Triangulation. **Triangulation** is a part of data collection that cuts across two or more techniques or sources. Essentially, it is qualitative cross-validation. It can be conducted among different data sources or different data-collection methods. As Denzin (1978) points out: "Triangulation can take many forms, but its basic feature will be the combination of two or more different research strategies in the study of the same empirical units" (p. 308).

Figure 12.5 illustrates triangulation in two cases—one involving data sources and the other involving data-collection procedures. The figure applies to the social interaction example.

Basically, triangulation is comparison of information to determine whether or not there is corroboration. It is a search for convergence of the information on a common finding or concept. To a large extent, the triangulation process assesses the sufficiency of the data. If the data are inconsistent or do not converge, they are insufficient. The researcher is then faced with a dilemma regarding what to believe.

> *Triangulation* is qualitative cross-validation. It assesses the sufficiency of the data according to the convergence of multiple data sources or multiple data-collection procedures.

Consider an instance of triangulation from the social interaction example. The observation data in Figure 12.4, concerning ninth-grade students, led the researcher to a tentative hypothesis that there was more social interaction across the races for boys than for girls at this age. Some information collected from individual interviews with a ninth-grade boy and a ninth-grade girl was as follows:

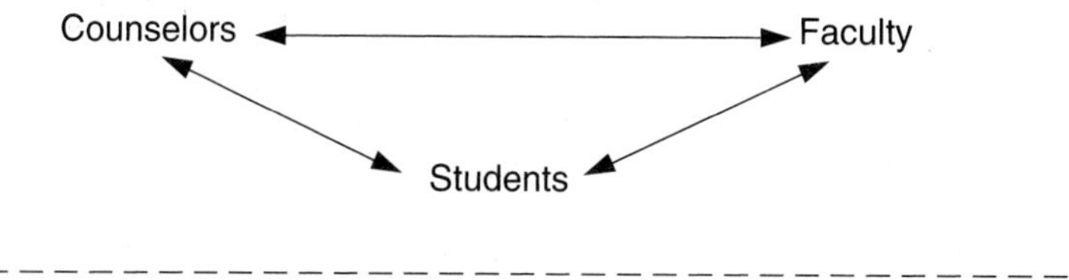

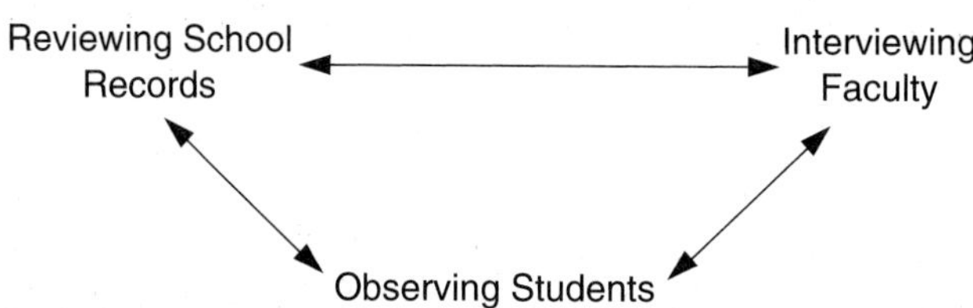

FIGURE 12.5 Triangulation (the Process of Qualitative Cross-Validation) for the Social Interaction Example

> *Ninth-grade boy:* Yes, I do things at school with both African American and white boys. We practice basketball together and sometimes eat lunch together. When we talk in the halls it is mostly about sports. There are not many white kids in my neighborhood, but sometimes on Saturday we get together on one of the playgrounds at the big park and shoot baskets, and the white guys come over. One time a bunch of us went to a movie that the coach wanted us to see, but only guys went.
>
> *Ninth-grade girl:* The African American girls in school pretty much stick together. We have nothing against the white girls, but they do different things. If we have a party or something outside of school, it's for the neighborhood, which is mostly African American. Sometimes in science class the teacher has us do projects together, and I might work with a white girl or guy, which is OK.

This information from the interviews supports the hypothesis based on the observation data.

In reviewing school records, one type of information checked was the composition of the races in extracurricular activities, such as athletics and clubs. For activities in which ninth-grade students participated, the records showed that the proportional incidence of both African American and white ninth-grade boys being involved in predominantly male-oriented activities was greater than the corresponding proportional incidence for African American and white ninth-grade girls in predominantly female-oriented activities. Although this was relatively weak supportive evidence for it, there were no data to refute it. The results of the triangulation appear to be consistent.

Analysis

Analysis in ethnographic research consists of synthesizing the information from the observation, interviews, and other data sources. Typically, no hypotheses are tested using statistical procedures as is often the case with experimental and survey data. However, there may be some quantitative measures computed, such as proportions and percentages, based on classifications of items from interviews or types of activities and events observed.

The quantity of data to be analyzed may seem overwhelming, at least initially. There are the field notes from observation and interviews, data from records, etc. To begin with, it can be helpful to make some classifications of the data just to get a feel for what they contain. Becker et al. (1961) suggest a number of ways information can be classified, including the following:

1. Dichotomous categories indicating whether information obtained was directed by the observer's activities or was volunteered spontaneously by those being studied.
2. Number of responses to direct queries.
3. Dichotomous categories indicating whether information was obtained in the presence of the observer alone or when other individuals were present.
4. Proportions of information that consist of activities observed versus statements made.

Classifying data in such a manner is far from a complete analysis, but it does provide some direction. Presenting results in tabular form may be helpful, both frequencies and proportions. An example format for the social interaction example is given in Figure 12.6.

Bogdan and Biklen (2003) suggest two mechanical procedures for sorting through the data. The first suggestion is to number all the pages of material sequentially, most likely in chronological order. The numbering may be done separately for different types of data,

Statements	***Volunteered***	***Directed***	***Total***
To observer alone			
To other students with observer present			
To other students with observer and faculty present			

Activities	***Same Race***	***Mixed Race***
With one other student		
With more than one other student		
With one or more faculty		
With both other student(s) and faculty		

FIGURE 12.6 An Example Format for Classifications of the Data from the Social Interaction Example

such as observation data, interview data, etc. Page numbering helps to locate data. The second procedure is to take long undisturbed periods of time and read through the data at least twice. This procedure should give a sense of the scope and holistic nature of the data. By the second reading some preliminary ideas for developing a coding system should come to mind, and a tentative list of codes might be forthcoming. Because the quantity of data usually is large, it is useful to take notes about the data.

> Numbering the data pages and at least two readings of the data are two procedures to get the analysis under way.

Coding. **Coding** the data is a necessary analysis task of practically any qualitative research study. Coding was discussed in Chapter 10, and it may be useful for the reader to review that section. Coding is a quite subjective activity and the codes basically come out of the data. Chapter 10 also suggests some general codes such as context codes or process codes.

Coding categories may be modified as the analysis proceeds. Major codes and subcodes may be used. The number of codes or categories in a system should be limited, but that does not mean that there will be only a few codes. Bogdan and Biklen (2003, p. 173) suggest limiting the number of codes from thirty to fifty. It is important that the codes cover all the data, yet provide a meaningful separation of the information.

A coding system that might apply to the social interaction example is "relationship codes." Relationships include friendships, cliques, leader/follower roles, and so forth, essentially the groupings and their interactions that make up the social structure of the school. Because the high school is racially mixed, the racial composition of relationships would be of interest, as would the composition across the sexes.

Codes may be divided into major codes, subcodes, and supplemental codes. Major codes are broad categories and subcodes divide the major codes into more detailed categories. Supplemental codes are categories somewhat peripheral to the primary focus of interest, but, nonetheless, representing an influence on the phenomenon being studied.

In the social interaction example, a major category of the relationship codes would be friendships. Subcodes would be within the same race and within the same sex, and these could be further subdivided by African American, Hispanic, and white. A supplemental code would be student/faculty friendships. This code is not directly a part of student interaction, but it may impact on such interaction. Table 12.1 contains relationship codes for the social interaction research study. This is not an exhaustive list, but it does illustrate codes that focus the analysis on the research problem.

> Codes are used for categorizing the information in the data. Major codes, subcodes, and supplemental codes may be used.

Coding is a means to an end, not an end in itself. Codes should be useful for organizing and synthesizing the data. They may be modified as necessary while the analysis is in

TABLE 12.1 Example Relationship Codes for the Social Interaction Research Study

Major Code: Friendships

Subcodes:

1. Within same race, same sex
- **1a.** African American girls
- **1b.** African American boys
- **1c.** White girls
- **1d.** White boys

2. Across races, same sex
- **2a.** Girls
- **2b.** Boys

3. Within same race, different sex
- **3a.** African American
- **3b.** White

4. Across races, different sex
- **4a.** African American boy, white girl
- **4b.** African American girl, white boy

Major Code: Cliques

(repeat same type of subcodes, and continue this breakdown through the major relationship codes)

Supplemental Code: Student/faculty mentor

Subcode:

1. Within same race, same sex
- **1a.** African American woman faculty, African American girl
- **2b.** African American man faculty, African American boy
- **3c.** White woman faculty, white girl
- **4d.** White man faculty, white boy

The subcodes may be continued as above. A second supplemental code category might be Student/faculty, nonmentor friendship.

process. Although some coding systems may be apparent due to the phenomenon under study, the data themselves, such as field notes, imply applicable systems and categories.

Use of Numbers. In ethnographic research, terms such as *large, a long time,* or *quite rapid* often are used in describing phenomena. For certain types of phenomena, such as length of time, quantitative measures are available, and their use can increase the precision of the description. To say that the observation periods averaged about three hours is more precise than saying that they were "quite long" or that they lasted "most of the afternoon." In a study of high schools, if size of class is a characteristic used in the description, numbers such as averages are more informative than simple descriptive terms.

Ethnographic researchers engage in what is sometimes called **ballparking**—providing a very rough estimate of a phenomenon. An example of ballparking is, "Many students of both sexes engaged in conversations in the halls." For some activities and situations, it is impossible or undesirable to obtain numerical estimates, and ballparking is adequate. However, confusion can be introduced if numbers are specific when in fact they represent only ballpark estimates. Researchers should be clear about whether numbers are ballpark estimates or more specific estimates. If they are ballpark estimates, they may be indicating only order of magnitude.

Researchers should use caution in classifying individuals on variables whose frequency or existence involves a subjective perception. Schofield and Anderson (1984, p. 13) cite an example of ethnic identity: "Ethnic identity is, after all, a construct referring to one's subjective sense of self rather than to certain physical or cultural criteria that someone else might use to label one as belonging to a particular group."

A problem arises when certain counts or categorizations are based on operational definitions that are not in agreement with the perceptions of the individuals being studied. For example, "official classification" may not be in agreement with the way the individuals studied perceive themselves, in which case numbers based on official classification would be misleading.

> Numbers are useful in ethnographic research for providing more specific information than descriptive terms alone. Researchers must be clear about the level of precision contained in the numbers.

The analysis in ethnographic research relies heavily on description; even when statistics are used, they tend to be used in a descriptive rather than an inferential manner. Inferential statistics might be appropriate if random sampling of events or of some characteristic of the study had been done. But we would not expect the research context to be a random sample of some larger population of contexts. The ethnographic researcher is probably more willing than other types of researchers to accept the uniqueness of the research context and its conditions.

Drawing Conclusions

Experimental and survey research typically leave drawing conclusions as one of the final steps. In ethnographic research, drawing conclusions is integrated much more with other parts of the research process, especially the fieldwork. In fact, to the extent possible, it is a good strategy to incorporate the writing into the fieldwork even to the point of preparing a first draft while the fieldwork is in process.

Tentative hypotheses, theories, and explanations are generated during the fieldwork, but the ethnographic researcher guards against drawing final conclusions prematurely. Thus we have a successive approximation procedure of coming to conclusions when conducting ethnographic research. We should allow as much time for analyzing and writing as was spent in the field. It is not the fieldwork that produces the ethnography, but the analysis and writing. What has been said and done does not have educational, psychological, sociological, or other meaning until such meaning is ascribed by the researcher. Producing the ethnographic account requires insight, reflection, and, typically, some rethinking of initial conclusions.

The conceptual schema for ethnographic research helps clarify the components involved in a specific study and aids in identifying the focus of the research.

Examples of Ethnographic Research in Education

There are classic examples of ethnographic research, such as the Becker et al. (1961) study, *Boys in White: Student Culture in Medical School.* However, not many educators are likely to conduct studies of such magnitude—not even for a doctoral dissertation. The extensive classic studies can provide useful information about methodology, but at this point it should be helpful to consider examples of less extensive studies—those that are feasible for practicing educators and graduate program research. When considering examples, it is not feasible to reproduce entire reports, but the discussion below provides an overview of the nature of the research.

EXAMPLE 12.1

Creating Classroom Cultures: One Teacher, Two Lessons, and a High-Stakes Test

Valli and Chambliss (2007) compared the classroom cultures of two reading lessons taught by the same teacher. One lesson was from a regular reading class and the other from a supplementary reading intervention class that was designed to help students pass a high-stakes state assessment. They found that the teacher developed a child-centered culture in the first instance and a test-centered culture in the second.

The target teacher had thirty-five years of experience and was teaching fifth grade. The researchers were interested in the teacher's perspectives on teaching, testing, and literacy that guided her actions and the instructional processes that occurred during the two lessons.

The researchers engaged in what they called interpretive fieldwork research to understand teacher and student "sense making" within the culturally organized activities and its relation to the broader social and political context. They selected the school in the study because it had a moderate to high level of poverty and higher than expected levels of achievement. The teacher had been identified as exemplary.

Data were gathered with a time-sampling standardized protocol that was done six times a year, running field notes, an audiotape of a class session, and an interview after the taped lesson. The taped session occurred near the end of the school year. The audiotapes provided a record of what was said, in what sequence, and to whom. The field notes described class composition, organization, interactions, movement, and body language. The field notes also contained the observer's impressions of the teacher and her relationship to her students. The interview asked how groupings, texts, and content were determined.

Analysis of the data revealed that the reading lesson was "child centered" in that it built on children's experiences, expanded their knowledge, and encouraged them to be analytical and metacognitive. The reading intervention lesson was found to be strikingly different. In pursuing the differences, the researchers independently analyzed transcripts of tapes, field notes, and handouts. Using recursive rounds of coding, memo writing, and drafting thick descriptions of lesson segments, they identified literacy activities on which the lessons differed: text choice and vocabulary, comprehension, and composition instruction.

The following is a very brief overview of their findings. The researchers stated:

> Although Ms. G.'s passion and involvement was the same in both lessons, instructional goals and tasks, classroom discourse, and teacher–student roles and relationships were strikingly different. This was evident in both vocabulary activities and in comprehension and composition activities; creating, in our mind's eye, images of distinctly different classroom cultures. (p. 62)

With regard to the selection of reading materials, the teacher chose books for the reading course that the students would enjoy and that would allow the students to identify with the characters and learn from them. The books were matched to the students' English proficiency, prior knowledge, and cultural experience. She chose materials for the intervention course that lent itself to short-response questions, the format of questions that the students would encounter on the state assessment. The lessons mirrored the state test topics of main idea, sequencing, cause and effect, inferencing, fact and opinion, author's purpose, figurative language, and summarizing.

Vocabulary activities also differed in the two classes. The students in the reading class selected words that they did not know that seemed important to text meaning, noted each word on the page to see it in context, and used the words in a chapter organizer and in a vocabulary web. They looked up the definition of the words in the dictionary, found synonyms and antonyms, and used each word in a sentence. They then discussed the words as a group activity. The vocabulary activities in the intervention class became a session on test-taking strategy. She taught the students to eliminate options on multiple-choice items to arrive at the correct answer.

When comprehension and composition activities were compared, the researchers found that in the reading lesson the students were taught to use background knowledge to understand setting, characters, and plot. The instruction in the intervention class focused on comprehending the test questions and evaluating the quality of student answers.

Additional results are provided, but are not presented here. The overall conclusion is well supported by the comparisons that were made of the two lessons. The researchers clearly found that the same teacher used very different methods in the two classes. The activities in the reading course were child centered and had substantial support in the literature. The activities in the intervention were test centered and did not represent best practices.

EXAMPLE 12.2

Students Serving Christ: Understanding the Role of Student Subcultures on a College Campus

Magolda and Ebben (2007) studied the Students Serving Christ (SSC) student organization to examine the role of student subcultures in higher education. They explored how a subculture is formed and sustained, what counts as normal within a subculture, different forms of student resistance, and the tensions and paradoxes in the subculture. It is an interesting study because it clearly shows how the researchers are immersed in the context in ways that are very different from what is done in quantitative research.

The researchers shared that ignorance and curiosity about Evangelical collegiate Christians influenced their decision to conduct an ethnographic study of the organization. They describe their study as follows:

> First, we infused the issue of power into an interpretive tapestry; specifically, the article focuses on subculture power relations that reveal how power operates within the SSC context. Second, we acknowledge our own presence, politics, and subjectivity and that we are intimately involved with the research context and SSC participants in the creation of knowledge. Third, we use difference and conflict, rather than similarities and consensus, as organizing concepts in our analysis. (p. 141)

The researchers were participant–observers who observed more than thirty-five events and programs; conducted over twenty formal interviews or focus groups; had a large number of informal interviews; and reviewed documents, publications, the SSC website, and e-mail announcements to members.

An interesting anecdote described one of the researcher's experiences while conducting the research:

> I wonder if Matthew, aware that I am not a Christian, is making purposeful eye contact with me as he talks about non-Christians and sinners. I flash back to a scene from *Taxi Driver*, where the alienated Travis Bickle stands alone in a room and calls out, "You talkin' to me? . . . Well, I'm the only (non-Christian) here." I repress my urge to recite this classic line and ponder the arguments Matthew advances in the name of Christ. (p. 139)

This is not the kind of comment made by quantitative researchers. It is useful, though, because it emphasizes the very personal lens through which the ethnographer views the research context.

The researchers describe the operations, activities, conversations, and interactions within the SSC organization. The language of the participants is captured and reported verbatim to give the reader a feeling of being present in the meetings. Observations are related to the professional literature on subcultures to enhance and support the researchers' interpretations.

The conclusions are not presented in a step-by-step list associated with hypotheses or research questions. They need to be extracted from the discussion. The conclusions, in an oversimplified version, are:

1. Subcultures form in reaction to the hegemony of dominant groups. Marginalized groups resist the normalizing expectations of the dominant group and form communities of support.

2. SSC opposes the public higher education that steers clear of religious teachings as well as opposing the large-scale, high-tech Christian organizations.

3. SSC members develop their own language, using *disciple* as a verb, for example. They develop a purposeful style with its own meaning and structures.

4. Tensions and paradoxes exist. SSC positions itself as an outsider, yet Christianity is the most popular religious preference for students at that university. Efforts to reach out to non-Christians are sincere, but their dichotomy of Christian versus non-Christian or followers of Christ versus sinners undermines their reconciliation agenda.

One of the tasks associated with reporting ethnographic research, or any research for that matter, is synthesizing the data into a manageable amount. Because of the quantity of data collected when conducting ethnographic research, this is an extensive and demanding task, probably more so than when reporting on surveys or experimental research. Reports of ethnographic research in periodicals tend to be quite long, sometimes exceeding twenty pages. Reports are characterized by quite long narratives and limited use of tables.

The Reliability and Validity of Ethnographic Research

As indicated in Chapter 1, the **reliability** of research involves the extent to which studies can be replicated. The concept applies to both procedures and results. If a study is reliable, another researcher who uses the same procedures, variables, measurements, and conditions should obtain the same results. The **validity** of research involves the interpretation of research results with confidence and the generalizability of the results. The former is called *internal validity* and the latter *external validity.* Reliability and validity influence the credibility of the research and the confidence that can be placed in the findings.

> *Reliability* is concerned with replicability of both procedures and findings. *Validity* refers to the interpretation and generalizability of results.

Chapter 10 has a discussion of reliability and validity of qualitative research in general, and those concepts also apply to ethnographic research. The following discussion of reliability and validity elaborates on these concepts as they apply to ethnographic research.

Reliability

Goetz and LeCompte (1984) distinguish between two types of reliability in ethnographic research—external and internal. External reliability involves the extent to which independent researchers working in the same or similar context would obtain consistent results. Internal reliability involves the extent to which researchers concerned with the same data and constructs would be consistent in matching them. Because it is conducted in naturalistic settings and often focuses on processes, ethnographic research is susceptible to problems of replication. However, these problems have been addressed and procedures have been suggested for averting them.

Ethnographic research usually is focused, not on the tabulation of frequencies of events or behaviors, but on obtaining an accurate description of the phenomena under study. In a specific study, internal reliability would depend on the extent to which two or more observers agree on what they saw and how they interpret what they saw. How can observers be made to agree? Basically, the way to enhance reliability (and validity, for that matter) in ethnographic research is no different from the way to do so in any other type of research—that is, through applying good methodology.

Ethnographic researchers may not be able to begin a study with as much design specificity as exists for other research, but the context of the research and the overall problem addressed should be specified as much as possible. Then, access to data is an important factor, in terms of not only availability of the data but also the status of the researcher. As one of the potential problems of fieldwork, Erickson (1986) identifies the limiting of the researcher's access to data due to inadequate negotiation for entry into the field setting. The researcher must develop a relationship with the participants that will provide access to data from the perspectives of the participants.

The use of multiple data-collection procedures, along with triangulation, tends to enhance internal reliability. There should be a variety of sources—observation, interviewing, site documents, and possibly other supporting sources—for data, and data must be in adequate quantity to have confirmed any assertions with confidence. Disconfirming evidence must also be sought and explained if such evidence exists. Videotaping, when it is applicable, can be useful. It allows the repeated viewing of situations or the phenomenon under study until underlying concepts can be identified consistently and with confidence. Also, if two or more observers are involved, repeated viewing can be a check on consistency of interpretation across observers, and it provides an opportunity for the resolution of differences.

The extensive description used in ethnographic research is a plus in terms of internal reliability; if there seems to be a lack of observer agreement, the sources of disagreement can be identified from the description. If observers are in disagreement, there should always be an opportunity for discussion to resolve the disagreement. Ethnographic research is often a cooperative effort among several individuals. There always should be opportunities for sharing insights, discussing interpretations, and reviewing the descriptions of others.

External reliability is a matter of degree, and some would argue that nothing can be replicated exactly. Many ethnographic researchers are not very concerned about whether or not others can replicate their studies. But, because ethnographic procedures are varied and are applied with varying degrees of sophistication, the ethnographic researcher must be particularly comprehensive in describing the methodology. It is not sufficient to use a shorthand description and then assert that data collection and analysis were carefully conducted. Goetz and LeCompte (1984) summarize this point:

> The researcher must clearly identify and fully discuss data analysis processes and provide retrospective accounts of how data were examined and synthesized. Because reliability depends on the potential for subsequent researchers to reconstruct original analysis strategies, only those ethnographic accounts that specify these in sufficient detail are replicable. (p. 217)

Validity

Attaining reliability does not assure the validity of research—either internal or external. For example, observers could agree on their conclusions and yet the conclusions could be in error. If conclusions cannot be drawn with confidence, there are deficiencies in the research procedures and the study lacks internal validity. If the results of a study do not generalize, the study lacks external validity, even if results were consistent internally and the study is replicable.

> A research study may be both internally and externally reliable yet lack validity.

Consider internal validity first. In experimental design, we control extraneous variables to the extent possible—for example, through randomization or by including additional independent variables in the design. Because ethnographic research is conducted in the natural setting, it does not have this option of control. However, the naturalness of the data enhances validity. Smith and Glass (1987, p. 278) identify naturalness of the data as one of the qualities by which to critique a naturalistic study. The natural state of a study should be without reactivity and artificiality and should have a minimum of observer effects. There should be checking for possible observer effects.

Ethnographic research studies typically cover relatively long time periods, which increase the possibility of extraneous effects. However, longevity in the research context does enhance the search for causes and effects. The temporal ordering of events, the perspectives of various informants, and the possible effects of confounded variables are examples of factors that may affect internal validity, yet they are factors that tend to become better understood with exposure in the situation. Of necessity, in order to obtain adequate amounts of data, the data-collection period is quite long. There is no designated time period for ethnographic research; the length of time required for a specific study depends on the extent and complexity of the phenomenon being investigated. In summary, establishing internal validity is a process that involves both deduction and induction; the researcher systematically reasons through the possible causes for the data.

The concern of external validity is generalization: To what populations, conditions, contexts, and situations do the results generalize? LeCompte and Goetz (1982) identify the problem as one of demonstrating "the typicality of a phenomenon, or the extent to which it compares and contrasts along relevant dimensions with other phenomena" (p. 51). There is no difficulty with this concept of generalization; the difficulty comes in attempting to use the concepts of random sampling or a formal mathematical model for argumentation, the latter being used either knowingly or inadvertently. External validity in ethnographic research is, as the research itself, grounded in phenomenology and not in the positivism approach of quantitative research.

So, how then do we argue the generalizability of ethnographic research results? To take an extreme position that there is no generalization is not a functional position. Polkinghorne (1991) makes a very useful distinction between two types of generalizations:

Aggregate-type—generalizations limited to statements about the population considered as an entirety.

General-type—generalizations in which assertions are made that something is true for each and every member of a population (p. 5, paraphrased).

Quantitative research uses the **aggregate-type generalization,** although sometimes there is confusion and group results are interpreted as individual results. Ethnographic research uses **general-type generalization.**

This latter type of generalization is based on what is called **assertoric argumentation** (Polkinghorne, 1983). Such argumentation is based on the reasonableness of its claim given that its assumptions and evidence are acceptable. Assertoric argumentation accepts a full range of rationality. As examples, generalization may be based on the logic of similarity or dissimilarity in which something is understood as more or less like a prototype, and the logic of narrative relationships of events to a plot in which the meaning of an event is understood by its relationship to a designated outcome (Polkinghorne, 1991, p. 7).

> External validity in ethnographic research is general-type generalization based on assertoric argumentation.

The study concerning the subculture Students Serving Christ (Magolda and Ebben, 2007), described in Example 12.2, provided a discussion of generalizability. The subculture was chosen as a purposeful sample. The selection was influenced by the researchers' ignorance of and curiosity about the organization.

> The stories provide readers a vicarious experience, offering access into the collegiate worlds of these students and their spiritual leader. The interpretation illuminates the foundational values that guide this unique organization and how members perceive the other, and vice versa. Although we make no claims that SSC's practices and values generalize to other Christian collegiate organizations, these stories and this analysis sensitize readers to issues that numerous Christians (and other marginalized groups) encounter and come to grips with on a daily basis on college campuses. (p. 154)

Although the authors do not use the term *assertoric argumentation*, essentially this is what is being used. The opening sentence recognizes that a sampling argument cannot be used, but then the authors make a logical case for the generalizability of the results.

Another way of considering external validity in ethnographic research is that it is established through **a posteriori judgment,** which means an argument based on actual observation. In this type of generalization, the argument is that the results represent a reasonable possibility of being applicable in other situations. The generalization of the results is not conclusive until the results are actually tested in the situation to which the results are believed to apply. (This is sometimes called a generalization test.) This brings up another point about the responsibility of the reader of ethnographic research reports in establishing the external validity of the research. Lincoln and Guba (1985) comment on the transfer of findings from qualitative research:

> The burden of proof (for the generalizability of results) lies less with the original investigator than with the person seeking to make application elsewhere . . . the responsibility of the original investigator ends in providing sufficient descriptive data to make such similarity judgments (with the "new" situation) possible. (p. 298)

Thus, with ethnographic research—as with all qualitative research—the reader, or potential user, of the research results has a responsibility of interpreting the results and making judgments about its generalizability. This responsibility is greater than it would be for most quantitative research results. However, it is the responsibility of the researcher to specify conditions of the research setting and procedures, so that the basis for comparison (or lack thereof) can be established.

> External validity of ethnographic research typically is argued on the basis of a posteriori judgment.

As a procedural matter, external validity can be strengthened by multisite studies. If a phenomenon seems to be consistent across a number of studies, its generalizability is increased. Even if there is inconsistency in the phenomenon, a study of the differences between the sites may reveal the limitations or specific conditions of generalization. Certainly, not all ethnographic studies in education can be multisite studies; in fact, few would meet that criterion. But the external validity can be enhanced by including variations of the research context in the same study. For example, if writing instruction in the elementary schools is being studied, including two or more elementary classrooms in the same study would enhance external validity.

Absolute reliability and validity are impossible to attain in any research study, regardless of type. Yet researchers establish reliability by using appropriate research procedures and through careful documentation of the research. This strategy applies to ethnographic research, and external validity is established, for the most part, by a logical argument.

The Role of Ethnographic Research

Ethnographic research involves a variety of procedures, giving it considerable flexibility and applicability in education. Ethnographic research emphasizes context, making it especially suitable for inquiry into educational issues that are heavily context-dependent. Many of the important educational issues and questions are quite context-dependent; at least they are raised in the instructional context of the schools. Educational reform efforts at the local level, for example, are directed at the naturalistic, instructional level. So, ethnographic research can contribute not only to solving problems but also to identifying the most important issues or questions that should be addressed.

Because of the extensive and rich description coming from ethnographic research, such research provides a good potential for theoretical contributions, certainly theory development and, to some extent, theory testing. Extensive description provides a reservoir of evidence; if the fieldwork is well done, just from its sheer volume, it provides a preponderance of information about educational phenomena. Ethnographic research is appropriate for large-scale studies about the nature of education.

However, it should not be inferred that ethnographic research is applicable only for large-scale studies or for studies with extensive funding resources. The phenomenon under study requires observation to be understood, and teachers, part of whose role is that of classroom observer, are in an advantageous position for conducting research in the schools. Kantor, Kirby, and Goetz (1981) address this point, along with collaboration between teachers and researchers:

> Experienced teachers have knowledge of children and classroom settings which makes them potentially strong researchers; ethnography allows them to use that knowledge and opens opportunities for dialogue between teachers and researchers. Especially promising are collaborative efforts between teachers and researchers. (p. 305)

Johnson (2000) makes the case for involving teachers in research on teaching.

> One alternative to over-reliance on the findings of large-scale studies is for educators to assume the role of the researcher. By studying their students, teachers can bring the academic findings down to earth and discover what works in their specific classroom. Susan Black (1996) equates teacher research to the work done by anthropologists or ethnographers. "They are able to observe the cultural scene closely . . . and create a research record of the people, places, events and objects within it, as well as their own personal interactions and responses." By using the classroom as a laboratory, teachers can, for example, learn whether interdisciplinary teaching is as effective with their remedial students as with their high achievers. (online)

Wagner (1990) makes the case that school administrators can serve effectively as ethnographers, especially in collaborative efforts with other educational researchers. In this article, the author examines several parallels between the work of educational administrators and school ethnography. Cited are examples of successful, collaborative research in which educational administrators have assumed the role of ethnographer. Accepting these arguments for the participation of teachers and administrators in ethnographic research implies that this area of research is amenable to action research. Ethnographic research, by its very nature, requires a considerable time commitment, but teachers and school administrators are in an advantageous position to participate in such research.

However, just as any research approach has its limitations, ethnographic research should not be expected to be all things to all people. As Wolcott (1988, p. 203) points out, ethnographic research tends to focus on how things are and how they got that way. Of itself, ethnographic research does not prescribe courses of action; these are left for the researcher to develop, and the ethnographic account may or may not be helpful in this endeavor. Ethnographic research tends to reveal the complexity of educational phenomena, and, in the long run, this should be helpful in improving education. As more ethnographic research is done, the educational community should become better informed and become more sensitive to the importance of context in educational research.

> Ethnographic research makes contributions to education through empirical description of phenomena, the development of grounded theory, and theory testing. Ethnographic research focuses on how things are and how they got that way.

Summary

This chapter discussed ethnographic research in education, its rationale, and its methodology. Ethnographic research is conducted in a natural setting with emphasis on understanding the phenomenon under study from the perspective of those being studied. The product of ethnographic research is an ethnography, an account that might be described as a portrait of a culture or a **portraiture.** The ethnography is cultural description and interpretation.

Ethnographic research is concentrated heavily in fieldwork, and includes observation, interviewing, and other data-collecting procedures. The pre-fieldwork stage consists of focusing in on the research problem and selecting a research site. The ethnographic researcher does not necessarily formulate specific questions or hypotheses until the fieldwork is begun, but the available knowledge base relative to the problem is explored. The research site is not selected at random; it is selected because of characteristics that make it appropriate for the research.

Data are collected in the field, which necessitates on-site observation using field-based instruments. Observation may be more or less structured, and the results of observation are recorded in field notes. The processes of generating hypotheses, collecting data, and drawing conclusions are highly integrated. The research process is an attempt to enter into the conceptual world of those being studied in order to understand how and what meaning they construct about the phenomenon under study. The objective is to attain a holistic description of the phenomenon.

A conceptual schema for ethnographic research was discussed, involving the concepts of perspectives, cultures, and organizations. Such a conceptual schema aids in understanding the general characteristics of an approach to research. The methodological steps in ethnographic research include the usual activities of conducting research. These steps or activities tend to overlap and are more extensively integrated than they are in other types of research. For example, an experimenter typically begins with a specified set of hypotheses that will be tested by conducting the experiment. In contrast, the ethnographic researcher identifies the phenomenon to be studied and then develops the hypotheses through the data collection. Subsequently, the hypotheses may be retained, modified, or discarded. Theory may be generated from the data; this is known as grounded theory.

Ethnographic research's contribution to education is through "rich," empirical description. Through this description understanding is enhanced, and there is a potential for theoretical contributions. As a mode of inquiry, ethnographic research is inductive, which means that the analysis is based on the information that emerges from the data rather than being imposed on the data according to some prior theory or hypotheses. Ethnographic research emphasizes context, and, because so many educational phenomena appear to be context-specific, ethnographic research has many applications in educational research.

KEY CONCEPTS

Ethnography
Phenomenology
Grounded theory
Field research
Contextualization
Organization
Culture
Perspective
Foreshadowed problems
Privileged observer
Limited observer
Participant–observer
Field notes
Descriptive field notes
Analytic field notes
Key informant
Triangulation
Coding
Ballparking
Reliability
Validity
Aggegate-type generalization
General-type generalization
Assertoric argumentation
A posteriori judgment
Portraiture

EXERCISES

12.1 Contrast the nature of ethnographic research and the nature of experimental research. Identify differences in orientation and methodology. What are some conditions under which each type is appropriate?

12.2 Identify two research questions that would be better addressed through ethnographic research than through experimental or quasi-experimental research.

12.3 If we identify the conceptual components of ethnographic research as perspectives, cultures, and organizations, describe how these components are related or connected. Select an example (either real or hypothetical) of ethnographic research in education, and identify these components for the example.

12.4 Define the process of triangulation. Suppose a researcher is conducting ethnographic research on instruction in elementary school mathematics. Describe how triangulation might be used.

12.5 A study is being conducted on student life in a private, residential prep school (assume grades 9–12). Identify the perspectives, cultures, and organization for this study. Develop two or more sample hypotheses that might be generated, based on the observation.

12.6 A fourth-grade teacher is interested in conducting research, essentially action research, on the nature of instruction in arithmetic compared to the nature of instruction in reading–language arts, from the students' viewpoints. The research is conducted with this teacher's class of twenty-seven students, beginning in October and concluding the next June. As an ethnographic study, identify the organization, cultures, and possible perspectives in this study. What phenomena would be observed within the instruction? Would interviewing be conducted, and, if so, what types of questions would be asked and of whom? Comment on the external validity of the study. How important is generalizability of results, and on what basis could external validity be established?

12.7 For the study described in Exercise 12.6, suppose the teacher designates an hour each week for observation of instruction in each of the two subjects. At the completion of the hour, the teacher writes field notes about the instruction observed. Suggest possible coding systems that might be used for classifying the information in the field notes. What might be useful major codes and subcodes? Is it necessary to use the same coding system for instruction in both arithmetic and reading–language arts?

12.8 Compare the process of having one researcher conduct an ethnographic study to the process of having a team of researchers conduct the same study. For example, at what points in the study should the solo researcher ask for feedback and review from others? What should be considered when assigning tasks to members of the research team? What are the strengths and weaknesses of doing this kind of research alone or as a team?

12.9 Describe the differences between a participant–observer, a privileged observer, and a limited observer. Provide an example of each that applies to ethnographic research in education.

12.10 An ethnographer is conducting a study of the "nature of foreign language instruction" in a senior high school, specifically instruction in French, Spanish, and German. Over the period of a school year, the researcher observes classes in each language on a continuing basis, observing at least two classes in each language each week. Describe what may be the content of the researcher's field notes. Develop three or four questions that might be included in a student interview. Do the same for a teacher interview.

12.11 Distinguish between the reliability and the validity of ethnographic research.

12.12 Describe what is meant when we say that external validity in ethnographic research is based on assertoric argumentation and is general-type generalization. Contrast this with aggregate-type generalization typically used for establishing external validity for most quantitative research.

12.13 Why is it sometimes difficult to establish external validity of ethnographic research? What can be done to enhance external validity in ethnographic research?

12.14 Locate an ethnographic study from a professional journal. Review the article carefully, identifying the research problem and the hypotheses. Is the methodology described in adequate detail so that the reader can understand how the study was conducted? How is the issue of generalizability addressed? Do the conclusions follow from the results?

12.15 What problems or issues might an ethnographer face when doing research in a Head Start program for preschoolers as compared to doing research on a group of adults such as student teachers?

12.16 Ethnographic studies tend to be more fun to read than quantitative studies. What are the elements that contribute to this? Do these elements make the studies less scientific?

NOTES

1. The schema discussed in this section is based on concepts discussed in Becker et al., *Boys in White: Student Culture in Medical School* (Chicago: University of Chicago Press, 1961). Although the Becker et al. book is based on an extensive study, one beyond the scope of most research conducted for a thesis or dissertation, the concepts underlying that study are useful for conceptualizing ethnographic research regardless of the scope of a specific study.
2. The term *informant* is not used as in police circles, when it means a person who informs on other people. Ethnographic researchers use informants for their knowledge, opinion, and interpretation.

REFERENCES

Becker, H. S., Geer, B., Hughes, E. C., and Strauss, A. L. (1961). *Boys in white: Student culture in medical school.* Chicago: University of Chicago Press.

Bogdan, R. C., and Biklen, S. K. (2003). *Qualitative research for education: An introduction to theory and methods* (4th ed.). Boston: Allyn & Bacon.

Denzin, N. K. (1978). *The research act: A theoretical introduction to sociological methods* (2nd ed.). Chicago: Aldine.

Erickson, R. (1986). Qualitative methods in research on teaching. In M. C. Wittrock (Ed.), *Handbook of research on teaching* (3rd ed., pp. 119–161). New York: Macmillan.

Geertz, C. (1973). *The interpretation of cultures.* New York: Basic Books.

Goetz, J. P., and LeCompte, M. D. (1984). *Ethnography and qualitative design in educational research.* New York: Academic Press.

Johnson, J. H. (2000). Data-driven school improvement. *Journal of School Improvement, 1,* Online. Retrieved July 22, 2007, from www.ncacasi.org/jsi/2000v1i1/data_driven

Kantor, K. J., Kirby, D. R., and Goetz, J. P. (1981). Research in context: Ethnographic studies in English education. *Research in the Teaching of English, 15,* 292–309.

Lancy, D. F. (1993). *Qualitative research in education: An introduction to the major traditions.* New York: Longman.

LeCompte, M. D., and Goetz, J. P. (1982). Problems of reliability and validity in ethnographic research. *Review of Educational Research, 52,* 31–60.

Lincoln, Y. S., and Guba, E. G. (1985). *Naturalistic inquiry.* Beverly Hills, CA: Sage.

Magolda, P., and Ebben, K. (2007). Students Serving Christ: Understanding the role of student subcultures on a college campus. *Anthropology and Education Quarterly, 38,* 138–158.

Polkinghorne, D. E. (1983). *Methodology for the human sciences: Systems of inquiry.* Albany, NY: State University of New York Press.

Polkinghorne, D. E. (1991). *Generalization and qualitative research: Issues of external validity.* Paper presented at the annual meeting of the American Educational Research Association, Chicago.

Schofield, J. W., and Anderson, K. (1984). *Integrating quantitative components into qualitative studies: Problems and possibilities for research on intergroup relations in education settings.* Paper presented at the annual meeting of the American Educational Research Association, New Orleans.

Smith, M. L., and Glass, G. V. (1987). *Research and evaluation in education and the social sciences.* Englewood Cliffs, NJ: Prentice-Hall.

Valli, L., and Chambliss, M. (2007). Creating classroom cultures: One teacher, two lessons, and a high-stakes test. *Anthropology and Education Quarterly, 38,* 57–75.

Wagner, J. (1990). Administrators as ethnographers: School as a context for inquiry and action. *Anthropology and Education Quarterly, 21,* 195–221.

Wolcott, H. F. (1988). Ethnographic research in education. In R. M. Jaeger (Ed.), *Complementary methods for research in education* (pp. 187–210). Washington, DC: American Educational Research Association.

CHAPTER 13 Mixed, Modeling, and Delphi Methods

The immediately preceding seven chapters have addressed quantitative and qualitative research design in general, and specific methods typically associated with these two types of research design. This chapter addresses methods, generally less used, that do not fit exactly into either quantitative or qualitative design categories. Many, probably most, educational research studies are somewhat complex and may involve multiple measures and two or more groups. It may be that a survey, generally considered quantitative research, involves collecting some qualitative data if one or more open-ended items are included in the survey. An ethnographic study may include quantitative data among those collected, even though the majority of field notes typically consist of qualitative information. These are examples of situations in which the data are not all quantitative or qualitative, both types of data are collected to meet the needs of the studies.

Mixed Methods

Mixed methods is a convenient term for describing research studies involving two or more methods. It is a term probably more commonly associated with evaluation than with educational research. Research studies conducted in school settings, especially those involving multiple school sites, may use mixed methods. Several issues may be investigated simultaneously, requiring multiple methods. Research associated with comprehensive school reform projects is an example of research often involving mixed methods.

> Mixed methods research involves two or more methods used in the same research study.

For practically all research studies directed toward school improvement or reform, student achievement is measured. Improvement in student achievement is the ultimate goal, the bottom line for the research. The intervention designed to improve achievement takes on the form of an experimental treatment. This part of the research is an experiment or, more likely, a quasi-experiment. Another part of the research may be directed toward teachers' perceptions of the intervention. Suppose the intervention is implemented for the period of an academic year. The teachers would be surveyed at the close of the year about their perceptions of the intervention, questions dealing with factors such as ease of implementation. Thus, such research includes both experimental and survey research.

A mixed methods study may involve both quantitative and qualitative methods. In a Kentucky project, "Study of Writing Instruction in Kentucky Schools" (Coe et al., 1999), student writing achievement was the dependent variable being affected by the writing instruction. Implementing writing instruction took the form of an experimental treatment. By identifying forty-two schools with consistently improving scores in writing achievement and eighteen schools with consistently declining scores, there were two "levels" of performance differentiated by student writing achievement. This part of the research took on the characteristics of a quasi-experiment.

Site visits were conducted in both types of schools, those improving and those declining, that consisted of ethnographic research. Researchers spent several days in classrooms observing the instructional program, with emphasis on the implementation of the writing program.

In addition, samples of teachers, students, and administrators were interviewed. These interviews focused on the perceptions of the writing instruction program and its implementation from the different perspectives. This was an extensive research project, conducted over several years. The study involved mixed methods as described above.

> Mixed methods research may include both quantitative and qualitative methods in the same study.

A Mixed Methods Example: Quasi-Experiment and Survey

In a research and evaluation study designed to close the achievement gap between African American students and the student population,[1] AEL, Inc., the regional educational laboratory for Kentucky, Tennessee, Virginia, and West Virginia, investigated the effect of a supplementary program on student achievement. The students involved in the study were in their regularly assembled classes; they were not selected at random so this was a quasi-experiment. The experimental period was the academic year and the dependent variables were the various measures of student achievement, taken in May, near the end of the school year. Student achievement was measured using a standardized published test. The program was implemented in four schools and there were four comparison schools that did not participate in the program.

In an attempt to better understand the success (or lack thereof) of the program, the teaching staffs of the participating schools were administered the AEL Measure of School Capacity for Improvement (MSCI) at the beginning of the year. The MSCI is a survey instrument with several subscales (e.g., Collective Teacher Efficacy) designed to measure the capacity of a school staff for improvement. When administered at the beginning of the school year, it might be viewed as a "Readiness for Improvement" inventory, readiness measured on several factors by the subscales. Scores on the subscales of the MSCI are important in this context. If the program lacked success, it may be that the school staff had little capacity for improving instruction. The subscale scores provide information on the factors a school staff might lack.

In addition, a twenty-seven-item student survey was administered to the students as a measure of their perceptions of school. This survey was administered twice: before the program was implemented and at the closing of the school year. Thus, a measure of change in perception of school was obtained for the students in the program.

This was a study involving surveys and a quasi-experiment. Implementation of the program, the numerous schools involved, and various measures taken on teachers and students made for considerable complexity of the research. Such complexity is often the case with mixed methods research. A diagram of the basic design of the research is provided in Figure 13.1.

Advantages of Mixed Methods

There are a number of advantages of mixed methods research. It avoids possible unimethod bias. Each research method has its strengths and weaknesses. For example, experiments are believed to provide the strongest cause-and-effect evidence, but sometimes the conditions of an experiment are a bit artificial. Self-report surveys get at information that is known only to the respondent, but the responses may not always be true. Using more than one method in the same research study allows the researcher to capitalize on the strengths of each method.

Another advantage is that mixed methods appeal to different audiences. Some people will be persuaded only by the results of "rigorous," experimental research, while others are more convinced by the rich information provided by ethnographic research. Using mixed methods will increase the likelihood that a wider audience will find the conclusions convincing and use the findings.

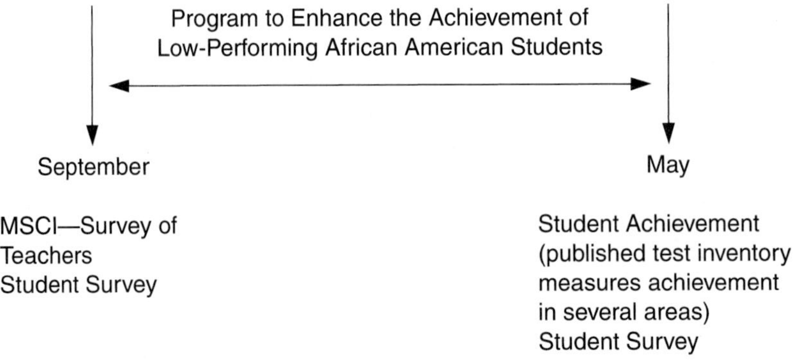

FIGURE 13.1 Design of a Mixed Methods Research Study

Mixed methods provides different sight lines; that is, it enables the researcher to look at something from a variety of perspectives, for a more comprehensive understanding. Educational outcomes are complex and often influenced by a variety of factors. A limited research design may provide only part of the picture. Mixed methods can give a more complete understanding of the phenomenon being investigated.

Probably the greatest advantage of mixed methods research is that it addresses multiple questions, so often the situation in education research. Quantitative research methods are appropriate for answering questions about variables such as "Did second graders using Direct Instruction have higher reading comprehension scores than similar students taught with the America's Choice reading program?" Questions about processes such as "How did the teachers implement the Direct Instruction approach in their classrooms?" are better addressed by qualitative methods. Using mixed methods allows the researcher to explore diverse questions.

Considering the breadth and magnitude of much of educational research, it is not surprising that a single study may require mixed methods. Evaluation research associated with school reform and improvement efforts typically requires mixed methods to meet the objectives of the research. But mixed methods are by no means limited to evaluation research. Many research studies include multiple measures, some of which provide quantitative data and others qualitative results. So, there are any combination of conditions that may require the researcher to use mixed methods.

Modeling Methods

Model building, or the use of **modeling methods,** has received increased attention within recent years in educational research and more generally in social sciences research. Economists have used **models** for some time in attempts to determine the relationships among a variety of economic factors such as money supply, interest rates, and economic growth. In essence, models are hypothesized or conceptualized descriptions of the relationships (connections) between a number of variables. They are attempts to explain phenomena; when used in educational research, they are explanations of educational variables operating in a context, most likely an educational context.

However, simply conceptualizing a model is not an adequate research endeavor. The model must be specified in terms of its variables and tested with observed data. These parts of model building require a statistical model to fit the conceptual theory. Statistical models commonly consist of **linear equations** or additive equations that show the linkages between the variables. The statistical analyses involved are complex and beyond the scope of this text.[2] The discussion here focuses on the underlying concepts of modeling methods when used for research.

> Modeling methods involve conceptualizing relationships between a number of variables and fitting a statistical model to the conceptual theory.

The Steps in Modeling

Modeling methods are intended to result in models that represent the hypothesized structures of a set of observed variables. The variables may include **latent variables,** variables that are present (or potentially present) but not visible. A latent variable in a study of school achievement might be parental attitude toward academic activity. Theory and statistical methods are combined to produce and test a model. Modeling methods involve steps as described below.[3]

Developing the Conceptual Model. The initial step in model building is to develop one or more models from the existing theory. The model must be clearly specified, showing the underlying causal structure or at least the relationship structure of a set of variables as hypothesized from the theory. A path diagram might be drawn showing the theoretical linkages between the variables. The linkages represented in the diagram must be justified by the theory.

Model Specification. Assuming that the observed data can be represented adequately by a linear model, the conceptual model is then represented by a system of simultaneous linear equations, sometimes referred to as "structural equations." Two types of assumptions are made at this point:

1. those about relationships between observed test variables and latent variables (not observed), and
2. those about causal relationships between latent and observed variables.

Of course, equations can be quite complex, depending on the phenomena being researched, but linear equations have the general form:

$$X_1 = A_1Y_1 + A_2Y_2 + \dots + A_kY_k + e_1$$

where k is the number of variables that are associated with variable X_1; e_1 is an error component.

As Ferguson (1997, p. 877) describes, an important and often complicated part of model building is identifying the proposed model. Identification requires that it can be demonstrated that the parts of the linear equations that represent the model can be estimated from the data, that is, the measures of the observed variables. There may be certain conditions required for model identification such as the number of parts to be estimated relative to the number of observed variables.

Model Fitting. The data are then fitted to the proposed model. At this point the statistics become somewhat complex, using correlation and partial correlation, and a computer program utilizes an algorithm for estimating the parts (coefficients) in the equations. There may be assumptions about the distributions of the observed variables that are required when applying the algorithm.

The next step that can be included with model fitting is to test the model for how well the data fit it. At this point, an ill-fitting model can be rejected. A model whose fit is good, or at least adequate, is consistent with the data. It may not be the only model appropriate for the data, but at least it has passed the test of consistency with the data.

Model Appraisal. The model essentially is a statistical model and its complete appraisal requires more than an adequate fit between the model and the data. Ferguson (1997) summarizes the requirement for model appraisal as:

> It requires showing that, within the limits of available evidence and knowledge, the proposed model is likely to be the best or most informative account of the data that can be constructed. This requires placing the structural equations into the broader context of evidence and theory that examines the likely realism of the model (p. 877).

The following steps, in order, are involved in modeling methods:

1. Developing the conceptual model
2. Model specification
3. Model fitting
4. Model appraisal

A Modeling Example

Unrau and Schlackman (2006) conducted a modeling study of motivation and its relationship with reading achievement in a middle school. They developed a research-based theoretical model of how students' ethnicity, gender, grade level, intrinsic motivation, and extrinsic motivation are related to reading achievement. Self-determination theory was used to conceptualize the interrelationships among the variables. This theory essentially says that each student's need for personal development and self-regulation affects his or her motivation to read. Intrinsic motivation arises from personal interest and self-regulated activity. Extrinsic motivation arises from participation to achieve rewards or to be released from some external social demand such as a teacher's or parent's rebuke. Unrau and Schlackman's model of how intrinsic and extrinsic motivations are related to each other and to reading achievement is shown in Figure 13.2. Note that the model generally flows from left to right, from characteristics of the students to the dependent variable, reading achievement. The intrinsic motivation and extrinsic motivation factors are placed in the middle of the model, as they may or may not serve as mediating variables in the theoretical framework.

The authors used structural equation modeling (SEM), a complex statistical approach, to estimate the direct and indirect relationships among the variables in the model. The SEM calculations are well beyond the scope of this book, but the technique did allow the researchers to test the following questions:

1. To what extent does intrinsic and extrinsic motivation relate to the reading achievement of students in middle school?
2. What are the relationships among gender, grade, intrinsic and extrinsic motivation to read, and reading achievement?
3. To what extent do the variables and their relationships in the structural models arising from Questions 1 and 2 differ across Hispanic and Asian middle school students?
4. Does intrinsic and extrinsic motivation change significantly across ethnicities, school grade, and gender? (p. 85)

The modeling approach yielded several interesting results. Intrinsic motivation had a stronger positive relationship with reading achievement for Asian students than for Hispanic students. There was also a significant decrease in overall motivation to read during the middle school years.

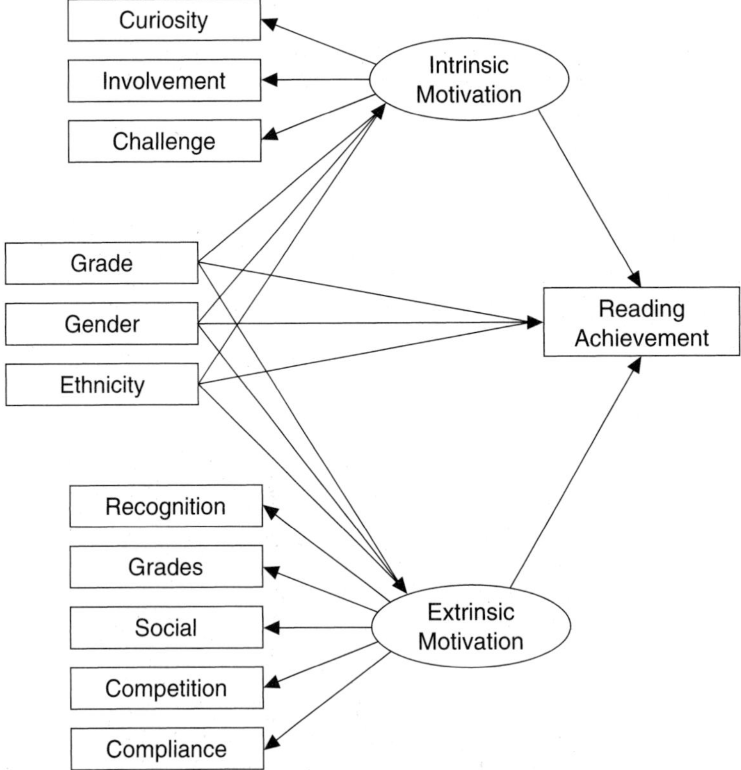

FIGURE 13.2 Unrau and Schlackman's (2006) Theoretical Model of Motivation and Reading Achievement

Source: Journal of Educational Research, 100, 81–100, 2006. Reprinted with the permission of the Helen Dwight Reid Educational Foundation. Published by Heldref Publications, 1319 Eighteenth St., NW, Washington, DC 20036-1902. Copyright © 2006.

Modeling Summary

Model building is a useful approach to researching complex educational phenomena. The example described above was one for reading achievement. For some situations hierarchical models might be fitted. Generally, a hierarchy is a system in which persons or things are ranked or ordered in some "lower to higher" fashion. A hierarchical model in education is students in classes, classes in schools, and schools in a school district or system. For example, a school district might compare the reading performance of students who were taught with Direct Instruction to the performance of students taught with other approaches. They might simply compare the students who had Direct Instruction to all of the other students. However, students are in separate classrooms that are, in turn, in separate school buildings. A hierarchical analysis would compare schools and classrooms as well as students within classrooms within schools. Such an analysis is more likely to provide an understanding of the complexity of the situation. Hierarchical regression analysis, which is beyond the scope of this book, would be more appropriate in this situation. Models develop from a conceptual or theoretical base through a statistical analysis using simultaneous linear equations. The statistics and underlying mathematics are complicated but they are performed by computer. However, the computer does not interpret the models. That task, along with understanding the parts and whole of the model, is left to the researcher.

Delphi Methods

There are many educational issues and problems that are not amenable to being researched by typically identified methods such as an experiment or an ethnographic study. Curriculum research often has this characteristic. For example, what should be the mathematics requirements in a college-prep curriculum and what are the justifications for these requirements? It would be impossible to design an experiment and randomly assign students to various levels of mathematics instruction over a four-year high school period. To initiate research in such areas, we need insights and informed judgments of experts in the field.

There are research situations for which there is insufficient information and/or data, including insufficient theory. Policy-related research is an area in which some issues or research problems simply have an insufficient information base on which to initiate research efforts. For such situations, it is possible to use a research approach known as the **Delphi method** or Delphi technique.

> There are educational research situations for which the research cannot be initiated through typical methods. These include situations for which there are insufficient data.

There are several definitions of the Delphi method in the literature, which, as might be expected, are essentially the same. A good definition, and one that has been around for a while, is that given by Delbecq, Van de Ven, and Gustafson (1975):

> [The Delphi method is] a method for the systematic solicitation and collection of judgments on a particular topic through a set of carefully designed sequential questionnaires interspersed with summarized information and feedback of opinions derived from earlier responses (p. 10).

The definition summarizes succinctly the process involved when using the Delphi.[4] It is a structured process that involves collecting and synthesizing knowledge from a group of experts.

The Delphi is quite often viewed as a method of qualitative research, and, to a large extent, it is qualitative in nature. It involves using expert opinion to generate research data. This process and the data obtained are inherently subjective. However, in summarizing the data, quantitative results may be obtained through quite objective methods. So, if one were classifying the Delphi as a method, it probably fits most closely in the qualitative sphere.

The Delphi Process

The Delphi originated in the 1950s as the name for an Air Force–sponsored project conducted by the Rand Corporation, hence, its name. Delphi is a group communication process in which the members of the group do not interact face-to-face but through a series of interactions, that is, rounds of questionnaires, in which they receive controlled feedback of group response. The members of the group are referred to as the Delphi panel and they are considered experts on the issue under consideration.

> The Delphi is a group communication process with controlled feedback, but no face-to-face interaction among group members.

Although there are variations of the Delphi, depending on the research situation, we can describe the general process. For this description we will use the step definitions given by Wilhelm (2001):

1. Question definition
2. Delphi panel creation
3. First-round questionnaire: Initial subject consideration
4. First-round analysis: Data synthesis
5. Second-round questionnaire: Subject exploration
6. Second-round analysis: Data synthesis
7. Third-round questionnaire: Consensus or conclusion reaching
8. Third-round analysis: Conclusion drawing
9. Final report preparation (pp. 13–21)

The above sequence of steps includes three rounds of questionnaires. Seldom would more than three rounds be used, although there could be additional rounds if necessary. For some studies the questions and issues might be defined in enough detail by the researchers so that the first round is not necessary and the process begins with the subject exploration questionnaire. When this is done, the process is typically called a modified Delphi.

Question Definition. This step, which is the starting point of the process, is completed by those conducting the research. The research problem is identified at this point. Information about the philosophical and theoretical bases of the problem is collected and synthesized, suitable for circulation to the panel. Individuals that are likely to use the research results may be interviewed as to what would be useful information. The information should be such that panel members can evaluate it, and provide their insights, criticisms, and any other relevant comments.

Delphi Panel Creation. The **panel of experts** makes up the respondents to the questionnaires. Explicit criteria should be established for panel membership and these should be adhered to for the selection of panel members. Selection should not be based on personal acquaintance with individuals somewhat knowledgeable about the research problem. Typically, a homogenous group of experts comprises the panel. However, there may be situations, such as with policy research, for which it is desirable to have experts with opposing views of policy. If possible, it is desirable to have panel members with different perspectives. For example, with evaluation research it would be useful to have stakeholders on the panel, those that will use results. There might be other experts concerning the theory and application. For curriculum research it would be well to have teachers on the panel who will implement the curriculum, as well as curriculum experts in the area.

It would be difficult to overemphasize the importance of panel selection. Duboff and Spaeth (2000) suggest selecting what is called a lead user. These are users of the product or service on which the research is focused who will adapt it to meet their needs. They are the trendsetters of the users. Examples from education would be curriculum innovators and instructional innovators.

> Panel selection should be based on specific criteria. Among other criteria, the key requirement for panel membership is expertise in the area being researched.

There is no optimal size for a Delphi panel. The panel should be representative of the experts in the area, but the number must be feasible from the standpoint of time and effort required. Parenté and Anderson-Parenté (1987) suggest a minimum number of 10 panel members, and with homogenous panels 10–15 members may be sufficient. Other authors (see, for example, Delbecq et al., 1975) suggest 25 to 30 panel members as a maximal number. As panel size is increased, reliability is enhanced up to a point. In a study by Murry and Hammonds (1995), in which the presidents of 906 public community and technical colleges comprised the population of experts, 35 presidents were selected randomly to serve on the panel. Three of those initially selected declined participation and alternatives were selected as replacements. Parker, Akira, and Cogan (1999) conducted a multinational curriculum development study covering several fields. They identified a multinational panel of 182 members. The members were scholars, practitioners, and policy leaders in their respective fields. This was an exceptionally large panel due to the breadth of the study. In contrast, McCoy (2001), in identifying competencies in computer technology for business education teachers, used a panel of 23 experts. With substantial resources and an extensive study, a large panel may be necessary, but for most studies a more modest-sized panel will be adequate.

There is no specified number of panel members to serve all research situations. The typical suggested range of numbers for the panel is ten to thirty, although some studies will have considerably more.

Those conducting the research should contact potential panel members individually to ensure (1) that they are adequately motivated to serve on the panel, and (2) that they understand the commitment of time and effort required of panel members. Each potential panelist should be committed to serve through the entire process, which may require several months. Panel attrition is certainly undesirable, but it does occur, and only a little can be tolerated before the process is in jeopardy of being deficient.

Of course, panel members' identities are known to the researchers and the communications require feedback to individuals. However, panel members should be assured confidentiality to the extent that their individual responses will not be shared with other panel members.

First-Round Questionnaire: Initial Subject Consideration. This first of the **questionnaires rounds** is somewhat open-ended in that the panel members are sent the information generated in the first step. This information includes background information issues, objectives, theory, problems, and solutions relative to the research problem under study. Essentially, panel members are asked to expand the data based on their expert knowledge. Responses will be used to develop the content of subsequent questionnaires. At each round of questionnaires, panel members should be given directions for completing the task and guidelines for responses, if appropriate. Panel members should be provided a telephone contact in case clarification is necessary concerning the process.

Subsequent-Round Questionnaires and the Analysis of Responses. The first-round questionnaires should provide substantive ideas about the research problem. The panelists' responses will deal with their personal views and concepts as well as those of the greater population. The overall scope of opinions about the research problem should be covered by these first-round responses. This scope should include any divergent views.

The analysis of the first-round responses requires a synthesis that will provide the basis for the content of subsequent questionnaires. The analysis should provide overall feedback for the next questionnaire including specific areas of convergence and divergence, that is, the areas of agreement and disagreement from the first-round responses.

Each subsequent questionnaire is constructed from the responses of the preceding questionnaire, with appropriate synthesis. The second round is called the "Subject Exploration" round, and the panel members respond to specific items. Typically, they are asked to rate and rank items. Rating tasks commonly use Likert-scale response options. At each round, to the extent appropriate, panel members are provided a summary of their individual responses compared to the group responses. In this way, individual panel members can see their points of agreement and disagreement with the panel as a whole. On points of disagreement they are asked to explain their positions or given the opportunity to modify them. Panel members may elaborate on the assumptions underlying their positions.

As appropriate, the summaries of responses at any round include statistical information. Means, medians, and measures of variability of ratings may be presented. Diagrams, graphs, and charts may be used. These not only facilitate communicating results, but may stimulate respondents' thinking about the issues.

> The second-round questionnaire is the subject exploration round. Its content is based on the first-round responses. The content of all subsequent-round questionnaires is based on the responses to the preceding questionnaire.

At this point it should be mentioned that only panel members who responded to the preceding questionnaire receive the next questionnaire. Panel attrition is undesirable and, therefore, it is important to obtain panel member commitment when the panel is selected.

The data from the second round of questionnaires are again summarized and synthesized for the next round. Similar procedures are again used, such as statistical analysis. The third round usually is the final round, so the content of the third-round questionnaire should set the stage for final ratings and rankings. Each panel member should clearly understand his or her position on each item compared to that of the entire panel. Any panel member whose final responses remain outside the range of consensus should justify his or her position in this third round, which is the "Consensus or Conclusion Reaching" round.

The responses of the third-round questionnaire provide the basis for drawing conclusions about the research problem. The points of convergence and divergence that emerged from the Delphi are identified and explained. The final report, of course, includes the conclusions. However, the final report should be comprehensive, describing the research problem, goals and assumptions, and the process. Textual, statistical, and graphic presentations typically are included in the final report. Explanations of points on which there was agreement or disagreement are very important. The responses of any individual panel member should remain anonymous in the final report.

> The third-round questionnaire is the consensus or conclusion-reaching round. The conclusions are based on the responses of this round.

The Delphi involves a somewhat complex process in communication and analysis. It is a communication process that does not involve face-to-face interaction among panel members. Therefore, the responsibility for adequate communication at the various questionnaire stages is the researchers'. The Delphi is summarized in the flowchart of Figure 13.3. The figure contains three questionnaire rounds, which, for most research studies using the Delphi, is an adequate number. Additional rounds could be included if, for example, adequate consensus had not been reached. The content of additional questionnaires would be based on the preceding questionnaire. Additional rounds would be used only if necessary. They tend to extend the research to an undesirable length, put additional demands on the panel, and increase the likelihood of panel attrition.

Under the figure boxes representing the questionnaire rounds are mentioned the major emphases of the analyses at the rounds. When analyzing questionnaire response, researchers are interested in the convergence and stability of response. Convergence is the panel members coming to an agreed-on response, the extent to which they come to a common result. The individual responses center around a median response, for example, and there is little divergence. Stability is the extent to which responses no longer change, that is, the positions of the panel members have become static. For example, two or more panel members may not agree, but they are not changing their results. When convergence and/or stability is reached, the Delphi questionnaire rounds terminate.

Delphi studies require considerable time because of the turnaround for the questionnaires and the effort required of the panel members. Sometimes one or two panel members are late in responding and this slows the entire process. A national study mentioned earlier by Murry and Hammonds (1995) took about six months for completion. Few studies can be done adequately in less time, and, indeed, one of the possible disadvantages of the Delphi is its required time span.

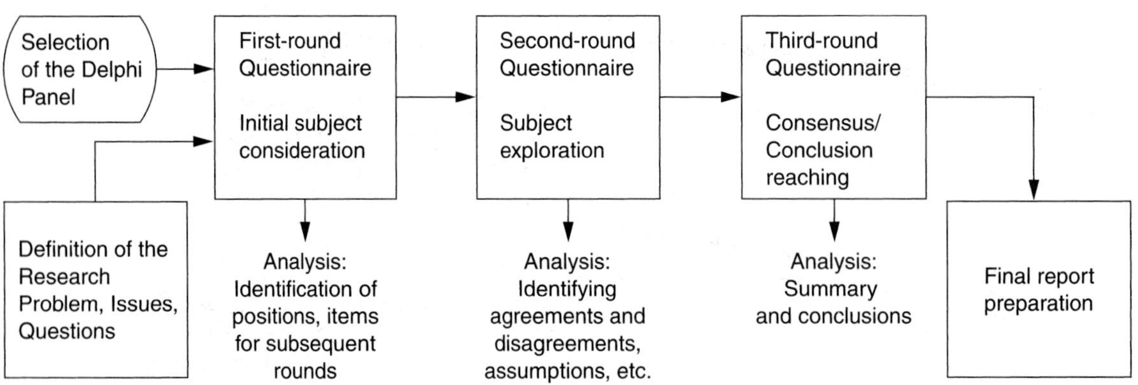

FIGURE 13.3 Flowchart of the Delphi Process

Variations of the Delphi

The conventional Delphi is a paper-and-pencil questionnaire procedure directed toward a convergence or consensus of expert opinions. The **consensus Delphi** tends to be the most applicable for educational research.

The area of policy research might involve what Bjil (1992) calls the **Policy Delphi.** This situation does not aim for convergence or consensus, but rather aims for opposing views. The purpose is to uncover the variety of positions. The process should reveal the pros and cons of each position.

Somewhat similar to the policy Delphi in that it does not necessarily seek consensus, is the **Adversary Delphi** as described by Helmer (1994). As the name implies, this Delphi applies to decision making in adversarial situations. Again, the reasons underlying the two or more positions are of paramount importance. If consensus cannot be attained, the majority of opinion takes precedence in reaching a decision.

Finally, a variation of the Delphi is not a conceptual variation but a way of conducting the study, the **e-Delphi** or Real-time Delphi. Instead of a paper-and-pencil approach, the e-Delphi is conducted electronically. The questionnaire construction and communication with panel members is conducted using the Web. Applied correctly, this does enhance the efficiency of using the Delphi. For more information about the e-Delphi system, the reader is referred to Chou (2002).

> There are variations on the Delphi that are not necessarily directed to consensus but toward opposing opinions or positions. The Delphi can also be conducted electronically through e-Delphi.

A Delphi Example

Bulger and Housner (2007) conducted a modified Delphi investigation of the critical exercise science competencies that would be recommended for inclusion in the physical education teacher education curriculum. Their purpose was to determine which of the competencies on the list of knowledge, skills, and abilities that was recommended by the American College of Sports Medicine in 2000 for people working in the field of exercise science would be judged to be of theoretical importance and have pedagogical relevance for physical education teachers.

This is a modified Delphi study because the participants did not generate the list of competencies that were rated. Instead, they worked from a list of competencies that was provided to them. The study consisted of two rounds, which correspond to the second and third rounds of Figure 13.3.

The panel consisted of ten university faculty members who were specialists in exercise science, seven university faculty members who were physical education teacher educators, and three physical education teachers who had completed the Physical Best Health-Fitness Instructor Certification. Another study that could have been done would be to have three separate panels, run three separate Delphi studies, and then see whether the three groups endorsed the same competencies.

A pilot study was done in which experts, similar to the panel members, evaluated the questionnaire items for content validity and completeness. Some items were eliminated and some new ones were generated. There were 222 competencies that were eventually sent to the panel for rating.

Round 1 procedures included the mailing of the questionnaire along with a cover letter and a stamped, self-addressed return envelope. Follow-up of nonrespondents was done two weeks and four weeks after the initial mailing. Follow-ups were by e-mail and by telephone. When the Round 1 questionnaires were returned, responses were recorded and means were calculated for each item.

In Round 2, the panel members were sent their item ratings and the group average ratings and asked to reevaluate their ratings based on the group means. Mailings and follow-ups were done as they had been in Round 1.

The returns were analyzed item by item. A competency was judged to be valuable if it had a mean rating of 4 or higher on the 5-point scales for importance and for relevance. Additionally, the competency had to have been rated a 4 or a 5 by at least 75 percent of the panel members. There were 109 of the 222 competencies that met these criteria. Note that the Delphi process accomplished two goals. First, it reduced the number of competencies that were deemed to be important and relevant, and second, it formed a "consensus" about those competencies.

Considerations When Conducting a Delphi Study

As with any research method, conducting a Delphi requires attention to detail. After the research problem has been identified, panel selection takes place, and it is crucial to have an appropriate panel of experts. A possible problem is having panel members who are not experts in the area. Experts typically are considered to be those who have special skills and knowledge, can identify problems in their area of expertise, and, if the problem is solvable, can suggest possible solutions.

Panel attrition is a problem if panel members begin dropping out after the initial and subsequent rounds. A panel member cannot join again if a round is missed. Prospective panel members should be completely informed of the magnitude of the task, its approximate duration, and they should be committed to completing the task.

> Panel selection is very important. Panel members must be experts in the area under study, and they must be committed to participation in all the Delphi questionnaire rounds. The quality of the Delphi questionnaire responses depends on the caliber of panel members.

The researchers conducting a Delphi have major responsibility for the success of its use, from panel selection through the entire process, including the report preparation. Linstone and Turoff (1975) have listed difficulties that can cause Delphi failure:

> Imposing monitor views and preconceptions of a problem upon the respondent group by overspecifying the structure of the Delphi and not allowing for the contribution of other perspectives related to the problem.
>
> Assuming that Delphi can be a surrogate for all other human communications in a given situation.
>
> Poor techniques of summarizing and representing the group response and ensuring common interpretations of the evaluation scales utilized in the exercise
>
> Ignoring and not exploring disagreements, so that discouraged dissenters drop out and an artificial consensus is generated
>
> Underestimating the demanding nature of a Delphi and the fact that the respondents should be recognized as consultants and properly compensated for their time if the Delphi is not an integral part of their job function (p. 6)

Nevertheless, despite possible difficulties, when properly conducted the Delphi is a viable research method. It has some definite positive characteristics such that it provides an opportunity for the participation of experts who cannot meet as a group. Although panel members work on the same issue, they are not influenced by group interaction dynamics, such as domination by a strong personality. The Delphi provides focus on the research problem. Finally, the process provides complete documentation of responses, and so forth, as consensus on the final conclusions is reached. Thus, the final report of the study should be comprehensive and complete.

The Delphi is a research method in which a panel of experts working individually and anonymously provide the data. The method applies to areas such as curriculum research and policy research, areas in which much of what is done is guided by expert (or possibly not-so-expert) opinion. The process of the Delphi is a multistep process conducted through successive questionnaire rounds distributed through the mail or through e-mail. For most Delphis conducted in educational research the desired outcome is consensus, although there may be situations that conclude with diverse positions. The summaries of panel responses may be quantitative, but the Delphi, at least in its initial round, is considered to be qualitative research.

Summary

This chapter has addressed three research methods that do not fit completely into the traditional methods such as experiment and survey. With some educational research studies being quite extensive, it is not uncommon to find more than one research method used in a single study, a mixed methods situation. Modeling methods are receiving increased attention, especially with the availability of complex computer programs for sophisticated analysis in fitting models. Linear equation modeling is a sophisticated, quantitative analysis.

Finally, most of this chapter was devoted to the Delphi method. This method has been around for about five decades, but its increased use in educational research has been more recent. The Delphi sometimes is used as the initial research method to generate data, followed by another method such as a survey. As with all research methods, these methods are used when they meet the purposes and needs of the research study.

KEY CONCEPTS

Mixed methods
Model building
Modeling methods
Models
Linear equation
Latent variable
Delphi method
Panel of experts
Questionnaire rounds
Consensus Delphi
Policy Delphi
Adversary Delphi
e-Delphi

EXERCISES

13.1 A large school system has adopted a new mathematics curriculum for its middle school students. Evaluative research of the curriculum is to be done during the second semester of the academic year. The research will address three questions:

a. How is the mathematics achievement of the students affected by the new curriculum?
b. What are the characteristics, features, and so forth, of mathematics instruction with the new curriculum?
c. What are teacher perceptions of the new curriculum and its implementation?

Describe how this research will involve mixed methods. Identify each method used, when it would be used during the second semester, and provide specific examples of the data that might be collected for each method.

13.2 A historian at a large university (over 30,000 students on campus) is doing historical research on the football program from 1945 to the present. The research focuses on factors such as expenditures, conditions and support of athletes, and emphasis on the sport in the university community. In addition to the historical part of the study, the historian, along with two colleagues, is interested in present faculty perceptions of the football program.

a. Identify the types of research necessary to complete both parts of the study.
b. Describe what is necessary to complete the second part. Assume that the faculty and administration of the university number over 1400. How would you go about conducting this research? Specifically, identify data to be collected from the faculty.

13.3 The application of linear models in educational research involves sophisticated conceptualization and complex statistical analysis. For a discussion of an application of hierarchical linear methods, the reader is referred to: Bryk, A., and Raudenbush, S. W. (1987). Application of hierarchical linear models to assessing change. *Psychological Bulletin, 101,* 147–158. If you have an interest in this topic, review this article and discuss its content with others who are familiar with the topic.

13.4 Suppose you were planning to identify effective school leadership characteristics of school principals. Describe the criteria you would use in selecting "expert" principals to serve as members of a Delphi panel. How many experts would be selected for the panel? Describe the information you would provide the panel for the first questionnaire round.

13.5 Dropout prevention is an important issue for educators in large school systems, especially those with inner-city schools or schools with high proportions of minority students. Suppose you were designing a Delphi intended to identify effective dropout prevention practices. How would you go about selecting panel members for the Delphi? What criteria would be used for panel membership? How many members would serve on the panel?

13.6 Identify three advantages of using a mixed methods approach that include both qualitative and quantitative research techniques over using only quantitative or only qualitative methods.

13.7 Develop a hypothetical conceptual model for understanding the dropout phenomenon in a small rural school district. Suggest a causal structure that might be tested. Use a diagram to depict your model.

NOTES

1. Maximizing the Achievement of African American Children in Kanawha County (MAACK). A project conducted at AEL, Inc., 1031 Quarrier Street, Charleston, WV 25301–2314. The study is described in various project-related papers.
2. There are any number of texts that address the statistics involved. See, for example, K. A. Bollen, *Structural equations with latent variables* (New York: John Wiley, 1989), and A. S. Bryk and S. W. Raudenbush, *Hierarchical linear models: Applications and data analysis methods* (Newbury Park, CA: Sage Publications, 1992).
3. The sequence and description of the steps generally follow those presented by D. M. Ferguson, Annotation: Structural equation models in developmental research, *Journal for Child Psychology and Psychiatry, 38*, 877–887 (1997).
4. We will use the convention of most authors by simply referring to the Delphi method as the Delphi.

REFERENCES

Bjil, R. (1992). Delphi in a future scenario study on mental health and mental health care. *Futures, 24*, 232, 250.

Bulger, S. M., and Housner, L. D. (2007). Modified Delphi investigation of exercise science in physical education teacher education. *Journal of Teaching in Physical Education, 26*, 57–80.

Chou, C. (2002). Developing the e-Delphi system: A Web-based forecasting tool for educational research. *British Journal of Educational Technology, 33*, 233, 236.

Coe, P., Keyes, M., Meehan, M., Orletsky, S., Lewis, S., Rigney, S., Runge, C., and Whitaker, J. (1999). *Development validation of successful writing program indicators based on research in continuously improving and continuously declining schools. Report of the Kentucky state writing project: A study of writing instruction in Kentucky Schools.* Charleston, WV: AEL, and Frankfort, KY: Kentucky State Department of Education.

Delbecq, A. L., Van de Ven, A. H., and Gustafson, D. H. (1975). *Group techniques for program planning: A guide to nominal group and Delphi processes.* Glenview, IL: Scott Foresman.

Duboff, R., and Spaeth, J. (2000). *Market research matters: Tools and techniques for aligning your business.* New York: John Wiley.

Ferguson, D. M. (1997). Annotation: Structural equation models in developmental research. *Journal for Child Psychology and Psychiatry, 38*, 877–887.

Helmer, O. (1994). Adversary Delphi. *Futures, 26*, 79–88.

Linstone, H. A., and Turoff, M. (1975). *The Delphi method: Techniques and applications.* Reading, MA: Addison-Wesley.

McCoy, R. W. (2001). Computer competencies for the 21st century information systems educator. *Information Technology Learning and Performance Journal, 19*, 21–35.

Murry, J. W., and Hammonds, J. O. (1995). Assessing the managerial and leadership ability of community college administrative personnel. *Community College Journal of Research and Practice, 19*, 209–218.

Parenté, F. J., and Anderson-Parenté, J. (1987). Delphi inquiry systems. In G. Wright and P. Ayton (Eds.), *Judgmental Forecasting* (pp. 129–156). New York: John Wiley.

Parker, W. C., Akira, N., and Cogan, J. (1999). Educating world citizens: Toward multinational curriculum development. *American Educational Research Journal, 36*, 117–145.

Unrau, S. M., and Schlackman, J. (2006). Motivation and its relationship with reading achievement in an urban middle school. *Journal of Educational Research, 100*, 81–101.

Wilhelm, W. J. (2001). Alchemy of the oracle: Delphi technique. *Delta Pi Epsilon Journal, 43*, 6–26.

CHAPTER

14 Sampling Designs

The preceding chapters discussed research designs for various types of studies and mentioned samples and random assignment from time to time. On occasion, an entire population of individuals may be included in a research study, but in many educational research studies, it is simply not feasible to include all members of a population. The time and effort required would be prohibitive. This is certainly true in survey research when large populations are concerned. Thus, a sample is used much more commonly. This chapter describes procedures for selecting samples.

A **sample** is a subset of the population to which the researcher intends to generalize the results. To do this, the researcher wants the sample, or the individuals actually involved in the research, to be representative of the larger population. Selecting a random sample ensures representativeness from a mathematical perspective. However, it is not possible to select random samples for all possible educational research studies so, at times, purposeful samples are used. A sample either is or is not random, and a random sample must incorporate some aspect of random selection. Obtaining a random sample may be a relatively complex procedure, especially if large (and possibly diverse) populations are to be sampled. The first part of this chapter is devoted to a discussion of random sampling procedures, followed in the second part by a discussion of purposeful sampling.

The Concept of a Random Sample

A random sample involves what is called **probability sampling,** which means that every member of the population has a nonzero probability of being selected for the sample. In other words, all members of the population have some chance of being included in the sample. In complex sampling designs, the probabilities of selection may *not* be the same for all members, but the probabilities are all nonzero. A simple random sample is such that when it is selected, all members of the population have the same probability of being selected.[1]

A **random sample** is an unbiased sample, which means that those individuals selected vary only as they would due to random fluctuation. There is no systematic variation in the sample that would make this sample different from other samples. Of course, a random sample is representative of the population from which it was selected.

> A *random sample* is a probability sample in that every population member has a nonzero probability of selection. In a simple random sample, this probability is the same for all population members.

Random Selection and Random Assignment

Random selection and random assignment are not quite the same, but they are both used to obtain representativeness and eliminate bias. In **random selection,** the individuals are selected randomly as representing a population; in **random assignment,** commonly used in experiments, the individuals are randomly assigned to different groups or treatments. They may or may not have been initially selected randomly from a larger population to participate in the experiment. Some examples follow.

An institutional researcher at a university selects a random sample of 250 from the freshman class of 6821 students, who are then surveyed about their attitudes toward certain factors of college life. This example involves random selection. The 250 students of the sample are representative of the 6821 in the freshman class.

A psychologist has 90 students in a sophomore-level psychology course. The psychologist is conducting a learning experiment using three different types of materials. All 90 students will participate, and 30 will be randomly assigned to each of the types of materials. In this way, the three groups of students assigned to the different materials vary only on a random basis. As the students are assigned, any student has the same probability of being assigned to any one of the three materials—namely, one in three or one-third.

In the latter example, what population do these 90 students represent? They were not randomly selected from a larger population. Their reason for participating in the experiment is that they enrolled in the psychology course. In a sense, they have self-selected themselves. In this situation, the psychologist would likely argue that the 90 students are representative of young adults attending college. If sophomore students at this university are much like those at other universities, the results may generalize to other populations of university students. It is not likely that the results would generalize to all young adults everywhere. Often, in studies of this type, representativeness is argued on a logical basis, depending on the individuals and variables involved.

The contrast between random selection and random assignment is diagrammed in Figure 14.1. When a defined group (such as the psychology class) is used, and the members are randomly assigned to treatments, there is no question about the assignment being unbiased or the results generalizing to the group involved. But the generalizability of the results to larger populations is done on a logical basis, in which questions of unrepresentativeness may be raised. Of course, this is a matter of external validity, and the extent of representativeness and, correspondingly, the generalizability are always a matter of degree. Yet random assignment is commonly used in this way in educational research. Knowledge about the variables and individuals of the study is then used to make valid generalizations.

It might be mentioned that in a situation in which the number of individuals in the intact group does not equal the number required, the excess individuals are eliminated at

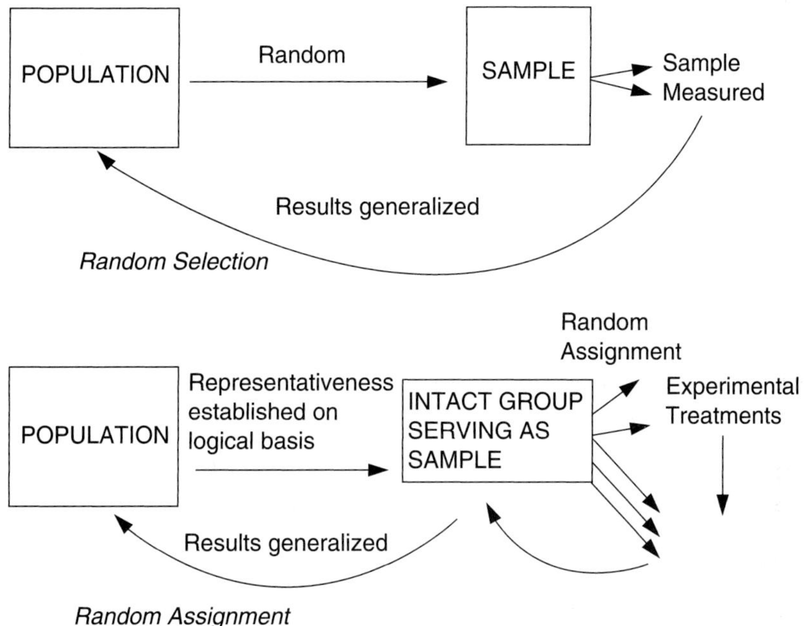

FIGURE 14.1 Contrast Between Random Selection and Random Assignment

random. (This is conceptually the same as selecting those for inclusion at random.) In the learning experiment example, if there were 94 students in the class and only 90 were required, 4 would be randomly selected not to participate. To avoid causing any apprehension, the psychologist could use all 94 in the experiment and then randomly eliminate the data of 4 individuals with the condition that each type of material would still have the data of 30 individuals.

Use of a Random Number Table

A simple random sample can be obtained by using a table of random numbers. (Table 14.1 is a sample page from a random number table.) Each member of the finite population is assigned a number, and then as many numbers as comprise the sample size are selected from the table. If there is a population of 70 members and 10 are to be selected at random, each of the 70 members is assigned a number from 1 to 70. The first 10 numbers that appear, wherever one begins in the random number table, determine the 10 sample members. Because there are only 70 members in the population, two-digit random numbers are used. Beginning with the first row in Table 14.1 and going across, taking two-digit numbers in sequence gives the following 10 numbers.

> 59, 39, 15, 80 (which is ignored, since our highest number is 70), 30, 52, 09, 88 (also ignored), 27, 18, 87 (also ignored), 02, and 48.

TABLE 14.1 Sample Page from a Table of Random Numbers

	50–54	55–59	60–64	65–69	70–74	75–79	80–84	85–89	90–94	95–99
00	59391	58030	52098	82718	87024	82848	04190	96574	90464	29065
01	99567	76364	77204	04615	27062	96621	43918	01896	83991	51141
02	10363	97518	51400	25670	98342	61891	27101	37855	06235	33316
03	86859	19558	64432	16706	99612	59798	32803	67708	15297	28612
04	11258	24591	36863	55368	31721	94335	34936	02566	80972	08188
05	95068	88628	35911	14530	33020	80428	39936	31855	34334	64865
06	54463	47237	73800	91017	36239	71824	83671	39892	60518	37092
07	16874	62677	57412	13215	31389	62233	80827	73917	82802	84420
08	92494	63157	76593	91316	03505	72389	96363	52887	01087	66091
09	15669	56689	35682	40844	53256	81872	35213	09840	34471	74441
10	96116	75486	84989	23476	52967	67104	39495	39100	17217	74073
11	15696	10703	65178	90637	63110	17622	53988	71087	84148	11670
12	97720	15369	51269	69620	03388	13699	33423	67453	43269	56720
13	11666	13841	71681	98000	35979	39719	81899	07449	47985	46967
14	71628	73130	78783	75691	41632	09487	61547	18707	85489	69944
15	40501	51089	99943	91843	41995	88931	73631	69361	05375	15417
16	22518	55576	98215	82068	10798	86211	36584	67466	69373	40054
17	75112	30485	62173	02132	14878	92879	22281	16783	86352	00077
18	80327	02671	98191	84342	90813	49268	95441	15496	20168	09271
19	60251	45548	02146	05597	48228	81366	34598	72856	66762	17002
20	57430	82270	10421	05540	43648	75888	66049	21511	47676	33444
21	73528	39599	34434	88596	54086	71693	43132	14414	79949	85193
22	25991	65959	70769	64721	86413	33475	42740	06175	82758	66248
23	78388	16638	09134	59880	63806	48472	39318	35434	24057	74739
24	12477	09965	96657	57994	59439	76330	24596	77515	09577	91871
25	83266	32883	42451	15579	38155	29793	40914	65990	16255	17777
26	76970	80876	10237	39515	79152	74798	39357	09054	73579	92359
27	37074	65198	44785	68624	98336	84481	97610	78735	46703	98265
28	83712	06514	30101	78295	54656	85417	43189	60048	72781	72606
29	20287	56862	69727	94443	64936	08366	27227	05158	50326	59566
30	74261	32592	86538	27041	65172	85532	07571	80609	39285	65340
31	64081	49863	08478	96001	18888	14810	70545	89755	59064	07210
32	05617	75818	47750	67814	29575	10526	66192	44464	27058	40467
33	26793	74951	95466	74307	13330	42664	85515	20632	05497	33625
34	65988	72850	48737	54719	52056	01596	03845	35067	03134	70322
35	27366	42271	44300	73399	21105	03280	73457	43093	05192	48657
36	56760	10909	98147	34736	33863	95256	12731	66598	50771	83665
37	72880	43338	93643	58904	59543	23943	11231	83268	65938	81581
38	77888	38100	03062	58103	47961	83841	25878	23746	55903	44115
39	28440	07819	21580	51459	47971	29882	13990	29226	23608	15873
40	63525	94441	77033	12147	51054	49955	58312	76923	96071	05813
41	47606	93410	16359	89033	89696	47231	64498	31776	05383	39902
42	52669	45030	96279	14709	52372	87832	02735	50803	72744	88208
43	16738	60159	07425	62369	07515	82721	37875	71153	21315	00132
44	59348	11695	45751	15865	74739	05572	32688	20271	65128	14551
45	12900	71775	29845	60774	94924	21810	38636	33717	67598	82521
46	75086	23537	49939	33595	13484	97588	28617	17979	70749	35234
47	99495	51434	29181	09993	38190	42553	68922	52125	91077	40197
48	26075	31671	45386	36583	93548	48599	52022	41330	60651	91321
49	13636	93596	23377	51133	95126	61496	42474	45141	46660	42338

Source: Reprinted by permission from *Statistical Methods* (6th ed.), by G. W. Snedecor and W. G. Cochran, © 1967 by the State University Press, Ames, Iowa.

If a number exceeding 70 appears, it is ignored. If a number appears that has already been selected, it, too, is ignored, because a single member of the population is not included twice in the sample. Any kind of sequencing in the table is random, and it is not necessary to go across the rows. The numbers could be selected in columns or by blocks. In Table 14.1, the numbers are grouped by fives to make it easier to locate them.

The random number table can also be used for random assignment. If 10 individuals are to be assigned at random, 5 to each of two treatments, single-digit numbers can be used, because (instead of 10) zero can be assigned to one individual. Using the random numbers of Table 14.1, if one begins with the first row of the second major block of five rows, the individuals with the first five numbers would be assigned to Treatment 1: 9, 5, 0, 6, and 8. This leaves the individuals with the following numbers for Treatment 2: 1, 2, 3, 4, and 7. If an individual's number repeats, it is passed over, because an individual can be assigned only once to a treatment.

Random number tables can be used for random selection and random assignment.

Use of the Computer in Sample Selection

Before discussing the use of the computer, a couple of terms need to be defined. One is **sampling frame,** which is the list of units or elements from which the sample is selected. For example, in a school survey the sampling frame may consist of the names of all registered voters in the district. When conducting a survey, the sampling frame may be called the survey population.

The second term is **sampling fraction.** This fraction is the ratio of sample size to population size, often designated n/N. Thus, if a sample of size 300 is selected from a population of size 2000, the sampling fraction would be 300/2000 or 3/20, which equals 0.15. The sampling fraction also may be expressed as percent, for example, 15 percent. For a simple random sample, the sampling fraction equals the probability of any member of the population being selected for the sample.

The *sampling fraction* is the ratio of sample size to population size, expressed as n/N.

There are several websites that will generate random numbers for you. One that is very easy to use is www.randomizer.org. This site leads you through a series of questions such as how many random numbers to generate, what the range of values should be limited to, and how many sets of random numbers to produce.

Many statistical software packages include programs for selecting a random sample. One such package is SPSS for Windows 15.0 (SPSS, Inc., 2006). Of course, as with any program, the sampling frame, probably a large data set, must be available for analysis. The sampling frame might be a list converted to numbers, a number for each name. If a data set contained the achievement scores of several thousand high school students, grades 9–12, the sampling frame could be defined as all tenth-graders. The SPSS program has a Data—Select Cases dialogue box that allows you to specify that you want to select a random sample. In this box the conditional expression for selection can be specified. The conditional expression can use any existing variable names or constants, such as all tenth-graders in the data set.

SPSS allows two options for specifying the size of the random sample:

- **Approximately.** A user-specified percentage. SPSS generates a random sample of approximately the specified percentages of cases.
- **Exactly.** A user-specified number of cases. You can also specify the number of cases from which to generate the sample. This number should be less than or equal to the total number of cases in the data file. If the number exceeds the total number of cases in the data file, the sample will contain proportionally fewer cases than the requested number.

The first option specifies the sampling fraction. In the example above, 20 percent of all tenth-graders could be selected. Or for a specified number, we could specify 200 selected from the 1596 tenth-graders listed.

The second option also allows for selection in subpopulations. Suppose in the example, there are four high schools but we want to select the tenth-grade sample from only two schools. We could list those schools first in the database and have the selection made only from the first number of tenth graders listed that would equal the total number in these two schools.

When the sample size is specified, click on *Continue* and the sample will be selected. There are two ways to designate those of the population that are *not* selected for the sample. One way is called "filtered," which simply draws a diagonal (/) in front of the cases not selected. The second way is called "deleted," which eliminates cases not selected. In the tenth-grade example, filtered likely would be used because it may be important to retain the entire database for later use. If a sample is selected from a voter list for a school survey, we likely would delete those not selected because the information would not be used again. Either way, those cases remaining or without a diagonal comprise the random sample.

Other software packages have programs for selecting a random sample. Additional conditions may be included so that the sample selected is a random sample other than a simple random sample. Whatever program is used, the procedure should be implemented as described in the manual for the software.

Sampling Error and Sampling Bias

Sampling error and **sampling bias,** two terms associated with sampling, at times are confused, although they have very different meanings. Sampling error is associated with random sampling and the term *error* does not mean making a mistake. Suppose we have a population of 1675 fifth-graders and we select a random sample of 150 from this population. The sample is administered a science achievement test and the mean score on the test is 86.3. Would we argue that the mean of the population is *exactly* 86.3? No, but we are confident that the mean is a value around 86.3. The difference between the sample mean of 86.3 and the population mean, whatever it is, is an example of sampling error. Sampling error is related to variation, a concept introduced in Chapter 6 and discussed more fully in the chapters on statistical analysis. Sampling error is variation due to random fluctuation. In specific situations in which statistical analyses are used, we can obtain an estimate of sampling error. Generally, as sample size increases, the variation due to random fluctuation, and hence sampling error, decreases.

> Sampling error is variation due to random fluctuation when random samples are used to represent populations.

Sampling bias is a different matter. Bias enters in when a sample fails to represent the population it was intended to represent. Bias can be due to any number of sources, and it is a threat whenever nonrandom (or nonprobability) sampling is used, or when random sampling is used with a biased source.

Consider again the previous example of the fifth-grade population. Suppose, instead of selecting a random sample, we selected five classes of fifth-graders, each class from a different school. The classes average 30 students per class so we again have 150 students in the sample. But the classes selected are the high-ability classes within the schools. For this sample the mean on the science achievement test is 103.8. Does this mean represent the science achievement of the population? Absolutely not. Sampling bias has occurred and this is a biased sample because of the way in which the sample was selected, in this case in a nonrandom manner.

Even though random sampling is used, sampling bias can occur if we have a biased source. The commonly cited survey in which a biased source was used was the 1936 survey by the *Literary Digest*, which predicted that Alf Landon would win the presidential election over Franklin Roosevelt. Random sampling was used but the sample was selected primarily from telephone directories and automobile registration lists. In 1936 these lists were not representative of the voting population.

Consider another example. Suppose someone wanted to select a sample of the general population of U.S. adults. Country club membership lists are used for the source, and a random sample selected from such lists. This sample is not representative of the general adult population. It was selected from a biased source.

> Sampling bias is a distortion caused by the way the sample was selected or formed, so that the sample is no longer representative of the population.

As was discussed in Chapter 9, questionnaire surveys cause concern about possible bias due to nonresponse. Even though the original sample was selected randomly, the respondents, in essence, self-select themselves into the sample, possibly becoming a biased source. This may bias the sample causing those who respond to be no longer representative of the population. This, too, is an example of sampling bias.

Criteria for a Sampling Design

There may be any number of reasons why a researcher would depart from simple random sampling to use a more complex sampling design. Probably the most common reason is that the population from which the sample is to be selected is so large that simple random sampling cannot be conducted. The population may also be quite diverse and may consist of several subpopulations. Populations whose members are grouped or clustered are more readily sampled than individual members. If the population is very heterogeneous, an alternative to simple random sampling will tend to control some of the sampling variation.

Whatever the reason for using a more complex sampling design, a good sampling design should meet certain requirements. Kish (1965) identified four broad criteria for a good sampling design: (1) goal orientation, (2) measurability, (3) practicality, and (4) economy.

The first criterion, goal orientation, means that the sampling design should be tailored to the research design and should be based on the study's goals or objectives. The measurement necessary to obtain the data and the anticipated analyses, based on the research problem, also have important implications for sampling. These factors are considered in deciding what sampling design will best meet the goals and objectives of the study.

The criterion of measurability means that the sampling design provides the data for the necessary analyses. If a design has measurability, valid estimates of sampling variability, which are essential for the use of inferential statistics, can be made. (Inferential statistics are discussed in Chapter 17.) Measurability enables valid inferences to be made from the sample data to the population from which the sample was selected.

It is one thing to sketch a sampling design on paper theoretically and another to apply the design in a real situation. The criterion of practicality means that the actual activities of applying the sampling design have been identified and are feasible in the real situation. Practicality also means attempting to anticipate problems and devising methods for avoiding or circumventing them, and it involves making the conceptual design conform with the actual situation.

The criterion of economy is largely self-explanatory. Expenditures for educational research projects are usually limited, and economy requires that the research objectives be met with available resources: time, financial, personnel, and any other necessary resources. Because obtaining data for a research project can be time-consuming and expensive, a good sampling design is not wasteful of data-collection efforts.

Because it is not likely that all four criteria can be met maximally, attempting to meet these four criteria when developing a sampling design often becomes a matter of balance. For example, to enhance measurability, the researcher may increase the sample size to the extent that some economy is sacrificed. It may not be possible to anticipate all problems, but even with problems a design may be feasible and thus attain adequate practicality. The important overall criterion is that the design be feasible and adequately accommodate the research problem.

Stratified Random Sampling

In some cases, the population to be sampled is not homogeneous but, in essence, consists of several subpopulations. Rather than selecting randomly from the entire population, the researcher might divide such a population into two or more subpopulations, called *strata.* This approach to sampling is called **stratified random sampling** because the population is stratified into its subpopulations. All strata are represented in the sample, and the sample members are selected from each stratum at random. Thus, the condition of random selection is included by the selection within the strata.

Allocation of Sample Size Among Strata

The decision must be made as to the number (that is, allocation) that will be selected from each stratum for the sample. One method of allocation, called **equal allocation,** is to select equal numbers from the strata. Thus, if there were five strata, one-fifth of the sample would be selected from each stratum. Unless the strata had equal population sizes, the sampling fraction would vary among strata.

A more commonly used method is **proportional allocation,** whereby each stratum contributes to the sample a number that is proportional to its size in the population. The allocation of strata members in the sample is proportional to the numbers of members in the strata of the population. Suppose that there are k strata to be sampled and that the respective population sizes of the strata are $N_1, N_2, \ldots N_k$. Total population size can be indicated by N and total sample size by n. We can let $n_1, n_2, \ldots n_k$ be the sample sizes for the respective strata. Then:

$$\frac{n}{N} = \frac{n_1}{N_1} = \frac{n_2}{N_2} = \cdots = \frac{n_k}{N_k}$$

where $N_1 + N_2 \ldots + N_k =$ and $n_1 + n_2 \ldots + n_k = n$. The sampling fraction is n/N, and this fraction (proportionality) is held constant for the allocation of the sample to the k strata.

Stratified sampling guards against wild samples, ensures that no subpopulation will be omitted from the sample, and avoids overloading in certain subpopulations. Stratified random samples are sometimes called **self-weighting samples.** Simple random samples have a tendency to distribute themselves according to the population proportions, and stratified random sampling with proportional allocation will build this proportionality into the sample.

> *Proportional allocation* in stratified random sampling distributes the sample in such a way that the sampling fraction is the same for all strata.

Other allocations could be used if there is a compelling reason to do so. For example, if there is a stratum in which the scores are much more variable than for the other strata, a decision might be made to give that stratum a much larger allocation than the other strata.

But, from a practical standpoint, equal allocation and proportional allocation are by far the most frequently used allocations, with proportional allocation often preferred because of its self-weighting characteristic.

Stratified random sampling is used often in educational research. Duncan and Noonan (2007) used this technique when investigating the factors that affect teachers' grading and assessment practices. They were interested in determining whether class size, school size, and subject matter had any impact on teachers' practices, so they stratified on those three factors when selecting their sample to ensure adequate data to address their research questions. Their final sample included 513 teachers from 66 high schools in one Western Canadian province.

EXAMPLE 14.1

We will present an example using proportional allocation. The director of institutional research at a university is conducting a survey of student opinion on the adequacy of facilities—the student union, the library, and so forth. The questionnaire is quite extensive, so rather than administer it to all students, a 5 percent stratified random sample will be selected. The university contains seven colleges, with a total enrollment of 15,823 students. The definition of an enrolled student is one who is presently registered to be taking at least one course for degree credit. College is the stratifying variable, and proportional allocation will be used. Because a 5 percent sample is selected, the sampling fraction is 1/20, or .05. The information for this sampling example is presented in Figure 14.2.

Strata (college)	Strata sizes		Sample size by strata
Arts & Sciences	5461		273
Business Administration	1850		93
Community Services	2092	A 1/20 random sample is selected from each stratum	105
Education	3508		175
Engineering	2112		106
Law	318		16
Pharmacy	482		24
	15,823 = N		792 = n

.05 of the total university population equals 15,823 × .05 = 791.15.
The n of 792 includes any rounding off.

FIGURE 14.2 Sample Selection Using Proportional Allocation—University Example

Note that all strata (colleges) contribute to the sample. The sample members for each college are randomly selected within the college. Because colleges vary greatly in size, equal allocation would not be desirable if the opinions varied considerably among colleges.

The question might be raised, "What variables and how many can be effectively used for stratification?" More than one stratifying variable could be used, but this can substantially increase the number of strata because it involves combinations of the two variables. In the example, if the colleges of Arts and Sciences, Business Administration, Education, and Engineering have graduate as well as undergraduate programs, it might be desirable to stratify on the dichotomous variable undergraduate–graduate in these four colleges. Law would likely be considered a graduate program and thus would have no undergraduates. Community Services and Pharmacy have only undergraduates. If stratification were done in this manner, there would be 11 instead of 7 strata.

The number of strata that can be conveniently accommodated depends to some extent on the sample size. The larger the sample size, the more strata can be used. However, strata are not identified simply for the sake of having a large number of them. Unless a large survey is being conducted, stratification seldom involves more than two stratifying variables (usually only one), and the total number of strata would seldom exceed 20 and usually is considerably less.

Cluster Sampling

When the selection of individual members of the population is impractical or too expensive, it may be possible to select groups or clusters of members for the sample. **Cluster sampling** is a procedure of selection in which the unit of selection, called the cluster, contains two or more population members. Each member of the population must be uniquely contained in one, and only one, cluster. Cluster sampling is useful in situations where the population members are naturally grouped in units that can be used conveniently as clusters. For example, pollsters doing surveys sometimes use city blocks as the cluster unit for selecting a sample. In educational research, a class can serve as a cluster. A school building, or possibly even a school system, might serve as a cluster in a large-scale study.

Cluster sampling differs from stratified random sampling in that the random selection occurs not with the individual members but with the clusters. The clusters from the sample are randomly selected from the larger population of clusters, and, once a cluster is selected for the sample, all the population members in that cluster are included in the sample. This is in contrast to stratified random sampling, in which the individual members within strata are randomly selected. In cluster sampling, before selecting the sample, not only must all population members be identified in their clusters, but all the clusters must be identified. It is not necessary that all clusters have the same number of population members.

> *Cluster sampling* involves the random selection of clusters from the larger population of clusters. All the population members of a selected cluster are included in the sample.

In cluster sampling, the exact sample size may not be known until after the sample is selected. This is because clusters usually are not the same size, and the final sample size depends on those clusters that are randomly selected. However, clusters are often somewhat similar in size, and if the researcher has a sample size in mind, the number of clusters required can be estimated.

Cluster sampling appears in the literature less often than stratified random sampling and sometimes the two techniques are used together. House (2003) did research on the relationship between self-beliefs and reading achievement in elementary school students in Hong Kong and in the United States. Data were obtained from the Progress in International Reading Literacy Study (PIRLS) 2001 Assessment. The PIRLS sample design involved a two-stage stratified cluster design in which schools were sampled during the first stage and classrooms were selected in the second stage. The United States' sample was stratified on school size, metropolitan/nonmetropolitan, public/private; minority status for public schools, high/low; and religious denomination for private schools, Catholic/other religious/nonsectarian. The Hong Kong sample was stratified on gender status, boys/girls/mixed; school type, whole day/non–whole day; and district. When a school was selected, classrooms were randomly selected within the school and all of the students in that classroom were tested. The classrooms were the clusters in this design.

EXAMPLE 14.2

An example of a research situation for which cluster sampling would be appropriate is a survey of fourth-grade achievement in mathematics, using a standardized achievement test, conducted by the research director of a city system that contains thirty-three elementary schools. It is too expensive to administer the test to all fourth-graders in the system, and the logistics of selecting a simple random sample and administering the test would be quite extensive. Stratified random sampling might be feasible, but it has one disadvantage: the fourth-graders are in classes, and it is inconvenient to test some members of the class and not others. Because the fourth-graders are "naturally" assembled in classes, cluster sampling is to be used, using class as the sampling unit. Then all students in a selected class are to be tested.

There are 83 fourth-grade classes throughout the system, with an average enrollment of 27.3 students per class. A sample size of approximately 550 students is desired, so it is decided to select 20 classes or clusters. The sampling design is diagrammed in Figure 14.3.

All members of the 20 selected classes are tested on mathematics achievement. It so happens that 561 students are tested, which is a slightly larger than anticipated sample. (Some students may be absent on the testing day, but this is of no concern if the absence pattern is typical.)

The tendency is for cluster sampling to be used with large populations. Whatever the sampling unit, it is usually something that groups the population members naturally. As the size of the cluster increases, however, the sample size also becomes large, because all members of a selected cluster are in the sample. The sampling unit should be carefully selected and well defined so that there is no confusion as to what comprises a cluster. Cluster sampling has implications for the analysis of data in that the cluster may be used as the unit of analysis. That would mean that, instead of 561

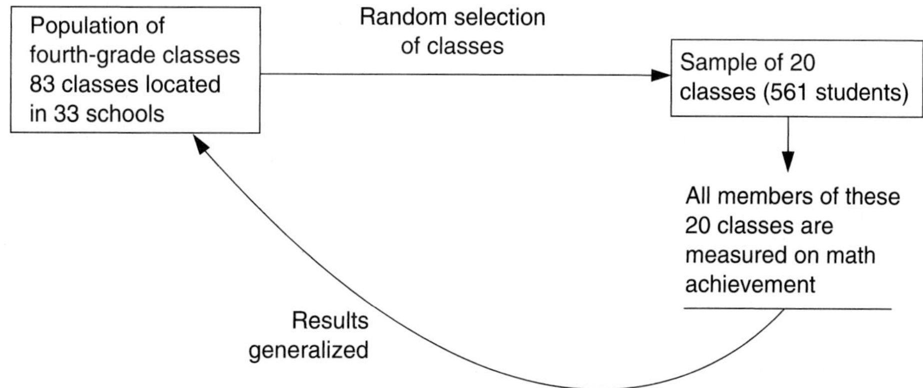

FIGURE 14.3 Sample Selection Using Cluster Sampling—Fourth-Grade Example

observations, quite a large sample, we would really have only 20 observations, the means of the students in each of the clusters.

Systematic Sampling

The use of systematic sampling is quite common in educational research in which large populations are studied and alphabetical or possibly other lists of the population members are available. Directors of institutional research often use this technique in selecting a sample. The primary advantage of systematic sampling in educational research is convenience.

Systematic sampling is a procedure by which the selection of the first sample member determines the entire sample. The population members (that is, their names or identification numbers) are in some type of order; for example, the names of the population members may be placed in alphabetical order on a list. The sample size is chosen and the sampling fraction determined. If the sampling fraction is 1/10, the first member of the sample is randomly selected from the first ten names on the list. Following this first selection, every tenth member of the population is selected for the sample. In the general case, if the sampling fraction n/N equals $1/k$, the first member of the sample is randomly selected from the first k names on the list, and after that, every kth name on the list is selected. When the list is exhausted, the sample will have n members.

Possible Problem of Periodicity

Although the first member of a systematic sample is randomly selected, it is possible that this sampling design will yield a biased sample. The most serious and really the only threat of bias in systematic sampling is the existence of some type of periodicity in the ordering of the population members. **Periodicity** means that every kth member of the population has some unique characteristics that are related to, or have an effect on, the dependent variable. In that case, the sample becomes biased.

The likelihood of periodicity entering a list is generally quite small, though it could enter inadvertently.

> *Systematic sampling* involves randomly selecting the first member of the sample from a list and from that point on taking every *k*th name on the list if 1/*k* equals the sampling fraction.

Ma and Crocker (2007) used systematic sampling in a study investigating differences among the Canadian provinces on the 2000 Programme for International Student Assessment (PISA). A two-stage sampling plan was used. In the first stage schools were selected systematically from a national list of schools. The probabilities of selection were proportional to the number of fifteen-year-olds in the school. In the second stage, students were systematically sampled from a list of all students in the school. The researchers found that the provinces differed significantly in the effects that disciplinary climate and sense of belonging to the school had on reading achievement.

EXAMPLE 14.3

A sample of fifth-graders is being selected from a large school system population. The sample is to be measured on an ability test to estimate the ability level of the fifth-grade population of the school system. The researcher in charge of the study decides to take a 1-in-30 sample and notes that class lists can be used conveniently, because the fifth-grade classes all contain about thirty students. The researcher calls for class lists, but instead of sending alphabetical lists, the fifth-grade teachers send lists on which the student names in each class are arranged from high to low according to performance on a recent achievement test. The researcher puts the lists together, one class following another, and selects the systematic sample. Because achievement and performance on an ability test are quite conclusively related, periodicity has entered into the sampling list. If the first random selection gives the third name on the list, it would mean that the third, thirty-third, sixty-third, and so forth students on the list would comprise the sample. This sample would differ from other samples, especially, for example, one beginning with the twenty-sixth name on the list. Whatever sample is selected would have the effect of periodicity in it.

The foregoing example of periodicity, though possible, is quite unlikely, because, for that type of research situation, another sampling design, possibly cluster sampling, would likely be used. Systematic sampling is convenient, for example, for an institutional researcher in a university who is to survey the student body (or some part of it) with a brief questionnaire to be returned by mail. Alphabetical lists of students for whatever population is being surveyed could be used.

Systematic sampling provides the condition of sampling throughout the population due to its spacing of selections over the entire list. A definite advantage of systematic sampling over, say, simple random sampling is that it requires less work. However, the researcher should be aware of how the list is ordered and check for the possibility of periodicity.

Considerations in Determining Sample Size—Random Sampling

Several factors can influence the size of the sample used in a research study, but, with the exception of cost, information about such factors is often incomplete and it becomes difficult to set an exact size. Cost refers not only to the expenditure of money but also to the time and effort required to obtain the sample data. In any survey, the actual cost of obtaining the data per unit in the sample should be estimated as accurately as possible. If standardized tests are used, what is the cost per test? How much does it cost to score the tests and summarize the data? What, if any, costs will be encountered in locating the sample for testing? What is the cost of test administration? These are all examples of questions that can be raised. A researcher who is securing funds for a project from a funding agency usually is required to produce quite accurate cost estimates. Researchers who are university professors (and possibly graduate students) often receive funds from a funding agency or from a source within the university; thus, cost estimates are required. Even in the rare instances when facilities and resources are available through a university at no hard-dollar costs, costs of proposed projects should be estimated; at least time and effort estimates should be made.

Sample size is also related to the statistical analysis of quantitative data. Two important concepts here are **statistical precision** and **statistical power.** The concepts are related but will be explained separately. The simplest example of statistical precision is when polling agencies are estimating the percentage of the voters who will vote for a school tax. They would like their estimate to be as precise as possible. Suppose that 55 percent of a random sample of voters said that they would vote for the tax. If the 55 percent were based on a small sample, the estimate might range from 40 percent to 70 percent (55 percent ± 15 percent). If a large sample were used, the estimate might range from 52 percent to 58 percent (55 percent ± 3 percent). Note how much more useful the latter estimate is.[2] The statistical precision of the estimate is directly related to the sample size. Larger samples yield greater statistical precision.

Statistical power deals with whether a result is statistically significant, that is, not merely due to chance. In an experiment, for example, a statistical test is conducted to see whether the mean of the experimental group is significantly different from the mean of the control group. We hypothesize (null hypothesis) that the population means of the experimental and control conditions are equal. We then compute the difference between the means of the experimental and control groups (our data). Suppose the mean of the experimental group is five points higher than the mean of the control group. We then run a statistical test to see whether the five-point difference is more than we would expect from mere random fluctuations. The results of the statistical test will cause us either to (1) reject the null hypothesis and conclude that the five-point difference is statistically significant, or (2) not reject the null hypothesis and conclude that the null hypothesis is very possibly true. The power of the statistical test is defined as the probability of declaring that the experimental and control group means differ significantly if the population means that they represent are not equal.[3] Statistical power is directly related to sample size. The larger the sample(s), the greater the statistical power. In practical terms, this means that we are more likely to find statistical significance with large samples than with small samples.

Large samples provide greater statistical precision and greater statistical power than small samples.

When the researcher can express the **effect size** that is a meaningful difference, we can determine how large the sample should be. Suppose a researcher would like to see whether a certain intervention would increase the average scores on a self-concept measure by eight points. She believes that a difference of at least this amount is necessary to affect academic performance. When we know the effect size that she wants to detect (eight points), the significance level (possibly .05), and the desired level of statistical power (possibly .80), we can find the necessary sample size. Multiple factors must be considered simultaneously, but if enough prior information is available, such as the variability in the self-concept scores, sample size can be estimated for a desired level of statistical precision. Prior information would include knowledge about the variability of the dependent variable. Hinkle and Oliver (1983) discuss estimating the necessary sample size when certain characteristics are given.

The general procedure for determining sample size involve the following steps:

1. There must be a designation of what is expected of the sample in terms of statistical precision, power, or error. This is the responsibility of the researcher. Information from related studies may be useful and certainly knowledge of the dependent variables is helpful.

2. An equation is specified connecting sample size with the desired precision of Step 1. If parts of the equation are unknown they must be estimated. Solving this equation provides an estimate of sample size (n).

3. In many studies, more than one dependent variable is involved; for example, a survey may contain two or more subscales. If a desired degree of precision is specified for each subscale, a sample size will be estimated for each. There must be some resolution for these various n values. If feasible, selecting the largest n would be the optimal solution in terms of precision.

4. Finally, whatever n is selected must be considered to determine whether it is consistent with the resources for conducting the research, the costs of data collection, time, and effort required.

Although the determination of sample size can be somewhat complex statistically, there are some general guidelines, more or less based on empirical studies conducted over the years. Sudman (1976, p. 87) suggests that for regional or special surveys (such as for a thesis or dissertation), with few subgroups, a sample of 200–500 is typical. Krejcie and Morgan (1970, p. 608) suggest sample sizes based on population sizes. Their numbers are based on a formula developed by the U.S. Office of Education. As population size increases, sample size also increases, but sample size becomes a decreasing percentage as population size increases. For example, for a population of size 700, the suggested n is 248, and for a population of size 75,000, n equals 382.

There may be several groups in a research study, such as an experiment for which the experimental variable has several levels forming several experimental groups. Generally, the more variable the dependent variable the greater the number required in each group. If a field experiment had several groups, say 8 or 10, 15 to 30 individuals per group should be adequate for sample size. However, if there were only two groups, we usually would not consider 15 or so per group an adequate sample. It would be desirable to get the total sample size across the groups to at least around 100. On the other hand, for a tightly controlled experiment, in a learning lab, for example, 15 or so subjects per group, and a total of 60 or so subjects, might be adequate.

If a complex design is used, such as a factorial with two or more independent variables, and the number of cells or groups is large, 10 or so subjects per cell may be an adequate minimum sample size. However, increasing the sample size does enhance the statistical analysis, and a total sample size of 240 would be preferred to one of size 120. Again, effect size or desired statistical precision for the specific research would need to be considered in determining the minimum sample size.

It should not be inferred that it is always desirable to increase the sample size to its maximum, because this may be unduly costly and wasteful of effort and information. For some surveys, the time required for the data collection of large samples may be so long that the timeliness of the results is ruined. Increasing sample size is not necessary to attain adequate representation. The method of selection and ensuring that selection is from unbiased sources are the important determiners of attaining adequate representation. Probability sampling must include some aspect of random selection. The *Literary Digest* survey predicting the outcome of the 1936 presidential election mentioned earlier was based on a sample size of 2.4 million, which did nothing to counter the biased source. The annual Phi Delta Kappa/Gallup polls of the public's attitudes toward the public schools are national surveys, yet total sample sizes typically are around 1000 to 1500.

With some types of research studies, there is the possibility that data will not be obtained from all sample members. Questionnaires mailed in survey research are susceptible to nonresponse, and studies conducted in a laboratory may lose subjects because of inability to perform. Replacement procedures may be implemented for individuals failing to participate in the study. However, if the likelihood of substantial nonresponse or nonparticipation by sample members is great, a certain percentage of *oversampling* may be included. This, of course, has direct implications for sample size. The percentage of oversampling to be used in a specific project will need to be estimated, possibly on the basis of previous experience or information from the research literature. It should be noted that oversampling does not solve the problem of possible sampling bias caused by nonresponse; it only tends to keep the amount of data at an originally desired level.

In the final analysis, it is not uncommon for research studies to make trade-offs on sample size. Sometimes statistical precision is reduced because the cost of collecting data beyond a certain point is prohibitive. For some types of studies the number of available subjects is limited, or there is limited access to subjects. There is little point in developing a research design with a large sample size if the costs are prohibitive, not only in money but also in terms of time and effort. On the other hand, there is little point in conducting a study with such limited statistical precision that decisions about hypotheses and so forth cannot be made with confidence. The researcher has to decide what trade-offs are necessary and if making those trade-offs maintains a viable research study.

This discussion is just an overview of sample size, a relatively complex concept in quantitative research. There are numerous references that discuss this issue in detail, some of which have already been mentioned.

Purposeful Sampling

Probability sampling procedures that include some form of random selection are not always appropriate or desirable. We have seen that quasi-experimental designs are used when it is not possible to apply random assignment for an experiment. Ethnographic research and historical research, those toward the qualitative end of the research continuum, typically are not amenable to random sampling, at least not for the site selection.

There are a number of reasons why random sampling may not be appropriate or feasible. Sometimes a researcher simply does not have access to an entire group. It would be almost impossible logistically to select a random sample from all graduating high school seniors in the United States. Sampling or random assignment may not be appropriate for ethical reasons. In medical research, it is unethical to randomly assign patients for treatment or nontreatment. Generalizability of the results may not be of great importance; at least it is not argued on a statistical basis. Most ethnographic research, for example, is more concerned with describing the specific situation than with generalizing the results. External validity then is argued on a logical basis. Finally, there may be only one or a limited number of sites or groups relevant to the research problem, and sampling is not feasible.

> Random sampling is not appropriate or feasible in all educational research situations, for any of a number of reasons, both practical and conceptual.

When random sampling is not used, the researcher selects a sample to meet the purpose of the research, called a **purposeful sample.** Purposeful samples are very different from random samples, not only in how they are selected but also in the logic of their use. The logic of random sampling is based on the sample being statistically representative of the population, thus allowing generalization to the population. The individuals of the population are assumed to be equivalent data sources. The logic of purposeful sampling is based on a sample of **information-rich cases** that is studied in depth. There is no assumption that all members of the population are equivalent data sources, but those selected are believed to be information-rich cases. Key informants in ethnographic research are examples of such selected individuals. Polkinghorne (1991) identifies two requirements of an adequate qualitative database that are met by purposeful sampling:

> intense descriptions of the phenomenon under investigation and enough variation in the data to develop a comprehensive structural description. (p. 11)

Generalization is then based on assertoric argumentation as discussed in the ethnographic research chapter.

> Random sampling and purposeful sampling differ in their selection procedures and in the logic of their use.

It should not be inferred that purposeful sampling is haphazard. Selection of units is based on prior identified criteria for inclusion. Researchers must be knowledgeable about the characteristics of the units, such as variability and the existence of extreme cases. Units, whether sites or individuals, are selected because the data they can provide are relevant to the research problem. There are variations on purposeful sampling as discussed in the following sections.

Comprehensive Sampling

Comprehensive sampling is used when every unit is included in the sample. This type of sampling applies when the number of units is small. For example, six or so students might be in a special counseling program in a high school, and all would be included in the research. A study of one type of severely handicapped children in a school system likely would include all such children. When historians do biographies of individuals or do an analysis of a single event or issue, they essentially are using comprehensive sampling.

Comprehensive sampling was done by Menard-Warwick (2007) when she did research on a Nicaraguan immigrant extended-family household in California. She focused on two sisters-in-law who shared a home and whose daughters attended the same elementary school. Both women were from the same hometown, attended the same junior secondary school, and attended the same ESL family literacy program. They differed substantially though, in the personal, familial, and community resources they used to support their daughters' success in school. Note that to study two sisters-in-law from the same household required Menard-Warwick to use all of the units in a narrowly defined population.

> Comprehensive sampling includes all units with specified characteristics in the sample.

Maximum Variation Sampling

Maximum variation sampling is a strategy by which units are selected for the sample because they provide the greatest differences in certain characteristics. An ethnographic researcher working in three high schools might select three that are quite different in terms of student characteristics, location, and other demographics. Maximum variation sampling is intended to generate two types of information: (1) the detailed descriptions of the cases that highlight their differences, and (2) the commonalities across the cases in spite of their variations.

Sometimes maximum variation sampling is associated with *quota sampling* because specified numbers of units are designated for the various categories of units. For example, in a study of social interaction among students in a racially mixed high school, an ethnographic researcher might designate certain numbers of African American males, African American females, white males, and white females to be interviewed as key informants.

Fisherkeller (1997) conducted a study in a New York City middle school of young adolescents learning about identities in television culture. The students were a racially and ethically diverse group. The researcher was a participant–observer at the school and conducted informal interviews. Also, the homes of eight students were visited and three students were identified for in-depth study as to their lifestyles, their television experiences, and their preferences for television personae. The selection of these students is described as follows:

> In this article, I situate three young adolescents in their home, neighborhood, school and peer cultures. . . . The three students I selected to portray in depth were chosen for their diversity of experiences. Wolverine was the only boy I was able to interview in both years of the study so he was selected by default . . . Dezeray and Samantha were the most different from each other and from Wolverine with respect to race and ethnicity. . . . Furthermore, their personalities and demeanor contrasted. (abbreviated, pp. 469–470)

The report then provides in-depth descriptions of the home situations and school life of each student. In a limited sense, because only three students were selected for in-depth study, this is an example of maximum variation sampling. The researcher wanted variation among these students, but there was no indication that these were considered extreme cases of the factors studied.

> Maximum variation sampling is a selection process that includes units so that differences on specified characteristics are maximized.

Extreme Case Sampling

Extreme case sampling involves units that have a special or unusual characteristic. Studies of effective or exemplary schools typically involve extreme case sampling. The schools are included because they have been successful based on some specified criteria. The logic of using extreme case sampling is that what is learned from the extreme cases may be applied to typical cases.

Selecting extreme cases on both ends of a continuum may provide confirming and disconfirming units, so that comparisons can be made about the consistency or lack of consistency in characteristics and patterns. For example, a study of exemplary schools might involve one or more schools considered poor or unsuccessful based on the criteria used to define an exemplary school. Comparisons could be made to determine which practices, characteristics, and so on are relevant to an exemplary school. In essence, selecting on both ends for extreme case sampling becomes a special case of maximum variation sampling.

Pressley, Mohan, Raphael, and Fingeret (2007) used extreme case sampling in their study "How Does Bennett Woods Elementary School Produce Such High Reading and Writing Achievement?" By studying a school with exemplary results, they were able to cast some light on the practices that were used to attain success. They found, among other things, that the faculty focused on reading and writing. The students experienced many books as they received instruction in how to read words, to comprehend meanings, and to write. The instruction was connected to content learning in a motivating environment.

> Extreme case sampling includes units with special or unusual characteristics.

Typical Case Sampling

In contrast to maximum variation and extreme case sampling, **typical case sampling** takes the "middle road," selecting units that are considered typical of the phenomenon under study. In a study of schools, in contrast to selecting very good or very poor schools, typical schools would be selected. Students interviewed in such a study would not be the extremely gifted or poorly performing students. Those interviewed would be typical on those characteristics under study.

Homogeneous Sampling

Homogeneous sampling is used when the purpose of the study is to focus on a particular subgroup, which in some sense is considered homogeneous. For example, in a study of teaching practices it may be decided to involve only a sample of beginning teachers. This is considered a homogeneous subgroup of the teacher population. From the sampling perspective, homogeneous sampling is considered the opposite of maximum variation sampling.

Other Variations of Purposeful Sampling

There are other variations of purposeful sampling, all of them involving a judgment as to who or what should be included in the sample. Chain, **network, or "snowball" sampling** is a process by which individuals initially selected suggest the names of others who might be appropriate for the sample. For example, in a survey of teachers who have strong pro-teacher union views, teachers initially selected suggest the names of others who have similar views on the issue.

Patton (1990) discusses **critical case sampling** and defines critical cases as:

> those that can make a point quite dramatically or are, for some reason, particularly important in the scheme of things. (p. 174)

Critical cases may not be easy to find, but when used they are identified on some logical basis. Critical cases may be viewed from two perspectives. For example, suppose a study is done on the implementation of a "new" instructional organization in an elementary school. One approach would be to select a school that has operational difficulties, poor student achievement, and low teacher morale. The idea is that, if the instructional organization works in this school, it will work in any school. Another approach would be to do the implementation in a "highly" successful school: one with high teacher morale, good student achievement, and many resources. Selecting such a school would maximize the likelihood of the instructional organization's success.

Qualitative research often involves what Polkinghorne (1991, p. 12) calls the "**intermittent selection** of subjects." That is, individuals may be selected for the sample as the research is in progress. Sometimes when getting into the research it becomes apparent that additional individuals or individuals initially not anticipated can provide useful data.

When case studies of an organization or institution are conducted, the organization is selected for a given reason, such as being a typical example of such organizations. Suppose a case study of a school district is being conducted, the case study focusing on the instruction in the academic and skills areas. Likely, it would be impractical to interview everyone involved, review all possible related documents, and observe all instruction. It would be necessary to do what Bogdan and Biklen (2003, p. 61) refer to as "internal sampling." **Internal sampling** would identify the individuals to be interviewed, the documents to be reviewed, and the classes to be observed. Students to be interviewed and classes to be observed might be selected at random. However, more likely, selections would be made on the basis of individuals (key informants) that would be rich sources of information. Individuals interviewed and materials reviewed would be selected so that the range of diversity and the range of quality are represented. These selections would be made on a logical basis.

Although commonly used types of purposeful sampling have been described above, it should not be assumed that these types are always used in their "pure sense," so to speak. There may be variations and combinations. For example, typical case sampling or extreme case sampling may involve snowball sampling to extend the number of subjects with similar characteristics.

There may be random selection in connection with purposeful sampling. For example, in an ethnographic study, which had available fifty, equally qualified subjects for interviewing, five might be selected randomly. When random sampling is used in this manner, it is done to keep the data collection within feasible limits.

An example of purposeful sampling that contained elements of quota sampling, internal sampling, and intermittent selection of subjects was done by Taut and Alkin (2003). They were attempting to identify barriers to the implementation of program evaluations through in-depth interviews with program staff.

> Because we were interested in personal insights that reach well beyond placing checkmarks or even writing a few lines on a questionnaire, we decided to conduct a qualitative study based on face-to-face interviews as the data collection method. The first author conducted eighteen semi-structured, confidential, 45-minute interviews. The interview protocol enabled the interviewer to be adaptive to each individual at the expense of fully comparable

> results. The interviewees included staff from different hierarchical levels of the program: four academic and four administrative staff in high-level university positions, one administrative staff in a lower-level university position, six program implementation personnel, and three school district employees. An original list of interviewees was slightly altered and expanded as the study proceeded. In the end we succeeded in completing all the intended interviews. (p. 216)

This sample spanned the positions of interest and, in all but one instance, had multiple respondents from each position to search for differences and commonalities in the responses. It is interesting to note the trade-off between adapting to each interviewee and having comparable information. Choosing the adaptive interviews is consistent with the qualitative nature of the study.

> Purposeful sampling has several variations and those used are done so in order to obtain information-rich units in the sample.

Sample Size of Purposeful Samples

Sample sizes in qualitative research are typically small. The number of sites at which the research is conducted is often one or a very limited number. But how many individuals or subjects are necessary? There is no general answer to this question. Very likely it is not possible at the beginning of the research to specify a number and intermittent sampling is common. Lincoln and Guba (1985) make the following comment about sample size:

> In purposeful sampling the size of the sample is determined by informational considerations. If the purpose is to maximize information, the sampling is terminated when no new information is forthcoming from new sampled units; thus redundancy is the primary criterion. (p. 202)

Although generally sample size cannot be specified as a number, it may be useful to consider sample selection in examples of qualitative research.

Summary

Sampling is an important consideration in any study in which there is concern about the sample providing adequate representation of a population. When probability sampling is used, some procedure of random selection must be applied in order to generalize from the sample to the population. When surveys are conducted, it is often necessary for logistical reasons to use some approach other than simple random sampling. This chapter described four approaches to sampling involving random selection. A summary of the general characteristics of those designs is provided in Table 14.2.

TABLE 14.2 Summary of General Characteristics of Random Sampling Designs

Design	Random Selection	Other Characteristics
Simple random sampling	Sample members individually from the population.	The entire population serves as a single unit from which the sample is selected.
Stratified random sampling	Sample members individually within each of the subpopulations or strata.	All strata are represented in the sample; strata are allocated sample members, usually by one of two allocation systems: equal or proportional allocation. Proportional allocation is most frequently used.
Cluster sampling	Clusters of members selected from the larger population of clusters.	All members of a selected cluster are included in the sample. Not all clusters are included. Clusters need not be of equal size.
Systematic sampling	The initial sample member is individually selected.	The population is ordered in some manner and the designation of the initial sample member determines the entire sample.

Purposeful sampling is associated with qualitative research and it is important to note that the logic of purposeful sampling differs from that of random sampling. Several variations on purposeful sampling were described in this chapter, variations designed to meet the needs of different research purposes.

Representativeness of the sample deals with the populations to which a researcher intends to generalize results. Random samples are representative, but what about nonrandom samples such as purposeful samples? When nonrandom samples are used, generalization cannot be argued on a probability basis. It must be argued on a logical basis. In some studies, generalizing to populations is not a big concern. In any event, when generalizing on a logical basis, how well the case can be made depends on the specifics of the study.

The discussion of this chapter essentially is an overview of some of the more common sampling designs used in educational research. Complex designs can be developed in which sampling procedures are used in combination and the sample is selected in multiple stages. The discussion here was intended to provide the researcher with a basic knowledge of design characteristics, differences among designs, and the conditions under which they might be applied.

KEY CONCEPTS

Sample
Probability sampling
Random sample
Random selection
Random assignment
Sampling frame
Sampling fraction
Sampling error
Sampling bias
Stratified random sampling
Equal allocation
Proportional allocation
Self-weighting sample
Cluster sampling
Systematic sampling
Periodicity
Statistical precision
Statistical power
Effect size
Purposeful sampling
Information-rich cases
Comprehensive sampling
Maximum variation sampling
Extreme case sampling
Typical case sampling
Homogeneous sampling
Network or "snowball" sampling
Critical case sampling
Intermittent selection
Internal sampling

EXERCISES

14.1 Suppose a researcher has a population of 839 members, and a simple random sample of size 50 is to be selected. Describe how a random number table would be used for selecting the sample. Use Table 14.1 to select the first ten members for the sample.

14.2 Describe the procedures involved in stratified random sampling using proportional allocation. Provide an example of a situation for which the sampling procedure might be used.

14.3 A study is proposed to determine the mathematics achievement of high school seniors in a statewide area. A sample of seniors is to be measured. Discuss some of the sampling difficulties that would be likely with such a large population. Discuss the possibilities of using stratified or cluster sampling. What would be possible stratifying variables if a stratified random sample were selected?

14.4 Discuss how the condition of random selection differs between stratified random sampling and cluster sampling in terms of including strata, clusters, and the members of the strata or clusters.

14.5 A population is divided into four strata. The population sizes of the four strata are 830, 660, 480, and 1030 for stratum 1 through stratum 4, respectively. A sample of size 450 is to be selected, using stratified random sampling with proportional allocation. What is the sampling fraction? Distribute the sample among the four strata using proportional allocation.

14.6 An educational psychologist has a population of 690 undergraduates available for participation in a concept-attainment experiment to be conducted in the learning lab. The experiment requires 120 individuals, including 60 men and 60 women. The population contains 381 women and 309 men. Describe how the individuals would be randomly selected for participation in the experiment. Suppose the experimental variable has four levels and equal numbers of men and women are to be assigned to each level. Describe how the individuals would be randomly assigned to levels.

14.7 The education department of a state containing approximately 500 school districts is planning a survey of the reading achievement of entering senior high school students (tenth grade). A sample of students is to be tested around mid-September. Develop a sampling plan using cluster sampling. What would be possible cluster sampling units and possible difficulties with this approach? Estimate the total sample size using your plan.

14.8 Describe the differences, both logistically and conceptually, between probability sampling, which involves some form of random selection, and purposeful sampling.

14.9 Describe the differences between comprehensive sampling and maximum variation sampling when using purposeful sampling. Provide an example for each type of sampling.

14.10 Describe the differences between typical case sampling and homogeneous sampling when using purposeful sampling. Provide an example for each type of sampling.

14.11 An educational research center of a state university has a contract to do a statewide ethnographic study of the nature of compensatory reading programs for first-graders deficient in reading performance. Basically, there are three different compensatory reading programs found throughout the 453 school districts of the state. The districts range in size from small rural districts to large city districts. The study has resources for including 50 sites for periodic observation, interviewing, and so on on a regular basis during one school year. Describe how a purposeful sample of sites would be selected for this study. After the study is under way, describe how intermittent sampling might be used.

14.12 A school or community survey is to be conducted in a district and a list of 3215 registered voters is available. This list is to be the sampling frame. A sample of size 300 is to be selected. What is the sampling fraction? A simple random sample could be selected but, with the available list, it may be more convenient to select a systematic sample. Describe how this would be done, including the selection of the first sample member, and the identification of the remaining members. In addition to convenience, what is another advantage of a systematic sample over simple random sampling in this situation?

14.13 A large population is to be surveyed, and this population contains five strata. The population sizes of the strata are 5000, 16,000, 7000, 5000, and 9000. The sampling fraction is .02 or 1 in 50. Stratified random will be used.

a. Distribute the sample using equal allocation.

b. Distribute the sample using proportional allocation.

14.14 Use Research Navigator to locate a research study that uses purposeful sampling. Are there descriptions of the site selection (if applicable) and the unit selection? Are the descriptions for selection adequate? Is the sample size given? Does the author address generalizability or external validity and, if so, does the case seem adequate?

14.15 Explain how the concept of external validity applies when a stratified random sample is obtained and when a purposeful extreme case sample is obtained.

14.16 Explain why an ethnographer would almost never use random sampling to select a target site.

NOTES

1. If sampling is from a finite population without replacement, a slight adjustment in the definition is necessary. A sample is then considered to be a simple random sample if it is drawn in such a way that all possible samples of a given size have the same probability of being selected.

2. This is an example of building a 95-percent confidence interval for a proportion. Confidence intervals are discussed in Chapter 17.

3. Inferential statistics are discussed in Chapter 17, which contains an elaboration of these concepts.

REFERENCES

Bogdan, R. C., and Biklen, S. K. (2003). *Qualitative research in education* (4th ed.). Boston: Allyn & Bacon.

Duncan, C. R., and Noonan, B. (2007). Factors affecting teachers' grading and assessment practices. *The Alberta Journal of Educational Research, 53*, 1–21.

Fisherkeller, J. (1997). Everyday learning about identities among young adolescents in television culture. *Anthropology and Education, 28*, 467–492.

Hinkle, D. E., and Oliver, J. D. (1983). How large should the sample be? A question with no simple answer? Or . . . *Educational and Psychological Measurement, 43*, 1050–1051.

House, J. D. (2003). Self-beliefs and reading achievement of elementary-school students in Hong Kong and the United States: Results from the PIRLS 2001 assessment. *Child Study Journal, 33*, 195–212.

Kish, L. (1965). *Survey sampling.* New York: John Wiley.

Krejcie, R. V., and Morgan, D. W. (1970). Determining sample size for research activities. *Educational and Psychological Measurement, 30*, 607–610.

Lincoln, Y. S., and Guba, E. G. (1985). *Naturalistic inquiry.* Beverly Hills, CA: Sage Publications.

Ma, X., and Crocker, R. (2007). Provincial effects on reading achievement. *The Alberta Journal of Educational Research, 53*, 87–109.

Menard-Warwick, J. (2007). Biliteracy and schooling in an extended-family Nicaraguan immigrant household: The sociohistorical construction of parental involvement. *Anthropology and Education Quarterly, 38*, 119–137.

Patton, M. Q. (1990). *Qualitative evaluation and research methods* (2nd ed.). Newbury Park, CA: Sage Publications.

Polkinghorne, D. E. (1991). *Generalization and qualitative research: Issues of external validity.* Paper presented at the annual meeting of the American Educational Research Association, Chicago.

Pressley, M., Mohan, L., Raphael, L. M., and Fingeret, L. (2007). How does Bennett Woods elementary school produce such high reading and writing achievement? *Journal of Educational Psychology, 99*, 221–240.

SPSS, Inc. (2006). *SPSS for Windows: Base System User's Guide: Release 15.0.* Chicago: SPSS Inc.

Sudman, S. (1976). *Applied sampling.* New York: Academic Press.

Taut, S. M., and Alkin, M. C. (2003). Program staff perceptions of barriers to evaluation implementation. *American Journal of Evaluation, 24*, 213–226.

CHAPTER

15 Measurement and Data Collection

When doing educational research, sooner or later something is measured, and this something includes the dependent variable. For example, if an experiment is conducted on different instructional approaches to teaching mathematics to sixth-graders, some measure of mathematics achievement or performance is necessary. The score on such a measure is the dependent variable of the study. The measure might be the mathematics subtest of a standardized achievement test or it might be a mathematics test constructed specifically for the experiment. Dependent variables may take on a variety of forms, so there are many different types of **measurement** used across the spectrum of educational research.

Because educational research encompasses a vast diversity of variables that are measured, a large variety of measurement devices is used in educational research—tests, inventories, observation schedules, and others. In some research projects, the measurement requirements can readily be met through the use of existing tests or instruments. For others, developing adequate measurement procedures may involve a substantial portion of the research effort. Whatever the case, the measurement instruments must adequately measure the variables, concepts, or phenomena under study, because a research study is only as well done as the measurement that generates the required data.

The areas of educational measurement, indeed the measurement of educational variables such as achievement and attitude, are of themselves disciplines of study. It is the intent of this discussion to provide an overview of measurement as it is a part of conducting research, including basic measurement concepts. There are suggestions about sources of tests and other measurement instruments, sources that can be very helpful in locating examples of the more commonly used measurement instruments in educational research.

> The questions of measurement in the context of educational research are basically twofold: What is to be measured and how is it to be measured?

Concepts of Measurement

A straightforward and widely accepted definition of measurement is given by Kerlinger (1986, p. 391):

> The assignment of numerals to objects or events according to rules.

A numeral is a symbol, such as 1, 2, or 3, that is devoid of either quantitative or qualitative meaning unless such meaning is assigned by a rule. The rules for a particular measurement are the guides by which the assignment of numerals proceeds. These may include, for example, the assignment of points for certain kinds of responses or the summing of numerals that have been assigned to the responses of two or more items.

> Measurement is a process of assigning numerals according to rules. The numerals are assigned to events or objects, such as responses to items or to certain observed behaviors.

Types of Measurement Scales

The four general levels of measurement scales—nominal, ordinal, interval, and ratio—are briefly reviewed here. The four **scales of measurement** comprise a hierarchy of measurement levels based on the amount of information contained in the score or the measure generated by the scales. The scales go from nominal to ratio in order from least to the most information contained. The four scales are defined as follows; in each case, an example of a variable that could be measured by the type of scale is given:

Nominal: This gives categorization without order; whatever is being measured is categorized into two or more classifications that indicate only differences with respect to one or more characteristics. Example: gender of the individual.

Ordinal: In addition to indicating difference, this scale also orders the scores on some basis, such as low to high or least to most. Although the scores are ordered, equal intervals between scores are not established. Example: attitude toward school.

Interval (also called equal unit): In addition to order, equal units or intervals are established in the scale such that a difference of a point in one part of the scale is equivalent to a difference of one point in any other part of the scale. Example: scale scores on an achievement test.

Ratio: In addition to an equal unit, the scale contains a true zero point that indicates a total absence of whatever is being measured. Example: monetary expenditures for various school functions.

Although the descriptions of the scales seem straightforward enough, it is not always easy to categorize a variable into the hierarchy. The difficulty, when it appears, usually comes between the ordinal and interval scales. For example, Likert-scale items were introduced in Chapter 9. The scale of an individual item is ordinal; responses may be ordered but there is no equal unit. Later in this chapter a semantic differential is introduced. Like Likert-scale items, individual scales on a semantic differential are ordinal scale measurement. But suppose there is a substantial number of Likert-scale items, say 20 or so, that all measure a single concept such as a student's attitude toward school. Each item is scored 1 to 5 on a scale of "strongly dislike" to "strongly like," so that the higher the score the more positive the attitude. If the item scores (the numerals assigned to responses) are summed across the 20 items we have a total score that can range from 20 to 100. Does this total score attain interval scale measurement? It might be argued that the total score at least approaches having an equal unit in the scale, and thus could be considered interval scale measurement. Correspondingly, semantic differentials typically have several sets of bipolar adjectives (which correspond to items in Likert scales) applied to a single concept. The responses are then summed across the sets and the total score is treated as interval scale measurement.

Intervals in measurement scales such as those just described are established on the basis of convention and usefulness. The basic concern is whether the level of measurement is meaningful and that the implied information is contained in the numerals. The meaning depends on the conditions and variables of the specific study.

Many variables measured in educational research are human characteristics, attributes, or traits that are somewhat subtle. However, whatever is being measured must be defined operationally. This means that the variable will be represented or described by the score of the test or whatever measurement device is used. For example, mathematics achievement may be defined as the mathematics subtest score on the Iowa Test of Basic Skills. A student's perception of instruction may be the score on a ten-item rating scale developed specifically for the instruction under consideration. In doing research, such variables are operationally defined in terms of what is used to measure them.

> The operational definition specifies the instrument or the operations to be used for measuring the variable.

Reliability of Measurement

Two essential characteristics of measurement that must be considered in establishing the appropriateness and usefulness of measurement instruments are reliability and validity. In a word, **reliability of measurement** means consistency—consistency of the instrument in measuring whatever it measures. In a conceptual sense, an observed score can be seen as consisting of two parts: one part the individual's "true" score and the other part an "error" score, which is due to the inaccuracy of measurement. Reliability is related to these parts. If scores have large error components, reliability is low; but if there is little error in the scores, reliability is high. Reliability is a statistical concept based on the association between two sets of scores representing the measurement obtained from the instrument when it is used with a group of individuals. **Reliability coefficients** can take on values from 0 to 1.0, inclusive. Conceptually, if a reliability coefficient were 0, there would be no "true" component in the observed score. The observed score would consist entirely of error. On the other hand, if the reliability coefficient were 1.0, the observed score would contain no error; it would consist entirely of the true score. Clearly, in educational measurement, it is desirable to obtain high reliability coefficients, although coefficients of 1.0 are very rare indeed.

Reliability is the consistency of the instrument in measuring whatever it measures. Reliability coefficients can take on values of 0 to 1.0, inclusive.

Empirical Procedures for Estimating Reliability

Several procedures can be used to estimate reliability. All of them have computational formulas that produce reliability coefficients. The commonly used procedures are described as follows:

Parallel forms or alternate forms: The **parallel forms procedure** involves the use of two or more equivalent forms of the test. The two forms are administered to a group of individuals with a short time interval between the administrations. If the test is reliable, the patterns of scores for individuals should be about the same for the two forms of the test. There would be a high positive association between the scores.

Test-retest: In this procedure, the same test is administered on two or more occasions to the same individuals. Again, if the test is reliable, there will be a high positive association between the scores.

Split-half: The **split-half procedure** requires only one administration of the test. In computing split-half reliability, the test items are divided into two halves, with the items of the two halves matched on content and difficulty, and the halves are then scored independently. If the test is reliable, the scores on the two halves have a high positive association. An individual scoring high on one half would tend to score high on the other half, and vice versa.

Kuder-Richardson procedures: For the **Kuder-Richardson procedures,** two formulas for estimating reliability, developed by Kuder and Richardson (1937), require only one administration of a test. One formula, KR-20, provides the mean of all possible split-half coefficients. The second formula, KR-21, may be substituted for KR-20, if it can be assumed that item difficulty levels are similar.

Cronbach alpha: The **Cronbach alpha procedure,** a formula developed by Cronbach (1951), based on two or more parts of the test, requires only one administration of the test.

Although all reliability coefficients are estimates of test consistency, there are different types of consistency. Procedures that involve only one test administration (split-half, KR-20, KR-21, Cronbach alpha) generate coefficients of internal consistency. The Kuder-Richardson procedures (KR-20 and KR-21) are applicable to binary data; for example, responses to items on achievement tests for which the response to an item is either correct or incorrect. The Cronbach alpha coefficient is a generalization of KR-20 to multipoint data. An example of multipoint data is an attitude scale item that has five response options. For this reason, the Cronbach alpha coefficient commonly is used to estimate internal consistency of attitude scales.

When two or more parallel forms of the test are used, the reliability coefficient is a coefficient of equivalence—the extent to which the forms are equivalent. Using the test-retest procedure gives a reliability coefficient that is a coefficient of stability—the extent to which the scores on the single test remain stable. Coefficients of equivalence and stability are based on more than one test administration.

If published tests or inventories are used, the accompanying manuals should contain information about reliability, such as the type of reliability and the size of the reliability coefficients. When locally constructed instruments are used, reliability estimates should be computed. For example, suppose a group of teachers is conducting a study on students' attitudes toward school, measured by a locally constructed attitude inventory. The reliability of interest would most likely be internal consistency reliability. If the inventory contained forty items, they could be divided into two halves of twenty items each, and the scores on the two halves could be correlated. (Correlation procedures are discussed in the next chapter.) The correlation coefficient between the scores on the two halves would then be used for estimating the reliability of the attitude inventory.

> There are a number of procedures by which reliability can be empirically estimated. Those procedures that involve only one test administration give reliability coefficients of internal test consistency. If there is more than one test administration, the reliability coefficients are estimates of test equivalence or stability.

Expected Reliability Coefficients for Various Types of Tests

Although it is desirable to obtain reliability coefficients as close to 1.0 as possible, reliability is affected by a number of factors. One factor is the length of the test. Increased length tends to increase reliability, which is one reason total test reliability tends to be greater than the reliability of subtests that may be contained in the total test.

Size of the reliability coefficient also is affected by the variable being measured. Achievement tests in academic and skills areas, for example, tend to have higher reliability than interest and attitude inventories. Table 15.1 contains examples of typical reliability coefficients found with selected tests and scales. When a range is given for the reliability coefficient (r), it indicates reliability estimates from multiple administrations of the test, or from two or more subscales.

Validity of Measurement

Another essential characteristic of measurement is *validity*—**validity of measurement** refers to the extent to which an instrument measures what it is supposed to measure. Simply stated, validity of measurement addresses the question, "Does the instrument measure

TABLE 15.1 Examples of Reliability Coefficients Reported for Selected Tests and Scales

Test	r
Basic Early Assessment of Reading—Initial Skills	.82 to .85
Bennett Mechanical Comprehension Test	.75 to .93
Canadian Achievement Tests (3rd ed.)	.64 to .92
Cognitive Abilities Test—Form 6	.90
Devereaux Early Childhood Assessment—Clinical Form	.88 to .94
Gates-MacGinitie Reading Tests (4th ed.)	.90
Home & Community Social Behavior Scales	.91 to .97
Kindergarten Diagnostic Instrument	.87 to .91
Multiple Affect Adjective Checklist—Revised	.62 to .95
Reynolds Bully-Victimization Scales for Schools	.93 to .95
School Social Behavior Scales (2nd ed.)	.94 to .98
STAR Math Version 2.0	.79 to .88
TerraNova (2nd ed.)	.90

Note: These coefficients were obtained from the *Sixteenth Mental Measurements Yearbook*, edited by R. A. Spies and B. S. Plake, 2005, Lincoln: University of Nebraska.

the characteristic, trait, or whatever, for which it was intended?" Validity refers to the appropriateness of the interpretation of the results of a test or inventory, and it is specific to the intended use. A test may be highly valid for some situations and not valid for others. For example, a science achievement test may be valid for measuring science knowledge but not valid for measuring logical reasoning skills.

There are basically two approaches to determining the validity of an instrument. One is through a logical analysis of content or a logical analysis of what would make up an educational trait, construct, or characteristic. This is essentially a judgmental analysis. The other approach, through an empirical analysis, uses criterion measurement, the criterion being some sort of standard or desired outcome. The criterion measure might be performance on a task or test, or it could be a measure such as job performance. Validity is then a measure of the association or correlation between the test being validated and the criterion measure.

Validity is a unitary concept but there are different types of evidence of validity. This is essentially a conceptual difference; the procedures for establishing validity are the same whether we consider different types of validity or different types of evidence for establishing validity. In the following discussion, the types-of-evidence view is used.

> *Validity* of measurement is the extent to which the instrument measures what it is designed to measure.

Content-Related Evidence. Content validation is the process of establishing the representativeness of the items with respect to the domain of skills, tasks, knowledge, and so forth of whatever is being measured. Thus, **content-related evidence** deals with the adequacy of content sampling. Content validation is a logical analysis of the items, determining their representativeness. Validity of achievement tests is commonly based on content-related evidence.

Criterion-Related Evidence: Concurrent and Predictive. **Criterion-related evidence** establishes validity through a comparison with some criterion external to the test. The criterion is, in essence, the standard by which the validity of the test will be judged. If the scores of the measure being validated relate highly to the criterion, the measure is valid. If not, the measure is not valid for the purpose for which the criterion measure is used.

Concurrent and predictive validation are empirical approaches to establishing validity in which the relationship between the test scores and measures of performance on an external criterion are determined. Concurrent validation is used if the data on the two measures, test and criterion, are collected at or about the same time. Predictive validation involves the collection of the data on the criterion measure after an intervening period—say, six months—from the time of data collection for the test being validated. This is the basic operational distinction between the two. There also is a distinction in the objectives of validation. Concurrent validation is based on establishing an existing situation—in other words, what is—whereas predictive validation deals with what is likely to happen. Specifically, the question of concurrent validation is whether or not the test scores estimate a specified present performance; that of predictive validation is whether or not the test scores predict a specified future performance.

The criterion measure of concurrent validation is not necessarily the score on another test given at the same time as the test being validated. It may consist of concurrent measures, such as job success or grade-point average. The criterion measures used with predictive validation often are some types of job performance—certainly subsequent performance. Predictive validation is especially relevant when test results are used for the selection of personnel to fill positions. In school, predictive validation is associated with readiness and aptitude tests, such as reading readiness tests.

Construct-Related Evidence. Construct validation can involve both logical and empirical analyses. The term *construct* refers to the theoretical construct or trait being measured, not to the technical construction of the test items. A construct is a postulated attribute or structure that explains some phenomenon, such as an individual's behavior. Because constructs are abstract and are not considered to be real objects or events, they sometimes are called hypothetical constructs. Theories of learning, for example, involve constructs such as motivation, intelligence, and anxiety.

Quite often, one or more constructs are related to behavior, in that individuals are expected to behave (or not behave) in a specified manner. A theory of frustration might include specific behavior patterns. For example, frustration increases as the individual unsuccessfully persists in a problem-solving task. The construct may be conceptualized informally with only a limited number of propositions, or it may be part or all of a fully developed theory. When using construct validation, the researcher initially suggests which constructs might account for test performance based on a logical analysis. Empirical procedures of construct validation involve relating scores on other tests that reflect the same general theory or constructs. Personality tests, for example, commonly are validated on the basis of **construct-related evidence.**

The different types of evidence all have their function in educational measurement and, correspondingly, in educational research because measurement is involved. If published tests or inventories are used, validity information should be provided in the accompanying manual. However, published tests, especially those for school-age children, often are prepared for broad populations, and the validity (and reliability) information may not be generalizable to the subjects of the research study. Researchers should determine the validity and reliability of the test for the specific situation. The types of validity evidence and their characteristics are summarized in Table 15.2.

Reliability is a necessary but not sufficient condition for validity. That is, a test or measuring instrument could be reliable but not valid. In that case, it would be consistently measuring something for which it was not intended. However, a test must be reliable to be valid. If it is not consistent in what it measures, it cannot be measuring that for which it was intended. If it doesn't measure something consistently, it's not going to be useful or valid.

The discussion of reliability and validity in this chapter is only an overview and it is necessarily brief. Although procedures were named and described, no computational examples were given. Specific procedures can be quite extensive and can be found in several measurement and testing books.[1]

TABLE 15.2 Types of Evidence and Their Characteristics Used in Establishing Validity

Type	How Analyzed	Example of Use
Content	Logical analysis of item content	Achievement tests in academic and skills areas; a test of computational skills in fifth-grade mathematics
Criterion, Concurrent	Empirical analysis—establishing the relationship between scores on the test and those on another measure obtained at the same time	Validation of a short history test against a long, standardized history exam that is known to be a valid measure of history achievement
Criterion, Predictive	Empirical analysis—establishing the relationship between scores on the test and those on another measure obtained at a later time	A comparison of performance on a screening test for word processing specialists to a measure of job performance taken six months later
Construct	Logical and empirical analyses	Analysis of a personality test to determine whether it measures the major traits of a neurotic personality

The Variables Measured in Educational Research

Because educational research covers a broad spectrum of phenomena, many different variables are measured. Research on student learning often focuses on student achievement in cognitive and skills areas, intelligence or some measures of inherent ability, and student attitudes. Sometimes observations are made of student behavior in a classroom. The variables measured may include different behaviors that occur as well as the frequency of occurrence of certain behaviors. When field notes are taken in ethnographic research, they contain descriptions of numerous variables as found in the specific context. Educational research may involve the measurement of opinions or perceptions. Some examples are studies of teachers' perceptions of administrative practices and students' opinions of teaching effectiveness.

Sometimes attempts are made to measure relatively abstract phenomena, such as how individuals learn to learn or how an individual's personality develops and changes. Many times, what is measured is very specific to the study. This is especially characteristic of surveys in which self-constructed questionnaires are used. Sometimes, physical skills or characteristics are measured. For example, a survey might be conducted on differences in personal habits related to health promotion. The list could go on. Individuals in practically any age range might be included in the measurement, although those measured are often of school age.

Tests and Inventories Used for Measurement

Tests, inventories, and scales commonly are used for obtaining the data in educational research studies, especially with research that is quantitative in nature. Often an available test or measuring instrument can be used; if this can be done, it greatly reduces the effort required to prepare for data collection. Many tests are available through commercial publishers of education tests, including achievement tests, intelligence tests, attitude inventories, self-concept inventories, and personality tests, among others. Sometimes, measuring instruments are available from other researchers who are working with similar variables.

In many situations, however, the researcher must construct an instrument because of the specific nature of the dependent variable. Sometimes, an existing instrument can be modified by changing the content of items, or a general format for the items can be used with only the content of the items being specific to the study. For example, a general form for an attitude scale may be used, but the items must be constructed for the study. In this section, some general forms are described and examples are included. Because construction of items for questionnaires was given considerable attention in Chapter 9, that discussion will not be repeated here. However, a questionnaire might include several items comprising an attitude scale, for example, and the comments on attitude scales would be relevant for a questionnaire as well as for an inventory administered in a classroom.

Achievement Tests in Academic and Skills Areas

Because achievement (or lack of it) is one of the principal outcomes of schooling, much research is done on this topic. Multitudes of **achievement tests,** commonly known as standardized achievement tests, are commercially available. These are generally norm-referenced tests; that is, performance on the tests is compared to the performance of some group, called the *normative group*. Information about the normative group is contained in the manual accompanying the test.

Achievement tests that focus on a particular set of skills without reference to a norm group are called criterion-referenced tests. A third type of achievement test that has become the driving force in education is proficiency tests. Proficiency tests specify a standard of acceptable performance. The No Child Left Behind legislation requires that states use some form of proficiency tests. When a researcher uses a published test for a research study, the task is to select a test that measures what he or she wants to measure. This requires a careful review, preferably of the potential tests themselves, but at least of sources that describe the tests. The typical college library contains a number of sources that describe available tests.

Extensive sources of information about tests are the materials of the Buros Institute of Mental Measurements at the University of Nebraska at Lincoln, specifically the *Mental Measurements Yearbooks* (*MMY*) and *Tests in Print* (*TIP*). The *Sixteenth Mental Measurements Yearbook* (Spies and Plake, 2005) contains reviews of 283 tests, tests that are new or have been significantly revised since the previous edition of *MMY*. Many of these tests have more than one review to provide balanced perspectives on the tests. In addition, *MMY* provides descriptive listings, technical information, and references for the tests. *MMY* has been published at irregular intervals since 1938, with supplements between publication dates. It is currently updated about every two years without supplements. Each *MMY* supplements, but does not replace, the preceding one. Test reviews from the *Mental Measurements Yearbook* are now available online at http://buros.unl.edu. This resource should be used carefully because there is a fee for the search.

Tests in Print VII (*TIP*), edited by Murphy, Spies, and Plake (2006), contains descriptive listings of, and references to, commercially available tests in about twenty major classifications. *TIP* serves as an index to all *TIP*s and *MMY*s up to the publication date. It contains the following indexes:

Index of Titles	allows searching by title
Classified Subject Index	allows searching by subject
Publishers Directory and Index	addresses of test publishers
Index of Names	authors of tests, reviews, and references
Index of Recently Out-of-Print Tests	lists the last volume the test was in
Index of Acronyms	spells out acronyms
Score Index	description of scores the test provides

Each entry in *TIP* contains a basic description of the test including:

purpose	population	publication date	acronyms
scores	administration	price	time limits
comments	authors	publisher	

MMY and *TIP* should be consulted when selecting a commercially available test when doing research. The information allows for careful consideration of competing tests.

When using a standardized achievement test, the researcher should check carefully to determine the appropriateness of the test. If the researcher intends to use normative data, the manual should be carefully reviewed to make certain the norms are appropriate. Often it is not necessary to have norms, because comparisons are made between or among groups in the study, not with external groups.

> Published standardized tests often can be used effectively for research in achievement. The content of the test should be reviewed, as should any norms that may be used.

Published achievement tests are usually very well constructed—at least technically—and of course their use greatly reduces the effort needed to prepare for the measurement, compared to a study for which the test must be constructed. However, in some studies, the researcher may want to measure achievement in a very limited area for which a test is not readily available. Also, it may be that the standardized test is much longer than is actually needed and, therefore, would not be desirable. A self-constructed achievement test may then be used.

When a self-constructed achievement test is used, the items of the test should very closely reflect the objectives of the research. Usually, in achievement testing, finding an adequate fit between research objectives and test content is not very difficult because validity can be established through a logical analysis (content analysis). However, if at all possible, a pilot run of the test should be made, and reliability should be checked prior to the use of the test for the project. Then reliability can be checked using the research data. If reliability has not been previously checked and then turns out to be undesirably low, the entire project is in jeopardy.

Attitude Inventories

Achievement tests generally are designed to measure an individual's best or maximum performance, whereas an attitude inventory is intended to measure typical performance. Attitudes involve an individual's feelings toward such things as ideas, procedures, and social institutions. Note that the attitude is toward something. Most people think of attitudes in such terms as acceptance–rejection or favorable–unfavorable; however, the intensity of a person's feelings usually is not dichotomous but is on a continuum between the extremes. Measurement of the attitude is intended to place individuals on this continuum.

Attitude inventories are available from commercial publishers. The sources for information about tests discussed in the preceding section also contain information about available attitude inventories. However, it is usually more difficult to find an available attitude inventory than an achievement test for a research project. This is because attitude inventories used for research tend to be quite specific, and more general inventories may not be adequate. Often, it is necessary to construct an attitude scale. Several item formats may be used.

Likert Scale.[2] The **Likert scale** is a scale with a number of points or spaces, usually at least three but not more than seven. Five-point scales are common. The points represent a set of related responses, one for each point. The individual responds by checking a point, circling a letter (or number), or writing the number in a blank preceding the item. The points or checks are assigned numerical values, for example, with a 5-point scale, values 1 to 5, or 0 to 4. These values are then totaled over the items to give the individual an attitude score.

The Likert scale was introduced in Chapter 9, and that chapter contained some example responses. There are any number of possible sets of Likert-scale responses. The important characteristics of a set are that the number of responses is adequate for the measurement, and that the responses are appropriate for the items. Following are some sample sets of Likert-scale responses:

Very satisfactory	Very good
Satisfactory	Good
Undecided	No opinion
Unsatisfactory	Poor
Very unsatisfactory	Very poor
Highly appropriate	Highly favorable
Appropriate	Favorable
Neutral	No opinion
Inappropriate	Unfavorable
Highly inappropriate	Highly unfavorable
Very supportive	Definitely yes
Supportive	Probably yes
Neutral	Uncertain
Unsupportive	Probably no
Very unsupportive	Definitely no

The Rosenberg Self-Esteem Scale is an example of a Likert scale and is presented in Figure 15.1. There are ten items on the scale and the wording is reversed in five of the items. The scoring is explained in the figure. Each of the items may appear to be more ordinal than interval, but the summed scores for the ten items can be reasonably thought of as interval scaled data.

> A *Likert scale* contains a number of points on a scale, quite often five, but typically an odd number. The points have designations such as "strongly agree" to "strongly disagree."

Constructing an attitude inventory using Likert-scale items requires identifying the major topics or points to be addressed by the scale and then generating statements. These undoubtedly will need some revision to ensure clarity and relevance. Usually, items of both

- To score the items, assign a value to each of the 10 items as follows:
  - For items 1, 2, 4, 6, 7: Strongly Agree = 3, Agree = 2, Disagree = 1, and Strongly Disagree = 0.
  - For items 3, 5, 8, 9, 10 (which are reversed in valence, and noted with the asterisks** below): Strongly Agree = 0, Agree = 1, Disagree = 2, and Strongly Disagree = 3.
- The scale ranges from 0–30, with 30 indicating the highest score possible. Other scoring options are possible. For example, you can assign values 1–4 rather than 0–3; then scores will range from 10–40. Some researchers use 5- or 7-point Likert scales, and again, scale ranges would vary based on the addition of "middle" categories of agreement.

Present the items with these instructions. ***Do not print*** the asterisks on the sheet you provide to respondents.

BELOW IS A LIST OF STATEMENTS DEALING WITH YOUR GENERAL FEELINGS ABOUT YOURSELF. IF YOU **STRONGLY AGREE**, CIRCLE **SA**. IF YOU **AGREE** WITH THE STATEMENT, CIRCLE **A**. IF YOU **DISAGREE**, CIRCLE **D**. IF YOU **STRONGLY DISAGREE**, CIRCLE **SD**.

		1. Strongly Agree	**2. Agree**	**3. Disagree**	**4. Strongly Disagree**
1.	I feel that I'm a person of worth, at least on an equal plane with others.	SA	A	D	SD
2.	I feel that I have a number of good qualities.	SA	A	D	SD
3.	All in all, I am inclined to feel that I am a failure.**	SA	A	D	SD
4.	I am able to do things as well as most other people.	SA	A	D	SD
5.	I feel I do not have much to be proud of.**	SA	A	D	SD
6.	I take a positive attitude toward myself.	SA	A	D	SD
7.	On the whole, I am satisfied with myself.	SA	A	D	SD
8.	I wish I could have more respect for myself.**	SA	A	D	SD
9.	I certainly feel useless at times.**	SA	A	D	SD
10.	At times I think I am no good at all.**	SA	A	D	SD

FIGURE 15.1 The Rosenberg Self-Esteem Scale

Source: Rosenberg, Morris. 1989. *Society and the Adolescent Self-Image*. Revised Edition. Middletown, CT: Wesleyan University.

directions are used to provide more variety and breadth in the items. It also may make the items more interesting for the respondents. A pool of items is generated, and these items should be administered in a pilot run. On the basis of the pilot run, those items to be used in the inventory can be identified and put into final form.

The data from the pilot run should be reviewed carefully. Items with little variance in the responses will not differentiate between individuals or groups. Similarly, items that are frequently omitted may be unclear or offensive to the respondents. It is often helpful to have the people in the pilot run explain their understanding of the items and their reasons for answering as they did. This technique will inform the researcher whether the items are truly yielding the information that is sought.

Unlike achievement tests, it is possible for an individual to fake responses when taking an attitude inventory. The direction of the more positive attitude usually can be identified from the item, and the individual could deliberately respond in that direction regardless of true feelings. However, if the researcher is primarily interested in groups of scores, such as those for a class, and the respondent is aware of this, there is no reason to fake. Sometimes, very similar items are put in different parts of the inventory so that the consistency between responses can be checked.

Some individuals may develop a response set or tendency to respond in a certain manner as a reaction to the construction of the scale, independently of the item content. For example, the middle-of-the-roader will respond near the center of the scale regardless of true feelings. Sometimes, reversing the direction of items is used as a deterrent to response set.

It should be noted that Likert scales can be used for measurements other than attitude inventories. For example, a Likert scale could be used to measure teachers' perceptions of a program.

Semantic Differential. The **semantic differential** (Osgood, Suci, and Tannenbaum, 1957) is a measuring instrument that focuses on a single word or concept at a time to measure the connotative meaning of that concept. Then a series of bipolar adjective scales are given, and the respondents are asked to indicate their feelings (perceptions) on each scale with respect to the word or concept. Figure 15.2 contains an example of a semantic differential, taken from a study by Nussel, Wiersma, and Rusche (1988). This semantic differential was developed to measure professors' perceptions of college teaching as a profession. The pairs of bipolar adjectives were based on descriptors found in the job satisfaction literature. The semantic differential was tried out in a pilot run prior to its use in the research study.

> The *semantic differential* provides a series of bipolar adjective scales relative to a word or concept; the respondents indicate their feelings on the continuum of each scale.

Scoring of the semantic differential can be done in different ways. The important thing about scoring is that it is consistent and meaningful. The usual scoring procedures are such that the greater the score, the more positive the attitude or perception.

One approach to scoring is to list all pairs of adjectives in a consistent direction, usually low to high or negative to positive. The position of the adjectives (whether the right or

SEMANTIC DIFFERENTIAL: COLLEGE TEACHING AS A PROFESSION

We are interested in how you feel about college teaching as a profession. Please respond to the items below, indicating your perception of your professional position. Mark *one X* and *one X only* for each pair of words. Place the *X* in the center of a space, not on the boundaries. For example:

If you feel your position is very stimulating, place the *X*

stimulating ___*X*___ : ______ : ______ : ______ : ______ : ______ : ______ dull

If you feel your position is very dull, place the *X*

stimulating ______ : ______ : ______ : ______ : ______ : ______ : ___*X*___ dull

Or if you feel your position is neither very stimulating or very dull, place the *X* closer to the middle of the line, but on the side that you favor.

MY PROFESSIONAL POSITION

stimulating	___	: ___	: ___	: ___	: ___	: ___	: ___	dull
rewarding	___	: ___	: ___	: ___	: ___	: ___	: ___	unrewarding
exciting	___	: ___	: ___	: ___	: ___	: ___	: ___	monotonous
bad	___	: ___	: ___	: ___	: ___	: ___	: ___	good
secure	___	: ___	: ___	: ___	: ___	: ___	: ___	insecure
fair	___	: ___	: ___	: ___	: ___	: ___	: ___	biased
tiresome	___	: ___	: ___	: ___	: ___	: ___	: ___	interesting
menial	___	: ___	: ___	: ___	: ___	: ___	: ___	challenging
same	___	: ___	: ___	: ___	: ___	: ___	: ___	varied
stable	___	: ___	: ___	: ___	: ___	: ___	: ___	fluctuating
trivial	___	: ___	: ___	: ___	: ___	: ___	: ___	important
orderly	___	: ___	: ___	: ___	: ___	: ___	: ___	confused
active	___	: ___	: ___	: ___	: ___	: ___	: ___	passive
unpleasant	___	: ___	: ___	: ___	: ___	: ___	: ___	pleasant
simple	___	: ___	: ___	: ___	: ___	: ___	: ___	rigorous
valuable	___	: ___	: ___	: ___	: ___	: ___	: ___	worthless
nice	___	: ___	: ___	: ___	: ___	: ___	: ___	awful
tense	___	: ___	: ___	: ___	: ___	: ___	: ___	relaxed
flexible	___	: ___	: ___	: ___	: ___	: ___	: ___	rigid
routine	___	: ___	: ___	: ___	: ___	: ___	: ___	demanding
successful	___	: ___	: ___	: ___	: ___	: ___	: ___	unsuccessful
relevant	___	: ___	: ___	: ___	: ___	: ___	: ___	irrelevant
stereotyped	___	: ___	: ___	: ___	: ___	: ___	: ___	original
disorganized	___	: ___	: ___	: ___	: ___	: ___	: ___	systematic
vague	___	: ___	: ___	: ___	: ___	: ___	: ___	defined
autonomous	___	: ___	: ___	: ___	: ___	: ___	: ___	controlled
common	___	: ___	: ___	: ___	: ___	: ___	: ___	distinctive
boring	___	: ___	: ___	: ___	: ___	: ___	: ___	fun
satisfying	___	: ___	: ___	: ___	: ___	: ___	: ___	unsatisfying
isolated	___	: ___	: ___	: ___	: ___	: ___	: ___	interactive
noncompetitive	___	: ___	: ___	: ___	: ___	: ___	: ___	competitive
career	___	: ___	: ___	: ___	: ___	: ___	: ___	job

FIGURE 15.2 An Example of a Semantic Differential

Note: Reproduced with permission of the authors.

left side is negative) is an arbitrary choice, but if the negative adjectives are on the left, and the positive ones are on the right, then the values 0-1-2-3-4-5-6 (or any sequence of seven consecutive numbers) are assigned to the slots from left to right. Values of −3, −2, −1, 0, +1, +2, +3 could also be used, although this gives a possibility of a total score that is negative. Either way, the score is the sum of the values across the pairs of adjectives.

In the example of Figure 15.2, the adjective pairs are listed in both directions, and the order of direction was assigned randomly. For example, items 4 and 5 have reversed directions. Scoring was done by reversing the direction of assigning the numerical values, always keeping the 6 on the positive end and the 0 on the negative end. Because this semantic differential had 32 items, the maximum total score was 192; the greater the score the more positive the perception of college teaching as a profession.

Another scoring procedure can be used in which the values 6-5-4-3-2-1-0 are assigned left to right regardless of item direction. Then the score for the item is weighted either positive or negative, depending on its direction. A disadvantage of this procedure is the possibility of a negative total score. Sometimes semantic differentials are constructed to contain two or more subscales, called *dimensions* or *constructs*. For example, a semantic differential could be constructed to measure teachers' professional attitudes that might contain a subscale on feelings toward children and a subscale on feelings toward the school administration. A subset of the items in the semantic differential would make up the items for a subscale. Subscale scores would be generated in a manner similar to generating a total score. Of course, a subscale would involve fewer items than the total scale.

Aptitude Tests

Aptitude is considered to be the potential for achievement. Although actual achievement and the potential ability for achievement are not the same thing, operationally they may be difficult to separate. Intelligence tests are the most commonly known measures for aptitude in academic and skills areas, but other terms such as *general scholastic ability* and *general mental ability* are being used increasingly to replace the term *intelligence*. The difficulty with the term *intelligence* comes with the long-standing belief that intelligence tests somehow measure an inborn capacity, regardless of the individual's background, experience, and the like. Cronbach (1984) comments on the problem with this perception of intelligence.

> In British and American discourse, "intelligence" seemed usually to refer to potentiality as if the test score foretold what level the person would reach if given every educational advantage. The evidence is necessarily one-sided. Good ultimate performance proves capacity, but poor performance does not prove incapacity. The typical school-age test is best identified as a "test of general scholastic ability." It measures a set of abilities now developed and demonstrated (not a "potential"). It emphasizes abilities helpful in most schoolwork. (p. 198)

The importance of Cronbach's remarks to the educator is that one must be cautious when using an aptitude test and not assume that the test is measuring inherent ability independent of other factors, such as existing achievement (or the lack thereof). When diverse groups, possibly those from subcultures within the larger culture, are being measured by aptitude tests, it should not be assumed that the tests are equally valid for all groups.

Aptitude tests come in a variety of forms, commonly designated as individual or group tests. Individual tests tend to be more elaborate and may involve manipulation of objects, whereas group tests are usually limited to items on paper. The Wechsler Adult Intelligence Scale (WAIS) is an example of an individual test, and the California Test of Mental Maturity is an example of a group test.

The tests mentioned here are largely designed to measure global intelligence or ability. There also are aptitude tests that focus more on specific abilities. For example, the Scholastic Aptitude Test (SAT) is highly oriented to the types of abilities learned in formal schooling, with an emphasis on verbal and mathematical abilities. Numerous batteries of aptitude tests measure multiple aptitudes through a series of subtests or subscores, an example being the Differential Aptitude Test. Such tests contain subtests of abilities, such as mechanical reasoning, numerical ability, and spatial relations, to mention just a few.

Scores on aptitude tests sometimes are used in educational research as control variables. For example, scores on an aptitude test may be used to classify individuals according to levels of ability if ability is used as an independent variable in the research design. Aptitude test scores also may be used as statistical controls.

The development of an aptitude test is a difficult task that requires a good deal of information, effort, and measurement expertise. For this reason, aptitude tests are seldom self-constructed for a research project. There are numerous aptitude tests available for both general and specific aptitudes. Information about specific aptitude tests can be found in sources such as the *Mental Measurements Yearbook* mentioned earlier in this chapter.

Aptitude is the potential for achievement. It may be difficult in the measurement to separate potential from actual achievement. In essence, an aptitude test gives indirect evidence of the existence of the potential.

Rating Scales

Rating scales are used frequently in educational research, and indeed they have already been introduced in connection with Likert scales. A rating scale presents a statement or item with a corresponding scale of categories, and respondents are asked to make judgments that most clearly approximate their perceptions. Rating scales may have three, four, five, or conceivably any finite number of points, and they may be presented in different formats. We have seen the Likert scale given with five points or options.

Figure 15.3 shows an example of rating scale items that use a common set of responses. Note that this particular set of questions obtains two pieces of information: (1) whether the information was gathered and (2) a rating of the usefulness of the information.

Any number of variables can be measured using rating scales, including perceptions of instruction, adequacy of facilities, perceptions of program effects, and so forth. The

7. Below is a list of sources of potential evaluation information. Please rate the usefulness of the evaluation information that your project gathered.

Potential Evaluation Information	Data We Gathered	Degree of Usefulness			
	Check (✓) those that apply	Not Useful	Somewhat Useful	Useful	Very Useful
Course level student satisfaction data					
End of program student satisfaction data					
Student course grades					
Date regarding student dropout rates					
Data on student or industry referrals to the program					
Postprogram follow-up data from students (e.g., employment status, preparedness for industry)					
Postprogram follow-up data from supervisors of students (e.g., re. skills, knowledge, preparedness for industry)					
Testing of students' knowledge and skills against established business/industry work standards					
Comparison of students' knowledge and skills against other critical competitors (e.g., personnel from other colleges or military programs or other course options)					
Faculty feedback on course and program implementation					
Course records/logs (e.g., syllabi, content taught, sample assignments, etc.)					
Feedback from instructional experts regarding content and instruction of courses and program (e.g., comparisons of program content and instruction against critical competitors)					
Feedback from companies that employ your students and graduates					
Expert panel review of program and/or products					
Other (describe):					

FIGURE 15.3 Sample Items from a Rating Scale

Source: These materials were created as part of Project ATE 07–08, funded by the National Science Foundation, Award #0702981. Reproduced by permission of Arlen R. Gullickson, project director.

descriptors used for the categories of the scale are selected to fit the particular variable being rated. Rating scales also can be used by observers who are observing an activity such as teaching.

Rating scales can vary in length, but usually they contain several statements, called *items*, that use the same descriptors and relate to a single concept, activity, phenomenon, experience, or physical object. If it is desirable to obtain a total score over all items or groups of items, this can be done in the usual manner by summing the item scores. The scoring usually is done so that the greater the score the higher the respondent's rating.

> *Rating scales* contain items related to a concept, phenomenon, activity, or physical object; the respondent is asked to select a descriptor on a scale that most closely approximates his or her assessment of whatever is described in the item.

Observation Systems

Tests and inventories used for measuring achievement, attitudes, scholastic ability, and so forth, are for the most part paper-and-pencil instruments, many of them administered simultaneously to an entire group. There also are educational research situations in which the data are collected through an **observation system**—a procedure by which an observer records what is occurring in some situation or setting, such as a classroom.

Observation systems can take a variety of forms; however, those for observing student and teacher behavior or classroom interaction roughly fall into two categories. One category consists of rating scale items for which observed behaviors are judged qualitatively. Usually, the observer must use considerable judgment to infer the proper rating; hence these types of systems sometimes are called "high inference." Then the ratings are combined in some manner in an attempt to quantify behavior. An example of a rating scale type of observation system is the Teacher Observation Form that is used in the Houston schools to identify students who might participate in the gifted/talented program (www.houstonisd.org/GiftedTalented/Home/Forms). Figure 15.4 contains the first part of that observation system. The observations include three subscales: General Intellectual Ability, Creative Ability, and Leadership Ability. There is also a section on Additional Traits Which Could Affect Giftedness that consists of separate items, not scales. Each rating requires some degree of judgment concerning the amount of time that the student displays the rated behavior.

The second type of observation system consists of "low-inference" observations in which the observer notes the presence or absence of a particular behavior without having to judge how much or how well something is done. Figure 15.5 (on p. 353) contains items from an observation system used to assess the development of infants and toddlers. Parents or other caregivers can use these criteria to judge whether a child is delayed in its development. The observation system comes from the New York Department of Health, which provides

TEACHER OBSERVATION FORM

Student Name: ______________________ **Current Grade Level:** ______________

Form should be completed by the current teacher, or teacher from the previous school year only. Submit only one teacher observation form with your application.

Evidence of Possible Giftedness
Please circle the number that best indicates the degree to which the student exhibits the following characteristics.

	RARELY	LESS THAN HALF THE TIME	ABOUT HALF THE TIME	MORE THAN HALF THE TIME	CONSISTENTLY MOST OF THE TIME
A. General Intellectual Ability					
1. Shows a preference for complex tasks and "why" of things	1	2	3	4	5
2. Has knowledge and vocabulary unusual for age or grade; has fluent verbal ability	1	2	3	4	5
3. Demonstrates abstract and critical thinking ability, an ability to think things out, to think things through logically or analytically	1	2	3	4	5
4. Is a keen and alert observer; often "sees more" in a learning situation than others; may show evidence of long, detailed memory	1	2	3	4	5
5. Shows an interest in problem solving and is flexible and resourceful in problem solving	1	2	3	4	5
6. Has a quick grasp of concepts and underlying principles and can see relationships between ideas, events, people, and things; may ask provocative questions	1	2	3	4	5

FIGURE 15.4 Items from the Teacher Observation Form for Rating Characteristics of Giftedness

(continued)

	RARELY	LESS THAN HALF THE TIME	ABOUT HALF THE TIME	MORE THAN HALF THE TIME	CONSISTENTLY MOST OF THE TIME
B. Creative Ability					
1. Is curious and asks many questions	1	2	3	4	5
2. Produces work which is fresh, vital, and unique; creates new ideas, products, and processes; does the unexpected	1	2	3	4	5
3. Exhibits playfulness and a keen sense of humor, may make jokes, puns, etc., at times	1	2	3	4	5
4. Shows unusual capacity for concentration, imagination, and originality on tasks that interest him or her	1	2	3	4	5
5. Bores quickly with routine tasks, memorization of facts and details; prefers talking about ideas and problems	1	2	3	4	5

FIGURE 15.4 (***Continued***)
Source: (© Copyright, 2008). Reproduced by permission of the Advanced Academics Department, Houston Independent School District, Houston, TX.

early intervention assistance when developmental delays are identified. Low-inference observations tend to be somewhat more reliable than high-inference observations because there is much less subjective judgment.

Some observation systems, usually low-inference systems, consist of a matrix of cells representing observed behaviors or combinations of behaviors. Often a check mark is used to record the presence of behaviors and possibly the frequency or duration of behaviors within or at specified time intervals is indicated. The Preschool Observation Code (Bramlett and Barnett, 1993) is an example of this kind of matrix. This observation is used to assess children's behaviors and their interactions with others within contexts such as classrooms. Recordings of behaviors and events are made at thiry-second intervals over a ten-minute period. Initially, the behavior is checked in the "states" matrix and then the remainder of the interval is used to record the event behaviors in the "events" matrix.

Collecting data using observation systems is a demanding task. Regardless of the type of system, observation requires training of observers, who must be consistent in

At three months of age, most babies:	At six months of age, most babies:	At 12 months of age, most babies:
• turn their heads toward bright colors and lights • move both eyes in the same direction together • recognize bottle or breast • respond to their mother's voice • make cooing sounds • bring their hands together • wiggle and kick with arms and legs • lift head when on stomach • become quiet in response to sound, especially to speech • smile	• follow moving objects with their eyes • turn toward the source of normal sound • reach for objects and pick them up • switch toys from one hand to the other • play with their toes • help hold their bottle during feeding • recognized familiar faces • imitate speech sounds • respond to soft sounds, especially talking • roll over	• get to a sitting position • pull to a standing position • stand briefly without support • crawl • imitate adults using a cup or telephone • play peek-a-boo and patty cake • wave bye-bye • put objects in a container • say at least one word • make "ma-ma" or "da-da" sounds

At 1 1/2 years of age, most children:	At two years of age, most children:	At three years of age, most children:
• like to push and pull objects • say at least six words • follow simple directions ("Bring the ball") • pull off shoes, socks, and mittens • can point to a picture that you name in a book • feed themselves • make marks on paper with crayons • walk without help • walk backwards • point, make sounds, or try to use words to ask for things • say "no," shake their head, or push away things they don't want	• use two-to-three-word sentences • say about 50 words • recognize familiar pictures • kick a ball forward • feed themselves with a spoon • demand a lot of your attention • turn two-to-three pages together • like to imitate their parent • identify hair, eyes, ears, and nose by pointing • build a tower of four blocks • show affection	• throw a ball overhead • ride a tricycle • put on their shoes • open the door • turn one page at a time • play with other children for a few minutes • repeat common rhymes • use three-to-five-word sentences • name at least one color correctly

FIGURE 15.5 Checklist for Growing Children

Source: Reprinted from *Early Help Makes a Difference*, 2006, with permission of the New York State Department of Health.

recording what they observe, both across observers and for a specific observer across observations. Most available observation systems have detailed procedures for training observers and manuals for the use of the system.

> An *observation system* is used for recording preselected behaviors in an attempt to quantify behavior in the situation being observed.

Where to Find Test Information

There are any number of sources for information about tests and inventories that are used in various areas of education. Two of these, *Tests in Print VII* and the *Mental Measurement Yearbooks*, have already been described and these are available from the Buros Institute at the University of Nebraska. There are other testing publications available from the Buros Institute. One of these is *Buros Desk Reference: Psychological Assessment in the Schools* (Impara and Murphy, 1994). This desk reference highlights 112 tests used by school psychologists and others when assessing children from early childhood through late teens. Also, the Buros Institute provides a computerized database service, Bibliographic Retrieval Service (BRS), which is useful for obtaining information about new and revised tests. Libraries that offer the BRS service can conduct computer searches of the database. Libraries that offer the BRS service often provide searches of the Buros Institute's materials through Silver Platter.

As might be expected, Educational Testing Service (ETS) of Princeton, New Jersey, has a lot of information about tests in its ETS Test Collection. This collection, which is continually growing, presently contains information about some 15,000 tests. Annotated test bibliographies that provide information about tests in many testing areas can be obtained from the collection. ETS publishes a monthly newsletter, *News on Tests*, which provides a lot of information, such as announcements of new tests added to the collection. ETS will provide, on request, a listing of major U.S. test publishers and their addresses and telephone numbers. ETS also provides a service, Test Link, which makes available tests not published commercially. The ETS test database is available at www.ets.org.

A less likely **test information source,** but one that may have some potential, is tests used in dissertations. *Dissertation Abstracts International* (*DAI*) can be searched online for test information, but the abstracts have been included online only since 1980. For tests used in dissertations prior to 1980, Fabiano (1989) has compiled a volume titled *Index to Tests Used in Educational Dissertations,* which lists over 40,000 tests used in dissertations from 1938 to 1980. The tests cover achievement, aptitude, personality, physical fitness, vocational ability, and almost any other area of educational testing.

Many test publishers provide promotional brochures and catalogs about their tests. An example is the Publishers Test Service of CTB/McGraw-Hill. Virtually all published tests are accompanied by a manual, which is a valuable source of detailed information about the test under consideration. Many school systems and universities have counseling centers or testing centers in which such manuals are available and, sometimes, examples of tests.

Information about tests is contained throughout the periodical literature. Tests occasionally are reviewed in professional journals. Journals such as the *Journal of Educational Measurement* often contain reports about the use of exploratory approaches to measurement. Thus, there is a good deal of test information available, much of which can be located through the use of indices (see Chapter 3).

Scoring and Data Preparation

Measuring instruments, such as tests and inventories, require scoring before the analysis can be done. Scoring must be accurate and consistent and defined procedures should be followed for the scoring. When standardized instruments are used, especially those from test publishers, scoring procedures usually are well-defined in the manual. In fact, for most standardized tests, scoring service is available, and if the answer sheets or tests are completed properly, such scoring is very accurate. If hand-scoring is used, accuracy checks and routine precautions for errors are necessary.

Research projects that involve considerable data from standardized tests or inventories can greatly reduce scoring time through the use of machine-scored answer sheets. Many universities have a scoring service available on campus. It is important to make arrangements prior to data collection so that appropriate answer sheets can be used, and the form of the data is compatible with the scoring procedure. Companies such as IBM sell standardized, machine-scored answer sheets and these may be useful.

If self-developed instruments are used and they cannot be machine-scored, the researcher must define and operationalize the scoring procedure. Scoring responses to open-ended items can be complex, and it may be necessary to follow some of the procedures for holistic scoring described earlier. Typically, objective-type items, such as multiple-choice items, are easier to score than open-ended items, but the scoring does require specific rules for arriving at the score and accuracy checks.

Coding Data

Any research project that involves even a small amount of quantitative data or requires anything but very simple statistical analysis will have the data analyzed by computer. Scores on standardized tests and inventories of various types usually are considered quantitative data. In addition to scores on measuring instruments, there are data that describe the subjects of the research, identifying data, and sometimes what is called demographic information. A format for all the data must be specified in order to transfer the data into the computer.

Commonly used programs such as Excel or SPSS can accommodate many variables and many cases. The standard spreadsheet format for the data puts cases in the rows and variables in the columns. The process of developing the format for identifying the variables in the columns is called **coding data.** Different types of data are coded such as identification numbers; characteristics of the subjects such as age, grade, and gender; group identifiers such as experimental/control; and dependent variables such as test scores, survey responses, and observation data. The order of the variables is arbitrary, so it is important to develop a codebook that lists the variables and contains a key for the different variable codes such as 1 = male and 2 = female or 1 = experimental group and 2 = control group. The codes of 1 or 2 for gender and group are completely arbitrary because these are nominal data. They could just as easily have been reversed.

> *Coding data* consists of developing the format by which the data are specified and organized in preparation for the analysis.

Column	Data			
1.	Gender	M = Male	F = Female	
2.	Lunch	F = Free	R = Reduced	N = Neither
3.	IEP	Y = Yes	N = No	
4.	Speech Disability	Y = Yes	N = No	
5.	Gifted	F = False	T = True	
6.	ELA Scale Score 05–06			
7.	ELA Performance Level 05–06	BBAS = Below Basic	BAS = Basic	
		Prof = Proficient	ADV = Advanced	
8.	ELA Scale Score 04–05			

FIGURE 15.6 An Example of a Codebook

An example of coding information is given in Figure 15.6 for the Palmetto Achievement Challenge Test (PACT) data set that accompanies this book. Some of the variables have letter codes such as *M* for *Male* and *F* for *Female*. Most computer programs will allow you to recode these letters into numerical values if computations are needed. Using letters allows you to quickly scan and understand the information instead of trying to remember whether males were coded 1 or 2. The scale scores are numerical so they do not need further explanation.

An Example of a Data File

The data should be organized so that a minimum of effort is required to transform the data from their original form to the computer software that will be used for the analysis. Often the data can be imported directly from a database or from another program. Moving data from Excel to SPSS, for example, is as simple as a "copy" and "paste" command. It is essential to confirm that the data have been transformed accurately before proceeding with the analysis though, because there are times, especially with large data sets, when data get lost in the transformation. An important part of the data processing is ensuring the accuracy of the data at each step in the process.

When data are taken from survey or observation forms and entered into the analysis software, it is important to process the data systematically and to make sure that they are accurate. A random sample of entries should be checked for accuracy. The more steps that are involved in the data processing, the more chances there are for errors to slip in. The statistical software has no defense against bad data; it will analyze whatever data it is given. When all the data are entered, we have a **data file.**

Figure 15.7 contains the beginning portion of the PACT data set. This information was taken from the Excel spreadsheet that accompanies this book. Note that each row

Gender	Lunch	IEP	Speech Disab.	Gifted	ELA Scale Score 05–06	ELA Perf. Level 05–06	ELA Scale Score 04–05
F	F	N	N	F	799	BAS	701
F	F	N	N	F	785	BBAS	684
F	R	N	N	F	804	BAS	710
M	F	N	N	F	805	BAS	708
F	F	N	N	F	800	BAS	685
F	F	N	N	F	805	BAS	706
M	F	Y	N	F	175	BBAS	94
F	F	N	N	T	819	PROF	714
M	N	N	N	F	809	BAS	713
F	F	Y	N	F	781	BBAS	673
M	F	N	N	F	785	BBAS	784
M	F	N	N	F	798	BAS	710
F	F	N	N	T	808	BAS	709
M	F	N	N	F	782	BBAS	684

FIGURE 15.7 Sample Data File for the PACT Data Set

contains the data for an individual student and the columns specify the variables. Note the correspondence of the coding sheet in Figure 15.6 and the data file in Figure 15.7.

Summary

This chapter provided an overview of some of the more common types of measurement used in educational research. For many research studies, adequate measurement devices—in the form of tests, inventories, scales, or observation schedules—are available, and suggestions were provided about information sources. Because the measurement instruments used provide the operational definition of the data, their selection merits attention.

Because some research projects have measurement needs that cannot be met readily by existing instruments, it is sometimes necessary to construct the instruments, and this increases the total research effort. Commonly constructed instruments such as rating scales were discussed. Before embarking on the development of an instrument, however, the researcher should check for available instruments and estimate the magnitude of the development task. In some areas, such as the measurement of personality, instrument development requires sophisticated knowledge and skills.

The concepts of reliability and validity of measuring instruments were discussed. Whenever an instrument is used, its validity in the context of its use—the extent to which the instrument is measuring what it is intended to measure—must be considered. Reliability is consistency of measurement. There are a number of procedures for establishing reliability, as discussed in this chapter.

Because education includes so many variables, measurement is very broad and varied. Entire books are written on even limited areas within measurement, so this chapter did not go into detail about the theoretical concepts of measurement or some of the infrequently used procedures. The amount of effort that must be put into obtaining the measurement instrument and collecting the data depends on the conditions of the specific research study.

It is important to plan the data collection carefully and to identify the specific measurement requirements of the research study. Collecting a mass of data and then trying to fit a research problem to it is not acceptable practice. After data are collected, they must be assembled for analysis. Coding and construction of a data file were illustrated in this chapter; these procedures are done so that analysis can proceed in an appropriate and efficient manner. Although good measurement does not ensure good research, it is a necessary but not sufficient condition for good research.

KEY CONCEPTS

Measurement
Scales of measurement
Reliability of measurement
Reliability coefficient
Parallel forms procedure
Split-half procedure
Kuder-Richardson procedures
Cronbach alpha procedure
Validity of measurement
Content-related evidence
Criterion-related evidence
Construct-related evidence
Achievement tests
Likert scale
Semantic differential
Aptitude tests
Rating scales
Observation systems
Test information sources
Coding data
Data file

EXERCISES

15.1 Discuss the distinction between the concepts of validity and reliability. Why do we say that measurement can be reliable without being valid, but that the reverse cannot be true?

15.2 A researcher plans to do a study about the extent of hostility in upper elementary classrooms taught by teachers classified as autocratic or democratic. Discuss the problem of establishing validity in measuring hostility. Assume that hostility can go both ways: from students to teachers and vice versa. What are possible approaches to measuring hostility? For example, would observation be used? If so, what would be included in the observation schedule? What is a possible operational definition of hostility? Is it possible to quantify hostility in any way?

15.3 Suppose a guidance counselor wants to do a study on the attitudes of junior high students toward a compulsory "orientation to the school" program. Students who have completed the program are to respond to an attitude inventory. Construct five items for such an inventory. Designate the scoring for your items.

15.4 A researcher is doing research on the science achievement of students in grades 5–7. Another researcher is doing research on personality characteristics of junior high students. Contrast the measurement of these two research studies with respect to the:
a. availability of published measuring instruments.
b. type of validity of major concern.
c. data-collection procedures.

15.5 Suppose a researcher is doing research on the attitudes of junior high school students toward their teachers. Construct a semantic differential that might be used to measure such attitudes.

15.6 Construct five items for a rating scale that might be used with high school teachers to measure faculty perceptions of the central administration of the school system.

15.7 Contrast the use of a Likert scale and a semantic differential. In what ways are they operationally different in terms of the manner in which an individual responds? Describe any differences and similarities in the scoring procedures.

15.8 Identify two to three problems with using self-reports of behavior on sensitive topics such as academic cheating, drug use, or bullying. Then suggest alternative measures that would eliminate or minimize the problems that you identified.

15.9 What should you do with answers to your survey questions that do not adhere to your directions, such as:
a. Marking the space halfway between the 3 and the 4 on a 5-point rating scale?
b. Ranking two or more things the same when you told respondents that tied ranks were not allowed?
c. Circling more than one answer on the 1 to 5 rating scale?
How would your suggestions change your spreadsheet entries?

15.10 Why would you expect the reliability coefficient for a third-grade test of arithmetic facts to be higher than the reliability coefficient for a measure of self-esteem for the same group of students?

NOTES

1. See, for example, N. E. Gronlund, R. L. Linn, and K. M. Davis, *Measurement and Assessment in Teaching* (8th ed.). (Englewood Cliffs, NJ: Prentice-Hall, 1999) or A. J. Nitko, *Educational Assessment of Students* (3rd ed.). (Englewood Cliffs, NJ: Prentice-Hall, 2000).
2. The terms *index* and *scale* commonly are used interchangeably, although some authors make a technical distinction between them. Both scales and indices are composite measures of variables based on responses to more than one item, and both typically provide ordinal measurement for the individual items. An index is obtained through the simple cumulation of scores to responses over the items. A scale is obtained through the assignment of scores to response patterns, thus taking into account any intensity structure that may exist in the items. By these technical definitions, most of the scales used in educational research are indices, but this discussion will continue with the more common term *scale*.

REFERENCES

Bramlett, R. K., and Barnett, D. W. (1993). The development of a direct observation code for use in preschool settings. *School Psychology Review, 22,* 49–62.

Cronbach, L. J. (1951). Coefficient alpha and the internal structure of tests. *Psychometrika, 16,* 297–334.

Cronbach, L. J. (1984). *Essentials of psychological testing* (4th ed.). New York: Harper & Row.

Fabiano, E. (1989). *Index to tests used in educational dissertations*. Phoenix, AZ: Oryx.

Houston Independent School District. (2007). Teacher Observation Form. Retrieved October 20, 2007, from www.houstonisd.org/GiftedTalented/Home/Forms.

Impara, J. C., and Murphy, L. L. (1994). *Buros desk reference: Psychological assessment in the schools.* Lincoln, NE: Buros Institute.

Kerlinger, F. N. (1986). *Foundations of behavioral research* (3rd ed.). New York: Holt, Rinehart and Winston.

Kuder, G. F., and Richardson, M. W. (1937). The theory of the estimation of test reliability. *Psychometrika, 2,* 151–160.

Murphy, L. L., Spies, R. A., and Plake, B. S. (Eds.). (2006). *Tests in print VII.* Lincoln: University of Nebraska Press, Buros Institute for Mental Measurements.

Nussel, E. J., Wiersma, W., and Rusche, P. J. (1988). Work satisfaction of education professors. *Journal of Teacher Education, 39,* 45–50.

Osgood, C. E., Suci, G. J., and Tannenbaum, P. H. (1957). *The measurement of meaning*. Urbana: University of Illinois Press.

Spies, R. A., and Plake, B. S. (Eds.). (2005). *Sixteenth mental measurements yearbook*. Lincoln: University of Nebraska Press, Buros Institute for Mental Measurements.

CHAPTER

16 Data Analysis: Descriptive Statistics

This chapter and the following chapter describe a variety of statistical procedures used for data analysis. Data can take many forms, and when they take numerical forms such as scores or frequencies, the usual course of action is to perform an appropriate type of statistical analysis.

When data are presented as numbers, they are usually accorded some level of quantitative meaning. Not surprisingly, statistical analyses are commonly associated with quantitative research. In the chapters dealing with experimental, quasi-experimental, and survey research, specific analysis procedures were not emphasized because statistical procedures have broad application. That is, a specific procedure is not unique to experimentation, for example.

Analysis in qualitative research relies heavily on induction, and the product, rather than being a statistical result, is description. However, statistical procedures may be appropriate for some parts of data analysis in historical and ethnographic research, but they certainly are not the major thrust of analysis in qualitative research.

Statistical analysis has been greatly facilitated by the availability of computers. With the use of computer programs, computational accuracy is pretty well assured, and the student can concentrate on the underlying reasoning of the procedures and the meaning of the results. There are many computer programs available for statistical analysis. Later in this chapter and in the next chapter, there will be some illustrations of computer analyses using SPSS, the Statistical Package for the Social Sciences.

The Multiple Meanings of Statistics

The term **statistics** has multiple meanings in educational research, but probably its simplest meaning is "bits of information." If one says that 632 students are enrolled in a specific school, this can be considered a statistic. The salary schedule and the numbers of teachers at each salary level for a district are sometimes called salary statistics.

Statistics has a much broader meaning than simply bits of information, however. It also refers to the theory, procedures, and methodology by which data are summarized. It has been suggested that to some people the terminology of statistics seems like a foreign language. Although this may be true, the understanding and use of statistics is not so much a matter of identifying new terminology and symbols for already known concepts as it is a way of reasoning and drawing conclusions. Although the layperson often views statistics as an accumulation of facts and figures, the researcher sees statistics as the methods used to describe data and make sense of them.

Many different specific statistical analyses are available to the educational researcher, but it is not the intent of this discussion to cover statistical analysis in detail. Rather, the following two purposes will be addressed by this chapter and Chapter 17: (1) to provide the reasoning underlying the use of statistical analysis, and (2) to list the more commonly used statistical procedures and the conditions under which they apply. The discussion is intended to emphasize the logic of analysis, not computational procedures.

Descriptive statistics, discussed in this chapter, are exactly what the name implies: procedures and measures by which we describe quantitative data. Suppose values or scores on some variable have been collected; one of the first tasks is to describe these scores. If fifty fourth-grade students have been tested on arithmetic achievement and their fifty scores comprise the data of the research study, how will these scores be described? Simply listing them on a sheet of paper is not adequate. They must be summarized somehow. Certain information is generated that describes these scores as a group. This information and the process by which it is obtained are called **descriptive statistics.**

Distributions

The group or set of all scores or observations on a variable is called a **distribution.** The fifty arithmetic achievement scores mentioned earlier would be a distribution. If measurement were on an interval scale, rather than listing all fifty scores individually, one would tabulate them according to frequency. That is, each possible score would be listed, and the frequency of its occurrence would be listed, as in Table 16.1. The *f* stands for frequency, and the content of Table 16.1 is called a **frequency distribution.**

Arranging the scores as in Table 16.1 does not provide much information. The largest and smallest scores, sixty and ninety-nine, can be determined, and they cover a total of

TABLE 16.1 Frequency Distribution of Arithmetic Test Scores

Score	*f*	Score	*f*	Score	*f*	Score	*f*
60	1	70	0	80	2	90	1
61	1	71	0	81	2	91	1
62	0	72	4	82	3	92	1
63	0	73	0	83	2	93	2
64	0	74	2	84	2	94	1
65	0	75	3	85	1	95	2
66	3	76	1	86	2	96	0
67	1	77	1	87	1	97	1
68	0	78	2	88	0	98	2
69	1	79	1	89	2	99	1

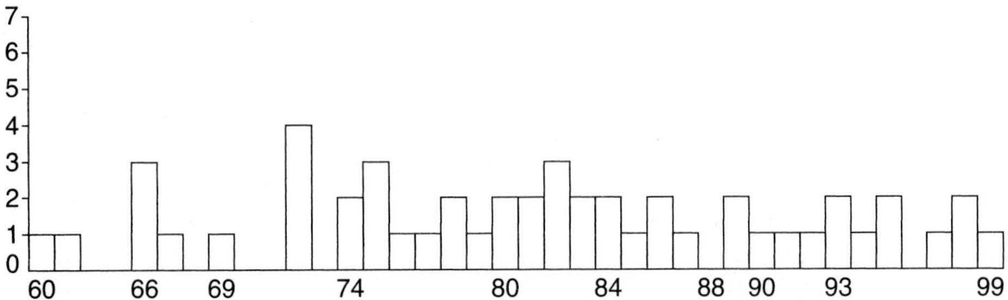

FIGURE 16.1 Histogram for the Frequency Distribution of the Raw Scores on an Arithmetic Test

forty points on the scale of measurement. Thus, the scores have a range of forty points. Instead of a tabular form, the scores could be put into graphic form by indicating frequency on the vertical axis and the values of the scores on the horizontal axis. Such a representation is called a **histogram.** The histogram for the arithmetic test scores is quite flat and spread out because of relatively small frequencies and a wide range of scores. The histogram brings out the general shape of the distribution, as illustrated in Figure 16.1.

Describing a Distribution of Scores

Although a frequency distribution and a histogram pull together the scores, they are hardly adequate for describing a distribution. All research results cannot be reported by merely producing frequency distributions and constructing related histograms. Measures that more efficiently and fully describe a distribution are needed.

Basically, there are three requirements for describing a distribution of scores or observations. One is that something must be known about where the distribution is located on the scale of measurement. Second, there must be information about how the distribution is spread out—how it is dispersed. The third requirement is the identification of its shape.

> To describe a distribution is to provide information about its location, dispersion, and shape.

Statistics called *measures of central tendency* indicate the location of a distribution. Correspondingly, statistics can be computed to indicate the dispersion of the distribution; these are called *measures of variability.* A histogram could be generated to determine the shape of a distribution, but it is more common to infer a shape from knowing something about the variable under study. Many educational variables—for example, achievement scores in academic areas—tend to have symmetrical, bell-shaped distributions, which approximate what is known as a normal distribution.

Measures of Central Tendency. Measures of **central tendency** are commonly referred to as *averages.* In this sense, they give an indication of what a typical observation in the distribution is like. Measures of central tendency are locators of the distribution; that is, they locate the distribution on the scale of measurement. They are points in the distribution that derive their name from a tendency to be centrally located in the distribution.

The mean, median, and mode are the most commonly used measures of central tendency. **Mean,** used in this context, refers to the arithmetic mean. The mean is determined by simply adding the scores in a distribution and dividing by the number of scores in the distribution. The **median** is the point on the scale of measurement below which one-half of the scores of the distribution lie. The *mode,* which is used less often, is simply the score with the greatest frequency. Although the focus of this chapter is not on computation, the measures of central tendency for the data in Table 16.1 are:

Mean = 81.26
Median = 81.5
Mode = 72

The following illustrates the idea of a locator. There are two distributions of weights, one for adult men and one for adult women. The mean weight of the distribution is 170 pounds for the men and 132 pounds for the women. Both distributions have the same measurement scale—pounds—and both can be located on the measurement scale by their means. If the distributions are set on the measurement scale, the distribution for the men would be located to the right—that is, farther up the scale—than the distribution for the women.

> Measures of *central tendency* are points in the distribution used to locate the distribution. The *mean* is the most commonly used measure of central tendency; it is the arithmetic average—the sum of all the scores divided by the number of scores. The *median* is the point below which one-half of the scores lie.

Measures of Variability. In describing a distribution, it also is necessary to know something about its dispersion, or the spread of the scores; dispersion is indicated by measures of **variability.** In contrast to measures of central tendency, which are points, measures of variability are intervals (or their squares); that is, they designate a number of units on the scale of measurement.

There are several measures of variability. The *range* is a crude measure, because it provides little information. It gives the number of units on the scale of measurement necessary to include the highest and lowest scores, but it provides no information about the pattern of variation between these scores.

The measures of variability most commonly used are the **variance** and the **standard deviation.** Before these measures can be defined, the meaning of a deviation must be considered. *Deviation* means the difference between an observed score and the mean of the distribution. To determine the variance, the squares of these deviations are summed and divided by the number of scores.[1] If n is the number of scores and $\overline{X}$ (read "*X*bar"), the mean of the distribution, the variance, is then given in symbol form by:

$$\text{Variance} = \frac{\Sigma(X_i - \overline{X})^2}{n}$$

That is, the deviation of each score from the mean is squared, the squares of these deviations are then summed, and this sum is divided by the number of observations in the distribution. Thus, the variance is the average of the squared deviations from the mean. The *standard deviation* is defined as the positive square root of the variance.

The measures of variability for the data in Table 16.1 are:

Range = 40
Variance = 100.31
Standard deviation = 10.01

> The *variance* and the *standard deviation* are the most commonly used measures of variability. They are intervals (or their squares) on the scale of measurement, and they indicate the dispersion in the distribution.

This discussion of measures of central tendency and measures of variability has indicated the need for both types of measures, as well as knowing something about the shape, for describing distributions. When distributions are described as being alike, for example, it is important to specify in what way they are similar. Figures 16.2 and 16.3 illustrate distributions that are alike in one respect yet very different in the other.

Shapes of Distributions. Distributions may take on a variety of shapes. The shape of the histogram in Figure 16.1 has no specific name, but there are distributions whose shapes have been named. A distribution that (at least theoretically) occurs frequently in educational research is the *normal distribution.* The normal distribution is not a single distribution with a specific mean and standard deviation. Rather, it is a smooth, symmetrical distribution that

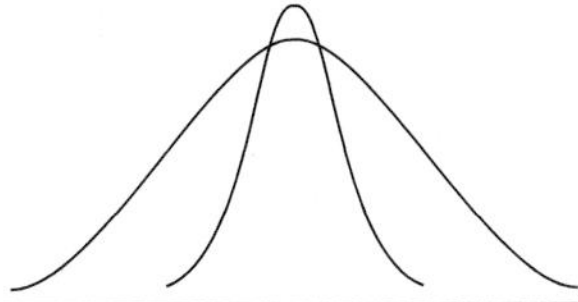

FIGURE 16.2 Distributions with Like Central Tendency but Different Variability

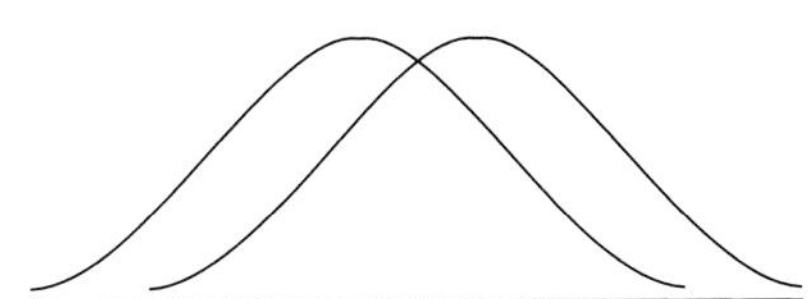

FIGURE 16.3 Distributions with Like Variability but Different Central Tendency

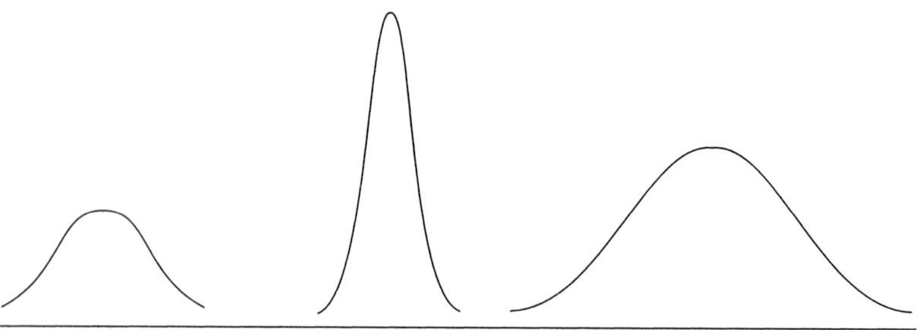

FIGURE 16.4 Examples of Normal Distributions

follows the general shape of the distributions in Figure 16.4 (sometimes called bell-shaped). The specific normal distribution depends on characteristics such as its variability.

When considering the **shape of a distribution** of scores comprising the data of some research study, the important consideration is not identifying the exact shape of the distribution of the sample but whether the data from the sample seem to conform to some theoretical shape. For example, there are many statistical tests that assume that the data have been randomly drawn from a population of values that have a normal distribution, that is, a bell-shaped curve as its shape. The easiest way to look at the shape of the data for the sample is to use Excel, SPSS, or some other statistical software to graph the histogram. These programs allow you to graph the separate scores, as was done in Figure 16.1, or to group the scores into intervals so that the general shape is more clearly seen. Unlike the measures of central tendency and variability, for which specific values are computed, a researcher is less concerned about the actual shape of the distribution of observed scores and more concerned with its assumed or theoretical shape.

When a distribution is not symmetrical, it is called skewed. The first distribution in Figure 16.5 is a negatively skewed distribution where most of the values are near the top of the range. Examples of negatively distributed variables would be scores on a mastery test where only a few subjects have low scores or the times of finishers in a marathon where a small number of elite runners finish in much less time than most of the group. The second distribution in Figure 16.5 is a positively skewed distribution where most of the values are grouped and only a few of the values are extremely high. Incomes are positively skewed, as are the number of library books read by the students in a third-grade class.

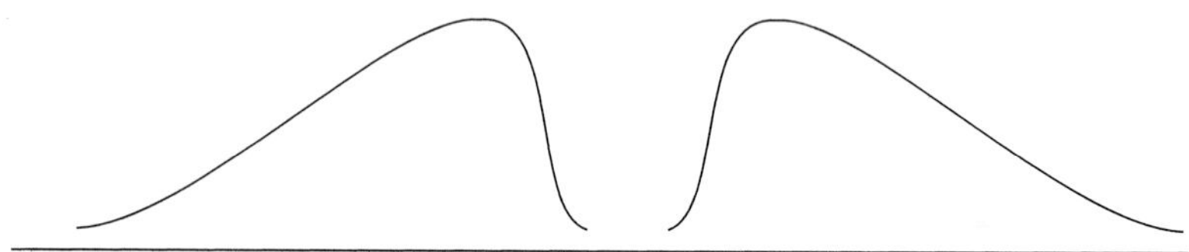

FIGURE 16.5 Skewed Distributions

Standard Scores

Suppose an instructional experiment is being conducted, and there are two dependent variables, performance on a mathematics test and performance on a science test. If a subject in the experiment has a score of 78 on the mathematics test and a score of 92 on the science test, which is the better performance? There is no way to tell simply from the raw or observed scores because the tests may be on different scales and have different numbers of items. What can be done is to transform the scores to a common equal-interval scale, and such scores are called standard scores. Standard scores are obtained by using the standard deviation as the unit of measure and then indicating the relative position of a single score in the entire distribution of scores in terms of the mean and standard deviation. Specifically, a standard score is the number of standard deviations that an observed score is located from the mean.

> Standard scores are obtained by a transformation so that the unit of measurement is the standard deviation and the score is expressed in standard deviation units from the mean.

Properties of Standard Scores. The commonly used symbol for a standard score is a lowercase z (z-score). When converting to standard scores, a z-score is calculated for each score in the original distribution. The distribution of z-scores has the following properties:

1. The shape of the distribution of z-scores is identical to that of the original distribution of scores.

2. The mean of the distribution of z-scores equals zero regardless of the value of the mean in the original distribution.

3. The variance of the distribution of z-scores is 1, and, because the standard deviation is the positive square root of the variance, it too is 1. This is true regardless of the value of the variance of the original distribution.

> The distribution of standard scores has the same shape as the original distribution, a mean of zero, and a standard deviation of 1.

Determining Standard Scores. A z-score is computed by subtracting the mean from the observed score and dividing the result by the standard deviation. This process can be expressed by:

$$\text{Standard score} = \frac{\text{Observed score} - \text{mean}}{\text{Standard deviation}}$$

or in symbol form:

$$z = \frac{X - \overline{X}}{s}$$

where:

X is the observed score
$\overline{X}$ is the mean of the observed distribution
s is the standard deviation of the observed distribution

Going back to the two dependent variable scores mentioned earlier, the 78 on the mathematics test and the 92 on the science test, what would these scores be as standard scores? First we need to know the means and standard deviations of the original distributions of scores. Suppose the distribution of mathematics test scores has a mean ($\overline{X}_m$) of 76 and a standard deviation (s_m) of 4. The science test score distribution has a mean ($\overline{X}_{sc}$) of 94 and a standard deviation (s_{sc}) of 6. Converting the subject's scores of 78 and 92, respectively, to z-scores we have:

for the mathematics test score:

$$z_m = \frac{X_m - \overline{X}_m}{s_m}$$

$$z_m = \frac{78 - 76}{4}$$

$$z_m = +.50$$

for the science test score:

$$z_{sc} = \frac{X_{sc} - \overline{X}_{sc}}{s_{sc}}$$

$$z_{sc} = \frac{92 - 94}{6}$$

$$z_{sc} = -.33$$

These are the two standard scores of one individual or subject. Note that the relative position of the mathematics test score with a z-score of $+.50$ is considerably better than that of the science test score with a z-score of $-.33$, even though the original scores were 78 and 92, respectively.

The above illustration shows that z-scores take on both positive and negative values. In fact, in a symmetrical distribution there will be as many negative as positive scores. A score at the mean of the original distribution will be a z-score of zero. So, attractive as z-scores are, they do have some undesirable features.

To avoid negative and zero scores we can transform a distribution of standard scores to a distribution with an arbitrarily selected mean and standard deviation. A transformation sometimes used is one to a distribution with a mean of 50 and a standard deviation of 10. This way negative scores are avoided and the scores tend to locate around 50. The transformation process is expressed by:

$$\text{Transformed score} = (10)(z) + 50$$

Transforming the previous science test score in this manner would give:

$$\begin{aligned}\text{Transformed score} &= 10\,(-.33) + 50 \\ &= -3.3 + 50 \\ &= 46.7\end{aligned}$$

So now, instead of a negative z-score, the original score of 92 is transformed into a score of 46.7.

Test publishers often transform standard scores to a distribution with a designated mean and standard deviation. A mean of 500 and a standard deviation of 100 are sometimes used. Distributions with a mean of 100 and a standard deviation of 15 have been used for intelligence test scores.

Standard scores are useful for showing the relative positioning of scores in a distribution. They also are used for finding values in statistical tables, as will be discussed later.

Correlation: A Measure of Relationship

Thus far, this discussion has been concerned mainly with describing the scores on a single variable, those of one distribution or set of data. However, in education researchers are often interested in two variables simultaneously to determine how they relate to one another. An example might be the relationship between student achievement in language arts and scores on a self-concept inventory.

This extent of relationship is approached through the distributions of scores that represent the two variables. The two distributions are commonly made up of paired scores from a single group of individuals. In any event, the distributions make up sets of ordered pairs of scores. The researcher is interested in how the scores in the distributions correlate or covary. To *covary* means "to vary together"—high scores with high, low with low, high with medium, whatever the case may be. The relationship between the two distributions (and, hence, the variables represented by the distributions) is based on how the pairs of scores vary together, that is, how changes in one variable compare with changes in the other. The degree of relationship or association between two variables is referred to as **correlation.** Thus, correlational studies are concerned not with a single distribution but with two distributions of scores.

The measure of correlation is called the *correlation coefficient* or the *coefficient of correlation.* The correlation coefficient is an index of the extent of relationship between two variables that can take on values from -1.00 through 0 to $+1.00$, inclusive. The greater the absolute value of the coefficient, the stronger the relationship. The end points of the interval indicate a perfect correlation between the variables, whereas a correlation of 0 indicates no relationship between variables, in which case it is said that the variables are independent. The sign on the coefficient, plus or minus, indicates the direction of the relationship. If the sign is plus, high scores on one variable go with high scores on the other variable. The same is true for low scores on both variables going together. If the sign is minus, the relationship is reversed. That is, low scores on one variable go with high scores on the other variable, and vice versa.

There are several formulas for computing the correlation that are algebraically equivalent. The simplest one is:

$$r = \Sigma z_x \cdot z_y / n$$

where the pairs of scores are converted to standard scores (z-scores), the cross-products are summed, and that total is divided by n, the number of paired scores.

The *correlation coefficient* is a measure of the relationship between two variables. It can take on values from -1.00 to $+1.00$, inclusive. Zero indicates no relationship.

A plot of the scores of the two variables in a two-dimensional space or plane illustrates the concept of correlation. Each individual has two scores, one for each variable. For the scores to be plotted, the scale of one variable is assigned to the horizontal axis and the scale of the other variable to the vertical axis. The variables may be called X and Y, and each individual's pair of scores may be plotted as a point in the plane. There will be as many points as there are individuals measured on both variables. Such a plot is called a *scattergram.*

Figure 16.6 illustrates a positive relationship between variables and, hence, a positive correlation coefficient. The high values of variable X are associated with high values of variable Y. The opposite situation is true for a negative correlation; that is, high values of variable X go with low values of variable Y, and vice versa, as shown in Figure 16.7. To have a perfect correlation ($+1.00$ or -1.00), the points of the scattergram must fall on a straight line, although such a relationship is extremely rare in education.

For example, intelligence and achievement in science are two variables that seem to be positively correlated; that is, students who score high on IQ tests tend to be the highest scorers on science tests. An example of a negative correlation coefficient might be the relationship between intelligence scores and time to perform a learning task. That is, the more intelligent individuals should tend to perform the task in less time. Two variables that probably have zero correlation are foot size of fourteen-year-old girls and performance on a mathematics test.

The scatter or dispersion of the points in the scattergram gives an indication of the extent of relationship. As the positions of points tend to deviate from a straight line, the correlation tends to decrease. If a relationship exists but is not $+1.00$ or -1.00, the points

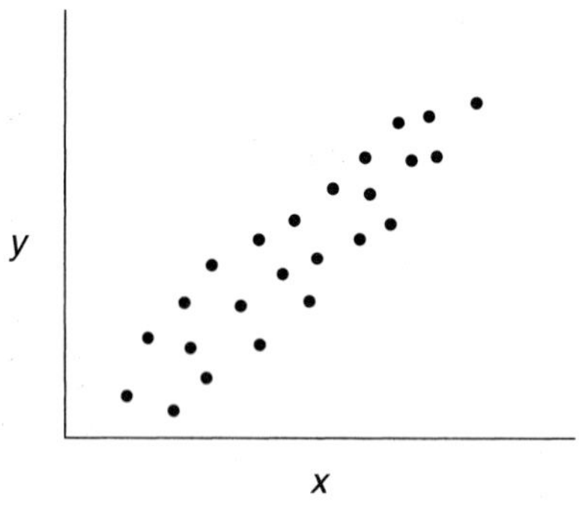

FIGURE 16.6 Scattergram Indicating a Positive Correlation Coefficient

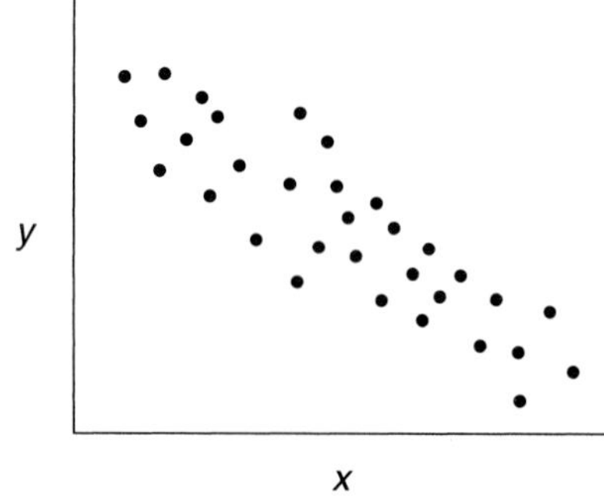

FIGURE 16.7 Scattergram Indicating a Negative Correlation Coefficient

generally fall in an elliptical ring. As the ring becomes narrower—that is, approaches a straight line—the relationship becomes stronger, and the absolute value of the correlation coefficient increases. The direction of the ring indicates whether the relationship is positive or negative, lower left to upper right being positive and upper left to lower right being negative. When the points of the scattergram fall within a circle, there is a correlation of zero. Figure 16.8 presents some examples of scattergrams, with the corresponding magnitude of the correlation coefficient given by *r*.

The correlation coefficient does not necessarily indicate a cause-and-effect relationship between the two variables. That is, it does not necessarily follow that one variable is causing the scores on the other variable. For example, there usually exists a positive correlation between the salaries paid to teachers and the percentage of graduating seniors going on to college in a particular school or system; that is, schools with higher teachers' salaries tend to have greater percentages of graduating seniors going on to college. However, it would be difficult to argue that paying higher teachers' salaries is causing greater percentages of seniors to go on to college or, conversely, that sending seniors to college increases teachers' salaries. A third factor or a combination of external but common factors may be influencing the scores on both variables. Multiple causation is not uncommon when dealing with educational variables.

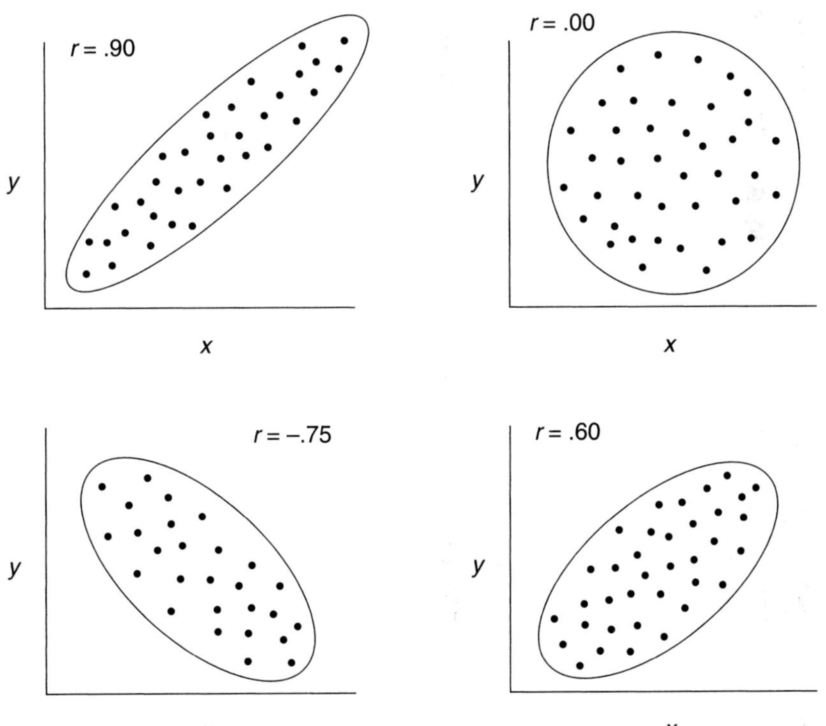

FIGURE 16.8 Examples of Scattergrams and Corresponding Correlation Coefficients

Uses of Correlation

The correlation coefficient is used extensively as a descriptive statistic to describe the relationship between two variables. It is also used for **prediction**—the estimation of one variable from knowledge of another variable. The variable from which one predicts is called the *predictor variable,* and the variable being predicted is called the **criterion variable.**

For a prediction study, an equation of the form $Y = bX + a$ can be developed in which Y is the criterion variable and X is the predictor variable. This is the equation of a straight line that is fit to the scattergram of points representing the scores of the two variables. (It is also called the equation of the regression line of Y on X.) The values of b and a are constants for a given set of data.

The simplest formulas for calculating b (the slope) and a (the intercept) are these:

$$b = r \cdot s_y / s_x$$

$$a = \overline{Y} - b\overline{X}$$

or, in words,

slope = correlation times the standard deviation of Y divided by the standard deviation of X

intercept = the mean of Y minus the slope times the mean of X

The correlation between X and Y has a definite effect on the prediction—specifically, the errors of prediction. The greater the absolute value of the correlation coefficient, the more accurate the prediction. What is meant by accuracy of prediction? Consider the criterion variable, Y. For each Y score, there is a paired X score that can be used in the prediction equation to generate a predicted score, say $\hat{Y}$. Then the difference would be symbolized by $(Y - \hat{Y})$, and this difference is an error in prediction. If all the errors of prediction are computed, these would comprise a distribution of error scores. This distribution has a standard deviation, called the **standard error of estimate.** The smaller this standard deviation, the more accurate the prediction. Correspondingly, the greater the correlation between the criterion and predictor variables, the smaller the standard deviation of the distribution of error scores.

> *Prediction* is the estimation of one variable from a knowledge of another. Accuracy of prediction is increased as the correlation between the predictor and criterion variables increases.

Prediction in education is used in a multitude of ways, for example, predicting achievement (criterion) from scores on an intelligence test (predictor). Guidance counselors often use prediction equations composed of more than one predictor variable in attempting to predict success in college or success on a job. Scores on tests such as the Scholastic Aptitude Test (SAT) and the American College Testing (ACT) program are considered predictors of success in college. Often, predictor variables are used in combination rather than singly; for example, SAT score and high school grade-point average are used to predict success in college. The correlation coefficient also can be used in inferential statistics, which are discussed in the next chapter.

Different Correlation Coefficients

Although the concept of correlation is consistent, different correlation coefficients are used under varying conditions. The most commonly used correlation coefficient is the *Pearson product-moment*, which requires at least interval scale measurement because the means of the distributions must be computed. The most important consideration affecting the choice of a coefficient is the level of measurement of the variables. Table 16.2 lists five of the more commonly used correlation coefficients and the minimum measurement scales required of the variables being correlated.

EXAMPLE 16.1

Use of Descriptive Statistics: Means and Standard Deviations

Three sixth-grade teachers in a school are conducting a study involving two types of instruction: individualized and traditional. Both boys and girls are involved in the study; thus, type of instruction and sex of the student are independent variables. The dependent variable is the score on a reading achievement test.

The purpose of the study is to describe the distributions of reading achievement scores. It would be important to know the means of those distributions to determine the relative positions. However, knowledge about the variability or dispersion of the distributions is also important. It may be that individualized instruction spreads out the students more than traditional instruction. This would be evidenced by a greater standard deviation for the distribution of reading test scores

TABLE 16.2 Correlation Coefficients and Minimum Required Measurement of the Variables

Correlation Coefficient	Measurement of Variables (Minimum Required)
1. Pearson product-moment	**1.** Both variables on interval scales.
2. Spearman rank order	**2.** Both variables on ordinal scales.
3. Point biserial	**3.** One variable on interval scale; the other a genuine dichotomy on a nominal or ordinal scale.
4. Biserial	**4.** One variable on interval scale; the other an artificial dichotomy on an ordinal scale. The dichotomy is artificial because there is an underlying continuous distribution.
5. Coefficient of contingency	**5.** Both variables on nominal scales.

of those taught by individualized instruction. The research questions can be stated as follows:

1. What are the means and standard deviations of the distributions of reading test scores for type of instruction: individualized and traditional?
2. What are the means and standard deviations of the distributions of reading test scores for sex: boys and girls?
3. What are the means and standard deviations of the distributions of reading test scores for the four types of instruction and sex combinations?

There is a total of 86 sixth-grade students enrolled in the school, 47 girls and 39 boys. The teachers can accommodate 40 students in the individualized instruction, so 20 boys and 20 girls are randomly assigned to this type of instruction. (This means that the remaining 46 students are also randomly assigned to traditional instruction.) The instruction proceeds and after one semester all students are measured on reading achievement. Because type of instruction is an experimental variable, the research design can be described as a posttest-only control group design.

Using the notation developed in the chapter on experimental designs, the experiment can be diagrammed as follows:

R G_1 (boys)........................X.. O_1
R G_2 (girls) ....X.. O_2
R G_3 (boys).. O_3
R G_4 (girls) .... O_4

In this design, X represents individualized instruction. Although boys and girls within the type of instruction were not separated, they are in the design to show that sex of the student is an independent variable. The Os represent the measurement on the reading achievement test.

The following results appeared.

Distribution	*Mean*	*Std. Dev.*
Individualized inst.—both boys and girls	82.1	12.6
Traditional inst.—both boys and girls	76.0	17.2
Individualized inst.—boys	80.6	14.1
Individualized inst.—girls	83.6	11.3
Traditional inst.—boys	71.8	8.0
Traditional inst.—girls	80.2	6.8
All boys	76.2	16.3
All girls	81.9	12.7

Various combinations generated eight distributions that contained varying numbers of scores. For example, the first distribution, individualized instruction for both boys and girls, contained 40 scores, but the second distribution, for traditional instruction, contained 46 scores.

Although distributions with 40 scores and 46 scores would not be distributed as exact normal distributions, the teachers probably would not be much concerned about the distribution shapes because there would be adequate evidence from previous use of the reading test that sixth-grade scores tend to be normally distributed. Thus, attention would focus on the location and variability of the distributions of scores.

The scores of those students receiving individualized instruction had a higher mean than the scores of those receiving traditional instruction. Overall, girls had a mean score higher than boys, and this pattern was consistent for both individualized and traditional instruction. However, the gap between boys and girls was much greater for traditional instruction than for individualized instruction, the difference between the means being 8.4 and 3.0 points, respectively.

The scores of the boys were more variable than those of the girls overall, and again this pattern was consistent for the two types of instruction. Considering the distributions of boys and girls singly within the types of instruction, the scores for individualized instruction were more variable. However, when the scores of boys and girls were combined, traditional instruction had the greater standard deviation. This was most likely caused by the fact that, within traditional instruction, the girls' performance was considerably higher than that of the boys.

Data Analysis by Computer

Unless the quantity of data from a research study is very limited, most statistical analyses are done on a computer. Although some analysis can be done on a hand calculator, computers generally facilitate data analysis. In more complex analyses the computer will be much faster and more accurate than hand computations. Statistical software tends to be easy to use and offers a multitude of choices of statistical procedures. In fact, the beginning student can be intimidated by the number of sophisticated analyses that are available. High-quality research studies can be conducted with basic statistical analysis. You probably will never use 80 percent or more of the statistical programs that are available. Use what you need and leave the rest for those who specialize in statistics.

The computer facilitates the analysis of large data sets. Hundreds and even thousands of cases can be analyzed quickly. Those analyses would probably not even be attempted if they had to be done with a calculator. The statistical software allows the researcher to conduct multiple analyses on the same data to provide different looks at the data. The researcher is not limited to a single statistical analysis.

Computers are extremely useful for data analysis because of their functionality, speed, accuracy, and accessibility. Functionality deals with the variety and sophistication of what the computer can do through its hardware (that is, the actual machines) and the software (the programs that give the computer instructions). Speed concerns the time, often in fractions of seconds, it takes the computer to perform the analysis. If the data are prepared without error and the appropriate analyses are used, the solution will be errorless. So, we have complete accuracy. Finally, computers generally are accessible.

> Computers are extremely useful for data analysis because they are functional, fast, accurate, and accessible.

Probably the three most commonly used statistical packages for behavioral sciences research are:

Excel, available at www.Microsoft.com/office/Excel

Statistical Package for the Social Sciences (SPSS), available at www.SPSS.com

Statistical Analysis System (SAS), available at www.SAS.com

There are manuals, user's guides, and often online help available for these software packages. The software and accompanying publications are updated almost continuously. Universities tend to have the latest editions, but it is not necessary to have the latest edition to run statistical analyses. All of the commonly used statistical analyses can be run on all of these software systems, but some analyses are easier to run on one system than on another.

This text is accompanied by a data disk that contains three data sets. The first data set, Ohio Teachers, contains district-level data on teachers' years of experience, degrees held, and salaries. This information was taken from the Ohio Department of Education's website, www.ode.state.oh.us. The second data set is the NC-SAT data, which lists the per-pupil expenditures, total expenditures, and SAT scores for school districts in North Carolina. The data are from the website of the North Carolina Department of Public Instruction, www.ncpublicschools.org. The third data set, PACT, lists the scores of over 100 ninth graders in a school in South Carolina on the Palmetto Achievement Challenge Test across three years. The file also contains information about the students such as gender, free/reduced lunch status, and whether they have an IEP. The variables in each data set are listed in Figure 16.9. The files are provided as Excel files and as SPSS files. Some examples are explained in the text, but the reader is encouraged to practice different analyses with these data sets. Run the analyses and then write an interpretation of the results.

The analyses of this chapter and those in Chapter 17 were run using SPSS for Windows, Version 15.0. Because there are many statistical software packages available, the data sets are not tied to one version or release. Frankly, the formula for computing a mean does not change from one version to another. Readers may use any software at their disposal, and the results should be the same although the format of the output may differ.

Potential data for statistical analysis abounds now that it can be downloaded from the Internet. Some words of caution are needed, though:

1. Question the accuracy of the data unless it is from a trusted source such as the National Center for Educational Statistics, state departments of education, or similar sources.
2. Check for missing data. This can be entire cases or scattered variables within cases. If there are substantial missing data, consider abandoning the analysis.

FIGURE 16.9 Variables in the Data Sets

Ohio Teachers			
DIST	District		
COUNTY	County		
ATT	Teacher attendance rate 2005–06		
EXP	Average years of teacher experience		
NUM	Number of full-time teachers		
NBACH	Number of full-time teachers who have at least a bachelor's		
NMAST	Number of full-time teachers who have at least a master's		
CERT	% of teachers who are fully certified		
NOTQ	% of teachers who are not highly qualified		
PBACH	% of full-time teachers who have at least a bachelor's		
PMAST	% of full-time teachers who have at least a master's		
SALARY	Average teacher salary		
TEMP	% of core courses taught by teacher with temporary certificate.		
NC-SAT-2006			
district	District		
math	Average SAT Mathematics Score		
reading	Average SAT Reading Score		
writing	Average SAT Writing Score		
perpupil	Per pupil expenditures		
total	Total expenditures		
PACT			
gender	M = Male	F = Female	
lunch	F = Free	R = Reduced	N = Neither
iep	IEP	Y = Yes	N = No
speech	Speech disability	Y = Yes	N = No
gift	Gifted	Y = Yes	N = No
elass05	English/Language Arts Scale Score 2005–06		
elapf05	English/Language Arts Performance Level 2005–06 (Below Basic, Basic, Proficient, Advanced)		
elass04	English /Language Arts Scale Score 2004–05		
elapf04	English/Language Arts Performance Level 2004–05		
elass03	English/Language Arts Scale Score 2003–04		
elapf03	English/Language Arts Performance Level 2003–04		
matss05	Math Scale Score 2005–06		
matpf05	Math Performance Level 2005–06		
matss04	Math Scale Score 2004–05		

(continued)

FIGURE 16.9 ***(Continued)***

matpf04	Math Performance Level 2004–05
matss03	Math Scale Score 2003–04
matpf03	Math Performance Level 2003–04
sciss05	Science Scale Score 2005–06
scipf05	Science Performance Level 2005–06
sciss04	Science Scale Score 2004–05
scipf04	Science Performance Level 2004–05
socss05	Social Studies Scale Score 2005–06
socpf05	Social Studies Performance Level 2005–06
socss04	Social Studies Scale Score 2004–05
socpf04	Social Studies Performance Level 2004–05

3. Clean the data, if needed, by eliminating duplicate records and values that are "out of bounds" such as a "6" on a 5-point rating scale. Decide how to handle missing data.

EXAMPLE 16.2

Use of Descriptive Statistics: Analysis of Selected Variables on the Ohio Teachers Data Set

Suppose we select four variables from the Ohio Teachers data set. There are data from 610 school districts and the selected variables are:

EXP	average number of years of experience
NUM	number of teachers in the district
PMAST	percent of teachers with at least a master's degree
SALARY	average teacher salary

We compute descriptive statistics for the variables that include the maximum and minimum values, the means, and the standard deviations. Then we compute the correlations between the pairs of variables. Finally, we present the results for the regression line for predicting salary from the percent of teachers with master's degrees. The regression results include b, the slope of the regression line, and a, the intercept. The SPSS output is in Figure 16.10.

The mean for years of experience is about 15. Remember that this is the district average. The lowest average years of experience was 6 and the highest was 27. There was quite a bit of variability across districts in terms of average years of teacher experience. The mean number of teachers in a district was 172.78 with a standard deviation of 272.28. Once again, the maximum and minimum values of 3436 teachers and 14 teachers, respectively, indicate that Ohio has some very large districts and some very small districts. When we look at the statistics for the percentage of teachers with at least a master's degree,

FIGURE 16.10 SPSS Output for the Ohio Teachers Data Set

Descriptive Statistics

	N	Minimum	Maximum	Mean	Std. Deviation
EXP	610	6.00	27.00	15.0213	2.91835
NUM	610	14.00	3436.00	172.7852	272.28861
PMAST	610	.00	85.40	54.7879	12.97147
SALARY	610	32056.00	69307.00	48043.848	6235.70435
Valid N (listwise)	610				

Correlations

		EXP	NUM	PMAST	SALARY
EXP	Pearson Correlation	1	−.110**	.307**	.044
	Sig. (2-tailed)		.006	.000	.275
	N	610	610	610	610
NUM	Pearson Correlation	−.110**	1	.056	.335*
	Sig. (2-tailed)	.006		.169	.000
	N	610	610	610	610
PMAST	Pearson Correlation	.307**	.056	1	.435**
	Sig. (2-tailed)	.000	.169		.000
	N	610	610	610	610
SALARY	Pearson Correlation	.044	.335**	.435**	1
	Sig. (2-tailed)	.275	.000	.000	
	N	610	610	610	610

**Correlation is significant at the 0.01 level (2-tailed).

Coefficients[a]

Model	Unstandardized Coefficients		Standardized Coefficients		
	B	Std. Error	Beta	t	Sig.
1 (Constant)	36586.424	988.324		37.019	.000
PMAST	209.123	17.555	.435	11.913	.000

a. Dependent Variable: SALARY

we see that the districts range from 0 percent to 85 percent with a mean of 54.78 percent. The districts, on average, report about half of their teachers as having master's degrees. Finally, the district average salary data indicate a mean of about \$48,000 with a standard deviation of about \$6200. Most readers will note that the maximum district average salary was \$69,307. These results are useful when studying teachers in Ohio, but they are also useful for comparisons with other states. Additional analyses could be run to check for differences across different regions of the state, between large and small districts, and between urban and rural districts, just to mention a few.

The correlation matrix shows the extent of relationships among these variables. In the correlation matrix part of the figure, the 610 for N indicates that the correlation was based on 610 districts. The "Sig. (2-tailed)" values can be ignored because they apply to using the correlation in an inferential manner, which will be discussed in Chapter 17. The diagonal values are all 1 because any variable correlated with itself generates a correlation coefficient of 1.00. Finally, the two parts of the matrix above and below the diagonal are mirror images, because, for example, the correlation of EXP and NUM is the same as the correlation of NUM and EXP.

The variable with the largest correlation with SALARY is PMAST, a value of .435. This is a positive correlation indicating that districts with more of their teachers with master's degrees also tend to have higher salaries. Higher salaries and having a master's degree are positively correlated. Years of experience correlate about 0.00 with salary. Having a master's degree is more predictive of salary than is just years of experience. Note too that larger districts tend to have higher average salaries as indicated by a correlation of .335. None of these correlations is especially high, nowhere near the possible maximum value of 1.00, but the correlations of SALARY with PMAST and NUM are large enough to indicate a predictive association between these variables.

The regression results indicate the equation of the straight line that can be used to predict district average salary from the percent of teachers with at least a master's degree. The SPSS output uses labels that are a bit different from our notation. We used:

$Y = bX + a$ where b is the slope of the line and a is the Y-intercept

In the SPSS output the intercept is found on the row labeled "Constant" and the column labeled "B." So for these data the intercept is 36586.424. The slope is in the row labeled "PMAST" and the column labeled "B." The value of the slope is 209.123. The regression equation for predicting district average salary from the percent of teachers with at least a master's degree is:

$$Y = (209.123)X + 36586.424$$

You can now substitute any value for X (the percentage of teachers with master's degrees) and find the predicted value of the district average salary.

Summary

This chapter has provided an overview of descriptive statistics, one of the broad categories of statistics used in analyzing quantitative data. Descriptive statistics are used to describe distributions and relationships between variables. In general, descriptive statistics are measures of central tendency, measures of dispersion, and measures of relationship. To describe a distribution adequately we need to know its shape, its location on the scale of measurement, and its variability. We can plot the scores and develop a histogram to determine shape, but more commonly we know from the research literature, or other sources, the shape of distributions. For example, many educational variables are either known or assumed to have normal distributions. Measures of location are points on the scale of measurement, and the most commonly used are the mean and median, measures of central tendency. Finally, the most commonly used measures of variability, also called measures of dispersion, are the variance and the standard deviation. Measures of variability are intervals (or their squares) on the scale of measurement.

The relationship between two variables is described by the correlation coefficient. Correlation coefficients can take on values from -1.00 to $+1.00$ inclusive; the greater the absolute value of the coefficient, the stronger the relationship. A correlation coefficient of zero indicates no relationship or independence of the variables.

If descriptive statistics are being computed, "What is being described?" includes central tendency, dispersion, relationship—any or all three of these descriptors. The specific descriptive statistics that can be computed depend on the level of measurement of the variables. Table 16.2, presented earlier, indicates the levels of measurement that correspond with specific correlation coefficients. With nominal scale measurement, the lowest level, we can determine the mode, the category of greatest frequency, but, because nominal scales only categorize without order, the concept of dispersion does not apply. As we go up in the hierarchy of measurement scales, the statistics become more sophisticated; that is, they contain more information. Ordinal measurement can provide a mode and possibly a median. For dispersion we may designate a range in terms of the descriptors used for the ordinal data. Essentially, the same statistics can be computed for interval scale and ratio scale measurement: mode, median, and mean for central tendency; range, standard deviation, and variance for dispersion.

Descriptive statistics are useful in analyzing data, but they are only part of the statistics story. Inferential statistics comprise another broad category of statistics and these are discussed in the next chapter. Often descriptive and inferential statistics are used in combination when analyzing research data. It is not the intent of this text to provide computational procedures or have the reader perform statistical analysis. Rather the intent is to provide a rationale for statistical analysis of data and to describe the reasoning of some of the more commonly used statistical procedures. Numerous applied statistics texts are available that describe computational procedures for both descriptive and inferential statistics commonly used in educational research. A sampling of such texts is provided at the close of Chapter 17.

KEY CONCEPTS

Statistics
Descriptive statistics
Distribution
Frequency distribution
Histogram
Central tendency
Mean
Median
Variability
Variance
Standard deviation
Shape of a distribution
Correlation
Prediction
Criterion variable
Standard error of estimate

EXERCISES

16.1 Discuss the difference between measures of central tendency and measures of variability. Why are both types of measures necessary in describing a distribution? Present some examples of educational variables that are alike in measures of central tendency but different in variability, and some that are alike in dispersion but different in location.

16.2 Suppose a small company has around fifty employees working in the plant and office who earn around $30,000 per year. However, there are five executives, the president and four vice presidents, who earn over $175,000 each per year. Why would the median be a more informative measure of central tendency than the mean for this salary distribution?

16.3 Identify the three types of information necessary to describe a distribution.

16.4 The fourth-grade teachers in an elementary school want to compare the relative performances of individual students on tests of reading, mathematics, and science. Why is it necessary for them to use some type of standard score? Would the z-score be a desirable score? Why or why not? If the z-score is not used, what would be a desirable and useful transformed score?

16.5 The correlation coefficient is an index of the relationship between two variables. A positive correlation coefficient indicates a direct relationship, a negative correlation coefficient an inverse relationship, and a correlation coefficient of zero no relationship. For the following pairs of variables, indicate whether the correlation between the two variables would be expected to be positive, negative, or zero.

a. Performance on an intelligence test and time required to solve concept attainment problems.

b. Scores on an anxiety measure and those on a statistics test.

c. Scores on the reading and mathematics subtests of a standardized test battery.

d. Scores on an intelligence test and distance a baseball can be thrown.

e. Shoe size and performance on a high school geometry test.

16.6 In a small high school, an attitude toward mathematics and mathematics-related professions scale is administered to the students. The mean score on the scale is 52.6 for boys and 50.9 for girls. The standard deviation of the distribution of scores for boys is 5.7, and that for girls 14.6. The maximum possible score on the scale is 130. The scores in each distribution are normally distributed. Interpret these descriptive statistics.

16.7 The research office of a school system conducts a survey of 366 teachers in the system, comprised of 172 elementary school teachers, 102 junior high school teachers, and 92 senior high teachers. All teachers respond to an "attitude toward the central administration" scale. This scale contains 18 items, each scored from 1 to 5, so total scores on the scale can take on possible values from 18 to 90 inclusive. The greater the score, the more positive the attitude toward the central administration.

Total scores are computed for all teachers and then separated by level taught, elementary, junior high, and senior high school, giving three distributions of scores. The three distributions are plotted and they all are approximately normally distributed.

The means ($\overline{X}$) variances (s^2), and standard deviations (s) for the three distributions are as follows:

Elementary	*Junior High*	*Senior High*
$\overline{X}_E = 73.2$	$\overline{X}_{JH} = 71.6$	$\overline{X}_{SH} = 50.3$
$s_E^2 = 44.9$	$s_{JH}^2 = 151.3$	$s_{SH}^2 = 240.3$
$s_E = 6.7$	$s_{JH} = 12.3$	$s_{SH} = 15.5$

Interpret these results in terms of the attitudes toward the central administration of these teachers and how the attitudes differ by level taught.

16.8 Use the data in NC-SAT-2006 to correlate the average scores on the SAT with per-pupil expenditures. What is the conclusion that you can draw regarding the association of per-pupil expenditures and district SAT scores?

16.9 Use the PACT data set to find the percentage of students eligible for free lunch, the percentage with an IEP, the percentage with a speech disability, and the percentage labeled gifted.

16.10 Show the means and standard deviations of the PACT ELA standard scores across the years 2003–2004, 2004–2005, and 2005–2006.

NOTES

1. The symbol Σ is the summation operator and indicates to sum what follows, in this case the deviations. The i on the X_i indicates the individual scores used, in this case the first through the nth. When no numbers are indicated over the Σ, it indicates that i takes on values 1 through n.

CHAPTER 17 Data Analysis: Inferential Statistics

Chapter 16 discussed data analysis through the use of descriptive statistics and, certainly, a lot of information can be gained about distributions of scores through descriptive statistics. However, for several decades behavioral sciences research, including research in education, has relied heavily on the use of inferential statistics for analyzing data. Much analysis has centered around testing null hypotheses, hypotheses of no difference or no relationship, and there have been criticisms of behavioral sciences research indicating that it is too oriented to testing null hypotheses.

Estimation is another important and major part of inferential statistics. In fact, there have been instances of reported research in the past in which null hypothesis testing was overused when estimation would have been more appropriate. As will be seen later, this chapter considers estimation as one of the more important procedures of inferential statistics.

Context for Using Inferential Statistics

In many research situations, a specific group is studied with the intention of generalizing to some larger group. For example, surveys are conducted of large populations, not by surveying everyone in the population, but by surveying a subgroup of that population, called a *sample,* and then using the sample data to generalize to the population. As another example, a research director for a large city school system might set up five third grades and expose them to some experimental treatment with the purpose of generalizing to all third-grade students in the system. A university might sample 200 or so of its students rather than administer a questionnaire to all of its several thousand students. In these situations, the analysis is an attempt to infer something about the large group by using the data from a subset of that group.

> The context for inferential statistics is one of using data from a subset (sample) of a larger group (population) to make inferences about the larger group.

Inferential statistics are based on random sampling. Essentially, the logic is that the data of the sample, the only data available, reflect the population data within random sampling fluctuation. For example, if a sample mean is 85, then the population mean is something around 85. If we know the characteristics of the data due to random sampling fluctuation, we can make generalizations to the population based on the sample data.

Thus, the researcher has a distribution consisting of sample scores. The descriptive measures, such as the mean and standard deviation computed from the sample data, are called statistics. Correspondingly, there are descriptive measures of the population (these measures are called *parameters*). Of course, parameters are not computed, because data are not collected from the entire population. Rather, inferences are made and conclusions are drawn about parameters from the statistics of the sample—hence, the name inferential statistics.

In *inferential statistics,* statistics are measures of the sample and parameters are measures of the population. Inferences are made about the parameters from the statistics.

The basic idea in making inferences from statistics to parameters is to obtain the sample distribution and then to use accepted statistical techniques to make the inferences to the population. Statistics are computed from the sample data; on the basis of these statistics, generalizations to the parameters (population measures) are made. The theory and methodology underlying this procedure are known as inferential statistics. To construct the reasoning for inferential statistics, some basic concepts of probability and distributions (for the most part theoretical) related to probability must be employed. In this way, the researcher arrives at an established and conceptually sound procedure for making inferences from research data now summarized by statistics—inferences made from the sample to some larger population.

Testing Hypotheses and Estimating Parameters

In analyzing data by means of inferential statistics, we can use one or both of two general procedures: **testing hypotheses** or **estimating parameters.** Hypothesis testing is the more common procedure reported in the research literature. A hypothesis in the context of inferential statistics is a statement (conjecture) about one or more parameters. The researcher goes through a procedure of testing the hypothesis to determine whether or not it is consistent with the sample data. If it is not consistent, the hypothesis is rejected (note that the sample data are not discarded). If the hypothesis is consistent with the sample data, the hypothesis is retained as a tenable value for the parameter.

For example, a researcher might hypothesize that the population means of males and females are equal for the dependent variable "attitude toward independent reading." When the mean of a random sample of boys is compared to the mean of a random sample of girls, there are two possible conclusions. If the sample means are fairly similar, within reasonable sampling fluctuation, we will conclude that the hypothesis is plausible; we cannot reject it. If the sample means are extremely different from each other, we will reject the hypothesis that the population means are equal. We will state that the sample means differ significantly. The term *significantly* will be explained later when we discuss sampling distributions.

> In inferential statistics, a hypothesis is a statement about one or more parameters.

A second general procedure of inferential statistics is estimating a parameter. Given a set of sample data, the question can be asked, "What are tenable estimates of the parameter?" There are actually two types of estimates, a *point estimate* and an **interval estimate,** also called a *confidence interval.* A point estimate is simply a single-value estimate of the parameter. It is the value of the corresponding statistic from the sample. An interval estimate is an interval on the scale of measurement that contains tenable estimates of the parameter. Interval estimation is used much more than point estimation.

For example, a researcher who is studying childhood obesity might want to estimate the average weight in the population of fourth-graders in some state. If she can get the weights of a random sample of fourth-graders in the state, she can then use estimation to infer the population mean. Suppose that the mean for her random sample is 70 pounds. The best point estimate of the mean weight of fourth-graders in the state would be 70. Inferential statistics can be used to get an interval estimate such as 70 ± 8. The interval estimate provides more information than the point estimate.

> Estimating a parameter in inferential statistics can be done by point estimation or interval estimation. Point estimation consists of estimating the parameter by a single value. Interval estimation consists of defining an interval (confidence interval) on the scale of measurement that contains tenable values of the parameter. Either way, the estimate is made from sample data.

The procedures of hypothesis testing and related concepts are discussed in the following section and illustrated with examples.

Hypothesis Testing and Sampling Distributions

Developing the chain of reasoning in inferential statistics uses some concepts of random sampling fluctuation and probability. For example, suppose that the researcher in the example above, who was studying childhood obesity, hypothesized that the mean weight of fourth-graders in the state is 75 pounds. Note that the hypothesis is defined before the researcher gathers the data. She then obtains the weights of a random sample of 225 fourth-graders. The mean for her sample is 77. What should she conclude? Is 77 different enough from the hypothesized value of 75 so that she can reject the hypothesis as most probably being a false statement?

The process of testing the hypothesis can be expressed in five steps:

1. State the null and alternate hypotheses.
2. Establish the sampling distribution for the null hypothesis.
3. Compute the sample statistics.
4. Reference the sample statistic in the sampling distribution.
5. State the conclusion.

Step 1. The null hypothesis in this example is that the population of fourth-graders in this state has an average (mean) weight of 75 pounds. The alternate hypothesis is that the mean weight is not equal to 75 pounds. Note that these two hypotheses cover all possible outcomes. Also note that the alternate hypothesis allows the population's mean to be greater than 75 or less than 75. Allowing both outcomes makes this a "two-tailed" test of the hypothesis.

The hypotheses can be expressed in symbols as follows:

$$H_0 : \mu = 75$$
$$H_0 : \mu \neq 75$$

If the researcher were familiar with the literature concerning weights of fourth-graders and had reason to believe that the population's mean weight was actually greater than 75, she could have conducted a "one-tailed" test of the hypothesis and her hypotheses would be:

$$H_0 : \mu \leq 75$$
$$H_0 : \mu > 75$$

Step 2. The **sampling distribution** for the sample mean, the statistic of interest here, is established by the **central limit theorem.** This theorem was developed by mathematical statisticians and we can use it without going into the mathematics. Essentially it says:

> Given any population with mean μ and finite variance σ^2, as the sample size increases without limit, the distribution of the sample mean approaches a normal distribution with mean μ and variance σ^2/n where n is the sample size.

This tells us that the sampling distribution is a **standard normal distribution** (the familiar bell-shaped curve) and its mean is the number that we specified in the null hypothesis, 75. The standard deviation of the sampling distribution is found by dividing σ, the population standard deviation, by n, the sample size.

> Conceptually, a *sampling distribution* consists of the values of a statistic computed from all possible samples of a given size.

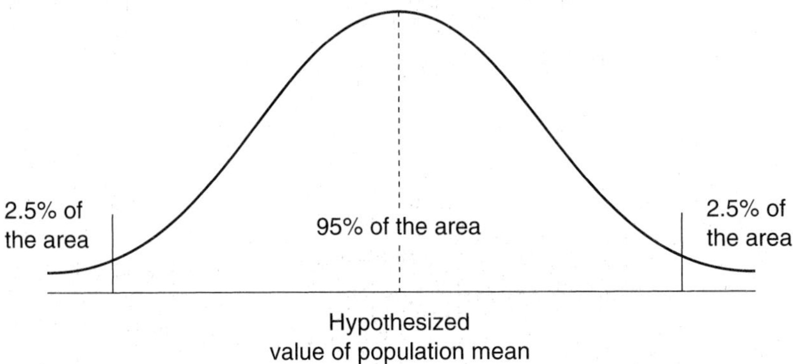

FIGURE 17.1 Area of the Sampling Distribution of the Mean with a Significance Level of .05

For the sake of developing the example, suppose that information from other states indicates that $\sigma = 12$ is an appropriate number. If the researcher uses a sample size of 225, then we can describe the sampling distribution because we have μ, σ, and n. It is a normal distribution, as shown in Figure 17.1. The mean of the sampling distribution is 75, taken from the null hypothesis. The standard deviation of the sampling distribution, called the standard error of the mean, is $\sigma/\sqrt{n}$, which for this example is $12/\sqrt{225}$, or 0.80.

Step 3. Now we gather the data from the random sample. Suppose that the mean for the random sample of 225 fourth-graders turns out to be 77.

Step 4. We reference the sample mean in the sampling distribution by determining how many standard errors away from the hypothesized population mean is the sample mean. Because the properties of the normal curve have been established by mathematical statisticians, we can use this information to determine the probability of obtaining a sample mean that is discrepant from the population mean.[1]

The sample mean is 2 pounds above the hypothesized value, found by $77 - 75$. This is 2.50 standard errors above the hypothesized population mean, found by 2/0.80.

In other terms: $$\frac{77 - 75}{0.80} = 2.50$$

Table A of Appendix 3 lists the areas under the normal curve that correspond to these values. The number 2.50 has a corresponding area of .4938. The .4938 is the percentage of sample means in the sampling distribution between 75 and 77. So, $.5000 - .4938$, or .0062, is the percentage of sample means in the sampling distribution that are greater than 77. Remember that this is a two-tailed hypothesis test, so we need to allow for means 2.50 standard errors below the hypothesized mean too. Thus our final probability is $2 \times .0062$, or .0124. This result can be interpreted as the probability of getting a sample mean this discrepant from the hypothesized value is .0124. This result is depicted in Figure 17.2.

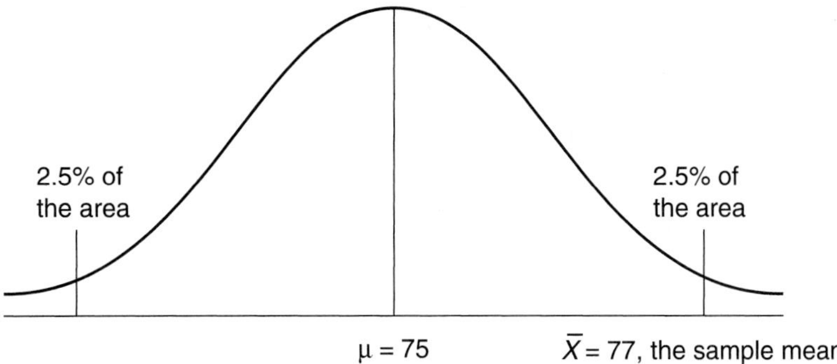

FIGURE 17.2 Location of the Observed Sample Mean in the Sampling Distribution for the Example

Step 5. What probability level do we need to obtain before we can reject the null hypothesis? This critical probability is called the **level of significance** and it is set by the researcher. The most commonly used levels in educational research are .05 and .01. If the researcher in this example chose the .05 level of significance, we would reject the null hypothesis because our calculated probability, .0124, is *less than* the level of significance, .05. A shorthand notation for this result is $p < .05$. On the other hand, when the calculated probability exceeds the significance level, we say that we fail to reject the null hypothesis.

> The *significance level* (α-level) is a probability used in testing hypotheses. Commonly used α-levels are .05 and .01.

Building a Confidence Interval: The Example Continued

Developing the concept of sampling distribution was done in the context of a hypothesis testing example. Another procedure in inferential statistics is building a confidence interval, which is an interval estimation of a parameter.

Consider again the example of the 77 sample mean on the weights of fourth-graders. Instead of testing hypotheses about the population mean, we want to obtain an interval estimate of it. This requires a **confidence level,** which is a defined probability that the interval will span the population mean.[2] Commonly used confidence levels in educational research are .95 and .99.

When a confidence interval for the mean is constructed, the interval is constructed symmetrically around the sample mean. If a 95 percent confidence interval (confidence level .95) for the example is constructed, the researcher wants an interval on the scale of measurement such that it includes 95 percent of the area of the sampling distribution. Because the sampling distribution is the normal (known from the discussion of hypothesis testing), it is necessary to go 1.96 standard deviation units on either side of the mean. The standard deviation of the sampling distribution of the mean was 0.80. Therefore, to construct the interval, the two points are determined by:

$$77 \pm 1.96\ (0.80)$$

This gives the interval 75.43 to 78.57, and we are 95 percent confident that this interval spans the population mean.

In general, when constructing confidence intervals, the researcher constructs the interval around the statistic by using the following formula:

Statistic ± (C.V.) (standard deviation of the statistic)

The C.V. is the critical value from the sampling distribution in standard score form, which is required to include the proportion of area equal to the confidence level. Then this critical value is multiplied by the standard deviation of the sampling distribution of the statistic to convert from the standard distribution to the scale of measurement for the particular variable. This product is one-half the span of the confidence interval, because its length is contained on either side of the statistic.

Possible Errors in Hypothesis Testing

As mentioned earlier, in inferential statistics a hypothesis is a statement about one or more parameters. The term **null hypothesis** is often used in statistical analysis to describe the hypothesis of no relationship. (The hypothesis of no relationship is the hypothesis of independence of the variables.) In testing a hypothesis about a population mean, mu (μ), a researcher might have the null hypothesis, H_0: $\mu = 56$, which can be rewritten H_0: $\mu - 56 = 0$, which technically is a hypothesis of no difference. If a researcher is testing a hypothesis about two population means being equal, the hypothesis can be written in the null form as H_0: $\mu_1 = \mu_2$ or H_0: $\mu_1 - \mu_2 = 0$. The null hypothesis is used to locate the sampling distribution for the statistical test.

> The *null hypothesis,* often called a *statistical hypothesis*, is the hypothesis of no difference or no relationship.

Whenever a statistical test is used to test a hypothesis, a decision is made either to reject or not to reject the hypothesis. In either case, there is the possibility that an error has been made because the true value of the parameter(s) will not be known, because the entire population is not measured. If a researcher rejects the hypothesis, it is possible that a true hypothesis is being rejected. If a hypothesis is not rejected, it is possible that a false hypothesis is not being rejected.

The test of a specific hypothesis will yield one of four possible results, based on the actual situation in the population and the decision of the researcher. This may be

		True	False
Researcher's Decision	Accept	Correct	Error
	Reject	Error	Correct

FIGURE 17.3 The Four Possible Outcomes in Hypothesis Testing

diagrammed in a 2 × 2 table, as in Figure 17.3. The columns in this figure represent the situation in the population, which will never be known for certain. The rows indicate the researcher's decision relative to the hypothesis, and the statements in the box indicate whether the researcher's decision is correct or in error.

If a true hypothesis is not rejected or a false hypothesis is rejected, there is no error. The other two alternatives result in errors—namely, a true hypothesis is rejected or a false hypothesis is not rejected. The error of rejecting a true hypothesis is referred to as a **Type I error,** or alpha (α) error. This is because if a null hypothesis is rejected, the probability of having made an error equals the significance (α) level. The error of failing to reject a false hypothesis is called a **Type II error,** or beta (β) error. Its probability is somewhat complicated to calculate and depends on a combination of factors. In any one statistical test, there is the possibility of making only one type of error, because the researcher either rejects or fails to reject the hypothesis. Generally, when a statistical test is computed, reducing the risk of one type of error increases the risk of the other type of error.

> In hypothesis testing there are two possible errors, rejecting a true hypothesis or failing to reject a false one. Once the decision is made on the hypothesis, there is the possibility of having made only one type of error.

Inferences from Statistics to Parameters: A Review

Considerable space has been devoted to the discussion of the basic ideas of inferential statistics and relatively elementary examples. The reason for this is that these concepts provide the foundation for testing hypotheses using statistical analyses, which are used so extensively in educational research. There are many specific inferential statistical procedures, and there are numerous statistics texts that describe these very well. Some statistical procedures are quite complex, at least computationally, but whenever inferential statistics are used the basic reasoning is the same. It is a chain of reasoning used to make decisions when testing hypotheses and estimating parameters. Any reader who masters this reasoning is well on the way to understanding statistical analysis.

When a random sample is used to represent a population, the inference is from the statistics of the sample to the parameters of the population. The chain of reasoning, illustrated

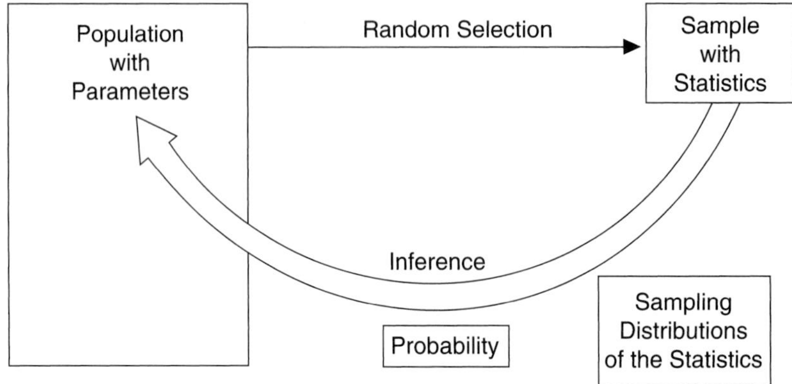

(1) We have a population and we want to make decisions about measures of the population, namely, parameters.

(2) We select a random sample and compute measures of the sample, which are statistics.

(3) The statistics reflect the corresponding parameters and sampling fluctuation.

(4) We observe the statistics, which are the facts that we have, and infer back to the parameters in the light of the sampling distributions and probability.

FIGURE 17.4 Chain of Reasoning for Inferential Statistics

in Figure 17.4, is linked as follows: The researcher has a population and wants to know something about the descriptive measures of this population—the parameters. It is not feasible to measure the entire population, so a random sample is drawn. The descriptive measures of the sample are statistics, which are calculated. Because the sample is a random sample, the statistics reflect the parameters within the limits of random sampling fluctuation. It is at this point that the sampling distributions of statistics come in. If the sampling distribution of a statistic is known, it is also known how the statistic behaves—that is, how it fluctuates due to random sampling. The appropriate sampling distribution for a specific statistic has been determined by mathematical theory, and commonly used sampling distributions have been tabled in standard form.

From the information of the statistic and its sampling distribution, we reason back to the parameter. The parameters are never known for certain (unless the entire population is measured, in which case there is no inference or need for inferential statistics). Decisions about parameters are made through testing hypotheses and estimating parameters, the latter with a confidence interval.

As mentioned earlier, there are many specific statistical tests used in analyzing data. There are also numerous sampling distributions that are used, depending, of course, on the specific statistic. This is not a statistics text, so there is no intent to develop statistical mastery. However, in the remaining part of the chapter, a compendium of some of the more commonly used statistical procedures is provided. The different statistical tests that apply under different conditions are discussed. Sampling distributions other than the normal distribution are also mentioned as they apply for specific tests. In each case, the hypothesis will be indicated. Most data analyses for research projects are done on a computer, so the important point for any researcher is to understand the analysis.

Parametric Analyses

Undoubtedly the most frequently used analyses in educational research are **parametric analyses,** so called because a set of assumptions, called the **parametric assumptions,** are required for their application. The example of testing the hypothesis about the mean weight of fourth-graders, discussed earlier, involved a parametric analysis.

The parametric assumptions can be summarized as follows:

1. Measurement of the dependent variable, the variable whose data are being analyzed, is on at least an interval scale.

2. The observations or scores are independent, which means that the score of one individual is not influenced by the score of any other.[3]

3. The scores (dependent variable) are selected from a population distribution that is normally distributed. Actually, this assumption is required only if sample size is small—less than thirty.

4. When two or more populations are being studied, they have homogeneous variance. This means that the populations being studied have about the same dispersion in their distributions.

With more complex parametric procedures, additional assumptions may be required, but those listed here are the basic assumptions. (Any assumptions involving distributions refer to the population distributions.)

The *t*-Distribution: Another Sampling Distribution

In the discussion about a hypothesized population mean, the normal distribution was used as the sampling distribution of the sample mean—the statistic. Actually, if the sample standard deviation is used to estimate the population standard deviation, the appropriate sampling distribution is not the normal distribution. Rather, it is a family of distributions called the student *t*-distributions or, simply, ***t*-distributions.**

The *t*-distributions are identified by *degrees of freedom* (*df*) values. In an analysis, the degrees of freedom are the number of ways the data are free to vary. Operationally, degrees of freedom are determined by subtracting the number of restrictions placed on the data from the number of scores. When testing a hypothesis about a population mean, the sample mean is computed, which requires the summing of the sample scores. Once $n - 1$ of the scores are determined, the nth score, too, is uniquely determined, because it must provide the remainder for the sum. Thus, the degrees of freedom are $n - 1$.

Like the normal distribution, the t-distributions are symmetrical and bell-shaped. As degrees of freedom increase, the t-distributions become more and more like the normal. Usually, if the degrees of freedom exceed 120, the normal distribution is used as an adequate approximation for the t-distribution. The t-distributions are given in standard form in Table B of Appendix 3. Degrees of freedom must be considered in their use; this will be illustrated in the following example.

> The t-distributions comprise a family of distributions that are the sampling distributions for many statistics. Each t-distribution is determined by a degrees-of-freedom value.

EXAMPLE 17.1

A Science Achievement Example Involving the t-Distribution

Suppose that it is known that over the years the science achievement of seventh-graders in a school has stabilized, and this is evidenced by a mean performance of 82.5 on a standardized end-of-the-year science test. The teachers are interested in whether or not individualized science instruction will affect this measure of achievement. A random sample of 31 seventh-graders is selected for a class taught by individualized instruction. At the close of the school year, these students are tested using the standardized test.

The null hypothesis being tested is "The population science test mean of seventh-graders taught by individualized instruction equals that of seventh-graders taught by the usual instruction in this school." The mean of students taught by usual instruction is known to be 82.5, so the null hypothesis can be written:

$$H_0: \mu_1 = 82.5 \text{ or } H_0: \mu_1 - 82.5 = 0$$

It should be noted that the population of seventh-graders taught by individualized instruction is a hypothetical population, but the thirty-one students in the class so taught do comprise a sample of that population. Also, at the beginning of the study, it was not hypothesized that individualized instruction would be less or more effective than the usual instruction. So, when testing the null hypothesis, the rejection region will be located in both tails of the sampling distribution. The .05 level of significance is used.

The sample data are as follows: the mean, $\overline{X} = 87.0$, and the standard deviation of the thirty-one science test scores is 9.5. The statistic to be tested is the sample mean, and the standard error of this statistic (the standard deviation of its sampling distribution) is found by:

$$s_x = \frac{s}{\sqrt{n}} = \frac{9.5}{\sqrt{31}} = \frac{9.5}{5.56} = 1.71$$

The appropriate sampling distribution is the *t*-distribution with $n - 1$, or 30, degrees of freedom.

The computation for the statistical test is:

$$t = \frac{\overline{X} - \mu}{s_x} = \frac{87.0 - 82.5}{1.71} = \frac{4.5}{1.71} = 2.63$$

The μ is the hypothesized value of the population mean if H_0 is true. The computation provides a value (sometimes called the *t*-value) in standard score form. It is the standard score of the statistic, in this case the sample mean, in its sampling distribution.

To check the value of 2.63 in the *t*-distribution table we use the *t*-distribution with 30 degrees of freedom. Going to Table B and to the row for 30 *df*, we find the critical value for level of significance .05, two-tailed test (the rejection region for H_0 is in both tails as noted above), to be 2.042. The computed test statistic (the *t*-value above) of 2.63 exceeds this critical value, hence, the statistical test is statistically significant and we reject the null hypothesis.

The probability statement is:

> The probability that the sample mean of 87.0 would have appeared due to random sampling fluctuation, if the population mean of seventh-graders taught by individualized instruction is 82.5, is less than .05.

Hence, we reject the null hypothesis and conclude that the population mean on the science test is not 82.5. The difference of 4.5 points between the sample mean and the hypothesized value of the mean is too great to attribute to chance (random sampling fluctuation). Because the sample mean is different from the mean for the usual instruction, and the statistical test was significant, we can conclude that the effect of individualized science instruction is not the same as the effect of the usual method of instruction for seventh-graders in this school.

Before converting seventh-grade instruction in the school to individualized instruction, the teachers might ask, "How much of a difference from the usual instruction may we expect?" The mean for the sample was 4.5 points greater than the established mean, but the sample mean is subject to random sampling fluctuation. So, we build a 95 percent confidence interval for the mean of the seventh-graders taught by individualized instruction. This interval provides an estimate of the performance on the test that might be expected if instruction is individualized in the future.

We have all the information that is needed to construct the confidence interval. The formula is:

$$\overline{X} \pm (\text{C.V.})s_{\overline{x}}$$

and substituting in we have:

$$87.0 \pm 2.042\ (1.71)$$

$$87.0 \pm 3.49$$

or essentially, the interval goes from 83.5 to 90.5. We are 95 percent confident that the interval 83.5 to 90.5 contains the population mean of seventh-graders taught by individualized instruction.

On the low end of this interval, the estimated mean is only one point greater than the established mean; on the high end eight points greater. It appears that individualized instruction does improve performance on the science test. However, it remains for the teachers to decide whether such improvement is worth the added effort and resources required for individualizing instruction. The confidence interval provides information for making that decision. The gain in the mean performance may be only around one point, and it is very unlikely that it is greater than eight points.

Analysis of Variance (ANOVA)

Analysis of variance (ANOVA) is an inferential statistics procedure by which a researcher can test the null hypothesis that two or more population means are equal (H_0: $\mu_1 = \mu_2 = \ldots = \mu_k$). Usually, it is not used for only two means, because a *t*-test for the difference between two means can be used. The sample means, one corresponding to each population mean, are computed and tested simultaneously for any statistically significant differences between them.

The null hypothesis in ANOVA is tested by comparing two estimates of variance.[4] These are put into a ratio form, called the *F*-ratio or *F*-value. The sampling distribution for the ratio of two variances is the ***F*-distribution** (named after R. A. Fisher). The *F*-distribution is a family of distributions that are generally not symmetrical. They are located between zero and plus infinity, so the numerical values of the distribution are all positive. It requires two degrees-of-freedom values, one for each of the variance estimates in the ratio, to determine the correct distribution. The *F*-distributions are given in Table D of Appendix 3; their use is illustrated with a subsequent example.

> ANOVA tests the null hypothesis that two or more population means are equal. A ratio of two variance estimates is computed, and this ratio has as its sampling distribution the *F*-distribution, determined by two degrees-of-freedom values.

ANOVAs can include one or more independent variables. If one independent variable is included, the ANOVA is a *one-way* ANOVA. If an experiment were conducted in which there were four experimental treatments, there would be four levels of the independent variable, experimental treatment. The null hypothesis would be H_0: $\mu_1 = \mu_2 = \mu_3 = \mu_4$; a sample mean for each of the four treatments would be computed and these means would be tested. This would be a one-way ANOVA because only one independent variable is included.

If two independent variables are included simultaneously in an ANOVA, the analysis is called a *two-way* ANOVA. In this case, there is a null hypothesis for each of the independent variables, and an *F*-ratio is computed for each of the groups of sample means from the two independent variables. It may also be possible to compute a statistical test for the interaction between the two independent variables. (Interaction is a combined effect of the independent variables on the dependent variable.) If this is done, the null hypothesis of no interaction is tested. As many F-ratios are computed as there are null hypotheses tested. In a two-way ANOVA, there are at most three null hypotheses, one for each independent variable and one for the interaction.

There are also three-way and more complex ANOVAs, which means that more independent variables are included in a single analysis. When more complex ANOVAs are used, increasing numbers of independent variables are included, although in educational research it would be rare to include more than four or five independent variables in a single analysis. The numbers of possible interactions and their complexities (including more than two independent variables in a single interaction) also increase. Data from the factorial designs discussed in the chapter on experimental designs are usually analyzed by what are called *factorial ANOVAs*. This simply means including the two or more independent variables simultaneously in the same analysis.

EXAMPLE 17.2

One-Way ANOVA: A Teaching History Example

Consider an experiment in which three types of instruction are used for teaching American history—T_1, T_2, and T_3. Random samples of history students are assigned to the three types and, after a period of instruction, are tested on a common history exam. The independent variable is type of instruction. The dependent variable is performance or score on the history exam. The three random samples contain 25, 30, and 33 students, respectively, for T_1, T_2, and T_3.

The null hypothesis is H_0: $\mu_1 = \mu_2 = \mu_3$; that is, the population means of students taught by the three types of instruction are equal. The level of significance is set at .05. The sample means are found to be $\overline{X}_1 = 83$, $\overline{X}_2 = 72$, and $\overline{X}_3 = 80$, and the F-ratio from the ANOVA is $F = 4.93$.

To determine whether or not this F-ratio is statistically significant, we first need to identify the appropriate degrees of freedom associated with it. In this case, the *df* for the numerator of the F-ratio is 2, one less than the number of sample means. In determining the variance among sample means, the mean of all scores (called the *grand mean*) is computed, so one restriction is introduced. In general, for a one-way ANOVA, there are $k - 1$ *df* for the numerator if k is the number of sample means.

The *df* associated with the denominator of the F-ratio is 85. There is a total of 88 scores in the entire ANOVA. When computing the variance estimate for the denominator of the F-ratio, all 88 scores are used, but the mean for each sample is also used in the computation, so three restrictions are introduced. For a one-way ANOVA, there are $N - k$ *df* for the denominator of the F-ratio if N is the total number of scores in the analysis and k is the number of sample means.

Now we have a computed F-ratio of 4.93, with 2 and 85 degrees of freedom. Turning to Table D in Appendix 3, we go down the column for 2 *df* (the *df* for the numerator) to the row for 85 *df* (the *df* for the denominator). There is no row for 85 *df*, but there are rows for 60 *df* and 120 *df*. For each of these *df* values, there are actually four rows of critical values given, one for each of four significance levels. We select

α-level .05 and find that the critical value for 60 *df* is 3.15 and that for 120 *df* is 3.07. Because we have 85 *df*, the critical value is about 3.12, based on a straight-line interpolation between the two table values. Our computed F-ratio exceeds 3.12; therefore, it is statistically significant and the null hypothesis is rejected. The probability statement and the conclusion are as follows:

> *Probability statement:* The probability that the sample means would have occurred due to random sampling fluctuation, if the null hypothesis is true, is less than .05.
>
> *Conclusion:* The null hypothesis is rejected, and it is concluded that the population means are not all equal. This is the inference to the parameters. The types of instruction are not all equally effective, and we can conclude, at least, that T_1 is more effective than T_2.

If more than two sample means are tested and if the F-ratio is statistically significant, the ANOVA does not indicate where the significance lies; that is, only one pair of means may be significantly different, all pairs may be significantly different, or some pairs may be different. We know that at least the two extreme sample means are significantly different (hence, the foregoing conclusion). However, subsequent tests, *post hoc tests*, can be computed to determine specifically which means are significantly different from others. Statistics texts such as those listed near the end of the chapter contain descriptions of such post hoc tests.

A summary ANOVA table commonly is used for presenting results of an analysis of variance in a research report. A summary ANOVA table for the example above is found in Table 17.1. The content is described below the table. The "total" line may or may not be included. It shows that the *SS* and *df* of "between" and "within" add to those of "total." We do not compute a mean square for "total" because it is not used.

TABLE 17.1 Example Summary ANOVA Table

Source	*SS*	*df*	*MS*	*F*-Value
Between	36.48	2	18.24	4.93*
Within	314.50	85	3.70	
Total	350.98	87		

$^*p < .05$

In a one-way ANOVA the total variation is partitioned into two sources: (1) between the levels (groups) of the independent variable, in the example T_1, T_2, and T_3; and (2) within the groups of the independent variable.

SS stands for sum of squares, the numerator of a variance estimate.

Dividing SS by *df* gives a mean square, *MS*, which is a variance estimate.

The F-value is obtained by dividing the *MS* Between by the *MS* Within. The $p < .05$ (probability less than .05) indicates the F-value, 4.93, is statistically significant at the .05 level of significance.

EXAMPLE 17.3

ANOVA Computer Solution

Consider the PACT data set from the accompanying data disk. This is a random sample of 123 ninth-graders who took the PACT test. Suppose that a researcher was interested in knowing whether eligibility for the free or reduced price lunch program was related to performance on the science portion of the PACT test. Students were separated into three groups. Group 1 consisted of students who were eligible for free lunch, Group 2 was eligible for reduced price lunch, and Group 3 was students who were eligible for neither free nor reduced price lunch. The null hypothesis is:

$$H_0 : \mu_1 = \mu_2 = \mu_3$$

that is, the population means on the science test, variable SCISS05 on the data disk, are equal for the three groups of students.

Figure 17.5 contains SPSS output for the one-way ANOVA solution. The Descriptives indicate that the free lunch students (Group 1) have the lowest mean, the

FIGURE 17.5 SPSS Output for the ANOVA

Descriptives
SCISS05

Lunch	Mean	N	Std. Deviation
F	782.6186	97	30.2429
N	801.2000	10	13.0111
R	797.0833	12	9.2781
Total	785.6387	119	28.3969

ANOVA
SCISS05

	Sum of Squares	*df*	Mean Square	*F*	Sig.
Between Groups	4878.059	2	2439.029	3.134	.047
Within Groups	90275.403	116	778.236		
Total	95153.462	118			

Multiple Comparisons
Dependent Variable: SCISS05
LSD

		Mean			95% Confidence Interval	
(I) FRL	(J) FRL	Difference (I – J)	Std. Error	Sig.	Lower Bound	Upper Bound
1.00	2.00	−14.4648	8.5367	.093	−31.3729	2.4433
	3.00	−18.5814*	9.2653	.047	−36.9326	−.2303
2.00	1.00	14.4648	8.5367	.093	−2.4433	31.3729
	3.00	−4.1167	11.9447	.731	−27.7747	19.5414
3.00	1.00	18.5814*	9.2653	.047	.2303	36.9326
	2.00	4.1167	11.9447	.731	−19.5414	27.7747

*The mean difference is significant at the .05 level.

reduced price students (Group 2) have the middle mean, and those eligible for neither (Group 3) have the highest mean. In other words, the students who are the poorest economically have the lowest mean on the science test. The group with the highest economic level, as indicated by not being eligible for free or reduced price lunch, has the highest average score.

The ANOVA results show an F-ratio of 3.134 and a "Sig" of .047. The Sig value is the probability that the differences in the sample means would have occurred by chance if the null hypothesis were true. We compare the Sig value to the significance level to decide whether to reject the null hypothesis. The value .047 is less than the significance level of .05. Therefore, we reject the null hypothesis and conclude that the population means are not all equal.

We then conduct follow-up tests to see which pairs of sample means differ significantly. The Multiple Comparisons output indicates that, using the LSD method, only one pair-wise comparison had a Sig value that was less than .05. This is the comparison of Group 1 and Group 3. Our conclusion is that the population mean of students who were eligible for free lunch is different from the population mean of the students who were not eligible for free or reduced price lunch. Notice that the confidence interval for the difference in the means of Groups 1 and 3 does not span zero, but zero is within the other two confidence intervals.

Nonparametric Analyses

As indicated earlier, the use of parametric analyses requires certain assumptions about the populations under study. Interval scale measurement is also required so that means can be computed. If these assumptions are not met, it is more appropriate to use nonparametric analyses. These analyses do not require interval scale measurement; ordinal and nominal scale data can be analyzed. Also, for most nonparametric analyses, assumptions about the shape of the population distribution are not required. For that reason, they are often used when small sample sizes are involved.

Nonparametric analyses are part of inferential statistics, so the chain of reasoning for inferential statistics applies. Hypotheses are tested and can be stated in null form. The statistics involved are not means but statistics such as frequencies. Whatever the case, the statistics are still measures of the one or more samples.

> *Nonparametric analyses* require few if any assumptions about the population under study. They can be used with ordinal and nominal scale data.

The Chi-Square (χ^2) Test and Distribution

The most commonly used sampling distribution for statistics generated by nonparametric analysis is the **chi-square (χ^2) distribution.** Like the t-distribution, the χ^2 distribution comprises a family of distributions, each specific distribution identified by one degrees-of-freedom value. Unlike the *t*-distribution, the χ^2 distribution is not symmetrical. Theoretically, it extends from zero to plus infinity. The basic reasoning for using the sampling distribution is the same for the χ^2 distribution as for other distributions, such as the normal and *t*-distributions. However, because of the nonsymmetrical nature of the χ^2 distribution, the rejection region when testing hypotheses is usually contained entirely in the right-hand tail of the distribution.

Numerous hypotheses can be tested by computing a statistic called the χ^2 value. This statistic involves the comparison of observed and expected frequencies—the latter being anticipated on the basis of a null hypothesis—within categories. The χ^2 value is then distributed as the χ^2 distribution with the appropriate degrees of freedom. If a computed χ^2 value exceeds the tabled value (critical value) for a designated significance level, the statistical test is significant and the null hypothesis being tested is rejected.

A χ^2 test can be used to test hypotheses about how well a sample distribution fits some theoretical or hypothesized distribution. Such a test is also called a *goodness-of-fit test;* that is, it tests how well the sample distribution fits the hypothesized distribution. For example, we could test a hypothesis that a population distribution from which a sample was selected is normally distributed. The null hypothesis is that the population distribution is normally distributed or stated as a hypothesis of no difference: "There is no difference between the population distribution and the normal distribution." The statistical test tests whether the sample observations are within random sampling fluctuation of coming from a normal distribution. If the χ^2 value is statistically significant, we would reject the null hypothesis.

One common use of the χ^2 test is with **contingency tables,** which are two-dimensional tables with one variable on each dimension. Each of the variables has two or more categories, and the data are the sample frequencies in the categories. The null hypothesis of independence—that is, no relationship—between the variables is tested. The following example involves a contingency table.

EXAMPLE 17.4

Contingency Table Using the χ^2 Test

At a liberal arts college, a researcher is interested in student attitudes toward compulsory attendance at college convocations. A random sample of students is drawn from each of the four undergraduate classes at the college. Equal numbers need not be selected from the classes. The students in the sample then respond to "agree," "undecided," or "disagree" to compulsory attendance.

The null hypothesis is that the four class populations do not differ in their attitude toward compulsory attendance. Another way of stating the null hypothesis is that class and attitude toward compulsory attendance are independent. This hypothesis does not imply what the extent of agreement or disagreement is; it implies only that the class populations do not differ. Table 17.2 represents sample data in a 3×4 contingency table.

Table 17.2 contains observed frequencies or sample data. To compute a χ^2 test, expected or theoretical frequencies are required. These expected frequencies are calculated from the sample data by using the marginal totals. The calculations will not

TABLE 17.2 Observed Sample Frequencies of Response to Compulsory Attendance at College Convocations

	Category			
Class	*Agree*	*Undecided*	*Disagree*	*Total*
Freshman	12	48	20	80
Sophomore	7	20	33	60
Junior	6	19	35	60
Senior	5	3	32	40
Total	30	90	120	240

be presented here, but Table 17.3 contains these expected frequencies, based on what would be expected if the null hypothesis is true.

The expected frequencies are found by this formula:

$$E = \text{(Row total) (Column total) / Grand total}$$

There is an expected frequency for each row–column combination.

In general, contingency tables have $(r - 1)$ times $(c - 1)$ degrees of freedom, where r and c are the number of rows and the number of columns, respectively, in the contingency table. For the example, the χ^2 test has 6 degrees of freedom. Suppose that we set the significance level at .05. The formula for computing the χ^2 value is given by:

$$\chi^2 = \sum_{i=1}^{k} \frac{(O_i - E_i)^2}{E_i}$$

TABLE 17.3 Expected Frequencies of Response to Compulsory Attendance at College Convocations

	Category			
Class	*Agree*	*Undecided*	*Disagree*	*Total*
Freshman	(12) 10	(48) 30.5	(20) 40	80
Sophomore	(7) 7.5	(20) 22.5	(33) 30	60
Junior	(6) 7.5	(19) 22.5	(35) 30	60
Senior	(5) 5	(3) 15.5	(32) 20	40
Total	30	90	120	240

Note: Observed frequencies from Table 17.2 are in parentheses.

where O = observed frequency
E = expected frequency
k = number of categories, groupings, or cells

When a contingency table is used, $k = r \times c$, the number of cells in the table, which for the example is 12.

The computed χ^2 value for testing the null hypothesis is 33.59, based on the data in Table 17.3. We turn to Table C of Appendix 3, which contains the χ^2 distributions. This table contains critical values. The columns represent area to the right of the critical value point. The rows vary by degrees of freedom. The drawing of the distribution shows how the area is divided.

We set the level of significance at .05, so we go down the column headed .05 to the row corresponding with 6 *df* and find a critical value of 12.59. Thus, the statistical test is significant and the probability statement and conclusion are as follows:

> *Probability statement:* The probability that the sample responses would have occurred by chance if class and attitude toward compulsory attendance at college convocations are independent in the population is less than .05.
>
> *Conclusion:* Class and attitude toward compulsory attendance at college convocations are related (not independent) in the college student population. The null hypothesis is rejected.

An inspection of the frequencies shows that upper-class students tend to have higher frequencies of "disagree" than expected, and lower-class students have higher frequencies of "undecided" than expected.

The foregoing example illustrates the use of a nonparametric analysis involving the χ^2 test. There are numerous nonparametric analyses, some of which are listed in a table later in this chapter. Specific formulas for computation can be obtained from any applied statistics text. However, the underlying reasoning of inferential statistics still applies.

Correlational Analysis

Correlation was discussed in the previous chapter as a descriptive statistic that is a measure of the relationship between two variables. We can conduct inferential **correlational analyses** on correlation coefficients and regression coefficients to test hypotheses concerning them. The most frequently tested hypothesis is that the correlation in the population is zero. This is the hypothesis that two variables are independent, that there is no correlation between them.

Whether correlation from the sample is statistically significant is largely a function of the sample size. The critical values of the correlation coefficient for rejecting the hypothesis that the population correlation is zero are given in Table E of Appendix 3. The levels of significance are given in the columns and the degrees of freedom are in the rows. The degrees of freedom for this hypothesis are $n - 2$ because two variables are being considered. If the absolute value of the correlation coefficient equals or exceeds the tabled value, then the null hypothesis is rejected at the specified level of significance. The interesting point is that a particular correlation coefficient may be statistically significant for one sample size and not for another. Even correlations near zero can be significant with a large sample size.

EXAMPLE 17.5

Testing the Hypothesis of No Correlation in the Population

In the preceding chapter we discussed correlation as a descriptive statistic using the Ohio Teachers data set. We correlated the average teacher salary in the district (SALARY) with the average years of teacher experience (EXP), the number of teachers in the district (NUM), and the percent of teachers who had at least a master's degree (PMAST). The matrix of correlations is repeated here as Figure 17.6.

In order to test the hypotheses about the correlations, we need to consider the probabilities, *p*-values, which SPSS labels as Sig. The correlations are based on 610 school districts. This is a large number so we can expect that some relatively weak correlations may still be statistically significant. Inspection of Figure 17.6 reveals that four of the six correlations are significant and two are not. Salary is significantly correlated with the percent of teachers with master's degrees and the number of teachers in the district. The percent with master's degrees is significantly correlated with teacher experience. Finally, average years of experience is significantly correlated with the number of teachers, although this correlation coefficient is very near zero and the significance is due to the large sample size.

We should note that the 610 districts are really the population of districts in Ohio. Inferential statistics are used with random samples and not with population data. Strictly speaking, the only way that inferential statistics would be appropriate in this example would be if we were to consider the data as coming from a randomly representative year.

FIGURE 17.6 SPSS Output for Analysis of Correlations

Correlations

		PMAST	SALARY	EXP	NUM
PMAST	Pearson Correlation	1.000	.435**	.307**	.056
	Sig. (2-tailed)		.000	.000	.169
	N	610	610	610	610
SALARY	Pearson Correlation	.435**	1.000	.044	.335**
	Sig. (2-tailed)	.000		.275	.000
	N	610	610	610	610
EXP	Pearson Correlation	.307**	.044	1.000	−.110**
	Sig. (2-tailed)	.000	.275		.006
	N	610	610	610	610
NUM	Pearson Correlation	.056	.335**	−.110**	1.000
	Sig. (2-tailed)	.169	.000	.006	
	N	610	610	610	610

**Correlation is significant at the 0.01 level (2-tailed).

Analysis of Covariance

A parametric statistical analysis that involves correlation is the **analysis of covariance.** In Chapter 6, the matter of using a statistical adjustment to enhance control when conducting research was discussed. Analysis of covariance is a procedure for statistical adjustment or statistical control over variation.

Analysis of covariance is closely related to analysis of variance. Essentially, it is analysis of variance with the dependent variable scores adjusted on the basis of the dependent variable's relationship to some other relevant variable. This relationship, of course, involves the correlation between the dependent variable and the other variable. The adjusted dependent variable scores are adjusted so they are independent of the influence of this other relevant variable, called the *covariate.*

> *Analysis of covariance* is a procedure by which statistical adjustments are made to a dependent variable. These adjustments are based on the correlation between the dependent variable and another variable, called the covariate.

The null hypothesis in the analysis of covariance is that the *adjusted* population means are equal. It can be written as the null hypothesis in analysis of variance, $H_0: \mu_1 = \mu_2 = \ldots = \mu_k$, except that now the μ's represent adjusted population means. As in the analysis of variance, the statistic generated is the ratio of two variances, and the appropriate sampling distribution is the F-distribution. The statistical reasoning is the same, except that conclusions and inferences are now made to adjusted population dependent variable means.

Analysis of covariance is especially useful for situations in which experimental or design control over an extraneous or mediating variable is impossible or undesirable. A researcher, especially one who works in a school setting, often must take intact groups such as classes for research studies. Analysis of covariance may be used to make adjustments, although it should be noted that analysis of covariance does not make the groups equivalent.

Selecting an Appropriate Statistical Analysis

Selecting an appropriate statistical analysis depends on a number of factors, which can be summarized by the answers to three questions:

1. What information do we want?
2. What are the levels of measurement of the variables, especially the dependent variable?
3. What assumptions are met?

The answer to the first question determines whether descriptive statistics or inferential statistics will be used, or possibly both. The statement of the research problem usually gives adequate direction to answer this question. The answers to questions (2) and (3) determine the kinds of analyses (the statistics and statistical tests that can be computed) appropriate given the data.

When inferential statistics are to be used, the specific statistical analysis or statistical test depends on the hypotheses to be tested, the levels of measurement of the variables, and the assumptions that can be met. If the dependent variable is measured on an interval scale and the independent variable is categorical, either ordinal or nominal measurement, parametric analyses would be used. Testing hypotheses about means would be examples of using a parametric analysis. When less than interval scale measurement is attained or the parametric assumptions cannot be met, nonparametric analyses are used. If we are testing hypotheses about the relationship of two variables, we would use a correlation test, the specific test depending on the measurement of the variables. Table 17.4 contains a summary of statistical tests and hypotheses that can be tested by the tests. When a *t*-test is indicated, a statistical test involving the *t*-distribution as the sampling distribution is being used. If sample size is large (around 120), the normal distribution is used as an adequate approximation for the *t*-distribution. The table also contains two nonparametric tests not discussed earlier.

Figure 17.7 contains a decision tree for selecting an appropriate statistical test. There are many statistical tests in inferential statistics, and this figure presents a limited number

TABLE 17.4 Some Common Statistical Tests Used in Inferential Statistics

Statistical Test	Hypothesis Tested
Parametric Tests	
t-test (or use of normal distribution)	About a single mean $H: \mu = \alpha$ Difference between two means $H: \mu = \mu_2$ or $H: \mu - \mu_2 = 0$, used for both independent and dependent samples but formulas differ.
Analysis of variance (one-way)	Two or more population means are equal. $H: \mu_1 = \mu_2 = \cdots = \mu_k$, from the levels of a single independent variable.
Analysis of variance (two-way)	Two or more population means are equal; two independent variables included, and there is a hypothesis for each and their interaction.
Analysis of covariance	Two or more population means are equal after being adjusted for the effect of the covariate.
Nonparametric Tests	
χ^2 test, goodness of fit	A population distribution has a hypothesized shape.
χ^2 test, independence (contingency table)	Two variables are independent in the population.
χ^2 test, median test	The medians of two or more populations are equal.
Mann-Whitney *U*-test	There is no difference in the scores from two populations.
Correlational Tests	
t-test (or use of normal distribution)	The population correlation coefficient is zero. $H: \rho = 0$
Fisher's *z*-transformation test, which uses the normal distribution	The population correlation coefficient is a specified value. $H: \rho = \alpha$ Two population correlation coefficients are equal. $H: \rho_1 = \rho_2$ or $H: \rho_1 - \rho_2 = 0$.

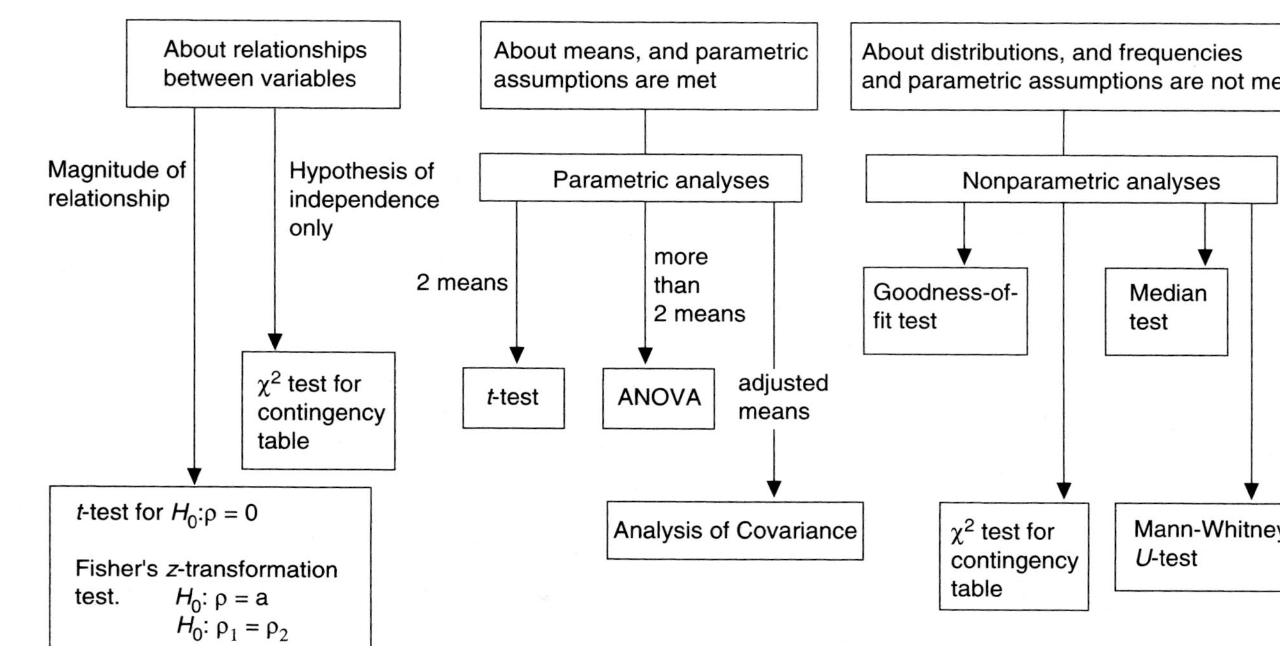

FIGURE 17.7 Decision Tree for Selecting an Appropriate Statistical Test

of those most commonly used. The top row of boxes indicates what the hypotheses are about. For example, if we are testing a hypothesis about four means, the parametric assumptions are met, and we are not adjusting the means, we would use ANOVA. Whatever the statistical test used, the underlying reasoning of inferential statistics remains the same, that of making inferences from the sample statistics to the population parameters. It is important to keep this reasoning in mind and not lose it in the technicalities of doing the statistical test.

Comments about Statistical Analysis

Statistical analysis is a tool for understanding data. Inferential statistics are used to project the sample results to the populations from which the random samples were chosen. Working with random samples rather than the entire population is tremendously cost effective and most research would never be done if we were limited to using population data. However, there are some areas of concern that should be mentioned.

Assumptions underlie each inferential technique. Often the assumptions are that the sample is random, that measurement of the dependent variable is on an interval scale, and that comparison groups have equal population variances. The assumptions vary across different statistical techniques. When the assumptions of an inferential statistical test are not met, the results of the analysis can be inaccurate and misleading.

Practical significance is not the same as statistical significance. **Statistical significance** means that the results are not likely to be due to sampling fluctuation. The results may or may not have practical importance. Statistical significance is a necessary but not sufficient condition for practical significance. Citing earlier examples in this chapter, the researcher who was studying childhood obesity had a sample mean of 77 and the hypothesized value of the population mean was 75. This difference was statistically significant, but a 2-pound difference probably has no practical importance. On the other hand in the ANOVA example, students who were eligible for free lunches had a mean on the science section of the PACT test that was roughly 20 points less than the mean of students who were not eligible for free or reduced price lunch. This difference is statistically significant and most likely is of practical significance.

Statistical power refers to the probability of rejecting the null hypothesis when it is false. Researchers want to have sufficient power to detect differences between comparison groups. It would be a shame to conduct a randomized comparative experiment and then not be able to find significant differences between the treatment group and the control group when the treatment really did make a difference. Statistical power can be increased by using large samples rather than small samples, minimizing the variance within comparison groups with control variables such as gender or ability level, and eliminating extraneous variables. When designing a study it is wise to consult a statistics textbook such as one of those listed at the end of the chapter to ensure that your proposed sample size has adequate statistical power.

The foregoing discussion of statistical analysis was brief and considered only more commonly used and relatively elementary procedures. In fact, the analyses discussed in

A misinterpretation of statistical results is to routinely interpret statistical significance as of practical importance.

this chapter are limited to **univariate analyses,** which means that only one dependent variable is included in an analysis. There are analyses, called multivariate analyses, that include two or more dependent variables simultaneously. Multivariate analyses require quite complex statistical calculations, and the interpretations of results also are complicated because often the analyses create artificial variables from combinations of the dependent variables. Such analyses appear quite frequently in the research literature, in part because the availability of computers and software has greatly enhanced their application. Advanced statistics texts and entire books address multivariate analysis topics.

The original analysis of the data from a research study is called a **primary analysis,** and often this is the only analysis ever done. **Secondary analyses** may be useful, and these are basically of two forms. One is to reanalyze the data for the purpose of addressing the original research questions with better statistical procedures. The other form is to answer new research questions by additional analysis of the original data—in essence, extracting more information from the data. Doctoral dissertation research often produces large quantities of data, and not all of the information is used for the dissertation. Secondary analysis can be useful for extended analyses of such data.

Meta-Analysis

Meta-analysis is a statistical procedure for synthesizing research results across studies that address a common topic or issue. The term essentially means analysis "after or beyond" the original analyses. Meta-analysis is the analysis of analyses, completed on a rather large collection of quantitative studies. The findings from the studies are synthesized in order to draw general conclusions.

Meta-analysis requires a common measure for expressing the results across studies, and the measure typically used is **effect size** (*ES*), as suggested by Glass (1977). Essentially, an effect size is a standard score (*z*-score) of the mean of one group referenced in the distribution of another group, often a control group. Thus, an effect size is a score expressed in standard deviation units. When results are being summarized across studies involving experimental and control groups, the effect size may be defined as:

$$ES = \frac{\overline{X}_E - \overline{X}_c}{S_c}$$

where $\overline{X}_E$ = mean of the experimental group
$\overline{X}_c$ = mean of the control group
S_c = standard deviation of the control group

One of the advantages of meta-analysis is that it provides this common measure, effect size. Studies on the same research topic typically vary in the measures, designs, and statistics used, and meta-analysis provides a common base for comparing results. However, not all meta-analyses use the standard deviation of one group in computing effect size. In a meta-analysis of the effectiveness of after-school programs, Scott-Little, Hamann, and Jurs (2002) computed effect size by subtracting the mean of nonparticipants from the mean of participants, and dividing by a "pooled" standard deviation, which was the average of the standard deviations of the two groups.

One possible difficulty with meta-analysis is that results may be combined from studies so different that they should not be combined. In an attempt to avoid this difficulty, it is necessary to establish criteria for the inclusion of studies in a meta-analysis. Criteria are necessary in order to ensure some level of similarity across studies, and also to avoid including poorly done studies that may bias the results of the meta-analysis.

Rohrbeck, Ginsburg-Block, Fantuzzo, and Miller (2003) conducted a meta-analysis of studies of the effects of peer-assisted learning interventions done with elementary school students. The review of the literature yielded ninety studies that met their selection criteria:

1. The study was published in a peer-reviewed journal article.
2. Participants were elementary school students.
3. The focus was on peer tutoring.
4. There was an empirical intervention and a reported outcome.
5. The intervention was conducted in a school.
6. The targeted subject matter was academic.

Additionally, the studies had to meet certain design criteria:

7. The study evaluated a peer tutoring intervention (as opposed to simply describing one).
8. The study used an experimental or quasi-experimental design.

There were eighty-one studies that met all eight criteria.

Effect size was defined as the difference between treatment and comparison group scores divided by the pooled standard deviation. An average effect size was found for each study and these were weighted by the inverse of its variance to account for differences in sample sizes.

The overall average effect size was 0.59, which is a moderate effect size.[5] The researchers determined that differences in effect sizes were associated with minority status, location, and grade level, but not with SES or content area. Many other theoretically derived hypotheses were tested. The results were informative and yielded implications for further research and for practice.

> Meta-analysis requires a quantitative measure of effect size and criteria should be established for including studies in the meta-analysis.

Meta-analyses have advantages, one already mentioned being the common measure, or metric, effect size. Because of this, the focus is on the magnitude of an effect if one exists. Studies included in a meta-analysis usually have enough information about study characteristics so that the effects of different characteristics can be determined. Meta-analyses in education are quite easily located because "meta-analysis" is an ERIC descriptor. So, it can be combined with the descriptor of a topic to search *CIJE* and *RIE* databases. Meta-analyses not only provide synthesis of results but also contain quite extensive reference lists that can be explored.

However, meta-analysis is not without potential pitfalls. Research results in education are sometimes inconsistent, at times even contradictory, and studies must be reviewed carefully for possible explanation of inconsistent results. There may be a tendency to exclude studies that do not support the conclusions of interest to the person doing the meta-analysis. Statistically nonsignificant results may be overlooked or, indeed, not reported in the literature.

Conducting a meta-analysis requires a substantial effort. Meta-analysis is not done by including five or so studies; some include upwards of sixty to seventy studies. Yet meta-analysis has proven useful and there is continued interest in conducting meta-analysis and extending its methodology.

> Meta-analysis is a statistical procedure used to synthesize the results across numerous independently conducted research studies.

Summary

This chapter provided an overview of inferential statistics, undoubtedly the most widely used collection of procedures for analyzing quantitative data in educational research. In inferential statistics, we attempt to infer from statistics, computed from sample data, to parameters, the measures of the population from which the sample was selected. In general, hypotheses about parameters are tested or parameters are estimated. The chain of reasoning in inferential statistics was identified and discussed in the chapter.

Descriptive statistics (discussed in Chapter 16) and inferential statistics provide for the researcher effective means for analyzing quantitative data. Statistics are a means to an end; they are not ends in themselves. In this sense they have a service function in educational research. Data analysis is greatly facilitated by the use of computers, and within recent years computers have become widely accessible.

As with Chapter 16, the intent of this chapter was to provide a rationale for the analyses of data and to review some of the more common analyses. There was no intention to elaborate on computational procedures or to have the reader perform statistical analyses. Numerous applied statistics texts are available that include detailed discussions of statistical procedures including computational formulas. The following is a sampling of such texts:

1. Glass, G. V., and Hopkins, K. D. (1995). *Statistical methods in education and psychology* (3rd ed.). Boston: Allyn & Bacon.

2. Hays, W. L. (2007). *Statistics* (6th ed.). New York: Holt, Rinehart and Winston.

3. Heiman, G. W. (2006). *Basic statistics for the behavioral sciences* (4th ed.). Boston: Houghton Mifflin.

4. Hinkle, D., Wiersma, W., and Jurs, S. (2003). *Applied statistics for the behavioral sciences* (5th ed.). Boston: Houghton Mifflin.

KEY CONCEPTS

Testing hypotheses
Estimating parameters
Interval estimate
Sampling distribution
Central limit theorem
Standard normal distribution
Level of significance
Confidence level
Null hypothesis
Type I error
Type II error
Parametric analyses
Parametric assumptions
t-distribution
Analysis of variance (ANOVA)
F-distribution
Nonparametric analyses
Chi-square (χ^2) distribution
Contingency table
Correlational analyses
Analysis of covariance
Statistical significance
Univariate analysis
Primary analysis
Secondary analysis
Meta-analysis
Effect size

EXERCISES

17.1 The end-of-year reading level of approximately 1000 first-grade students of a city school system is to be estimated. The entire population cannot be tested. Discuss how sampling and inferring from statistics to parameters would be used. Identify the statistic and parameter involved in this situation. Reconstruct the chain of reasoning used to arrive at some conclusion about the level of the entire first-grade population.

17.2 Distinguish between a statistic and a parameter in the context of inferential statistics. Discuss the role of the sampling distribution. Describe what is meant by a sampling distribution, and give an example of a sampling distribution.

17.3 Suppose a group of 150 teacher education students has been measured on three measures of scholastic achievement and a measure of performance on a professional knowledge exam. Thus, there are four dependent variables. In connection with what research questions would we do the following:

a. Compute only descriptive statistics for the four dependent variables?

b. Use inferential statistics?

c. Compute correlation coefficients between pairs of the dependent variables?

17.4 The mean science achievement on an objective test of a ninth-grade student population is hypothesized to be 85. A sample of twenty students is randomly selected from the population and given the science test. A *t*-test is then computed using the sample data, and the *t*-value is found to be 3.12. Using the .05 level of significance, find the appropriate *t*-distribution and decide whether or not you would reject the hypothesis. What value of *t* is necessary to reject the hypothesis at the .05 level?

17.5 A researcher is estimating the mean performance score of a large fifth-grade population on a science achievement test. A large sample of size 400 is selected and tested, and the sample mean is found to be 88. A 95 percent confidence interval is constructed to be 86.5 to 89.5. Suppose the standard deviation of the population was estimated by the sample standard deviation. What is the appropriate sampling distribution for constructing the interval? Would this sampling distribution change if the sample size had been 25? If so, how? Suppose, with the given mean, the researcher had constructed a confidence interval of 85.5 to 89.5. Do you think there might have been an error and, if so, why? If a 90 percent confidence interval had been constructed, would this interval be shorter or longer than three units?

17.6 A study is being done in which the professional attitudes of four different populations of teachers are being surveyed. Random samples are selected from the populations and measured on an attitude inventory that has interval scale measurement. Thus, means are computed for all samples. An analysis of variance is used to analyze the data. What is the null hypothesis being tested? Suppose we are interested not only in differences in attitudes among the four populations but also in differences between male and female teachers. Could the possibility of such a difference be determined in the same analysis? If so, explain how the ANOVA would be extended.

17.7 Suppose we have a variable measured on an ordinal scale with five categories. Four independent samples are measured on this variable. The hypothesis is that these four samples were drawn from a common population. A chi-square test is computed and found to be statistically significant at $\alpha = .05$. What is the conclusion about the populations from which the samples were selected? Give the associated probability statement.

17.8 Suppose in Exercise 17.7 the variable is attitude toward school and that the four samples were students selected from grades four through seven. (The data are in a 5×4 contingency table.) State the hypothesis of independence. If the χ^2 test is significant at $\alpha = .05$, what is the conclusion? What if the χ^2 test is not statistically significant?

17.9 For the following situations, identify the descriptive statistics or the statistical test that would be computed. If a statistical test is used, identify the hypothesis being tested.

a. All fifth-grade students in a school are measured with an achievement test, and the teachers want to know where the scores are located on the scale of measurement and the spread of the scores. The test scores have interval scale measurement.

b. Math test scores are available for all students in a junior high school, and an attitude-toward-school inventory is administered to the entire student body. The teachers want to know if there is a relationship between math test performance and attitude.

c. A random sample of fifty students enrolled in a high school is administered a math test and an attitude-toward-school inventory. The teachers want to know if there is a relationship between math test performance and attitude.

d. An experimenter selects a random sample of one hundred individuals and randomly assigns twenty-five to each of four experimental treatments. After participating in the treatments, the individuals perform a cognitive task that is measured on an interval scale. The parametric assumptions are met. The experimenter wants to know whether the treatments have differing effects on ability to perform the task.

e. Researchers measure a random sample of 200 students, aged 8 to 17 years, on a physical performance test. They want to know if the population distribution of test scores is uniformly distributed, that is, follows a flat, boxlike distribution.

17.10 Define the two possible types of errors in hypothesis testing. Why is there always a possibility of making an error when a decision is made about a hypothesis in inferential statistics?

17.11 Briefly review the meaning of a correlation coefficient and describe how the correlation coefficient can be used as a descriptive statistic and how it can be used in inferential statistics.

17.12 A researcher tests the performance of two random samples of individuals on a task. The performance of each is scored as poor, fair, good, or excellent. A *t*-test for the difference between means is then computed on the sample data. This result is interpreted as being significant at the .01 level but not at the .05 level. However, it is decided to reject the null hypothesis and conclude that the sample measures are, in fact, different. The researcher is then concerned about the probability of having made a Type II error. There are several errors in reasoning and procedures in this example. Identify these errors.

17.13 A researcher conducts an experiment in which there are five experimental treatments. The dependent variable is a performance score measured on an interval scale. Twenty individuals are assigned at random to each of the experimental treatments. The data are analyzed by an ANOVA and the summary ANOVA table is as follows:

Source	***SS***	***df***	***MS***	***F*-Value**
Between Exp. Treatments	122.76	4	30.69	3.11
Within Exp. Treatments	937.65	95	9.87	
Total	1060.41	99		

a. What is the null hypothesis tested by this ANOVA?

b. Using the .05 level of significance, complete the statistical test of the ANOVA. Give the conclusion about the null hypothesis.

c. Give the probability statement after the completion of the ANOVA.

17.14 Locate a research report that includes inferential statistics for the analysis of the data. Identify the hypotheses tested and the statistical procedures for testing the hypotheses. Were those procedures appropriate? Were the conclusions from the statistical analyses appropriate? Is the author's chain of reasoning in using inferential statistics apparent and correct?

17.15 Briefly review the chain of reasoning in hypothesis testing. Consider such points as the meanings of *statistic* and *parameter*, the *probability,* and the *inference to the population.*

17.16 Locate a report of a meta-analysis. (Journals, such as the *Review of Educational Research*, are good sources.) Review the meta-analysis. Does it seem to be well done? How many studies were included? Is effect size discussed? Do the summary conclusions follow from the results of the individual studies reviewed?

17.17 Correlate per-pupil expenditures and total expenditures with the average SAT Reading scores using the NC-SAT-2006 data set. Then test the hypotheses that the population correlations are zero. Set the significance level at .01.

17.18 Conduct a chi-square test to see whether gender is independent of having an IEP. Use the variables gender and IEP from the PACT data set. Set the significance level at .05.

NOTES

1. The standard deviation of the sampling distribution of the mean also is called the *standard error of the mean.* In general, the term *standard error* is used in inferential statistics to indicate the standard deviation of the sampling distribution of a statistic.
2. This probability statement is not quite technically correct. If there is a 95 percent confidence level, for example, and if all possible intervals for a given sample size are constructed, 95 percent of those intervals would span the population mean. In practice, for a specific problem, only one interval is constructed, and that interval either does or does not span the population mean. However, there is 95 percent confidence that it does span the population mean.
3. Scores from the same individual in a repeated measures analysis violate this assumption, but there are ways to deal with the lack of independence in the analysis.
4. Estimates of variance in ANOVA are called *mean squares,* commonly symbolized by *MS.*
5. Assigning descriptions of magnitude to effect sizes is somewhat subjective. Effect sizes from .05 to .20 are quite small. An effect size approaching 1.0, say .75 to .80, indicates a powerful effect. Effect sizes from .25 to .70 or so are considered modest to moderate to substantial. Seldom do effect sizes exceed 1.0, although such effect sizes are possible.

REFERENCES

Glass, G. V. (1977). Integrating findings: The meta-analysis of research. In L. Shulman (Ed.), *Review of research in education.* Itasca, IL: Peacock.

Rohrbeck, C. A., Ginsburg-Block, M. D., Fantuzzo, J. W., and Miller, T. R. (2003). Peer-assisted learning interventions with elementary school students: A meta-analytic review. *Journal of Educational Psychology*, *95*, 240–257.

Scott-Little, C., Hamann, M. S., and Jurs, S. G. (2002). Evaluations of after-school programs: A meta-evaluation of methodologies and narrative synthesis of findings. *American Journal of Evaluation, 23*, 387–420.

APPENDIX 1

Ethical and Legal Considerations in Conducting Research

Educational research often involves people as participants in experiments, respondents to surveys, or the focus of observations. Even the use of school records involves people. Because human participants are involved, ethical and legal considerations are of concern.

Researchers need access first to the research site and then to the individual participant. Whenever research is conducted in an educational setting, it is necessary to obtain permission from the site's "gatekeeper," who may be the principal, the superintendent, or a committee that is charged with this responsibility. It is important to know and follow the approval policies of the agency.

The Family Education Rights and Privacy Act of 1974 and the set of regulations called the Common Rule[1] that was issued in 1991 by the U.S. Department of Health and Human Services apply to educational research. The federal regulations require that universities and agencies engaging in research with human participants have an institutional review board (IRB) for the review and approval of research proposals. This includes the research proposals of students.

IRBs are required to review research proposals and certify that the proposed research will be conducted in accordance with the law and will protect the human subjects who are involved in the research. Typically, each institution has a standard form for IRB review that is available from an Office of Research or its equivalent. Criteria for IRB approval of research projects can be summarized generally as:

- Projects should identify anticipated risks to subjects and be designed to minimize such risks. Risks are reasonable relative to expected benefits.
- Participation of subjects is voluntary and equitable.
- Informed consent will be obtained from each prospective subject and properly documented.
- Additional safeguards must be taken for the inclusion of potentially vulnerable subjects such as children.
- Adequate provisions are made as appropriate for ensuring the safety of subjects, monitoring data collection, and maintaining privacy and confidentiality of subjects and data. (Paraphrased from the Protection of Human Subjects 46.111)

There is some controversy about the role and practice of IRBs in practitioner research, such as action research, because practitioner research is usually an integral part of ordinary educational practice, and thus is not subject to IRB review. Pritchard (2002) provides an excellent discussion of IRBs and practitioner research.

The Common Rule defines research as:

> A systematic investigation, including research development, testing, and evaluation, designed to contribute to generalizable knowledge. (45 CFR 46.102d)

The definition of generalizable knowledge is left to the researcher or the IRB, but practically all educational research falls within this definition of research. The definition of human subject is also broad:

> A living individual about whom an investigator (whether professional or student) conducting research obtains (1) data through intervention or interaction with the individual, or (2) Identifiable Private Information. (45 CFR 46,102D)

The researcher is obligated to protect participants from risk. Risk has a broad definition as exposure to the possibility of physical, social, or psychological harm. Harm can occur in a variety of ways. Any studies dealing with the effects of drugs have potential for social or psychological harm because they alert participants to possible illegal or antisocial behavior. Studies of sexual behavior run a high risk of causing harm because of the sensitive nature of the data. Magolda and Weems (2002) argue that harm is an inevitable outcome of much qualitative research. They say the inquiry process in ethnographic research increases the probability of harm because of the intrusive inquiry into the feelings and perceptions of participants. Two ways to limit the risk of harming human subjects are participant consent and confidentiality/anonymity.

Participant Consent

Informed Consent

The National Research Act requires that research participants are informed about their role in the research and that they give their written consent for participation. Consent forms should not contain any exculpatory language that may cause subjects to waive, or appear to waive, their legal rights. Consent forms must comply with local, state, and federal laws or regulations, and they cannot place limits on the authority of professionals, such as police officers or physicians in case of an emergency.

Informed consent must address the purposes and procedures of the research, and a description of any possible risks or negative consequences. The subject must be informed of the likely duration of the research and the necessary commitments of the participants. The subject should know whom to contact if any questions arise

Passive Consent

An example of passive consent would be sending a description of a questionnaire or activity that is to be used to parents, asking them to indicate in writing whether they do not want their child to participate. Failure to respond is considered as informed consent.

Hughes and Gutkin (1995, pp. 320–321) point out that there may be other reasons than consent why some parents don't reply. The letter may not have arrived home or it may have been dismissed as junk mail from the school. There may have been language problems or other reasons why parents did not understand the nature of the study. So in some cases, it may be difficult to argue that passive consent is informed consent.

Implied Consent

The requirement of informed consent may be waived under certain conditions. Surveys involving questionnaires, for which only group results are reported, usually have what is called implied consent. That is, respondents have the option of refusing participation (failure to return the questionnaire), and if they return a completed questionnaire they have, in essence, given consent to participation.

Ethical Guidelines

Confidentiality

Confidentiality refers to the researchers not disclosing the identity of the participants or indicating from whom the data were obtained. Note that the researcher does not have lawyer–client or doctor–patient privilege. A court order could require disclosure of identities, but this would be a very unlikely event.

Anonymity

Anonymity means that the names of the participants from whom the data have been obtained are not known.

Federal legislation protects the privacy of students' educational records. The researcher must guard against unauthorized identification of students. Written consent must be obtained if it is necessary to have personal identification and the identification information must be destroyed following its use for research.

Other Guidelines

We provide the seven guidelines given by Bogdan and Biklen (2003) for meeting the legal and ethical requirements for conducting educational research. These guidelines were developed for qualitative research, but they generally apply to all educational research.

1. Avoid research sites where informants may feel coerced to participate in your research.
2. Honor your informants' privacy.
3. There is a difference in informants' time commitment to you when you do participant observation in public places (where people are spending the time they would normally spend there) and when they do an interview with you.
4. Unless otherwise agreed to, the subjects' identities should be protected so that the information you collect does not embarrass or in other ways harm them.
5. Treat subjects with respect and seek their cooperation in the research.

6. In negotiating permission to do a study, you should make it clear to those with whom you negotiate what the terms of the agreement are, and you should abide by that contract.
7. Tell the truth when you write up and report your findings.

Professional associations have standards and codes of conduct for conducting research. The American Psychological Association (2002) has a comprehensive statement that addresses ethical principles of psychologists. Ten areas of ethical standards are addressed, one of which is "Research and Publication" (pp. 1069–1071). Fifteen research-related issues are discussed, from obtaining institutional approval through publication and review. As well as applying to psychologists conducting research, these standards apply to any behavioral science researchers.

The American Educational Research Association has published *Ethical Standards of the American Educational Research Association: Cases and Commentary* (Strike et al., 2002). This is a comprehensive publication, developed by an ad hoc committee of the Association. Standards are categorized into six parts and conducting research is addressed. A very desirable feature is that standards are interpreted and their application described with issues and cases, including difficult cases.

Protecting the rights of research participants and conducting research in an ethical manner are, to a large extent, common sense. The researcher must protect the dignity and welfare of the participants. The individual's freedom to decline participation must be respected, and the confidentiality of the research data must be maintained. The researcher must guard against violation or invasion of privacy. The responsibility of maintaining ethical standards remains with the individual researcher, and the principal investigator also is responsible for actions of coworkers and assistants. When human participants are involved, the rules and procedures of that institution must be reviewed and followed. Generally, these will be in keeping with the federal legislation.

NOTES

1. The formal title of the Common Rule is "Protection of Human Subjects," and it is part 46 of Title 45 of the Code of Federal Regulations (1991) (45 CFR 46).

REFERENCES

American Psychological Association. (2002). Ethical principles of psychologists and code of conduct. *American Psychologist, 57*, 1060–1073.

Bogdan, R. C., and Biklen, S. K. (2003). *Qualitative research for education: An introduction to theory and methods* (4th ed.). Boston: Allyn & Bacon.

Hughes, J., and Gutkin, T. (1995). Legal and ethical issues in conducting research on alcohol and drug use with children: A reaction to Havey and Dodd. *Journal of School Psychology, 33*, 319–326.

Magolda, P., and Weems, L. (2002). Doing harm: An unintended consequence of qualitative inquiry? *Journal of College Student Development, 43*, 490–505.

Pritchard, I. A. (2002). Travelers and trolls: Practitioner research and institutional review boards. *Educational Researcher, 31*, 3–13.

Strike, K. A., Anderson, M. S., Curren, R., Van Geel, T., Pritchard, I., and Robertson, E. (2002). *Ethical standards of the American Educational Research Association: Cases and commentary*. Washington, DC: American Educational Research Association.

APPENDIX 2

Solutions to Exercises

Note: Solutions are not provided here for exercises (1) that have flexible answers; (2) that direct the reader to some type of extended activity, such as reading a journal article; or (3) that indicate considerable discussion. The purpose of this appendix is to help the reader make the solution of exercises a more profitable learning experience. Answers are brief; not all possible discussion is presented for some exercises.

Chapter 1

1.1 The essential difference between basic and applied research is in the orientation of the research. Applied research is oriented to the solution of a specific, often immediate, problem. Basic research is oriented to the extension of knowledge in the discipline.

1.2 Internal validity involves the extent to which we can interpret the results of a research study. It considers the conditions of the study that make the results interpretable (or uninterpretable). External validity involves the extent of generalizability of the results—the populations, conditions, and so forth to which the results can be generalized.

1.3 If the results cannot be interpreted, they cannot be validly generalized.

1.4 **a.** Internal
b. Internal
c. External
d. Internal

1.5 Reliability means consistency; when applied to research, it is the extent to which research is replicable (the methods, conditions, results). For (a) there may be inconsistency in the way the four experimenters administer the treatment; for (b) observers may not be consistent when interpreting the teacher behaviors.

1.6 In an experiment, at least one variable is deliberately varied or manipulated by the researcher.

1.7 Inductive inquiry involves reasoning from the specific (situation, etc.) to the general situation, and so on. When conducting qualitative research something specific such as an educational phenomenon, issue, and so forth is studied in detail and holistically, and to the extent possible, generalizations are made to similar phenomena, issues, and so on.

1.8 Grounded theory is theory generated from data. To develop a grounded theory of principal evaluation, descriptions of evaluation systems used for evaluating principals would be obtained, along with data that might have been collected when the systems were used. The descriptions and the data would be analyzed for similarities and differences in methods, kinds of data, purposes, outcomes, and so forth. Possible components might be: (1) the extent of interaction with students, (2) methods and skills in conducting faculty meetings, and (3) public relations efforts with parents of students and the community in general.

1.9 Historical research focuses on a description and interpretation of past events or facts; ethnographic research focuses on a holistic description of some present phenomenon.

1.12 One difficulty would occur if the group receiving written praise and the group receiving verbal praise were students in the same classroom who compared their comments from the teacher. The experimental treatments would be known to both groups, which could have an effect. Another problem might be that the teacher would have an ethical dilemma if she knew that a particular student responded well to verbal praise but was randomly placed into the written-praise treatment group.

Chapter 2

2.1 The constants are grade level, gender, and school. The independent variable is instructional materials. The teacher is an intervening variable, and the effect of the teacher variable cannot be separated from the effect of instructional materials because each teacher uses only one type of instructional material with only one group. The dependent variable is reading achievement.

2.2 Gender of the student is a variable that may also serve as a control variable if the reading scores for boys and girls are separated. School and grade level are likely to be included as control variables. (In essence, they become additional independent variables.) Class and method cannot be separated within schools, so within the schools, class (and also teacher, assuming that each teacher uses only one method) is an intervening variable.

2.3 Hypotheses would be directed to the variables under study. An example is, "The reading achievement of fourth-grade girls is equal to that of fourth-grade boys." This is a nondirectional hypothesis. A directional hypothesis might be, "The reading achievement of fifth-graders is higher than that of fourth-graders." There are other possible hypotheses.

2.4 Examples of foreshadowed problems might be:
a. Extent of play among children of different races.
b. Social interaction among children and teachers.

2.5 A nondirectional hypothesis does *not* specify a direction for the results; for example, it does not specify that one mean score will be greater than or less than another. A directional hypothesis specifies the direction (or order) of the results, for example, that one mean score will be greater than another.

2.6 It would be more appropriate to use directional hypotheses because the science educator is interested in whether or not the constructivist approach improves science achievement, not whether its effect simply is different from that of other approaches. The dependent variables are achievement scores (possibly final exam scores) in biology, chemistry, and physics. Certainly the approach to science instruction (constructivist versus other approaches) is the independent variable of primary interest. The gender of the student might be another independent variable, included as a control variable. The school is a constant. Student learning style and student study habits are intervening variables.

2.7 *Open classroom* is a rather general term that may have varied meanings, so it would need to be defined specifically for this study. Scholastic performance is the dependent variable, but most likely there would be several dependent variables such as the scores on specific tests of scholastic subjects, for example, reading. The grade levels of elementary school students included in the study would need to be specified.

2.9 The researchable problem would not contain the word *should* because that is a value judgment. One possibility is: What percent of parents think that physical education should be required in grades 2–6?

2.10 One possibility is: When similar students are given low, moderate, or highly anxiety-producing instructions on a test, their average test scores will differ such that the low-anxiety group will have the highest average performance and the high-anxiety group will have the lowest average performance.

2.11 The problem is deciding whether supporting the overall hypothesis requires that all three independent variables are supported by the data. What should you conclude if only two of the three are supported by the data?

Chapter 3

3.2 The major descriptors to use are Instruction, Curriculum, and Education. More specifically, use Mathematics Curriculum (subheadings Arithmetic Curriculum and Elementary School Math), Curriculum (Mathematics Curriculum and Elementary School Curriculum), Education Programs (International Programs), and Comparative Education (International Education). The forgoing descriptors would be used in combination when referencing in the following ERIC publications: *Educational Documents Index, Resources in Education* (Subject Index), and *Current Index to Journals in Education* (Subject Index).

3.3 Descriptors to use are Teacher Behavior, Teacher Performance, Teacher Competency, Science, and Science Achievement. To broaden the search, suppose that the results of searching on Teacher Behavior and Science Achievement produced few references. Then Teacher Behavior or Teacher Performance or Teacher Competency and Science Achievement could be used. An example of narrowing the search would be to use High School and Science Achievement. Note the connectors: *and* generally narrows the search; *or* broadens it.

Chapter 4

4.4 This situation suggests a considerable quantity of results. Because there are ten test scores, four grades, and two groups within each grade, there are 80 means and 80 standard deviations ($10 \times 4 \times 2$). Forty *t*-tests are computed, so there are 40 *t*-values. There are 45 correlation coefficients to report. Thus, to avoid excessively large or complicated tables, the minimum number of tables necessary is four. One way to organize the results would be a table for means, with eight columns for the four grades (experimental and control columns for each grade). The means for a specific test would then be in a row. We would have a similar table for standard deviations; a table of *t*-values containing four columns, one for each grade (it would be well to have this table near the table of means, because the difference between means is being tested); and a table (sometimes called a matrix) of correlation coefficients. The following is an example of a title and headings for the table of means:

TABLE A.1 Means for Experimental and Control Groups by Grade and Test

	Grade							
	3		4		5		6	
Test	E	C	E	C	E	C	E	C

4.5 More than one table would be necessary. A table for the means might be organized as follows:

TABLE A.2 Means on Four Professional Measures by Level Taught and Gender of Teacher Education Graduates

	Elementary		**Secondary**	
Professional Measure	Males	Females	Males	Females
Prof Rel				
Ped-Know				
Ped-Appl				
Hist of Ed				

If a table could accommodate eight columns of numbers, both means and standard deviations could be placed in the same table. Similar tables could be constructed substituting race for gender and age for gender. Age could be dichotomized into two categories: 22 years and less and greater than 22 years.

Chapter 5

5.1 If the survey involved a mailed questionnaire, failure to report the response rate is an error. Using a sample that was not selected at random and then assuming that the sample was random is an error. Inappropriate measurement or inappropriate analysis are possible errors.

5.2 Possible errors related to both genders participating:
a. Failure to balance the experimental treatments relative to gender
b. Failure to compute a gender effect

5.4 The title does not provide information about the research problem or the variables that are investigated. It cannot be electronically or manually identified as being relevant to a researcher's literature search.

5.5 Warranted means that the results and conclusions are based on the data that are presented. Research is transparent when the logic and procedures of the research are explained in sufficient detail to be readily understood by one who is competent in the field of study.

Chapter 6

6.1 Possible variables that may contribute to the variance in performance test scores are age, general physical health, differences in physical "shape," strength, weight, height.

6.2 **a.** Built into the design as an independent variable
b. Constant
c. Built into the design as an independent variable
d. Randomization
e. Randomization
f. Constant

6.3 To some extent, level of school is confounded with school as is age of the students. The "geographic region," which includes socioeconomic factors, and so forth may have some impact on attitude, and region is confounded with school. Any effects that individual teachers, administrators, counselors, and so on, have on attitude would be confounded with school.

6.4 No independent variables are manipulated by the researcher; attitude is measured as it occurs in the natural setting.

6.5 The following points should be noted in developing the research design: (a) Because each teacher teaches two classes, each teacher should use both packets, one for each class; in this way, teacher and instructional materials are not confounded. (b) Unless some measure of learning style is available, learning style would likely be controlled by randomization. (c) Gender of the student and teacher could be included as independent variables, although gender of the student could also be controlled through randomization. (d) The available GPA could serve as a measure of ability and could be used as a statistical control.

6.6 The ability level of the participants is a likely variable that may have an effect on the dependent variable. An ability-level measure could be administered to the participants and then a statistical adjustment made on the basis of ability-level score. There may be some difference in the performances of boys and girls or in the manner in which they respond to the motivational techniques. Therefore, the gender of the participant could be included as an independent (control) variable.

6.7 When two or more variables are confounded in a research study, their effects cannot be separated.

6.9 Any variables that might affect reading performance and that vary across schools would be confounded with the reading programs. Possible confounded variables are the quality of instruction and the amount of time spent on reading instruction. If the socioeconomic characteristics of the areas served by the schools are different, there may be factors in the home environment that affect reading performance and are confounded with the reading programs.

6.10 To limit the age variable, only students 18 to 22 years of age could be included. Seventy-five women and 75 men are selected at random and 25 of each gender randomly assigned to each of the three levels of physical training. In this way, gender would be controlled as an independent variable. Variables such as prior physical training and extent of physical activity outside of the training would be controlled by the random assignment to the training levels.

6.11 The discussion should include the fact that students are not randomly assigned to schools, so the comparison groups would not necessarily be equivalent. Some of the variables on which they are likely to differ should be identified and the implications of those differences should be explained.

Chapter 7

7.1 (This exercise is similar to Exercise 1.2.) Internal validity concerns the basic minimum control, and so forth, that is necessary for the results of the experiment to be interpretable. External validity is the extent to which the results of the experiment are generalizable to existing conditions, populations, and the like. Internal validity is often enhanced by increasing control, which may include reducing the number of factors operating in the situation. This tends to jeopardize external validity. The reverse may also occur when the experiment is essentially a replication of the real situation (has high external validity), but so many factors are operating that it is impossible to interpret the cause and effect.

7.2 The fact that the teachers can assign students at random within the school gives a measure of control that would be missing if existing classes had to be taken. Existing classes may differ on ability and on other factors related to achievement. Control can be enhanced by building school into the design as an independent variable. Because each teacher teaches four classes, one of each size can be assigned per teacher. However, the teacher variable would be confounded with the independent variable school, because any one teacher would teach in only one school. The school variable might have several uncontrolled but relevant variables associated with it, such as extent of lab facilities. These variables are essentially confounded with the school variable.

7.4 The primary gain in internal validity is being able to check on an effect of pretesting. A possible interaction between pretesting and experimental treatment can also be checked.

7.5 The pretest-posttest control group design applies. Because the teacher is interested in the amount of algebra learned during the semester, pretesting is necessary. The pretest score may also be used as a statistical control. This experiment would most likely be quite high in external validity, because testing could occur at natural times and the experiment would be carried on in a natural educational setting. The population to which the results are generalized would have to be carefully defined in terms of the students enrolled in advanced algebra classes in this specific type of high school.

7.6 **a.** No, because the groups have been formed by random assignment.
b. No, because there is no pretesting of any groups.
c. (1) There are experimental treatment effects: the four experimental treatments all have differing effects. (2) There are experimental treatment effects: X_1 and X_3 have equal effects: X_2 and X_4 have equal effects (or the same effect), but their effects differ from those of X_1 and X_3. (3) X_1 and X_2 have effects and they are the same. (4) X_4 is the only treatment that has an experimental effect.

7.7 **a.** The researcher can determine the possible effect of X extended in time, along with a comparison group extended in time. Also, a possible diminishing effect of pretesting could be checked.
b. Compare O_2 and O_9; compare O_4 and O_{10}.
c. (1) If an experimental effect exists, it is a function of time. There is no long-term experimental effect. No pretesting effect appears in the short-run posttest results of experimental groups. (2) There is an experimental effect that is not affected by the different posttest times of the design; the experimental effect is the same in the short and long run. (3) In the short run, there is no change due to experimental treatment for pretested groups. (4) In the short run, there is no experimental effect, nor is there an effect of pretesting; there is an experimental effect in the long run with the pretested groups.

7.8 **a.** Gain scores can be analyzed; if necessary, we could also check on subject mortality.
b. No; an effect of pretesting cannot be checked because there are no nonpretested groups with which to make a comparison.
c. O_3 and O_6 compared with O_9; O_1 with O_3, and O_4 with O_6; O_2 with O_3; and O_3 with O_6.
d. No, because random assignment was used.
e. We would conclude that some external factor is causing the control group to change between measurement occasions.

f. (1) There are experimental effects in the short run, and they are the same for X_1 and X_2. The effects do not persist for the long run. (2) There are experimental effects in the short run that are not the same for X_1 and X_2. (3) There are no experimental effects in the short run. There are experimental effects in the long run, but we cannot tell whether or not X_1 and X_2 effects are the same. We know that $O_2 \neq O_3$ and $O_5 \neq O_6$, but it is possible that $O_3 = O_6$. (4) There are experimental effects in the short run, and the effects are different for X_1 and X_2. There are also effects in the long term, but they do not remain constant between the short and long terms. The long-term effects of X_1 and X_2 are not the same.

7.10 There are many advantages to using a repeated measures design. You can get the same number of data points with fewer subjects because each subject is assessed several times. You also get a clear picture of development or change across time, clearer than a cross-sectional design would provide.

7.11 The effects of the treatments vary depending on whether the subjects are male or female. Males do best with treatment T_3 and females do best with treatment T_1.

7.12 There are many possible correct answers. One would be 24, 34, 40. No interaction means that the difference between the male and female means would be roughly the same for every treatment group.

Chapter 8

8.1 The primary difficulties that may be introduced when using intact groups are associated with possible lack of equivalence of the groups on factors related to the dependent variable. Such factors may be confounded with experimental treatments, threatening the internal validity of the research.

8.2 There are three sets of laboratory materials, and one set could be designated the traditional or control set, because it is unlikely that a class would do the lab work with no materials. The design can be diagrammed as follows:

$$G_1\text{—}X_1\text{—}O_1$$
$$G_2\text{—}X_2\text{—}O_2$$
$$G_3\qquad O_3$$

The pretest-posttest, nonequivalent control group design would be applied by administering a pretest at the beginning of the semester. The pretest might cover biology content, but if this study were conducted during the first semester of the school year, it might be a Scholastic Aptitude Test or a science achievement test. The advantages of pretesting are (1) that the preexperiment equivalence of the classes on the pretest can be checked, and (2) that pretest scores may be used as a statistical control in the analysis. Internal validity is threatened if the classes are not equivalent, and other variables affecting the dependent variable are confounded with the materials. There is also the possibility that contamination across the classes may occur if students from different classes discuss or share materials. Assuming that the results can be interpreted, they generalize to the biology students in this school taught by this teacher, probably over a period of years if the characteristics of the student body do not change. Generalization to other schools, students, and teachers would have to be argued on a logical basis.

8.3 There is no random assignment of students to the practice treatments. The teacher variable is very apparent and essentially uncontrolled. The assumption is that teachers are most effective with the techniques they prefer. Even if this is true, there is no evidence that different teachers, independent of practice method, are equally effective. With only three schools, it would be difficult to make a case for the assumption that the teachers of each method are a representative sample of fifth-grade teachers, either in general or as a more specific group. There may be other relevant uncontrolled factors within the schools, and, because the method is optional to the teacher, there is no reason to assume a balance between schools on such factors. Thus, internal validity is low because of lack of control. External validity is also low because of poor internal validity and questions that might be raised about the representativeness of the teachers. It would be important to have information about the characteristics of the teachers and their similarities across the two practice methods.

8.4 This is an example of a time series design. A design such as this is susceptible to multiple-treatment interference. In this case, detailed effects may begin appearing on subsequent observations. The pattern of results may be difficult to interpret. The advantage of using such a design is that it can be applied in a natural setting and can provide information on the reading achievement profile of a specific class. A special measurement problem would be attaining equivalent difficulty levels for the various tests given at four-week intervals. Suppose that there was a marked drop in performance after one period. This would be interpreted as an effect of the method of instruction, when in fact the drop might be due to a more difficult test.

8.5 **a.** There are short-term effects of the training programs but no long-term effects. In the short term, the effects of the programs are not the same, with X_1 being most effective and X_3 least effective.

b. There are short-term effects that persist for the long term, and the effects are the same for the three training programs.

c. The groups were not equivalent initially, and they retain their relative positions in the short term. We cannot tell if there is a short-term effect. Apparently, there is no long-term effect, and the long term has also eliminated initial differences among the groups.

d. O_3 with O_1 and O_2, O_6 with O_4 and O_5, and O_9 with O_7 and O_8.

e. No, because all groups are pretested. There is no comparison group that was not pretested.

8.6 **a.** The experimental treatment has a positive effect, at least an immediate effect, and the effect increases over time.

b. There is a short-term effect of the experimental treatment, which continues for an additional three weeks but then disappears.

c. Check G_2 across O_8 to O_{14}. If there are changes in the attitude scores, normal class instruction is having an effect.

8.7 The study would be conducted over an eight-week period, with four observations (O_1 through O_4) taken when no logs were being kept and four observations (O_5 through O_8) taken when logs were kept. If O_5 through O_8 showed improvement in the student's subjects over performance from O_1 through O_4, the treatment is having an effect. If it were a one-time effect, O_5 would be greater than O_1 through O_4, but consistent with O_6, O_7, and O_8. If there were an accumulative effect, O_5 would be greater than O_1 through O_4, and O_6 would be greater than O_5, O_7 greater than O_6, and O_8 greater than O_7.

8.10 A group not receiving the experimental treatment is a control group and serves as a basis for comparison to determine whether there is any experimental effect at all. Many quasi-experimental situations are limited to the number of available groups and there may be only one group available, the one receiving the experimental treatment.

8.12 This design could work when the nonequivalent groups are elementary and secondary teachers attending an in-service workshop on using a new student database software program. The dependent variable might be scores on a criterion test after a two-hour training session. Of course, there are many other possible examples.

8.13 The response to this question should include the difference in internal validity when participants are randomly assigned to comparison groups versus when intact groups are used. There should also be discussion of the role of the pretest in the nonequivalent group design.

Chapter 9

9.1 There may be any number of independent variables of interest (some would serve as control variables). Examples are grade level, sex of the student, at the high school level, subject taught, location of the school in terms of socioeconomic level of the community, size of the school, region of the state. Scholastic achievement in numerous subjects and areas would serve as dependent variables, at least some dependent variables measured by standardized achievement tests. Scores on attitude inventories could serve as dependent variables. One value of a longitudinal study is that there may be a check on long-range effects.

9.2 One advantage of the longitudinal study is the option of studying change occurring in the class as it goes through college. The longitudinal study would take four years or so to complete; the cross-sectional could be done in a much shorter time period, requiring data collection at only one point in time.

9.3 As a cohort study, the present freshman class would be the cohort and a random sample of this class would be selected each year as it goes through its four-year college experience. As a panel study, a random sample (the panel) of the present freshman class would be selected, and this same sample or what remains of it would be surveyed each of the four years. A disadvantage of the panel study is possible attrition in the panel, especially if the college has a high dropout rate. An advantage of the cohort study is avoiding the attrition problem. An advantage of the panel study is that individual change could be checked, whereas a cohort study would measure only group change.

9.4 The panel study allows for the opportunity of collecting data from the same group of teachers at different times. In this way, changes over time within specific teachers could be detected. A panel study is always susceptible to the difficulty of keeping the panel intact, and five years is a long period for maintaining a panel. It is also possible that over time the remaining members of the panel are no longer representative of the teacher population. The stability of the teacher population in this school system would impact the effectiveness of the panel.

9.5 To the extent possible, it would be well to use selected-response items because students who have dropped out would have little motivation for devoting much thought to responding to the questionnaire. For this reason, nonresponse very likely would be a problem. Some procedure for personal contact with nonrespondents, such as a telephone call, may be necessary.

9.6 The cover letter should be signed by the director of, or assistant superintendent in charge of, the Department of Guidance and Counseling.

9.7 Because all schools or guidance offices have telephones, all guidance counselors selected could be contacted by telephone. The advantage of using the telephone over a mailed questionnaire is the direct contact, which might increase response rate and would allow for more flexibility in the questioning, if this is desirable. Using the telephone would essentially shift the study from a questionnaire to an interview. A disadvantage of the telephone survey is that it may interrupt the work of the guidance counselors and responding by telephone may not allow adequate time for thinking about responses. It would be desirable—almost necessary—to provide prior information and to schedule the telephone call in advance. The additional effort of the telephone survey may not be merited, because the response rate with a mailed questionnaire would probably be quite good for this professional sample.

9.8 Very likely an independent variable would be position of the educator, teacher, principal, superintendent, and so on. Their opinions would have policy implications and the implications would be different if such groups had similar opinions versus diverse opinions.

9.9 Possible sources of nonresponse that should be identifiable: position of the educator, region of the state, location of the school—rural, city, suburban, size of the school system.

9.10 In order to provide more focus for the items (on the curriculum, student issues) and to make response easier, use selected-response items to the extent possible. The president of the board of education likely would sign the cover letter.

9.11 A longitudinal design would be used if there were an interest in opinion change over time. In the interest of positive school–community relations, it would be well to survey the entire parent population.

9.12 There would be little likelihood of success with mailed questionnaires (or distributed for students to take) because many would not be returned and those that were returned most likely would be completed as a group activity, or at least in consultation with others. It might be possible to administer the questionnaire to a "captive audience" such as a class, but the members of the class would not be a random sample of the student population. Careless or dishonest response might be a problem; for one reason, students might report more variable or positive eating habits than are being followed. Checking for possible careless or dishonest response could be done by checking for impossible or implausible responses or unlikely response combinations. The respondents could be asked how honest (or accurate) they were when responding.

9.13 The most likely recipient of the questionnaire would be someone at the central office of the school district. In small districts, this would likely be the superintendent. Sending the questionnaire to the superintendents in all districts may be the best strategy. Large district superintendents would delegate completion of the questionnaire to someone else, but for most districts it would be unlikely that the state department staff would know the identity of that person. The cover letter for the questionnaire should be signed by the chief state school officer to draw attention to the importance of completing the questionnaire.

9.17 **a.** Other variables might include parent education level, parent involvement with the child's reading instruction, and other variables related to socioeconomic status such as nutrition and enrichment experiences.

b. Correlation does not necessarily imply causation, but we could probably tentatively conclude that putting books into bedrooms that had no books might increase reading scores. Adding more books when there are already quite a few is not likely to increase reading scores.

Chapter 10

10.1 Among the decisions that would be made at this initial step of the research design are (a) the site selection, that is, the specific school(s) whose principal(s) will be observed; (b) who in addition to the principal will be observed or interviewed, that is, school staff and students; and (c) duration of the study (at least a tentative decision) and the schedule for data collection in the school(s). One of the initial decisions would be whether data collection will be done in one or more schools.

10.2 A working hypothesis might be, "The principal's role is more that of policy implementor than instructional leader." A foreshadowed problem might be, "The professional interaction between the principal and teachers."

10.3 Examples of documents that might be collected are (a) minutes of faculty meetings, and (b) copies of reports prepared by the principal for the central administration of the school system. The principal would be observed conducting routine activities, and certainly a faculty meeting would be observed when the opportunity arises.

10.4 **a.** A general question might be, "What are teacher perceptions of the efficiency effectiveness and feasibility of site-based management?"

b. Schools—elementary, secondary, and so forth—where site-based management has been implemented would be candidates for sites. Because a limited number of schools could be included, criteria for inclusion would need to be considered. Possible subjects include teachers, principals, students, and the like. Interview data, observation, and school records are examples of potential sources of data.
c. The funnel approach would begin with general questions and, as data collection proceeds, it would become increasingly focused on specific phenomena.
d. An example of a specific phenomenon is the principal's role (tasks) in site-based management.

10.6 The modified analytic approach works from a specific research problem, in this case a study of teachers' perceptions about a model for teacher evaluation, to a comprehensive description of the "phenomenon." As the study is conducted in this school system, a grounded theory of teacher evaluation as applied or practiced may emerge from the data. This theory, undoubtedly, would have several components, thus providing a comprehensive description.

Chapter 11

11.2 **a.** Survey
b. Experiment
c. Historical
d. Survey (ex post facto in nature)
e. Historical
f. Survey (ex post facto in nature)
g. Survey

11.4 An educational term that may have a problem of definition over the years is *progressive education.*

11.9 Primary sources might include interviews of people who were actually involved in the desegregation, police and court records from that time period, and video recordings of demonstrations. Examples of secondary sources would include books written about the events, editorials from newspapers in other states, and the reflections of correspondents on television news shows such as *Dateline* or *60 Minutes.*

11.10 It would be difficult to develop a historical perspective on recent events or issues because the consequences of the events or issues have not yet manifested themselves. Historical analysis would be premature and narrowly defined. The conclusions would not likely hold up over time.

Chapter 12

12.1 Experimental research involves the direct manipulation of at least one independent variable; ethnographic research focuses on variables as they occur in the natural setting without any intervention by the researcher.

12.3 Perspectives form the cultures and the cultures collectively make up the organization.

12.4 Triangulation is qualitative cross-validation; it involves comparisons (among sources or data-collection procedures, for example) to determine the extent of consistency.

12.6 Relative to external validity, it probably would not be of much direct concern, and any external validity would need to be argued on a logical basis.

12.9 As a participant–observer, the researcher assumes the role of an active participant in the situation. A privileged observer does not assume the role of participant but has access to the activities of the situation. Limited observers are not participants, and they can observe only some of the activities. A young adult, actually enrolled in law school, doing research on what it is like to be a law school student is an example of a participant–observer. A researcher in a school observing all aspects of school operation—instruction, faculty meetings, lunchroom activity, and so on—but not actually being a teacher or student would be a privileged observer. A researcher in a school who observes only junior high science instruction two days per week would be considered a limited observer.

12.11 The concepts of reliability and validity are consistent with their meaning for types of research other than ethnographic research. Reliability is concerned with replicability of research procedures and results. Validity concerns the interpretation of results (internal) and their subsequent generalizability (external).

12.12 Assertoric argumentation is general-type generalization, applying to every member of a group or population rather than to the entire population as a whole. Such argumentation is based on reasonableness and rationality given acceptable assumptions and evidence. Aggregate-type generalizations are made about the entire population, not individuals, and they are often based on random sampling probability models.

12.13 Because ethnographic research is so situation- or context-specific, generalizability and, hence, external validity may be limited. Broadening the scope of an ethnographic research study to multiple sites tends to enhance external validity. Generalizability usually is not as big a concern as with quantitative research studies, and in ethnographic research the case for generalizability typically is made on a logical basis.

12.15 Doing an ethnographic study with young children may require getting informed consent from their parents. This is not always a simple matter. It is also true that when adults are studied they can provide diaries or written reflections that help the ethnographer to understand their perceptions of the situation. Young children will not provide written documents.

Chapter 13

13.1 If the school system uses a standardized, published mathematics achievement test or a state-mandated mathematics proficiency test (at least one of which is highly likely), the students would be surveyed as to math achievement at the close of the second semester to address question (a). Results would consist of scores on the mathematics test, including subtest scores. The results could be compared to those of previous years. However, the surveys should continue into subsequent years because the effect of the curriculum likely would be more long-range than just one year. To address question (b) would require observation, possibly a limited ethnographic study of the nature of mathematics instruction under the new curriculum. Data could be collected on factors such as amount of time spent in discovery activity. The final question, question (c), would be addressed through a teacher survey. Teachers would be asked about factors such as appropriateness of materials with the new curriculum and the ease of adjustment to teaching the curriculum.

13.2 **a.** Historical and survey research

b. Rather than survey the entire faculty, a random sample may be selected, with sample size around 300 or so. The survey would include factual items, for example, how many of the university's football games the faculty members attend during the season. Perception items would include, for example, opinions about the emphasis placed on football.

13.6 The mixed methods approach can use quantitative methods to establish significant differences between comparison groups or regression equations that are used to predict some outcome from student or school characteristics. The qualitative methods can then be used to provide a thick description of the culture or context in which these variables are operating. The mixed methods also allow the researcher to pursue different research questions within the same study. It is true that some audiences are more convinced by qualitative studies than by quantitative studies. The reverse is also true. Using both approaches in the same study means that you will be responding to the information needs of both kinds of audiences.

Chapter 14

14.1 Because there are 839 population members, three-digit random numbers are necessary. Any numbers selected between 840 and 999 inclusive can be disregarded.

14.2 For stratified sampling, we divide the population into nonoverlapping subpopulations called strata. When proportional allocation is used, the sample sizes selected from the strata are proportional to the sizes of the corresponding strata populations.

14.4 In stratified sampling, all strata are represented in the sample, and the random sampling is done within strata according to some allocation. Thus, individuals, not strata, are randomly sampled. In cluster sampling, the clusters are randomly selected from the population of clusters, but if a cluster is selected, all its members are included in the sample.

14.5 The sampling fraction is $\frac{450}{3000}$, which equals $\frac{3}{20}$ or .15. Sample sizes for strata 1 through 4, respectively, are 124.5, 99, 72, and 154.5. Because partial units probably cannot be included, the researcher must arbitrarily decide whether to select 125 from stratum 1 or 155 from stratum 4.

14.6 Sixty men and 60 women would be randomly selected from their respective populations. There would be 15 men and 15 women assigned to each of the four levels of the experimental variable. Because selection is random from each population, the first 15 of each sex selected could be assigned to level 1, the second 15 to level 2, and so on.

14.9 Comprehensive sampling is such that all units with specified characteristics are included in the sample. Maximum variation sampling includes units in the sample so that they provide the greatest differences in specified characteristics.

14.10 Typical case sampling involves selecting units judged to be the "average or middle road" units relative to the phenomenon under study. Homogeneous sampling involves selecting units that are similar; they may not be typical units, but are units belonging to some defined subgroup.

14.12 The sampling fraction is $\frac{300}{3215}$ or about .093. In selecting a systematic sample, we divide 3,215 by 300, which is 10.72, which may be called the sampling interval. The first sample member is determined by a random selection of the first 11 names on the list. Then 10.72 would be added to the number of this selection and all subsequent selections until the list is exhausted. At each step, the fraction would be rounded to the nearest integer. An advantage of systematic sampling in this situation is that it is extremely unlikely that two members of the same household would be selected.

14.13 The total population size is 42,000 and, with a sampling fraction of .02, sample size is 840.

a. Each stratum would receive 1/5 of 840, or 168.

b. $n_1 = 100, n_2 = 320, n_3 = 140, n_4 = 100, n_5 = 180.$

14.15 The results that are obtained from a stratified random sample can be projected to the population from which the random sample was drawn. The results from an extreme case sample cannot be statistically projected beyond the sample. An argument could be made that the extreme case is similar to like cases and that cautious generalization might be made to like cases.

14.16 A site that has been randomly selected from a large population of sites is not likely to be an information-rich site. If for some strange reason the researcher had six similar information-rich sites, random selection could be used to select a single site for the research.

Chapter 15

15.1 Validity has to do with whether or not a test measures what it is supposed to measure; reliability concerns whether or not it is consistent in measuring whatever it does measure. A test can be reliable but not valid by consistently measuring something it was not designed to measure or by failing to measure what it was designed to measure. An unreliable test cannot be valid because lack of consistency eliminates the possibility of measuring what it is supposed to measure.

15.4 **a.** Published measuring instruments are available to both researchers, but the one working on achievement would have greater choice. It would likely be easier to find an instrument specifically suited to the needs of the science achievement study.

b. Content-related evidence would be of concern in establishing validity for the measurement of achievement; construct-related evidence would be of most interest for the validity of personality measurement. Evidence for the former would come from a logical analysis; evidence for the latter would most likely be based on information from the test manual, especially if the researcher is attempting to establish the constructs that underlie the junior high personality.

c. Achievement could be measured by a paper-and-pencil test; personality data might be obtained by some type of written group test or might require individual testing.

15.7 A Likert scale is a scale used with individual items; it contains a number of points, usually four or more, with intervals between the points assumed to be equal. The respondents respond to individual items. The semantic differential, on the other hand, contains a series of pairs of bipolar terms (usually adjectives); each pair is located on the endpoints of the scale (continuum), usually with seven or nine intervals. The respondent is asked to judge the word or phrase (which represents a concept) at the top of the page by checking the scale for each of the bipolar pairs.

15.8 Informants might underreport their behaviors to make themselves look good. This can be addressed by using anonymous questionnaires so that the responses cannot be traced back to particular informants. Another problem can occur when informants tell you what they think you want to hear. This may require alternative data gathering such as observation rather than self-report.

15.9 **a.** The researcher could count this as a 3.5 and enter that number into the spreadsheet of data.

b. The researcher could toss out all rankings that do not adhere to the instructions. The problem with this approach is that a lot of data could be lost. Perhaps a different item format would work better in the first place.

c. The researcher could randomly pick one of the circled answers, making sure that there were no systematic bias in selecting the answer, for example, not always selecting the left-most circled response. The other choice would be to treat it as missing data because you cannot tell which is the true response.

15.10 The domain of third-grade arithmetic facts is well defined and the test items will match the domain. Students who do well on the test are likely to do well when retested or administered a parallel form of the test. What constitutes self-esteem for third-graders is less well defined. The students may have day-to-day fluctuations in self-esteem. Both factors imply that the reliability coefficient of a self-esteem measure will be lower than the reliability coefficient of the arithmetic facts test.

Chapter 16

16.1 Measures of central tendency are points that locate the distribution on the scale of measurement. Measures of variability are intervals that indicate the dispersion or spread in the distribution. In describing a distribution, measures of central tendency indicate where the distribution is located on the scale of measurement; measures of variability are indicators of the spread of scores in the distribution.

16.2 The mean is sensitive to extreme scores and the median is not. The salaries of the president and vice presidents are bunched at the extreme end of the distribution and would put the mean salary around $45,000. The median salary would be around $30,000 or so, which is more indicative of what most employees earn in this company.

16.3 To describe a distribution, it is necessary to know (1) its shape, (2) its location on the scale of measurement, and (3) its dispersion or variability.

16.4 Some type of standard score is necessary in order to put the scores from the school subjects on a common measurement scale so that the scores of an individual student can be compared. The *z*-score would not be desirable because its distribution has a mean of zero and many scores (about one-half) would be negative. Any number of transformed scores could be used; for example, one with a mean of 100 and a standard deviation of 20.

16.5 **a.** Negative; those scoring higher on the intelligence test would likely require less time.
b. Possibly a low, negative correlation.
c. Positive
d. Zero
e. Zero

16.6 The mean scores show little difference, that for the boys being less than two points greater than the mean for girls. However, the distribution for girls is more variable (spread out more) than that for boys. This indicates that, relatively speaking, some girls have very positive attitudes and others quite negative attitudes. The boys are more homogenous in attitude. However, with a total possible score of 130, both means are more than ten points below the midpoint of the scale, indicating in absolute terms quite low or negative attitudes.

16.7 Considering the means of the total scores, it is apparent that the elementary and junior high school teachers have substantially more positive attitudes toward the central administration than the senior high school teachers. The means of 73.2 and 71.6 average to be about four on the five-point scales of the individual items. (An average of four on individual items would give a total score of 18 times 4, or 72.) So, in absolute terms, the elementary and junior high school teachers have quite positive attitudes.

However, the junior high school teachers' scores are more variable than those of the elementary school teachers. The standard deviation of 12.3 is almost twice that of 6.7. This result indicates that there are some junior high school teachers with quite low scores on the attitude scale, and some with quite positive scores. But, as a group, the junior high teachers are not as uniformly positive as the elementary school teachers. The small standard deviation of the elementary school teachers' scores indicates that their scores are bunched around the mean. The scores of the senior high teachers have the largest standard deviation. Although they have the lowest mean, with a large standard deviation there are some high scores among those of the senior high teachers.

16.8 The correlations of per-pupil expenditures with the SAT Math Test, Reading Test, and Writing Test are −.199, −.121, and −.172, respectively. This indicates a negative correlation where higher test scores are associated with lower per-pupil expenditures. The correlations are fairly near zero, indicating weak associations between the pairs of variables.

TABLE A.3 Correlations

		Math	Reading	Writing	Per Pupil
MATH	Pearson Correlation	1.000	.962**	.954**	−.199*
	Sig. (2-tailed)	.	.000	.000	.034
	N	114	114	114	114
READING	Pearson Correlation	.962**	1.000	.969**	−.121
	Sig. (2-tailed)	.000	.	.000	.200
	N	114	114	114	114
WRITING	Pearson Correlation	.954*	.969**	1.000	−.172
	Sig. (2 tailed)	.000	.000	.	.068
	N	114	114	114	114
PER PUPIL	Pearson Correlation	−.199*	−.121	−.172	1.000
	Sig. (2-tailed)	.034	.200	.068	.
	N	114	114	114	115

16.9

TABLE A.4 Lunch

		Frequency	Percent	Valid Percent	Cumulative Percent
Valid	F	101	82.1	82.1	82.1
	N	10	8.1	8.1	90.2
	R	12	9.8	9.8	100.0
	Total	123	100.0	100.0	

TABLE A.5 IEP

		Frequency	Percent	Valid Percent	Cumulative Percent
Valid	N	98	79.7	79.7	79.7
	Y	25	20.3	20.3	100.0
	Total	123	100.0	100.0	

TABLE A.6 Speech

		Frequency	Percent	Valid Percent	Cumulative Percent
Valid	N	123	100.0	100.0	100.0

TABLE A.7 Gift

		Frequency	Percent	Valid Percent	Cumulative Percent
Valid	F	116	94.3	94.3	94.3
	T	7	5.7	5.7	100.0
	Total	123	100.0	100.0	

16.10

TABLE A.8 Descriptive Statistics

	N	Minimum	Maximum	Mean	Std. Deviation
ELASS05	123	175.00	827.00	761.5285	112.1483
ELASS04	123	94.00	807.00	675.9350	114.7922
ELASS03	123	102.00	804.00	577.2846	102.2461
Valid N (listwise)	123				

Chapter 17

17.1 A random sample would be selected and statistics computed from this sample. The sample measures would reflect the population measures within the limits of sampling fluctuation. Hence, the statistics are used to infer to the parameters, again within the bounds of sampling fluctuation. The statistic involved would be the mean reading level of the sample of first-graders measured; the corresponding parameter is the mean reading level of the entire first-grade population. The chain of reasoning follows the implied inference. The population has certain measures, called parameters. The statistics are determined, and from them we reason back to the corresponding parameters and draw conclusions about the parameters. In this situation, conclusions are drawn about the population mean from the observed sample mean.

17.2 A statistic is a measure of a sample, and a parameter is a measure of a population. The sampling distribution is the distribution of the statistic, usually a theoretical distribution. (It is the distribution of all possible values of the statistic for the given sample size.) The sampling distribution provides the theoretical base for how the statistic under study behaves; that is, it identifies the shape, location, and dispersion of the distribution of the statistic of which the researcher has one observation.

17.3 **a.** If we were interested only in describing the distribution of scores for these 150 students.

b. If inferences were being made to a larger population of teacher education students and the 150 students consisted of a random sample of this population.

c. If the relationships between the variables were of interest.

17.4 We would reject the hypothesis because with 19 degrees of freedom and a two-tailed test (no direction is hypothesized) a *t*-value of 2.09 is required for significance at the .05 level.

17.5 The sampling distribution of the mean is used; this would be the *t*-distribution with 399 degrees of freedom (*df*), but, because the *df* are so large, the normal distribution would be used. If sample size were 25, the *t*-distribution with 24 *df* would be used. There would be an error, because the confidence interval is constructed symmetrically about the sample mean; therefore, it must be the midpoint of the interval. The interval would be shorter if it were a 90 percent confidence interval.

17.6 In this case, the difference between the four sample means could be analyzed simultaneously, rather than analyzing only the difference between two means at a time with a *t*-test. The null hypothesis is that the four population means are equal—H_0: $\mu_1 = \mu_2 = \mu_3 = \mu_4$. Differences between male and female teachers also could be analyzed by extending the ANOVA to a two-way ANOVA.

17.7 Because the χ^2-value was significant, the conclusion is that the four samples were not drawn from a common population, or that the population distributions differ with respect to this variable. The probability that the sample distributions would have appeared due to random sampling fluctuation if the population distributions were the same is less than .05.

17.8 Grade level and attitude toward school are independent. If the χ^2-test is significant, we conclude that grade level and attitude toward school are related (not independent) in the student population sampled. If the χ^2-test is not significant, we cannot reject the hypothesis of independence and conclude that grade level and attitude toward school are not related to the population.

17.9 **a.** The mean would be computed as a measure of central tendency and the standard deviation as a measure of dispersion. The teachers also might compute the median and mode as additional information about central tendency, and the range as a second measure of dispersion.

b. The correlation coefficient between math test performance and attitude inventory score.

c. In contrast to the situation in (b) above, a random sample was selected so this situation involved inferential statistics. The correlation coefficient between math test scores and attitude inventory scores would be computed. This coefficient is a statistic and it would be used to test the null hypothesis that in the high school population the correlation is zero.

d. The cognitive task means of the four groups would be computed and used to test the null hypothesis, H_0: $\mu_1 = \mu_2 = \mu_3 = \mu_4$, by computing an ANOVA.
e. A goodness-of-fit test is called for; use a chi-square test, testing the sample distribution against the uniform distribution.

17.10 The two types of possible errors are rejecting a true hypothesis and failing to reject a false hypothesis. In inferential statistics, we do not know the values of the parameters about which we are hypothesizing; therefore, there is always the possibility of making an error. Inferences are made to the parameters from the statistics on the basis of probability. Although the probability of making an error may be very small, it is never zero.

17.12 Errors of reasoning or procedure:
a. A *t*-test does not apply to data measured on an ordinal scale, and means should not have been computed with ordinal data.
b. There is confusion on significance; a test that is significant at the .01 level is also significant at the .05 level.
c. Rejecting the null hypothesis would result in concluding that the population measures, not the sample measures, are different.
d. Because the null hypothesis is rejected, there is no probability of having made a Type II or beta error. The possibility does exist of having made a Type I or alpha error—that is, rejecting a true hypothesis.

17.13 **a.** H_0: $\mu_1 = \mu_2 = \mu_3 = \mu_4 = \mu_5$. The population means of the five experimental treatments are equal. The null hypotheses also could be stated as: The five experimental treatments are equally effective in the population.
b. The computed *F*-value of 3.11 exceeds the critical value of *F* from Table D in Appendix 3, for four and 95 *df* and a significance level of .05. The critical value is about 2.49. Therefore, we reject the null hypothesis and conclude that the population means are not all equal.
c. The probability that the five sample means would appear by chance, if the population means are all equal, is less than .05.

17.15 We want to make some decisions about the population characteristics, which are parameters. We draw a sample and compute characteristics of the sample, which are statistics. The statistics reflect the corresponding parameters within the bounds of random sampling fluctuations. We hypothesize about parameters, and the statistics have a certain probability of appearing by chance if the hypotheses are true. It is not necessary to determine the exact probability, only whether it is less than or greater than the significance level. We infer from the statistics and the results of hypothesis testing to the parameters and thus make decisions about the population.

17.17 The average SAT Reading scores and per-pupil expenditures correlate −.121. The associated *p*-value (labeled Sig. in the SPSS output) is .200. This value is greater than .01, so we fail to reject the hypothesis that the population correlation is zero.

The average SAT Reading scores and total expenditures correlate .192. The associated *p*-value (labeled Sig. in the SPSS output) is .041. This value is greater than .01, so we fail to reject the hypothesis that the population correlation is zero. Note that if we had been using the .05 level of significance, we would have rejected the null hypothesis.

TABLE A.9 Correlations

		Reading	Per-Pupil	Total
Reading	Pearson Correlation	1.000	−.121	.192*
	Sig. (2-tailed)	.	.200	.041
	N	114	114	114
Per-Pupil	Pearson Correlation	−.121	1.000	−.230*
	Sig. (2-tailed)	.200	.	.013
	N	114	115	115
Total	Pearson Correlation	.192*	−.230*	1.000
	Sig. (2-tailed)	.041	.013	.
	N	114	115	115

*Correlation is significant at the 0.05 level (2-tailed)

17.18 The chi-square value is found to be 5.423. The *p*-value (noted as Sig. in SPSS) is .020. This value is less than .05 so we reject the null hypothesis. Having an IEP is related to gender. Inspection of the table reveals that proportionally more boys have IEPs than girls do.

TABLE A.10 Gender * IEP Cross-Tabulation

		IEP		
		N	**Y**	**Total**
Gender	F	53	7	60
	M	45	18	63
Total		98	25	123

TABLE A.11 Chi-Square Tests

	Value	*df*	Asymp. Sig. (2-sided)	Exact Sig. (2-sided)	Exact Sig. (1-sided)
Pearson Chi-Square	5.423[b]	1	.200	.	.
Continuity Correction[a]	4.429	1	.035	.	.
Likelihood Ratio	5.590	1	.018	.	.
Fisher's Exact Test	.	.	.	.025	.017
N of Valid Cases	123	.	.	.	.

[a]Computed only for a 2 × 2 table

[b]0 cells (.0%) have expected count less than 5. The minimum expected count is 12.20.

APPENDIX 3

Tables

TABLE A Ordinates and Areas of the Normal Curve (in terms of σ units)

$\frac{x}{\sigma}$	Area	Ordinate	$\frac{x}{\sigma}$	Area	Ordinate	$\frac{x}{\sigma}$	Area	Ordinate	$\frac{x}{\sigma}$	Area	Ordinate
.00	.0000	.3989	.35	.1368	.3752	.70	.2580	.3123	1.05	.3531	.2299
.01	.0040	.3989	.36	.1406	.3739	.71	.2611	.3101	1.06	.3554	.2275
.02	.0080	.3989	.37	.1443	.3725	.72	.2642	.3079	1.07	.3577	.2251
.03	.0120	.3988	.38	.1480	.3712	.73	.2673	.3056	1.08	.3599	.2227
.04	.0160	.3986	.39	.1517	.3697	.74	.2703	.3034	1.09	.3621	.2203
.05	.0199	.3984	.40	.1554	.3683	.75	.2734	.3011	1.10	.3643	.2179
.06	.0239	.3992	.41	.1591	.3668	.76	.2764	.2989	1.11	.3665	.2155
.07	.0279	.3980	.42	.1628	.3653	.77	.2794	.2966	1.12	.3686	.2131
.08	.0319	.3977	.43	.1664	.3637	.78	.2823	.2943	1.13	.3708	.2107
.09	.0359	.3973	.44	.1700	.3621	.79	.2852	.2920	1.14	.3729	.2083
.10	.0398	.3970	.45	.1736	.3605	.80	.2881	.2897	1.15	.3749	.2059
.11	.0438	.3965	.46	.1772	.3589	.81	.2910	.2874	1.16	.3770	.2036
.12	.0478	.3961	.47	.1808	.3572	.82	.2939	.2850	1.17	.3790	.2012
.13	.0517	.3956	.48	.1844	.3555	.83	.2967	.2827	1.18	.3810	.1989
.14	.0557	.3951	.49	.1879	.3538	.84	.2995	.2803	1.19	.3830	.1965
.15	.0596	.3945	.50	.1915	.3521	.85	.3023	.2780	1.20	.3849	.1942
.16	.0636	.3939	.51	.1950	.3503	.86	.3051	.2756	1.21	.3869	.1919
.17	.0675	.3932	.52	.1985	.3485	.87	.3078	.2732	1.22	.3888	.1895
.18	.0714	.3925	.53	.2019	.3467	.88	.3106	.2709	1.23	.3907	.1872
.19	.0753	.3918	.54	.2054	.3448	.89	.3133	.2685	1.24	.3925	.1849
.20	.0793	.3910	.55	.2088	.3429	.90	.3159	.2661	1.25	.3944	.1826
.21	.0832	.3902	.56	.2123	.3410	.91	.3186	.2637	1.26	.3962	.1804
.22	.0871	.3894	.57	.2157	.3391	.92	.3212	.2613	1.27	.3980	.1781
.23	.0910	.3885	.58	.2190	.3372	.93	.3238	.2589	1.28	.3997	.1758
.24	.0948	.3876	.59	.2224	.3352	.94	.3264	.2565	1.29	.4015	.1736
.25	.0987	.3867	.60	.2257	.3332	.95	.3289	.2541	1.30	.4032	.1714
.26	.1026	.3857	.61	.2291	.3312	.96	.3315	.2516	1.31	.4049	.1691
.27	.1064	.3847	.62	.2324	.3292	.97	.3340	.2492	1.32	.4066	.1669
.28	.1103	.3836	.63	.2357	.3271	.98	.3365	.2468	1.33	.4082	.1647
.29	.1141	.3825	.64	.2389	.3251	.99	.3389	.2444	1.34	.4099	.1626
.30	.1179	.3814	.65	.2422	.3230	1.00	.3413	.2420	1.35	.4115	.1604
.31	.1217	.3802	.66	.2454	.3209	1.01	.3438	.2396	1.36	.4131	.1582
.32	.1255	.3790	.67	.2486	.3187	1.02	.3461	.2371	1.37	.4147	.1561
.33	.1293	.3778	.68	.2517	.3166	1.03	.3485	.2347	1.38	.4162	.1539
.34	.1331	.3765	.69	.2549	.3144	1.04	.3508	.2323	1.39	.4177	.1518

Source: Educational Statistics, by J. E. Wert. Copyright 1938 by McGraw-Hill Book Company. Used by permission of McGraw-Hill Book Company.

TABLE A ***(Continued)***

$\frac{x}{\sigma}$	Area	Ordi-nate	$\frac{x}{\sigma}$	Area	Ordi-nate	$\frac{x}{\sigma}$	Area	Ordi-nate	$\frac{x}{\sigma}$	Area	Ordi-nate
1.40	.4192	.1497	1.80	.4641	.0790	2.20	.4861	.0355	2.60	.4953	.0136
1.41	.4207	.1476	1.81	.4649	.0775	2.21	.4864	.0347	2.61	.4955	.0132
1.42	.4222	.1456	1.82	.4656	.0761	2.22	.4868	.0339	2.62	.4956	.0129
1.43	.4236	.1435	1.83	.4664	.0748	2.23	.4871	.0332	2.63	.4957	.0126
1.44	.4251	.1415	1.84	.4671	.0734	2.24	.4875	.0325	2.64	.4959	.0122
1.45	.4265	.1394	1.85	.4678	.0721	2.25	.4878	.0317	2.65	.4960	.0119
1.46	.4279	.1374	1.86	.4686	.0707	2.26	.4881	.0310	2.66	.4961	.0116
1.47	.4292	.1354	1.87	.4693	.0694	2.27	.4884	.0303	2.67	.4962	.0113
1.48	.4306	.1334	1.88	.4699	.0681	2.28	.4887	.0297	2.68	.4963	.0110
1.49	.4319	.1315	1.89	.4706	.0669	2.29	.4890	.0290	2.69	.4964	.0107
1.50	.4332	.1295	1.90	.4713	.0656	2.30	.4893	.0283	2.70	.4965	.0104
1.51	.4345	.1276	1.91	.4719	.0644	2.31	.4896	.0277	2.71	.4966	.0101
1.52	.4357	.1257	1.92	.4726	.0632	2.32	.4898	.0270	2.72	.4967	.0099
1.53	.4370	.1238	1.93	.4732	.0620	2.33	.4901	.0264	2.73	.4968	.0096
1.54	.4382	.1219	1.94	.4738	.0608	2.34	.4904	.0258	2.74	.4969	.0093
1.55	.4394	.1200	1.95	.4744	.0596	2.35	.4906	.0252	2.75	.4970	.0091
1.56	.4406	.1182	1.96	.4750	.0584	2.36	.4909	.0246	2.76	.4971	.0088
1.57	.4418	.1163	1.97	.4756	.0573	2.37	.4911	.0241	2.77	.4972	.0086
1.58	.4429	.1145	1.98	.4761	.0562	2.38	.4913	.0235	2.78	.4973	.0084
1.59	.4441	.1127	1.99	.4767	.0551	2.39	.4916	.0229	2.79	.4974	.0081
1.60	.4452	.1109	2.00	.4772	.0540	2.40	.4918	.0224	2.80	.4974	.0079
1.61	.4463	.1092	2.01	.4778	.0529	2.41	.4920	.0219	2.81	.4975	.0077
1.62	.4474	.1074	2.02	.4783	.0519	2.42	.4922	.0213	2.82	.4976	.0075
1.63	.4484	.1057	2.03	.4788	.0508	2.43	.4925	.0208	2.83	.4977	.0073
1.64	.4495	.1040	2.04	.4793	.0498	2.44	.4927	.0203	2.84	.4977	.0071
1.65	.4505	.1023	2.05	.4798	.0488	2.45	.4929	.0198	2.85	.4978	.0069
1.66	.4515	.1006	2.06	.4803	.0478	2.46	.4931	.0194	2.86	.4979	.0067
1.67	.4525	.0989	2.07	.4808	.0468	2.47	.4932	.0189	2.87	.4979	.0065
1.68	.4535	.0973	2.08	.4812	.0459	2.48	.4934	.0184	2.88	.4980	.0063
1.69	.4545	.0957	2.09	.4817	.0449	2.49	.4936	.0180	2.89	.4981	.0061
1.70	.4554	.0940	2.10	.4821	.0440	2.50	.4938	.0175	2.90	.4981	.0060
1.71	.4564	.0925	2.11	.4826	.0431	2.51	.4940	.0171	2.91	.4982	.0058
1.72	.4573	.0909	2.12	.4830	.0422	2.52	.4941	.0167	2.92	.4982	.0056
1.73	.4582	.0893	2.13	.4834	.0413	2.53	.4943	.0163	2.93	.4993	.0055
1.74	.4591	.0878	2.14	.4838	.0404	2.54	.4945	.0158	2.94	.4984	.0053
1.75	.4599	.0863	2.15	.4842	.0395	2.55	.4946	.0154	2.95	.4984	.0051
1.76	.4608	.0848	2.16	.4846	.0387	2.56	.4948	.0151	2.96	.4985	.0050
1.77	.4616	.0833	2.17	.4850	.0379	2.57	.4949	.0147	2.97	.4985	.0048
1.78	.4625	.0818	2.18	.4854	.0371	2.58	.4951	.0143	2.98	.4986	.0047
1.79	.4633	.0804	2.19	.4857	.0363	2.59	.4952	.0139	2.99	.4986	.0046
									3.00	.4987	.0044

TABLE B Critical Values of *t*

	Level of significance for one-tailed test					
	.10	.05	.025	.01	.005	.0005
	Level of significance for two-tailed test					
df	.20	.10	.05	.02	.01	.001
1	3.078	6.314	12.706	31.821	63.657	636.619
2	1.886	2.920	4.303	6.965	9.925	31.598
3	1.638	2.353	3.182	4.541	5.841	12.941
4	1.533	2.132	2.776	3.747	4.604	8.610
5	1.476	2.015	2.571	3.365	4.032	6.859
6	1.440	1.943	2.447	3.143	3.707	5.959
7	1.415	1.895	2.365	2.998	3.499	5.405
8	1.397	1.860	2.306	2.896	3.355	5.041
9	1.383	1.833	2.262	2.821	3.250	4.781
10	1.372	1.812	2.228	2.764	3.169	4.587
11	1.363	1.796	2.201	2.718	3.106	4.437
12	1.356	1.782	2.179	2.681	3.055	4.318
13	1.350	1.771	2.160	2.650	3.012	4.221
14	1.345	1.761	2.145	2.624	2.977	4.140
15	1.341	1.753	2.131	2.602	2.947	4.073
16	1.337	1.746	2.120	2.583	2.921	4.015
17	1.333	1.740	2.110	2.567	2.898	3.965
18	1.330	1.734	2.101	2.552	2.878	3.922
19	1.328	1.729	2.093	2.539	2.861	3.883
20	1.325	1.725	2.086	2.528	2.845	3.850
21	1.323	1.721	2.080	2.518	2.831	3.819
22	1.321	1.717	2.074	2.508	2.819	3.792
23	1.319	1.714	2.069	2.500	2.807	3.767
24	1.318	1.711	2.064	2.492	2.797	3.745
25	1.316	1.708	2.060	2.485	2.787	3.725
26	1.315	1.706	2.056	2.479	2.779	3.707
27	1.314	1.703	2.052	2.473	2.771	3.690
28	1.313	1.701	2.048	2.467	2.763	3.674
29	1.311	1.699	2.045	2.462	2.756	3.659
30	1.310	1.697	2.042	2.457	2.750	3.646
40	1.303	1.684	2.021	2.423	2.704	3.551
60	1.296	1.671	2.000	2.390	2.660	3.460
120	1.289	1.658	1.980	2.358	2.617	3.373
χ	1.282	1.645	1.960	2.326	2.576	3.291

Source: Abridged from Table III, p. 46 of R. A. Fisher and F. Yates, *Statistical Tables for Biological, Agricultural and Medical Research,* 6th edition. Copyright © 1974. Reprinted by permission of Pearson Education.

TABLE C Upper Percentage Points of the χ^2 Distribution

$1 - \chi$

χ

0

χ_α^2

df	.99	.98	.95	.90	.80	.70	.50	.30	.20	.10	.05	.02	.01	.001
1	$.0^3157$	$.0^3628$	.00393	.0158	.0642	.148	.455	1.074	1.642	2.706	3.841	5.412	6.635	10.827
2	.0201	.0404	.103	.211	.446	.713	1.386	2.408	3.219	4.605	5.991	7.824	9.210	13.815
3	.115	.185	.352	.584	1.005	1.424	2.366	3.665	4.642	6.251	7.815	9.837	11.345	16.266
4	.297	.429	.711	1.064	1.649	2.195	3.357	4.878	5.989	7.779	9.488	11.668	13.277	18.467
5	.554	.752	1.145	1.610	2.343	3.000	4.351	6.064	7.289	9.236	11.070	13.388	15.086	20.515
6	.872	1.134	1.635	2.204	3.070	3.828	5.348	7.231	8.558	10.645	12.592	15.033	16.812	22.457
7	1.239	1.564	2.167	2.833	3.822	4.671	6.346	8.383	9.803	12.017	14.067	16.622	18.475	24.322
8	1.646	2.032	2.733	3.490	4.594	5.527	7.344	9.524	11.030	13.362	15.507	18.168	20.090	26.125
9	2.088	2.532	3.325	4.168	5.380	6.393	8.343	10.656	12.242	14.684	16.919	19.679	21.666	27.877
10	2.558	3.059	3.940	4.865	6.179	7.267	9.342	11.781	13.442	15.987	18.307	21.161	23.209	29.588
11	3.053	3.609	4.575	5.578	6.989	8.148	10.341	12.899	14.631	17.275	19.675	22.618	24.725	31.264
12	3.571	4.178	5.226	6.304	7.807	9.034	11.340	14.011	15.812	18.549	21.026	24.054	26.217	32.909
13	4.107	4.765	5.892	7.042	8.634	9.926	12.340	15.119	16.985	19.812	22.362	25.472	27.688	34.528
14	4.660	5.368	6.571	7.790	9.467	10.821	13.339	16.222	18.151	21.064	23.685	26.873	29.141	36.123
15	5.229	5.985	7.261	8.547	10.307	11.721	14.339	17.322	19.311	22.307	24.996	28.259	30.578	37.697
16	5.812	6.614	7.962	9.312	11.152	12.624	15.338	18.418	20.465	23.542	26.296	29.633	32.000	39.252
17	6.408	7.255	8.672	10.085	12.002	13.531	16.338	19.511	21.615	24.769	27.587	30.995	33.409	40.790
18	7.015	7.906	9.390	10.865	12.857	14.440	17.338	20.601	22.760	25.989	28.869	32.346	34.805	42.312
19	7.633	8.567	10.117	11.651	13.716	15.352	18.338	21.689	23.900	27.204	30.144	33.687	36.191	43.820
20	8.260	9.237	10.851	12.443	14.578	16.266	19.337	22.775	25.038	28.412	31.410	35.020	37.566	45.315
21	8.897	9.915	11.591	13.240	15.445	17.182	20.337	23.858	26.171	29.615	32.671	36.343	38.932	46.797
22	9.542	10.600	12.338	14.041	16.314	18.101	21.337	24.939	27.301	30.813	33.924	37.659	40.289	48.268
23	10.196	11.293	13.091	14.848	17.187	19.021	22.337	26.018	28.429	32.007	35.172	38.968	41.638	49.728
24	10.856	11.992	13.848	15.659	18.062	19.943	23.337	27.096	29.553	33.196	36.415	40.270	42.980	51.179
25	11.524	12.697	14.611	16.473	18.940	20.867	24.337	28.172	30.675	34.382	37.652	41.566	44.314	52.620
26	12.198	13.409	15.379	17.292	19.820	21.792	25.336	29.246	31.795	35.563	38.885	42.856	45.642	54.052
27	12.879	14.125	16.151	18.114	20.703	22.719	26.336	30.319	32.912	36.741	40.113	44.140	46.963	55.476
28	13.565	14.847	16.928	18.939	21.588	23.647	27.336	31.391	34.027	37.916	41.337	45.419	43.278	56.893
29	14.256	15.574	17.708	19.768	22.475	24.577	28.336	32.461	35.139	39.087	42.557	46.693	49.588	58.302
30	14.953	16.306	18.493	20.599	23.364	25.508	29.336	33.530	36.250	40.256	43.773	47.962	50.892	59.703

For $df > 30$, the expression $\sqrt{2\chi^2} - \sqrt{2df - 1}$ may be used as a normal deviate with unit variance.

Source: Abridged from Table IV, p. 47 of R. A. Fisher and F. Yates: *Statistical Tables for Biological, Agricultural, and Medical Research,* 6th edition.

TABLE D Upper Percentage Points of the *F*-Distribution

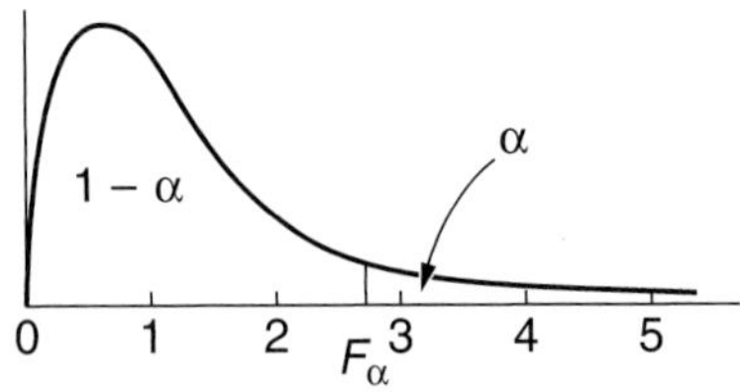

df *for denominator*	α	df *for numerator* 1	2	3	4	5	6	7	8	9	10	11	12
	.25	5.83	7.50	8.20	8.58	8.82	8.98	9.10	9.19	9.26	9.32	9.36	9.41
1	.10	39.9	49.5	53.6	55.8	57.2	58.2	58.9	59.4	59.9	60.2	60.5	60.7
	.05	161	200	216	225	230	234	237	239	241	242	243	244
	.25	2.57	3.00	3.15	3.23	3.28	3.31	3.34	3.35	3.37	3.38	3.39	3.39
2	.10	8.53	9.00	9.16	9.24	9.29	9.33	9.35	9.37	9.38	9.39	9.40	9.41
	.05	18.5	19.0	19.2	19.2	19.3	19.3	19.4	19.4	19.4	19.4	19.4	19.4
	.01	98.5	99.0	99.2	99.2	99.3	99.3	99.4	99.4	99.4	99.4	99.4	99.4
	.25	2.02	2.28	2.36	2.39	2.41	2.42	2.43	2.44	2.44	2.44	2.45	2.45
3	.10	5.54	5.46	5.39	5.34	5.31	5.28	5.27	5.25	5.24	5.23	5.22	5.22
	.05	10.1	9.55	9.28	9.12	9.01	8.94	8.89	8.85	8.81	8.79	8.76	8.74
	.01	34.1	30.8	29.5	28.7	28.2	27.9	27.7	27.5	27.3	27.2	27.1	27.1
	.25	1.81	2.00	2.05	2.06	2.07	2.08	2.08	2.08	2.08	2.08	2.08	2.08
4	.10	4.54	4.32	4.19	4.11	4.05	4.01	3.98	3.95	3.94	3.92	3.91	3.90
	.05	7.71	6.94	6.59	6.39	6.26	6.16	6.09	6.04	6.00	5.96	5.94	5.91
	.01	21.2	18.0	16.7	16.0	15.5	15.2	15.0	14.8	14.7	14.5	14.4	14.4
	.25	1.69	1.85	1.88	1.89	1.89	1.89	1.89	1.89	1.89	1.89	1.89	1.89
5	.10	4.06	3.78	3.62	3.52	3.45	3.40	3.37	3.34	3.32	3.30	3.28	3.27
	.05	6.61	5.79	5.41	5.19	5.05	4.95	4.88	4.82	4.77	4.74	4.71	4.68
	.01	16.3	13.3	12.1	11.4	11.0	10.7	10.5	10.3	10.2	10.1	9.96	9.89
	.25	1.62	1.76	1.78	1.79	1.79	1.78	1.78	1.78	1.77	1.77	1.77	1.77
6	.10	3.78	3.46	3.29	3.18	3.11	3.05	3.01	2.98	2.96	2.94	2.92	2.90
	.05	5.99	5.14	4.76	4.53	4.39	4.28	4.21	4.15	4.10	4.06	4.03	4.00
	.01	13.7	10.9	9.78	9.15	8.75	8.47	8.26	8.10	7.98	7.87	7.79	7.72
	.25	1.57	1.70	1.72	1.72	1.71	1.71	1.70	1.70	1.69	1.69	1.69	1.68
7	.10	3.59	3.26	3.07	2.96	2.88	2.83	2.78	2.75	2.72	2.70	2.68	2.67
	.05	5.59	4.74	4.35	4.12	3.97	3.87	3.79	3.73	3.68	3.64	3.60	3.57
	.01	12.2	9.55	8.45	7.85	7.46	7.19	6.99	6.84	6.72	6.62	6.54	6.47
	.25	1.54	1.66	1.67	1.66	1.66	1.65	1.64	1.64	1.63	1.63	1.63	1.62
8	.10	3.46	3.11	2.92	2.81	2.73	2.67	2.62	2.59	2.56	2.54	2.52	2.50
	.05	5.32	4.46	4.07	3.84	3.69	3.58	3.50	3.44	3.39	3.35	3.31	3.28
	.01	11.3	8.65	7.59	7.01	6.63	6.37	6.18	6.03	5.91	5.81	5.73	5.67
	.25	1.51	1.62	1.63	1.63	1.62	1.61	1.60	1.60	1.59	1.59	1.58	1.58
9	.10	3.36	3.01	2.81	2.69	2.61	2.55	2.51	2.47	2.44	2.42	2.40	2.38
	.05	5.12	4.26	3.86	3.63	3.48	3.37	3.29	3.23	3.18	3.14	3.10	3.07
	.01	10.6	8.02	6.99	6.42	6.06	5.80	5.61	5.47	5.35	5.26	5.18	5.11

TABLE D (*Continued*)

df for numerator													df *for de-nomi-nator*
15	20	24	30	40	50	60	100	120	200	500	χ	α	
9.49	9.58	9.63	9.67	9.71	9.74	9.76	9.78	9.80	9.82	9.84	9.85	.25	
61.2	61.7	62.0	62.3	62.5	62.7	62.8	63.0	63.1	63.2	63.3	63.3	.10	1
246	248	249	250	251	252	252	253	253	254	254	254	.05	
3.41	3.43	3.43	3.44	3.45	3.45	3.46	3.47	3.47	3.48	3.48	3.48	.25	
9.42	9.44	9.45	9.46	9.47	9.47	9.47	9.48	9.48	9.49	9.49	9.49	.10	2
19.4	19.4	19.5	19.5	19.5	19.5	19.5	19.5	19.5	19.5	19.5	19.5	.05	
99.4	99.4	99.5	99.5	99.5	99.5	99.5	99.5	99.5	99.5	99.5	99.5	.01	
2.46	2.46	2.46	2.47	2.47	2.47	2.47	2.47	2.47	2.47	2.47	2.47	.25	
5.20	5.18	5.18	5.17	5.16	5.15	5.15	5.14	5.14	5.14	5.14	5.13	.10	3
8.70	8.66	8.64	8.62	8.59	8.58	8.57	8.55	8.55	8.54	8.53	8.53	.05	
26.9	26.7	26.6	26.5	26.4	26.4	26.3	26.2	26.2	26.2	26.1	26.1	.01	
2.08	2.08	2.08	2.08	2.08	2.08	2.08	2.08	2.08	2.08	2.08	2.08	.25	
3.87	3.84	3.83	3.82	3.80	3.80	3.79	3.78	3.78	3.77	3.76	3.76	.10	4
5.86	5.80	5.77	5.75	5.72	5.70	5.69	5.66	5.66	5.65	5.64	5.63	.05	
14.2	14.0	13.9	13.8	13.7	13.7	13.7	13.6	13.6	13.5	13.5	13.5	.01	
1.89	1.88	1.88	1.88	1.88	1.88	1.87	1.87	1.87	1.87	1.87	1.87	.25	
3.24	3.21	3.19	3.17	3.16	3.15	3.14	3.13	3.12	3.12	3.11	3.10	.10	5
4.62	4.56	4.53	4.50	4.46	4.44	4.43	4.41	4.40	4.39	4.37	4.36	.05	
9.72	9.55	9.47	9.38	9.29	9.24	9.20	9.13	9.11	9.08	9.04	9.02	.01	
1.76	1.76	1.75	1.75	1.75	1.75	1.74	1.74	1.74	1.74	1.74	1.74	.25	
2.87	2.84	2.82	2.80	2.78	2.77	2.76	2.75	2.74	2.73	2.73	2.72	.10	6
3.94	3.87	3.84	3.81	3.77	3.75	3.74	3.71	3.70	3.69	3.68	3.67	.05	
7.56	7.40	7.31	7.23	7.14	7.09	7.06	6.99	6.97	6.93	6.90	6.88	.01	
1.68	1.67	1.67	1.66	1.66	1.66	1.65	1.65	1.65	1.65	1.65	1.65	.25	
2.63	2.59	2.58	2.56	2.54	2.52	2.51	2.50	2.49	2.48	2.48	2.47	.10	7
3.51	3.44	3.41	3.38	3.34	3.32	3.30	3.27	3.27	3.25	3.24	3.23	.05	
6.31	6.16	6.07	5.99	5.91	5.86	5.82	5.75	5.74	5.70	5.67	5.65	.01	
1.62	1.61	1.60	1.60	1.59	1.59	1.59	1.58	1.58	1.58	1.58	1.58	.25	
2.46	2.42	2.40	2.38	2.36	2.35	2.34	2.32	2.32	2.31	2.30	2.29	.10	8
3.22	3.15	3.12	3.08	3.04	3.02	3.01	2.97	2.97	2.95	2.94	2.93	.05	
5.52	5.36	5.28	5.20	5.12	5.07	5.03	4.96	4.95	4.91	4.88	4.86	.01	
1.57	1.56	1.56	1.55	1.55	1.54	1.54	1.53	1.53	1.53	1.53	1.53	.25	
2.34	2.30	2.28	2.25	2.23	2.22	2.21	2.19	2.18	2.17	2.17	2.16	.10	9
3.01	2.94	2.90	2.86	2.83	2.80	2.79	2.76	2.75	2.73	2.72	2.71	.05	
4.96	4.81	4.73	4.65	4.57	4.52	4.48	4.42	4.40	4.36	4.33	4.31	.01	

(*continued*)

TABLE D (*Continued*)

df *for de-nomi-nator*	α	df *for numerator* 1	2	3	4	5	6	7	8	9	10	11	12
	.25	1.49	1.60	1.60	1.59	1.59	1.58	1.57	1.56	1.56	1.55	1.55	1.54
10	.10	3.29	2.92	2.73	2.61	2.52	2.46	2.41	2.38	2.35	2.32	2.30	2.28
	.05	4.96	4.10	3.71	3.48	3.33	3.22	3.14	3.07	3.02	2.98	2.94	2.91
	.01	10.0	7.56	6.55	5.99	5.64	5.39	5.20	5.06	4.94	4.85	4.77	4.71
	.25	1.47	1.58	1.58	1.57	1.56	1.55	1.54	1.53	1.53	1.52	1.52	1.51
11	.10	3.23	2.86	2.66	2.54	2.45	2.39	2.34	2.30	2.27	2.25	2.23	2.21
	.05	4.84	3.98	3.59	3.36	3.20	3.09	3.01	2.95	2.90	2.85	2.82	2.79
	.01	9.65	7.21	6.22	5.67	5.32	5.07	4.89	4.74	4.63	4.54	4.46	4.40
	.25	1.46	1.56	1.56	1.55	1.54	1.53	1.52	1.51	1.51	1.50	1.50	1.49
12	.10	3.18	2.81	2.61	2.48	2.39	2.33	2.28	2.24	2.21	2.19	2.17	2.15
	.05	4.75	3.89	3.49	3.26	3.11	3.00	2.91	2.85	2.80	2.75	2.72	2.69
	.01	9.33	6.93	5.95	5.41	5.06	4.82	4.64	4.50	4.39	4.30	4.22	4.16
	.25	1.45	1.55	1.55	1.53	1.52	1.51	1.50	1.49	1.49	1.48	1.47	1.47
13	.10	3.14	2.76	2.56	2.43	2.35	2.28	2.23	2.20	2.16	2.14	2.12	2.10
	.05	4.67	3.81	3.41	3.18	3.03	2.92	2.83	2.77	2.71	2.67	2.63	2.60
	.01	9.07	6.70	5.74	5.21	4.86	4.62	4.44	4.30	4.19	4.10	4.02	3.96
	.25	1.44	1.53	1.53	1.52	1.51	1.50	1.49	1.48	1.47	1.46	1.46	1.45
14	.10	3.10	2.73	2.52	2.39	2.31	2.24	2.19	2.15	2.12	2.10	2.08	2.05
	.05	4.60	3.74	3.34	3.11	2.96	2.85	2.76	2.70	2.65	2.60	2.57	2.53
	.01	8.86	6.51	5.56	5.04	4.69	4.46	4.28	4.14	4.03	3.94	3.86	3.80
	.25	1.43	1.52	1.52	1.51	1.49	1.48	1.47	1.46	1.46	1.45	1.44	1.44
15	.10	3.07	2.70	2.49	2.36	2.27	2.21	2.16	2.12	2.09	2.06	2.04	2.02
	.05	4.54	3.68	3.29	3.06	2.90	2.79	2.71	2.64	2.59	2.54	2.51	2.48
	.01	8.68	6.36	5.42	4.89	4.56	4.32	4.14	4.00	3.89	3.80	3.73	3.67
	.25	1.42	1.51	1.51	1.50	1.48	1.47	1.46	1.45	1.44	1.44	1.44	1.43
16	.10	3.05	2.67	2.46	2.33	2.24	2.18	2.13	2.09	2.06	2.03	2.01	1.99
	.05	4.49	3.63	3.24	3.01	2.85	2.74	2.66	2.59	2.54	2.49	2.46	2.42
	.01	8.53	6.23	5.29	4.77	4.44	4.20	4.03	3.89	3.78	3.69	3.62	3.55
	.25	1.42	1.51	1.50	1.49	1.47	1.46	1.45	1.44	1.43	1.43	1.42	1.41
17	.10	3.03	2.64	2.44	2.31	2.22	2.15	2.10	2.06	2.03	2.00	1.98	1.96
	.05	4.45	3.59	3.20	2.96	2.81	2.70	2.61	2.55	2.49	2.45	2.41	2.38
	.01	8.40	6.11	5.18	4.67	4.34	4.10	3.93	3.79	3.68	3.59	3.52	3.46
	.25	1.41	1.50	1.49	1.48	1.46	1.45	1.44	1.43	1.42	1.42	1.41	1.40
18	.10	3.01	2.62	2.42	2.29	2.20	2.13	2.08	2.04	2.00	1.98	1.96	1.93
	.05	4.41	3.55	3.16	2.93	2.77	2.66	2.58	2.51	2.46	2.41	2.37	2.34
	.01	8.29	6.01	5.09	4.58	4.25	4.01	3.84	3.71	3.60	3.51	3.43	3.37
	.25	1.41	1.49	1.49	1.47	1.46	1.44	1.43	1.42	1.41	1.41	1.40	1.40
19	.10	2.99	2.61	2.40	2.27	2.18	2.11	2.06	2.02	1.98	1.96	1.94	1.91
	.05	4.38	3.52	3.13	2.90	2.74	2.63	2.54	2.48	2.42	2.38	2.34	2.31
	.01	8.18	5.93	5.01	4.50	4.17	3.94	3.77	3.63	3.52	3.43	3.36	3.30
	.25	1.40	1.49	1.48	1.46	1.45	1.44	1.43	1.42	1.41	1.40	1.39	1.39
20	.10	2.97	2.59	2.38	2.25	2.16	2.09	2.04	2.00	1.96	1.94	1.92	1.89
	.05	4.35	3.49	3.10	2.87	2.71	2.60	2.51	2.45	2.39	2.35	2.31	2.28
	.01	8.10	5.85	4.94	4.43	4.10	3.87	3.70	3.56	3.46	3.37	3.29	3.23

TABLE D ***(Continued)***

df *for numerator*													df *for denominator*
15	20	24	30	40	50	60	100	120	200	500	χ	α	
1.53	1.52	1.52	1.51	1.51	1.50	1.50	1.49	1.49	1.49	1.48	1.48	.25	
2.24	2.20	2.18	2.16	2.13	2.12	2.11	2.09	2.08	2.07	2.06	2.06	.10	10
2.85	2.77	2.74	2.70	2.66	2.64	2.62	2.59	2.58	2.56	2.55	2.54	.05	
4.56	4.41	4.33	4.25	4.17	4.12	4.08	4.01	4.00	3.96	3.93	3.91	.01	
1.50	1.49	1.49	1.48	1.47	1.47	1.47	1.46	1.46	1.46	1.45	1.45	.25	
2.17	2.12	2.10	2.08	2.05	2.04	2.03	2.00	2.00	1.99	1.98	1.97	.10	11
2.72	2.65	2.61	2.57	2.53	2.51	2.49	2.46	2.45	2.43	2.42	2.40	.05	
4.25	4.10	4.02	3.94	3.86	3.81	3.78	3.71	3.69	3.66	3.62	3.60	.01	
1.48	1.47	1.46	1.45	1.45	1.44	1.44	1.43	1.43	1.43	1.42	1.42	.25	
2.10	2.06	2.04	2.01	1.99	1.97	1.96	1.94	1.93	1.92	1.91	1.90	.10	12
2.62	2.54	2.51	2.47	2.43	2.40	2.38	2.35	2.34	2.32	2.31	2.30	.05	
4.01	3.86	3.78	3.70	3.62	3.57	3.54	3.47	3.45	3.41	3.38	3.36	.01	
1.46	1.45	1.44	1.43	1.42	1.42	1.42	1.41	1.41	1.40	1.40	1.40	.25	
2.05	2.01	1.98	1.96	1.93	1.92	1.90	1.88	1.88	1.86	1.85	1.85	.10	13
2.53	2.46	2.42	2.38	2.34	2.31	2.30	2.26	2.25	2.23	2.22	2.21	.05	
3.82	3.66	3.59	3.51	3.43	3.38	3.34	3.27	3.25	3.22	3.19	3.17	.01	
1.44	1.43	14.2	1.41	1.41	1.40	1.40	1.39	1.39	1.39	1.38	1.38	.25	
2.01	1.96	1.94	1.91	1.89	1.87	1.86	1.83	1.83	1.82	1.80	1.80	.10	14
2.46	2.39	2.35	2.31	2.27	2.24	2.22	2.19	2.18	2.16	2.14	2.13	.05	
3.66	3.51	3.43	3.35	3.27	3.22	3.18	3.11	3.09	3.06	3.03	3.00	.01	
1.43	1.41	1.41	1.40	1.39	1.39	1.38	1.38	1.37	1.37	1.36	1.36	.25	
1.97	1.92	1.90	1.87	1.85	1.83	1.82	1.79	1.79	1.77	1.76	1.76	.10	15
2.40	2.33	2.29	2.25	2.20	2.18	2.16	2.12	2.11	2.10	2.08	2.07	.05	
3.52	3.37	3.29	3.21	3.13	3.08	3.05	2.98	2.96	2.92	2.89	2.87	.01	
1.41	1.40	1.39	1.38	1.37	1.37	1.36	1.36	1.35	1.35	1.34	1.34	.25	
1.94	1.89	1.87	1.84	1.81	1.79	1.78	1.76	1.75	1.74	1.73	1.72	.10	16
2.35	2.28	2.24	2.19	2.15	2.12	2.11	2.07	2.06	2.04	2.02	2.01	.05	
3.41	3.26	3.18	3.10	3.02	2.97	2.93	2.86	2.84	2.81	2.78	2.75	.01	
1.40	1.39	1.38	1.37	1.36	1.35	1.35	1.34	1.34	1.34	1.33	1.33	.25	
1.91	1.86	1.84	1.81	1.78	1.76	1.75	1.73	1.72	1.71	1.69	1.69	.10	17
2.31	2.23	2.19	2.15	2.10	2.08	2.06	2.02	2.01	1.99	1.97	1.96	.05	
3.31	3.16	3.08	3.00	2.92	2.87	2.83	2.76	2.75	2.71	2.68	2.65	.01	
1.39	1.38	1.37	1.36	1.35	1.34	1.34	1.33	1.33	1.32	1.32	1.32	.25	
1.89	1.84	1.81	1.78	1.75	1.74	1.72	1.70	1.69	1.68	1.67	1.66	.10	18
2.27	2.19	2.15	2.11	2.06	2.04	2.02	1.98	1.97	1.95	1.93	1.92	.05	
3.23	3.08	3.00	2.92	2.84	2.78	2.75	2.68	2.66	2.62	2.59	2.57	.01	
1.38	1.37	1.36	1.35	1.34	1.33	1.33	1.32	1.32	1.31	1.31	1.30	.25	
1.86	1.81	1.79	1.76	1.73	1.71	1.70	1.67	1.67	1.65	1.64	1.63	.10	19
2.23	2.16	2.11	2.07	2.03	2.00	1.98	1.94	1.93	1.91	1.89	1.88	.05	
3.15	3.00	2.92	2.84	2.76	2.71	2.67	2.60	2.58	2.55	2.51	2.49	.01	
1.37	1.36	1.35	1.34	1.33	1.33	1.32	1.31	1.31	1.30	1.30	1.29	.25	
1.84	1.79	1.77	1.74	1.71	1.69	1.68	1.65	1.64	1.63	1.62	1.61	.10	20
2.20	2.12	2.08	2.04	1.99	1.97	1.95	1.91	1.90	1.88	1.86	1.84	.05	
3.09	2.94	2.86	2.78	2.69	2.64	2.61	2.54	2.52	2.48	2.44	2.42	.01	

(continued)

TABLE D ***(Continued)***

df *for de-nomi-nator*	α	df *for numerator* 1	2	3	4	5	6	7	8	9	10	11	12
	.25	1.40	1.48	1.47	1.45	1.44	1.42	1.41	1.40	1.39	1.39	1.38	1.3
22	.10	2.95	2.56	2.35	2.22	2.13	2.06	2.01	1.97	1.93	1.90	1.88	1.8
	.05	4.30	3.44	3.05	2.82	2.66	2.55	2.46	2.40	2.34	2.30	2.26	2.2
	.01	7.95	5.72	4.82	4.31	3.99	3.76	3.59	3.45	3.35	3.26	3.18	3.1
	.25	1.39	1.47	1.46	1.44	1.43	1.41	1.40	1.39	1.38	1.38	1.37	1.3
24	.10	2.93	2.54	2.33	2.19	2.10	2.04	1.98	1.94	1.91	1.88	1.85	1.8
	.05	4.26	3.40	3.01	2.78	2.62	2.51	2.42	2.36	2.30	2.25	2.21	2.1
	.01	7.82	5.61	4.72	4.22	3.90	3.67	3.50	3.36	3.26	3.17	3.09	3.0
	.25	1.38	1.46	1.45	1.44	1.42	1.41	1.39	1.38	1.37	1.37	1.36	1.3
26	.10	2.91	2.52	2.31	2.17	2.08	2.01	1.96	1.92	1.88	1.86	1.84	1.8
	.05	4.23	3.37	2.98	2.74	2.59	2.47	2.39	2.32	2.27	2.22	2.18	2.1
	.01	7.72	5.53	4.64	4.14	3.82	3.59	3.42	3.29	3.18	3.09	3.02	2.9
	.25	1.38	1.46	1.45	1.43	1.41	1.40	1.39	1.38	1.37	1.36	1.35	1.3
28	.10	2.89	2.50	2.29	2.16	2.06	2.00	1.94	1.90	1.87	1.84	1.81	1.7
	.05	4.20	3.34	2.95	2.71	2.56	2.45	2.36	2.29	2.24	2.19	2.15	2.1
	.01	7.64	5.45	4.57	4.07	3.75	3.53	3.36	3.23	3.12	3.03	2.96	2.9
	.25	1.38	1.45	1.44	1.42	1.41	1.39	1.38	1.37	1.36	1.35	1.35	1.3
30	.10	2.88	2.49	2.28	2.14	2.05	1.98	1.93	1.88	1.85	1.82	1.79	1.7
	.05	4.17	3.32	2.92	2.69	2.53	2.42	2.33	2.27	2.21	2.16	2.13	2.0
	.01	7.56	5.39	4.51	4.02	3.70	3.47	3.30	3.17	3.07	2.98	2.91	2.8
	.25	1.36	1.44	1.42	1.40	1.39	1.37	1.36	1.35	1.34	1.33	1.32	1.3
40	.10	2.84	2.44	2.23	2.09	2.00	1.93	1.87	1.83	1.79	1.76	1.73	1.7
	.05	4.08	3.23	2.84	2.61	2.45	2.34	2.25	2.18	2.12	2.08	2.04	2.0
	.01	7.31	5.18	4.31	3.83	3.51	3.29	3.12	2.99	2.89	2.80	2.73	2.6
	.25	1.35	1.42	1.41	1.38	1.37	1.35	1.33	1.32	1.31	1.30	1.29	1.2
60	.10	2.79	2.39	2.18	2.04	1.95	1.87	1.82	1.77	1.74	1.71	1.68	1.6
	.05	4.00	3.15	2.76	2.53	2.37	2.25	2.17	2.10	2.04	1.99	1.95	1.9
	.01	7.08	4.98	4.13	3.65	3.34	3.12	2.95	2.82	2.72	2.63	2.56	2.5
	.25	1.34	1.40	1.39	1.37	1.35	1.33	1.31	1.30	1.29	1.28	1.27	1.2
120	.10	2.75	2.35	2.13	1.99	1.90	1.82	1.77	1.72	1.68	1.65	1.62	1.6
	.05	3.92	3.07	2.68	2.45	2.29	2.17	2.09	2.02	1.96	1.91	1.87	1.8
	.01	6.85	4.79	3.95	3.48	3.17	2.96	2.79	2.66	2.56	2.47	2.40	2.3
	.25	1.33	1.39	1.38	1.36	1.34	1.32	1.31	1.29	1.28	1.27	1.26	1.2
200	.10	2.73	2.33	2.11	1.97	1.88	1.80	1.75	1.70	1.66	1.63	1.60	1.5
	.05	3.89	3.04	2.65	2.42	2.26	2.14	2.06	1.98	1.93	1.88	1.84	1.8
	.01	6.76	4.71	3.88	3.41	3.11	2.89	2.73	2.60	2.50	2.41	2.34	2.2
	.25	1.32	1.39	1.37	1.35	1.33	1.31	1.29	1.28	1.27	1.25	1.24	1.2
χ	.10	2.71	2.30	2.08	1.94	1.85	1.77	1.72	1.67	1.63	1.60	1.57	1.5
	.05	3.84	3.00	2.60	2.37	2.21	2.10	2.01	1.94	1.88	1.83	1.79	1.7
	.01	6.63	4.61	3.78	3.32	3.02	2.80	2.64	2.51	2.41	2.32	2.25	2.1

TABLE D (*Continued*)

df *for numerator*													df *for de-nomi-nator*
15	20	24	30	40	50	60	100	120	200	500	∞	α	
1.36	1.34	1.33	1.32	1.31	1.31	1.30	1.30	1.30	1.29	1.29	1.28	.25	
1.81	1.76	1.73	1.70	1.67	1.65	1.64	1.61	1.60	1.59	1.58	1.57	.10	22
2.15	2.07	2.03	1.98	1.94	1.91	1.89	1.85	1.84	1.82	1.80	1.78	.05	
2.98	2.83	2.75	2.67	2.58	2.53	2.50	2.42	2.40	2.36	2.33	2.31	.01	
1.35	1.33	1.32	1.31	1.30	1.29	1.29	1.28	1.28	1.27	1.27	1.26	.25	
1.78	1.73	1.70	1.67	1.64	1.62	1.61	1.58	1.57	1.56	1.54	1.53	.10	24
2.11	2.03	1.98	1.94	1.89	1.86	1.84	1.80	1.79	1.77	1.75	1.73	.05	
2.89	2.74	2.66	2.58	2.49	2.44	2.40	2.33	2.31	2.27	2.24	2.21	.01	
1.34	1.32	1.31	1.30	1.29	1.28	1.28	1.26	1.26	1.26	1.25	1.25	.25	
1.76	1.71	1.68	1.65	1.61	1.59	1.58	1.55	1.54	1.53	1.51	1.50	.10	26
2.07	1.99	1.95	1.90	1.85	1.82	1.80	1.76	1.75	1.73	1.71	1.69	.05	
2.81	2.66	2.58	2.50	2.42	2.36	2.33	2.25	2.23	2.19	2.16	2.13	.01	
1.33	1.31	1.30	1.29	1.28	1.27	1.27	1.26	1.25	1.25	1.24	1.24	.25	
1.74	1.69	1.66	1.63	1.59	1.57	1.56	1.53	1.52	1.50	1.49	1.48	.10	28
2.04	1.96	1.91	1.87	1.82	1.79	1.77	1.73	1.71	1.69	1.67	1.65	.05	
2.75	2.60	2.52	2.44	2.35	2.30	2.26	2.19	2.17	2.13	2.09	2.06	.01	
1.32	1.30	1.29	1.28	1.27	1.26	1.26	1.25	1.24	1.24	1.23	1.23	.25	
1.72	1.67	1.64	1.61	1.57	1.55	1.54	1.51	1.50	1.48	1.47	1.46	.10	30
2.01	1.93	1.89	1.84	1.79	1.76	1.74	1.70	1.68	1.66	1.64	1.62	.05	
2.70	2.55	2.47	2.39	2.30	2.25	2.21	2.13	2.11	2.07	2.03	2.01	.01	
1.30	1.28	1.26	1.25	1.24	1.23	1.22	1.21	1.21	1.20	1.19	1.19	.25	
1.66	1.61	1.57	1.54	1.51	1.48	1.47	1.43	1.42	1.41	1.39	1.38	.10	40
1.92	1.84	1.79	1.74	1.69	1.66	1.64	1.59	1.58	1.55	1.53	1.51	.05	
2.52	2.37	2.29	2.20	2.11	2.06	2.02	1.94	1.92	1.87	1.83	1.80	.01	
1.27	1.25	1.24	1.22	1.21	1.20	1.19	1.17	1.17	1.16	1.15	1.15	.25	
1.60	1.54	1.51	1.48	1.44	1.41	1.40	1.36	1.35	1.33	1.31	1.29	.10	60
1.84	1.75	1.70	1.65	1.59	1.56	1.53	1.48	1.47	1.44	1.41	1.39	.05	
2.35	2.20	2.12	2.03	1.94	1.88	1.84	1.75	1.73	1.68	1.63	1.60	.01	
1.24	1.22	1.21	1.19	1.18	1.17	1.16	1.14	1.13	1.12	1.11	1.10	.25	
1.55	1.48	1.45	1.41	1.37	1.34	1.32	1.27	1.26	1.24	1.21	1.19	.10	120
1.75	1.66	1.61	1.55	1.50	1.46	1.43	1.37	1.35	1.32	1.28	1.25	.05	
2.19	2.03	1.95	1.86	1.76	1.70	1.66	1.56	1.53	1.48	1.42	1.38	.01	
1.23	1.21	1.20	1.18	1.16	1.14	1.12	1.11	1.10	1.09	1.08	1.06	.25	
1.52	1.46	1.42	1.38	1.34	1.31	1.28	1.24	1.22	1.20	1.17	1.14	.10	200
1.72	1.62	1.57	1.52	1.46	1.41	1.39	1.32	1.29	1.26	1.22	1.19	.05	
2.13	1.97	1.89	1.79	1.69	1.63	1.58	1.48	1.44	1.39	1.33	1.28	.01	
1.22	1.19	1.18	1.16	1.14	1.13	1.12	1.09	1.08	1.07	1.04	1.00	.25	
1.49	1.42	1.38	1.34	1.30	1.26	1.24	1.18	1.17	1.13	1.08	1.00	.10	χ
1.67	1.57	1.52	1.46	1.39	1.35	1.32	1.24	1.22	1.17	1.11	1.00	.05	
2.04	1.88	1.79	1.70	1.59	1.52	1.47	1.36	1.32	1.25	1.15	1.00	.01	

Source: Abridged from Table 18 in *Biometrika Tables for Statisticians,* Vol. 1, 3rd ed., E. S. Pearson and H. O. Hartley, eds. (New York: Cambridge, 1966). Used with permission of the editors and the Biometrika Trustees.

TABLE E Critical Values of the Correlation Coefficient

	Level of significance for one-tailed test			
	.05	.025	.01	.005
	Level of significance for two-tailed test			
df	.10	.05	.02	.01
1	.988	.997	.9995	.9999
2	.900	.950	.980	.990
3	.805	.878	.934	.959
4	.729	.811	.882	.917
5	.669	.754	.833	.874
6	.622	.707	.789	.834
7	.582	.666	.750	.798
8	.549	.632	.716	.765
9	.521	.602	.685	.735
10	.497	.576	.658	.708
11	.476	.553	.634	.684
12	.458	.532	.612	.661
13	.441	.514	.592	.641
14	.426	.497	.574	.623
15	.412	.482	.558	.606
16	.400	.468	.542	.590
17	.389	.456	.528	.575
18	.378	.444	.516	.561
19	.369	.433	.503	.549
20	.360	.423	.492	.537
21	.352	.413	.482	.526
22	.344	.404	.472	.515
23	.337	.396	.462	.505
24	.330	.388	.453	.496
25	.323	.381	.445	.487
26	.317	.374	.437	.479
27	.311	.367	.430	.471
28	.306	.361	.423	.463
29	.301	.355	.416	.456
30	.296	.349	.409	.449
35	.275	.325	.381	.418
40	.257	.304	.358	.393
45	.243	.288	.338	.372
50	.231	.273	.322	.354
60	.211	.250	.295	.325
70	.195	.232	.274	.303
80	.183	.217	.256	.283
90	.173	.205	.242	.267
100	.164	.195	.230	.254

Source: Abridged from Table VII, p. 63 of R. A. Fisher and F. Yates, *Statistical Tables for Biological, Agricultural and Medical Research,* 6th edition. Copyright © 1974. Reprinted by permission of Pearson Education.

GLOSSARY OF RESEARCH METHODS TERMS

analysis of covariance A method of statistical control through which scores on the dependent variable are adjusted according to scores on a related variable.

analysis of variance A statistical technique by which it is possible to partition the variance in a distribution of scores according to separate sources or factors; although variance is partitioned, the statistical test tests for differences between means.

a posteriori judgment A judgment based on actual observation (data), after the fact, so to speak.

applied research Research conducted for the primary purpose of solving an immediate, practical problem.

a priori decision A decision made prior to collecting data, for example, deciding what comparisons will be made before collecting data.

aptitude The potential for achievement.

assertoric argumentation Making the case for generalization (external validity) using a general argument that something is true for each and every member of a population.

attitude A tendency to possess certain feelings toward a specified class of stimuli.

basic research Research conducted for the primary purpose of adding to the existing body of knowledge, for example, research for theory development.

case study A study characterized by an investigation of a single individual, group, event, institution, or culture.

census (in survey research) A study that includes all members of a population.

central limit theorem A theorem that states that given any population with a mean and finite variance, as sample size increases, the distribution of the sample means approaches a normal distribution, with mean equal to the population mean and variance equal to the population variance divided by sample size.

cluster sampling The selection of groups of elements, called clusters, rather than single elements; all elements of a cluster are included in the sample, and the clusters are selected randomly from the larger population of clusters.

coding Process of organizing data, specifying designations and symbols as appropriate. Usually, the process results in data reduction.

cohort studies Longitudinal designs (in survey research) in which a specific population is studied over time by taking different random samples at various points in time.

concurrent-related validity of a test The extent to which scores on a test match performance scores on one or more criterion measures obtained at about the same time the test is given.

confidence interval An interval estimate of a parameter constructed in such a way that the interval has a predetermined probability of spanning the parameter.

confounded variables Variables operating in a specific situation such that their effects cannot be separated.

constant A characteristic that has the same value for all individuals in a research study.

construct-related validity of a test The extent to which a test measures one or more dimensions of a theory or trait.

content-related validity of a test The extent to which the content of the test items reflects the academic discipline, behavior, or whatever is under study.

contextualization (in ethnographic research) The requirement that data be interpreted only in the context of the situation or environment in which they were collected.

contingency table The array into which a set of numeration data may be grouped according to two or more classification variables.

continuous variable A variable that can take on any value within an interval on the scale of measurement.

control group (in an experiment) A group of subjects who do not receive any experimental treatment; the group is included for comparison purposes.

control variable A variable, other than the independent variable(s) of primary interest, whose effects are determined by the researcher. Control variables are included in designs as independent variables for the purpose of explaining variation.

correlation The extent of relationship between two variables.

correlation coefficient The measure of the extent of relationship between two variables.

covariate The measure used in an analysis of covariance for adjusting the scores of the dependent variable.

criterion-related validity of a test The extent to which scores on a test correlate with scores on some external criterion measure.

Cronbach alpha An internal consistency or reliability coefficient for a test, based on two or more parts of the test but requiring only one test administration.

cross-sectional studies Surveys in which the data are collected at one point in time from a random sample of a general population that contains two or more subpopulations, with the intention of comparing the data from the subsamples or noting trends across such subsamples.

data file The organized array of data and identification information commonly placed in a computer prior to analysis.

degrees of freedom The number of ways in which the data are free to vary; the number of observations minus the number of restrictions placed on the data.

Delphi method A method for systematic solicitation and collection of judgments on a topic through sequential questionnaires interspersed with summarized information and feedback.

dependent variable The variable being affected or assumed to be affected by the independent variable.

descriptive statistics That part of statistical procedures that deals with describing distributions of data and relationships between variables.

directional hypothesis A hypothesis stated in such a manner that a direction, usually indicated by "greater than" or "less than," is hypothesized for the results.

distribution The total observations or a set of data on a variable; when observations are tabulated according to frequency for each possible score, it is a frequency distribution.

ecological psychology Psychology focusing on naturally occurring human behavior and relationships between human behavior and the environment.

error variance (in a statistical context) Inherent or natural variance due to random assignment or random selection; also called *random variance.*

ethnographic research Research that is intended to provide scientific descriptions of (educational) systems, processes, and phenomena within their specific contexts.

ethnography A branch of anthropology that deals with the scientific description of individual cultures; also, the written account that is the product of an ethnographic study.

evaluation research Research procedures used for the process of evaluation, that is, collecting data and making decisions (value judgments) about an educational program, policy, and so forth.

experiment (in educational research) A research situation in which one or more independent variables are systematically varied according to a preconceived plan to determine the effects of this variation.

experimental mortality The dropping out of subjects participating in an experiment; the failure of certain subjects to continue in the experiment until its conclusion.

ex post facto research Research in which the independent variable or variables have already occurred and in which the researcher begins with the observations on a dependent variable, followed by a retrospective study of possible relationships and effects.

foreshadowed problems (in ethnographic research) Specific research problems, possibly stated in question form, that provide a focus for the research.

gatekeeper (in educational research) The individual or group of individuals (such as an IRB) that approves or rejects proceeding with research, and/or allows or prohibits access to the research site.

grounded theory Theory based on a study of the data rather than on some prior set of axioms and theorems.

hard copy The paper printout of computer output.

hardware Computer equipment including related equipment such as printers.

histogram A graphical representation, consisting of rectangles, of the scores in a distribution; the areas of the rectangles are proportional to the frequencies of the scores.

historical research Research directed to the study of a problem, event, and the like, of the past, using information from the past.

historiography The historical method of conducting research.

holistic ethnography The study of all or parts of a culture or community by describing beliefs and practices of the group and considering the various parts as they contribute to the culture as a unified, consistent whole.

hypothesis A conjecture or proposition about the solution to a problem, the relationship of two or more variables, or the nature of some phenomenon.

independent variable A variable that affects (or is assumed to affect) the dependent variable under study and is included in the research design so that its effect can be determined.

inferential statistics That part of statistical procedures that deals with making inferences from samples to populations.

informed consent The agreement, preferably in writing, to participate in a research study after being made fully knowledgeable about the purposes, procedures, and so forth of the study.

institutional review board (IRB) A group or committee of at least five individuals, representing an institution or agency, that has the authority to approve, require modifications of, or reject research that is subject to federal legislation.

interaction The effect of one independent variable on another; the lack of the effect of one independent variable remaining constant over the levels of another.

interval scale A measurement scale that, in addition to ordering scores, also establishes an equal unit in the scale so that distances between any two scores are of a known magnitude; also called *equal-unit scale.*

intervening variable A variable whose existence is inferred but that cannot be manipulated or measured.

key informant (in ethnographic research) An individual in whom one invests a disproportionate amount of time because that individual appears to be particularly well informed, articulate, approachable, or available.

Kuder-Richardson methods Procedures for determining the reliability of a test from a single form and single administration of the test without splitting the test.

level of confidence The probability associated with a confidence interval; the probability that the interval will span the corresponding parameter. Commonly used confidence levels in educational research are .95 and .99.

level of significance A probability associated with the test of a hypothesis using statistical techniques that determines whether or not the hypothesis is rejected. Commonly used significance levels in educational research are .05 and .01; also called *alpha level.*

Likert scale A scaling procedure, commonly associated with attitude measurement, that requires a graded response to each item or statement. In scoring, the alternative responses to items are assigned numerical values, and the individual's score is the sum of the numerical values.

linear relationship A relationship between two variables such that a straight line can be fitted satisfactorily to the points of the scattergram; the scatter of points will cluster elliptically around a straight line rather than some type of curve.

longitudinal studies Studies that involve measuring the same or different individuals two or more times during a period of time (usually of considerable length, such as several months or years), for example, measuring the mathematics performance of the same students at yearly intervals as they progress from the fourth grade through senior high.

maturation Psychological and biological processes operating and causing systematic variation within individuals with the passing of time.

mean The sum of the scores in a distribution divided by the number of scores in the distribution.

measurement The assignment of numerals to objects or events according to specific rules.

measures of central tendency Points in a distribution that locate the distribution on the measurement scale; points within the distribution about which the scores tend to group themselves.

measures of variability Measures of a distribution that indicate the amount of dispersion or spread in the distribution.

median The point in a distribution below which 50 percent of the scores lie.

meta-analysis A statistical procedure used to summarize the results across numerous, independently conducted research studies.

mode The point or score of greatest frequency in a distribution.

models (in the context of modeling methods) Hypothesized or conceptualized descriptions of relationships (connections) between variables.

modem A mechanism that converts computer language to audiotones allowing telephone communication between two computers.

moderator variable A variable that may or may not be controlled but has an effect in the research situation.

multiple-treatment interference Carryover or delayed effects of prior experimental treatments when individuals receive two or more experimental treatments in succession.

multivariate analyses Statistical data analyses in which two or more dependent variables are analyzed simultaneously.

nominal scale A measurement scale that simply classifies elements into two or more categories, indicating that the elements are different, but not according to order or magnitude.

normal distribution A family of bell-shaped, symmetrical distributions whose curve is described mathematically by a general equation; sometimes called the *Laplace-Gaussian normal probability function.*

norms Descriptive statistics that summarize the test performance of a reference group of individuals.

null hypothesis (in inferential statistics) A hypothesis stated such that no difference or no relationship is hypothesized.

operational definition A definition expressed in terms of the processes or operations that are going to be used to measure the characteristic under study.

optimum allocation (in stratified random sampling) Selecting the sample in such a manner that the strata contributions to the sample are proportional to the sizes of strata populations and the strata variances.

ordinal scale A measurement scale that classifies and ranks elements or scores.

organismic variable A variable that is an existing or natural characteristic of the individuals under study, for example, the sex of the individual.

panel studies Longitudinal designs (in survey research) in which the same random sample is measured at different points in time.

parallel forms of a test Two (or more) forms of a test that are equivalent in terms of characteristics.

parameter A characteristic or measure of a population, for example, the population mean.

participant–observer The role assumed by the researcher in ethnographic research such that the researcher becomes a participant in the situation being observed.

periodicity (in systematic sampling) A periodic characteristic that follows the listing of the elements and the selection interval so that a bias is introduced into the sample.

phenomenology The study of phenomena through observation and description.

pilot study A study conducted prior to the major research study that in some way is a small-scale model of the major study; conducted for the purpose of gaining additional information by which the major study can be improved, for example, an exploratory use of the measurement instrument with a small group for the purpose of refining the instrument.

population The totality of all elements, subjects, or members that possess a specified set of one or more common characteristics that define it; in inferential statistics, the group to which inferences are drawn.

portraiture An ethnography that is a descriptive account of a culture, in essence, providing a portrait of the culture through words.

prediction The estimation of scores on one variable from information about one or more other variables.

predictive-related validity of a test The extent to which predictions made from the test are confirmed by subsequent data.

primary source An original or firsthand account of an event or experience.

probability sample A sample selected in such a way that each member of the population has some nonzero probability of being included in the sample.

proportional allocation (in stratified random sampling) Selecting the sample in a manner such that the sample size is divided among the strata proportional to population sizes of the strata.

purposeful sample A sample selected in a nonrandom manner, based on member characteristics relevant to the research problem.

quasi-experimental research Research involving an experimental variable with intact groups, or at least with groups that have not been formed through random selection or random assignment; single subjects, not randomly selected, may also be involved.

random sample A sample selected in such a way that the selection of one member of the population in no way affects the probability of selection of any other member.

random (error) variance The inherent variance in a distribution of scores, which includes variance due to sources such as random sampling (or assignment) and intervening variables.

range One plus the difference between the two extreme scores of a distribution.

ratio scale A measurement scale that, besides containing an equal unit, also establishes an absolute zero in the scale.

regression (as a threat to experimental validity) A tendency for groups, especially those selected on the basis of extreme scores, to regress toward a more average score on subsequent measurements, regardless of the experimental treatment.

regression line The straight line of best fit (usually according to the least squares criterion) for a set of bivariate data.

reliability coefficient A measure of the consistency of a test. There are several methods of computing a reliability coefficient, depending on the test and the test situation.

reliability of measurement The consistency of the measurement.

reliability of research—external The extent to which research is replicable.

reliability of research—internal The extent of consistency in the methods, conditions, and results of research.

response set The tendency for an individual to respond to items or other stimuli in a consistent manner, regardless of the content or context of the stimuli.

sample A subset of the population under study.

sampling bias A distortion caused by the way the sample was selected or formed so that the sample is no longer representative of the population.

sampling distribution of a statistic The distribution (usually theoretical) of all possible values of the statistic from all possible samples of a given size selected from the population.

sampling error Variation due to random fluctuation when random samples are used to represent populations.

sampling frame List of units or elements of the population from which the sample is selected.

sampling ratio The ratio of sample size to population size; also called the *sampling fraction.*

scattergram The plot of points determined by the cross-tabulation of a set of bivariate data.

secondary analysis Reanalysis of the data for the purpose of (1) addressing the original research problem with better statistical procedures, and/or (2) answering new research questions.

secondary source An account that is at least one step removed from an event or experience.

semantic differential An attitude measuring technique in which the respondent is asked to judge a word or concept using a set of bipolar adjective scales.

significant statistic A statistic whose appearance by chance in the light of the hypothesis is less than the probability designated by the significance level, for example, a significant difference; a difference too large to be attributed to chance (random sampling fluctuation) if the hypothesis is true.

simple random sample A sample selected in such a way that all members of the population have an equal probability of selection; in the case of sampling without replacement from a finite population, all possible samples of a given size have the same probability of being selected.

software Programs used to provide instructions to the computer concerning analyses, procedures, or operations.

split-half method A procedure for determining the reliability of a test by which a single form of the test is divided into comparable halves, the scores on the halves are correlated, and the reliability coefficient is computed by applying a special formula known as the Spearman-Brown step-up formula.

standard deviation A measure of variability that is the positive square root of the variance.

standard error of a statistic The standard deviation of the sampling distribution of the statistic.

standard normal distribution The normal distribution with a mean of zero and a standard deviation of 1.0.

standard score A score given in terms of standard deviation units from the mean of the distribution. A negative score indicates below the mean and a positive score indicates above the mean.

statistics In descriptive statistics, measures taken on a distribution; in inferential statistics, measures or characteristics of a sample; in a more general sense, the theory, procedures, and methods by which data are analyzed in a quantitative manner.

stratified random sampling A sampling procedure in which the population is divided into two or more subpopulations, called *strata,* and elements for the sample are then randomly selected from the strata.

structural equations A system of simultaneous equations representing the conceptual model in model building.

survey research Research that deals with the incidence, distribution, and relationships of educational, psychological, and sociological variables in nonexperimental settings.

systematic sampling A selection procedure in which all sample elements are determined by the selection of the first element, because each element on a selection list is separated from the first element by a multiple of the selection interval.

test-retest method A procedure for determining test reliability by correlating the scores of two administrations of the same test to the same individuals.

trait A tendency to respond in a certain way to situations.

trend studies Longitudinal designs (in survey research) in which a general population is studied over time by taking different random samples at various points in time.

triangulation (in ethnographic research) Qualitative cross-validation of data using multiple data sources or multiple data-collection procedures.

two-stage sampling A general term referring to any sampling procedure that requires two steps in the sample selection.

Type I (or alpha error) In inferential statistics, the error of rejecting a true hypothesis.

Type II (or beta error) In inferential statistics, the error of failing to reject a false hypothesis.

unbiased statistic A statistic computed in such a manner that the mean of its sampling distribution is the parameter that the statistic estimates.

validity of measurement The extent to which a measurement instrument measures what it is supposed to measure.

validity of research—external The extent and appropriateness of the generalizability of results.

validity of research—internal The basic minimum control, measurement, analysis, and procedures necessary to make the results interpretable.

variable A characteristic that takes on different values for different individuals.

variance A measure of variability that is the average value of the squares of the deviations from the mean of the scores in a distribution.

NAME INDEX

SUBJECT INDEX

DISK INSTRUCTIONS

Hardware and Software Requirements

Any IBM PC or compatible computer, equipped with the memory and hardware specifications necessary to run:

SPSS for Windows, Version 6.1 or a later version or a PC statistical package other than SPSS.

Any Macintosh computer, equipped with the memory and hardware specifications necessary to run:

SPSS for Macintosh or a Macintosh statistical package other than SPSS.

Instructions for Using the Data Sets/Files

1. Create a copy of each master disk to be used as a working disk or put the files in a directory on your hard drive. Store the original master disk in the event that the working disk becomes damaged. Refer to your manual for specific instructions on manipulating the files.
2. Start your statistical program and choose a file and open it.

If your software is, for example, a different statistical program, just start your software, choose a text file, and open it. Your statistical software will automatically convert the file from ASCII. The text should also wrap to fit your screen. No further formatting will be necessary.

The Data Sets

Ohio Teachers

The Ohio Teachers Data Set contains information on school districts in Ohio.

DIST	District
COUNTY	County
ATT	Teacher attendance rate 2005–06
EXP	Average years of teacher experience
NUM	Number of full-time teachers
NBACH	Number of full-time teachers who have at least a bachelor's
NMAST	Number of full-time teachers who have at least a master's
CERT	% of teachers who are fully certified
NOTQ	% of teachers who are not highly qualified as defined by NCLB
PBACH	% of full-time teachers who have at least a bachelor's
PMAST	% of full-time teachers who have at least a master's

SALARY	Average teacher salary
TEMP	% of core courses taught by teacher with temporary certificate

NC-SAT-2006

The NC-SAT-2006 Data Set contains district level information on SAT scores and district expenditures.

district	District
math	Average SAT Mathematics Score
reading	Average SAT Reading Score
writing	Average SAT Writing Score
perpupil	Per-pupil expenditures
total	Total expenditures

PACT

The PACT Data Set contains student level demographic information and scores from the South Carolina Palmetto Achievement Challenge Test.

gender	M = Male	F = Female	
lunch	F = Free	R = Reduced	N = Neither
iep	IEP	Y = Yes	N = No
speech	Speech disability	Y = Yes	N = No
gift	Gifted	Y = Yes	N = No
elass05	English/Language Arts Scale Score 2005–06		
elapf05	English/Language Arts Performance Level 2005–06 (Below Basic, Basic, Proficient, Advanced)		
elass04	English /Language Arts Scale Score 2004–05		
elapf04	English/Language Arts Performance Level 2004–05		
elass03	English /Language Arts Scale Score 2003–04		
elapf03	English/Language Arts Performance Level 2003–04		
matss05	Math Scale Score 2005–06		
matpf05	Math Performance Level 2005–06		
matss04	Math Scale Score 2004–05		
matpf04	Math Performance Level 2004–05		
matss03	Math Scale Score 2003–04		
matpf03	Math Performance Level 2003–05		
sciss05	Science Scale Score 2005–06		
scipf05	Science Performance Level 2005–06		
sciss04	Science Scale Score 2004–05		
scipf04	Science Performance Level 2004–05		
socss05	Social Studies Scale Score 2005–06		
socpf05	Social Studies Performance Level 2005–06		
socss04	Social Studies Scale Score 2004–05		
socpf04	Social Studies Performance Level 2004–05